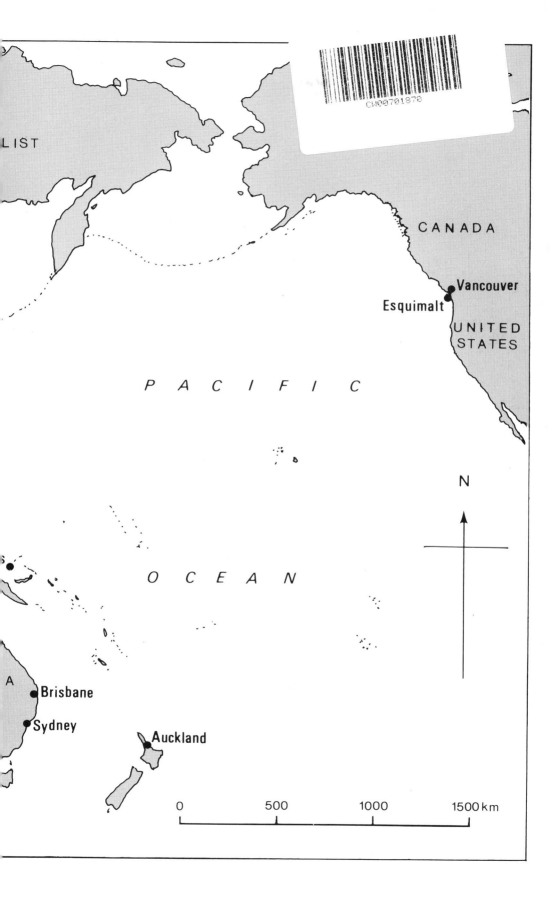

LIST

CANADA

Vancouver

Esquimalt

UNITED
STATES

P A C I F I C

N

O C E A N

A
Brisbane

Sydney

Auckland

0   500   1000   1500 km

BETWEEN TWO OCEANS

A Military History of Singapore From First Settlement to Final British Withdrawal

Malcolm H. Murfett • John N. Miksic
Brian P. Farrell • Chiang Ming Shun

UNIVERSITY PRESS
1999

Oxford University Press

Oxford   New York
Athens   Auckland   Bangkok   Bombay
Calcutta   Cape Town   Dar es Salaam   Delhi
Florence   Hong Kong   Istanbul   Karachi
Kuala Lumpur   Madras   Madrid   Melbourne
Mexico City   Nairobi   Paris   Singapore
Taipei   Tokyo   Toronto

and associated companies in
Berlin   Ibadan

Oxford is a trade mark of Oxford University Press

ISBN 0 19 588482 5

Printed by Seng Lee Press Pte. Ltd.,
Published by Oxford University Press Pte. Ltd.,
37 Jalan Pemimpin, #03-03 Union Industrial Building, Block A, Singapore 577177

TABLE OF CONTENTS

PROLOGUE

T his volume explores the military history of the island of Singapore from approximately 1275 to 1971. In so doing it seeks to dispel several myths that have over the course of time become so entrenched and believable that they have been accepted, often unreservedly, by many people as actual fact. Because comparatively little is known of the early history of Singapore, the popular view appears to be that Sir Stamford Raffles was the first person to discover the geo-strategic importance of this little diamond-shaped island lying off the southern coast of the Malayan peninsula. This assumption is well wide of the mark as Dr. Miksic, the noted regional archaeologist, reveals in his early chapters in this volume. Far from being a sleepy tropical island that escaped the attention of all but a few indigenous natives and isolated remnants of the Chinese diaspora and had only nineteenth and twentieth century significance, Dr. Miksic demonstrates that Singapore — in its various guises — was recognised as an important maritime location centuries before Raffles set foot on the banks of the Singapore River in 1819. By piecing together fragments of the historical record from an impressive range of sources, Dr. Miksic has reached the conclusion that Singapore probably first assumed an importance in regional mercantile trade in the last quarter of the thirteenth century. His own archaeological excavations in a few selected sites near the river or on Fort Canning Hill in Singapore have tended to confirm this supposition. Although these excavations have unearthed a relatively small number of thirteenth-century pieces, they have revealed a much richer source of artifacts from the fourteenth century. At a *prima facie* level, therefore, this would appear to be consistent with the contention that Singapore (Temasik) was used as a port for certain trading purposes in the thirteenth century and that it grew more populous and important thereafter. Dr. Miksic suggests that the precipitous fall in the fortunes of Temasik at the turn of the fifteenth century was inversely proportional to the rise of the Malayan port of Melaka. Although not abandoned entirely, Singapore's decline lasted well beyond the Portuguese conquest of Melaka in 1511 and was consolidated by its own defeat at the hands of the Portuguese in 1613, when much, if not all, of the ancient settlement of Singapore was burned to the ground. Singapore lurched on in an inferior position for another ninety years before the island was offered as a gift by the Sultan of Johore to a British sea captain who was visiting Johor on his way to China in 1703. Abdul Jalil's extraordinary offer may have been made as a convenient ploy to bring British power into the region and buttress his own faltering hold over his possessions in the area. Despite politely declining the Sultan's offer, news of its issue spread and was to have enormous influence one hundred and sixteen years later in 1819 when Sir Thomas Stamford Raffles was looking to establish a settlement south of the Malay peninsula for the purpose of protecting the expanding East India Company's trade routes between India and China. Although Raffles began his quest for the development of a British base south of the Melaka Straits by preferring Bangka, Bintan, Sambas and Pontianak (on the west coast of Borneo) and Karimun, he eventually opted for Singapore and came ashore for the first time near the mouth of the Singapore River on 29 January 1819.

Although far more is known of Singapore's post-1819 socio-economic and political history, the military and geo-strategic aspects of the island's development have with some notable exceptions received much less attention from the academic world. In the remaining chapters of this volume, the four authors have concentrated their attention on this relatively neglected sphere of Singapore's history. Both Dr. Miksic and Chiang Ming Shun have shown that British plans for the defence of the island passed through a series of phases in the nineteenth century — some enlightened, others not, but that the essential catalyst for action and effective preparedness was always the likelihood of attack by a superior regional power. At times when that morbid fear was high, defence plans took on a much more impressive form than when that factor was removed. Inconsistency and imperial arrogance reigned supreme in the days of *Pax Britannica.*

By the time the First World War broke out in Europe in August 1914, both the troops and defences of Singapore had become threadbare. This regrettable state of affairs worsened in the months thereafter and finally resulted in the ill-fated Sepoy Mutiny of February 1915. As Chiang reveals in his investigation of this dramatic incident, the symbolism of the British relying upon the Japanese amongst others to put down this mutiny was neither lost on the people of Singapore, nor on those who had been called into the breach in this emergency.

Unfortunately, the message that defending colonial territories in Southeast Asia under all circumstances was patently more difficult for all European powers to orchestrate than they might care to believe was lost totally on the British. There seemed to be a general unwillingness on their part to accept the fact that the days of Palmerston were gone forever. Being British no longer carried quite the same clout that it had done more than half a century before. This much ought to have been realised by the government in Whitehall if not by the rest of the country. Looking at the much-vaunted "Singapore Strategy" in the inter-war period, however, one is hard-put to see any such recognition save from an enlightened few who nonetheless found themselves outside the charmed circle of real influence in London. Indeed, and almost perversely, the

British policymakers in supporting this strategic plan virtually defied the logic of contemplating what would happen in a worst-case scenario, preferring instead to see imperial defence in the best possible light. It was seen as a duty that they could discharge even in dire emergencies. Sadly, it was as big a myth as the popular conception that Singapore had no significant pre-history before Raffles.

Even so the British did finally come to their senses after the fall of France in June 1940 and admit that Singapore was an ocean too far for them to defend under all circumstances and that other areas now took precedence over that of Singapore and its immediate environs. Notwithstanding the United Kingdom's belated brush with reality, the myth grew up that such a profound policy change was deliberately kept from both the Australasian dominions. Sinister talk of a great betrayal has been heard for over fifty years. Was this yet another example of *perfidious Albion?* Despite the passage of the years and the declassified information that is now in the public domain, the myth persists. This volume addresses the issue and demonstrates that although the British government did act disingenuously, the Australian ministers in Canberra displayed a strategic myopia that almost defies belief. In the end neither power had any real alternative but to trust to luck, and that particular commodity deserted both of them in December 1941.

Once the Japanese had launched their attack on southern Thailand and northern Malaya, the limp nature of British defence preparations was immediately shown in graphic relief. What the Commonwealth wistfully hoped would ultimately be a Fortress Singapore soon turned into a sick and cruel joke — instead of being an imperial redoubt it rapidly became a military internment camp. A combination of insufficient money and troops, inadequate military materiel, and a gross underestimation of the enemy's ability to wage war, would have been reasons enough for alarm at the best of times, but the British managed to compound these colossal mistakes with a command structure that lacked inspiration, élan and cohesion. In the heat of battle when decisive judgement was required, their military leaders either failed to lead or invariably chose the wrong option with catastrophic results. Explanations for this débacle are legion and popular misconceptions have rarely been far from the surface of most of these accounts. For years afterwards the fall of Singapore was often partly attributed to the fact that the guns pointed the 'wrong way' (out to sea) and could not be turned to bear on the enemy approaching from the northern landward side. Convenient scapegoats existed from the outset. British military folklore has portrayed the men of the Australian Imperial Forces (AIF) as a cowardly rabble who fled from the advancing Japanese, thus compromising what was left of a defensive strategy on the island of Singapore. For their part the Australians have not been slow to accuse Churchill, Percival and the entire British military establishment of both gross deception and utter incompetence. It is high time that an air of unbiased, dispassionate professionalism was brought to bear on this matter. Dr. Farrell, a Canadian military historian, has done just that. His research findings have separated both fact from fiction viii

and the rational from the irrational, while providing a balanced account of a tragic episode in Commonwealth military history.

In the end, of course, this humiliating defeat was to usher in an ignoble succession. From the outset, the Japanese Occupation of Singapore was discriminatory, merciless and excessive. What good the Japanese Military Administration may have accomplished in its thirty-month tenure of power, was undermined by the horrific deeds done on its behalf by members of the Imperial Japanese Army (IJA) and the dreaded *Kempeitai*. Sadly, there are few myths to be dispelled in this era. Claims against the Japanese of sadism, violence and malevolence are almost indisputable. One wishes it were not so for it appears that morality, conscience and justice must have stood in abeyance as the baser instincts of mankind revealed themselves to their hapless victims. Even those who escaped punitive sanctions were not spared some element of privation, such as insufficient food or medicine, so that all but a few simply had to endure the Occupation. While it may have been character building for some, the ordeal left an indelible impression on virtually all who experienced it.

Denied the chance of recapturing Malaya and Singapore by the sudden and dramatic ending of the war in August 1945, the British found themselves unprepared for peace when it actually arrived. Instead of being able to restore some of their military pride lost in the dark days of 1941–42 by making a success of Operation *Zipper*, the British forces were immediately required, amongst other things, to maintain civil order and discipline throughout Southeast Asia. Ironically, this task proved well beyond the limited number of British troops on station in the region. In Singapore and elsewhere, therefore, enemy troops were engaged to assist in carrying out these duties. There was clearly an air of chaotic improvisation about the whole business, providing yet another uncomfortable reminder, if such was needed, that the sterling qualities for which the British Empire had once been justly famous, notably, sound organisational principles and administrative flair, had somehow been lost in transit.

After these embarrassing hiccups, British military rule duly returned to Singapore in September 1945. It did so rather half-heartedly. For several years the three services scratched around in a vain search for an effective role to play in the region. Just when it looked as though Clement Attlee's Labour government had reconciled itself to a much-diminished role east of Suez, however, a succession of international crises spawned by the rise of communism in Malaya, China and Korea reversed the trend significantly. Singapore's pivotal strategic position was rediscovered in an era increasingly identified with preventing the "domino theory" from being realised in practice.

Although committed to maintaining a military presence in Southeast Asia through its operational base in Singapore, the British government had reason to believe that its colonial empire was coming apart at the seams. An ill-advised conspiracy against Nasser in 1956 ended up costing the United Kingdom far more than Egypt and the Suez Canal. A defiant wind of change — the demand for national self-determination — was blowing not only in Africa but also around the globe and the United Kingdom did not look to be positioned economically, militarily or morally to benefit from it. Appearances can on occasion be deceptive, however. Despite only yielding politically that which it could not hope to hold onto, the United Kingdom maintained its military presence in Singapore in the early 1960s and soon found that it could play a regional role in Southeast Asia with great distinction.

But hardly had the struggle for *Konfrontasi* ceased before the United Kingdom's seemingly perennial economic predicament came back to haunt Harold Wilson's Labour government in London. Substantial economies from across the broad spectrum of government ministries were now obligatory if the government was to avoid the stigma of devaluation. Far East Command became both a target and a casualty of this austerity drive. By April 1967 the British Cabinet had reluctantly conceded that a British military withdrawal from Singapore was inevitable and would take place in stages over several years. After the devaluation crisis broke in November 1967, however, even that timetable was compressed. Edward Heath's election at the head of a Conservative government in June 1970, failed to do more than make a few cosmetic changes to the overall picture. By midnight on 31 October 1971, Far East Command had ceased to exist. Even the token force that remained behind was finally removed between September 1975 and March 1976. Singapore was basically on its own. Another phase in its military history had begun.

In due course, the story of the military history of the Republic of Singapore needs to be told...but others with access to the definitive sources will have to tell it.

ACKNOWLEDGEMENTS

It has been more than seven years since the idea for this book was first mooted by Professor Peter Dennis in the course of numerous conversations he had with Dr. Malcolm Murfett of the History Department at the National University of Singapore. Although Professor Dennis's other academic and administrative duties as the chairman of the History Department at the Australian Defence Force Academy eventually assumed so great a burden that he relinquished his leading role in this project, Dr. Murfett was able to secure the willing services of his colleagues Dr. John Miksic, Dr. Brian Farrell and Chiang Ming Shun, a former graduate student of NUS, to complete the work that had been started in 1991.

All four authors should like to acknowledge their grateful thanks to many people and institutions who have assisted them in the conduct of their research in various countries. We are particularly grateful to Mr. Lee Seng Gee, Chairman, The Lee Foundation, Singapore, who has never failed to provide research funds and travel grants for this project over several years. In Singapore our gratitude is extended to Brian Bogaars; Mickey Chiang; Ms. Beatrice Chong Choy Hoong; Iskandar bin Mydin, Senior Curator, Singapore History Museum; Ms. Rajwant Kaur; Koh Lian What; Dr. Paul Kratoska; Ms. Asha Kumaran, Managing Editor, Oxford University Press; Kwa Chong Guan; Dr. Albert Lau; Associate Professor Edwin Lee, Head, Department of History, The National University of Singapore [NUS]; Clement Liew; Ms. Cheryl Lim; Clarence Lim, Managing Director, Oxford University Press; Lim How Seng, Director, Singapore History Museum; Ms. Cheryl-Ann Low; Mrs. Madeline Marcus, Ministry of Information and the Arts; Rudy Mosbergen; Ms. Vimala Nambiar, Head, Reprographic Services Department of the Central Library, NUS; Ms. Ong Su Chern; Ms. Seow Siok Mui; Shah Alam; Dr. Susan Sutton; Mrs. Lily Tan, Director, National Archives of Singapore; Gabriel G. Thomas; Ms. G. Uma Devi; Vinayagan s/o Dharmarajah; Victor A.P. Wong and Ms. Lucille Yap. Grateful thanks also go to those who helped us overseas. In Australia the staff at both the Australian War Memorial, and the Australian Archives in Canberra were very helpful, as were Dr. E.P. Hodgkin in Perth and Dr. Richard Pennell and Dr. Alan Warren in Melbourne. In India notable assistance was provided by Aidar Chakraverti in Calcutta; Chan Keng Howe and Dr. P. Perti in New Delhi; and Thiru Rangamani and Stephen

Soh in Madras. In the United Kingdom we were helped by Ms. Janet Chisholm; Anthony Farrington, India Office Library and Records; Major(ret.) Alan Harfield; the staff of the Liddell Hart Centre for Military Archives, King's College, London; Boris Mollo, National Army Museum; the staff of the Oriental and India Office Records section of the British Library; the staff of the Public Records Office, Kew Gardens; John Wenzel, Imperial War Museum Cabinet War Rooms, Dr. Conrad Woods, the Department of Sound Records and the Department of Documents, Imperial War Museum.

All Crown-copyright material in this book is reproduced by permission of the Controller of Her Majesty's Stationery Office. Material from other public archives and private collections is reproduced by permission of the appropriate authorities identified in the endnotes.

Finally, we should each like to thank our families and close friends for all they have done to support us as we worked on this project. While it may have taken longer to complete than we anticipated at the outset, we trust that *Between Two Oceans* will be seen as a fitting tribute to the late Professor Wong Lin Ken, to whom this work is dedicated.

Malcolm H. Murfett, John N. Miksic, Brian P. Farrell
& Chiang Ming Shun.
Singapore, 21 June 1998

NOTES ON AUTHORS

Chiang Ming Shun was born in Singapore in 1968. After graduating from the National University of Singapore [NUS] with a B.A. Hons. in History in 1994, he worked in the School of Arts at the National Institute of Education. He obtained his M.A. in Southeast Asian Studies from the NUS in June 1997. He is currently training for the Methodist ministry at Trinity Theological College in Singapore. Mr Chiang wrote chapters 4 and 5 of *Between Two Oceans.*

Brian P. Farrell was born in Montreal in 1960 and graduated with a B.A. from Carleton University, Ottawa before gaining his doctorate from McGill University in 1992. He was appointed a lecturer in Military History at the NUS in 1993. Dr. Farrell is the author of *The Basis and Making of British Grand Strategy 1940-1943: Was There a Plan?* (1998) He is currently working on a full length study of the defence and fall of Singapore in World War II. Dr. Farrell wrote chapters 7, 8, 10, 11, and Appendices 2 and 3 of this current volume.

John N. Miksic was born in Rochester, New York in 1946. After obtaining his B.A. from Dartmouth College in 1968, he joined the Peace Corps and spent four years in Malaysia. In 1979 he received his Ph.D. from Cornell University. Since that time he has lived in Sumatra (1979–81), Java (1981–87) and Singapore (1987 to the present). He has been historical consultant to Fort Canning Park since 1987. He is a senior lecturer in the Southeast Asian Studies Programme at the NUS. Dr. Miksic's research publications include *Archaeological Research on the 'Forbidden Hill' of Singapore* (1985) National Museum, Singapore; *Old Javanese Gold* (1990) Ideations, Singapore; *Borobudar: Golden Tales of the Buddhas* (1990) Periplus, Singapore. He wrote chapters 1, 2, 3 and Appendix 1 of *Between Two Oceans.*

Malcolm H. Murfett was born in Grove in the United Kingdom in 1948. After studying at both Keele and Leeds Universities, he won a scholarship to New College, Oxford to do graduate work leading to the award of a D.Phil in History in 1980. While at Oxford he was appointed the Principal Research Assistant to the Earl of Birkenhead and worked for five years on the officially commissioned single-volume life of Sir Winston Churchill. He joined the Department of History at NUS in June 1980 and was subsequently promoted to Senior Lecturer in 1986 and Associate Professor in 1995. He was elected a Fellow of the Royal Historical Society in 1990. Professor Murfett's publications include *Fool-proof Relations: The Search for Anglo-American Naval Cooperation During the Chamberlain Years, 1937–1940* (1984) Singapore University Press, Singapore; *Hostage on the Yangtze: Britain, China and the Amethyst Crisis of 1949* (1991) Naval Institute Press, Annapolis, Md; *In Jeopardy: The Royal Navy and British Far Eastern Defence Policy 1945–1951* (1995) Oxford University Press, Kuala Lumpur; *The First Sea Lords: From Fisher to Mountbatten* [ed.] (1995) Praegor, Westport, Conn. He wrote the Prologue and chapters 6 and 9 of this book.

GLOSSARY

benteng: Malay for "fort", usually signifying a site enclosed by an earthwork.

Bugis: a seafaring group of people originally from South Sulawesi (eastern Indonesia).

cakravartin: literally "wheel turner" in Sanskrit; a term used to refer to a notion of an ideal world ruler.

Dragon's Tooth Strait / Lungyamen: the narrow passage between Sentosa Island and Labrador Point at the west end of Keppel Harbour. A rock which once stood here was called by the Malays *Batu Berlayar*, "Sail Rock"; the British named it Lot's Wife.

Gutta percha: corruption of Malay *getah percha*, "Sumatra sap"; a kind of Indian rubber. It was replaced by Brazilian rubber for most purposes in the late nineteenth century.

Karimun: an island approximately 30 km west of Singapore, strategically located at the southern end of the Straits of Melaka.

Laksamana: a Malay title given to the leader of a kingdom's naval forces.

Malay Annals / Sejarah Melayu: a Malay text which tells the story of the origins and descent of the Malay rulers. Singapore plays a prominent role in the early part of the story.

Orang Laut: literally "sea people" in Malay. A general term used to describe the many scattered populations who until very recently inhabited most of the coastal areas of the Singapore area, Sumatra, and the Malay Peninsula. They were characterised by a life mainly spent aboard small boats, which they used to move in groups from place to place in search of food and other resources.

orang kaya: "rich person" in Malay; originally a reference to a class of nobility.

Pancur: "spring of water" in Malay; a fourteenth-century Chinese text gives this place-name as the political centre of Singapore.

Parameswara: a fourteenth-century Malay ruler of Singapore.

Riau: the archipelago south of Singapore; part of Indonesia.

Srivijaya: a trading kingdom centred in Southeast Sumatra which rose in the seventh century A.D. and controlled the Straits of Melaka for about four centuries.

Temasik: fourteenth-century name of Singapore.

Wang Dayuan: a fourteenth-century Chinese trader who visited Singapore.

LIST OF PLATES AND MAPS

Plates:

Maps:

1

Geography and Traditional Warfare in Pre-British Southeast Asia: The Place of Singapore

Military histories of particular places may be divided into two categories, depending on whether they focus on considerations of operations fought there, or on broader aspects related to the military experience and influence on that place. The authors of this book have found it necessary to employ both approaches in order to explore the military history of Singapore, albeit with particular emphasis on the strategic aspects of its military story. The word "strategy" implies considerations relevant to long-range planning to achieve a particular goal. In discussing the strategic significance of a site or area, the historian must be able to identify long-term trends, underlying factors which provide continuity over a long period of time, in order to reach beyond the surface flow of daily events. Important variables for those who hold this view of history include factors of geography, technology, economics, and cultural institutions. These contrast with the short-term phenomena which appear on the surface of history as the concrete manifestations of underlying structures.

The strategic importance of a place is not a timeless, unchanging quality. It varies from one period to another, in response to developments in weaponry, transportation, political conditions, and economic activities. Strategic considerations are not fixed characteristics of a place; they are dependent on the position of that place in a wide and often complex web of geographical and cultural relations. It must also be emphasised that strategic importance is not least a matter of psychological perception rather than objective reality. Psychological perception in turn is derived from the assumptions and beliefs, including religious ideas, of all groups with potential or actual influence on events in the place under study.

In discussing the evolution of perceptions of Singapore's military and strategic importance, several historical phases can be distinguished. The beginning of each phase is marked by changes in the perceptions of Singapore's strategic importance held by the group of people with most influence over the events which took place here. The indigenous people of Singapore have for much of its history not been the major group whose perceptions must be considered. In fact, whether Singapore's significance rose or fell at the start of a new phase has depended largely on trends and perceptions external to Singapore itself. Singapore's

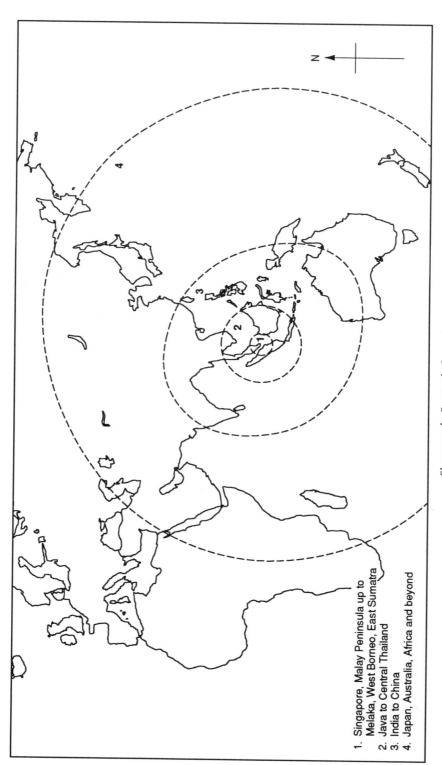

N

1. Singapore, Malay Peninsula up to
   Melaka, West Borneo, East Sumatra
2. Java to Central Thailand
3. India to China
4. Japan, Australia, Africa and beyond

Singapore's Strategic Importance

strategic significance has varied not only with time, but also according to the location of the person or group whose perception we are attempting to describe. Thus when we speak of Singapore's strategic significance, we must define not only the time period with which we are dealing, but also the point of view relative to which this significance is being evaluated. As we shall see, in the long sweep of Singapore's 700-year history there have been times when Singapore's strategic significance fell from the point of view of one category of observers, but remained steady or even rose from another perspective. Like the physical universe which Einstein revealed to us, the strategic universe lacks fixed reference points. Geographical relationships, which might be thought to be stable and constant, in the Singapore context turn out to be relatively unimportant determinants in and of themselves. Geography facilitates some developments and makes others less likely, but has not determined the course of Singapore's strategic history.

We may define concentric circles, each of which constitutes a different perspective from which Singapore's strategic importance may be viewed. The first circle extends from Singapore to the Riau and Lingga Archipelagoes, western Borneo, eastern Sumatra, and the Malay Peninsula as far north as Melaka. This circle encompasses one set of strategic relationships within which Singapore's strategic significance is likely to be seen in a similar light by all parties. The second circle extends to Java in the south and Thailand in the north. The third circle extends to India and China. The fourth is practically boundless, including Japan, the Near East, Europe, and North America.

Throughout the entire history of Singapore's strategic significance, military considerations have never been separable from economics. Singapore's stature in the strategic calculations of various parties has depended greatly on the shifting configuration of patterns of trade passing through the Straits of Melaka. Maritime traffic between the Indian Ocean and the South China Sea became firmly established 2000 years ago. Since that ancient connection was formed, at least one important seaport serving this trade has been located in the vicinity of the south entrance to the Straits of Melaka.

The precise location of the port has changed several times. The oldest port known to have existed in this region was located rather far to the south of the Straits, in the region of Palembang, South Sumatra.[1] Other locations have included Jambi, also in Sumatra; Bintan, in the Riau archipelago; Melaka; and several locations along the banks of the Johore River. Thus considerations of economic activity, including locations of external markets and favoured sailing routes, can never be far from evaluations of the strategic considerations of various parties in which Singapore played a part. For the moment, however, economic factors must be relegated to the background. The primary variable which has determined all other calculations regarding Singapore's military importance is of course the military context. It is this context that we must first establish before we investigate Singapore's part in the strategic pattern which prevailed when Singapore first came into existence.

The Nature Of Early Southeast Asian Warfare

In pre-fifteenth century Southeast Asia, warfare was endemic but fought on a small scale. The earliest clear references to events in the insular portion of western Southeast Asia come to us from Chinese documents. These sources consist of records of diplomatic missions to the Chinese court between 430 and 452, from a kingdom the name of which is preserved in Chinese transcription as *Ho-lo-dan* or sometimes *Ho-lo-to*.[2] This kingdom was probably located in West Java. The very first mission of which we have any knowledge brought with it a letter from the Indonesian king to the emperor of one of the kingdoms into which China was then divided, asking for help:

> My country once had a large population and was prosperous. My country was never bullied by other countries. But now the situation is different and we have become weak. My neighbours vie with each other in attacking me. I beg Your Majesty to extend your protection from afar . . . If you pity me I hope that you will send missions ordering these countries not to maltreat us so that Your Majesty's reputation as the protector of the weak will be known everywhere.[3]

This old Southeast Asian diplomatic note betrays the fact that at the dawn of regional history, considerations of inter-polity security were already a subject of great concern to local rulers. It is of course not possible to extrapolate back into the remote past of Southeast Asia such concepts as "states" defined by discrete boundaries which had to be defended. Early Southeast Asian polities were not organised on a territorial basis. Land was an abundant resource in early Southeast Asia. The major resource over which ambitious rulers contended for control was not land; it was people. Until the late nineteenth century, the principal factor which limited the aspirations of an ambitious ruler of a Southeast Asian kingdom was manpower: people to grow the food, manufacture the crafts, conduct the ceremonies, and perform all the other activities in which the ambitions of rulers are normally expressed.

The reasons for this general lack of population are still subject to debate,[4] but the overall situation was undeniably one of competition between ambitious people to accumulate followers, by force if necessary (or if possible). Thus a sixteenth-century Chinese source quotes Southeast Asians as saying that "it is better to have slaves than to have land."[5] Given a scarcity of people and an abundance of empty land, the obvious strategy to adopt when attacked is to decamp if possible rather than attempting to defend a fixed position with the probability that some defenders will be lost even if the battle is won. New towns could always be founded, and new lands cleared for agriculture, but people to inhabit them and work them were more difficult to come by. In many parts of the world, such as Mesopotamia, India and China, some of the oldest archaeological remains which can be connected with settlements are defensive walls, but in Southeast Asia it is debatable whether any such structures were built of permanent materials before the construction of the fourteenth-century Lines of Singapore.[6] Local languages contain numerous words for "fort, stockade" *(kubu, benteng, kota)*, but in all cases the image which these terms conjure up is that of a temporary defensive barrier built of nothing more substantial than wooden logs.

The mode of warfare in ancient Southeast Asia, particularly in the coastal and insular areas such as the one of which Singapore formed a part, therefore took the form of surprise attacks, raids aimed mainly at capturing moveable property and people with the objective of taking them back to one's own home territory rather than occupying new areas in order to expel the previous occupants and thus gain more room for one's own subjects. Some of the larger kingdoms based in rice-growing areas in Cambodia, Thailand and Burma did demonstrate an inclination toward a different system of values in which land tenure did play a role of some importance, but even there the major constraint on agricultural production always seems to have been lack of people rather than land.

It is for this reason that trade assumed an importance for societies of the Straits of Melaka and Java Sea beyond the ordinary level found in many other early civilisations. Maritime trade provided access to items which were not available locally. In Southeast Asian society, the possession of rare items in itself conferred on their possessor an aura of special power and status. This phenomenon was certainly not unique to Southeast Asia. Southeast Asian trade with China since its inception in the Three Kingdoms period in the third century A.D. had been motivated by a desire on the part of the imperial Chinese court for access to "rare and precious" items such as incense, pearls, kingfisher's feathers, ivory, fragrant wood, tortoise shell, and other items associated with the South Seas, the *Nanhai*. The Chinese court monopolised commerce in many of these items. The obvious connotation was that those who could display these items could use them to claim status. In Southeast Asia, a similar dynamic operated. Men became powerful in many cases because they could distribute tokens of status obtained from distant sources. Such tokens included Chinese silk and other textiles, and metal objects. As late as the seventeenth century, the Sultans of Palembang still maintained the loyalty of the hinterland peoples of South Sumatra, and extracted such important items as gold and ivory from them, in return for gifts of salt, cloth and iron, all imported commodities. The Palembang rulers situated in the estuarine zone along Sumatra's east coast had direct access to these items, whereas the mountaineers of the west coast did not. The balance of political power was largely determined by matters of access to foreign imported goods. Indigenous Malay sources specifically acknowledge this, in such bald statements as "where there is sovereignty, there is gold"[7]. Thus control over trade passing through the Straits of Melaka provided the surest means of acquiring followers, who were the most prized commodity in ancient Southeast Asia, the main measure of wealth. The use of military means to retain power or expand it had to be weighed very carefully in terms of costs versus benefits to be gained. Such equations determined the strategic deliberations of ancient Southeast Asians.

Little is known of the weaponry or strategy employed in the earliest Southeast Asian warfare. The main source of information now extant consists of literature, which cannot always be taken as an accurate reflection of what took place. The ideal which these sources depict is a fight between two champions. Standing armies did not exist. Military forces were raised by rulers passing demands on to their vassals. By the fourteenth century some sources suggest that some troops in Java were being paid, but this practice does not seem to have been adopted in the Malay realm of which Singapore formed a part. Military strife was depicted in traditional sources as a contest between individuals, the outcome to be determined not simply by skill and might, but by spiritual qualities. Thus the winner was deemed to have achieved success by right of superior moral and religious virtue. Victory was the sign that the winner possessed such virtue. It seems that rulers often personally led their troops in battle. Thus when a leader fell, the army with him might then crumble even though the rest of the battle might be in their favour. Even the first casualty might be seen as an omen of defeat.

Weaponry in ancient times consisted of a number of types. The best-known Malay weapon is the *keris*, the wavy-bladed short sword, which was normally used to stab rather than to slash. The *keris* and the spear or lance often had supernatural qualities attributed to them. They were often handed down through many generations as *pusaka*, heirlooms which could provide a special protective power to the descendants of an ancestor who made or used the weapon. Spears and *keris* could be highly decorative works of art, but were also known as being highly effective, well-wrought arms. Blowguns were however more feared by the Chinese traders. These weapons used by pirates could act at a distance, and were treated with vegetal poisons, making their effects particularly feared.

The *Malay Annals* of 1612 gives the impression that the Malays of Melaka were confounded by the Portuguese use of cannon in 1511. This is probably an anachronism; "Southeast Asians were familiar with firearms well before the arrival of the Portuguese." Why then did the annalist adopt this tone? One obvious answer is that he wished to explain away the Malays' defeat.

In the sixteenth century Southeast Asians began to cast bronze artillery pieces, but these too seem to have served more for ceremonial purposes than as effective weapons. "The most profound impact of the new [military] technologies, in Southeast Asia as in Europe, was in strengthening the authority of the regimes which possessed them over their hinterlands which did not."[8] During the seventeenth century, however, Southeast Asians became adept at producing their own flintlocks and muskets. These could be manufactured by villagers; the Bugis, Balinese and Minangkabau gunsmiths were best-known for their skills.[9] Thus by the end of the seventeenth century gunpowder had become a widespread commodity in Southeast Asia, not a monopoly of the elite.

The Srivijayan Era, A.D. 100–1000

After several centuries during which only vague reports from distant China are available to confirm the existence of several competing entrepots around the southern entrance to the Straits of Melaka, the kingdom of Srivijaya emerged in the late seventh century as a major political and commercial power. Between 672 and 689 Srivijaya's sway spread from its heartland at Palembang to encompass the entire Straits of Melaka and perhaps strategic points on the west coast of Borneo and western Java as well. By 775 isthmian Thailand was also part of this South Sumatra-centric sphere of influence. For the next 300 years Srivijaya's capital Palembang engrossed international shipping passing between the Indian subcontinent and the Chinese empire. The wealth from this seaborne equivalent of the Silk Road raised Srivijaya to a level of prosperity which elicited expressions of admiration and respect even from the imperial court of China. Some Srivijayan officials rose to become leaders in foreign merchant communities established in ports along the south coast of China, where the Chinese allowed foreign diplomatic missions to present tribute and engage in strictly controlled but highly lucrative trade with designated Chinese merchants.

Srivijaya's sphere of control extended to the northern entrance to the Straits of Melaka, but the nature of the kingdom's influence there is difficult to describe. The Chinese considered Srivijaya in the late first millennium A.D. to be a "double kingdom": one centre of authority lay at Palembang, the other somewhere in the area of northern Sumatra or on the opposite coast, in the region of Kedah and southern Thailand. Archaeologists have identified important trading sites dating from this period at Sungai Mas, Kedah, and Laem Pho and Takuapa, southern Thailand, with abundant remains of ceramics and glassware from both China and the Persian Gulf. While there is evidence that these areas acknowledged Srivijaya's suzerainty, the Chinese report that the part of the kingdom situated in the northern Straits had its own administration.

The nature of the early polities in the Straits of Melaka has been a subject of study for many years. Early commentators, impressed by Chinese descriptions of the kingdom's wealth and power, concluded that Srivijaya could be classified as an early centralised "state", an autocratic empire.[10] Subsequent refinements in the theory of political evolution and the study of inscriptions from early Southeast Asia have significantly altered the terms of this discussion. Most historians are now of the opinion that coarse generalisations such as "state", based on a theory of unilinear political evolution applicable worldwide, do not accurately convey the range of legal, social and economic relations which existed in early Southeast Asia. For the moment, most scholars dealing with the early kingdoms of Southeast Asia prefer to use special terms such as "galactic polity"[11] or "mandala"[12] to refer to the class of political institutions found in the region, without making any commitments regarding the comparability of this class to those found in other parts of the world.

In the first millennium A.D., Southeast Asia contained few concentrations of dense settled agrarian populations. In a few fertile zones — first and foremost central Java, the Tonle Sap region of Cambodia, the fringes of the Chao Phraya valley in Thailand, the coast of Vietnam, and the Irrawaddy of Myanmar — there formed centres of civilisation able to mobilise sufficient human resources to build religious monuments of impressive size. The largest of these, Borobudur in Java, was unchallenged as Southeast Asia's largest structure from its building around A.D. 800 until Angkor Wat was built over 300 years later.

These monument-building kingdoms were able to persuade large numbers of people to contribute their labour and other resources to common religious projects, but their rulers had little power to compel their subjects to engage in large-scale military conquests. One might speculate that they also lacked the inclination to do so, but this may be too charitable. The image of the "world conqueror" was well-known in both the versions of Hinduism and Buddhism which evolved in Southeast Asia. The ideal world would be ruled by a single *cakravartin* (literally "wheel-turner") who would attain supreme power through his superior spiritual qualities (although in mythology the *cakravartin*'s destiny still had to be played out on the battlefield). In Southeast Asia, the ambitions of would-be world conquerors were checked by the ability of those subjects who were disinclined to play the roles of the subordinate characters in the martial epics to move out of reach of the military recruiters. Fertile land suitable for agriculture was not scarce in the Southeast Asia of A.D. 1000.

The Javas and Cambodias of early Southeast Asia had few characteristics in common with the Frances and Germanys of medieval Europe, but those that did exist are highly instructive. In particular it is fascinating to observe that, just as the monument builders of both Europe and Southeast Asia were militaristic agrarian kingdoms in the hinterlands, in both regions the important trading kingdoms were situated on the margins of the land-based empires and left less conspicuous monuments.[13] It is also useful to note that medieval Europe possessed geographic analogues of ancient Southeast Asian maritime kingdoms, of which Venice is but the best-known.[14]

In strategic terms, it seems to have been in the interests of the major land-based empires of Europe to allow the small trading ports at the peripheries to maintain their own independent existence. If the old idea of the militaristic "state" is not a useful concept to use in describing ancient kingdoms in either Southeast Asia or Europe, the concept of symbiosis between extensive militaristic hierarchically-organised agrarian polities and smaller trading kingdoms with more flexible social structures may hold more possibilities for future comparative historical research, with implications for long-term strategic studies.

In ancient Southeast Asia, since manpower was a scarce resource, it was conserved as much as possible. In warfare, manpower was hoarded rather than expended; the objective of much military activity in Southeast Asia until the nineteenth century was to capture people, not land. Thus the whole nature of the strategic equation in early Southeast Asia has to be viewed in an entirely different light from the calculations used to formulate long-term plans in more familiar circumstances of over-population such as existed in ancient Europe, India, or China.

Contemporary documentary sources as well as descriptions of Southeast Asia from the period of early European contact suggest that one source of Srivijaya's ability to monopolise Southeast Asian maritime commerce, and indeed all shipping between the Indian Ocean and South China Sea, lay in her ability to attract the allegiance of skilled seafaring people. Although traders from other parts of Southeast Asia, India, and as far west as the Persian Gulf were found in South China's ports, all evidence suggests that the ships themselves which carried goods and people through the Straits were mainly if not exclusively built and sailed by Indonesians, principally the people of North Java, East Sumatra, western Borneo, and the islands off the southern tip of the Malay Peninsula denominated the Riau and Lingga Archipelagoes.

Srivijaya seems to have been born in a series of military actions. The first inscriptions from the late seventh century refer to military movements including an expedition against *bhumi jawa* "which had not yet submitted." This inscription was found at Kota Kapur, on the island of Bangka, which formed a primary source of skilled seafaring manpower in ancient Southeast Asia. Srivijaya's inscriptions all come from a brief period at the very beginning of the kingdom. Once the kingdom had established its suzerainty over the Straits of Melaka, and possibly western Borneo and western Java, carving of inscriptions ceased. No doubt other kinds of literary activity continued, but using perishable materials which have not survived. For the next three centuries, a kind of equilibrium seems to have existed in the Straits, whereby Srivijaya continued to reap the harvest of inter-Asian sea trade.

Although the Srivijayan inscriptions contain references to military commanders, using a Sanskrit term, their duties are not described. Judging from much later practices in effect when Europeans arrived, it would seem that there was no tradition of a standing army in any of the polities of the Straits of Melaka. As in ancient Europe, in times of need armed men were mobilised by the nobles faithful to the paramount ruler. In the Srivijayan domain, the significant source of armed force would have been found on the water, not on the land. The main fields of battle in the region were at sea. The main resources worth fighting over were the cargoes of trading ships and the populations of coastal and estuarine villages.

The unique drowned landscape of western Indonesia fostered the birth of a specialised ecological adaptation. Although we do not yet possess any archaeological data to date the inception of this way of life, it seems likely that for thousands of years the swampy coasts and offshore islands of the Straits have been exploited by specialised ethnic groups who live as nomads not in deserts, but at sea, spending most of their lives in boats migrating from place to place in search of food and goods for trade. In the nineteenth century these people consisted of many small groups, each with its own area and ethnic name. Although there are still many remnants of these groups, their way of life is rapidly vanishing. A generic term for peoples pursuing this way of life in the Straits is *Orang Laut*, Malay for "Sea People."[15]

The *Orang Laut* have formed a resource of potential strategic significance for much of the history of the Straits. Their importance is basically due to two factors: their military potential, and their economic role. As specialised hunters and gatherers of sea products, the *Orang Laut* have long been courted by coastal middlemen who have made significant profits by exchanging cloth, metal, and imported luxury goods for pearls, tortoise shell, coral, and seafood. From very early times, it would seem that the *Orang Laut* of the southern Straits had a special relationship with the ruler of Srivijaya and his successors. This relationship can be linked to the Kota Kapur inscription, set up in an area usually associated with this population, and traced through a series of semi-legendary chronicles, especially the *Sejarah Melayu* or "*Malay Annals*."[16] A common motif in the legends is the desire of the fragmented sea nomads for a focal point, a sense of cohesion, an intermediary with the outside world, a source of needed goods, and a means by which they could satisfy their desire for a ruler with divine protective powers.

When the *Orang Laut* were not under the direction of a strong ruler, they could change a formerly strategic place into one to be avoided. Although we lack sufficient historical documentation to tell the story, it is likely that the rise of Srivijaya was in part due to the success of the early ruler in discovering a mixture of ritual and commercial inducements which was able to convert the *Orang Laut* from a dis-organised population not averse to marauding and piracy, thus discouraging maritime trade, into a community which gave up their predatory propensities in return for a steady income derived from compelling ships to call at Srivijaya's ports to pay dues and delivering tribute in the form of sea products, in return for which they received *anugerah*, "tokens of esteem" from Srivijaya's ruler. The earliest source which describes trade routes in the Malay Peninsula is a fragment of a report written by two Chinese envoys sent to a major port in the southern Mekong Delta called Funan in about A.D. 250. The original report is lost, but citations of it in later works show that the route from the South China Sea to the Indian Ocean did not pass through the Straits of Melaka. Instead ships unloaded their cargoes on the east coast of what is now the Thai portion of the Malay Peninsula. From here the goods were transported across to the west coast, reloaded on other ships, and carried across the Bay of Bengal.

It is possible that such an arduous procedure was adopted because the route through the Straits of Melaka was unknown at this time. This seems quite unlikely, however, because at Funan the envoys obtained information about ports in western Indonesia, perhaps in South Sumatra, which had contact with India. It is quite likely that South Sumatran ports were in contact with both India and Funan at this time. It is also likely that the portage was undertaken because of unsafe conditions in the

Straits themselves, due to the piratical activities of the inhabitants. While it is true that several portage routes across the peninsula continued to be used until the twentieth century, the direct sea route was obviously superior in terms of time and effort needed to transport goods. When conditions in the Straits were safe, the transpeninsular routes were less used.

When the Malay court reformed itself in the Johore-Riau area after Melaka fell to the Portuguese in 1511, the *Orang Laut* are known to have formed one of the four main components of the Johore power structure — the others being the ruler himself; his ministers; and the council of nobles, *orang kaya*. It is probable that such a structure reflects the older system in the Straits as well, but we have no resources with which to study this period.[17] The various *suku* ("tribe") of the *Orang Laut* had specialised duties in the court. Positions as couriers and envoys obviously suited their ability to travel rapidly by water. Others were blacksmiths, including swordmakers; this specialty is less easy to account for, but is well attested. The swordmaking specialty may have been related to the other duty which they fulfilled: as armed levees.

The *Orang Laut* were mainly bound to the Malay rulers by ties of personal loyalty rather than desire for financial compensation. They rejected attempts by other individuals to purchase their loyalty. They voyaged from Johore and Riau as far as Thailand to avenge the "rude handling" of ships belonging to the Johore Sultan. The *Sejarah Melayu* shows however that they did expect some kind of generalised reciprocity of a material nature. Archaeological surveys in the Pulau Tujuh sector of the Riau Archipelago have recovered substantial evidence that *Orang Laut* burials of the thirteenth through fifteenth centuries contained large quantities of Chinese, Thai and Vietnamese porcelain and glassware. The Pulau Tujuh sector was not on the international trade route at the time; it thus seems probable that the *Orang Laut* obtained these prestigious items from the Malay rulers of Singapore. This would be but one example of the type of goods which the *Orang Laut* might have received as gifts from the Malay rulers in exchange for their loyalty. By directing the *Orang Laut*'s energies into more predictable channels, strong Malay rulers could keep piracy sufficiently in check to make the voyage through the Straits attractive to merchants.

A second focus of historic *Orang Laut* activity in addition to Bangka is found on the island of Karimun. This island is situated in the centre of the southern entrance to the Straits of Melaka, about 30 km west of Singapore. Karimun may well have been known to the Chinese as early as the Tang Dynasty (A.D. 618–906), under the name Luo-yue, which several scholars believe is a transcription for the Malay word *laut*, "sea". This place was not an important port, nor did it ever send any missions to China.[18] It is said to have lain on the northern shore of the Straits of Melaka, opposite Srivijaya,[19] according to the *Xin Tang-shu* of Jia Dan, A.D. 1060. The context of this and later references suggests that this place was a rendezvous for shipping, rather than a port of call.

There are two reasons for suspecting that Luo-yue is Karimun. The first is that in later centuries Karimun played the role of landmark where ships would rendezvous before sailing east. The second is the presence of an inscription on the north coast of Karimun. The inscription is undated but from the style of script epigraphers conclude that it was probably carved during the Srivijaya period, perhaps between A.D. 800 and 1000. The text is written in Sanskrit language and Nagari script. The first part of the inscription is not controversial; it mentions "the illustrious feet of the illustrious Gautama, the Mahayanist". References to feet in Hindu and Buddhist inscriptions are common; they are often used as symbols for the high and mighty, who could not be referred to directly, for it would be disrespectful to do so. The last phrase, although it is formed of Sanskrit roots, has not been found in any other Sanskrit text; its precise intention is still obscure.[20]

Karimun Island holds a commanding position at the southern entrance to the Straits: on the east it is only nine km from Johore on the Malay Peninsula, on the west it is 20 km from Pulau Rangsang, a large but swampy and sparsely inhabited island separated from Sumatra by only a narrow and shallow strip of water. Just south of Pulau Rangsang lies the mouth of the Kampar River which leads to the densely populated Minangkabau hinterland in West Sumatra. Several sites of ancient Buddhist monuments lie along the Kampar's course, the most famous being Muara Takus, a collection of ruins of brick temples built around A.D. 1000 or slightly later. The inscription itself is unique in Southeast Asia. It is carved in letters about 30 cm high on the side of a cliff on the north side of Karimun. From the top of the cliff one has a complete view of the Straits. It would be difficult to pass an obser-vation post here without being observed. Near the foot of the granite cliff is a stream of fresh water. A Portuguese author named Tome Pires who arrived in Melaka soon after its conquest in 1511 says that the people of Karimun were *Selates*, his word for *Orang Laut* (probably derived from *Orang Selat*, "People of the Strait"). Pires calls the small islands between Karimun and Rangsang the "Selates Islands".[21]

In the late nineteenth century Karimun's population was still largely composed of descendants of *Orang Laut*. The custom of dwelling permanently on boats was still followed by some *Orang Laut* of Karimun after World War II.[22] In the late 1980s a group called the *Orang Akit* resided a few kilometres west of the inscription site. They possessed wooden houses on land, but many families owned fishing boats which provided a major source of their livelihood. They described themselves as descendants of intermarriage between *Orang Laut* and Chinese, and belonged to a religion which they described as Buddhist. One of their ritual activities involved periodically decorating the site of the inscription with flags of coloured cloth. In the 1840s, Karimun was notorious as the base of a group of piratical *Orang Laut* of the *suku Galang*. The *Galang* pirates were a scourge of Singapore shipping. It seems likely that in earlier times Singapore, especially the Kallang Basin, had formed part of their range. When Raffles arrived in January 1819, the *Orang Laut* formed the majority of Singapore's population.

The significance of the Karimun inscription obviously derives not from its contents, which even if totally deciphered would not afford any important historical illumination. Its interest lies rather in the fact that as a late Srivijayan inscription it indicates that Karimun was more than an ordinary island for the southern Straits population. The chief of Karimun may have had special duties in the Srivijayan kingdom. It is likely that the island's role as a rendezvous for foreign shipping also made it a natural site for a lookout point.

The role of an intelligence-gathering position was vital to the Srivijayan system. In 1178 the Chinese author Zhou Qufei remarked that "If some foreign ship, passing this place [i.e. the capital of the southern Straits, then at Malayu-Jambi], should not enter here, an armed party would certainly come out and kill them to the last." A few years later, in 1225, the harbourmaster of Canton, Zhau Rugua, wrote in similar terms that "If a merchant ship passes by without entering, their boats go forth to make a combined attack, and all are ready to die [in the attempt]. This is the reason why this country is a great shipping centre."[23] The use of armed force to compel ships to enter a port was based on the requirement that all ships entering the harbour had to pay duties. It seems that the policy of using armed force to force ships to pay duties even if they had no desire to trade was an ancient feature of Asian maritime commerce. As early as the time of Ptolemy around A.D. 100, ships which called at ports where no foreign trade was permitted were escorted away under armed guard.[24] Such a system was found in Aceh (North Sumatra) as recently as the nineteenth century.[25]

Karimun's importance in the pre-European period of the Straits of Melaka can now be put in perspective. Karimun had no resources other than its *Orang Laut* and its location. Despite its potential as an intelligence-gathering station, it never became the centre of an important political entity. The island did however continue to play an important role in strategic calculations in the nineteenth century; as we shall see, Raffles considered it as a possible location for his planned base in the southern Straits.

A New Phase: The Rise of Malayu-Jambi, 1025–1275

At the start of the eleventh century Srivijaya was at the height of its prosperity. Its rulers in this period endowed temples in China and India. No ports in the Straits area had dealings with foreign merchants except with leave from the Srivijayan ruler. The wealth from port dues and other trade-related sources flowed to a very limited group of Sumatran nobles. In 1025 a calamity befell Srivijaya. The Chola kingdom of South India launched a naval raid which abducted the Srivijayan king. No more is heard of him; probably he died in captivity in India. For the next 100 years, most of Srivijaya's old domains in the area of the northern Straits of Melaka, from Barus on Sumatra's west coast to Kedah in north peninsular Malaysia and Takuapa in South Thailand, seem to have been dominated by representatives of powerful Tamil trading companies. These organisations combined commercial, military and diplomatic functions in a manner more than mildly reminiscent of the later European East India Companies.[26]

The Bujang Valley in Kedah seems to have been the central node of Tamil power in Southeast Asia. Numerous shrines were built there in typical South Indian style, and some sources suggest that the Chola crown prince was sent there as a kind of viceroy to learn the arts of ruling before returning to South India to assume the throne.[27] In the southern Straits, the center of trade during the late eleventh century shifted from Palembang to Jambi. The ancient kingdom of Malayu centred here had opened economic and diplomatic relations with China even before Srivijaya's rise.

For 250 years, from about 1025 to 1275, no single successor to Srivijayan thalassocracy appeared. Instead a number of busy ports evolved. Archaeological research along the east coast of Sumatra has identified several sites, some containing extensive and dense layers of broken Chinese porcelain, others with sizeable brick monuments mainly constituting ruined Buddhist structures. After the early twelfth century, Chola power shrank and disappeared from Southeast Asia due to the gradual decline of the kingdom in its home base in South India. Simultaneously a new phenomenon appeared which had a momentous impact on the Straits of Melaka: the arrival of the first Chinese immigrants.

The Song Dynasty came under increasing pressure from Mongols, and in 1126 the northern capital at Luoyang fell. The Chinese capital moved south, but for the next 150 years the court was under constant military pressure. Cut off from overland trade routes, and in need of funds for defense, the Song relaxed many of the old restrictions on contact between Chinese and foreigners. This enabled aspiring South Chinese to initiate their own commercial voyages. As a result, overseas Chinese settlements began to appear along the coasts of the Straits of Melaka in the twelfth century.

The inception of Chinese settlement overseas had two important effects on Southeast Asian society. It fostered the development of an urban-rural dichotomy, which does not seem to have previously existed in Southeast Asia; and it rendered impossible the reimposition of a Srivijayan-style monopoly on foreign trade. Chinese merchants, endowed with great commercial power and backed by the prestige of the Chinese court, could not be forced to confine their activities to one or two ports.

In 1225 Zhau Rugua mentioned for the first time a place in the Straits area called the "Dragon's Tooth Strait": "In the winter, with the monsoon, you sail a little more than a month and then come to Ling-ya-mon, where one-third of the passing merchants (put in) before entering this country (of San-fo-ts'i) [Malayu-Jambi]."[28] The translator-editors of the English text note that:

... some Chinese scholars, consulted on the meaning of this ambiguous phrase, think the passage may be mutilated and that it implies that a levy of one third ad valorem was made on merchandize at Ling-ya-mon (Lingga Strait and Island) before merchants were allowed to proceed to San-fo-ts'i. This interpretation seems forced; it appears much more likely that the Dragon's Tooth Strait was a convenient harbour for ships coming from the west and from Chan-ch'ong when sailing for San-fo-ts'i, and that many of them stopped there. Ling-ya-mon, "Dragon's Tooth Strait," thus would have referred to Berhala Strait, south of Lingga Island, in 1225, and signified a port of call where some dues were probably collected.[29]

Systematically acquired archaeological evidence from Lingga is not yet available, but unconfirmed reports suggest that Chinese ceramics of the Song Dynasty may be found there. This affords a preliminary reason to agree with Hirth and Rockhill that in 1225 the Dragon's Tooth may have been a Chinese name for the strait south of Lingga Island, where some ships stopped to pay duty, perhaps in preference to travelling to Jambi. The term "Ling-ya-mon" may have been used simply because of its resemblance to the local name "Lingga". The name reoccurs a century later, in a slightly different form, and possibly referring to a location in Singapore.

The Classical Singapore Phase, 1275–1400

When the story of Singapore begins, in the late thirteenth century, the societies of the Straits of Melaka area were in the process of adjusting to new social and commercial factors. The new presence of Chinese shipping played a strategic role, the effect of which was still in the process of making itself felt. Also a new type of Southeast Asian political expansion was beginning. The people of the Chao Phraya basin, mainly newly immigrant Thais, were in the process of forming a centralised kingdom which would eventually overthrow the Khmer and become the most powerful force on the mainland of Southeast Asia. More directly relevant to Singapore is the kingdom of Singhasari in East Java. In about 1275 Singhasari reached a new level of integration and reversed the centuries-old relationship with the Malays in which the Malays had usually had the upper hand in their rivalry.

It is not yet generally appreciated that Singapore even existed during the period before the arrival of Sir Thomas Stamford Raffles in January 1819; it is even less widely known that Singapore once possessed significant traces of ancient fortifications. These traces were however clearly described by Dr. John Crawfurd, during his first visit to Singapore.[30] Subsequently (in 1823) he became Singapore's second Resident. Dr. Crawfurd visited Singapore for the first time between 21 January and 25 February 1822, during the course of a voyage from India to Siam which he undertook on a diplomatic mission. Crawfurd had long been in the region; he had joined the East India Company in 1803, and was sent to Penang in 1808. He had worked in several positions during the British occupation of Java from 1811–1815, and in 1820 he published a long work, *A History of the Indian Archipelago*, which demonstrated his deep interest in history and antiquities.[31] He was therefore both naturally inclined to notice such aspects of his surroundings, and well qualified by experience in other parts of Asia to identify and make accurate observations of ruins.

In his journal's entry for 3 February, Crawfurd described a morning stroll "round the walls and limits of the ancient town of Singapore." His circuit began at the beach, probably along what is now the edge of the Padang, to "a wall" which he followed until it came to a hill (Fort Canning), thence back to his starting point by the Singapore River. He took pains to describe the wall in some detail. Its breadth he estimated at about sixteen feet (5 m) at its base; obviously it tapered to a narrower dimension at the top, but he does not describe the wall's cross-section. The wall's height he calculated as 8 or 9 feet (approximately 2.4 to 2.7 m), and its length a mile (1.6 km) from the shore to the foot of the hill. At that point the wall terminated.

The wall was paralleled for about two-thirds of its length by a little stream which flowed on its north side. At a certain point, about 1 km inland, near the site of the present National Museum, the wall seems to have terminated, while the stream continued in a more or less direct line. Where the wall ended, however, a dry ditch or moat began, and ran up the side of the hill. Crawfurd does not describe this moat any further; perhaps that area was still overgrown by vegetation. Crawfurd inspected the wall closely, noting that there were no signs of such refinements as embrasures or loop-holes for guns. Furthermore, there were no signs that similar walls had once defended the other borders of the "ancient town". From these details he concluded "that the works of Singapore were not intended against firearms, or an attack by sea; or that if the latter, the inhabitants considered themselves strong in their naval force, and therefore thought any other defences in that quarter superfluous." Although it is not expressly stated, the wall must have been constructed of earth, and could perhaps be better termed an embankment. There were ruins of structures on Fort Canning Hill, which Crawfurd describes as made of baked brick "of good quality", so one may take his silence on the matter of the wall's composition as evidence that it was not constructed of that material.

The "Old Malay lines" were used as a landmark and reference point in the 1820s. A letter from the Resident, Col. William Farquhar, to Lt. L.W. Hull, Secretary to Lt.-Governor T.S. Raffles, dated 23 December 1822 states that:

> The range to the westward of Government Hill towards Panglima Prang compound remains unoccupied with the exception of a portion of the North East side of the one near the western extremity of the old Malay lines where a Chinese gambier plantation had been commenced prior to our establishment at Singapore.[32]

The wall was still in existence in the mid-1820s. A map of Singapore drawn in 1825 clearly indicates a feature termed "The Old Lines of Singapore". The location of this feature corresponds precisely to Crawfurd's description of the old wall and stream, and it can therefore be concluded that the "Old Lines" and the "wall" are the same thing.[33]

There is a brief reference in an early tourist guide to Singapore to the dry ditch or moat on the slope of the hill.[34] The stream on the outside of the wall came to be called the Freshwater Stream, and a bridge was built across it near its mouth. Subsequently the stream was canalised and is now called the Stamford Canal. Most of its former course is now invisible; that which remains appears from beneath the ground beside the Cathay Building, between Orchard and Handy Roads, where it runs within concrete banks, appearing to be no more interesting than any other artificial drainage channel, until it disappears at the junction of Buyong Road and Buyong Lane. A small plaque commemorating the former bridge over the river's mouth is placed at the junction of Stamford Road and Connaught Drive, opposite the northeast corner of the Padang, but it is doubtful that one out of a thousand passers-by takes note of the unobtrusive black plaque, and even if one were to do so, it would be a mystery as to why a bridge should ever have existed there, since the old stream is now invisible as it courses to the sea kilometres further east, beyond Marina Park.

The course of the wall, or "Old Lines", is identical to that of modern Stamford Road. The embankment was undoubtedly levelled at an early stage of nineteenth-century Singapore's development. The map of 1825 is the only one to depict it. The former existence of this now-vanished landmark deserves to be more widely known and appreciated. The Old Lines demonstrate that ancient Singapore occupied an unusual position in early Southeast Asian history. By investigating the precise nature of this peculiarity, we obtain an instructive glimpse into the position of ancient Singapore in the political, economic and geographical contexts of early Southeast Asia. All these factors in turn are intimately associated with the particular topic of the history of military strategy in the environs of Singapore.

Since, as stated earlier, ancient Southeast Asian warfare was endemic but fought to capture people not land, why was a wall built in Singapore? When was it built? What was its purpose? That the date of the construction must be attributed to a time earlier than the beginning of the nineteenth century is clear; in 1819 Singapore's population totalled 500 at most. Many of these were boat-dwelling sea nomads who did not build houses on land, much less fortifications.

An archaeological survey of Sumatra identified seven sites of *benteng*, "earthworks/walled sites". Of these seven, two were judged to post-date European arrival; one was not studied. Another, Muara Takus, is a Buddhist site consisting of a number of religious structures surrounded by a low wall, in this instance built of brick; the wall's function is clearly symbolic. There is a second, earthen wall associated with the site, the function of which is unclear. There is however no evidence that the site, which lies in the centre of Sumatra, far from the sea, was ever a trading centre or occupied by a dense population, and so it would seem that the second wall's purpose was probably not defensive either.[35]

The site of Bawang, also known as Haur Kuning, in the province of Lampung, is associated with an inscription in Old Javanese dated A.D. 997, and a stone foundation. The site at the time of the survey was overgrown with jungle, so no firm interpretations of the wall's function, or even its extent, could be formed — but once again the site's location, in a hinterland location, argues against a defensive function.

The site of Mambang, in South Sumatra Province, lies on the bank of the Musi River, upstream from Palembang, Srivijaya's capital. Although pre-European statuary has been found approximately 4 km away from the site, only nineteenth-century ceramics have so far been found in association with the *benteng* itself. Finally, the site of Pugungraharjo, also in Lampung, consists of a very extensive complex of enigmatic remains enclosed by a large earthen rampart and trench. The remains include terraced pyramids of earth reinforced with stone, on top of one of which villagers discovered a statue of thirteenth-century style; a set of stone seats surrounding a stone pillar forming a complex associated with non- or pre-Indic religious practices; and some areas where Chinese ceramics dating from the fourteenth and fifteenth centuries have been found, brought to the surface during agricultural operations.[36] Once again, the site lies in the interior rather than near the coast, and does not seem to have been an important trading center. Zhau Rugua, harbourmaster of Canton in 1225, stated that the capital of Sanfoqi ("Three Vijayas", perhaps referring to Malayu's capital which probably then was located at a site now called Muara Jambi) was surrounded by a wall built of bricks.[37] No trace of such a wall now remains, although there are ruins of several brick religious complexes extant, each surrounded by walls.

From this data, we can conclude that in all Sumatra no sites with evidence of permanent fortifications dating from the pre-European (or pre-Islamic) period have yet been found. It is possible that such sites may yet be discovered, but they cannot have been common at best. This circumstance suggests that fourteenth-century Singapore was highly unusual among trading ports along the Straits of Melaka: its population cooperated to construct a permanent fortification, investing much labour in an immoveable asset. This can only mean that they believed Singapore to be a location with more than common potential as a trading port. The Singaporeans perceived threats; we can only speculate as to what they may have been, but it seems likely that they were the dual expanding mandalas of the Thai and the Javanese. To turn for a moment to a subject which may be more correctly termed tactical rather than strategic, one may ask why the Singapore wall was located along the north side of the settlement only. One can only speculate, but it would seem that the re-sidents of fourteenth-century Singapore considered their naval defenses adequate to meet any threat from that quarter, and that any invader would choose to land somewhere away from the settlement rather than launch a frontal attack from the sea. The fortification was therefore designed to forestall an invasion from the landward flank rather than the seaward frontage. It is suggestive to compare this pattern of threat perception with that which materialised much later, in the twentieth century.[38]

The name "Dragon's Tooth Strait" reappears in Chinese works on Southeast Asia in the fourteenth century. In 1320 a mission from the reigning Yuan Dynasty visited this place to obtain tame elephants. Perhaps stimulated by this attention from the imperial court, the people of the Dragon's Tooth Strait sent a diplomatic/commercial mission to China in 1325. About five years later a Chinese merchant, Wang Dayuan, visited Lung-ya-men and other places in Southeast Asia. Was this Dragon's Tooth Strait the same as the one mentioned a century earlier by Zhau Rugua? The two principal authorities who have discussed this question concur that at this time the Strait lay somewhere close to Singapore, though they disagree as to its precise location. C.A. Gibson-Hill concluded that the Strait which Wang described must have been the western entrance to Keppel Harbour, the narrow stretch of water which passes between Labrador Point and Sentosa Island.[39] Another scholar, J.V.G. Mills, suggested that the Strait was in fact that now known as Singapore Main Strait, about 15 km south of Singapore.[40] In either case, the Dragon's Tooth Strait now seems to have become the main artery for shipping entering the Straits of Melaka, whereas formerly the main route seems to have passed south of Lingga. This northward shift of the trade route must have occurred somewhere between 1225 and 1330. What was the reason for this change? No clear answer can be given. From 1275 until at least 1292, South Sumatra seems to have been dominated by the East Javanese kingdom of Singhasari. The most overt demonstration of Singhasari's claim to overlordship is a statue of the Buddhist deity Amoghapasha found in the Batanghari valley of Jambi, with an inscription stating that the statue was given to the people of Sumatra by King Kertanagara of Singhasari. This image is a near-exact replica of another found at Candi Jago, near Kertanagara's capital in East Java. The erection of a statue of a deity closely associated with the king was a common way of asserting claims to overlordship in ancient India; it seems likely that a similar intention explains this statue's presence in the heartland of the old Malay kingdom. Possibly the trade route moved further north to avoid interference from the Javanese. However, this explanation seems unsatisfactory. If the Javanese could reach Jambi, they could certainly reach Singapore. Also, foreign merchants would have no need to avoid Javanese-controlled areas; it made no difference to them whether the taxing authority was local or distant.

Certainly the use of the route near Singapore by ships intending to sail directly from the east through the Straits of Melaka was much more economical than the route further south. Possibly the Chinese sailors only learned of the existence of this route at about the beginning of the fourteenth century. The complex nature of the waters, winds and land features in the Riau Archipelago caused the early European mariners much difficulty. It took the British some time to discover the existence of the Keppel Harbour strait; Raffles was unaware of it when he founded the British settlement at the mouth of the Singapore River in 1819. Only the *Orang Laut* knew all the intricacies of the area, and they did not willingly share their knowledge with outsiders. Archaeological evidence suggests that settlement around the Singapore River only began in the second half of the thirteenth century. It is impossible to tell whether the inception of this settlement was the cause or the result of the shift in the trade route. The most that can be said in the present state of our knowledge is that the two developments were interrelated.

Wang Dayuan applies the name "Dragon's Tooth Strait" to a place which is "bordered by two hills of the Tan-ma-hsi barbarians which look like dragons' teeth, between them there is a waterway."[41] He describes the "fields" of this place as "barren", yielding little rice, indicating that his use of the term also included the land on either side of the Strait. Next he describes the custom of the "chief" who puts on ceremonial dress and a bejewelled crown, which was found in the ground "in ancient times", to mark the beginning of the new year. The common people, he says, wore cotton jackets and black sarongs. Chinese were already living "side by side" with the indigenous people. The items traded there by the Chinese were "red gold, blue satin, cotton prints, Ch'u-chou-fu porcelain, iron caldrons, and such like things."[42] Ch'u-chou (in modern transcription Quzhou) is the name of a prefecture in Jiangxi province, in the region of the famous Longquan pottery kilns.

This information would suggest that the Dragon's Tooth Strait was a typical port in the southern Straits which existed mainly due to trade rather than locally produced items. In fact the source explicitly states that "Neither fine products nor rare objects come from here. All are obtained from intercourse with Chuan-chou traders." Wang then goes on to add further information which shows that the intentions of the Dragon's Tooth Strait inhabitants were not at all peaceful, however:

> When junks sail to the Western Ocean the local barbarians allow them to pass unmolested but when on their return the junks reach Ji-li-men (Karimon), [then] the sailors prepare their armour and padded screens as a protection against arrows for, of a certainty, some two or three hundred pirate prahus will put out to attack them for several days. Sometimes [the junks] are fortunate enough to escape with a favouring wind; otherwise the crews are butchered and the merchandise made off with in quick time.[43]

It is difficult to reconcile the two images of Lung-ya-men which Wang presents. How could Chinese traders live side by side with the pirates who butchered Chinese traders? Is it possible that the references to the traders had been transposed from the description of the next port? This was called Pancur (Banzu), meaning "spring [of water]" in Malay.[44] He described it as "the hill back of Lung-ya-men, it is like a coil cut off [at the top], it rises to a hollow-topped summit enclosed in a series of [rising] slopes [lit., coils]; as a consequence the people live all around it."[45] Here too "The soil is poor and grain scarce." In contrast to the people of Lung-ya-men, the people here "By custom and disposition are honest." Their appearance also was much different from those at Lung-ya-men: they wore their hair short rather than long, with fancy head-cloths of gold-brocaded satin, and red "oiled-cloths" as sarongs. Their industries included making salt by boiling sea water, and brewing rice wine. Items offered for sale were the casques of hornbills, which the Chinese carved into decorative items; cotton; and laka wood, the latter possibly a local product. In exchange the Chinese traders offered green cotton cloth, iron, both in bars and in the form of pots, "native cotton prints", "dark red gold" and other items not specified.

The name *pan-tsu* is not used for the hill in any other source, but it is certainly derived from the Malay word for spring, *pancur*. Indeed in 1819 there was a spring on the west side of the hill, which according to the inhabitants had been the king's bathing place during the time when a Malay royal family had lived on the hill. This may be a reference to the fourteenth century. The spring was an important source of water for ships during the 1820s, when an aqueduct was built to collect the water and channel it from the spring to the bank of the river. Perhaps it was used in a similar manner during the fourteenth century, which would explain why this name of "spring" would come to stand for the hill.

It seems incontrovertible that the Lung-ya-men by this time was the strait between Labrador Point and Sentosa. This identification is reinforced by the nature of the topography there. Until it was blown up in 1848, a pillar of granite stood several metres from the south shore and rose several metres in the air. This distinctive feature was known in the early nineteenth century as "Lot's Wife" in English, and "Sail Rock" (Batu Berlayar) in Malay. To Chinese sailors, this rock might have reminded them of the two wooden pegs at the bows of their junks through which the anchor cables ran. In the Amoy language of Southeast China these pegs are also known as "Dragon's teeth".[46]

Sentosa Island was formerly known by several names, one of which is Blakang Mati. The meaning of the name is obscure; the words literally mean "Behind Dead". According to the Malay author Abdullah Munshi, in the early nineteenth century there were still many stories of the pirate lair which once existed there. His description is rather colourful, but may not be too greatly exaggerated:

> Now at this time the seas round Singapore so far from being navigated freely by men, were feared even by jinns and devils, for along the shores were the sleeping-huts of the pirates. Whenever they plundered a ship or a ketch or a cargo-boat, they brought it into Singapore where they shared the spoils and slaughtered the crew, or fought to the death among themselves to secure their gains.
>
> All along the shore there were hundreds of human skulls rolling about on the sand; some old, some new, some with hair sticking to them, some with the teeth filed and others without... The Sea Gypsies were asked 'Whose are all these skulls?' and they replied 'These are the skulls of the men who were robbed at sea. They were slaughtered here. Wherever a fleet of boats or a ship is plundered it is brought to this

place for a division of the spoils. Sometimes there is wholesale slaughter among the crews when the cargo is grabbed.'[47]

The similarity of Munshi Abdullah's reported conversation to Wang Dayuan's fourteenth-century account of the Dragon's Tooth Strait is striking. It is difficult to understand why the Chinese sailors would have chosen to sail through this narrow passage, which has several natural hazards, as well as the human one, in preference to the broad Main Strait only 15 km south. One can only assume that once again incomplete knowledge was responsible.

Thus there were three place-names associated with the Singapore area in the fourteenth century. Lung-ya-men was the western entrance to Keppel Harbour and surrounding shores; Pancur was "the hill behind" this strait; archaeological and other evidence shows that this could be no other place than Fort Canning Hill. The third name, Dan-ma-xi, is a Chinese transliteration of Temasik. Wang's reference to Lung-ya-men as the strait between "two hills of the Dan-ma-xi barbarians" suggests that Temasik was a larger inclusive term. It must have been meant as a general toponym covering the south coast of Singapore and the offshore islands.

The name Temasik was relatively well-known in the fourteenth century. In 1330, perhaps precisely when Wang was visiting Pancur, a Vietnamese prince, Tran Nhat Duat, died. In his memorial, the Vietnamese annals mention that he could serve as an interpreter for the Malay envoys from Sach-ma-tich, the Vietnamese transcription of Temasik.[48] A Javanese poem written in the sixteenth century, the *Pararaton*, records that the famous Prime Minister of Majapahit, Gajah Mada, swore to unify the Indonesian archipelago by conquering a number of countries, among them Temasik. Although this source is not unimpeachable, indisputable confirmation for Majapahit's interest in and claims over Temasik is found in a Majapahit court poem dated 1365 in which Temasik appears in a list of Majapahit's vassals.[49] It is therefore established that by the middle of the fourteenth century Temasik had become a port of some importance, known from Java to Vietnam and among the traders of South China. There is yet another party who was also interested in Temasik: the expanding Thai.

To return now to the subject of Singapore's ancient fortification wall, it is quite possible that the wall already existed at the time of Wang's visit around 1330. In a section of his account describing the people of Hsien/Xian (usually interpreted as a Chinese transcription of "Siam"), he notes how a group of them had besieged Temasik for over a month. The people of Temasik however "shut up their gates" and held off the invaders. A stalemate ensued which was only relieved when a Chinese mission happened to pass by the place. This illustrative anecdote concerning ancient Temasik provides two useful pieces of evidence. First, it indicates that Chinese vessels not intending to call at Temasik regularly passed by close enough that they were able to see what was going on at the port. The normal sea lane thus ran very close to Temasik at this time. Second, it shows that the people of Temasik were in fact prepared for such an eventuality as a siege, a type of encounter which seems to have been rare in ancient Southeast Asia; in fact, the only other known description of such a military encounter also concerns Singapore. This is the Malay depiction of the attack on Singapore by the ruler of Majapahit during the reign of the last of the five kings mentioned in the *Sejarah Melayu*. The Javanese defeat Singapore due to treachery when a Singapore official, embittered against his ruler for an injustice done him, opens the gate of Singapore's fort after the battle had continued for several days without result. The fort itself is not described; it could have been a wooden stockade. However, the official and his wife were turned into stone in the moat of Singapura. This reference to the moat is reinforced by the statement that the rock could still be seen "to this day". This account corresponds to the Freshwater Stream on the north of the Old Lines of Singapore still visible in the early nineteenth century. The concern of the chronicler to point out a visible landmark which would confirm his version of events in early Singapore is interesting because it is unique; this is the only instance of such a reference to an existing trace of the past to be found in the entire *Sejarah Melayu*. Apparently the *parit Singapura* or "Singapore moat" was a feature of some renown in the Malay society of its time, as one would expect of an unusual defensive work.

The version of events leading to the fall of Singapore found in other works differs from that in the *Sejarah Melayu*. The Portuguese authors in Melaka recorded several versions of the history of Singapore's downfall. One of the most reliable in other matters, Tome Pires, who was writing only about 120 years after the event took place, says that Temasik's last ruler was a usurper from Sumatra named Parameswara. Parameswara had tried to declare independence from Java, but fled after the Javanese destroyed settlements on Bangka (probably these were his *Orang Laut* supporters). He came to Temasik, assassinated the local ruler, and "governed the channel and the islands...and he had not trade at all except that his people planted rice and fished and plundered their enemies, and lived on this the said channel of Singapore." This remark seems to be a reference to the piratical tendencies of the inhabitants. Parameswara had been accompanied by *Orang Laut* when he evacuated Palembang. While he stayed in Temasik, they occupied the waters around Karimun. According to another Portuguese author, Joao da Barros, the Singapore population hated the *Orang Laut* who came with Parameswara,[50] possibly because they had murdered a local man.

The murdered ruler of Singapore had been related to the king of Siam by marriage; probably Singapore at this time was a Siamese vassal. In revenge, after five years the Siamese attacked and drove Parameswara away. Another possibility is that he refused to pay tribute to Siam. The Chinese author Ma Huan in the early fifteenth century noted that Melaka in its early years paid tribute to them; failure to do so "would have provoked an attack".[51]

Parameswara evaded capture once again and fled into the jungles of the southern Malay peninsula. A few years later, his faithful *Orang*

Laut discovered the advantages of the site of Melaka and invited Parameswara there to start a third kingdom.[52] Da Barros also wrote that the Siamese, not the Javanese, were responsible for expelling Parameswara from Singapore to a place about 35 or 40 km upstream in what is now Johore.[53] The son of Alfonso d'Albuquerque, conqueror of Melaka, says that Parameswara was driven from Sumatra by a Javanese attack and came to Singapore; he adds the detail that a large town already existed there.[54]

Thus it seems clear that the attackers who invaded Singapore in about 1396 or 1397,[55] whether Javanese or Siamese, intended not to destroy Singapore but to punish one man, Parameswara. He successfully evaded capture twice, before founding a third centre north of the entrance to the Straits of Melaka. Here he seems to have found a site which was still sufficiently close to the south entrance to the Straits to enable him to regulate shipping, while simultaneously being remote from the attentions of both the expanding mandalas of the Javanese and the Siamese.

It seems that Melaka's rise was tied to Singapore's fall. Da Barros wrote that when Parameswara's old enemy the king of Siam died, Parameswara:

> began to compel the ships which formerly navigated in the Strait between Malacca and Sumatra that they should no longer go to Singapore and also the ships from the East which used to come there to exchange merchandise with those from the West, according to old custom; as a result of this Singapore began to become empty of merchants who came to live in Malacca.[56]

Nevertheless Temasik was still known to the Chinese of the early fifteenth century. The name appears on the Wu Bei Zhih sailing charts compiled from the records of the Zheng He voyages of 1403–1433, which in turn had been copied from an Arab original.[57] A Chinese author, Shun-feng, writing around 1430, mentions Dan-ma-xi Strait as a place where passengers could change ship.[58]

The name "Singapura" is first known from an Arab source of 1462.[59] It may however have been introduced by Parameswara after his usurpation, in order to give his new capital a grander-sounding name with a Sanskrit derivation. Parameswara seems to have considered Temasik to be the most eligible location to establish a successor to the old royal capital at Palembang which had represented a main political centre for a very long time: 700 years. The selection of Temasik as a plausible replacement for this ancient centre from which the trade of the Straits of Melaka could be controlled says much about the perception of Singapore's location in the eyes of the Malays. It seems probable that Parameswara was successfully dislodged from his position in Singapore because he was unable to muster support from among the local population. Nevertheless once Melaka became an alternative, trade was slowly drawn there from Singapore, and the population gravitated northward as well.

Factors which probably contributed to Singapore's fourteenth-century rise included the settlement of Chinese there; probably they established themselves there in small numbers when it was still a rather small settlement, and their interaction with local resource gatherers contributed to the port's growth. Perhaps some Chinese sailors discovered the shorter route through the Dragon's Tooth Strait around this time. Unsettled conditions in South Sumatra after the Javanese Pamalyu expedition of 1278 may also have made a more northerly approach an attractive option. Singapore itself possessed several advantageous features. One of these was the spring of water on Fort Canning Hill which gave the place its name in Wang Dayuan's *Dao I ji lue*. Water was always a critical resource both for settlements and for ships in pre-modern times. A dependable and plentiful source was a valuable asset; Raffles' concern for developing the spring in 1819 indicates the perpetuation of the prominence which thoughts of water occupied in strategic thought of that period as well. Another asset which Singapore possessed was its nautical manpower. Although difficult to control, manpower of any type was so scarce in early Southeast Asia that any cluster of people would automatically attract the attention of political leaders. The *Orang Laut* had special talents as well which made them potentially prized subjects: knowledge of local waterways, ability to travel quickly to transfer messages (intelligence has always been highly prized by both soldiers and merchants), and familiarity with and ability to harvest sea produce which formed an important part of the long-distance trade. The estuary of the Singapore River also provided a safe anchorage.

Had Parameswara not alienated the local population by assassinating their chief, it seems likely that Singapore and not Melaka would have been the great spice port of the fifteenth century which attracted the Portuguese attack of 1511. As a noted historian has asked rhetorically, "Would the Portuguese have been able to conquer and retain possession of a Malay capital in the heart of the offshore islands?"[60] At Singapore, the Malay ruler would have occupied a more formidable defensive position than at Melaka, with the strongholds of his naval forces the *Orang Laut* all around, from Karimun to Bintan. History however is replete with such opportunities for speculation, which must remain no more than interesting but untestable hypotheses.

The Melaka Phase, 1400–1511

Singapore was not abandoned after the foundation of Melaka. Several Arab, Chinese and Malay works of this period continue to mention it. In addition to Shun-feng's report that passengers could change ship at Dan-ma-xi Strait around 1430, Fei Xin, who accompanied several of Zheng He's voyages to Southeast Asia between 1403 and 1433, also mentioned that Lung-ya-men and its piratical inhabitants still existed. At least one of Zheng He's voyages, the sixth, which took place in 1421–1422, went through the Singapore Strait.[61] Dan-ma-xi is prominently shown on the Mao Kun map which derived from Zheng He's voyages.[62] In 1436 Singapore was still paying tribute to Siam.[63] The *Ming-Shih* reports that around 1415 some members of a party of Chinese envoys were going to Java, but were driven ashore at Pan-tsu-erh by a storm.[64] The Javanese had to ransom them from the inhabitants. In 1418 the Javanese ruler conveyed them back to China with an embassy of his own. A country named Ku-li-pan-tsu sent tribute to China frequently during the reign of the Yung-lo emperor (1403–1424).[65] *Ku-li* may be an incorrect transcription of *pulau* (meaning island, in Malay); this might therefore imply that Singapore was still a tributary of China during the early fifteenth century.

In the *Sejarah Melayu*, Singapore reappears after its fall to the Javanese, as the fief of the leader of Melaka's naval forces, the *Laksamana*. The *Sejarah Melayu* describes a sea battle between the fleets of Melaka and of the kingdom of Haru, Melaka's main Sumatran adversary. The *Laksamana*, Sri Bija 'diraja, defeated the Haru fleet though outnumbered three to one. His fief is not specifically mentioned, but his son, Tun Kudu, who succeeded to his position as *Laksamana*, is stated to have come from Singapore to attend a court ceremony at Melaka. Tun Kudu was eventually put to death for arriving late for another court festival; the *Sejarah Melayu* does not state where he had been on this occasion. It is however stated that Tun Kudu's son, Sang Stia Bentayan, was then given Singapura as his fief.[66] It would seem that in the early Melaka sultanate period, Singapore was the fief and fixed residence of the *Laksamanas* of Melaka. This indicates that Singapore was still the main source of seafaring manpower for the Melaka sultanate, a highly strategic resource. In a later period, however, the *Sejarah Melayu* records that the fief of the *Laksamana* was Sungai Raya.[67]

From the post-1511 period, the very last section of the Raffles Manuscript 18 version of the *Sejarah Melayu*[68] gives us the story of Pateh Ludang (or Adang), a Singapore chief who offended Sang Stia, fled to Pahang with his "tribesmen", but was treacherously killed there on the royal barge.[69] Thus during the fifteenth century Singapore continued to play a considerable role in the strategic considerations of the Melaka sultanate.

The Johore-Riau Phase 1511–1780

After the Portuguese capture of Melaka in 1511, the Malay court retreated to the Singapore area, but not onto Singapore itself; for the next several centuries the capital migrated back and forth between the upper reaches of the Johore River and the island of Bintan. Singapore may have been considered to be too exposed to attack. Bintan had been mentioned in Arab accounts of the thirteenth century; Ibn Said called it a pirate lair. Marco Polo, who passed through the area without stopping in 1292, mentioned Bintan, and called it a spice-exporting port. Bintan sent a mission to China in 1323, around the same time as Lung-ya-men.[70]

Pires in about 1515 knew of Singapore, but did not give it much prominence. He described the population of the Singapura channel as consisting of a few unimportant Selates villages. He did call it a "kingdom", though it controlled little territory. It did however continue to attract Chinese traders, with "infinite quantities of the black wood that grows in Singapore".[71] Alfonso d'Albuquerque in 1557 however gave Singapore more respect, describing it as having once been "a large and populous town, as is attested by the great ruins still visible today".[72] According to d'Albuquerque, after Melaka fell, the *Laksamana* moved to Singapura;[73] this would represent no more than his return to the *Laksamana*'s traditional appanage. In fact, one Portuguese source of approximately 1526, Joe de Lisboa, states that a *povoao* or "town" on Singapore had been destroyed by the Portuguese.[74]

Pigafetta, who accompanied Magellan's fleet around the world, heard of *Cinghapola* at the cape of *Malacha*.[75] In 1562 the Venetian scholar Josephus Moletius published a Latin translation of the first-century *Geography* of Ptolemaeus; he identified *Malaeucolon* promontory with *Cimcapula* cape.[76] In Luiz Vas de Camoes' epic *Os Lusiadas*, 1572, Singapore appears: "But on the land's end there, Cingapura you espy, where the sea lane narrow grows..." Francisco de Sa de Meneses, born at the end of the sixteenth century, in his epic poem *The Conquest of Malacca* (*Malacca Conquistada*), mentions Singapore several times. He repeats the story that Parameswara had killed the rightful ruler of Singapore and usurped his place.[77] Another verse contains the lines "Singapore thickly populated in previous times remains behind us beyond where the land ends there on the horizon. Malacca has grown to Singapore's disadvantage."[78]

During the sixteenth century, several sea fights took place near Singapore's shores. Godinho de Eredia sketched a maritime battle between Portuguese and Acehnese forces off the coast of Tanjong Rusa (now Changi) in 1577.[79] Another is shown on a map of 1603.[80] A rather detailed Portuguese map of Singapore from 1604 places a Xabandaria at the mouth of the Singapore River.[81] A *syahbandar* was one of the most important officials in a Malay court. The term (derived from Persian) can be translated literally as "lord of the harbour". The *syahbandar* collected duties from foreign merchants entering port, and had general authority over most aspects of foreign trade in the harbour, including transport and warehousing. He also exercised authority over the quarter where the foreign merchants resided, and acted as the intermediary in negotiations between them and the ruler. Thus the existence of a *syahbandar* in Singapore was noted by the Portuguese as a sign that foreign trade was conducted and taxed here. In 1603 a Dutch voyager mentioned a village named Sincapura on a creek just past a strait which corresponds to the waterway between Blakang Mati and Batu Berlayar.[82] In the same year the Dutch and Portuguese fought a sea battle in the Singapore Straits.[83]

In 1611 the Portuguese reported that the Dutch were trying to build a fort "in the Singapore Strait, on a small island that divides the old from the new strait."[84] This may have been a reference to Blakang Mati. The Portuguese attacked and burned Singapore in 1613, as part of their running battles against the heirs of Melaka. According to one British historian, "It is likely at this point, and not earlier, that the ancient settlement of Singapura went up in flames." Still, as late as 1686 the Dutch still mentioned "the Shahbandar of Singapura, Sri Raja Negara."[85]

Although the Malays of 1515 perhaps nostalgically still referred to Southeast Sumatra (rather than the Malay Peninsula) as *Tanah Melayu*, according to Tome Pires, when the Portuguese attacked them the only call for help the Melakans issued was sent to Riau, fief of the *Laksamana* and centre of local seafaring manpower. Some Palembang people took part in an unsuccessful counterattack, but as part of a Javanese force mustered by Demak. This particularly dramatic episode from Malay history underlines the strong alliance between the people of the Straits of Melaka, in particular those who called themselves *Orang Malayu*, and the people of the Riau Archipelago. This far-flung group of islands extends from the east coast of Sumatra to the island group of Natuna, 700 km to the northeast.

Within this extensive realm, there are of course subgroupings of islands and culture. A crude division would distinguish the western cluster which includes the large islands of Batam, Bintan and Lingga, from the eastern region. The latter is traditionally termed the Pulau Tujuh, "Seven Islands" after a nineteenth-century administrative system. Geographically there are three groups in eastern Riau: Anambas, Natuna and Tambelan. Historically the western group has been by far the more prominent of the two. In the *Sejarah Melayu*, Bintan is the home of Queen Sakidar Shah, who becomes the adopted mother of the first great Malay ruler, variously known as Sri Tri Buana or Sang Nila Utama. Symbolically this must have been a very important association in ancient Malay culture, given the importance attached to descent in the female line. After the fall of Melaka in 1511, the main political centre of the *Orang Melayu* was either found on Bintan or up the Johore River on the Malay Peninsula's southern tip. Bintan remained a political centre until 1911, although in the nineteenth century it had to share its primacy with Lingga.

Bintan appears in Chinese sailing directions as early as the early fifteenth century.[86] There is abundant archaeological and historical evidence that Bintan continued to play an important role as a shipping centre for Asian trade during most of the subsequent 600 years, and still continues to play that role today. In 1687 the Dutch observer Valentijn observed 500–600 boats in the estuary of the Riau River, on the west side of Bintan. These ships mainly came from from Jemaja, Siantan, Bunguran, Laut, Sarasan, Subi, and Tambelan, parts of the Pulau Tujuh.[87] These islands were rarely visited by outsiders. This was partly the effect of their greater distance from the southern end of the Straits of Melaka, and thus from the meeting-point of ships from the Indian Ocean, South China Sea, and Java Sea. Another, possibly more significant reason, was the reputation of the Pulau Tujuh inhabitants as being fierce pirates. As early as the thirteenth century the Chinese source *Zhufanzhi* mentions the people of Sha-hua kung as fierce pirates. "The farther one penetrates among these islands, the worse the robbers are."[88] Sopher inferred that Sha-hua kung probably refers to the Natuna Islands. Hirth and Rockhill merely equated this reference with *Orang Laut*, "People of the Sea."[89]

During the seventeenth century, Singapore was probably practically deserted. This does not mean that it had no strategic potential; rather it was perhaps not occupied precisely because no group had a strong enough position in the region to utilise it. The Malay courts had to maintain a fragile existence by nimbly retreating back and forth from the Johore River to the island of Bintan. The court did not possess the power to maintain a settlement there in the face of Portuguese raids. The Portuguese may not have considered Singapore worth occupying, but their relative disinterest in the island may also have been due to the probability that they would have been unable to defend it either.

The Dutch-Bugis Phase 1700-1819

The link between the Malay ruler and the *Orang Laut* lasted until the beginning of the eighteenth century. At that time several new factors contributed to the break-up of the old system; these included the assassination of the Malay ruler who was believed to have descended from the original divinely appointed king, the arrival of the Bugis from South Sulawesi, providing a new source of maritime manpower, and the increasing influence of the Dutch. The bond between the Malay rulers and the faithful People of the Sea was severed in 1699 when the last sultan of the ancient line was assassinated. During the eighteenth century their cohesion gradually broke down, probably due in large part to the lack of a single symbolic figure to provide unity for a mobile population scattered over a vast area of sea now that there was no longer a descendant of the ancient kings with whom their original pact of loyalty had been sealed. Also during the eighteenth century other groups, in particular the Dutch and Bugis, were making the situation in the Riau region more complex. The fragmented People of the Sea fell prey to attacks from better-organised groups and new diseases, and their erstwhile overlords the Malays even fell to raiding their islands for slaves. By 1900 they were looked down upon as backward primitives.

That Singapore had not been forgotten by the Malays, and that it was perceived as a place of some strategic importance is indicated by the interesting experience of the British sea captain who was actually offered Singapore as a gift! This episode may have had some direct influence in the next century; it is at least possible that either T.S. Raffles or the Malays or both remembered that Singapore had once been offered to the British. The facts of the matter are recorded in straightforward words by the English captain concerned:

> In Anno 1703 I called at Johore on my way to China, and he (the Sultan) [Abdul Jalil] treated me very kindly, and made me a present of the Island of Singapura, but I told him it could be of no use to a private person tho' a proper Place for a Company to settle a Colony on, lying in the Center of Trade, and being accomodated with good Rivers and safe

Harbours, so conveniently situtated, that all Winds served Shipping both
to go out and come into these rivers.[90]

Hamilton went on to describe the soil and products of Singapore's forest:

> The Soil is black and fat: And the Woods abound in good Masts for
> Shipping, and Timber for building. I have seen large Beans growing
> wild in the Woods, not inferior to the best in Europe for Taste and
> Beauty; and Sugar-cane five or six inches round...

Obviously he had spent some time inspecting the site, and may have
given the offer serious consideration.

Why would a Malay ruler take the unusual step of offering the island
as a gift to a European? Again we can do no more than speculate, but
it would seem that the changed situation since the assassination of the
former Sultan in 1699, the disarray between the Malays and their *Orang
Laut* allies, and the Malay desire to find a counterbalance to Dutch
dominance in the region, led the Sultan to make this offer. He obviously
calculated that a British establishment on this island had a fair chance
of success, and that his offer might be accepted. The significance of a
British post there for the Malays would be that it would establish a friendly
party there, and deny it to enemies. It would be interesting to speculate
what might have happened had Hamilton had more capital, or the
ambitions of a Brooke. During the eighteenth century, however, the
attentions of the British were focussed on India, and beyond their little
settlement at Bengkulu they had little interest in Southeast Asia.

It was only in 1786 that the British began to take new measures to
expand their role in Southeast Asia. Due to Captain Francis Light's
initiative, they occupied the island of Pulau Pinang (Penang, Prince of
Wales Island). A few years later Melaka came into their temporary
possession as a result of the Napoleonic Wars and the flight of the Prince
of Orange to England. Trade between India and China was taking on
increasing significance. It was therefore not surprising that new British
initiatives were gradually formed which led to the founding of an East
India Company settlement at Singapore, 116 years after another Briton
had declined it.

Notes

1. It is possible that a very early port did exist in the general area of Singapore.
Thirteenth-century cartographers drew a map of the Indian Ocean using in part data
collected by an Alexandrian Greek named Claudius Ptolemaeus around A.D. 100 and
compiled by a Byzantine monk around A.D. 1000. The map depicts the southern end
of the Malay Peninsula as an emporion, that is, a place where international trade was
conducted. Due to the vague nature of this map and its sources, however, it is not
possible to use it as a source for ancient Singapore. See P. Wheatley, *The Golden
Khersonese*, Kuala Lumpur, 1961, 151-52.

2. G. Coedes, *The Indianized States of Southeast Asia*, Honolulu, 1968, 54-55.

3. O.W. Wolters, *Early Indonesian Commerce*, Ithaca, 1967, 151.

4. A. Reid, *Southeast Asia in the Age of Commerce 1450-1680*, vol. 1, New Haven,
1988, 7, has proposed that frequent deliberate abortion by women and intentional

birth spacing may have been responsible for the low population density of Southeast Asia. The motivation for these measures in turn he suspects to have been the frequency of warfare in early Southeast Asia. Small families would have been advantageous under such conditions, due to the means of defense most frequently adopted by Southeast Asians: flight.

5. Ibid, 121, quoting Hwang Chung, who wrote in 1537.

6. There are numerous traces of circular earthen embankments and trenches surrounding mounds in northeast Thailand which appear to date back over 2000 years, and it has been postulated that the purpose of these may have been to serve as fortification walls. Other possibilities have however been suggested, particularly the idea that the object of this activity was not to erect embankments but to create moats or depressions in which water could be collected, either from rainfall or by tapping streams flowing nearby. The water thus collected may have served either agricultural or symbolic purposes. Around A.D. 1000 these sites ceased to be constructed. The reason for this change in practice is unknown; perhaps water management techniques were altered. See E.H. Moore, *Moated Sites in Early Northeast Thailand*, Oxford, 1988.

7. C.C. Brown (translated and annotated), *Sejarah Melayu or Malaya Annals*, Kuala Lumpur, 1970, 187.

8. Reid, Vol.2, 1993, 220.

9. W. Marsden, *History of Sumatra*, Kuala Lumpur, 1966 [original edition 1783], 347; J. Crawford, *History of the Indian Archipelago*, vol. 1, 1820, 191-92.

10. See for example F.H. van Naerssen, "The economic and administrative history of early Indonesia," *Handbuch der Orientalistik, Dritte Abteilung, Siebenter Band*, Leiden/Koln, 1977, 35-36.

11. S.J. Tambiah, "The galactic polity: the structure of traditional kingdoms in Southeast Asia," in S.A. Freed (editor), *Anthropology and the Climate of Opinion*, New York, 1977, 69-97.

12. O.W. Wolters, *History, Culture and Region in Southeast Asian Perspectives*, Singapore, 1982.

13. E.W. Fox, *History in Geographic Perspective: The Other France*, New York, 1971.

14. H.C. Darby, "The medieval sea-state," *Scottish Geographical Magazine*, 48/3, 1932, 136-49.

15. For a summary of historical sources describing these people, see David Sopher, *The Sea Nomads*, Singapore, 1977.

16. See note 7.

17. L. Andaya, *The Kingdom of Johor 1641-1728*, Kuala Lumpur, 1975, 41-49, provides this and other information not found in Sopher which is useful in forming an understanding of the historical relationship between Malay royalty and the *Orang Laut* before 1750.

18. O.W. Wolters, *The Fall of Srivijaya in Malay History*, Ithaca, 1970, 10-11.

19. According to the *Xin Tang-shu* of Jia Dan, AD 1060.

20. I. Caldwell and A.A. Hazlewood, "The Holy Footprints of the Venerable Gautama: A New Translation of the Pasir Panjang Inscription," in *Bijdragen tot de Taal-, Land-en Volkenkunde* 150, 1994, 457-80.

21. A. Corteso (editor/translator), *The Suma Oriental of Tome Pires*, vol.2, London, 1944, 156.

22. Sopher, 93-94, 403.

23. F. Hirth and W.W. Rockhill, *Chau Ju-Kua: His Work on the Chinese and Arab Trade in the Twelfth and Thirteenth Centuries, Entitled Chu-Fan-Chi*, St. Petersburg, 1911, 60-67.

24. E.H. Warmington, *The Commerce Between the Roman Empire and India*, Cambridge, 1928, 56, 113-14.

25. J. Anderson, *Acheen, and the Ports on the North and East Coasts of Sumatra*, London, 1840, 38.

26. K. Indrapala, "South Indian merchant communities in Ceylon, 950-1200," in *Ceylon Journal of Historical and Social Studies*, #'s 1-2, 1971, 101-113; D.D. Kosambi, "Indian feudal trade charters," in *Journal of the Economic and Social History of the Orient*, #'s 2-3, 1959, 281-93; K.A.N. Sastri, "A Tamil merchant-gilde in Sumatra," in *Tijdschrift voor Indische Taal-, Land-, en Volkenkunde uitgegeven door het (Koninklijk) Bataviaasch Genootschap van Kunsten en Wetenschappen*, #72, 1932, 314-27; B. Stein, "Coromandel trade in Medieval India," in J. Parker (editor), *Merchants and Scholars*, Minneapolis, 1965, 47-62.

27. For a discussion of the convoluted data regarding this episode, see J.N. Miksic, "Hubungan sejarah antara Srivijaya Palembang dan Lembah Bujang," in I. Hussein et al. (editors) *Tamadan Melayu*, vol.3, Kuala Lumpur, 1995, 894-917.

28. Hirth and Rockhill, 60.

29. Ibid, 63. Dragons are water symbols in Chinese mythology, and dragons were often used as metaphors for aquatic features of the landscape in Chinese literature. For example, a classical Chinese source refers to the Song Giang River in north Vietnam as the "Scream of the Nine Coils of the Dragon": "The head [of the dragon] looks toward the unsettled abyss, its tail constitutes the Stream of Gems...Water flows from the Head and from the Tongue of the Dragon..." Quoted in P. Wheatley, *Negara and Commander*, Chicago, 1983, 414.

30. *Journal of an Embassy from the Governor General of India to the Courts of Siam and Cochin China*, Kuala Lumpur, 1967 [1828], 44-45.

31. C.M. Turnbull, *A History of Singapore 1819-1975*, Singapore, 1975, 27.

32. Singapore National Archives (SNA), Straits Settlements Records, Vol. L 11.

33. The use of the expression "Lines" to refer to a city wall was common in the nineteenth century.

34. G.M. Reith, *Handbook of Singapore*, Singapore, 1985 [original edition 1907], 65.

35. B. Bronson, Basoeki, Machi Suhadi, and J. Wisseman, *Laporan Penelitian Arkeologi di Sumatera 20 Mei-8 Juli 1973*, n.p.: Lembaga Purbakala dan Peninggalan Nasional/ The University of Pennsylvania Museum, n/d, mimeographed.

36. Ibid.

37. Hirth and Rockhill, *Chao Ju-Kua*, 60.

38. See below, chs. 6-8.

39. C.A. Gibson-Hill, *Singapore Old Strait and New Harbour 1300-1870*, Memoirs of the Raffles Museum, vol. 3, 1956, 36.

40. J.V.G. Mills (translator and editor), *Ma Huan Ying-yai Sheng-lan: "The Overall Survey of the Ocean's Shores"*, 1433", Cambridge, 1970, 328.

41. W.W. Rockhill, "Notes on the relations and trade of China with the eastern archipelago and the coast of the Indian Ocean during the fourteenth century. Part II." *T'oung Pao*, 1915, 129. Rockhill tends to identify this strait with the Singapore [Main] Strait, but as he notes in a footnote on the same page, others have identified it with the entrance to Keppel Harbour. For further discussion, see C.A. Gibson-Hill, "Singapore Old Strait and New Harbour, 1300-1870", 35-37.

42. Rockhill, "Notes on the relations and trade of China", 132.

43. *Dao i ji lioh*, translated by Wheatley, *The Golden Khersonese*, 82.

44. The name "Pancur" is a common Malay placename. There is also another example of its use for the site of a Malaya capital in the area; a location about 15 km up the Johore River with this name was the seat of the Sultan of Johore, the successor to the Sultanate of Melaka — and thus indirectly the ruler of Singapore — from 1700 to 1708, and again from 1715 to 1718. C.A. Gibson-Hill, "Johor Lama and other ancient sites on the Johore River," in *Journal of the Malayan Branch of the Royal Asiatic Society* (JMBRAS), vol. 28, #2, 1955, 127-97, 160-65.

45. Rockhill, "Notes on the relations and trade of China," *T'oung Pao* 15, 1914, 133. Rockhill was unsure of the location of Pancur, suggesting Batam or Bintan, two islands near Singapore. The archaeological remains discovered by this author on Fort Canning

Hill and along the north bank of the Singapore River however make identification with Fort Canning Hill highly likely.

46. Kwa Chong Guan, "Appendix, Records and Notices of Early Singapore," in J.N. Miksic, *Archaeological Research on the "Forbidden Hill" of Singapore: Excavations at Fort Canning, 1984*, Singapore, 1985, 101.

47. Full citation of A.H. Hill, "The founding of Singapore described by 'Munshi Abdullah'" in JMBRAS 28, #3, 125-32, 137-49; page number of quote beginning with "Now at this time the seas round Singapore so far from being navigated freely by men, were feared... Sometimes there is wholesale slaughter among the crews when the cargo is grabbed."

48. Wolters, *History, Culture and Religion in Southeast Asian Perspectives*, n. 45, 48. As early as the seventh century a north Vietnamese monk was said to have been fluent in Malay; Wheatley, *Negara and Commandery*, 372. Obviously the study of ancient Vietnamese sources may teach us more about the Singapore area, and possibly Singapore itself.

49. T.G. Th. Pigeaud, *Java in the Fourteenth Century. A Study in Cultural History*, Vol. III, The Hague, 1960, 14/2.

50. Sopher, 316.

51. Wheatley, *The Golden Khersonese*, 321.

52. Cortesao, vol. II, 230-42.

53. M.J. Pintado, "Some Portuguese historical sources in Malacca history", in *Heritage*, vol. 3, 1978, 20-62.

54. G.P. Rouffaer, "Was Malaka emporium voor 1400 AD genaamd Malajoer?", in *Bijdragen tot de Taal-, Land-, en Volkenkunde van Nederlandsch-Indie*, vol. 77, 1921, 27-28.

55. For the calculation of the date of Singapore's fall, see Wolters, *The Fall of Srivijaya*,147.

56. Sopher, 317.

57. Wheatley, *The Golden Khersonese*, 96; P. Pelliot, cited in Gibson-Hill, n. 73, 2.

58. Mills, 325.

59. Wolters, *The Fall of Srivijaya*, 133; Wheatley, *The Golden Khersonese*, 233, 237, 242.

60. Wolters, *Fall of Srivijaya*, 246.

61. Gibson-Hill, 39.

62. Mills, 312.

63. Wolters, *Fall of Srivijaya*, 161.

64. W.P. Groeneveldt, *Historical Notes on Indonesia & Malaya Compiled from Chinese Sources*. Jakarta, 1960, 37.

65. Mills, *Ma Huan*, 200, #265.

66. Brown, *Sejarah Melayu*, 112-18.

67. Ibid, 150.

68. There are two main published versions of the *Sejarah Melayu*: the Shellabear version, published in Singapore in the nineteenth century, and the Raffles MS 18 version. The Shellabear rescension was probably composed in Bintan in the mid-eighteenth century. The Raffles MS 18 version is probably a copy of an older text, and is preferable for use here because the Shellabear version gives many signs of having been re-edited by the Riau court.

69. Brown, *Sejarah Melayu*, 198.

70. Gibson-Hill, "Singapore Old Strait and New Harbour, 1300-1870," n. 58, 37; Wolters, *The Fall of Srivijaya*, 77.

71. Cortesao, vol. II, 262.

72. R.O. Winstedt, "Tumasik or Old Singapore," in *Singapore 150 Years*, 10.

73. W. de G. Birch, *The Commentaries of the Great Alfonso Dalboquerque*, London, 1875-1884, 4 vols.

74. Rouffaer, 388-389.

75. J.A. Robertson, *Magellan's Voyage Around the World*, Cleveland, 1906, 3 vols.

76. Wheatley, *The Golden Khersonese*, 173.

77. Francisco de Sa de Meneses, translated by E.C. Knowlton Jr, *The Conquest of Malacca*, Kuala Lumpur, 1970, 61. This poem makes the interesting suggestion that a Melakan sea captain, Nakhoda Beguea, was a descendant of Parameswara, and wanted to avenge his death on his descendants now ruling there. The same episode is referred to again in another passage, 69.

78. Ibid, 123.

79. P-Y. Manguin, "The vanishing jong: insular Southeast Asian fleets in trade and war (fifteenth to seventeenth centuries)," in A.R. Reid (editor), *Southeast Asia in the Early Modern Era: Trade, Power and Belief*, Ithaca, 1993, figure 8, 207.

80. Theodore and Johannes de Bry, ca. 1605, *Collectiones peregrinationum in Indian Orientation et Occidentalem; Grandes et Petites Voyages*, Frankfurt, 1607.

81. J.V. Mills, "Eredia's description of Malacca, Meridional India, and Cathay," in *JMBRAS*, vol. 8, #1, 1930, plate 6.

82. Journal of Wybrand von Warwyck, discussed by Rouffaer, 400-402.

83. D.F.A. Hervey, "Valentyn's description of Malacca," in *Journal of the Straits Branch of the Royal Asiatic Society (JSBRAS)*. vol. 15, 1885, 128ff.

84. C.A. Gibson-Hill, "Singapore: Notes on the history of the Old Strait, 1580–1850," in *JMBRAS*, vol. 27, #1, no. 33a, 179.

85. Gibson-Hill, "Singapore Old Strait and New Harbour," 20.

86. Ma Huan, *Ying-yai Sheng-lan: The Overall Survey of the Ocean's Shores*. Translated and edited by J.V.G. Mills, Cambridge, 1970.

87. Andaya, 148-49.

88. Hirth and Rockhill, *Chua Ju-kua*, 150.

89. Sopher, 341.

90. Alexandar Hamilton, *A New Account of the East Indies*, Vol. 2, 53.

2

Why the British came to Singapore

B etween 1682 and 1786 the British possessed only one foothold in all of Southeast Asia: the settlement of Bencoolen (in modern Indonesian orthography Bengkulu), on the southwest coast of Sumatra. This possession was originally obtained as a reaction to the Dutch attainment of supremacy over the port of Banten, West Java. Banten had been for over a century the main spice mart in Asia, and both the Dutch and the British made it the objective of their first voyages to the East Indies in 1596. The British established a factory there, and had good relations with the rulers. However in 1682 the Sultan fell out with his son and appointed heir, and the Dutch seized the opportunity to rid themselves of the main rival to their own commercial centre a mere 120 km to the east, at Batavia (modern Jakarta).

In 1685 the Dutch obtained exclusive rights to Banten's foreign trade, and all other Europeans were expelled. The British then formulated the strategy of trying to implant another factory in the centre of one of the main pepper-producing areas which had formed the foundation of Banten's prosperity: Bengkulu. This they succeeded in doing, only to be bitterly disappointed by the results. The settlement was located far off the main trade routes, had a sparse population, and few resources. For the 140 years of British occupation, the settlement constituted a near-constant drain on the East India Company's budget.[1] The logic of competition with the Dutch however made the British loath to abandon it, and so they continued to invest resources there with little to show for it. The most efficient Governor to serve in Bengkulu, Joseph Collett, supervised the construction of a large fort, Fort Marlborough, in 1715, but none of his successors had his talent or energy. Bengkulu became one of the distant colonial outposts where the ne'er-do-wells of the Company were sent to die or blend into the local population.

To this dismal setting a new Governor was sent in 1818: Sir Thomas Stamford Raffles. This self-educated man of common parentage had risen through sheer dint of intellect and energy through the ranks of the East India Company. He was born at sea near Jamaica in 1781, one of six children of a sea captain. At the age of 14 he had to leave school because of poverty, and went to work for the Company as a temporary clerk. In 1805 he was posted to Penang as a junior merchant. Just before departing he married Olivia Fancourt, a widow ten years older than he. During the voyage Raffles learned Malay. He used the language, at which he seems to have become quite proficient, in many ways. He carried on a voluminous correspondence with Malay nobles. Through these letters he developed an appreciation for their culture and literature. These accomplishments, and his interest in collecting old Malay manuscripts, played a vital part in his choice of Singapore as a base.

In 1806 Raffles was appointed Acting Secretary of Penang. The next year he also took over the duties of official translator. While visiting Melaka on sick leave, he met William Farquhar, Resident (whom he later made first Resident of

Sir Thomas Stamford Raffles

Singapore). In 1810 he met the Governor-General of India, Lord Minto, and became one of his main advisers for plans to invade Java in order to deny it to the French under Napoleon. Minto made him Agent to the Governor-General of the Malay States. He moved to Melaka to begin preparations for the invasion, which took place in 1811. On the way the fleet passed through the Straits of Singapore but did not touch land. Raffles made no reference to Singapore at that time. His mind was obviously preoccupied with the future activities on Java.

In the aftermath of the successful military operations in Java, Raffles was appointed Lieutenant Governor. He was thus the supreme authority in the Netherlands Indies for the next four years. In 1814 Olivia Raffles died and was buried in Java. When in 1816 Napoleon was safely defeated and Java was returned to the Dutch, Raffles returned to England. In 1817 he married Miss Sophia Hull and was elected a Fellow of the Royal Society; his *History of Java* was published; he received a knighthood; and he was appointed to take over the British outpost at Bengkulu.

Crossroads of Empire: The Sea Route to China

In 1818, plans for increasing British prosperity relied heavily on expansion of the China trade. The route from British possessions in India to China had to pass through Southeast Asian waters. Since 1682 Southeast Asia's sea lanes had been dominated by the Dutch, Britain's bitter commercial rival. Holland had succeeded in forcing the British to close all of their trading posts except for Bencoolen on the isolated southwest coast of Sumatra.

Raffles arrived in Bencoolen in 1818. His thoughts however were aimed at a much larger scope of action. Even before reaching Sumatra he had begun to plan a two-pronged strategy to protect British shipping between India and China passing through the Dutch-dominated seas of Southeast Asia. One prong was his attempt to make a treaty with Aceh, on the north coast of Sumatra opposite Penang. Penang had turned out marginally better than Bengkulu. It was on the sea route between India and China. However, it was discovered that the real fulcrum of power in the maritime realm of Southeast Asia lay further south, where the Straits of Melaka narrowed to a small opening. It had once been planned to make Penang a naval arsenal for building ships for the Royal Navy, and "a marine station for the rendezvous, refitting and supply of His Majesty's squadrons in the eastern seas". These projects were however abandoned.[2] Penang's location was not sufficiently strategic to ensure that British ships might pass unhindered by the Dutch into the South China Sea.

The second objective therefore was to establish a British settlement at the south end of the Straits of Melaka. At this time the capital of the Johore kingdom, the dominant indigenous political force in the South Straits region, was located on Bintan, near Tanjung Pinang, where it had been since 1722. Territories technically subordinate to the Bintan sultans included Riau-Lingga, Johore and Pahang. Raffles had been in touch with the rulers of Riau and Lingga since 1809. As early as 1786, Warren Hastings had sent a mission to Bintan, but the Dutch had prevented the British from establishing a post there.

In the early nineteenth century the court of Johore-Riau was in disarray. A group of people descended from Bugis immigrants had held real power in the sultanate for a century. The Sultan was a Malay, but he was little more than a puppet of the Bugis minister who held the title *Yamtuan Muda*. In 1784 the Dutch drove the *Yamtuan Muda* out and installed a resident there. However the *Yamtuan Muda* returned in 1795 when the British took over Melaka, one of the Asian repercussions of the war in Europe against the French.

The Malay Sultan of Riau, Mahmud, died in 1812, and two brothers laid claim to the throne: Tengku Hussein, and Tengku Abdul Rahman. The Bugis and the Dutch both supported Abdul Rahman, but Hussein was supported by two high Malay officials: the Temenggong and the Bendahara. The Malay Sultans established a royal residence at Daik, on the island of Lingga, in the southern group of islands making up the Riau-Lingga archipelago, and left the Bugis to enjoy their supremacy in Bintan. In 1818, the Temenggong, also named Abdul Rahman, was the third highest official in the traditional hierarchy, technically in charge of the port, police and markets. His traditional appanage was Johore, Singapore and the nearby islands. The Bendahara's fief was Pahang. The Bugis and Dutch allied to oppose Temenggong Abdul Rahman, who moved to Singapore where he enjoyed some autonomy. Munshi Abdullah, the Malay author and teacher of Raffles, quotes the Temenggong as explaining the situation to Farquhar in 1819 thus:

Sir, I am an exile parted from my real home in Riau...I withdrew myself
to this Island in the middle of the sea, [i.e. Singapore] which in fact
is my own lawful inheritance. For under the customs and laws of the
Malays it is the Temenggong who holds power over all these islands,
the real sovereign, Sultan Mahmud, being dead. He had two sons; Abdul
Rahman, and Husain who possessed the title of Tengku Long; but neither
of them is of full royal birth. Since the death of the Sultan there has
been much argument among the chiefs in Daik and in Riau and in Pahang
over who shall be appointed by the Bendahara to succeed, for they are
both children of the late Sultan. Tengku Puteri, the widow of the late
Sultan, wishes Tengku Long to succeed while some of the chiefs wish
to have Tengku Rahman...Tengku Abdul Rahman has taken offence
and gone to Trengganu, while Tengku Long remains in Riau. That is
how the whole affair started, sir.[3]

Raffles had at one time thought seriously of establishing a British
base further south, on Bangka.[4] While in England in 1817, he began
working to arouse the East India Company's interest in the idea of
developing a new port in the Sumatra area:

This leads me to the second measure which I propose for the protection
of our commerce in the Eastern Archipelago against the power of the
Dutch to exclude us from it, viz. our taking immediate possession of
a port in the Eastern Archipelago, the best adapted for communication
with the native princes, for a general knowledge of what is going on
at sea and on shore throughout the Archipelago, for the resort of the
independent trade and the trade with our Allies, for the protection of
our commerce, and all our interests and more especially for an entrepot
for our merchandise. The station which I would recommend if obtainable
is the Island of Banca.[5]

Raffles' reasons for this suggestion included the fact that Bangka had
no history of prior Dutch occupation; a large population; valuable tin;
a good harbour; and a location on the direct passage between the Straits
of Sunda and Melaka. If Bangka were not agreeable to the Company's
powers, however, he had a second option in mind — Bintan:

It possesses one of the best harbours in the eastern seas, a considerable
population (not less than 10,000 souls) and is perhaps more favourably
situated for a general commercial entrepot than Banca. It is now the
general resort of pirates and smugglers, and the circumstance of its
being the principal station of the Arab and Bugis traders on the western
side of the Archipelago is a proof of the facilities which it possesses
for trade. It would be a commercial station for communication with
the China ships passing either through the Straits of Sunda or Malacca,
completely outflank Malacca and intercept its trade in the same manner
as Malacca has already intercepted that of Prince of Wales Island...[6]

Yet a third option he suggested was the western coast of Borneo, the
area of Sambas and Pontianak.

Thus the man with the most information, the strongest motivation
to make a decision, and the most steadfast willpower to see the decision
implemented, seemed to have no clear preference for any of these sites

over another. The place eventually chosen, Singapore, was not mentioned at all. This might be interpreted as an indication that Singapore was an afterthought, a lower priority. In fact, there is some evidence that he had already decided upon Singapore at the time these words were written, as shall be seen below.

For the East India Company no less than for the Malay kingdoms of the fourteenth century, commercial and military considerations were inextricably linked. Raffles had to incorporate plans for the use of the Company's military wing into his overall strategy. Too little is known about the sources from which Raffles drew his knowledge of military affairs, but as his role in the invasion of Java showed, he was more than a rank amateur in this field. His correspondence on the subject of his plans for a British commercial base which was eventually to take place on Singapore contains frequent references to military factors. Already in 1817, he wrote:

> A military force merely sufficient for the respectability of the flag and the security of the station is all that would be required ... It is not likely that a force exceeding five hundred men would under any circumstances be required.[7]

The powers in India gave Raffles cautious encouragement to explore the area around the southern tip of the Malay Peninsula. The Chief Secretary to the Governor-General-in-Council in December 1818 advised Raffles that the government of India was willing to consider a treaty with Johore "on the same footing as is now contemplated with Rhio and Lingen" if the Dutch re-established a post in Riau. But the Indian authorities emphasised the need for caution, since they knew so little of Johore's political situation, town and harbour. Its position however was thought to be "nearly, or perhaps entirely, as convenient a post for our purpose as Rhio."[8]

Yet another candidate for the choice of British base in the southern Straits which received serious consideration was the island of Karimun. As noted in the previous chapter, Karimun had been an important navigational landmark and rendezvous for over a thousand years. Col. William Farquhar, who had much experience in the region, having lived long at Melaka, favoured Karimun. Its location could not be more "strategic": it lies directly in the middle of the south end of the Straits of Melaka like a cork in the neck of a bottle. The expedition which eventually met the Temenggong in Singapore in January 1819 and secured a preliminary agreement to occupy the site indeed visited Karimun first.

As late as 1820, when Singapore was already beginning to grow, some British still wished the decision to be reconsidered:

> The Penang merchants objected to the position of Singapore, and recommended the Carimons, and Colonel Farquhar was sent again to visit them. Their argument was that, while Singapore only commanded one entrance to the Straits of Malacca, the Carimons commanded four, namely, Sabon, Dryon, the Old Straits round by Johore, and the New Straits round by St. John's Island.[9]

All this information would seem to confirm that Raffles had not given a thought to Singapore as a site for this projected port. However, according to Raffles' second wife, Sophia, even before he left England in 1817, Raffles had already decided that Singapore would be the most advantageous place to develop a stopping-off point to ensure that British ships were unhindered in their navigation between India and China. Why Singapore? In 1817 Raffles had never visited the island. As Raffles' biographer Wurtzburg wrote, "it was characteristic of Raffles that in his political planning he loved to have a historic background for his actions."[10] The Dutch possessed Melaka, the famous fifteenth-century port. The British could outdo the Dutch by attracting Malay trade to Singapore, which Malay literature depicted as Melaka's predecessor.

Raffles collected many Malay manuscripts as part of his study of Malay history and culture. One of these is particularly famous. Known as Raffles Manuscript (MS) 18, it is the oldest known version of the work known as the *Sejarah Melayu* or *Malay Annals*. Manuscript 18 preserves a description of the Malay royal line from its origins in Palembang, through the moves of capital to Singapore, Melaka and Bintan. According to the *Malay Annals*, Singapore was the first great Malay trading port.

Another of Raffles' many interests concerned antiquities. Although the science of archaeology did not yet exist, Raffles was more perceptive than most of his contemporaries who collected antiques as curiosities. Raffles had a truly anthropological cast of mind. He saw in the remains of the art and culture of the past peoples of Southeast Asia a means to understand their contemporary descendants.

While living in Java and Bengkulu, in addition to hiring people who scoured the forests for natural samples for him, Raffles encouraged others to bring him relics of the past. He organised teams of draftsmen to visit ancient ruins to sketch them. Raffles' collections included ancient Javanese statuary. He made attempts to decipher ancient inscriptions and manuscripts; this research plays a prominent part in his *History of Java* and is obviously connected with his choice of Singapore as a site for a new port.

Raffles' letters support this idea. On 12 December 1818, while on board the *Nearchus*, off the Sandheads, he wrote to an English friend, "you must not be surprised if my next letter to you is dated from the site of the ancient city of Singapura."[11] A few months after Singapore was founded, he wrote to another correspondent, "But for my Malay studies I should hardly have known that such a place [as Singapore] existed: not only the European, but the Indian world was also ignorant of it."[12] Further on in the same letter he wrote:

> You will probably hàve to consult the Map in order to ascertain from what part of the world this letter is dated. Refer to the extremity of the Malay Peninsula where you will observe several small Islands forming the Straits of Singapore. On one of these are the ruins of the ancient Capital of 'Singapura'...[13]

An interesting additional piece of anecdotal information on this subject comes from the pen of Capt. J.G.F. Crawford, in charge of the surveying vessel *Investigator*, which had accompanied Raffles and his party to Singapore in January 1819. His words seem to preserve something of the conversations which Raffles may have had with his contemporaries on the subject:

> This spot of ground is the site of the very ancient city and fort of Singapore, whose sovereigns, upwards of a thousand years ago, gave laws to Java, Sumatra and their adjacent islands and a great part of the Malay Peninsula. No remnants of its former grandeur exist, not the slightest vestige of it has ever been discovered... This place once so great, once so powerful, is now a petty fishing village, until our coming here unknown in modern history or geography, for Sir Stamford found accounts of it in a very old Malay work.[14]

Upon completion of the ceremonies on 6 February, Raffles wrote with gratification that he now expected the neighbouring local rulers to "hail with satisfaction the foundation and the rise of a British Establishment on the central and commanding situation once occupied by the Capital of the most powerful Malayan empire then existing in the East."[15] This phrase suggests yet another possible motive for Raffles' choice of Singapore: the hope that some prestige from Singapore's ancient position might accrue to its new British rulers. That Singapore still retained a special aura emanating from its previous role is borne out by the name given to the hill later known as Fort Canning when the British arrived: Bukit Larangan, the "Forbidden Hill".

In a letter written shortly after Singapore's founding to his patron, the Duchess of Somerset, Raffles described Singapore's location in these terms: "this is the spot, the site of the ancient maritime capital of the Malays, and within the walls of these fortifications, raised not less than six centuries ago, on which I have planted the British flag..."[16] On a subsequent visit, Raffles was able to console himself with his visions of Singapore's former greatness during a period of grave illness. He was subject to violent headaches, which were to result in his death at the age of 45. While in Singapore he sometimes took Chinese medicine which contained mercury; this could not have done him any good. In a letter to William Marsden dated 21 January 1823 he reported that he had built a small bungalow on "Singapore Hill" (Fort Canning), where he found the atmosphere much more comfortable, and the view both interesting and beautiful. Another source of comfort was the proximity to remnants of ancient Singapore: "The tombs of the Malay Kings are close at hand, and I have settled that if it is my fate to die here I shall take my place amongst them; this will at any rate be better than leaving my bones at Bencoolen." Two days later he wrote to the Duchess of Somerset that:

> Since I last wrote to your Grace about a month ago, I have had another very severe attack in my head, which nearly proved fatal, and the Doctors were for hurrying me on board ship for Europe, without much ceremony. However, as I could not reconcile myself to becoming food for fishes,

I preferred ascending the hill of Singapore, where if my bones must remain in the East, they would have the honour of mixing with the ashes of the Malayan Kings: and the result has been that, instead of dying, I have almost entirely recovered.[17]

By this time Raffles must have come to believe that some of the brick ruins on the hill were tombs. This interpretation of the ruins did not exist in 1819 when the hill was first cleared; indeed, the Temenggong and other inhabitants of Singapore seem to have been unaware that such remains existed. Soon after the jungle on the hill was cut down, a belief arose that the largest ruin was the *keramat* of Iskandar Shah, last of the five kings of ancient Singapore. The basis for this belief is unknown. The word *keramat* is derived from Arabic *karama*, "blessed". In Islam, especially in Sufi philosophy, sites or objects associated with holy people are believed to be legitimate as a focus for meditation. Muhammad himself meditated in caves. The goal of such activities in orthodox Islam is simply to assist the worshipper in furthering his submission to Allah.

In some expressions of popular, heterodox Islam, such practices became mixed with a cult of graves of devout Muslims as locations where spirits of the dead could be contacted in order to obtain specific favours. This is what seems to have happened at the *keramat* of Iskandar Shah. There is no evidence to support the theory that the *keramat* on Fort Canning was a grave; no tombstones have been recovered there. It is also unlikely that Iskandar Shah was buried in Singapore; he died in the year 1412 or 1413, according to Chinese records, and he had been living in Melaka since 1400. No record of his burial place exists, but it was probably in Melaka. Furthermore, during the fourteenth century the Malay ruling class had not converted to Islam. Iskandar may have been the first, but it was not until the reign of the third ruler of Melaka that Islam became firmly entrenched as the dominant Malay religion. Thus Raffles' assumption that the "tombs of the Malay kings" lay near his house is probably mistaken, based on a tradition which only appeared soon after his own arrival on the island in 1819.

1819 and Early Growing Pains

On 16 January, 1819, Raffles instructed Major William Farquhar[18] to:

> ...embark on the brig *Ganges* and proceed to the Straits of Singapore, communicating by the readiest means you have in your power with Captain Ross of the *Discovery* who has been requested to await your arrival on the N.E. end of the Little Carimon in order to submit his surveys of those islands. Having ascertained the capability of Singapore and its vicinity, and the result being satisfactory, you will make such arrangements for securing to us the eventual command of that important station as circumstances...may dictate.

The *Ganges* was accompanied by the *Mercury* and *Nearchus*, both troop carriers. Two survey ships, the *Discovery* and *Investigator*, were already mapping the waters around Karimun Island, 30 km west of Singapore.

Raffles had managed to have them slip out of Penang some time earlier. The schooner *Enterprise*, the cruiser *Minto*, and Raffles' own ship *Indiana*, together with a Malay *kora-kora*, a kind of war canoe capable of carrying more than a dozen men, completed the fleet which first rendezvoused at Karimun on 26 January 1819.

As Farquhar later wrote to the East India Company: "Having surveyed the Carimon Islands which did not afford advantages for the settlement, it was resolved to proceed to Johor but on the way at the suggestion of your Memorialist they stopped on 19 January at Singapore." This date was a slip of the pen; the true date, as other sources prove, was 29 January 1819. Raffles himself made a similar mistake, writing in his *Statement of Services* in 1824 that he had landed on 29 <u>February</u>. There was no such date in 1819. The fleet of eight ships and the Malay war canoe anchored off Singapore "near a fine sandy beach" at 1600 hrs on 29 January 1819. A group of Malays came on board, then went ashore to convey Raffles' message to the local chief authority, the Temenggong, that Raffles would like to meet him the next morning.

Farquhar's statement implies that he was the source of the decision to inspect Singapore. All other sources however point to the reverse: that the intention to settle on Singapore had been made much earlier by Raffles, and the visit to Karimun was intended more to humour Farquhar, and perhaps to throw any watching Dutch off the scent, than from a genuine intention to give Karimun serious consideration. The next day Raffles landed at a point near the mouth of the Singapore River, exact location unknown, called Kampong Temenggong. A week later, on 6 February 1819, an official ceremony of treaty-signing between the British and the Sultan of Singapore took place. Raffles then departed for Penang.

When Raffles first set foot on Singapore in 1819, there were about 500 people living on the island: approximately 100 Malay houses on the north bank of the Singapore River, and 30 families of Sea Nomads living on boats moored in the estuary. About 30 Chinese were also living on the island, largely employed in planting *gambir*, a shrub with leaves useful in tanning leather and making batik. The exact site of the house of the Temenggong is unknown, but one account places it "back from the river, between the sea and the river, near the obelisk."[19] The chief authority in Singapore was called the Temenggong, Abdul Rahman. He was officially subject to the Sultan of Riau, the capital of which was 100 km to the south on the island of Bintan. He had moved to Singapore only five years earlier, in 1814, mainly as an act of protest at the conduct of political affairs in Riau. Raffles, Farquhar and an Indian soldier made the first landing and proceeded to the Temenggong's house. The next day Raffles made a provisional treaty with the Temenggong, and British soldiers began to land. The treaty signed with Tengku Long from Riau in Singapore stated that the Governor-General of India had appointed Tengku Long to be "Sultan of Singapore and all the territories comprised in it, with the title of Sultan Husain Shah ibni Al-Marhum Sultan Mahmud."[20]

On 31 January Raffles wrote to his friend William Marsden: "Here I am at Singapore, true to my word, and in the enjoyment of all the pleasure which a footing on such classic ground must inspire." By "classic ground" he is again alluding to the historical role Singapore plays in the *Malay Annals*. This association with classical Malay literature obviously made an important contribution to Raffles' satisfaction in establishing a new port on this site. There would seem to be no other explanation for Raffles' fixation with establishing a British base there other than his desire to revive in some sense a port which he believed, and which archaeology has confirmed, did experience an earlier period of fluorescence.

Singapore was founded not for purely commercial reasons, but also because commercial operations were impossible in this area without a military presence to safeguard them. When the British established a port at Singapore, they were in imminent danger of having to defend it against a Dutch attack. Dutch military forces in the region were far superior to those of the British. Dutch forces, Raffles wrote, consisted of 10,000 European troops in Java, plus others in the Moluccas and other outer islands. Dutch warships stationed in the Netherlands Indies included one of 90 guns, another of 74, plus 3 frigates, 8 corvettes, and "innumerable smaller vessels; manned with upwards of 1700 Europeans, [this force] strikes terror through all the adjacent countries."[21]

R. Ross, Captain of HEIC *Discovery*, one of the surveying ships in Raffles' expedition, wrote on 6 March 1819 that he had been told that Melaka, at this time back under Dutch rule, had sent a recommendation to Batavia to seize the British at Singapore. The Dutch threatened to take Singapore by force, and put Farquhar "in chains". Thus it was not surprising that one of Raffles' first instructions to Farquhar concerned the defence of the settlement. Even the Temenggong of Johore, who was in fact quite glad to have the British as his backers, needed to make preparations to reconcile himself with the Dutch should they strike. He wrote to the Dutch authority at Melaka, "Tuan Raja Muda Adrian Koek," very soon after Raffles' arrival, reporting that the British had landed and assuring the Dutch that this had occurred without his approval.[22]

Thus it is not surprising that on 6 February 1819, while still in Singapore, Raffles wrote a detailed set of instructions for the future Resident, Col. Farquhar:

> Sir, Herewith I have the Honor to transmit to you one of the copies of the treaty this day conducted between the Honble the East India Company, and their Highness the Sultan of Johore, and the Tummungung of Singapoora and its dependencies...
>
> **13.** In determining the extent and nature of the works immediately necessary for the defence of the Port and Station my judgement has been directed in a great measure by your professional skill and experience. With this advantage, and from a careful survey of the Coast by Capt Ross, aided by my own personal inspection of the nature of the ground in the vicinity of the Settlement, I have no hesitation in conveying to you my authority for constructing the following works with the least delay practicable: on the hill overlooking the Settlement,

and commanding it and a considerable portion of the anchorage, a small Fort, or a commodious block-house on the principle which I have already described to you, capable of mounting eight or ten 12 pounders and of containing a magazine of brick or stone, together with a barrack for the permanent residence of 30 European artillery and or the temporary accommodation of the rest of the garrison in case of emergency. Along the coast in the vicinity of the Settlement one or two strong batteries for the protection of the shipping and at Sandy Point a redoubt and to the east of it a strong battery for the same purpose. The entrenchment of the Cantonment by lines and a palisade, as soon as the labor can be spared from works of more immediate importance.

14. These defences, together with Martello tower on Deep Water Point, which it is my intention to recommend to the Supreme Government, will in my judgement render the Settlement capable of maintaining a good defence.[23]

The "hill overlooking the settlement" was the place now known as Fort Canning Hill. In 1819 it was termed Bukit Larangan, the "Forbidden Hill" by the local inhabitants because according to local legend the palace of an ancient kingdom had once stood there. This story no doubt represents a residual memory of fourteenth-century Singapore; that its former role was still vividly enough remembered 400 years after the hill was abandoned and that it was still respected suggests that the Malays had a strong sense of it as a historic site.

Once again Munshi Abdullah has a colourful account of the way in which the story was told. Although he may not have witnessed the scene personally, his depiction of the beliefs surrounding the hill are probably accurate:

One day Colonel Farquhar wanted to ascend the Forbidden Hill, as it was called by the Temenggong. The Temenggong's men said 'None of us have the courage to go up the hill because there are many ghosts on it. Every day one can hear on it sounds as of hundreds of men. Sometimes one hears the sound of heavy drums and of people shouting.' Colonel Farquhar laughed and said, 'I should like to see your ghosts' and turning to his Malacca men 'Draw this gun to the top of the hill.' Among them there were several who were frightened, but having no option they pulled the gun up. All who went up were Malacca men, none of the Singapore men daring to approach the hill...When they reached the top Colonel Farquhar ordered the gun to be loaded and then he himself fired twelve rounds in succession over the top of the hill in front of them.[24]

Despite the emphasis which Raffles laid on the construction of a fort there as soon as possible, nothing was done to implement this instruction until the late 1850s. Raffles' insight in advocating that a defensive position be established on the hill eventually was ratified by the military decision to construct an artillery fort, called Fort Canning, on the site he had chosen 40 years earlier. By June, if not sooner, Raffles' plans had slightly altered: he envisioned the provision of a house for the settlement's governor on the hill. He wrote to Farquhar on 25 June 1819 that "The whole of the hill extending to the fort within the two rivers and the fresh water cut is to be reserved for the exclusive accommodation of the Chief Authority and is not to be otherwise appropriated except for defences." In another letter he wrote that "as soon as other more immediate works are complete a good bungalow for the residence of the chief authority may be constructed on the hill."[25] Another version of Raffles' instruction describes the area to be reserved for official purposes as the "whole space included within the Old Lines and the Singapore River."[26] The "Old Lines" refers to the old earth wall which Raffles found when he arrived, on the ground now corresponding to Stamford Road and part of Clemenceau. Together with the sea, the hill, the Singapore River, and the swampy ground in the Tank Road area, it formed a defensive bulwark against attack. This fort wall is mentioned in the *Dao i ji lue*, a fourteenth-century Chinese account of Singapore, and in the *Malay Annals*. Traces of it were still visible in 1819. It is not surprising that Raffles took an interest in the remains of old fortifications on the site of his new port. Aside from his interest in antiquities, he was obviously aware that an analysis of defensive preparations from an earlier period might assist him in designing as rapidly as possible a new defensive strategy for the settlement which he envisioned.

Not all of the British visitors were as impressed as Raffles and later John Crawfurd, second Resident of Singapore. In January 1819 J.G.F. Crawford, captain of the *Investigator*, saw little to excite the eye in the old rampart:

> Where the tents are pitched, the ground is level above one mile, partly cleared of the jungle, with a transparent fresh water brook or rivulet running through it ... This spot of ground is the site of the very ancient city and fort of Singapore ... No remnants of its former grandeur exist, not the slightest vestige of it has ever been discovered. As for the strength of the fortifications, no remains are to be seen excepting by those possessing a fertile imagination and can trace the foundation or parts of earthen bastions in a mound of earth that lines the beach and winds round the margins of the creek.[27]

None of the defensive works he envisioned — neither the "strong batteries" nor the Martello tower, let alone the entrenchment and palisade which would have enclosed the area at the foot of Fort Canning in the area of Hill Street — and which Raffles ordered, were erected. The only small fortifications built were at the mouth of the Singapore River, approximately on the site of the later Fort Fullerton, and a small battery at Scandal Point, now the northeast corner of the Padang.[28]

On the day after issuing this order, 7 February, Raffles left for Penang where he arrived on 13 February. He asked the Governor, Col. Bannerman, to send two companies of sepoys for the new settlement's defense against an anticipated Dutch attack, but Bannerman refused (for which he was later censured by the Calcutta authorities). Raffles had expected this, however, because he and Bannerman had long been on bad terms, and because Bannerman no doubt saw Singapore as a threat to the prosperity of Prince of Wales Island. Raffles then ordered a detachment of the 20th Regiment, Bengal Native Infantry, to move from Bencoolen to Singapore.[29]

Bannerman, believing that he had the support of the Indian government in disavowing Raffles' act in assuming responsibility for Singapore, wrote to Calcutta that:

> ...any force we are able to detach to Singapoor could not resist the overpowering armament at the disposal of the Batavia Government, although its presence would certainly compel Major Farquhar to resist the Netherlands even to the shedding of blood... Neither Major Farquhar's honour as a soldier nor the honour of the British Government now require him to attempt the defense of Singapoor by force of arms...[30]

But Hastings soon realised that the British merchant community in India was very enthusiastic about the foundation of Singapore. He then changed his tack, and wrote a nasty letter to Bannerman, now excoriating him for his cravenness in pandering to the Dutch: "we fear you would have difficulty in excusing yourselves should the Dutch be tempted to violence by the weakness of the detachment at Singapore and succeed in discharging it."[31] Bannerman then sent 200 more soldiers to Singapore. Bannerman also wrote to London, arguing that Singapore would be expensive to maintain and defend, and would not repay the costs. Though he lost the bureaucratic battle, Bannerman's prophecy did anticipate the conflict of interests and priorities between the need for defence, the amount of expenditure which should be devoted to it, and the distribution of the burden of paying for it which was to constitute a continuous theme of colonial Singapore's history.

The British establishment on the coast of Singapore came under the authority of the government of Fort Marlborough (Bengkulu) as of 6 February 1819, the date of the signing of the official agreement with Tengku Long. For the next three and a half years William Farquhar was Resident and also Commandant of the military forces, and operated as a virtually independent ruler although occasional orders came from Raffles in Bengkulu and the Governor-General at Fort William. The military played a dominant role in Singapore's early administration. In addition to Major (later Col.) William Farquhar, who held his commission from the Madras Engineers, other important appointments included Lt. Ralfe as Assistant Engineer, and Commander of Ordnance, and Lt. Low of 20th Native Infantry (NI), Cantonment Staff Officer. The original area under the control of the British did not include the entire island of Singapore, but only a small part of it. According to the "Arrangements Made for the Government of Singapore, In June 1819," Article 1, the boundaries of the area under the control of the British ran from Tanjong Malang on the west, to Tanjong Katong on the east, and as far inland as the range of a cannon shot.[32]

On 6 March 1819, Capt. Ross told Farquhar that the Dutch Governor of Melaka, Timmerman Thyssen, had sent a recommendation to his superiors in Batavia (Jakarta) that they attack Singapore. Farquhar had only about 150 sepoys, and they were unhappy because they were due to be rotated home to Bengal. He also had some artillery: a brigade of 12 pounders, and one brigade of 6 pounders manned by 30 Europeans of the Bengal Artillery. These light weapons would have been useless against a determined European man-of-war. The ship *Nearchus*, an East India Company cruiser, was leaky because of termites and could not be used. It had to be beached for repair. Food was also running out. There was no surplus production of food by the local population of Singapore which the soldiers could buy; the local people ate dried fish, fried sago and occasionally rice. The Temenggong ordered the Sea Gypsies to sell fish to Col. Farquhar, but they could not produce large quantities of this.

Farquhar sent a *prau* to Penang to ask for reinforcements against the possible Dutch attack, but Bannerman only advised that he escape before the attack came. The Dutch did not attack, however, and after a tense month things were looking up. On 1 April a detachment of 485 soldiers arrived from Bencoolen, and traders in Melaka managed to ship in food supplies despite threats from pirates and the Dutch. By early April, 100 small Malay trading vessels were said to have been anchored in the harbour. On the evening of 9 April the first junk arrived from Siam with an important cargo of food: rice, sugar, palm oil and fish. The new settlement was now on the Southeast Asian trading map.

The feared attack from the Dutch did not materialise. They did station a gunboat in the Straits to interdict shipping to Singapore. Pirates also took their toll; according to Munshi Abdullah, 40 Melaka Malays in one boat were killed by pirates. But during April 1819 the appearance of the site began to change. The troops set up their encampment at the foot of the future Fort Canning Hill. A bazaar and quarters for the camp followers also appeared. Bukit Larangan was cleared of forest after Farquhar had a cannon hauled up to the top and some rounds fired to reassure the local population that no ghosts remained of the former rulers. The brick ruins of the fourteenth-century structures mentioned in Chapter One were then revealed. Lt. Ralfe of the H.E.I. Company's artillery, appointed Executive Engineer, laid a road around the hill (creating much of the road which is now Canning Rise). Farquhar began to build a house for himself by the beach, somewhere near the present site of Empress Place.

Raffles arrived back in Singapore on 31 May 1819, but only stayed a short while. In the four months he had been absent, Singapore's population had grown from 400 to 5000, mainly Chinese. Bugis settlers had cleared ground to the east, in the Geylang area. On 28 June he left Singapore for his main post, which remained the isolated Fort Marlborough in Bengkulu. He was to visit Singapore only once more, after a lapse of three-and-a-half years. During that time much was to change.

The early history of the British occupation of Singapore inevitably revolves around the acts of T.S. Raffles. There are few other cities whose founding is so closely identified with the acts of an individual. Even now the name Raffles to most Singaporeans, who are of Asian rather than British ancestry, stands for the inauguration of Singapore history; all that had gone before, especially the fourteenth-century period which is only imperfectly known in myth and archaeology, to them is irrelevant to what Singapore was about to become. In a way this is a pity, because it suggests that modern Singapore would not exist were it not for the genius of Raffles and the military might of the East India Company. As we have seen, this is not true. A completely indigenous Singapore, comprising a cosmopolitan trading population, did exist and prosper here much earlier, owing nothing to external influence.

On the other hand, it is true that in the context of the early nineteenth century, the revival of an ancient port such as Singapore could only be undertaken by a group who had both the military resources and the commercial orientation of the British East India Company. The Dutch were content to stifle trade which they could not control rather than allow it to take its course even though the general level of prosperity would rise. Raffles insisted on free port status for Singapore, and this condition alone was largely responsible for the new settlement's explosive growth. The problem with this policy was that it meant funds for military protection would always be scarce, because there would be less revenue available to any local authorities to provide for defence.

The Dutch remained a threat to the settlement for the next five years. During this formative phase the Indian government regarded Singapore more as a military outpost rather than a future metropolitan entrepot.[33] Then a treaty was concluded in 1824, under the terms of which the British were to evacuate Bengkulu and acknowledge the primacy of Dutch interests in Sumatra in return for the right to develop a sphere of influence in the Malay Peninsula and Singapore, immune from Dutch interference. For the next quarter century, the most important threat to the settlement came not from a European, but from a local source; and not from a government, but from a disorganised set of violent men: the sea raiders whom the British termed "pirates".

It has long been recognised that the term "piracy" can be subjective; one person's pirate may be another's privateer. In Southeast Asia, the practice of raiding at sea existed at least as early as the fourteenth century, when Wang Dayuan gave an account of the pirate's lair at the Dragon's Tooth Strait.[34] No doubt it had existed much earlier than that. An inverse relationship has been observed between the incidence of piracy and the strength of government in the southern Straits of Melaka.[35] It seems that when political organisation in this area has been strong, the various independent groups of seafaring peoples have been organised by the ruling elite and used as naval forces. When political organisation has been lax, the volume of trade has declined, and individual groups of seafarers have turned to piracy.

Sea raiding was not perceived as a disreputable occupation. In fact Malay royalty in the early nineteenth century saw it as more honourable than honest trade. According to Munshi Abdullah:

The Sultan complained several times that the allowance paid him by the British was insufficient. Raffles suggested that he start a trading agency house, but 'When the Sultan and the Temenggong heard Mr. Raffles's words they laughed and said 'It is not the custom of rulers to engage in trade for they would lose dignity before other rulers.' When Mr. Raffles heard this the look on his face changed and his brow was dark, though he was smiling as he replied 'Your Highness, I am surprised to hear of such an extraordinary custom. Why should trading be so wicked that it brings disgrace when piracy brings no such disgrace?' the Sultan replied 'Piracy is our birthright and so brings no disgrace.'"[36]

In the period between 1820 and 1850, piracy formed the major threat to Singapore's trade and even its existence. Near the end of his last visit to Singapore, in June 1823, Raffles applied for a vessel to cruise against pirates. On 27 August 1823 Resident John Crawfurd hired a ketch, *Bona Fortuna*, to proceed against pirates but without success. In 1826 the fifth number of the *Singapore Chronicle* had a sketch of Malay piracy, probably by Crawfurd himself. The pirate ships of the time were quite large: usually 40–50 feet long, with a 15-foot beam. Their decks were made of split *nibong* wood. Smaller pirate craft put up thick plank bulwarks when fighting, while larger ones like those of the *Lanun*[37] had bamboo ledges hanging over their gunwales, with a protecting breastwork of plaited rattan about 3' [1m] high. A crew might consist of 20–30 men, augmented with oarsmen of captured slaves. Small craft would have nine oars a side; larger ones would be double-banked, with an upper tier of oarsmen seated on the bulwark projection hidden behind rattan breastwork.

Pirate armament included a stockade near the bow, with iron or brass 4 pounders, and another stockade aft, generally with two swivel guns. They also might have four or five brass swivels, or *rantaka*, on each side. Pirates carried bamboo shields, and were armed with spears, *keris* and such muskets and other firearms as they could get. Piracy continued on its course, in fact becoming worse, until the 1850s.[38] Ironically, one of the main factors which led to the elimination of piracy was the inception of the gutta-percha industry. This new source of income which the Sultan of Johore controlled was so lucrative that it finally convinced that noble to turn from a sponsor to a scourge of piracy.

Thus the main force which early Singapore had to fear was not the organised attack of a European-led foe, but the random raid of the pirate season. Fortunately, an assault on Singapore itself never took place. Despite the several threats to its survival, Raffles' creation lived through its earliest growing pains and took hold on Singapore Island. Situated as it was between two oceans and astride what seemed destined to become the most important British trade route, the new settlement seemed bound to become not only an important commercial port but a necessary military bastion as well.

Notes

1. J. Bastin, *The British in West Sumatra 1685–1825*, Kuala Lumpur, 1965; J. Kathirithamby-Wells, *The British West Sumatran Presidency (1760–85): Problems of Early Colonial Enterprise*, Kuala Lumpur, 1977.

2. Court of Directors of the East India Company to the Governor-General, Bengal, 7 April 1829, in V. Harlow and F. Madden (editors), *British Colonial Developments 1774–1834*, Oxford, 1953, 77.

3. A.H. Hill, "The founding of Singapore described by 'Munshi Abdullah,'" in *JMBRAS*, vol. 28, #3, 125-132, 137-149; *Singapore 150 Years*, 94-111.

4. Harlow and Madden; Bexley Papers, B.M. Add. MSS. 31, 237, ff244-57 passim. This paper was intended for Canning; a copy was enclosed in Raffles to Vansittart, 23 October 1817.

5. C. Wurtzburg, *Raffles of the Eastern Isles*, Singapore, 1986 (1954), 435.

6. Ibid.

7. Bexley Papers, 68-69.

8. Public Record Office (PRO), Bengal Secret Consultations, Vol. 307, John Adam to Sir Stamford Raffles, 5 December 1818. The "Governor-General-in-Council at Fort William in Bengal" was the official term for the "government of India" under British rule from 1774 to 1947.

9. C.B. Buckley, *An Anecdotal History of Old Times in Singapore*, Kuala Lumpur/Singapore, 1965, 63.

10. Wurtzburg, 454.

11. D. and J. Moore, *The First 150 Years of Singapore*, Singapore, 1969.

12. Harlow and Madden, 73. This letter was written on 10 June 1819 to Col. Addenbrooke, equerry to HRH Princess Charlotte, one of Raffles' main royal backers.

13. T.S. Raffles, "The Founding of Singapore," in *JSBRAS*, vol. 2, 175-182; reprinted in Tan Sri Dat' Mubin Sheppard (editor), *Singapore 150 Years*, Singapore, 1982, 87-93.

14. Wurtzburg, 486.

15. Singapore National Library (SNL), microfilm NL 57, series L 10, General Order, By the Honourable the Lt.-Governor, Singapore, 7 February 1819.

16. Moore and Moore, 31.

17. Wurtzburg, 620-21.

18. Farquhar was present at Melaka's surrender to the British in 1795, and was appointed supreme authority of that port for several terms. He died in Scotland as a Major-General in 1839, at the age of 68.

19. H.T. Haughton, "The Landing of Raffles in Singapore by an Eyewitness", in *JSBRAS*, 10, 1882, 285-86; *Singapore 150 Years*, 74-75. This article contains a statement by Wa Hakim, of the Kelumang "tribe" of Sea Nomads, who claimed to have been 15 years old when Raffles arrived. In 1882, when this statement was taken, he lived on Pulau Brani.

20. Hill, "The founding of Singapore," 103.

21. Moore and Moore, 9-10.

22. W.E. Maxwell, "The founding of Singapore", in *JSBRAS*, 4, 104-113; reprinted in *Singapore 150 Years*, 77-86.

23. Wurtzburg, 495, 498.

24. Hill, "The founding of Singapore," 99.

25. Buckley, 57-58.

26. SNA, Letters to Bencoolen, February 1819-June 1820, L 10, folio 73.

27. Wurtzburg, 486.

28. The advice to build a "Martello tower" needs some explanation. These were a relatively new form of defensive work in 1819. Raffles must have made a study of current theories of coastal defense in Europe to advocate such a structure. No Martello towers seem to have been built anywhere in Asia; none was in fact erected in Singapore. The Martello towers derived their name from a stone tower at Mortella, an old watch tower at the Golfe de Ste Florent, Corsica. In 1794 two large British ships with a total of 106 guns were defeated by this tower with three cannon. The British were so impressed that in 1805 they began building a series of 103 towers on the English coast, which were finished in 1812. They were built of brick, averaged 10 m high, with walls 4 m thick at base, 1.8 m thick at the parapet. Others were built in North America, and South Africa. They only had one gun, a 32 pounder. They were usually oval, surrounded by a dry ditch, and had a 30-man garrison. Martello towers were adopted around 1804 as defensive works for British coasts. Though none were built in Asia, several were erected elsewhere in the British empire, for example in Canada. See A. Charbonneau, Y. Desloges and M. Lafrance, *Quebec the Fortified City: From the 17th to the 19th Century*, Ottawa, 1982. The authors quote one source, p. 171, to the effect that "no other kind of works are, upon the whole, better adapted for the defence of an open beach against a hostile fleet."

29. Wurtzburg, 505.

30. Moore and Moore, 38.

31. Ibid, 40.

32. Buckley, 59.

33. B. Nunn, "Some account of our governors and civil service," in Makepeace.

34. Several excellent works on the cultural and historical context of piracy in the Singapore region have been written. Detailed discussions of the subject may be read in O. Rutter, *The Pirate Wind*, Singapore, 1984 (original edition 1910); N. Tarling, *Piracy and Politics in the Malay World*, Singapore, 1963; and C.A. Trocki, *Prince of Pirates*, Singapore, 1979.

35. O.W. Wolters, *Early Indonesian Commerce: A Study of the Origins of Srivijaya*, Ithaca, 1967.

36. Hill, 108.

37. *Lanun* or *Ilanun* were named after a pirate haunt in the southern Philippines. Until the late nineteenth century people still spoke of a *musim Lanun* or "pirate wind," a season when pirate raids were likely to take place. The *Lanun* were well organised, and able to capture whole settlements as well as individual ships.

38. G.E. Brooke, "Piracy," in Makepeace et al, 290-300.

3

From Fieldworks to Fort Canning 1823-1866

R affles was now in poor health. Three of his four children had died of illness in Bengkulu. In May 1820 Raffles' third child, Stamford Marsden, had been born; on 27 June 1821 Leopold Stamford died. Stamford Marsden died on 3 January 1822; his daughter Charlotte Sophia Somerset Tanjong Segara died on 14 January. The fourth and only surviving child, a young daughter named Ella, was hurriedly sent away without either parent to England on the next available ship in March 1822. News of her safe arrival reached her parents in April 1823.

Raffles left Bengkulu for Singapore on 17 September 1822, arriving on 10 October. Just before setting off, his close friend William Jack also died in Bengkulu. Despite this seemingly endless parade of tragedies, Raffles was cheered by what he found when he arrived after an absence of over three years. The economy of the settlement was thriving; the population had grown to 10,000. The day after he arrived, he wrote:

> The coldest and most disinterested could not quit Bencoolen and land at Singapore without surprise and emotion. What then must have been my feelings after the loss of almost everything that was dear to me on that ill-fated coast? After all the risks and dangers to which this, my almost only child, has been exposed, to find it grown and advanced beyond measure and even my warmest anticipations and expectations, in importance, wealth and interest — in everything that can give it value and permanence?[1]

Other aspects of Singapore's development he found less pleasing. He found that Farquhar had disregarded several of his instructions relating to the formal town plan he had drawn up. Storehouses and dwellings had been built on the ground reserved for government. Raffles ordered that they be moved to the south side of the Singapore River. This brought him into conflict with Farquhar and the European residents. Raffles noted that Farquhar was not dressing in military uniform, an indication that discipline was not being maintained. None of the fortifications he had ordered had been built.

As a result of this and other disagreements, on 27 January 1823 Raffles wrote to the Governor-General in Calcutta that he "considered Colonal Farquhar to be totally unequal to so important a charge as that of Singapore" and proposed that he be relieved by Dr. John Crawfurd of the Bengal Civil Service. Crawfurd arrived in Singapore on 27 May via the chartered brig *Hero of Malown*.[2] With his arrival, British Singapore moved into the second phase of its growth.

Creating a Defended Port

During Crawfurd's tenure, Singapore was transferred from a dependency of Bengkulu to a position directly under the government of Bengal. In 1824, two important treaties were signed with major consequences for Singapore's future. One, with the Dutch, the Treaty of London, finally removed one major threat to Singapore's security, that of a Dutch attack. The second, with the Temenggong and Sultan, negotiated by Crawfurd and signed on 2 August, extended British control of Singapore from the limited coastal strip around the Singapore River to include the entire island, except for some land at Telok Blangah. Singapore was now politically separate from Johore.

Other threats however remained. Not the least of these was internal. The rapid increase in population created a large body of rootless men out to seek their fortunes, a veritable Wild West frontier town. The possibility of civil unrest was ever present. One of the most severe incidents occurred while Raffles was present in 1823. Farquhar was stabbed by a Malay who, feeling himself permanently dishonoured, indulged in the custom of running amok. He stabbed a number of people to death, and managed even to wound Col. Farquhar while he was walking in the town before he himself was killed. Raffles decided that the body of the murderer should be hung from a gallows. The Malay authorities however objected and, according to one of Raffles' friends, Col. Nahuijs, "The natives adopted a threatening attitude and awakened considerable fear among the citizens."[3] Apparently the Chinese supported Raffles' policy, thus further inflaming the situation. After three days Raffles had the body handed over to his community for burial, and the immediate danger died down. This incident was perhaps the first example of a situation in which the mercantile community of Singapore felt a direct threat to their security. Concerns about the safety of the growing investments in the commerce of Singapore were already being voiced. This incident led directly to the introduction of a regulation according to which no one might carry a *keris* into the British-ruled settlement other than Malays of high social standing, and even they had to have their names registered at the police station.

The business community was already beginning to argue that Singapore needed a stronger defensive establishment. In the words of Col. Nahuijs:

> Two companies of Bengalis and a detachment of 25 European Artillery must hardly suffice to ensure the safety of their people and the large values that are lying in Singapore warehouses in the way of goods, especially opium and piece goods, two valuable articles which the natives

particularly prize. Many of the residents are not without anxiety that a man like the Malayan Temmengong, tempted by the large treasure, could easily be induced with the underlings and a great many of his friends, the pirates, to attack the weak garrison and citizens unexpectedly and then clear off with his booty to places where he could not be easily traced. People were hoping therefore that a good fort would be built, that the garrison would be strengthened and the port guarded by a couple of the company cruisers from Bombay.[4]

During Raffles' six-month stay in Singapore in 1822–23, he built himself a house on Singapore Hill (Fort Canning). When he left, Dr. John Crawfurd moved in and enlarged it. The house became the official residence of Singapore's chief authority. Thus the former Forbidden Hill obtained a new name: Government Hill. During this period of residence in Singapore, Raffles devoted himself mainly to civil administration. Despite the calls from some quarters of the public for more development of Singapore's defensive capability, he did not follow up his previous instructions that a fort be built on the hill where he now resided. Instead he had a botanical garden laid out, the boundaries of which can be seen on the map of 1825, and the settlement's European cemetery was established there as well.

The Singapore Institution (later renamed Raffles Institution) was founded as Raffles' last public act in Singapore. On 9 June, two weeks after Dr. Crawfurd arrived to take up the Resident's position, Raffles left Singapore for the last time. The garrison order issued the previous day read: "The troops in garrison to be in readiness to parade tomorrow at day-break to form a street leading from the landing place at the end of High Street in consequence of the embarkation of the Honourable the Lieutenant-Governor of Fort Marlborough."[5]

The rest of Raffles' life was short and held yet more disappointment. Another child, Flora, born 19 September 1823 in Bengkulu, died there 28 November 1823. On 2 February 1824 Raffles departed Bengkulu for England. The first night out, his ship, the *Fame*, caught fire and sank with all Raffles' property and collections aboard. He and his wife and crew had to make their way back to Bengkulu and await another ship. On 10 April Raffles left Bengkulu and reached England 20 August 1824, to be reunited with his daughter. He also learned that on 17 March 1824 a final settlement had been reached with the Dutch regarding Singapore. On 5 July 1826, Raffles was found dead in his house at High Wood, one day before his 45th birthday. An autopsy showed that he had been suffering from a brain disease, which caused the severe headaches of which he complained.

From 1819 to 1826 Singapore had been administered by the two Residents, Farquhar and Crawfurd, who reported to Calcutta. In 1826 a reorganisation took place. Robert Fullerton, a civilian from Madras, became President of the incorporated settlements of Prince of Wales Island (Penang), Singapore and Melaka, which together formed one of the four Presidencies of India. Penang was the largest settlement, and so became the centre of the Presidency's administration. First Prince, then Murchison, both of whom had served previously in Bengkulu when it was British, were chief authorities in Singapore during this period with the title Resident Councillor. Fullerton had trouble in getting the machinery of government to work smoothly, but he managed to start work on Fort Fullerton. Then in March 1827 he was suddenly recalled.

Meanwhile in 1827 Capt. Daniel Ross, B.M., surveyed the Singapore Strait officially and prepared a chart (published 1829), while G.D. Coleman was sent to survey Blakang Mati. In the same year, 1827, the first major study of Singapore's defensive potential to be conducted by a professional was carried out, by Capt. Edward Lake of the Bengal Engineers. He was given the dual task of reporting on Singapore's fortifications and civil public works. On the civil side, he recommended that a canal be cut from the Singapore River to Telok Blangah. In part he based his proposals on recommendations given him by Lt. Philip Jackson, Bengal Artillery, who had been in the settlement since 1822, and had drawn one of the earliest maps of the settlement; it seems probable that Jackson in turn received some of his ideas from Farquhar.[6]

Lake's inventory of the scanty defensive works then extant includes the following information:

> Magazine: In arched building / bombproof / of masonry. In good order.

> Lines of Fortification and Battery: A fieldwork formed entirely of earth. Have fallen in many places and are unserviceable in their present state but the battery may be reformed and will form one of the chain projected in my report on the defence of the place.

This latter work must have been "Battery Point", later Fort Fullerton. Interestingly, Lake called for the demolition of warehouses next to the site which belonged to Capt. Flint, Raffles' son-in-law.[7]

After concluding his research, Lake compiled a report advocating an elaborate scheme for Singapore's defence, incorporating a fortress with a vaulted chamber inside the wall (a "case mated redoubt") south of the Singapore River mouth, another similar fort at Tanjong Katong, on a spit of land at the entrance to the Kallang Basin then called Sandy Point, and three other batteries in between the two forts along the shore. He also envisioned a hilltop citadel as a fortified post and place of refuge for Europeans. Two sites were considered: Captain Pearl's Hill, south of the Singapore River, and Residency Hill (an alternative name for Government Hill, which in 1860 became the hill known as Fort Canning).

Residency Hill had the advantage that any enemy landing on the north side of the chain of batteries planned along the coast would have to pass under the fire of the hill to reach the town. The main disadvantages of the hill included its large size, and the broken nature of the ground around it, which might enable an enemy force to march from the town to the New Harbour west of the town unseen from the hill. Lake concluded by advocating Captain Pearl's Hill for the citadel. It had a more convenient size, was located in the midst of flat land, and was closer to the new harbour. Its principal disadvantage, that an enemy landing north of the town could attack it unimpeded, he felt was outweighed by the other factors.

The strategic perceptions demonstrated by this first report on Singapore's defences reveal a point of view which prevailed for the duration of the long British military presence in Singapore. Lake's main concerns were focussed on protecting the harbour from naval attack. The secondary concern of providing an internal strong point which might provide refuge in case of a local insurrection was a common one in the early colonial era, when Europeans and Chinese often found themselves in a small minority, surrounded by potentially hostile populations. Lake also considered fortifying Blakang Mati.[8]

The possibility of an attack from the landward side of the island was considered remote at this time, as it no doubt was. To reach the town through the jungle-covered swampy interior would have been a major task rendering any attempt at surprise fruitless. For the next 120 years the pattern envisioned by Capt. Lake continued to govern the construction of the defences of Singapore island itself, even though the possibility of an attack from the north was never forgotten. In the end, the only physical outcome of Lake's report was the building of Fort Fullerton. The rest of his plans lay in the archives for years. When other schemes for defence were contemplated in the middle decades of the nineteenth century, however, they followed generally similar lines to those he had envisioned in 1827. The discussion of the hilltop citadel in particular was revived, and the relative merits of Pearl's Hill and Residency Hill were to be reconsidered.[9]

Military activity continued to occupy a significant portion of the settlement. The main military cantonment occupied the area near what is now Short Street. The large exercising ground was roughly bounded by Prinsep St, Albert St, Queen St, and Bras Basah. Around 1827 the cantonments were moved to the Outram Road area. A military hospital stood in Selegie Road until February 1827; then it fell down. This occurrence seems to typify the gulf between the demands of the local residents for protection, and their willingness to pay for it. Between 1833 and 1845 all ill Europeans were treated in a gallery of the Pauper Hospital (a brick building which stood near the present Singapore History Museum).

On the side of civil administration, Singapore continued to perpetuate the fiction that it was part of a Malay sultanate. The Temenggong Abdul Rahman died at Singapore on December 1825, and was buried at the Telok Blangah Mosque. He was succeeded by his second son Ibrahim, then 15, who died in 1862, and was also buried there. Ibrahim was an energetic person who played an important part in establishing the position of Johore as a separate polity independent of Singapore. The Johore ruler continued to be called Temenggong until 1868, when the title changed to Maharajah until 1885. From that time on the title of Johore's chief authority has been Sultan.

The 1830s were a period of relative tranquillity and growing prosperity in Singapore. In 1830 Robert Ibbetson became Resident, and the Straits Settlements were reduced to a Residency under the government of Bengal. The title of Governor of the Straits Settlements was created in 1832. The holder of this position was responsible to the Indian government until 1867 when the Straits Settlements were transferred to the Colonial Office (CO). Kenneth Murchison occupied this position from 1833 to 1837, when he was succeeded by Samuel George Bonham (1837–43). According to one characterisation, Murchison "did not bring any very great ability to bear upon the affairs of the island, and his administration was distinguished for its singular immunity from anything in the shape of excitement."[10]

Sultan Hussein, Singapore's putative head of state, died at Melaka, in September 1835, and was buried at Tranquera Mosque, where his well-preserved grave may still be seen under a special roof, along with a plaque recording his biography: "On his death no steps were taken as to the succession."[11] In other words, the British, having no further need of a Malay ruler to give their settlement legitimacy in the eyes of the surrounding population or in international law, simply allowed the position to vanish. The remains of the old palace still stand in Kampong Glam, however, and are inhabited by descendants of the old royal line.

While Samuel G. Bonham was Governor (1837–43), the permanent residence of the supreme authority in the Straits Settlements was moved to Singapore. This was the era of the China Wars; Singapore became the point of departure and supply for British fleets heading there. This made it, for the first time, an important centre for distant British military operations. The first great fleet went to China from Singapore in April 1839. Two divisions containing 36 transports and 12 men-of-war set off, each led by a steamer. After his stint in Singapore, and the con- clusion of the China Wars, Bonham became Governor of Hong Kong, destined to rival Singapore as an imperial commercial and military post. But for the moment, despite the very incomplete state of its own defences, growing Singapore remained the only place in the region the British could develop fairly readily as a naval and military centre should they so choose.

Threats, Forts and the Basis of Defence

In 1843, after a succession of civilian Governors, a military man was appointed to the position, the first since William Farquhar: Col. William John Butterworth. There was some protest against his appointment; the *Singapore Free Press* wrote that the Governor-General, Lord Ellenborough, seemed "to place his special delight in depressing and mortifying the Civil Service, and bestowing all the lucrative and honourable posts on the Military."[12] Butterworth's accession to the governorship, it was said, was due to a friendship which he had formed with Lord Ellenborough whom he met at the Cape while Ellenborough was on his way to become Viceroy of India. Whatever the manner of his appointment, Butterworth was the first chief administrator of Singapore since 1827 to take an active interest in Singapore's defences. By 1844 Singapore's estimated population had grown to 50,000.[13] Thus the settlement's lack of any defences began to appear more and more glaring a weakness. Pressure to rectify it was slowly building from many quarters.

Butterworth in 1843 had Capt. Samuel Best of the Madras Engineers draw up an elaborate proposal for the defences of the island. These plans were however shelved. Only in 1859 would a revised plan by Capt. Collyer (after whom Collyer Quay is named) for constructing fortification works on the island finally be implemented. Nevertheless it is instructive to study Best's plans in order to appreciate the direction in which military thinking was evolving, and to obtain some indication of the strategic considerations which British military planners at that time perceived as relevant to Singapore's situation.

In August 1843 the government of Madras was informed by the government of India that Lake's plans were lost![14] Madras then sent Capt. Samuel Best to draw up plans for fortified works and a garrison of 600 men. Like Lake, he advocated the development of a citadel, plus minor redoubts on hills around the town, a continuous field entrenchment, sea batteries and Martello towers, and "a vast semicircle of floating batteries for the enclosure and protection of the anchorage."[15]

A proposal to fortify the New Harbour was also advanced in 1843 by Capt. James Bart, Madras Engineers. He wanted to place a redoubt at Tanjong Rhu. Seven batteries were to be sited to defend New Harbour, and five more at the waterfront from Telok Ayer to Kallang Basin. He also brought up the idea of moving the garrison to Blakang Mati (for which like Capt. Lake he used the alternative name of the Island of St. George). Nothing came of this proposal either. Blakang Mati was still believed to be too unhealthy for habitation away from the fringe along New Harbour. The only part of his elaborate plan that was implemented was the construction of a sea wall around Fort Fullerton.[16]

In May 1845 Maj.-Gen. Pollock, Commander of HEIC troops in the Straits Settlements, expressed "grave concern" at the defencelessness of Singapore. He informed the Bengal Presidency that Singapore's only defence was a "half sunken battery for six guns" on the Esplanade (the old Scandal Point battery) with insufficient range. Pollock suggested building four batteries with the latest pattern 56 pounder guns, which were 10 feet long, weighed 90 cwt, and had a range of 5000 yards. His reports were endorsed two years later by Rear-Admiral S.H. Englefield, Commander-in-Chief of HM Naval Forces in the East Indies and adjacent islands. The latter in turn drew the attention of the Governor-General-in-Council to the unsatisfactory defences of the island. Bengal's reply was that Singapore should depend on naval rather than land forces — suggesting the only apparent threat was external. Governor Butterworth lamented that there were no guns in position or batteries in Singapore.[17]

One reason for the lack of urgency in developing Singapore's defences was probably the invisibility of any other great power which might pose a threat to the settlement. Local disturbances, however, remained an important worry; in the 1840s piracy was still rampant, and posed a significant danger to the merchants of Singapore. During the 1820s and

1830s nearly every issue of the Singapore newspapers contained reports of pirate attacks. The situation became so bad in the 1830s that pirates could be seen attacking trading ships in broad daylight just outside the Singapore harbour. The potential for trade in Singapore was believed to suffer greatly from this problem. Merchants asked repeatedly for protection. In 1833 Chinese merchants themselves grouped together to charter a vessel to attack the pirates. The pirates were not confined to isolated bands; in 1830 a group of 30 pirate boats fought a battle with boats from the HMS *Southampton* and the East India Company schooner *Diamond*. Major pirate bases were located in the Dindings of Perak and on Galang Island south of Singapore. As a result of repeated requests, the British sloop *Wolf* plus two other gunboats were sent to Singapore. The *Andromache* was able to destroy many pirate boats because it was disguised as a trading ship carrying many animals on deck.[18]

The piracy problem in the immediate environs of Singapore was only significantly alleviated when a steamship, the *Diana*, arrived in 1837. In its first engagement with pirates, the attackers thought the ship was on fire and would be easy prey. The *Diana* however sailed into a pack of six pirate boats against the wind, and the surprise of this manoeuvre resulted in a major victory. This technological advance helped to alleviate, though not eliminate, the piracy problem.

In 1851 the HEIC's policy was to entrust Singapore's defence in the event of war to naval forces. The fixed defences of the Straits Settlements were to be limited to those facilities which could repel pirates "or for resistance against assault in the event of the temporary absence of Men of War and Steamers from the Port."[19] In 1851 no foreign navy posed a threat to Singapore. France, the only other major power in the region, was then extending its sway over Cochin China and Annam, but the British did not appear to consider this a serious threat.[20] In August 1851 the Madras Military Board sent to Singapore artillery supplies including eight heavy 8" iron guns (also known as 68 pounders), each to be equipped with 20 rounds of hollow shot, 250 common shells, and five cartridges of canister shot. This indicates that "the authorities were preparing against internal disturbances, as well as foreign naval attacks."[21] These guns were set up on the shore at either side of the main administrative area of the town: four at Fort Fullerton, four at Scandal Point.

The Indian government continued to discuss the advisability of expanding Singapore's defences, but gave no sign that they considered this an urgent matter. In 1852 the Indian authorities decided to approve the construction of two batteries of cannon and a magazine for gunpowder.[22] The Governor however thought that one of these batteries would prove useless and that more complex defences were needed. The Governor made his own suggestions for what he considered would be effective defensive works; in response the Military Board recommended sending a military engineer to review the situation in Singapore.[23] In August 1853 Lt. Henry Yule of the Bengal Engineers was detached to compile another study of the Singapore situation. He had studied the proposals of Lake and Best, and came to the wise conclusion that:

Both these able Officers appear to have been carried away by their schemes and to have forgotten that there are two kinds of impracticable projects, those that can't be executed and those that won't be executed. Under the latter head an observer would have classed both, but especially Capt. Best.[24]

Perhaps both Lake and Best had little expectation that their proposals would be executed, and so felt themselves free to indulge in schemes of a purely theoretical nature.

Already in October 1853 the Madras Military Board told Butterworth that they were sending him four 56 pounder cannon and three 8" gun platforms. Butterworth ordered work to commence on a Barbette Battery and mortar platforms at New Harbour.[25] A battery was set up at the end of Palmer's Road, thus forming the initial stage of what was to become Fort Palmer. Yule recommended that Singapore be defended by four batteries: at Fort Fullerton, Mount Palmer, Tanjong Katong, and Mount Faber.[26] The Governor-General-in-Council sanctioned the proposal[27] and in March 1855 the Governor of the Straits Settlements reported that Fort Fullerton, Mount Palmer and Mount Faber batteries had been completed.[28] A later report however informed India that the defensive work proposed at Tanjong Katong had not been undertaken because the sandy soil at the site was unsuitable.[29]

Not long after Yule was sent to Singapore, events emanating from far-off Europe again began to impinge on Southeast Asia, creating apprehension among the British population who resumed appeals for greater expenditure on security for the settlement. The Crimean War, which began in 1854, was one of the principal of these. A Russian naval squadron entered the South China Sea, calling at Manila and Batavia, and causing alarm in Singapore. Only one British naval vessel was present in the Straits of Melaka at the time: HM Sloop *Rapid*. Governor Butterworth again wrote to the Commander-in-Chief of the East India and China Station urging that renewed attention be paid to the exposed position of Singapore.

In May of the same year, 1854, major rioting broke out in Singapore. Several hundred people were killed during fighting between Chinese factions which lasted 12 days. The original stimulus was ostensibly the refusal of the Hokkien to join with the Teochew to contribute to a fund for rebel soldiers driven out of Guangdong by Imperial troops. The military events in Guangdong were part of the Taiping Rebellion, a popular revolt against the corruption of the Qing administration. Its leader considered himself an incarnation of Jesus Christ, but the majority of Taiping adherents considered their main goal to be the re-establishment of an ethnically Chinese empire in place of that ruled by the Manchu minority. The rebels achieved considerable success, nearly capturing Shanghai, before they were eventually put down after enormous bloodshed. But the real reason for the upheaval in Singapore was, as the British surmised, another dispute between rival secret societies.[30] When the battles had run their course, 400 people were dead and 300 houses burnt. One of the main concomitants of the fighting was the looting of

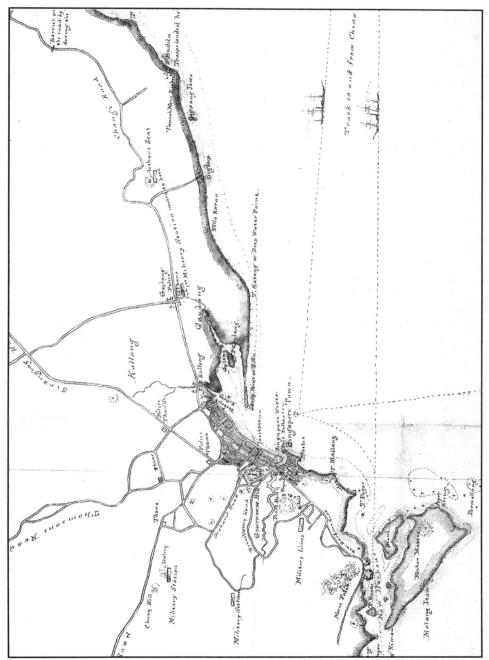

1854 riots

shops belonging to one faction which happened to be in an area controlled by another. The attentions of the Chinese rioters were completely devoted to each other; the British were neither harmed nor directly involved. The British forces marched through the riot-torn areas, and when they were visible disturbances ceased, but as soon as they left fighting resumed. The fact they were unable to quell the disturbances and restore order until the rioters themselves settled their dispute, nevertheless made the British aware that they were largely at the mercy of the indigenous population whom they presumed to rule.[31]

The total European population of Singapore was always miniscule in comparison with the Asian majority. In 1841 there were a grand total of 119 Europeans in Singapore. By 1871 this figure rose to 1329, out of a total population now numbering 96,087. By 1881 the proportion of Europeans remained only 2% of the total. This numerical inferiority explains some measure of the Europeans' concern over these large-scale battles despite their not being directly involved. The ease with which both troubles between the British and Chinese governments in China and secret society feuds there spilt over into Singapore, and produced unrest in response, fuelled such concern. This new threat added an important twist to the subsequent development of the defences of Singapore.

The Governor was now Edmund Augustus Blundell, who had been Commissioner of the Tenasserim provinces in Burma. On 21 April 1856 Governor Blundell wrote to the Secretary to the government of India, Fort William, to report on the progress of the defences of Singapore.[32] He pointed out that the absence of a battery in the Tanjong Katong area on the northeast end of the harbour left a hole in the defences. The soil there however he felt was not strong enough to support any sizeable structure.

One of the main points in his letter was to impress again upon the Indian authorities the necessity of providing "a place of refuge against any sudden attack of the enemy or an uprising amongst the Chinese population." He placed particular stress on the possibility of a rebellion by the Chinese and noted the comparatively small numbers of Europeans in Singapore. He reviewed the potential locations for such a refuge, and once again the choice came down to a consideration of the relative merits of Pearl's Hill and Government Hill. Like his precedessor, he and his subordinates — the Officer Commanding the Troops, Lt.-Col. Pooley, and Capt. Macpherson of the Madras Artillery — all thought Pearl's Hill the most suitable spot for such a work. The disadvantages of Government Hill were lack of space, even if Government House were to be moved, and the hill's distance from the military cantonment.

Other security matters which concerned Blundell included piracy. He argued that two gunboats ought to be sent to help clear the seas of pirates and to protect the town. Piracy had still not been completely eliminated as a source of danger to the settlement of Singapore itself, as well as its shipping.[33] Another theme which he repeated was the need for European artillerymen. Arguing that the Golundaze were not strong enough to work the 68 pounder guns, he suggested that the European regiment be transferred from Penang but noted that barracks would have to be built for them.[34] The extant arsenal he characterised as too small and in a dilapidated and dangerous state. A new commissariat godown was also needed; previously, a private house had been used for the store! This provides interesting evidence of the makeshift nature of Singapore's defensive infrastructure.

Yule agreed with the proposal for a citadel. On 25 June 1856 he wrote to Calcutta recommending that the place of refuge be located at Pearl's Hill, as Lake had recommended in 1827 (although Capt. Best preferred "Scott's Hill" [Mount Wallich]):

> Government Hill has some marked advantages of position in its ready accessibility from the town and adjoining villas [unobstructed] command over the greater part of the town and the roads leading to it and of some considerable extent of the beach and bay. Captain Macpherson objects to the restricted area of the summit, but from a rough sketch in my possession, I find the plateau on the top to measure about 100 yards by 200 which probably would be sufficient for the purpose, were the Government House removed.[35]

Pearl's Hill had similar advantages although it did not command the bay. More immediate points in favour of Pearl's Hill were that it was unoccupied and immediately available:

> To adopt the Government Hill would involve the removal of Government House from one of the most beautiful sites in the world for such a building; the removal of military lines to some position in the vicinity, and the construction of less destructable bridges between the Hill and the main body of the town than now exist or at least did exist three years ago.

However Yule recognised that he did not have the benefit of the latest information, since he had been away from Singapore for three years, and announced that he would agree to anything Macpherson recommended, since he was on the spot. An alternative proposed partial fortification of Government Hill with a few guns in position on it, without in any way interfering with the grounds or privacy of the Government House. This sensible suggestion does not seem to have received serious consideration.[36]

Yule disagreed with Blundell's criticism of the suitability of the soil at the site of the third battery recommended for Tanjong Katong, but agreed that steam gunboats would be a much better solution to the problem of the defences than this battery. Once again the theme of the desirability of dependence on a sea-based rather than land-based deterrent was sounded:

> It might not be out of place to refer to the limited scope of defences which were planned by me in 1853 in accordance with Lord Dalhousie's minute on the subject. Something very different in the scale both of defences and of Garrison would be required, were the main stay of

safety and that settlement to be anything but the preponderance and vigilance of the British Navy in these seas...[37]

The Governor-General-in-Council in August 1856 finally sanctioned the construction of the refuge. This letter discussed the sites for the refuge as suggested by Blundell in his letter of 21 April 1856.[38] Mounts Wallich and Palmer were private property; either would have to be purchased, and the price was apt to be expensive. To adapt Government Hill as a fort would mean the removal of Government House to some other site, the removal of the lines, and the construction of sturdier bridges between the hill and the town. In view of all this evidence, Pearl's Hill was judged to be the most appropriate site, and the Indian government sanctioned the construction of such a fort subject to the approval of the estimates and plans which he was to submit as early as was convenient. Blundell's request for European artillery for Singapore was approved in September 1856,[39] provided that suitable barracks were built.[40]

In 1857 Blundell forwarded a sketch of the work proposed at Pearl's Hill and reported that convict labourers had already begun work. But the sketch was very rough, without sections, scale or meridian.[41] Blundell had taken advantage of the presence of a detachment of Royal Engineers to lay out a small fort on the summit of the hill, but the detachment departed suddenly and the plan was left in a rough state. The government would not agree to begin work without better documentation, so it ordered that the work be stopped until the arrival in Singapore of an engineer officer who was ordered there from Madras.[42] With the sketch were forwarded estimates for barracks buildings but the Governor-General-in-Council did not approve of the designs, sent revised designs and estimates and asked that the buildings form part of the defences of Pearl's Hill.[43]

An important event which increased the sense of urgency to introduce a major programme of construction of defence works in Singapore was the Indian Mutiny, which broke out in May 1857. In the wake of the Mutiny, the HEIC was taken over by the British Crown, and by 1867 the old Company had been completely phased out. During the transitional period the Straits Settlements remained under the Bengal Presidency. The Bengal government instructed Capt. Collyer of the Madras Engineers to take on the job of making more professional plans for the fortifications of Singapore. In December 1857 Collyer wrote a "Report upon the works proposed to be erected on Pearl's Hill at Singapore as a citadel of strong place for refuge and defence against internal aggression." At this date the selection of Pearl's Hill seemed to have been finalised. A letter of 14 December 1857 included the statement that "the eminence called Pearl's Hill, has been selected as the site of the work and his Lordship in Council would not wish this selection to be disturbed."[44]

Blundell forwarded the first draft of these plans to India in February 1858.[45] These included a plan for a citadel, barracks, arsenal, and commissariat at Pearl's Hill. Collyer however felt that Pearl's Hill was not large enough to hold all these buildings. He suggested that Government Hill too should be partially fortified, which could be done without any extra cost by prisoners. Collyer began by assuming that Pearl's Hill would have to be exploited as best as possible given the fact that the barracks of the sepoy regiments and two new powder magazines had already been built under its protection. He therefore drew up plans for an earthen redoubt, excessive expense being avoided by "avoiding useless masonry." The earthen ramparts of the upper redoubt were to be 10 feet (3m) thick. In the lower redoubt the parapets were to be 10 feet thick at the part where the guns were sited, the other part only musket-proof. His report contained the strong statement that:

> I think that I am bound to state that had I been unfettered in my selection of a site for a citadel at Singapore for the defence of the European and other peaceable subjects against popular outbreak, I should have selected the Hill upon which Government House is built and the adjacent hill called Mount Sophia.
>
> Government Hill is the natural key of the whole place: with the other adjacent heights, it is sufficiently spacious to contain all the requisite buildings; it commands the dangerous part of the Town completely, it is easier of access as a place of refuge for the European community; and if suitably fortified, it could be made to form an important feature in the sea defences of the place. In fact it appeared to be the best site for the nucleus of defensive works for the protection of Singapore.[46]

Paragraph 6 of Collyer's report detailed the disadvantages of Pearl's Hill:

> Pearl's Hill is very limited in extent of summit surface, it is isolated, and has steep sides, it consists of ferugineous clay and gravel and from some way below the summit upwards it is of laterite of various degrees of hardness, its height is 170 feet above the level of the sea, and it has a command over all the hills in its immediate neighborhood except Mt. Faber, and another hill close to it, which are distant one and a half miles, and of the height above the sea of 300 feet and 265 feet respectively.

Pearl's Hill would have been suitable for the immediate aim of defence against a local rebellion but, in the longer term, he argued that Singapore should have a regular fort with effective sea defences to protect it. Furthermore, Collyer's original instructions already seem to have required him to combine the functions of refuge and fortress able to defend the settlement against external attack. The ammunition stores for example were supposed to be built inside the fort, "not merely under its guns".[47]

Government Hill and Mount Sophia together commanded both the town area of Singapore and most of the harbour. Pearl's Hill in his view was too far inland to be of any use in case of a naval attack. If Government Hill were fortified, the south end had space for a battery of seven 68 pounders:

...at a place where the solitary gun now stands. At the redan[48] there should be one 68 pounder and one 8" gun for the command of Kampong Glam. The redan and the battery being connected by a line of musket-proof parapet in front of the battery and below it, on the west of the steep cutting, there should be a light parapet extending as marked in the place from which the whole of the lease and the streets can be fired into and the redan should be connected with a light parapet with the burial ground wall which could be loop holed if necessary. There should be a battery for two guns, a 6 or 9 pounder and a howitzer at the point marked H[49] to sweep the road from Kampong Glam, Bukit Timah and up to Pearl's Hill. This battery should be connected with the corner of the burial ground by abbatis. The west corner of the battery should have an epaulment from which a musketry fire along the steep west face of Government House Hill along which a thick well-kept China Bamboo fence should be run to the shoulder marked F where another epaulment should be made and a connexion made between it and the seven 68 pounder battery.

8. It may be objected that seven 68 pounders in this position is unecessarily many. It is so simply for the defence against the populace but this position comes in as sea defences. Likewise as defending all the landing place from Fort Fullerton to Kampong Glam. In times of no fear of foreign aggression, 8" guns here would be sufficient.

11. Captain Best in his instructive report on the defences of the place which were for protection against foreign aggression proposed to raise and drill a local corps of Chinese and Malays who he considered good material for the purpose, but at the present moment, unfortunately it is against these very Chinese who were to have been a militia that the fortifications are being made.

Paragraph 12 of the letter estimated the manpower necessary for a garrison which would be able to withstand an assault of the entire population of 80 000 disaffected Chinese and the Indian convict labourers: a full company of European Artillery as well as another European Regiment.[50]

The fear of a Chinese insurrection remained rather strong in Singapore in the late 1850s, if the correspondence of the time is any indication. The Commissioner of Police worried that if there were a revolt, "the combined exertions of our present Military Force, the Police and European population would prove inadequate to the putting down of such a rising among the Chinese..."[51] The army however objected to being given the task of putting down a local insurrection in Singapore. One author wrote that "if the preservation of internal tranquillity is the main aim, then this should be done by the police."[52] On the other hand, if the proposed fortifications were built, to defend them it was estimated would require four complete companies of European Artillery, one reserve company of Golundaze, one full regiment of European Infantry and one regiment of Native Infantry of 1000 privates.

The idea of developing Singapore as a base for troops was beginning to take shape at this time, ironically stimulated in part precisely because the prosperity of Singapore's internal economy was increasingly becoming evident to London. The Commander-in-Chief in India concurred that:

> Whether with reference to the great and rising importance of Singapore as an emporium of trade to its forming a link in the chain of communications with China and Australia, to its position with respect to the neighboring foreign settlements, Duch (sic), French and Spanish, Sumatra, Java, Cochin China, Manilla etc., or lastly to the maintenance of due authority over the Chinese and other inhabitants of the place itself, it seems to Lord Clyde that, if possible, Singapore should be held by such Force (of Europeans in especial) as has been proposed by Sir Patrick Grant.
>
> Singapore is no doubt susceptible of easy defence from an external Force by our Naval Forces in the Indian Seas, but it is described to be a healthy place for Europeans, and to have a force quartered there, from which even half a Battalion could in emergency be thrown on the coast of China, might prove of vast consequence to our interests in that quarter.[53]

In his cover letter accompanying Collyer's report, Blundell noted that he was soon to leave the colony[54] and that therefore his comments would be brief. While he found himself to be in general agreement with Collyer, he still did not think that Government Hill was the best position for a fortified post. He argued that Pearl's Hill had never been designed as part of the defences of the harbour but merely as a place of refuge. He considered it "objectionable" to locate troops within the town:

> I do not quite agree in considering the Government Hill to be the best position for a fortified post. It is, or soon will be, in the centre of the Town of Singapore and is in that respect a bad location for European Troops. That Government Hill should be furnished with batteries on commanding points of its entourage is what I have always advocated and these may be connected by a parapet or thick hedge or palisade as may be deemed advisable.

Blundell pointed out that Collyer's plans were chiefly designed to deal with the defence of the settlement and also shipping in the harbour; Blundell contended that the protection of the harbour should be left to the Navy, in accord with long-standing policy. Blundell favoured erecting a small fort on Pearl's Hill and concentrating all military resources there under the cover of the fort's artillery. Blundell considered the batteries on Mount Faber and Mount Palmer to be useless, and even thought the guns should be withdrawn. One point on which Blundell emphatically agreed with Collyer was in scoffing at the idea that a corps of volunteers drawn from Singapore's Asian population would be useful: "The subject of a Local Corps of Chinese, Malay and other natives is one that need not be enlarged on here — In my opinion, no such Local Corps, if it could be raised which is extremely doubtful, would be of any service."[55]

Throughout their tenure in Southeast Asia, most British officials of the higher echelon resisted the idea of such a corps. As events in 1941–42 showed, they might have been repaid by risking greater reliance on the loyalty of the local population, or at least on their perception of a common cause with the British. Had this been cultivated at an early stage, could the defences of Singapore have been much stronger when they faced the ultimate test?[56] The traumatic experience of the Indian Mutiny affected the British so strongly that it greatly affected their planning for Singapore's defences. The refuge in Singapore was designed to protect against a similar occurrence. This concern overlooked the fact that the riots in Singapore had been entirely an internal affair of the local population, with no threats made to the British. The design of the fort was in the end largely determined by its function as a refuge, which in the end was never needed. Had the desire for a place of refuge been separated from the harbour fortifications, a more rational plan of defence might have been formed.

A partial compromise was envisioned, however. In the context of discussing the transfer of the Straits Settlements to the CO, a Malay regiment was proposed. The author of the report containing this recommendation believed that "There would be no difficulty in raising, on the spot, a couple of regiments of 1000 men each, provided it were for a local, limited service." The fact that the Malays were distinct from the Chinese, who formed the bulk of the inhabitants of the Straits Settlements, was enough to ensure that "a military force consisting of Malays...may be entirely relied on."[57]

The government in India called for a new general project to be prepared by Capt. Collyer. The Indian authorities felt that they had been led to believe there were difficulties with the proposal to use the site of Government Hill for a fort, and that there was some urgency in the work.[58] When Collyer's reports and plans were laid before the President-in-Council, it was decided that Pearl's Hill was not suitable. Collyer then set to work again, and soon formulated a new proposal to cover Government Hill with a fort, batteries, barracks, arsenal, magazine, workshops, and commissariat stores. If his plan had been fully carried out the commercial settlement of Singapore would have been converted into a heavily defended fortress.

Collyer's "Report on the Land Defences of Singapore," sent on 9 July 1858, was a 30-page appreciation of the situation.[59] In Collyer's view, Government Hill was unquestionably the best site for a defensive work against foreign aggressors regardless of whether it was the best place for a refuge against internal uprisings. The base of Government Hill was only 880 yards (.95 km) from the sea, and thus well-suited to defend against attack from that quarter. The best defence against internal insurrection, as Collyer believed, was a garrison of European troops. Collyer discussed the previous defence analyses, such as Lake's preference for Pearl's Hill, and Best's for Mount Wallich. Pearl's Hill had fewer existing buildings than Government Hill and was a defensible position but its area was very small, it did not command all the town and its approaches nor did it have any role to play in defence against attack from the sea. Collyer then discussed in detail all possible lines of attack of a foreign enemy and all means of defence to this.

Captain Faber in 1846 believed Government Hill was the best defensive position against a foreign attacker. Collyer elaborated on his reasons for choosing Government Hill and for putting batteries on Mount Sophia and Institution Hill which would be manned in the event of an external threat. The redoubt on Pearl's Hill should be a permanent post. Both hills presented some difficulty in supplying water "but I propose to have tanks and forcing pumps in the same way as suggested for Pearl's Hill":

> Available space on Government Hill is about 7 and a half acres, extreme length 1200 feet and an average breadth of 280 feet. This I have surrounded with a rampart, ditch and glacis and have given it the best of flanking fire...The Burial Ground is very much in the way and burial here for the future should be prohibited. The present wall and hedge round it might either be removed and an iron railing put or the wall left and converted into a post of loop holed defence.[60]

Collyer suggested that Government House be shifted to Bukit Timah, "the most commanding spot on the island", or Mount Caroline. He raised the possibility that government offices on the spot where Government House then stood could store property deeds, wills, surveys and treasure.[61]

Collyer's ambitious plan went on to make other suggestions: a building for state receptions, Governor's balls, breakfasts and dinners, where in time of alarm, the Governor and Resident Councillor might reside; it could also serve as a courthouse. The site intended as a courthouse could then be used as barracks. A wharf immediately below Government Hill could be used to load and unload stores for the fort. The area at the foot of the hill should also be incorporated into the fortified area. The sizeable garrison he had in mind would have comprised two companies on the top of the hill and four below, with two companies of Golundaze. Of course some houses at the foot of the hill would therefore have to be purchased by the government. That foothill area however he believed to be the best place of refuge, for "a crowd of refugees, women and children would be a terrible embarrassement in the fortress."

A week later, Collyer followed up his first report with a complimentary "Report on the Sea Coast Defences of Singapore."[62] This report also began with Collyer's reflections on previous reports on the defences of Singapore and discussed the possible location of a naval establishment. He preferred Pulau Brani as a site for a naval arsenal rather than New Harbour. As he summarised the problem, "The object in the defences is to secure the town against bombardment and to ensure the protection of New Harbour." When the single extant Guard Ship was out patrolling, the town was very vulnerable to naval attack, for the existing batteries were not powerful enough to beat off a determined European warship. He recommended batteries at new locations, at Katong and Kampong Glam to the east of the town, the extension of Fort Fullerton, and the improvement of Prince's Battery. His detailed plans for the defences of New Harbour envisioned batteries at Tanjong Pagar, Blakang Mati, Pulo Ayer Brani, and Mount Faber. He discounted widespread rumours that

Blakang Mati was an unhealthy spot. The jungle had been cut down a number of years ago and the whole of the island was then under cultivation with pineapples and coconuts by Malay inhabitants. There were two Malay villages on Ayer Brani Island and even a bungalow in which Europeans resided.

Most striking was a farsighted passage discussing the landward threat. The main potential threats to attack Singapore from the sea, which had to be countered by any defence system, were the French and the Russians. Yet even in this mid-nineteenth century period, Collyer did not fail to remark on the possibility of an enemy vessel landing on the north of the island "to take Singapore in reverse," although there were few roads and the whole of the northern coast was covered in mangrove jungle.

A stream of memoranda flowed from Collyer's pen, including estimates for the cost of the new batteries including the battery on the south end of Government Hill (208,389 Spanish dollars), additional magazines to accommodate the increased ordnance requirements (71,500 Spanish dollars), etc. The largest amount would be needed for the fortification of Government Hill: 525,795 Spanish dollars and 60 cents! But if the work could be carried out by convict labour, this would save two-thirds of the cost. The entire scheme, including barracks, powder, magazines, and the cost of the sea defences he estimated at 1,747,525 Spanish dollars.[63]

On 26 July 1858 Governor Blundell forwarded these new reports and plans to India. Blundell found the new plans to be "far removed" from the original proposition, a small earthwork on the top of Pearl's Hill for defence against the local population. Collyer's new plans were chiefly designed against a foreign enemy. Blundell now argued that the defence of the town and of the harbour were two different things which had to be considered separately. The batteries Collyer advocated would, Blundell saw, be ineffectual against a naval attack because they would have to fire through friendly shipping in the harbour. Therefore he restated his position that the safety of the shipping in the south harbour had to be left to the navy.[64]

The land defences were not designed to withstand any native hostility but against a foreign fleet which had temporarily driven the British fleet from the neighbourhood. In Blundell's view, "It is difficult to imagine such a contingency":

> To cover the extent of Government Hill with Batteries and Forts, with large buildings such as Barracks, Arsenal, Commissariat Stores, Hospitals, Magazines, Workshops, and all their appurtenances, will prove, as shown by Captain Collyer's Estimates, no slight or inexpensive undertaking in a place where labour and materials are already enormously dear and would soon be doubled in price under such a heavy demand for both on the part of the Government building.
>
> If these plans are carried out in their completeness, the hitherto peaceful and prosperous Commercial Settlement of Singapore will be, in great measure, converted into a great Military Fortress and it is a question

how far this conversion may effect the present rapid extension of the Trade.[65]

Despite his objections, Blundell gave orders to begin work on the battery on the south end of Government Hill, and on the enlargement of the battery at Fort Fullerton.

A decision came back from Allahabad, India, in a letter written on 16 October 1858. Charles Canning, of the Public Works Department, wrote to the Court of Directors, East India Company, noting a letter of 23 August which summarised the recent discussions of the defences of Singapore. The decision was to proceed with only a selection of Collyer's projects. The most important point in the letter was that in the end the Indian authorities decided to settle on Government Hill rather than Pearl's Hill as the central point of the fortification system:

> I consider that Captain Collyer has established this to be the true position for such a work, especially in regard to the aid which it will afford to defence from external aggression... I have sanctioned its construction. I have also sanctioned the construction of a battery at the south end of Government Hill commanding the town and part of the bay. And lastly I have sanctioned the construction of a barrack for two companies within the redoubt.[66]

No other buildings within the fort were to be built until further notice. Capt. Collyer's vision of such other works as the entrenchment of the space between Government Hill and the sea; the fortification of Pearl's Hill and some other adjoining heights; the construction of a number of detached batteries; the erection of a barracks for a complete regiment of European Infantry; and a floating battery and two gunboats, were still pending approval.

Since no proposal to build a naval base in the New Harbour had ever been seriously considered, more deliberation was also needed on that score before any more work could go ahead. But Allahabad underlined one point: that if New Harbour were to become a naval base, Blakang Mati would be the location for the headquarters, arsenal and stores. The whole question of the naval base was too big even for India to decide, and it was therefore referred to London.

Canning wanted clearer instructions on the scale which the defences of Singapore ought to assume. He commented that a naval establishment at New Harbour would have to be defended thoroughly. In time of war shipping would have to take shelter there. "If there is no naval base, then the present work, together with additions at moderate cost will probably suffice":

18 Work to be sanctioned:

Government Hill with gates etc.	36 685 Sp. Dollars
Barracks with offices etc.	38 069 Sp. Dollars
Battery at S. end of Government Hill with platforms	5 699 Sp. Dollars
TOTAL	80 452 Sp. Dollars
(or in rupees)	(176 996)[67]

The response from the Public Works Department in London was sent on 1 June 1859. London had several important points to make. First, since the transfer of Singapore and the other Straits Settlements to the CO was still under discussion, nobody was willing to take responsibility for such a major work programme. London noted that Collyer's plan was meant to defend against three separate threats: attack from land, internal unrest, and attack from the sea. The idea of a European attack from land was considered extremely remote. Protection of the Christian inhabitants of Singapore was not judged to require a citadel; much more moderate precautions consisting of a walled enclosure on a well-chosen site and the protection of a regiment of European Infantry and two companies of European Artillery would be sufficient "until reinforcements arrive."[68]

The protection of shipping would be best ensured by a couple of steam gunboats rather than building up the strength of the shore defences. This situation might however need reconsideration if a naval base were established in New Harbour. The typically bureaucratic conclusion was that:

> For the present it is sufficient to place you in possession of the views of H.M. Government with regard to the expediency of any large immediate outlay on the fortifications of Singapore to which, as may be perceived from the foregoing observation, they are decidedly opposed.[69]

It is clear that the powers in London felt that large fixed defences such as forts and heavy gun batteries in Singapore were unnecessary, and that the main defensive requirement was for a small mobile force able to protect shipping. Nevertheless, in August 1858 the government began to move forward with Capt. Collyer's plan to fortify Government Hill and to establish a battery there, with seven 68 pounder guns and two 13" mortars.[70]

An unusual insight into the deliberations which led to the decision to fortify Government Hill comes in the form of an unsigned fragmentary note found in the Madras archives. The tone is much less formal than the normal government correspondence of the time; it was obviously meant for limited internal circulation among a few officials:

> It appears to me that if Government persists in having the strong place of Singapore on Pearl's Hill, the permanent result will be very unsatisfactory. A large expenditure will be incurred, without obtaining now what is wanted, and without even approaching to an ultimate result which will be adequate to the objects in view. When Government decided on Pearl's Hill it was in the belief that Government Hill would not do; that all the buildings which it is urgently necessary to place in a secure place could be within the enceinte of Pearl's Hill; and that the fortification of this hill could be so contrived as to be susceptible of extension hereafter, whenever Government may think it advisable to have a larger and more complete and stronger fort at Singapore than is at present contemplated. Now the [illegible] before us shows that on all three points this was an erroneous belief.

All these three points are important. Contrary to what was formerly reported it now appears that Government Hill, if availed of, is capable of meeting the last mentioned requirements, but in all other respects, especially in the very important points of being the best protection to the town and roadstead and the place of refuge of easiest access to the European community it is infinitely preferable to Pearl's Hill.[71]

Another draft with the same general content, but in the form meant for general circulation, is also found in the same binding. After noting that it was now obvious that Pearl's Hill was not suitable for the government's objectives, acknowledging that "Government Hill is the natural key of the whole place", and admitting that the original purpose for which Pearl's Hill was chosen was mainly limited to a "means of defense against intestive commotion, rather than against foreign aggression," the memorandum noted that thinking had now begun to change, influenced by factors connected with regional strategic considerations rather than purely local affairs:

> But the Government of India having in view the position of Singapore and the future of China and the eastern Seas, feel confident that eventually it will be advisable to have a regular fort at that place with such sea defences as shall effectually protect it and in fact close the Straits as nearly as possible to an enemy.
>
> Viewing the matter in this light the Government of India, before coming to any conclusion on the subject, deem it expedient to have a new general project before them, prepared consistently with Captain Collyer's own ideas on the subject, and with reference to the views above expressed. In this manner by setting intelligently to work, there is reason to hope that design may be so drawn out that while present purposes are at once answered, something will be gained towards the larger ultimate object.[72]

At this juncture another party began to make its voice heard for the first time: the growing Singapore Chinese middle class. An echo of their concerns begins to appear in British documents in the late 1850s. It seems that influential local Chinese businessmen were in favour of a stronger land-based defence. This was probably due to their concerns about the safety of their own investments in case of further riots by their own compatriots. Thus in July 1858 one document contained the generalisation that:

> The large increase in the numbers of Chinese and the fact of Chinese emigrants in Tartary, Turkistan and in the Straits, having shown themselves to possess all the energy and determination of an active, enterprising race, accustomed to all management of their local affairs, with organising guilds and brotherhoods, should also have weight with the government as to the necessity of maintaining a powerful artillery for moving with some degree of certainty, so as to suppress with promptness all hostile movements on the island, and especially in the event of stockades being erected which a few thousand Chinese could easily effect in the course of a single night.[73]

The British administrators were not however entirely happy with the growing power of the Chinese mercantile class; they also suggested that Singapore needed to expand its water supply to help facilitate the growth of a population of Chinese farmers to counter-balance the traders.

Although the documents from time to time evidence some genuine concern that a Chinese insurrection against the British might develop, other glimpses into daily life suggest that this fear was more theoretical, even theatrical, than real. In 1858 it was necessary to suggest that the arsenal should be enclosed, as well as the rear of the gun batteries. By November 1858 the European artillerymen were installed in barracks at Pearl's Hill,[74] but there were complaints that locals were walking near the barracks and committing "nuisances of every description" right under the officers' houses![75] The general public used water from wells for washing and bathing which the sepoys wanted to reserve for drinking. Much to the disgust of the sepoys, much of the dirty water ran back into the wells. In other words, the barracks were unfenced and members of the public were free to wander around them. The division between military and civilian was not yet very firmly drawn in mid-nineteenth century Singapore society.

The problem of quartering the expanding troop population was alleviated when private landowners offered a 70-acre site at Tanglin to the government for the barracks at a cost of $15,000.[76] The site was then largely planted with nutmeg and fruit trees, and had a good stream of fresh water running through it. Furthermore it was near another area, called Clunie, which the government had already purchased, partly as an outpost in case of rioting breaking out again in the interior; many Chinese already lived in the vicinity. The area had been chosen by Col. W.C. Macleod, Commander of the Troops in the Straits, in 1857, because:

> When an outbreak was looked for last year amongst the Chinese, it was certain that they would be supported by large bodies of their countrymen from the rural districts in the direction of and from the mainland of Johore. The principal road from those parts, called the Bukit Timah Road, passes close to Clunie. It was to command this, to cover other roads, to give the European inhabitants in that neighborhood confidence, to protect their residences and property to a certain extent, and to afford them time to fall back on our main position, if obliged to abandon their houses, that Clunie was selected. I then proposed to place a company of Sepoys, some artillery men and two guns there.[77]

The area was found to be very healthy, and Collyer in his original report recommended it as a permanent post. The private land offered in Tanglin was first declined because it consisted of four hills which were considered too steep for buildings. Clunie, also then planted with nutmeg trees, was thought preferable.[78] Eventually in 1860 the Honourable President-in-Council, after considering all the proposed sites for the Infantry Barracks, decided upon Tanglin and authorised the purchase of the necessary land, including a portion of an estate belonging to the famous merchant Mr. Whampoa. By July temporary barracks at Tanglin were already nearly completed.[79] They turned out to be the nucleus of a substantial British commitment of resources and regular forces to the direct defence of Singapore. This commitment, started in such disorganised fashion, was never free from controversy, but lasted for over a century.

A First-class Field Fortification

In 1859 Singapore's urban area extended inland only as far as the foot of Government Hill. The north side of the hill, where lay the Christian cemetery established in 1823, was still a quiet, even remote area, even though Government House stood not far away on the hill's southern end. The hill was in some areas still covered with jungle, according to a request of 1860 for funds to clear the hill.[80] The cemetery ground was not very safe at night, as a complaint from the Chaplain of Singapore demonstrated. It was then the practice to employ convicts to guard the burial ground, but they were only on duty in the daytime. Reverend J.C. Smythe objected to this situation:

> The evil results of this arrangement were but too apparent a few days ago; when furniture belonging to the vestry of the cemetery was, during the night, removed by some person or persons unknown, and thrown upon the road. Such an outrage may be only the prelude to some desecration of the tombs or graves...

Smythe suggested that three burial ground peons be hired at 10 rupees a month, in place of the convicts.[81]

The somnolent, even desolate atmosphere of the hill started to change when construction of Fort Canning began on 1 March 1859. Formal orders to build the fort were issued in October 1858.[82] The Governor was then still living in Government House on the hill, so the first construction activity was initiated at its north end. It was decided to name the fort after Viscount George Canning, first Governor-General and later first Viceroy of India from 1857 to 1862. By May 1859 seven 68 pounder guns were already mounted in field redoubts on the south end of Fort Canning, facing the Straits, just below the Governor's residence.

Unfortunately, the Singapore public seems to have had little idea what was being done by the military and why. Indeed, it is hard to resist the conclusion that the decision to proceed with constructing a major permanent fort emerged in spite rather than because of any clear consensus on what threats Singapore faced and how they should be met. A fort established on Government Hill would be ideally placed to command Chinatown and the other Asian residential districts, and provide a refuge for the European community in case of trouble. In the shadow of the Indian Mutiny plus Chinese strife, this was obviously a major spur to the decision. But would that same fort also serve to protect the harbour and the town against an attack from the sea, as a last line of defence in case the navy was otherwise engaged? And what would it all cost, with what effect on trade, the lifeblood of Singapore? Those very questions were put with some asperity by the *Singapore Free Press* on 7 July 1859:

> It is rumoured that the estimates for the fortifications of Singapore are increasing in a most alarming manner, and that what it was originally intended should be confined to some millions of dollars will ultimately consume as many millions of pounds sterling…No fortifications that can be constructed will effectually protect the shipping in our open roadstead, or the warehouses of the merchants, from an attack by sea or from suffering severely from such an attack. It would therefore be desirable to ascertain the precise purpose for which such expensive fortifications are being designed. If they are to protect the docks and other works said to be projected at New Harbour for the use of the Navy, the outlay will be quite justifiable, but it will be otherwise if it is attempted to convert Singapore into a great fortification. Its trade has solely made Singapore what it is and without its trade it would soon be left to the sole occupancy of the tigers, that, even as it is, threaten to overrun it.

The army had no such qualms. Land-based defences were the order of the day, even if they contributed little or nothing to defence against the sea due to being sited too far back to protect the harbour. By February 1860 four 13" mortars and six 68 pounder cannon had been received and test-fired for deployment in the new fort.[83] By May, the Governor, Col. Cavenagh, reported much progress, with the completion of the expense magazines, platforms and making up room in the South Battery — the latter a "large arched room" for preparing gunpowder charges — as well as the posterns, scarp and counterscarp. The Governor pronounced the masonry "substantial and well finished." Work on the gateway was rapidly progressing.[84]

This report was soon followed by one from the indefatigable Capt. Collyer, the prime mover behind the fort. Collyer submitted a report in September 1860 which indicated that much had already been accomplished. The top of the hill was surrounded by a parapet 14 feet [4m] thick. Remains of the wall still existing consist of a granite facing on the exterior, and an interior facing of brick with an earth fill. The height of the wall on the interior of the surviving section is less than 2 metres. Beyond the parapet, the fort had a steep earthen bank about 20 feet [6.5m] high, then a dry ditch about 6 feet [2m] wide, then another bank of earth 6 feet high.[85]

No doubt many archaeological remains of fourteenth-century Singapore were destroyed at this time. The upper part of the hill where the fort was to be built was first levelled; this area must have been the site of the main palace area. Numerous remains of fourteenth-century activity were discovered by archaeologists in the 1980s and 1990s in a layer of dirt which was taken from the upper slopes and dumped along the edges to make the slope regular during the fort's construction.

The main fortification of the hill, the battery of 68 pounder guns, stood at the southern end overlooking the town, river and harbour. Buildings already here included Government House and a Flagstaff which carried signals giving information about ships entering and leaving the harbour. This was information of great interest and importance to Singapore's commercial community, and merchants in the town would have cast frequent glances at the banners to see which ships had recently arrived. On the southern end of the hilltop a broad terrace slightly lower than the summit where Government House stood had been a garden. According to paintings of the period, ceremonies such as the presentation of a sword to the Temenggong for his services in putting down piracy were conducted there. Now this area was converted into a battery with guns spaced at intervals facing southward, a large semi-subterranean magazine for ammunition, and other structures. This type of terrace in the military architecture of the period was called a banquette. Since no detailed plans of the fort have been located, it is impossible to determine the precise functions of these buildings.

The construction work required a force of 500-600 labourers. The entire force of convict labour, some of whom were described as "extremely skilled,"[86] was placed at Collyer's disposal. The quality of the work executed by the convicts was considered to be as good as, if not better than, that obtained from free Chinese labour. Construction went satisfactorily until August when unusually heavy rain caused a good deal of the newly landscaped escarpment to slide downhill. Collyer averred that had it not been for this setback, the fort would have been completed in November. He was forced to devote more attention to installing drainage to prevent future landslides. The angle of the slope also had to be made less steep. In addition to earthmoving, it was discovered that three quarters of an acre of sandstone boulders had to be removed, which required blasting work.[87]

Collyer had planned to make the hilltop into the barracks, hospital, parade ground, and other infrastructure, with the South Battery and the Redan or fortified area around the Keramat Iskandar Shah (which he termed the Fakir's Tomb) as separate outworks. For some reason perhaps connected with the diminished slope of the fort's outer ditch, he found this not to be feasible, and they were incorporated into the glacis, or outer slope beyond the ditch. "This work has been rather an embarrassment but I believe I have overcome it..." The fort only had one main entrance, on the north side of the hill. There was at least one sally port, a small side entrance, which ran beneath the northeast wall and communicated with the dry ditch. For unexplained reasons the main gate was made more elaborate than Collyer had intended. This gate still stands. It is a kind of miniature citadel, with an internal staircase leading to the flat roof which is surrounded by a parapet pierced by numerous loop holes. Despite these setbacks and deviations from his plan, in the end he pronounced himself satisfied: "Fort Canning may, I think, without presumption be considered a 1st class Field Fortification."[88]

A portion of the old fort wall still remains on the north side of the hill, running from the old fort gate along the edge of Dobbie Rise for about 150 m, until it reaches the site of the Underground Command Centre which was constructed in 1938. The exterior of the wall consisted of granite; the type and size of stone and the method of construction can still be seen in the sector of wall which remains. Most of the 1860 fort was torn down in 1926 when a reservoir was built on the hill's summit.

The main weapons on Fort Canning included seven 68 pounder guns on the south battery. In addition to these, other artillery pieces (eight 8" guns, two 13" mortars and a few 14 pounder carronades) were in due course mounted at a height of about 200 feet [66m] on the hill. When the fort was completed, it came to the attention of the authorities that Pearl's Hill overlooked Fort Canning Hill from a greater height. In order to ensure that enemies could not attack Fort Canning from Pearl's Hill, the Chief Engineer brought up a Chinese coolie force and cut off the top of Pearl's Hill.

In July 1860 it was estimated that Fort Canning would be completed "in about two months' time," and that gunpowder stores could then be moved there from the town.[89] Fort Canning was largely completed in 1861, according to Buckley, but the Governor's Diary of 23 January 1862 shows that the site had not yet been handed over to the military.[90] This may however refer to a mere formality. A detachment of the Royal Artillery had arrived in Singapore three months earlier. Until 1861 they stayed in Tan Tock Seng Hospital on Pearl's Hill, then in 1861 moved into barracks on Fort Canning. A note from the Governor confirms that much of the fortress was indeed already completed by May 1860.[91]

The move of the Artillery from Pearl's Hill to Fort Canning was complete by mid-1862, except for the ponies which drew the lighter field weapons. By 1864, Fort Canning was fully functional. Paintings of Singapore which depict the fort at this period show that the hill was almost completely denuded of vegetation. Trees were however planted in and about the Fort, and it was hoped that when they were fully grown, they would not only act as a screen to the present buildings but also shelter them in some degree from the effects of a cannonade. The walls of the fort were irregular in outline, following the natural configurations of Government Hill, the top of which had been slightly lowered to a height of 156 feet [52m]. The fortress consisted of two parts: the main fort and the south battery, which was an outwork about 30 feet [8.5m] below and seaward of the main fort, and connected to the main fort by a flight of steps which was in existence until the 1950s. The south battery held the seven 68 pounder cannon, while the main fort was equipped with eight 8" guns and two 13" mortars. Buildings in the fort included such amenities as quarters for two garrison batteries of Royal Artillery including married men, a canteen, a swimming pool (Plunge Bath), a Skittle Alley, School Room and Library, and quarters for two captains and four subalterns with out offices and stabling for their horses. By 1867 all the buildings of Fort Canning were lit with gas lamps.[92] According to one impartial report, "These barracks are indeed admirable, indeed perfect."[93]

So, nearly 50 years after Raffles had established a British presence in Singapore, the British military commitment to its defence was now crowned by a full-scale "first-class field fortification," manned by regular troops. Yet this indicated anything but a coherent appraisal of what threats Singapore faced, how to meet them, and how the military strategy for Singapore fit into the larger policy for imperial defence. The defence plans and capabilities for Singapore were instead enmeshed in a series of disputes between various authorities over cost and requirements, confused by reactions to several crises or near-crises in or near Singapore. The result was muddle. The Royal Navy was the main line of defence against any threat from the sea, but it was very frequently unable to station enough force to guarantee that any threat which might emerge would indeed be checked before Singapore could be attacked. That made coastal defence artillery necessary. But that was expensive. Moreover, the fear of an uprising by the Asian populations led to the construction of forts well-placed to face that threat, but expensive, undermanned and poorly placed to confront any external invasion. It also raised two vital questions: how future costs were going to be borne, and what could be done to make sure the defences of Singapore were effectively coordinated both to an assessment of threats and to broader British military strategy.

Those critics who feared that money would be wasted on ineffective defences now felt that was indeed what had come to pass. Instead of a small refuge for the European community, plus a regular naval force to protect shipping, Singapore received a large fortress, placed where it could not do much to protect the harbour. The *Straits Times and Singapore Journal of Commerce* noted scathingly on 21 June 1862 that the new fort was useless in both ways. On the one hand an enemy ship could ravage half the shipping in the harbour without fear of reply from the 68 pounders of Fort Canning, which could not reach the entire roadstead. On the other hand, it had these failings as a refuge: the locations of the guns were so exposed it was feared that a sharpshooter could make it impossible to man them; it was estimated there were at that point only enough gunners to man two of the 13 guns anyway; the cemetery on the northeast side of the hill gave excellent cover for the approach of any assault force; there were claims that the semi-sunken magazines were usually half full of water, with fish several inches long reportedly caught in one of them; and the fort's wells were said to be dry, making it useless in case of siege.

This muddle did not go unnoticed in London. One report to the CO had already summed up the essence of the problem:

> [the new fortifications of Singapore were] with very few exceptions, unsuitable and uncalled for: amounting in fact to a waste of public money in their construction, and a heavy military expenditure, should they be adequately garrisoned. The only effectual protection of the town and shipping of Singapore is a naval one...The principal fortification is situated on a hill 150 feet high, and about a mile inland from the shore, and consequently about three miles distant from the main anchorage, where there usually lie not fewer than 100 sail of square-rigged vessels. From such a distance or even from the nearer shore batteries, it is certain that the most powerful artillery would hardly be expected to injure an enemy...[94]

Fort Canning and the other forts built to protect the New Harbour were built as the outcome of a multitude of motivations, some which had their origins in conditions already existing in 1819, others of quite recent appearance. Singapore in fact had a dual strategic identity: a local collecting-point for Southeast Asian produce, with a turbulent populace and which also attracted seaborne marauders; and a focus of British power between India and China, two major arenas of Great Power contention. Despite the fact that these different attributes occasioned different sorts of threats to Singapore's long-term security, the cost factor tempted British authorities to try to combine measures to defend against local threats with the possibility that Singapore might be needed one day to play a role in imperial strategy, or in historical processes involving much of Asia. So Singapore now had expensive but ineffective fixed defences, despite the belief of a considerable body of opinion that the best strategy for its defence was to rely on a strong mobile naval force.

Militarily, it thus seemed that nearly a half century of reports, studies, expenditure, and effort had left Singapore possibly defenceless against any serious threat from any direction. To an extent, this reflected the general confusion of the era of the *Pax Britannica* — a strong sense of general security punctuated by alarms and panics both Imperial and external — and the particular confusion over responsibility for Singapore. But in retrospect, the themes which dominated the remainder of the British military presence in Singapore had all already emerged. The RN was the only real answer to any external threat; but could it be there when it was needed? If not, what could fill the gap? What other threats were there? How could they be met? How would the defence of Singapore be related to broader imperial defence? And who would pay, on what basis, for the defence of Singapore? The military future of what was now a thriving commercial entrepot and crucial way station on Imperial trade routes depended on political answers to these questions.

Fort Canning viewed from the High Street, 1870s

Notes

1. Wurtzburg, 606.

2. Crawfurd, formerly a medical doctor in the Bengal Medical Service, served in Penang and Java. "Crawfurd was famous both as an administrator and an author, but he was not a popular man; he succeeded two men of great popularity...Mr. Crawfurd's manner was against him and obscured the great qualities he undoubtedly possessed. He was a typical Scotchman [sic], and it was said of him that frugality, which is a virtue in a poor but high spirited people, is apt to degenerate into parsimoniousness." Buckley, 140. Crawfurd wrote a *History of the Indian Archipelago*, published in 1820, a *Descriptive Dictionary of the Indian Isles*, 1856, and accounts of missions to Ava (Burma), and Cochin-China (Vietnam).

3. Letters of Col. Nahuijs, 10 June 1824, in *JMBRAS*, vol. 19, 1941, 195-96.

4. See also a memorandum submitted to Raffles, now in the SNL: Microfilm NL57, Series L9, 1823.

5. L.T. Firbank, *A History of Fort Canning*, n/d, typescript in Central Library, NUS, 7.

6. In October 1822 Raffles appointed Jackson Assistant Settlement Engineer; in January 1823 he also became Surveyor of Lands. He returned to Europe in 1827.

7. SNL, Microfilm NL2467, A45, pp. 97-106, 1827.

8. See "Report on the Best Means of Fortifying Singapore," by Edward Lake, Inspector General, May 1827, in A. Harfield, *Britsh and Indian Armies in the East Indies 1685-1935*, Chippenham, 1984, 143-47.

9. Lake sailed from Singapore with his wife and two sons for England in 1830. Their ship was lost at sea and they were never heard from again. Harfield, 147.

10. J. Cameron, *Our Tropical Possessions in Malayan India*, Kuala Lumpur, 1965 (1865), 20.

11. Buckley, 44.

12. B. Nunn, "Some account of our governors and civil service," in Makepeace et al, 87.

13. This compares to a population of 39,589 for Penang; 51,509 for Province Wellesley; and 53,496 for Melaka. The total population of the British settlements in the Straits was thus 194,594.

14. SNA, Straits Settlements Records W8, no. 226, 11 August 1843.

15. SNA, Straits Settlements Records S21, no. 20, item 44, 13 March 1854.

16. Gibson-Hill, "Singapore: Notes on the history of the Old Strait 1580-1850," 200.

17. SNA, SSR, V9, no. 29, p. 159, 23 January 1844.

18. Buckley, 210.

19. Chiang M.S., "Military Defences and Threat Perceptions in Nineteenth Century Singapore, 1854-1891," Unpublished B.A. Hons. dissertation, Department of History, National University of Singapore, 1993.

20. B.L. Evans, "The Attitudes and Policies of Great Britain and China toward French Expansion in Cochin China, Cambodia, Annam, and Tongking: 1858-1883," Unpublished Doctoral Dissertation, School of Oriental and African Studies, University of London, 1961.

21. Chiang, 6.

22. PRO, CO273/2, Straits Settlements Original Correspondence, Letters from the Public Works Dept. Military, Fort William, India, Vol. 1; NUS microfilm, CO273/1, Letters 243 and 81, 7 October 1852 and 3 April 1854.

23. PRO, CO273/2, Straits Settlements Original Correspondence, Letters from the Public Works Dept. Military, Fort William, India, Vol. 1; NUS microfilm, CO273/1, Enclosure no. 81, 3 April 1854, report dated 3 May 1854.

24. SNA, Straits Settlements Records, S20, no. 725, item 77, 22 August 1853.

25. SNA, Straits Settlements Records T2, no. 5, item 58, 11 October 1853. A *Barbette*

Battery consisted of guns which could be mechanically elevated to fire over the crests of parapets instead of only through embrasures in walls.

26. PRO, CO273/2, Straits Settlements Original Correspondence, Letters from the Public Works Dept. Military, Fort William, India, Vol. 1; NUS microfilm, CO273/1, Enclosure no. 81, 3 April 1854, to report dated 3 May 1854.

27. PRO, CO273/2, Straits Settlements Original Correspondence, Letters from the Public Works Dept. Military, Fort William, India, Vol. 1, Construction of Defensive Works in Singapore; NUS microfilm CO273/1, Letter no. 520, 13 March 1854, enclosed in no. 11, 13 April 1854; PRO, CO2732/, f.11r, East India Company, London, to Governor of the Presidency of Fort William in Bengal, 19 July 1854, reply to Military Letter of 3 April 1854, no. 81, authorising implementation of Yule's plans.

28. SNA, Straits Settlements Records SSR U27, pp. 168-73.

29. PRO, CO273/2, Straits Settlements Original Correspondence, Letters from the Public Works Dept. Military, Fort William, India, Vol. 1, Construction of Defensive Works in Singapore; NUS microfilm, CO273/1, ff 15r-19v, Extract from the Proceedings of the Rt. Hon. the Governor-General-of-India-in-Council in the Military Dept, 11 August 1856, no. 282 (includes Blundell to the Secretary to the Government of India, letter no. 40, 21 April 1856).

30. Buckley, 585-95; Makepeace, 247-48.

31. Makepeace, 247; Buckley, 585-95. Col. Butterworth did make an attempt to restore order by riding into the midst of a fray near the foot of Government Hill, ie. near his own house, on his white horse, but found that the scale of the problem was too much for one man to put down. The rioters do not seem to have recognised the mounted man and even if they had it is doubtful whether they would have paid him any particular heed.

32. PRO, CO273/2, Straits Settlements Original Correspondence, Letters from the Public Works Dept. Military, Fort William, India, Vol. 1, Construction of Defensive Works in Singapore; NUS microfilm, CO273/1, ff. 15r-19v, Extract from the Proceedings of the Rt. Hon. the Governor-General-of-India-in-Council in the Military Department, 11 August 1856, no. 282 (includes Governor Blundell to the Secretary to the Government of India, 21 April 1856).

33. PRO, CO273/2, ff. 14r, 15v, Governor-General-of-India-in-Council, London, to Governor, Straits Settlements, 2 January 1857, no. 2, replied to a letter of 3 July 1856, no. 71, with a copy of a despatch sent to the government of Bombay ordering that six steam gunboats be built to form part of the Indian Navy. Further discussion was promised regarding the number of such boats needed by the Straits Settlements.

34. PRO, CO273/2, f. 238r, Extract Fort William Military Proceedings for October 1860. Secretary to Government of Madras Military Department to the Secretary to the Government of India, Military Department, Fort St. George, 11 September 1860, enclosing report by Adjutant General of the Army 30 August 1860, reporting that "it has been found that native artillerymen are physically unequal to the service of a 9 pounder field gun."

35. PRO, CO273/2, 19v-21r, Capt. Yule to the Secretary to the Government of India, Military Department, Calcutta, 25 June 1856.

36. Ibid.

37. Ibid.

38. PRO, CO273/2, no. 281, Secretary to the Government of India Military Department to Governor, Straits Settlements, 11 August 1856.

39. PRO, CO273/2, no. 308, ff. 23r-23v, Government of India Military Department to Fort William, 6 September 1856.

40. PRO, CO273/2, Public Works Dept. to Court of Directors of East India Company, Fort William Calcutta, 23 August 1858, citing PWD no. 4760, 12 December 1856.

41. PRO, CO273/2, no. 19, ff. 28v-29v, Blundell to Yule, in Secretary to the Government of India, 22 July, 1857. The letter encloses the plan and estimate for the barracks. CO273/2, no. 5533, ff. 33v-33r, Government of India to Blundell, 10 November 1857,

sanctioned the estimates for the construction of the barracks, and stressed that the barracks should form part of the defences of Pearl's Hill. The government of India however noted that the plans made no provision for married quarters or a hospital.

42. PRO, CO273/2, Public Works Dept. to Court of Directors of East India Company, Fort William Calcutta, 23 August 1858, citing PWD no. 6811, 2 October 1857.

43. PRO, CO273/2, PWD no. 6811, 2 October 1857.

44. National Archives of India (NAI), Extract from a letter No. 5965, Fort William, 14 December 1857, from the Secretary to the Government of India, Dept. of Public Works, in Report upon the Works to be erected on Pearl's Hll at Singapore as a citadel or strong place for refuge and defence against internal aggression, bound with Public Works Dept. 1858, Cons. 150-55, A Collection of Correspondence regarding the selection of a site for a citadel in Singapore, Consultations 23 April, no. 155, from Capt. Collyer, Superintending Engineer, to Government of India, Dept. of Public Works, 4 February 1858.

45. PRO, CO273/2, no. 23, ff. 34v-36v, Blundell to the Secretary to the Government of India, Singapore, 16 February 1858; see also SNA, Straits Settlements Records R 32, pp. 319-25.

46. PRO, CO273/2, no. 23, ff 34v-36v, Blundell to the Government of India, 16 February 1858, enclosing Capt. Collyer to the Government of India, 4 February 1858, 40r-59v.

47. Madras Archives (MA), Public Works Dept 1858, Consultations 23 April, from Capt. G.C. Collyer, Superintending Engineer, to Secretary, Government of India Dept. of Public Works, 4 February, quoting from a letter from the Secretary, no. 4396, 11 September 1857.

48. There seems to have been some sort of earthwork around the Keramat Iskandar Shah at this time. An earthen embankment completely encircling the Keramat can be seen in early photographs of Fort Canning from the late nineteenth century. It is not known when or for what purpose this earthwork was built.

49. Unfortunately it has not been possible to locate the plan which was enclosed with this proposal. All efforts to uncover drawings or detailed maps of the interior of the fortifications, planned or actually built, on Fort Canning Hill have so far proved fruitless. "Point H" must have been somewhere on the northeast side of the hill near the old cemetery, but without the map which accompanied this letter it is impossible to fix the spot, or other such reference points in this letter, with precision.

50. NAI, Public Works Dept. 1858, Cons. 150-155, Consultations 23 April, no. 155, Collyer to Government of India Dept. of Public Works, 4 February 1858.

51. PRO, CO273/6, ff. 235v-235r, Commissioner of Police to the Secretary to the Governor, 31 August 1858.

52. PRO, CO273/6, ff 236r-237v, Adjutant General to the Army, Fort St. George, to the Secretary to the Government of India Military Department, 30 March 1859.

53. PRO, CO273/6, f. 237r, Extract from Fort William Military Consultations for June 1859, Officiating Quarter Master of the Army to the Secretary to the Government of India Military Department, Simla, 6 June 1859.

54. Colonel Orfleur Cavenagh was appointed Governor of the Straits Settlements in 1858, but only took up his post in 1859.

55. SNA, Straits Settlements Records, R32, pp. 319-25, Blundell to the Secretary, Government of India, 16 February 1858.

56. See below, Chapter 8.

57. PRO, CO173/16, Straits Settlements Original Correpondence, Public Offices, Part II, 1867, Treasury Papers relating to the Straits Settlements: f. 115r, Notes on the proposal for annexing the settlements in the Straits of Melaka to the Colonial Administration of the Crown, by J. Crawfurd for the Rt. Hon. Lord Stanley [Colonial Secretary], 22 July 1858.

58. PRO, CO273/2, ff 65r-67v, PWD to Court of Directors, 1832, 23 April 1858; Secretary to the Government of India to Blundell, 23 April 1858.

59. PRO, CO273/2, no. 100, ff. 79r-94v, Singapore, 9 July 1858. This report was received via Marseilles on 19 November 1858, together with enclosure no. 3 from Alahabad, Public Works Department, 16 October 1858, no. 7. This routing information suggests that this report was sent along with the plans to the East India Company in London and therefore it plus the plans might be found in the India Office Records. Perhaps some researcher will eventually uncover the plans.

60. This plan was later changed. PRO, CO273/8, Straits Settlements Original Correspondence Individuals, 1863 to 1866, ff. 374v-376v, Report of Capt. Mayne, Chief Engineer, Straits Settlements, 20 January 1863 [held in microfilm at the Central Library, NUS], reports a new plan to re-site the reservoir three miles [five km] to the north of the town and to run a conduit along the streets of the town to the northwest of it. Collyer's plan to pump water up to the top of Government Hill before it could be distributed through the town was eventually put into effect, but only in 1926.

61. Coincidentally the National Archives of Singapore were first established on Fort Canning's east slope, then moved to Hill Street, and in 1997 moved again to Fort Canning Rise. Thus in a way Collyer's suggestion was eventually taken.

62. PRO, CO273/2, ff. 94r-110v, Report on the Sea Coast Defences of Singapore by Capt. Collyer, Singapore, 17 July 1858.

63. The Spanish silver dollar was the standard currency used throughout Southeast Asia in the early nineteenth century. One hundred Spanish Dollars was calculated by the British East India Company as being equal to £26 10 shillings, or 26 and a half pounds sterling: C. Trocki, *Prince of Pirates*, Singapore, 1979, xii.

64. PRO, CO273/2, no. 100, ff. 73r-78r, Blundell to Secretary to the Government of India, Singapore 26 July 1858. Extracts of this letter can be found in SNA, Straits Settlements Records R 33, pp. 187-206.

65. PRO, CO273/2, ff 73r-78r, Governor Blundell to Secretary to the Government of India, 26 July 1858.

66. PRO, CO273/2, ff. 8r-10r, Charles Canning, Public Works Dept. Military, to Court of Directors, East India Company, Allahabad, 16 October 1858.

67. PRO, CO273/2, ff. 122r-124v, Secretary to Government of India to Blundell, Alahabad, 9 October 1858.

68. PRO, CO273/2, ff. 125r-128r, Public Works Despatches to India, 1 June 1859 (no. 20).

69. Ibid.

70. Ibid, f. 479r. Inspector General of Ordnance to the Secretary to the Government, 18 August 1858.

71. MA, Unsigned fragmentary note bound with Public Works Dept. 1858, PWD Consultations, 150-55, 23 April 1858, no. 155, Collyer to Secretary, Government of India, 4 February 1858.

72. Ibid, another draft of the same unsigned note, with heading "From PWD to Governor Straits Settlements," 23 April 1858.

73. PRO, CO273/2, no. 25, ff. 473v, 474r-483r, Fort St. George Military Consultations, Collection of Documents referred to the Ordnance at Singapore 1858 to 1859: Inspector General of Ordnance to the Secretary to the Government of India, 13 July 1858, f. 478v.

74. Ibid, ff. 177v-178v, Extract of a letter from the Chief Engineer to the Officer Commanding the Troops, 12 November 1858.

75. PRO, CO273/3, f. 178r, Commanding Officer 14th Regiment to Staff Officer Singapore, 10 November 1858; ff. 175r-177v, Officer Commanding the Troops in the Straits to the Governor, Straits Settlements, Singapore, 4 December 1858.

76. Ibid, f. 201r, J.B. Leicester, Edward Leicester and W.S. Leicester to the Secretary to the Governor, Singapore, 2 February 1859; f. 202v, Acting Secretary to the Governor to the Chief Engineer Singapore, 10 February 1859, encloses the above together with a sketch.

77. PRO, CO273/2, no. 67, Colonel Commanding the Troops in the Straits to Governor, Straits Settlements, 15 February 1858.

78. Ibid, ff. 202v-203v, Chief Engineer to the Governor, Singapore, 11 February 1859;

f. 203r, Acting Secretary to the Governor to J.B. Edward and W.L. Leicester, Singapore, 12 February 1859, informed the three men that the Government wished to decline their offer as the land was not considered suitable.

79. PRO, CO273/3, ff. 1108r, 1109v, 1110r-v, 30 November 1859; CO273/6, f.238r, Office Commanding the Troops, Straits Settlements, to Quarter Master General Fort St. George, 30 July 1860.

80. PRO, CO273/4, ff. 1029r-1030r, no. 80: Col. Faber, Officiating Chief Engineer in Straits Settlements, to the Secretary to the Governor, 11 June 1860. This contains a plan and estimate of costs for clearing jungle and levelling the sides of the Government Hill, Fort Canning — amounting to $2,368 Spanish dollars. Collyer in his report of February 1860 also refers to changes in his plans which he made after seeing how different some parts of the hill looked after the jungle on it was cleared.

81. PRO, CO273/3, ff. 732r-733v, Residency Chaplain Singapore to the Secretary to the Governor, 10 February 1859.

82. PRO, CO273/2, ff 8r-10r, Charles Canning, Public Works Dept. Military, to the Court of Directors, East India Company, Allahabad, 16 October 1858; PWD Proceedings, Military, no. 16, 21 February 1860, with reference to Letter of the Governor General India, no. 7, 16 October 1858.

83. NAI, Proceedings, PWD, no. 7, 10 January, no. 369, 13 February 1860; Collyer to Secretary, Government of India, bound with Public Works Dept. 1858, Consultations 23 April, no. 155, 4 February 1858.

84. NAI, PWD Proceedings, Military, no. 33/77-558, Cavenagh to Officiating Secretary to Government of India, Public Works Dept., 1 May 1860. A *postern* was a gate at the end of a tunnel beneath the wall of a fort which led into the ditch or moat, also known as a *sally port*. A *scarp* was the interior wall of a ditch around a fort. A *counterscarp* was the exterior face of an earthern rampart beyond the ditch surrounding a fort, ie. the side facing the putative enemy.

85. NAI, PWD Proceedings No. 34, Military, Report by Capt. Collyer, Chief Engineer Straits Settlements, Upon Construction of Fort Canning, 7 September 1860.

86. PRO, CO273/16, ff. 128v, Straits Settlements Original Correspondence, Public Offices, Part II, Treasury Papers relating to the Straits Settlements, Extract Administrative Report for 1858-1859. This contradicts Buckley's assertion, p. 675, that most of the work was done by free labour.

87. NAI, Public Works Department Military, No. 34, Report by Capt. Collyer, Chief Engineer, Straits Settlements, Upon the Construction of Fort Canning, 25 February 1860.

88. Ibid.

89. PRO, CO273/6, f. 238r, Extract Fort William Proceedings for October 1860, enclosures for July and September 1860.

90. Harfield, 275.

91. SNA, Straits Settlements Records, R36, pp. 287-90, microfilm no. NL 76, Cavenagh to the Officiating Secretary to Government of India, Singapore, 1 May 1860. In this letter the Governor enclosed Collyer's report and confirmed the opinion of the Chief Engineer: "With the exception of the Gateway and the Gun Platforms (the former is rapidly progressing) the work may now be said to have been completed and may as stated by the Chief Engineer be considered as a first class Field Fortification."

92. PRO, CO273/10, ff. 350r-367r, Memorandum relative to the transfer of the barracks at Tanglin to the Royal Engineers Department and the works, lands and buildings that are to be transferred to the War Department on the withdrawal of the Indian troops, 22 April 1867.

93. PRO, CO273/10, ff. 273r-278r, Extract of a Report from the GOC Troops in Ceylon, Singapore, 23 April 1867.

94. PRO, CO273/16, ee. 136v-136r, J. Crawfurd, Suggestions for the Future Administration of the British Colonies in the Straits of Malacca, c. 1861.

4

Britannia Rules the Waves?
Singapore and Imperial Defence
1867-1891

T he Straits Settlements came under direct rule from the CO in London in 1865, with the War Office (WO) taking responsibility for military defences. One would expect that given the direct involvement of this more competent body — compared with the East India Company — Singapore's defences would at last have been integrated into a general colonial framework and be no cause for concern. Certainly, there remained many perceived threats, both internal and external. But there also remained chronic tension between local and colonial authorities over many military issues, not least money. It was inevitable that the local British population in Singapore would have a different view on local defence matters from that of British civil servants, soldiers and politicians halfway around the world in London. There were differences of opinion, sometimes severe, about what defences were actually required. It is important to understand these different concerns in order to plot the development not only of defence schemes, but also of the troops and equipment needed to make them work, in Singapore. In the end, internal disputes played as large a role in the military development of Singapore as any external threat — but the story is best told by combining the perspectives of local and imperial defence.

Defending a Crown Colony

The effort to escape from the East India Company began early, even before India was transferred to Crown rule. On 5 March 1857, the *Singapore Free Press* published a pseudonymous letter listing grievances against the East India Company. Among other things, the Honourable Company was accused of tampering with currency in the Straits Settlements and making repeated attempts to introduce port charges, which would damage Singapore's operation as a free port. These were all compared to the earlier Stamp Acts imposed on the North American colonies, which precipitated the Revolutionary War. The writer, "Fairplay", proffered secession as, again, the only solution for the Straits Settlements: he proposed the transfer of the Settlements from the government of the East India Company to the authority of the CO of the imperial government.[1] Buckley gives a full contemporary account of the transfer, which the imperial government decided in favour of as early as March 1858.[2] Pending the transfer, all questions on the defences of Singapore were deferred. The Secretary to the government of India in the Military Department noted in a letter to his counterpart in Madras that as early as August 1860, with regard to the defences of the Straits Settlements, the Secretary of State in the Public Works Department in London desired that "no expense should be incurred...beyond what was necessary to prevent their falling into an unserviceable condition..."[3]

In 1861, the Under-Secretary to the government of India in the Public Works Department reported that even with 29 heavy guns and five sea mortars in Singapore, the island was still short of 28 pieces of artillery to complete its complement. The following table shows the shortfall between the requirements of the Officer Commanding the Artillery in the Straits (submitted to the Governor-General of India) and the actual situation:[4]

	Actual Armament 1861	Proposed Armament
Fort Canning	none	16 x 8" guns 4 x 8" howitzers 2 x 13"mortars
Fort Canning South Battery	7 x 68 pounders	Same
Fort Fullerton	7 x 68 pounders 1 x 13" mortar	Same, plus 2 x 8" howitzers 4 x 8" guns 1 x 13" mortar
Mount Palmer	5 x 56 pounders	4 x 68 pounders 1 x 8" gun 2 x 13" mortars
New Harbour	2 x 56 pounders	2 x 68 pounders
Mount Faber	2 x 13" mortars	same
In Store	8 x 8" guns 2 x 13" mortars	—
Total	34 weapons	55 weapons

Table 1: Guns in Singapore 1861[5]

The requirement was for another six 68 pounders, thirteen 8" guns, six howitzers, and three mortars. The government of India decided that the 56 pounders should not be replaced and sent away, but even then to complete the indent would have required another 21 pieces of artillery. Two things can be seen from the table. The first is that 10 pieces of artillery were already in store. This was nearly one-third of the total guns actually available in Singapore. This comes as no surprise as there was only one company of artillerymen on the island.[6] In their haste to mount guns, the authorities seem to have forgotten about the men required to fire them. In his argument for complying with the indent, there is no mention by the Under-Secretary of sending additional artillerymen.

The manpower problem was in fact acute. Only 47 Europeans and 21 "natives" (probably Indians) were available to man the guns, compared with the force of two companies of Europeans — some 160 men — required for the new forts.[7] Some of Singapore's European gunners were sent to China as part of the British-French punitive expedition culminating in the destruction of the Summer Palace; in December 1860, officials in India proposed to divert them there rather than return them to Singapore, reducing its garrison further even as the forts were completed.[8] In 1861 officials in Calcutta again objected to losing any artillery to Singapore. But around the foot of the new fort on Fort Canning Hill, some 3000 men could be accommodated in the artillery barracks; in exasperation it was even suggested that some infantrymen should be trained to supplement the gunners if necessary.[9]

Why had the Officer Commanding the Artillery in the Straits been allowed to ask for 21 additional guns if he did not have enough men? The only simple answer is that another crisis had scared the powers-that-be into another impulsive flurry of rearmament. Blind action was preferred to any passivity in the face of a new threat, this time from the French. Prior to the joint British-French operations in China, the French were not strong in the region. That soon changed. In 1862, John William Reid, the officer in charge of the China Sea Survey then proceeding, wrote to the Hydrographer to the Admiralty, Admiral Washington, to report on his visit to Saigon. Reid's impression was that the French had a stronghold from which it would "be hardly possible to dislodge them."[10] He warned that the French could command the main route to China, and place Singapore and Hong Kong in constant dread of an attack:

> I can't help thinking, that both Singapore and Hong Kong ought at least to be placed beyond the fear of attack from small squadrons in the event of our ships being temporarily withdrawn from their protection, if nothing more is done; but I should be sorry to record it as my opinion that this would be at all sufficient to meet the exigency of our altered position in these Seas.[11]

How "altered" was this position? The French had 4000 men in Cochin China, both soldiers and sailors. They also had the *Duperee*, an old 74 gun ship from which most of the guns had been removed to shore. The transport *Muerthe* had been converted into a factory. The moored frigate *Didon* guarded the entrance to the river Mekong. Another frigate was stationed further up-river. Twelve small gunboats were also employed running up the river. Half a dozen steamers completed the list of the French Naval Force in Cochin China.[12] This was hardly a formidable force, as the British had 38 ships in China and the East Indies, and six more in Australia; a total of 5222 sailors alone.[13] Perhaps the British were not merely considering the threat at the time, but the potential threat that a stronghold like Saigon could support, if and when the French increased

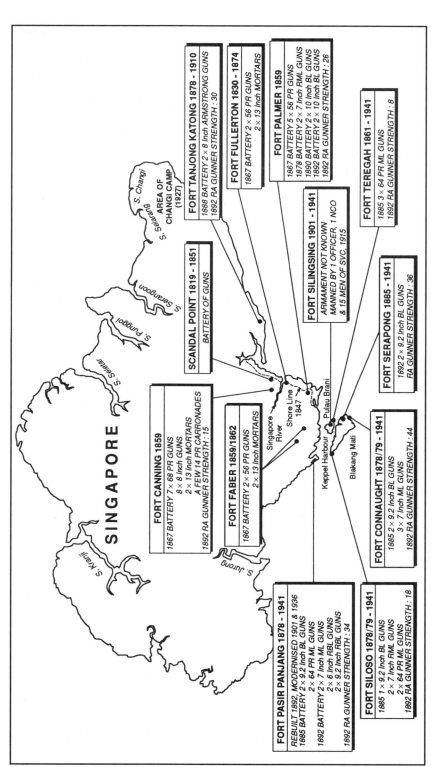

FORT TANJONG KATONG 1878 - 1910

1888 BATTERY 2 × 8 Inch ARMSTRONG GUNS
1892 RA GUNNER STRENGTH : 30

FORT FULLERTON 1830 - 1874

1867 BATTERY 2 × 56 PR GUNS
2 × 13 Inch MORTARS

FORT PALMER 1859

1867 BATTERY 5 × 56 PR GUNS
1878 BATTERY 2 × 7 Inch RML GUNS
1890 BATTERY 2 × 10 Inch BL GUNS
1892 BATTERY 2 × 10 Inch BL GUNS
1892 RA GUNNER STRENGTH : 26

FORT TEREGAH 1861 - 1941

1885 3 × 64 PR ML GUNS
1892 RA GUNNER STRENGTH : 8

FORT SILINGSING 1901 - 1941

ARMAMENT NOT KNOWN
MANNED BY 1 OFFICER, 1 NCO
& 15 MEN OF SVC, 1915

FORT SERAPONG 1885 - 1941

1892 2 × 9.2 Inch BL GUNS
RA GUNNER STRENGTH : 36

FORT CONNAUGHT 1878/79 - 1941

1885 2 × 9.2 Inch BL GUNS
3 × 7 Inch ML GUNS
1892 RA GUNNER STRENGTH : 44

FORT SILOSO 1878/79 - 1941

1885 1 × 9.2 Inch BL GUNS
2 × 7 Inch RML GUNS
2 × 64 PR ML GUNS
1892 RA GUNNER STRENGTH : 18

FORT PASIR PANJANG 1878 - 1941

REBUILT 1892, MODERNISED 1901 & 1936
1885 BATTERY 2 × 9.2 Inch BL GUNS
2 × 64 PR ML GUNS
1892 BATTERY 2 × 7 Inch ML GUNS
2 × 6 Inch RBL GUNS
2 × 9.2 Inch RBL GUNS
1892 RA GUNNER STRENGTH : 34

FORT FABER 1859/1862

1867 BATTERY 2 × 56 PR GUNS
2 × 13 Inch MORTARS

FORT CANNING 1859

1867 BATTERY 7 × 68 PR GUNS
8 × 8 Inch GUNS
2 × 13 Inch MORTARS
A FEW 14 PR CARRONADES
1892 RA GUNNER STRENGTH : 15

SCANDAL POINT 1819 - 1851

BATTERY OF GUNS

AREA OF CHANGI CAMP (1927)

SINGAPORE

S. Changi
S. Selarang
S. Serangoon
S. Punggol
S. Selatar
S. Kranji
S. Jurong
Singapore River
Shore Line 1847
Keppel Harbour
Pulau Brani
Blakang Mati

Location of forts in nineteenth-century Singapore

their naval deployment. It is useful to note at this point that the recommendation was for the capability of shore batteries to repel attack from small naval squadrons.

The British perspective on the problem was revealed in no uncertain terms in a letter by Sir James Graham, First Lord of the Admiralty, to Lord Bentinck, the Governor-General of India: "Trade with China is our only object…"[14] Any threat the French posed to trade with China had to be dealt with. As the British could not possibly fortify the coast of China, the only defence available to them was the RN. The possibility raised by Reid of the fleet being "temporarily withdrawn" from Southeast Asia became more of a certainty. Singapore would indeed have to look to gun batteries for its protection.

The whole question of Singapore's defences was given another airing in 1864 when Sir Hercules Robinson, Governor of Hong Kong, was asked by the Duke of Newcastle, Secretary of State for the Colonies, to sit in committee with the Governor of the Straits Settlements, Col. Orfeur Cavenagh, plus some of his senior officers, and report on the "Military Defence of the Straits Settlements," prior to the transfer of government. One of their first observations was that while the west was secure, the eastern approach to New Harbour was undefended. They urged that the long-contemplated Tanjong Katong battery be constructed.[15] Furthermore, they noted that Fort Fullerton was close to the most important commercial quarter of town, and that the bulk of the shipping in the roadstead — the anchorage in front of the town — would be anchored in front of and between the fort and any potentially hostile cruiser. The fort was not only useless, it was a liability. The Governors asked that Fort Fullerton be disposed of, the land sold, and the proceeds used to defray the cost of building Tanjong Katong Battery, and of improving Fort Palmer.[16] These two Batteries, along with Mount Faber Battery and Fort Canning, were deemed "due provision" for the defence of the town and roadstead "from the attack of one or possibly even two hostile cruisers should such escape the vigilance of our Squadrons, and visit the Port during the temporary absence of any of our own Naval Forces."[17]

Cavenagh also took the opportunity to submit a memorandum on the defence of the Straits Settlements. He rejected the possibility of a Russian assault as he thought Russian troops could not be sent so far from their nearest port. Cavenagh identified the main threat as a French squadron, with a land force of 2000 to 3000 men drawn from Saigon. What is also interesting was his report on the present defences. He reiterated that the artillerymen in Singapore, "even with the aid of seamen from the Merchant Shipping," would not be sufficient to man all the guns. Cavenagh asked for an extra European infantry regiment from which he proposed to take a certain number of men from each company to train in gun drill. These men could then cooperate with the artillery.[18] However, nothing much was done in this direction. Guns without gunners became more ornaments than weapons. Moreover, the Officer Commanding Troops, Straits Settlements, was less optimistic in his own assessment. He argued that Singapore's importance was enhanced by recent developments in Indochina; the French had just occupied Saigon, and now begun to fortify it. Thus they now presented a clear threat just five sailing days from Singapore. And the only British gunboat in the Straits, an 18 gun vessel, had to protect Singapore, Penang, Melaka, and patrol the waters of Sarawak and Bangka.[19] But at least the contradictions and gaps in Singapore's defences were now being discussed more systematically, at quite high levels.

On 1 April 1867, the transfer of the Straits Settlements to direct Crown rule was effected. What effect did this major change, from Company to Crown rule, have on the development of Singapore's defences, especially since the first colonial Governor was a colonel in the army? The main noticeable change was a shift in focus from the identification of enemies and calculation of defences required, to a more scrupulous calculation of money required, or more particularly, the amount that the colony should contribute to defence. This reflected a change in the approach of the new British government to imperial defence as a whole. On 8 October 1868, the Earl of Granville, Secretary of State for the Colonies, wrote to the Governor to discuss the garrisoning of the Straits with two small battalions of native irregular infantry, one company of native gun lascars and one battery of Royal Artillery.[20]

This question of the garrison and its expenses had of course already provoked acrimony between the resident European population and the home government. In long discussions in the years immediately prior to the transfer to Crown rule, the Europeans in Singapore sang one constant refrain: the government's plans called for more soldiers than they wanted to host, not because they felt no threat but because these plans asked them to pay a greater share of the cost than they were willing to bear. A public meeting on 22 May 1861 put the point bluntly: "that the greatly increased expenditure for military purposes entailed by the expensive system of fortifications now in progress should not be borne by these settlements, as it is undertaken for imperial and not local purposes."[21] In 1865, "merchants and others" wrote to the Under-Secretary of State for the Colonies arguing that there was no threat from any native power, any European threat would be met by the RN, and therefore the only garrison required was one that "gives confidence to peaceable inhabitants, preserves internal order, and gives security against lawlessness to property in goods, houses and warehouses." The authors suggested that a force of about 200 marines, on top of a native police force, would be enough.[22]

The main reason for this feeling can be summed up in one statistic: in 1863, nearly half of Singapore's local revenue was spent on military expenditure. The merchants in fact saw the military and its new fort as more of a threat than a guardian: "it was inexpedient, if not impractical to rely on the land works, as Fort Canning and Fort Fullerton would not protect the town from an attack by sea, and the probable result of their attempting to annoy a hostile fleet would be the destruction of the town."[23] Granville obviously assumed that his proposal would reduce the cost of the garrison and therefore hopefully end the problem. The Secretary of War later found that the £59,300 annual colonial payment could not cover the cost of upkeep of barracks for native troops and artillery.[24] The colonial government on the other hand was seemingly less concerned with cost and counter-proposed that the Royal Artillery battery be maintained, that one half-battery of native artillery be added, and that the defences of Singapore be re-modelled and re-armed according to plans approved by the War Office. All these at the expense of the colony! However, it was all a matter of re-distribution: the colonial subsidy was to remain at £59,300 of which £50,000 was to be the annual payment. The balance of not less than £9,500 was to be placed at the disposal of the colony.[25] In other words, the imperial government would in effect be receiving less money. The imperial government was not about to spend more money to maintain the defences of Singapore. It clearly was not going to release money from the colonial subsidy — money which would have to be made up from the Treasury's coffers. Again, nothing was done and the matter rested until February 1869, when the future of the defences was put in serious doubt.

The principal agent for change was Edward Cardwell, who was appointed Secretary of State for War in 1868. He immediately launched wide-ranging radical reforms in the Army.[26] On 27 February 1869 he sent the Secretary of State for the Colonies an astonishing memorandum from the Deputy Director of Works in the WO, Colonel William Drummond Jervois of the Royal Engineers, soon to be the Governor of the Straits Settlements. Jervois approached the question of the defence of the colony with the belief that there was "no great foreign military or naval power within easy reach of Singapore, and the defences of that place need only be on a small scale." He scorned the 6000 French troops in Saigon, confident that even if they had ships to transport them to either Hong Kong or Singapore, a mere portion of the army in India would be more than a match for them. The colony in the Straits need only concern itself with defence against "casual naval attack." Jervois recommended that both Fort Fullerton and Mount Palmer Battery be abandoned. He revived the suggestion that the Fort Fullerton land be sold and the money channelled into new works, this time at Mount Faber and on a floating battery in the harbour. The entire defence of the roadstead was to be entrusted to the navy, specifically a war steamer and three or four little gunboats with one gun each, and a proper sprinkling of torpedoes.[27]

Would the Navy have been up to the job? In October 1868, the RN had 52 ships in the Far East, with 7283 sailors. But one year later, the numbers fell to 39 ships, and 5655 men.[28] The decrease was due to the cessation of British interest in the suppression of piracy in Chinese waters, after the successes of Vice-Admiral Sir Henry Keppel's anti-piracy operations.[29] In other words, normal routine deployment of the fleet in Asia was probably around 39 ships.

Even with the naval presence, the role of shore batteries became more crucial. And yet the gun batteries had also not been improved. Buckley reports that Fort Fullerton began to be dismantled in 1865.[30]

It was a slow process. The Return of Heavy Ordnance in Store and Mounted in Forts of May 1869 seems to indicate that all 13" mortars were retired, and Mount Faber disarmed. The table shows a total of 31 artillery pieces distributed between Fort Canning, Fort Fullerton and Mount Palmer. This was a decrease of three guns from 1861. The largest gun in Singapore was the 8" gun and eight of these were mounted at Fort Canning. The reduction was perhaps not a very serious defect, as Singapore still did not have the men to operate all the guns.[31]

In a lengthy confidential letter, the then Governor in the Straits, Sir Harry St. George Ord[32], gave his opinion on Jervois' analysis. It was a very low opinion. Ord was the first colonial Governor appointed to the Straits Settlements and had been given to understand "by the highest Naval authority" that in event of war, the fleet would be solely occupied in the duty of harassing the enemy. Ord was certain that "No admiral would feel called upon to weaken the efficiency of his fleet by retaining an effective ship-of-war in what would be looked upon by naval men as inglorious idleness..." Help might not even come for months. Ord observed that an enemy cruiser could lie outside the three fathom mark and sink every ship in the anchorage. Ord's conclusion was that shore batteries were needed.[33] With the tide of opinion against him, all Ord could do was begin a re-organisation of the garrison in Singapore. On 17 June 1871, he personally explained his views in an interview at the WO in London. Ord preferred that the garrison be reduced and consist of only one British regiment and one battery, Royal Artillery, instead of one wing of a European regiment, one entire native regiment, and two artillery batteries. Ord was willing to split the cost of the European regiment with the imperial government, but Cardwell thought that the time had arrived "when the expenditure necessary for its protection should be defrayed by the Colony itself." Moreover, the policy of the country would be that of "concentration of force at home, and not its dispersion in distant colonies, even if the expense be thrown upon those colonies."[34] However, as Ord was in

Harry St. George Ord

London, the opportunity was present for yet another re-examination of the whole question of defence.

On Wednesday, 19 July 1871, both Ord and Jervois reported at the WO to sit in committee, with a naval officer, to consider the question.[35] The Committee eventually recommended that the colony be garrisoned by the substitution of one European regiment with a double force of gun lascars for the force then employed. The colony would pay half the cost of maintaining the European regiment. The imperial government would defray the other half on the supposition that a wing of the regiment be available for general service in the Eastern Seas, being in the meantime stationed cheaply on a healthy island.[36] The Under-Secretary of State in the CO, R.G. Herbert, was furious. He had received an unsigned copy of the report loaned by Ord so he was not entirely unaware of the recommendations, but he resented the report being adopted without any reference to Lord Kimberly, the Secretary of State for the Colonies. Herbert accused Cardwell of being eager to remove from the next defence estimate all costs of native infantry regiments both at the Straits and at Hong Kong.[37] He thought that too heavy a charge had been levied on the colony. Kimberly wrote that the arrangements were "quite as favourable as the colony is entitled to…But of course I cannot acquiesce in War Office decisions taken without concurrence of the Col. (sic) office."[38] Herbert was asked to write a letter to the WO requesting that no action at all be taken. It was now clear what the biggest threat to the defences of Singapore really was: office politics in London.

The situation was quickly resolved. On 28 October, the WO replied to Herbert admitting that Cardwell was eager to settle the question of the European regiment before the close of the financial year on 31 March. But if the question were postponed, the cost for troops in Hong Kong and Singapore would appear again in the Army Estimates, which Cardwell had pledged to reduce. The CO was fortunately in a conciliatory mood and Herbert announced, "We shall be ready to do all we can to facilitate matters…"[39] Events moved swiftly, and only a month later the WO promised that the 10th Regiment of Foot would arrive before the end of March. The Madras regiments would be returned to India and the artillery in the Straits reduced to one battery.[40] By the end of the year, the Treasury expressed approval of Cardwell's recommendation that the colonial contribution of the Straits be reduced to £51,595 and that the colony would undertake additional military expenditure of about £7000 per annum.[41] It was a small price to pay to relieve the imperial estimates of the cost of maintaining a Madras regiment.

Was the substitution of a European regiment of the line for two native regiments a worthwhile effort? It may have pleased the Europeans in Singapore. It certainly pleased Cardwell. Unfortunately the 10th Regiment did not acquit itself with too much honour during its tour of duty. Only one year later, on 21 July 1873, the *London & China Telegraph* carried the story that two soldiers from the 10th had entered the house of a Portuguese family and attempted to molest the women. Not only had the two soldiers failed in their attempt, they were "so severely punished [by passers-by] that it was deemed advisable to send them to hospital."[42] In 1875, out of 49 Europeans in jail, 23 were from the 10th Regiment.[43]

The same issue of the *London & China Telegraph* on 21 July 1873 also announced that news had been received in Singapore that Sir Andrew Clarke of the Royal Engineers had been appointed Sir Harry Ord's successor. It reported the incredible rumour that Sir Andrew had been specifically instructed to fortify Singapore at the colony's expense, and that he had been authorised to spend up to $300,000. The Straits inhabitants could "only promise His Excellency the most uncompromising opposition to, if not flat mutiny and rebellion against, such iniquitous and tyrannical folly."[44] Meanwhile, criticism of existing fortifications was still rife, the latest being from Maj.-Gen. Whitfield, Commanding Officer in China. On the New Year of 1873, he submitted a confidential report to the WO, dismissing the forts in Singapore as totally incapable of effective defence against modern artillery. As a means of cowing the non-European population, they were excessive: a few light field guns would have sufficed. Whitfield cautioned that any alterations had to be taken up as part of the general question of defence, including the remodelling of existing works and the construction of new ones.[45]

In the years immediately following the transfer of Singapore to Crown rule there was therefore no real improvement in the defences of Singapore. The shore batteries were loudly condemned but there was no attempt to rectify their defects. The only major activity undertaken was a shuffling around of troops. In the absence of serious threats of external attack, quibbling over costs, contrary opinions and office politics, all had their day.

Russians, Guns, Money, and Bureaucrats

Over the next two decades, British military strategy was influenced by Russian moves in Central Asia. The Russian thrust into Central Asia was both dramatic and constant. They took Turkestan and Chimkeat in 1864, Tashkent in 1865, and Samarkand in 1868. In 1873 the Khanates of Khiva and Bukhara became Russian protectorates, and Kokand was annexed in 1876. The primary motivation was the need for defensible frontiers, "conjoined with the excessive ambition of unruly local commanders willing to gamble that euphoria over early victories would expunge the consequences of insubordination."[46] Enthusiastic soldiers aside, the Russians were moving closer and closer to the jewel in the British crown: India. This inevitably impinged upon defence plans in Singapore.

In 1874, with the fall of Gladstone's Liberal government, the Tory Benjamin Disraeli became the British Prime Minister. Lord Salisbury was appointed Secretary of State for India. Both men were deeply distrustful of Russia and felt that British policy in the East had been too cautious and too prosaic.[47] Disraeli was determined to put right what he saw as a display of weakness towards the Russians, and relations between the two countries cooled rapidly.

At this time, for the British Army in general the lesser calibres of artillery were giving way to larger ones. Brigadier-General John Adye, Director of Artillery and Stores, reported in March 1878 that no 7" guns had been made since 1871, and no 9" guns since 1872.[48] Of course, there were still teething problems with the larger-calibre guns. Guns trials involving the 10" Rifled Muzzle Loading (RML) guns of 18 tons carried out in the U.K. showed that the common shells filled with sand tended to break up on striking strong parts of unarmoured ships made of either wood or iron. In Singapore, Sir William Drummond Jervois, late of the Department of Fortifications at the WO, was appointed Governor in April 1875. With the Russian problem bubbling to boil, he wrote to Vice-Admiral Alfred Phillipps Ryder, the Commander-in-Chief China Station, on 28 July 1876 for suggestions on improving the defences of Singapore. As subsequent events proved, Jervois was shrewdly seeking support for his own ideas. Jervois grumbled to Ryder that "These works [in Singapore] are weak and insignificant and in no way capable of affording effective defence against attack by a foreign enemy." In a long list of complaints, he pointed out that Fort Canning, "a weak straggling work, unprovided with flank defence", had only obsolete smoothbore weapons which were for the most part unserviceable. He noted that Fort Fullerton had been practically dismantled to make way for public buildings. He observed that the guns at Mount Faber were not yet in position. Finally, he complained that Fort Palmer was wrongly situated on the side of a hill and was in no way adapted for the requirements of modern warfare.[49]

Jervois suggested sweeping reforms. He wanted six 10" RML guns for a fort at Mount Siloso on Blakang Mati, and four 10" guns for a new battery at Palmer. Tanjong Katong was to have an open battery with five 11" RML guns, while citadels would be put on Mount Faber, and on Mount Serapong on Blakang Mati. Jervois also considered enrolling 200 artillery volunteers, and mining the harbour with electro-contact torpedoes. Of course, the imperial government should provide everything.[50] For once, a Governor of Singapore had asked not only for guns, but also for men to operate them. Moreover, Jervois had another card up his sleeve. On 31 August 1876, while awaiting Ryder's support, Jervois wrote to Lord Carnarvon, Secretary for the Colonies. He reminded Carnarvon that, while at the WO, he had written a memo on the defences of Singapore in which he argued the RN was the best means of defence. He remembered that the report had been "combated" by Ord, the Governor at that time. Now that Jervois was actually on the scene, with "intimate personal knowledge of the place itself...I have every reason to concur in [Ord's] view and to urge that local defences should be provided." Jervois took an oblique and novel approach to the touchy question, arguing that the best means of providing continuous employment for convict labour was to employ them on fortification works! This would provide remunerative labour for the convicts. At the same time, the colony would be contributing in an effort of great imperial importance.[51] The works should be on Pulau Brani and Pulau Blakang Mati. Jervois also mentioned in passing that he had consulted Ryder on the defences.

Not surprisingly, the CO reacted negatively. An official minuted:

> ...the best scheme from a military point of view, of defending Singapore & the mode in which the necessary expense should be provided, are questions belonging to a subject which has been now and then brought up for discussion ever since we took over the Straits Settlements from India, & I apprehend that it will long continue to be only a subject for discussion.[52]

But this anonymous official was wrong, because Jervois began extraordinary measures to build forts. Replying from Chefoo, China, on 15 August, Admiral Ryder entirely concurred with Jervois' opinion "as to the great importance of Singapore as a naval station and as to its present defenceless condition, should an Enemy attack it in the absence of an English [sic] squadron." However, he suggested that, instead of permanent fortifications, designs should be prepared for earthworks such as could be thrown up rapidly by unskilled labour in event of war. On the other hand, the guns could be demanded and supplied at once, but held in storage.[53] Temporary earthworks were not what Jervois wanted, but the partial support from Ryder was good enough. Jervois sent a despatch to Carnarvon to inform him that Ryder concurred with his own views. To offset Ryder's proposal for earthworks, Jervois enclosed an extract of a report dated 29 August 1870 by the Defence Committee with reference to the defence of the Principal Commercial Ports of the United Kingdom, chaired by His Royal Highness the Duke of Cambridge. Jervois felt that the observations there applied equally to the defence of Singapore. The report frowned on the idea:

> ...prevalent that batteries on shore for the defence of Commercial Ports can be improvised at short notice, and that it is unnecessary to construct works or to mount guns for this purpose until a time of expected attack. The Committee cannot, however, too strongly represent that considerable time is required for preparing the works necessary for the protection and service of the armament required to resist the attack of modern ships of war.[54]

The Committee felt that there was a necessity for introducing into the parapet material which would offer greater resistance than earth alone, and concluded that it was essential that batteries of a permanent character should be constructed and that guns should be mounted in them.[55]

This was a timely reminder, as events far away once again began to bear on the question of Singapore's defences. For on 12 April 1877, unable to reach agreement on affairs in the Balkans with other countries, Russia declared war on the Ottoman Empire. Russian troops crossed into Rumania and by 8 January 1878 were practically at the gates of Constantinople. London followed the series of Russian successes with great dismay. Queen Victoria wrote to Disraeli that, "If the Russians reach Constantinople, the Queen would be so humiliated that she thinks she would abdicate at once."[56] The British reacted sharply, ordering their Mediterranean Fleet to Constantinople. By the end of the month, five

British ironclads were in the Sea of Marmora.[57] The presence of the British did not affect the outcome of the war. With an enemy army at his doorstep, the Ottoman Sultan sued for peace.[58]

Russia's terms of peace dictated at San Stefano in March 1878 attempted to secure unrestricted right of passage for its Black Sea Fleet to the Mediterranean by demanding the creation of an independent Bulgaria stretching from the Black Sea to the Aegean Sea.[59] London refused to recognise the Treaty of San Stefano, and began openly preparing for war. Seven thousand Indian troops were ordered to Malta.[60] To add fuel to the fire, the Russians despatched Maj.-Gen. N.G. Stoletov to Kabul to secure an anti-British treaty with the Emir of Afghanistan. The British saw Stoletov's presence in Afghanistan as evidence of a conspiracy against India.[61] Britain's reaction was global. For instance, the British Minister in Japan, Sir Harry Parkes at Yedo, sent an extract from a Yokohama newspaper to the Secretary of State for Foreign Affairs. The article was a translation of a letter written by the Vladivostok correspondent of the naval newspaper *Yacht* giving account of a visit of Vice-Admiral Ryder and his officers to the port of Vladivostok. The article accused the British naval officers of spying on the defences there, but claimed that it was all futile since work was halted:

> Immediately after [the British] departure, the works were recommenced with unprecedented vigour... and now we are working at the defences, as though the hostile armaments of England were off our very shores. When it does come we shall give the officers a warmer reception than we gave the lot just gone.[62]

In May Vice-Admiral Hillyar, the C-in-C at Yokohama, reported that the Russians had mined Vladivostok, placing torpedoes at the entrance of the port.[63] Were the defences in Singapore equally prepared? In April 1877, the month when Russia declared war on the Ottoman Empire, 7 Battery of the 22 Brigade, Royal Artillery was stationed in Singapore. It had four officers and 110 men. But the Battery was only at half-strength with 55 men and one officer actually present in Singapore. Eight men were in hospital and the rest in Penang and elsewhere in Malaya.[64]

Meanwhile, Jervois retired in 1877. His successor, Sir William C.F. Robinson also took firm measures to improve defences. In a secret circular to the colonies dated 20 March 1878, the CO sent instructions that Governors were to consult the relevant authorities to frame emergency defence schemes with the means at their disposal. The danger was from an unexpected attack by a small squadron or a single unarmoured cruiser, rather than serious attempts to conquer colonies.[65] Robinson asked Col. C.A.S. Dickens, Commanding Officer of the 28th Regiment and Officer Commanding Troops in Singapore, to confer with Capt. C.F. Hotham, Senior Naval Officer, and Major J.F.A. McNair, Colonial Engineer, on the defences at Singapore given the "menacing aspects of European affairs." Robinson was not as optimistic as the CO and admitted that the colony could do little or nothing against an attack by two or more ironclad ships, but asked for preparations to repel an attack of a single vessel.[66]

Lt.-Col. L.F. Hall, the Commanding Officer of the Royal Artillery in China and the Straits Settlements, was not included. He was probably not in Singapore then, so he later sent a written report. In April 1878, this defence committee submitted a scathing report. Regarding armament, the report included observations like "practically useless against any war vessel that may be likely to approach;" "the only guns of any useful calibre, with one exception, are, with their carriages, quite unserviceable;" "any defence of the new harbour approaches with any of the present armament would be both futile and injudicious."[67] However, being fully seized of the fact that new armament was lacking, the committee could only advise that rifled guns and torpedoes be requested by telegraph. Until their arrival, the RN would have to defend Singapore. Fortunately, after writing the report, the committee was able to report to the Governor that seven 68 pounder guns were made serviceable. These were distributed between the positions at Tanjong Katong, Mount Palmer and Mount Faber.[68] Colonel Dickens of the 28th Regiment also wrote later to Robinson to say that he needed 25,000 pounds of gunpowder for the guns. Dickens dismissed the mortars as unreliable for service but useful for signalling. He then went on to make an astonishing remark:

> In thinking over the Tanjong Kutong (sic) position, I am not sure it would not be as well to have two 8" guns to protect the flanks in cases of boats landing and attempting to turn it, but as I have never been there I am unable to say for certain.[69]

One is left to speculate why Colonel Dickens never visited the defence works at Tanjong Katong — despite producing a report on defences there — and how accurate his report and recommendations for that position would be.

At the end of April, Lt.-Col. Hall gave his comments to Robinson in writing. He pointed out that Mount Palmer was beyond effective range of the northeast entrance to the harbour and unsupported by any other position. It therefore did not command the New Harbour at all. Moreover, the reserve magazine was a mile-and-a-half away. Fort Faber, in his position, was "in a very dilapidated condition, as far as can be seen through the brushwood and jungle that obscure the battery." Only one gun at Fort Faber could be brought to bear on a ship at the entrance of the New Harbour, and the firing of this gun would be too slow to cause much damage. Hall also noted that the embrasures at Palmer and Faber restricted the guns in their lateral range. But Hall suggested that even if the embrasures were removed, and the guns placed *en barbette*, their racers would still allow the same restricted degree of traverse. Hall reported that there were no emplacements or magazines for the guns at Tanjong Katong, and a boat attack could easily cut off the defenders.[70]

A report was even received from E.C. Saunder, the District Commissary of the Straits Settlements. He pointed out that he had no means whatsoever for transporting any heavy ordnance, "being solely dependent on the ordinary bullock gharry."[71] On a more positive note, the Defence Committee, in answer to a query from Robinson, recommended on 4

May 1878 that a launch be purchased immediately for torpedoes to be mounted. The Colonial Secretary, J. Douglas, the Senior Naval Officer, Capt. Hotham, the Master Attendant and the First Lieutenant of HMS *Charybdis* identified a 60-foot [18.5m] steam launch available for $6000.[72]

At the same time as Robinson formed his local defence committee, the Secretary of State for the Colonies also appointed a Colonial Defence Committee to consider the defences of the more important colonial ports from the imperial government's point of view. This was the first of three such bodies. Admiral Sir Alexander Milne, Sir Henry Barkly and General Sir Lintorn Simmons were directed to consider how to provide temporary defences in the event that hostilities broke out. They were specifically asked to propose defences to counter the four unarmoured Russian ships abroad at that time. These were armed with guns of equal power with the British 7" guns and, in one instance, with a 9" gun. Milne was the President of the Committee. In giving its recommendations, the Milne Committee stated that should heavier Russian ships from the Baltic or other ports join the squadron then abroad, their recommended defences would be inadequate.[73] The Committee limited its suggestions to the 7" gun which it considered a "thoroughly effective weapon." The Royal Gun Factory could manufacture this at the rate of two-and-a-half guns per week. The Milne Committee acknowledged that the trade and value of shipping in Singapore was valued at £74 million per annum — one-eighth of all British commerce — and placed Singapore third in relative importance on the list of all coaling stations. Ten 7" guns and six 64 pounders were recommended for this second runner-up coaling station. The Committee was quick to note that these batteries would only protect the New Harbour. The proposed guns would give no security to the outer harbour, roadstead or town. To protect lines of communication, a ship of war or two gunboats of the *Comet* class were suggested. The total cost involved was estimated at £69,400.[74]

Troops were also proposed. Milne had before him a report of the Imperial Defence Committee which stated that the number of troops, especially artillerymen, required merely for the defence of the coaling stations, was greater than could be spared in time of war. It is interesting to note the relative strengths of forces available and proposed:

	Regulars available			Regulars proposed		Local levies proposed	
	Arty	Eng	Inf	Arty	Inf	Arty	Inf
Cape Colony	241	72	3527	200	1000	400	2000
Mauritius	15	5	318	100	1000	150	—
Ceylon	295	4	900	300	800	100	400
Singapore	95	—	950	100	1000	150	—
Hong Kong	194	17	923	200	1800	100	1000
Total	940	98	6618	900	5600	900	3400

The desire to raise local troops to replace the more expensive British regiments is clear.

The Milne Committee recommendations do not seem to have been accepted unreservedly. The CO allotted Singapore six Whitehead torpedoes out of 25 put at its disposal.[75] But Milne was informed by the Director of Artillery and Stores Maj.-Gen. F.A. Campbell that only 30 to 40 6.5" guns could be appropriated. No other guns or torpedoes were available.[76] Milne then wrote to suggest that 10 of these 6.5 ton guns and 100 rounds of ammunition be sent to Singapore.[77] Finally, the imperial government authorised the expenditure of only £17,600 on defence works in Singapore.[78] Nonetheless, Robinson began constructing new defences to protect New Harbour. Alan Harfield has detailed the progress of the forts and batteries impressively.[79] Works were thrown up on Mount Siloso, Mount Blakang Mati East and Mount Serapong on Blakang Mati, at Pasir Panjang, and at Tanjong Katong, designed and constructed by Capt. Henry McCallum in 1878.[80] The works were to secure the western and eastern approaches to New Harbour with a withering crossfire. Fort Pasir Panjang was equipped with two 7" muzzle-loaders. At the same time, Fort Palmer exchanged its five 56 pounders for two 7" muzzle-loaders.[81]

Robinson served only two years and was replaced by Sir Frederick Augustus Weld. Makepeace records that Weld's efforts were mainly directed towards the consolidation of the welfare of the Malay States, and that he left the affairs of Singapore in the hands of others.[82] Even then, Weld was very much involved in defence matters. Soon after taking over the Governorship, Weld sent a telegram to the CO to say that he proposed to preside over the Local Committee on Defence unless otherwise instructed.[83] The committee was constituted to report on local defence for the consideration of the Royal Defence Commission on the Defence of British Possessions and Commerce Abroad.[84] Weld's offer was unusual as the normal procedure was for the committee to be appointed by the Governor, with the GOC China nominating the military members. Most of the committee members were military professionals. This was the model used in Hong Kong and the Cape in South Africa. Normally, the Governor would not preside.[85] Why was Weld so eager to do so?

Ever since the transfer of the Straits Settlements to Imperial rule, defence matters had been largely out of the purview of the Governor and civil authorities in Singapore. This can be clearly seen in the *Annual Reports on the Administration of the Straits Settlements*; after 1867, military matters ceased to be reported by the Governor. Public works pertaining to defence were given cursory mention and the total sum contributed to defence was simply stated, not explained. Now, Weld was attempting to regain some control over the direction of military defences in Singapore. There were no objections from the WO to Weld assuming the presidency of the committee, but the Secretary of State for War remarked that the Governor might be better placed for giving effect to recommendations if he were not the president. The CO thought it would be inconvenient were the Governor pledged to a scheme which might throw the whole burden of defence on the imperial government.[86] It finally informed Weld that it would be more desirable if he merely gave his views to the Committee.[87]

Weld's views are worth mention because they included the first serious consideration of an enemy landing. He proposed rifle-pits and earthworks extending from Pasir Panjang in the west to Fort Canning.[88] Weld showed a deep insight into defences, and his report was succinct and to the point. Unfortunately, the Committee largely ignored him, particularly on the issue of an enemy landing. The Committee worked fast, and on 29 April 1881 it submitted a comprehensive report. The importance of Singapore as a naval coaling station was emphasised, the Committee calculating that between 12,000 and 15,000 imperial tons of coal were loaded onto ships each month. Consequently, it was assumed that the object of any enemy attack would be the capture or destruction of the coal depots. The Committee accepted that Singapore might be attacked by two or more squadrons, but decided that, with regard to the state of the existing fleets of foreign powers, the defence works should be sufficient to resist and beat off two ironclads of medium strength and four or five lighter vessels.[89] The survey of existing defences in 1881 is tabulated below.

Site	Armament	Proposed Armament
Western Approaches	8 x 500lb. ground mines 6 x 100lb. electro-contact mines	
Mount Siloso	3 x 7" RML guns 2 x 64 pounders *en barbette* behind 1.75m parapet	2 x 7" RML guns 1 x 64 pounder 2 x armour-piercing guns
Eastern Approaches	8 x 500lb. ground mines 32 x 100lb. electro-contact mines	
Blakang Mati East (later Fort Connaught)	3 x 7" RML guns 2 x 64 pounders	2 x 7" RML guns 1 x 64 pounder 5 x armour-piercing guns 1 x rifled howitzer
Mount Serapong Redoubt	Nil	Nil
Mount Palmer	3 x 7" RML guns 2 x 64 pounders	3 x 7" RML guns 1 x 64 pounder 2 x armour-piercing guns
Tanjong Katong	3 x 7" RML guns	3 x armour-piercing guns

Table 2: Defences in 1881[90]

A few points are immediately obvious. The much-vaunted Fort Canning no longer had a role in laying down defensive fire. Only four forts were functional and these were all brand-new forts less than two years old. Fort Pasir Panjang for some unknown reason had had its 7" guns removed. The earlier batteries had all been disarmed. The number of guns was reduced from the impressive (but ineffective) total of 34 in 1861 to 19 in 1881. Armament was standardised into two models of the modern 7" gun, and the 64 pounder, one of the first rifled muzzle-loaders introduced in the 1860s. According to the report, the purpose of the works was primarily to defend the New Harbour, and secondarily to protect the town. The Committee ruefully observed that the latter object was imperfectly attained, because the "town lies upon an open bay and that any system...could not save it from distant bombardment." On the other hand, guns stretching from Tanjong Katong to Blakang Mati East adequately covered the approaches to the Harbour.[91] Yet, the Committee concluded, "the present defences are insufficient to beat off a squadron [of two ironclads and four or five lighter vessels]." The advent of armoured warships made the guns in Singapore all but obsolete. The Committee thus recommended that guns capable of piercing 8" of armour at 3000 yards should be provided. The Committee recommended the installation of unspecified armour-piercing guns and less reliance on the 7" and 64 pounders.[92] The defences of the roadstead should be strengthened by a floating sea fort anchored somewhere on the 2.5-fathom patch, or about half a mile [.95km] offshore.[93]

At the end of the year, Weld wrote to the Earl of Kimberly, Secretary of State for the Colonies, to urge that the scheme of works be carried out in its entirety, especially the sea fort. He tactfully dismissed the idea of the navy being the truest form of defence: "I do not think it at all safe to rely on convention, and believe that in any naval struggle priva-teering would be largely resorted to by any weaker naval power opposed to us... ."[94] Convention was, of course, the idea that the British fleet would be an adequate defence for Singapore. Response from the imperial government was slow. When it finally came, it was not even appropriate. In March 1883 the WO wrote to the CO asking for plans and surveys for the defence works in Singapore.[95] They did not state whether the plans and surveys were required for additional planning for improve-ments, or whether it was simply because the WO did not have copies.

The latter reason is more likely, as McCallum in Singapore designed the defences. In any case, the request showed the utter lack of coordina-tion between colonial and imperial authorities. Three months later, the WO suddenly realised "the present unsatisfactory condition of the arrangements for the maintenance of the Military works at Singapore." Apparently the colonial government maintained all military buildings built prior to 1879, and the WO maintained all subsequent defence works. In bureaucratic fashion, pending the report on the defences of the Straits Settlements by the Royal Commission, no steps were taken to make any general arrangement with the colonial government regarding maintenance of works. The WO chose this time to suggest that all works be handed over to the colonial government; in return the WO would undertake the submarine mining defences at Singapore.[96] The imperial government had decided that to defend the colonial stations in the East, it was necessary to establish a system of submarine mines and provide a staff. The headquarters of the Submarine Mining Corps would be in Singapore.[97] The WO scheme appears to have been accepted, because in January 1885 the CO was asked to instruct the colonial government to begin building accommodation at Pulau Brani for a submarine mining detail due in April.[98]

Before then, hostilities flared up at a remote oasis named Pandjeh, north of the Indian border and therefore, according to the British, belonging to Afghanistan. The Russians felt differently: they had occupied the nearby fortress of Merv in 1884, by virtue of which Pandjeh was clearly Russian. To press their claim, they began furtive troop movements in the area. The British became alarmed.[99] In London, the Straits Settlements Association in February 1885 asked the Secretary of the Colonies, the Earl of Derby, if he was "willing to inform the Association whether the necessary steps are being taken to insure the safety of the colony?" The Association persisted a fortnight later:

> ...the precarious condition of our relations with Russia has increased the feeling of anxiety with which the defenceless condition of the Straits Settlements is regarded by the large number of British subjects having interests at stake in the colony.[100]

The Association asked for some assurance that fortifications and ordnance were being prepared.

The anxiety was also present in Singapore. The Colonial Secretary and Acting Governor Cecil C. Smith, later himself to be Governor, gently chided the CO on 28 March that:

> ...the absence of definite information as to the intentions of Her Majesty's Government in regard to carrying out my (sic) scheme for placing the defence of the Settlements into a proper condition to resist an attack is creating an amount of excitement which it would be highly advisable to allay.[101]

There was certainly reason for excitement. A day earlier, the CO received from Singapore a ciphered telegram reporting that the Russian men-of-war *Vladimir-Momomac* and *Opritsnik* had arrived in Singapore and departed for Nagasaki, and that another ironclad named *General-Admiral* was expected after rounding the Cape of Good Hope.[102] Two weeks later, the Straits Settlements reported the imminent arrival of the *Minim*.[103] The Russians were reinforcing their fleet in Asia.

The FO also began receiving reports of Russian military activity: two army corps were mobilised in the Caucasus and all officers ordered back to their regiments.[104] The Russians apparently did not think the British seriously meant to go to war over what was to be known as the Afghan Boundary question. They felt that all warlike measures adopted in the U.K. and India were solely to intimidate Russia.[105] Confident of their appreciation of events, the Russians attacked Pandjeh on 30 March and routed the Afghan force, which suffered heavy losses.[106] The Russians were now dangerously close to India.

The excitement in Singapore remained at a high pitch. The imperial government feebly attempted some action. Sir Andrew Clarke, the former Governor, was now Inspector General of Fortifications in the WO. He submitted a proposal regarding the defences of Singapore, which, he thought, should be limited to secure New Harbour and deny the anchorage to an enemy. Needless to say, his proposal satisfied nobody in Singapore. An article in the 28 February 1885 issue of the *Army and Navy Gazette*, eagerly reprinted by the *Singapore Free Press*, pointed out that the enemy would be at perfect liberty to bombard the town so long as they kept out of New Harbour.[107] By May 1885, Singapore was very impatient. The short-hand report of the proceedings of the Legislative Council of Singapore on 20 May records that, with regard to the delay in improving defences, a Mr. Bond passionately inquired, "Who is the person, or what is the body, that stands in the way? Whom shall we hang?"[108] Cecil Smith, Acting Governor, sent a secret despatch to the Earl of Derby to suggest that Fort Tanjong Katong be supplied with better guns, preferably one 10" rifled breech-loader and two 9" RML.[109] Governor Weld, then in England, also urged the CO to send the guns at once. Indeed, Singapore was so anxious for guns that it was willing to order them from private firms if necessary.[110]

But the guns were not sent, probably the result of a bureaucratic muddle. The *Singapore Free Press* in March considered the matter and concluded that the blame lay elsewhere:

> ...because the men of eminent capacity at the head of the Army, the Navy, the Ordnance, and the Treasury, are fighting out some shadowy piece of patronage, or refusing to comply with a necessary request because some effete regulation of red tape has not been thoroughly complied with. The Military are all for the forts; the Navy for ships; the Ordnance cannot make up its mind as to the size or nature of the guns; whilst the Treasury does not seem to care a cowrie as to the ultimate upshot of all this disorganisation, provided the debit balance...is not increased.[111]

The WO explanation was that designs for defences for all the great harbours and ports of the Empire were being prepared, and Singapore was only one such port. Consequently, plans could not be drawn up as quickly as might have been possible if Singapore was alone under consideration.[112]

Nevertheless, some defence work was begun, both in Singapore and Hong Kong, the extent of which is not clear. The Colonial Engineer in Singapore superintended the works here as the Royal Engineers were fully occupied in Hong Kong. Either the WO felt that Maj. McCallum was capable, or the situation reflected Singapore's relative importance, or lack of it. Existing works were not to be disturbed as far as possible until the new works were completed.[113] Fort Palmer, for example, was to remain ready to defend the Harbour. In fact, it had the only guns available to cover the Eastern entrance of the Harbour.[114] The new works referred to could only be a fort on Mount Serapong in lieu of the infantry redoubt originally there. Otherwise it was only a question of improving and arming the existing forts. On an optimistic note, the guns were due in early 1886.[115] By then, the WO envisaged Singapore armed with 23 guns: two 10", five 9.2", and four 8" Breech-Loaders; five 7" RMLs; and seven 64 pounders.[116] Some 6 pounder Quick-Fire guns might also be added.[117] It looked like Singapore would finally be getting the armour-piercing weapons it had asked for back in 1881. Or would it?

In December 1885, a frustrated Weld sent the CO copies of correspondence involving an equally harassed Maj.-Gen. W. Gordon Cameron, the GOC China and Hong Kong. The 8" gun emplacements in Singapore were delayed for want of the holding-down bolts, which formed part of the gun mountings. Four 8" Armstrong guns and all accessories were in Hong Kong. Cameron attempted to ship the guns but surprisingly received no cooperation from the Navy. Finally, Vice-Admiral William Dowell, then C-in-C China Station, confessed that he had been ordered by the Admiralty to detain the guns.[118] It was an understandably very exasperated Weld who sent a terse telegram to the Colonial Office: "Urge Admiralty send eight inch guns from Hong Kong first government transport."[119] The only explanation for this seems to be fierce inter-service rivalry. Perhaps the article in the *Singapore Free Press* was precisely on the mark.

The Admiralty was not satisfied with merely detaining the guns. In July 1886, the Foreign Intelligence Committee of the Admiralty submitted a précis of existing and proposed defences in the China Station. Captain Armand Powlett of HMS *Champion* drew up a damning report on the land defences of Singapore in connection with this précis. Among other criticisms, Powlett observed that the iron fence surrounding all the forts except Tanjong Katong had bars far apart enough for an ordinary-sized man to squeeze through. Tanjong Katong itself was exposed to gunfire, and Fort Pasir Panjang could easily be overrun from the rear.[120] Furthermore, in a prophetic note, Powlett commented that "It does not appear, at present, as if the value of secrecy as regards the defences is thoroughly appreciated." There were no regular sentries, probably because the new guns were not yet mounted except at Tanjong Katong. Powlett mused that the Russians no doubt knew as much of the defences as the British did, particularly of Tanjong Katong, "where the butterfly hunting properties of the Russians took them frequently."[121] As was the case with previous reports, Powlett was ignored.

Nothing was done to improve security at the forts. The Russians, and other foreign officers, would have needed no pretext to visit the forts a year later. The new forts in Singapore then were still in various stages of completion and therefore in the charge of the Colony. They had not been handed over to the military.[122] European guards had been stationed for a time,[123] but in May 1887 they were suddenly withdrawn on the orders of General Cameron, on the grounds that guarding the forts was bad for the health of the troops. Displaying uncharacteristic concern for secrecy, Weld complained that foreign military officers were swarming all over the works.[124] Cameron then changed his tune, claiming that the soldiers were withdrawn because he had not received orders from the WO to post guards. The General was unconcerned about the foreigners examining the works, because they could have obtained the same information anyway by observation from public roads or from boats in the vicinity![125] The WO pronounced that the Field Marshal C-in-C and the Secretary of War both found Cameron's explanations satisfactory![126]

Cameron was not the utter incompetent this problem might suggest. It may be that the entire incident was a tactical manoeuvre by a bitter and sulking military to get even with the civil authorities. The colonial government built the forts. Neither Cameron nor his staff superintended the works, and the detailed drawings were not even sent to him for information, let alone approval.[127] The army responded in kind: when McCallum asked the Royal Artillery to take charge of one of the forts nearing completion, the military refused until alterations were carried out to their satisfaction. Furthermore, the Royal Artillery Headquarters in Hong Kong also insisted that proper procedure be followed: the Royal Engineers would take over the forts from the colonial government and hand them over to the artillery. Unfortunately, the Headquarters "regretted," there was no Royal Engineer detachment in Singapore![128] This bickering is even more difficult to understand when one remembers that the fortification plans were sent from the WO in the first place.

Despite all this squabbling, positive steps were taken by Singapore residents to improve the island's defences. A Local Defence Committee of the Straits Settlements was drawn up to consider and advise upon the question of defence in accordance with a secret memorandum of the Colonial Defence Committee in November 1886. On 8 October 1887, the committee made a very detailed preliminary report not only on the state of defences in Singapore, but also on measures to be taken in the event of war.[129] Moving beyond a mere discussion of forts and ordnance, and covering matters like food supply, evacuation of the population, lines of communications, and fire fighting, the report was the most comprehensive hitherto made on Singapore defences. The entire tenor of the report approximated the modern Singapore policy of "Total Defence." It was in effect a local war plan. Dealing mainly with matters well within the purview of the local authorities, much of the report was implemented. The report was published and revised annually.

There was also discussion on a proposed new dock for the navy. This was begun as early as 1883, when it was thought desirable to provide dock accommodation for ironclad ships at Pulau Brani. Although the Admiralty Board was loath to give any company a subsidy to construct the dock, they decided to let Pulau Brani to the Tanjong Pajar Dock Company for 21 years. Governor Weld was furious. He wrote to the Senior Naval Officer at Singapore, Capt. Pasley, to remind the Navy that the island was only let to the Admiralty and reverted back to the colony if it was not used for naval purposes. Weld also had the foresight to see that Pulau Brani would almost certainly be needed for military purposes in the event of war. Any private company holding a lease on the island would be able to claim compensation. He agreed, however, that it was "of national and local interest to have a dry dock that will admit the largest ship that is likely ever to need repairs at New Harbour."[130]

On 31 January 1885, the Director of Works of the RN wrote to Sir John Coode who was about to visit Ceylon and the Straits Settlements. Coode was asked for his opinion as to the best site for a dock for naval purposes at Trincomalee and Singapore, "in case it should be determined at any future time to construct one at each of those places... ."[131] Sir John Coode submitted his report in June 1886. He considered Blangah Bay "as the most eligible site in the locality on which a Dry Dock suitable for naval purposes could be constructed." The cost was estimated at £205,000, exclusive of the cost of the site. Coode thought that the site would be suitable for the construction of a first-class dock of a capacity similar to the docks at Devonport and Malta.[132] In 1887, the Admiralty asked the CO to have the Sultan of Johore confirm his promise that he would reserve the site for that use. To avoid the cost of purchasing the site, in August 1888, the CO submitted a proposal from the Governor of the Straits Settlements that the Admiralty should give the WO the Admiralty land at Pulau Brani. The WO could then give the colony their land at Pearl's Hill. The colony could in turn give up some land designated as the Colonial Government Reserve, adjacent to the P&O Yard, to the Admiralty. Finally the Admiralty could exchange this Reserve with the Sultan for Blangah Bay. The proposal was considered. Unfortunately the music for this real estate version of musical chairs petered out. The Admiralty told the WO that they intended to keep Pulau Brani. The WO told the CO that although the removal of the Arsenal from Pearl's Hill to Pulau Brani was desirable, the cost was a consideration and the top of Pearl's Hill could not be alienated or built on for reasons of defence.[133]

Elsewhere, matters beyond the scope of the local authorities remained stagnant; the military defences were still incomplete. At least the Russian threat faded, as tensions in both Afghanistan and the Balkans fell short of outright hostilities. But the British Empire remained in "splendid isolation" surrounded by perceived threats from envious rivals. The authorities in Singapore thus remained concerned about defences. In February 1888, Cecil C. Smith, succeeding Weld as Governor, grumbled that none of the 10" and 9.2" guns had been received. Indeed, nothing at all about the guns had been communicated to Singapore.[134]

The garrison did not fare any better. It was clearly too small. In the first revision of the report by the Local Defence Committee, the Commandant, Col. Cardew, gave in his covering letter the most serious and detailed analysis so far on a possible hostile landing. He projected a landing near Pasir Panjang by an enemy force of 500–1000 men.[135] The conclusion: the garrison of Singapore would not be able to oppose any landing, or successfully engage any enemy forces on the island of Singapore. There simply were not enough men. The Committee attempted to show this with simple calculations. It generously refused to consider the garrisoning of Fort Canning since it felt that this would require at least 1000 men to defend. Focussing solely on the other existing works, and calculating a rate of two men per yard of parapet while making allowance that not all forts would be attacked at once, the Committee's manpower requirements were 1650 infantry to man the walls. To oppose a sudden *coup de main*, a reserve of at least 800 men was required. This was a total of 2450 men. Unfortunately, there were only 536 men of the 2nd Battalion South Lancashire Regiment present on the island, with 166 men in Penang. The problem was unambiguously apparent in an exercise on 27 September 1888, when HMS *Firebrand* landed 500 men and guns under Fort Palmer. Cardew could only scrape up 217 men to oppose the landing, even though he filled the ranks with drummers and bandsmen.[136]

Strangely enough, Governor Cecil Smith dismissed Cardew's projections as not in accordance with any contemplated threat perception and altogether placing too much stress on the prospect of a landing. This persistent refusal to take measures to prevent a landing is hard to explain. Perhaps it was thought that the shore batteries could deal with any enemy transports that escaped the attention of the RN. Could they? Not when the artillery arm was also undermanned. With only 191 European gunners, there were just enough to furnish gun detachments but without any reliefs for the present armament. When and if the new breech-loaders arrived, there would be a desperate shortage, even if only 80 men from the Singapore Artillery Volunteers could be expected.[137]

To keep things in perspective, it is useful to note that conditions at Portsmouth, the greatest U.K. naval arsenal, were also appalling. The Adjutant General complained that the armament at Spithead and elsewhere was so inefficient that, in the absence of the British fleet, it would allow passage of a hostile fleet. Ten million pounds sterling was urgently needed to purchase guns for defences.[138] In the era of *Pax Britannica*, defence works had wasted away everywhere. On a lighter note, the year came to a close with Vice-Admiral Sir Howell Salmon providing some comic relief. The telegraph lines between Singapore and Hong Kong passed through French-held Saigon. Seizing on a proposal by the Local Defence Committee in Singapore to provide a direct telegraphic link to Hong Kong,[139] the Admiral went very much further in suggesting that a naval officer be put in control of the telegraph office in Singapore to intercept all messages intended for Saigon, and to delay suspicious ones. All such secret messages intercepted would then be put on fast cruisers at hand to be sent direct to Hong Kong. The CO could only surmise that "The Admiral seems to have gone off the rails."[140]

The CO certainly did not mince words. When in June 1889, the WO finally announced that two 9.2" guns were awaiting shipment to Singapore, with all the rest due towards the end of the year, the CO remarked that, "This may mean three months or more. This is the direct result of a rotten administration."[141] The delay of the 9.2" guns was due to alterations being required after the guns were supplied by the contractors. The liners were found to be defective and all the guns had to be re-lined.[142] The mountings for the 10" guns were not even ready. The WO received only one set of pivots for the guns, but even that was rejected because it was defective.[143]

Singapore once more became impatient. During its fifteenth meeting, the Local Defence Committee wondered that it was remarkable that "a neighbouring station" had been rated so highly as to be armed with the superior 6" breech-loading gun, whereas Singapore still had the 7" RML. The 7" gun had a short range, a low velocity and a long reloading time of four minutes minimum. Beyond 1800 yards [app. 1660m], its shooting was "extremely wild."[144] The list of complaints included again the warning that there were not enough men to man the guns. The total number of men available for operating the guns was 150, less those necessary to man range-finders and lamps, signallers, runners, and lookouts, but including the Singapore Artillery Volunteers — whereas the committee calculated that 367 men were needed to fire the guns. The "superior" 6" breech-loading gun referred to by the Local Defence Committee in fact failed its trials on board HMS *Excellent* in 1881. Capt. J.O. Hopkins of the *Excellent* reported that the gun was impossible to load with the battering charges supplied, and the breech could not close. Even after the charge was loaded, the channel for the flash to ignite the charge filled with powder, so that firing had to cease after two shots. By then, the jar of firing the gun had already caused the "Albini" sights to fly out of the socket.[145] One can only hope that improvements were made over the next eight years to justify its reputation with the Local Defence Committee.

For Singapore, the problems seemed to be mounting. At its meeting on 7 August 1890, the Local Defence Committee resigned itself to the fact that the defences had been "organised with a view of keeping hostile ships out of the New Harbour, but confers no power to turn a vessel out when once there." No guns could be brought to bear on much of New Harbour, and it was impossible to fire on a ship lying near the wharves without damaging the docks.[146] More problems began cropping up. The 10" guns[147] with their pivots finally arrived in April 1890. However a road had to be prepared as the existing road was unsafe for the heavy guns. The pivots easily reached Fort Palmer, but when they were placed on the brick piers that had been built, the piers gave way. "It was necessary to add a considerable amount of concrete to the foundations."[148] The pivots were not fixed till October, after which the new concrete was allowed to set for six months before mounting the guns. The WO in May 1885 had said the guns were due in early 1886. They were eventually mounted almost six years later, and about 15 years after Jervois first requested them! In 1891, an 8" breech-loading gun burst on firing. The WO then ordered all 8" guns at Singapore not to be fired except in an emergency, and that the guns now in place should be sent home to England to be strengthened.[149]

The nineteenth century thus drew to a close with a whimper as far as the defence of Singapore was concerned. Inter-service rivalry, interdepartmental politicking, and individual back-stabbing, prevalent at the highest levels within the British military and civil services, stymied, if not crippled, the effectiveness of the defences in Singapore. Fortunately, the same perceived threats that made the defences contentious in the first place never materialised. Although schemes were devised to improve defences, very little was actually done. The problem was compounded by the view that defences should be adequate to repel a single enemy ship, but anything more would be extravagant. Yet in the end, it was doubtful if even that could have been done. In military terms, Singapore's transition to direct rule as a Crown Colony turned out to be much smoke but no fire. The next two decades proved far more exciting.

Notes

1. *Singapore Free Press*, 5 March 1857.

2. Buckley, *Anecdotal History*, 755-58. Buckley claims that the resolutions passed in the public meeting on 15 September 1857 were the first mention in print of the desire for a transfer of government. The writer of the letter that appeared in the *Singapore Free Press*, "Fairplay," seems to pre-date them by six months.

3. PRO, CO 273/6, Letter from Secretary to the Government of India to the Secretary to the Government of Madras, 9 April 1862.

4. PRO, CO273/6, 1864 enclosed letter no. 877, 23 March 1861, pp. 608-09.

5. Buckley, *Anecdotal History,* 675, and Kathiravelu, "Fortifications," 12, show Fort Canning armed with eight 8" guns. They were probably referring to the guns in store. See also CO273/6, Governor's letter no. 333 of 1864 to the Governor-General of India, 23 March 1861.

6. PRO, CO273/6, no. 877, 23 March 1861, p. 609.

7. PRO, CO273/6, f. 238r, Extract Fort William Military Proceedings for October 1860, enclosures for September 1860; SNA, Straits Settlements Records FF 11 p. 333, microfilm no. NL 613, Letter 877, Undersecretary to the Government of India Public Works Department, Fort William, to Governor, Straits Settlements, 20 March 1861.

8. PRO, CO273/6, ff. 240r-247v, Extract of Fort William Military Proceedings for October 1861, enclosure for December 1860.

9. Ibid, Quarter Master General of the Army to the Officiating Secretary, Government of India Military Department, 9 February 1861. This officer claimed that Bengal itself was already six companies below strength.

10. G. Fox, *British Admirals and Chinese Pirates, 1832–1869*, London, 1940, 46.

11. PRO, CO273/6, no. 333 of 1864, enclosed letter no. 12, 3 December 1862, pp. 612-13.

12. Ibid., p. 612.

13. Fox, 62, 195. The Board of Admiralty stressed China as the most important part of the station, and the force there was to consist of "three captain's commands, two smaller vessels, besides gunboats."

14. Ibid., p. 46.

15. Collyer prepared a plan of a battery to be constructed there, including barracks for 80 men.

16. PRO, CO273/8/2131, pp. 506-08, 28 January 1864.

17. Ibid., pp. 508-09.

18. PRO, CO273/8/2131, Memorandum relative to the defence of the Straits Settlement (sic), pp. 527-29.

19. PRO, CO273/8, ff. 610r-611v, Officer Commanding Troops, Straits Settlements, to the Adjutant General, Fort St. George, Singapore, 8 March 1864. The OC Troops was

quite eloquent in his comments on grand strategy: "Since the establishment of the French in Saigon, however, the strategical value of [the Straits Settlements] has infinitely increased, commanding as they do, by the possession of Pulucondor, the main channel by which for several months is taken by our vessels en route to China. Singapore, and not Hong Kong, in case of war with that nation must in future, I conceive, be our *point d'appui* from India, from which the advantages of their position may be neutralised and with a climate well suited to Europeans and every facility for cantoning troops, it will naturally become as important a depot for military as it is likely to be for naval purposes."

20. The Settlements were still garrisoned by two full Madras Native Infantry Regiments and three garrison batteries of artillery, two at Singapore and one at Penang. See Robinson's report, CO273/8/2131, for more detail.

21. PRO, CO273/16, ff. 149r, 150v, Messrs. Read and others to the Duke of Newcastle, Singapore, 30 June 1861.

22. PRO, CO273/16, no. 21, ff. 170v-171r.

23. Buckley, 769-70.

24. PRO, CO273/29/7123, Summary of proposals from Governor, Straits Settlements, 13 May 1869.

25. Ibid., p. 346ff.

26. Cardwell, in an earlier tenure as Secretary of State for the Colonies, inaugurated a new policy of withdrawing all Imperial troops from the colonies in time of peace. In the WO, Cardwell pledged to reduce the defence budget. The "Cardwell System", in which one battalion of a regiment remained at home while the other served overseas, exchanging personnel until the battalions themselves switched over, became the basis of the organisation of the infantry until the Second World War. See Field Marshal Lord Carver, *The Seven Ages of the British Army*, London, 1986, 158, 178-85.

27. PRO, CO273/'35/2334, no. 15, p. 23, 24, 27, 28-30, February 1869. By casual naval attack, Jervois meant a possible attack by one cruiser only, or by a small squadron that might elude the RN.

28. Fox, 195.

29. Ibid., pp. 160-86. The anti-piracy operation was an international effort, with France and Russia also sending ships.

30. Buckley, 769.

31. PRO, CO273/29/7138, Return of Heavy Ordnance in Store and Mounted in Forts, 20 May 1869.

32. Ord was made a Major-General in the Royal Engineers after assuming the governorship and previously was the Lt.-Governor of Dominica in the West Indies. He retired as Governor of the Straits Settlements in 1873, and later became Governor of South Australia. See Sir Leslie Stephen and Sir Sidney Lee (eds.), *The Dictionary of National Biography*, Volume XIV, London, 1922, 1130; see also Appendix 1.

33. Ibid, 474ff. Ord did, however, give up a portion of the Fort to form an approach to a new bridge.

34. PRO, CO273/53/6062, Minute from WO to Under Secretary of State, CO, 17 June 1871. A CO official scribbled in the margin here, "& this it has been doing all along."

35. PRO, CO273/53/6993, Edward Lugard (WO) to Under Secretary of State, CO, 15 July 1871.

36. PRO, CO273/53/9733, Minute from WO to Treasury, 2 October 1871.

37. PRO, CO273/53/9733, Minute Paper, 2 October 1871.

38. Ibid., 411-12, 6 October 1871. Kimberly had spoken to Ord, and therefore expected the proposals.

39. PRO, CO273/53/10636, Minute from WO to Under Secretary of State, CO, 28 October 1871.

40. PRO, CO273/53/11538 and 10846, Minute from WO to Under Secretary of State, CO, 25 November 1871.

41. PRO, WO33/32, Colonial Contributions in aid of military expenditure report, June 1878. See also CO273/53/11954, Minute from Treasury to WO, 4 December 1871.

42. Reproduced in PRO, CO273/72/7908, copy of the *London & China Telegraph,* 21 July 1873.

43. PRO, CO273/82/5066, 58-68, 6 May 1875. This is a report of a premeditated outbreak among the Chinese in the same jail. The 23 soldiers were given arms and eagerly helped suppress the uprising.

44. PRO, CO273/72/7908, copy of the *London & China Telegraph,* 21 July 1873.

45. PRO, CO273/73/5718, pp. 381-84, 5 June 1873.

46. Fuller, 289-90.

47. E. Thompson and G.T. Garratt, *Rise and Fulfilment of British Rule in India,* London, 1934, 512-13.

48. PRO, WO33/26, Report of the Director of Artillery and Stores to the WO, March 1874.

49. PRO, ADM125/140, Letter from the Governor of the Straits Settlements to C-in-C China Station, 28 July 1876.

50. Ibid.

51. PRO, CO273/84/12075, Despatch from Jervois, Governor of the Straits Settlements to Earl of Carnarvon, Colonial Secretary, 31 August 1876.

52. PRO, CO273/84/12075, despatch 314, Minutes, 10 October 1876.

53. PRO, CO273/84/13267, 469ff, 15 August 1876.

54. PRO, CO273/84/13267, despatch 339, 466-70, 21 September 1876.

55. Earth forts showed great resilience: shot and shell buried themselves harmlessly in the embankments, and the garrison could easily rebuild any part of the parapets with pick and shovel. During the American Civil War, Battery Wagner, an earthwork on the mouth of Charleston harbour, survived a hail of 9000 rounds from Federal guns with its fighting capacity unimpaired: Roger F. Sarty, *Coast Artillery 1815–1914,* Bloomfield, Ontario, 1988, 13-14.

56. P. Hopkirk, *The Great Game: On Secret Service in High Asia,* Oxford, 1990, 379.

57. Ibid., 379-80. See also Fuller, 320. The Sea of Marmora was south of Constantinople. The mood in England is best summed up in a song that was doing the rounds in music halls:

> We don't want to fight, But, by jingo, if we do, We've got the men, we've got the ships, We've got the money too. We've fought the Bear before, And while we're Britons true, The Russians shall not have Constantinople.

58. Yapp, 77-80.

59. Ibid., 80.

60. Thompson, 513.

61. Fuller, 333. The Stoletov mission led directly to the second Anglo-Afghan War.

62. PRO, ADM125/81 no. 26, 156(132), 22 March 1878.

63. PRO, ADM125/81, no.15, 148-9(124-25), 4 May 1878.

64. PRO, WO10/2741, WO Form 377, Monthly Pay List of No. 7 Battery, 1 April to 30 April 1877. There were ten fines for drunkenness.

65. PRO, CAB7/1, Secret Circular to Colonies, 20 March 1878.

66. PRO, CAB7/1, Confidential Memo from Sir Robinson to Sir M.E. Hicks Beach, no. 224, pp. 113-14, 23 May 1878.

67. PRO, CAB7/1, Confidential Report to Governor, Straits Settlements, 8 April 1878.

68. PRO, CAB7/1, Enclosed minute no. 4 in letter to Sir M.E. Hicks Beach, 17 April 1878.

69. PRO, CAB7/1, Letter from Col. C.A.S. Dickens to Sir W. Robinson, 19 April 1878. Robinson subsequently requested the Governor of Hong Kong to send 700 68 pounder cartridges, 14,000 lbs. of powder in 15lb. bags and 800 8" empty cartridges. All the powder and most of the cartridges were sent. See CAB 7/1, telegraphic messages to

Governor of Hong Kong and Governor of Singapore, undated inclosures nos. 10 and 11 in undated letter to Sir M.E. Hicks Beach.

70. PRO, CAB7/1, Letter from Lt.-Col. L.F. Hall to Governor, Straits Settlements, 28 April 1878. Robinson showed Hall's letter to the defence committee, which damned it with faint praise. The committee felt that as Hall could offer no suggestions of more favourable sites for gun batteries, their plan was still the best. See CAB 7/1, Further Report of the Defence Committee, 1 May 1878.

71. PRO, CAB7/1, Inclosure no. 17 to letter to Sir M.E. Hicks Beach, 6 May 1878.

72. PRO, CAB7/1, Further Report of the Local Defence Committee, 4 May 1878.

73. PRO, CAB7/1, Secret and Confidential Report of a Colonial Defence Committee on the temporary defences of the Cape of Good Hope, Maurtius, Ceylon, Singapore and Hong Kong, 4 April 1878.

74. PRO, CAB7/6, Confidential Memorandum from C.H. Nugent, 1 April 1877. The *Comet* class gunboat mounted a single 18 pounder gun. The Cape Colony/Simon's Bay and Hong Kong were deemed more important than Singapore.

75. PRO, CAB7/1, Minute from Alexander Milne to CO, 20 May 1878.

76. PRO, CAB7/1, Minute from Major-General Campbell to Alexander Milne, 11 March 1878.

77. PRO, CAB7/1, Secret and Confidential Minute from Alexander Milne to CO, 14 March 1878.

78. PRO, CAB7/1, Confidential letter from Major-General G.W. Donovan, Commanding in China and the Straits Settlements, 28 May 1878.

79. Harfield, 282-307.

80. McCallum began his career as Private Secretary to Jervois.

81. Harfield, 282-307.

82. Makepeace, 106-07.

83. PRO, CO273/104/14804A, 23 September 1880.

84. PRO, CO273/108/10120, Minutes, 29 April 1881. See also CO273/112/11432, pp. 388-95, 29 June 1881.

85. PRO, CO273/106/9289, Minutes, p. 368, 19 June 1880.

86. PRO, CO273/106/15726, 8 October 1880.

87. PRO, CO273/108/10120, p. 328, 10 November 1880.

88. Ibid.

89. PRO, CO273/108/10120, paragraph 5, p. 320, 20 April 1881.

90. PRO, CO273/108/10120, Report on the Defences of Singapore, 29 April 1881.

91. Sarty, 14, 45, 321. The 7" guns at the Forts had a range of over 5000m.

92. PRO, CO273/108/10120, Report on the Defences of Singapore, 29 April 1881, pp. 322-23. A rifled howitzer was proposed for Blakang Mati East to command the redoubt on the much taller Mount Serapong just 750m away.

93. Ibid.

94. PRO, CO273/110/1142 Secret, paragraph 5, p. 421, 12 December 1881.

95. PRO, CO273/124/4133, pp. 428-31, 9 March 1883.

96. PRO, CO273/106/9334, pp. 435-39, 1 June 1883.

97. PRO, CO273/137/842, no. 15, 17 January 1885.

98. PRO, CO273/137/842, pp. 578-79, 14 January 1885.

99. Hopkirk, 408-10, 425-26.

100. PRO, CO273/138/4841, pp. 8-9, 18 March 1885.

101. PRO, CO273/133/7453, despatch 115, pp. 470-72, 28 March 1885. Cecil Smith was a member of the Local Defence Committee. Weld was at this time visiting England.

102. PRO, CO537/46, no.243 Secret, 27 March 1885.

103. PRO, CO537/46, no. 244, 10 April 1885.

104. PRO, FOCP5140/12, document 15, no. 72, pp. 154-55, vol. 12, 31 March 1885.

105. PRO, FOCP5140/80, document 18, pp. 157-58, vol. 12, 2 April 1885.

106. PRO, FOCP5140/33, document 22, p. 159, vol. 12, 7 April 1885.

107. Singapore Free Press, *The Defences of Singapore: being a series of articles reprinted from the Singapore Free Press*, Singapore, 1885, 29. Details of the actual proposal proved unattainable.

108. Ibid., p. 54.

109. PRO, CO537/46, no. 260, 13 May 1885. Tanjong Katong was armed with three 7" RMLs. The imperial government was prepared to send out nine new guns, including seven 9.2" and two 10". Smith was replying to the proposal for defence from the WO.

110. At the expense of the imperial government, of course: PRO, CO273/138/9233, pp. 342-43, 22 May 1885.

111. Singapore Free Press, "Defences," p. 31.

112. PRO, CO273/137/7026, no. 711, pp. 597-98, 20 April 1885.

113. Ibid., pp. 616-19, 15 April 1885, WO to GOC China and Hong Kong.

114. PRO, CO273/137/15602, pp. 642-45, 31 August 1885.

115. PRO, CO273/137/8404, no. 794, 27 May 1885.

116. PRO, CO273/137/12970, pp. 628ff, 24 July 1885, WO to CO. The WO details for the original arrangement are for nine 9.2" guns only. This figure seems less reliable than Singapore's own counting viz: CO537, vol. 46, no. 260, above, which lists seven 9.2" guns. See also CO273/137/10665, no. 758, pp. 610-11, 14 April 1885, which lists two 10", seven 9.2", eight 7" and seven 64 pounders. Either way, it is clear that the WO estimates fell short of the 18 armour-piercing guns the Local Defence Committee asked for.

117. PRO, CO273/137/10665, no. 758, pp. 610-11, 14 April 1885.

118. PRO, CO273/136/1373, despatch 469, 18 December 1885, pp. 319ff. The guns belonged to the Viceroy of Canton and had been purchased by the British government: pp. 323, 329-31.

119. PRO, CO273/136/21676, p. 315, 16 December 1885.

120. PRO, CO537/46, no. 362, 25 November 1887, paragraphs 4, 5, and 8, pp. 203-05. Vice-Admiral R. Vesley Hamilton, the C-in-C China Station, agreed with Powlett, believing the Russians would be eager to deal British prestige a heavy blow by treacherously attacking Singapore and holding it for a few days. The loss of a few cruisers would be a fair exchange: CO537/46, no. 362, Hamilton's submission no. 538, 23 August 1887.

121. PRO, CO537/46, no. 362, paragraph 6, p. 205, 25 November 1887.

122. PRO, CO273/145/8945, telegram, 7 May 1887.

123. PRO, CO273/145/8979, pp. 67-68, 21 May 1887.

124. PRO, CO273/150/9596, telegram, 6 May 1887.

125. PRO, CO273/150/18105, pp. 561-62, 12 May 1887, Cameron to Adjutant-General.

126. PRO, CO273/150/18105, pp. 558-60, 6 September 1887, WO to CO.

127. PRO, CO273/137/10665, pp. 616-19, 15 April 1885.

128. PRO, CO273/150/18105, p. 569-70, 9 April 1887.

129. PRO, CO537/46, no. 358, pp. 132-33, 8 October 1887.

130. PRO, ADM116/758, Straits Settlements No. 58, letter from Sir F.A. Weld, to the Earl of Derby, 12 February 1883.

131. PRO, ADM116/758, letter from Director of Works to Sir John Coode, 31 January 1885.

132. PRO, ADM116/758, Report of Sir John Coode to Director of Works, RN, pp. 1, 5, 15 June 1886.

133. PRO, ADM116/758, "Proposed New Dock" Report and Correspondence from the C-in-C Straits Settlements, dated 1 March 1889.

134. PRO, CO273/151/6402, no. 86, p. 744, 28 February 1888.

135. PRO, CO537/46, no. 426, 2 October 1888.

136. PRO, CO537/46, no. 426, pp. 301, 306, 316-17.

137. PRO, CO537/46, no. 426, pp. 283-85, 299-300, 2 October 1888.

138. PRO, WO33/48, Confidential Memorandum from Adjutant General to Under Secretary of State, WO, 22 February 1888.

139. PRO, CO537/46, no. 358, pp. 135-38, 11 October 1887.

140. PRO, CO537/46, Minutes, p. 270, no 425, pp. 275-76, 3 September 1888.

141. PRO, CO273/163/11303, no. 1840, p. 545, 3 June 1889.

142. PRO, WO33/51, Minute from WO to CO no. 150, 3 May 1888, and Minute from Ralph Thompson to CO, 24 August 1888.

143. PRO, CO273/164/16639, no. 1691, p. 572, 19 August 1889.

144. PRO, CO537/47, no. 479, Proceedings of the Local Defence Committee, Singapore, pp. 39-40, 14 October 1889.

145. PRO, ADM 116/198, reports from J.O. Hopkins to Director of Naval Ordnance, 1 June 1881 and 6 June 1881.

146. PRO, CO537/47, no. 587, p. 102, 21 October 1890.

147. The 10" Mk. 3 gun of 1888 weighed 132,090kg. It fired a 227kg shell with a muzzle velocity of 621 m/sec out to a maximum range of 10.5km. See I. Hogg, *The Illustrated Encyclopedia of Artillery*, London, 1987, 105.

148. PRO, CO273/178/14372, p. 174, 16 July 1891.

149. PRO, CO273/178/4846, 7 March 1891.

5

The Weakest go to the Wall: From Money to Mutiny 1892-1918

T he last decade of the nineteenth century saw Singapore embroiled in the usual disputes regarding defence expenditure, specifically the colony's share — the "Military Contribution." As the Empire moved into the twentieth century, it attempted to come to grips with the ever-changing military balance in the world. Military developments in the Far East affected British threat perceptions and disposition of forces worldwide. In Singapore, defence focus shifted away from fortifications. The defences were improved and strengthened. But for once the outbreak of war in Europe did not put the colonials in Singapore in fear of the island's safety. Conversely, Singapore was unusually eager to contribute to imperial defence abroad. Money was no longer a problem, the island was rich. What were the attitudes of the British in Singapore regarding defence? What was Singapore's contribution to the war effort in the Great War? Before these questions can be answered, the question of financial contributions must first be examined.

Paying for Defence: The Paper War

The basic principle of contribution was settled in 1889 at a conference between the Chancellor of the Exchequer, Lord Knutsford and the Secretary of State for the Colonies. Lord Knutsford admitted that it was difficult to lay down any broad principles except that of Britain providing the sea defence by means of the Navy and the colonies providing for their own land defences.[1] This formula cut no ice with the Europeans in Singapore. The Local Defence Committee's report stated that it was understood that in the event of hostilities, no cooperation was expected from the RN.[2]

Despite this, the disputes over money in Singapore became more intense. Everyone became involved, including the GOC Singapore in 1891. Maj.-Gen. Sir Charles Warren felt that the question was "How much can the Straits Settlements fairly pay?" and not "How much ought the Straits Settlements to pay?" Feeling that £100,000 was less than what the Settlements could fairly pay, Warren proposed to the Governor that an income tax be levied on the Settlements. The revenues from this tax, probably about £25,000 to £30,000, should then be added to the

Military Contribution. Warren could have been motivated in part by a sense of personal injustice: all imperial officers in the Straits Settlements were taxed on their income but, as he himself pointed out in a reminder to the Governor, "the Colonial Officers from His Excellency the Governor down to the Merchants and tradesmen, pay nothing."[3] Moreover, just three months earlier, in November 1890, Warren had written to the Governor to request a stable allowance, backdated till June 1890, of 20¢ a day for the first horse and 15¢ for subsequent horses for all officers ordered to be mounted. These included all field officers (officers above the rank of captain) and Warren himself. The Colonial Secretary in Singapore replied that the Governor had neither the authority nor the funds to provide for any stable allowance. The bickering went all the way up to the Under-Secretaries of State in the WO and CO.[4] The effects may still have been rippling in May 1891, when Warren absented all regular troops from the Queen's Birthday Parade at the Esplanade. The Singapore Volunteer Artillery had the whole parade ground to themselves. Warren was supposedly worried about the danger of letting British soldiers go out in the sun. Curiously, that had not been a concern the previous year when Warren marched the 58th Regiment of Foot, his artillerymen and the 7 pounder battery from Fort Canning to the Esplanade where the Royal Artillery fired the salute.[5]

Such friction between military and civilian authorities was not unusual, even in other colonies. In his report on the French in Indochina, the British Director of Military Intelligence easily "imagined that the lot of a General Commanding in Tonkin [was] by no means a happy one" as a result of friction with civilians. He also faced calls from the locals to retrench and reduce the number of troops.[6] In Singapore, the position regarding European troops was quite the opposite. The Europeans wanted more European troops; they just did not want to pay for them. Were additional European troops forthcoming?

In February 1892, the Colonial Defence Committee commented on the Defence Scheme proposed by the Local Defence Committee in Singapore. The concluding remarks of G.S. Clarke, the Secretary of the Colonial Defence Committee, reflect the underlying assumptions which dogged British threat perceptions and influenced the construction of defences in Singapore for most of the nineteenth century:

> The protection of Singapore from land attack necessarily depends upon Her Majesty's Navy. So long as an adequate strength is maintained in the China Seas, the risks of moving any considerable expeditionary force from Saigon, Tonquin, or Vladivostok are too great to be accepted by an enemy…In any case, however, the prevention of the transporting and landing on British territory of such an expedition would depend upon the maintenance of a sufficient naval force in these waters.[7]

Given this persistent mindset, there could be no additional troops for Singapore. In 1892, the authorised strength of the garrison at Singapore was:

	Officers	NCO's and Men
Royal Artillery	14	247
Native	2	118
Royal Engineers	6	89
Native Engineers	3	47
Infantry	28	985*
Staff etc.	12	29
Grand Total	65	1515

* Including a small force at Penang

Table 1: Singapore Garrison, 1892

Various schemes were devised to reduce costs. Most did not work. The Governor Sir C. Mitchell was told in 1894 that the Secretary of State for War did not think it practical to reduce the strength of the Royal Engineers in Singapore or substitute a regiment of colonial troops for the British regiment in order to reduce costs. The raising of a native contingent would only entail additional expenditure for the colony.[8] On the other hand, in 1895, Singapore received word that the WO would be sending proposals to replace the 7" RML guns with 6" Quick-Firing guns. Again the question of costs agitated the colony, which expected the imperial government to pay for the guns while the colony provided the new works to mount the guns.[9]

What were the costs involved? The annual costs of the military establishment in Singapore amounted to £154,730 in 1895. The charge levied on the colony was raised from £50,000 to £100,000 in 1890. But the storm of protests this created forced the imperial government to reduce the charge to £70,000 and £80,000 in 1894 and 1895 respectively. Then the colony received word that the charge for 1897 and 1898 would be increased to £110,000 and £120,000 respectively. The resulting grievance over charges assumed such serious proportions that all non-official members of the Legislative Council in Singapore resigned in protest. A pamphlet was circulated which summarised the Straits Settlement's case. The pamphlet argued that the defence requirements of Singapore were due to the importance of Singapore to other British communities and therefore the whole Empire should share the burden of expenditure. A table was drawn up with figures taken from published Parliamentary Returns for 1892-93, which showed most glaringly the inequality of contributions levied:

Colony	Men Stationed in Colony	Total Cost in £	Colony Contribution
Canada	1494	£124,547	Nothing
West Indies	3019	£198,704	Nothing
Cape Colony and Natal	3317	£293,336	Nothing £4000
West Africa	953	£57,155	Nothing
Hong Kong	2998	£140,333	£40,000
Straits Settlements	1558	£103,725	£100,000
Ceylon	1465	£94,914	£72,500
Gibraltar	5214	£324,594	Nothing
Malta	8809	£471,344	£5000

Table 2: Colonial Contributions

It is clear that Singapore, with the fourth smallest garrison and the third smallest defence costs of all British colonies, was being made to contribute the most money to defence. The authors of the pamphlet decried this want of system where small colonies were picked out to pay heavily and called it a case of "The Weakest go to the Wall."[10]

In May 1895, Mitchell wrote to "protest most earnestly" the demands upon the colony to contribute towards defence expenditure. Mitchell proposed in December 1894 that the Settlements should contribute 20% of the costs of the defence of Singapore. The imperial government would later generously suggest that only 17.5% would be preferable in the long run. Unfortunately, the system in 1895 required the colony to foot the bill for all defence works. The colony was then engaged in building additional barracks at Pulau Brani and Blakang Mati at an estimated cost of about £30,000. Furthermore, additional barracks were proposed at Tanglin and Fort Canning. Tanjong Katong Fort was also due to be demolished at a cost of £8000.[11]

In June 1897, Mitchell wrote to the Secretary of State for the Colonies, Joseph Chamberlain, gently complaining that the treatment of colonies on the question of defence expenditure had been unequal, with the Straits Settlements being called upon to shoulder a far larger proportion than any other colony. Mitchell produced figures to show that during the three years included in the new agreement, the amount paid by the colony considerably exceeded 20% of the total costs. He foresaw "ever-recurring demands of this nature involving friction between the civil and military authorities and discontent on the part of the Colony."[12] In 1897, the colony's contribution to the improved defences was $237,600 or £23,760. In order to meet this large expenditure without depleting the Treasury balances, Mitchell proposed delaying the construction of the Singapore-Johore railway.

The quarrel over costs dragged on into the twentieth century. The quibbling over costs was possible because there really was no serious threat to Singapore. The British considered even the Japanese benevolent. The Japanese naval and military authorities on their part supposedly gave the British "every facility for obtaining information about their port defences" and expected a degree of reciprocity.[13] In fact, certain portions of the Straits Settlements defence scheme may actually have been communicated to the Japanese government.[14] Why were relations so cordial?

In 1900, the Boxer Rebellion in China gave Russia an excuse to seize Manchuria. The Russians were already established in Port Arthur, Talienwan and the Liao-tung peninsula in China. They had a strong battle fleet in Port Arthur, just across the Yellow Sea from Japan. The fleet was reinforced from the Baltic. Naturally, the British did not like the idea of a strong Russian force in the Far East, so they sent a squadron of battleships to the China Station. Permeating European thought was a prevalent belief that Orientals were inferior to Europeans where martial skills were concerned. As one writer put it, "most Europeans were disposed to put their money on the Russians in the event of a Russo-Japanese clash."[15] But that very sentiment provoked the British to react; as Colonial Secretary Joseph Chamberlain put it, policy was clearly to encourage good relations with Japan and to "emphasize the breach between Japan and Russia." The British therefore gravitated towards the lesser of the two evils and concluded an Anglo-Japanese Alliance in 1902, to deter the Russians. This also suggested that the French and Germans would stay out of any Russo-Japanese conflict, as intervention would now mean going up against the British fleet. The British needed a friend to help deter threats to their Asian empire, Japan needed a friend to keep other Powers out of any clash with Russia. Singapore's position was duly affected.[16]

On 9 March 1901, the Secretary of State for War announced in the House of Commons some contemplated changes in the garrison of Singapore and other coaling stations that would involve the permanent withdrawal of the British regiment from the colony. It was already temporarily absent, sent in response to the outbreak of war in South Africa to reinforce the imperial armies there. The contemplated changes alarmed the colony. On 17 July 1901, the Chairman of the Straits Settlements Association wrote to Chamberlain and pointed out the arrangement of having native troops substituted for European troops was due to the outbreak of war in South Africa. The "temporary necessity of [the arrangement] was cheerfully recognised by the colony." However, the Singapore branch of the Straits Settlements Association viewed with apprehension the current proposed changes. A resolution was passed by the Singapore branch "to represent that the presence of a European Regiment in time of peace exercises a strong moral influence over the large Asiatic population, while their absence in time of war or crisis would be likely to produce a state of unrest and anxiety leading to disturbances which the substitution of Indian Infantry troops would not, in a country where so many different races are living side by side, adequately allay." Moreover, the Chairman felt that because foreign warships and transports with large bodies of European troops passed through Singapore from time to time, it was most important that the military forces in Singapore should be largely European.[17] Eventually, the colony regained its British regiment.

Europeans were also prominent in the local militia. In 1901, the Singapore Volunteer Artillery was 111 men strong. Only Europeans were allowed to enlist in it, and the force's principal armament consisted of a battery of six RML 7 pounder Mountain Screw guns and four Maxim machine guns. A Volunteer Rifle unit also existed. This comprised one company of 173 Europeans, one company of 100 Eurasians and a third company of 100 Straits-born Chinese. The unit was armed with Lee-Enfield rifles and there was even a Volunteer Engineer unit. In addition, there was a Constabulary Force of nearly 2000 men, of whom more than 300 were Sikhs.[18] The Volunteers had a long history, being first formed in 1854 after the Chinese riots. They took for their motto *Primus in Indis*, later changed to *In Oriente Primus*. Indeed, they were arguably the first official volunteer organisation in the British Empire.[19] The Volunteers certainly faced no problems with finances. Their four Maxim guns were purchased entirely with donations from the public. A total of $10,524 was collected, the Chinese community donating $7000. One individual, Mr Cheong Hong Lim, covered the cost of one gun with his donation of $2500. The Sultan of Johore covered the cost of another gun, and contributions from the Chinese, Arab, Malay, and Chetty communities paid for the other two guns.[20]

As it turned out, the Japanese did eventually fight the Russians. In February 1904, they launched a surprise torpedo attack on the Russian fleet in Port Arthur. By December, the Japanese had taken the port. The Japanese victory over the Russians gave rise to rumours of Japanese agents in the Straits Settlements. One rumour put a Japanese submarine in the Melaka Straits waiting to ambush the Russian Baltic Fleet reinforcements. Although the CO thought them "cock and bull stories," it nevertheless instructed the Governor in the Straits, Sir John Anderson, to keep watch on certain suspected Japanese agents.[21] In May the following year, the Japanese completed their victory by sinking the Russian fleet sent from the Baltic to intervene. The conclusion of the Russo-Japanese war saw the first major defeat inflicted by an oriental country on a European country in modern times. Japan was now a major naval force in the Far East.

What was the strength of the RN at this time? The fleet that the Russians lately maintained forced the British to attach five battleships to the China Squadron. In addition, there were smaller divisions of cruisers, sloops and gunboats in Australia, the East Indies, the Pacific, the South Atlantic, and at the Cape of Good Hope. Of course, the main fleet was concentrated nearer to home. Before 1904 and the Japanese victory at Port Arthur, the strongest fleet was maintained in the Mediterranean and the Channel Squadron was next in strength. In 1904, the

Admiralty inaugurated a new policy of striking off obsolete ships and reducing unnecessary foreign squadrons. The 1904 re-distribution of ships gave the Mediterranean Fleet eight capital ships and the Channel Fleet 10. At the same time, with the elimination of the Russian threat, the threat focus shifted to Germany, the only probable enemy. The five battleships in the China Squadron were thus no longer needed and were brought home.[22] The Admiralty's plan was to maintain a naval force at home twice the size of the German fleet, to which end they formed a new Home Fleet.[23]

The new distribution of ships seriously depleted British naval strength in the Far East. This did not worry the British. The conclusion of the Committee of Imperial Defence on 29 June 1909 was that British possessions in the Far East were secure as long as the Anglo-Japanese Alliance remained in force. The Committee observed that before the alliance was terminated, the British fleet in the Far East would have to be reinforced.[24] In fact, British defence needs were deemed to be met if the combined British and Japanese forces were superior to any other two naval powers in the region.[25] In 1910, the WO circulated a memorandum regarding a question referred to the Colonial Defence Committee by the Governor-General of Australia on whether the alterations in the balance of world power necessitated a modification of policy. The WO observed that:

1 In the early stages of a war between Great Britain and a combination of naval powers whose bases are far apart, the command of seas remote from our centres of naval strength may rest with the enemy.

2 In the event of Japan being one of the belligerents, we cannot count upon having a preponderance of naval force in the China seas on the outbreak of hostilities.

3 ... there will be a period of a month after the outbreak of hostilities during which Japan's command of the Pacific will be practically incontestable by our naval force in these waters.

It was noted on page four of the memo that "it is not unreasonable to suppose that the Commonwealth government may have no alternative to consenting to the Japanese terms...."[26] Yet for the moment, this was all hypothetical; the Anglo-Japanese Alliance had already been renewed and expanded, not abandoned.

While the naval presence may have been reduced, land forces in Singapore were beefed up. In 1910, there were a total of 155 officers and 3236 men garrisoning Singapore, including Volunteers. Of these, 26 officers and 534 men were artillerymen.[27] The men were to man defences at Mount Imbeah, Fort Siloso, Fort Connaught, Serapong Spur, Mount Serapong, and the Silingsing Battery. There was a drastic reduction in guns mounted compared with the earlier passion for them in the last half of the nineteenth century. Only nine guns were approved as armament for the Straits Settlements and defence works were expected to be completed by 1911.[28]

In 1912, the chain of artillery command at Singapore was as follows:

(a) two 6" Quick-Firing guns at Fort Siloso (gun group M) and one 9.2" Breech-Loader Mark X at Mount Imbeah (gun group L). The Fire Controller West at Imbeah directed these groups;

(b) two 9.2" Breech-Loader Mark X at Fort Serapong (gun groups A and B) and one each at Serapong Spur (gun group F) and Fort Connaught (gun group H), and two 6" Quick-Firing guns at Fort Silingsing (gun group O). The Fire Controller East at Serapong Spur directed these.

The Fire Controllers also had 10 direction finders and six Mark II depression range finders (with automatic sights) scattered along the coast to aid them.[29] Given the combination of the diplomatic and naval security provided by foreign policy, and the upgraded coastal defences, Singapore seemed secure.

The Great War and Singapore: Cruisers, Volunteers and Mutineers

World War I broke out in August 1914; the British Empire found itself at war not with Russia but with Germany. On 21 September 1914, the German cruiser *Emden* began her famous rampage in the Indian Ocean. She captured eighteen merchant ships, terrorised Penang where she sank the Russian cruiser *Zhemchug* and the French torpedo boat *Mousquet*, and bombarded Madras. All trade routes west of Singapore were closed. The *Emden's* defiant foray came to an end when the Australian cruiser *Sydney* sank her off the Cocos Islands, but not before Singapore and its residents received a nasty little scare in their brush with the European war.

The war remained concentrated in Europe, although Japan did take the trouble to intervene on the side of the Allies and overrun all German colonies in China and the Pacific. Down the road this played its part in altering the strategic position in the region. But for the moment Japan loyally supported the cause; indeed, by 1916 Japanese warships were in effect guaranteeing the security of Singapore and all other British colonies in the area. The Japanese patrolled the sea lanes, escorted convoys in the Indian Ocean, even sent ships to help in the Mediterranean. This allowed the RN to concentrate nearly all its strength in the main theatre. The enemy did not threaten Singapore. But as the war escalated beyond nearly everyone's worst nightmares, British survival did seem to be at risk. In this situation, the war became for Singapore a question of how it might help the mother country.

As far as recruitment was concerned, the European population in the Straits was very keen to do its part. On 27 October 1914, the WO received a telegram from the editor of the *Straits Times*, which read "Hundred ninety men offer for active service as Malayan Contingent. Age limit 35, average 27. 24 been regulars, 128 Volunteers, 10 seen active service. All given me written declaration willing serve any capacity. Several hold commissions, others suitable commissioned rank. Local Government will pay passages home. Men earnestly desire favour reply whether offer accepted still."[30] The WO did not respond immediately to the offer. However, they asked that regular troops be sent to England as reinforcements. Seven officers and 63 other ranks of the Royal Garrison Artillery (RGA), four 6" howitzers and six 15 pounder guns as well as all ammunition for these guns were ordered to embark on board the SS *Monmouthshire* for home.[31] The British regiment, the 1st King's Own Yorkshire Light Infantry, was also sent to the front at the end of 1914. At the same time, the WO thought it would be useful to send a regiment to Egypt. They preferred the Malay States Guides to the native 5th Bengal Light Infantry Regiment (5th L.I.) stationed in Singapore, which was felt to be "rather too Mussulman."[32] This raised the more troubling question of the fitness of non-British troops for duty either at the front or in Singapore. In the end, this problem, not the enemy, provoked the greatest threat Singapore faced during the war.

Although it was originally decided that the native 5th L.I. stationed in Singapore should be moved to Hong Kong, the GOC Straits Settlements, Maj.-Gen. Reade, felt that both the Malay States Guides and the 5th L.I. could not be spared at the same time. Reade also agreed that the Malay States Guides would be more suitable for service in Egypt "because 5th L.I. [were] very Mahometan (sic)." He alternatively offered detachments from each battalion or one complete battalion and a detachment from the other, a total of 950 to 1000 men, two guns and two mules.[33] Reade felt that the recent British naval victory at the Falkland Islands made it unlikely that enemy forces would bombard or raid Singapore. In his opinion, hostile action would be limited to action by enemy agents. He later suggested that even the 5th L.I. could be withdrawn for service elsewhere.[34] The Governor, Sir Arthur Young, regarded the risk of disturbance in Singapore to be so slight that he was prepared to release the 5th L.I. for front-line duty. Still, Young did feel that it was risky to allow the defence of the Malay Peninsula to devolve on the Malay States Guides. The Malay States Guides were "not altogether to be relied on."[35] Why not?

The Malay States Guides were organised in 1896 by Lt.-Col. B.S.F. Walker. Their establishment at the turn of the century consisted of 10 European and eight native officers and 613 NCOs and men organised in five infantry companies, a depot company and a detachment of artillery. The main headquarters were at Taiping, with local staff headquarters at Selangor and Pahang. In 1899, there were 541 Sikhs, 31 Pathans and 49 Muslim soldiers in the regiment. The annual report of the Commandant noted that the average age of the men was 26 years and seven months, with an average service of over four years. The average height was nearly 5'9" [1.77m].[36] But in 1914, however, the regiment was much less impressive. The list of complaints was a long one. The Commander of the regiment's Mountain Battery felt that there were many men who appeared too old to be good soldiers. The Regimental Commander, Lt.-Col. C.H.B. Lees, said it was easily apparent that the regiment had been pampered and had never been taught to look upon themselves as anything more than a "Sultan's toy." The men were not trained for anything else except drill. The Indian officers in the regiment were all low caste and therefore could not exercise command over their higher caste men. There were serious problems with the promotion system that chose the most unsuitable men. One officer had no military experience and had started his career as a High Court Hindustani interpreter. The British officers in the regiment were not in touch with their men at all.[37] Not surprisingly, there were disciplinary problems.

On 24 November 1914, the Commanding Officer of the Guides received an anonymous letter saying that some Indian officers were instructing the men not to go on service abroad if asked to. In anticipation of service abroad, the Guides had come to Singapore. On 3 December 1914, the Malay States Guides were told they were ordered to East Africa. The very next day, the men's unwillingness to go was evident. The Guides drew attention to the fact that their terms of agreement for service only required them to serve in Malaya. By 6 December, the Guides withdrew their offer to serve abroad. The men were also affected by talk of high casualties suffered by the British and by a rumour spread by German agents that the Germans had an electrical machine that could kill anyone within a ten-mile radius.[38] There was also the possibility of sedition. One officer, however, held the view that the men's monetary interests in the country were the cause of their refusal to serve.[39] Another officer, Capt. R.C.F. Schomberg, heard talk of the intention of the Guides to kill the officers, march on Tanglin, free the German prisoners and loot Singapore.[40] The situation was serious enough for a court of enquiry to be convened. The court found that it was indeed monetary interests and intrigues among the Indian officers that had led to the refusal to serve in East Africa. Sedition, German agents and fear of casualties were only contributory causes. The bad regimental spirit had allowed intrigues to take hold. The court also noted that the bad feeling was the result of mistakes in enlisting and promoting men who would have been refused by any other regiment in the Indian Army.[41] The regiment was sent back to Taiping, leaving only one battery in Singapore.

In Singapore, a soldier in that Malay States Guides Battery, Corporal Osman Khan, persuaded a trader named Mansur to write to the Turkish Consul at Rangoon. This was an attempt to persuade the Turks to send a warship to Singapore. The letter was intercepted and Mansur arrested on 23 January 1915. Osman Khan was on leave and managed to escape. But Mansur's treasonable letter cost him his life.[42] As events would prove, the Malay States Guides was not the only regiment in Singapore with serious problems.

The Governor did not think the 5th L.I. would be effective at the front either. Young believed that any threat from the Chinese could be dealt with by the police, but that the native regiment could not be trusted to deal with any trouble arising among the Sikhs and other northern Indians. On the other hand, no disturbance was anticipated. In a telegram to the Secretary of State for the Colonies, Sir Arthur considered that "if [there were] internal disturbance due to North Indians the present garrison could not cope with it. I do not anticipate any such disturbance and even if there is a slight risk consider that garrison should be reduced and the risk taken."[43] The authorities in Singapore were therefore prepared to send the 5th L.I. away.

The 5th L.I. was an old Indian regiment raised at Cawnpore in 1803 as the 2nd Battalion of the 21st Regiment. It was re-designated as the 5th Bengal Light Infantry in 1861. It was one of the Indian regiments that had remained loyal to the British during the Great Mutiny in India in 1857.[44] By World War I, however, the regiment was in complete shambles. In the opinion of Brigadier Dudley H. Ridout — who counted himself among Martin's friends — the 5th L.I.'s commanding officer, Lt.-Col. E.V. Martin, had "an unfortunate personality, was inactive, had no power of command, and did not inspire respect. He was no leader of men."[45] Martin was a company commander prior to his promotion and already made himself unpopular with the troops.[46] There was even trouble between Martin and his adjutant, Lt. W.A Strover. Both Strover and Captain L.P. Ball tried unsuccessfully to apply for transfers out of the regiment. Martin, when a company commander, had rows with other company commanders and the soreness remained after his promotion. In fact, he rarely spoke to his officers, choosing instead to use his second-in-command as a go-between. Brigadier Ridout's opinion was that:

> Lt.-Col. Martin commanded no respect, and exerted no real authority, and on the part of the Officers, some of them, notably Capt. Ball, Capt. Hall and Lt. Strover adopted a line of action wholly subversive to discipline, and this was made worse since the Commanding Officer did not appear to have checked it vigorously, but rather to have adopted the principle of "pin pricks," irritating interference.[47]

The bad feeling between the British officers was obvious to the sepoys and it lowered the standing of the officers in the eyes of their men. There was trouble as well with the sepoys. Several sepoys spread a rumour that the Regiment was being sent off to Mesopotamia to fight the Turks, fellow Muslims. Moreover, one havildar did not receive an expected Viceroy's Commission and this stirred up even more discontent. Unfortunately, all these problems were not known at that time. The 5th L.I. was a disaster waiting to happen.

As early as December 1914, there was official concern with regard to the 5th L.I. At the request of the Inspector General of Police, Sir Arthur Young asked India for an experienced European officer to investigate the matter of possible sedition amongst Indian troops in Singapore. A few seditious letters had been intercepted.[48] The WO also recognised "serious seditious tendencies" in the 5th L.I. and recommended that the composition of the regiment be changed. It even suggested that the regiment be disbanded when the situation permitted, although no immediate action was advocated.[49] With hindsight, this was clearly a mistake.

The WO felt that it was the Chinese who would be the most likely cause of any disturbance in Singapore. On 7 January 1915 it wrote to the Secretary of State for the Colonies to seek assurance that any reduced force would be sufficient to cope with "eventualities which might arise at a point of such importance where there is a large Chinese population, whose disposition might not always remain favourable." The WO accepted that the reduced force might be sufficient protection against external threats, so remote was the war from Singapore. The CO assured the Army Council that the reduced garrison would be sufficient to deal with any internal disorder.[50] As the WO did not recommend immediate disciplinary action with the 5th L.I, it was decided that the unit would embark on the troopship *Nore* for Hong Kong on 16 February 1915.[51] On the night of 14 February, one of the army's spies in the battalion received news that it was uneasy about being sent to fight against Turkey. The spy, a Punjabi, intended to make his report to the GOC on the night of 15 February. But he was too late. He was arrested out on the streets for suspicious behaviour on the evening of the 15th and only delivered his information on the 18th.[52] By then, the situation had long since exploded.

On the morning of 15 February, Brigadier Ridout, the new GOC, inspected the sepoys.[53] He spoke to the native officers who were very friendly. Ridout saw nothing unusual and felt that the battalion was in "a good frame of mind."[54] The regiment's left wing, however, noticed that the men in the right wing dismissed in a surly manner.[55] Harfield suggests that it was Ridout's failure to mention the regiment's destination that fuelled the sepoy's suspicion that they were indeed bound for Turkey.[56] Ridout gave authority for the sepoys to be told that they were going eastwards, and for the officers to be officially told the regiment was bound for Hong Kong.[57] Unimpressed, the sepoys planned to rise up at eight in the evening when all the officers would be in the mess for dinner. Their plans included freeing the German prisoners of war — mainly survivors of the *Emden* — and interned civilians at Tanglin and killing the Governor, before looting Singapore. The whole plan was upset by the fact that Martin's preparations for embarkation moved faster than expected. Lt.-Col. Martin ordered the ammunition (35,000 rounds of rifle and 10,000 machine gun rounds) and two machine guns to be moved into stores on the afternoon of the 15th, instead of the next day.[58] The mutineers were forced to advance their schedule.

In the afternoon of 15 February, during the last day of the Chinese New Year holiday, men of the 5th L.I. left Alexandra Barracks — about 8 km from town, across the road from the later Gillman Barracks — and went on a rampage. Only the 403 Rajput Muslims from the regiment's right or A wing mutinied. The men of the left wing remained loyal and began surrendering in batches.[59] The Malay States Guides Mountain Battery was in Alexandra Barracks when the mutiny started and some joined the mutineers.[60] The mutineers first looted the ammunition lorries. Dividing themselves into three bands, the mutineers sent one party towards the town and Keppel Harbour by Pasir Panjang Road and another party cross-country to Tanglin barracks, about 5 km away. The last group besieged their Commanding Officer's house.

The first group reached nearby Tanglin Barracks very quickly. There were 309 prisoners of war in the camp then. Breaking into the camp, the mutineers killed 13 British, Singapore Volunteer Corps and Johore Military Force soldiers and one German prisoner of war. They then fraternised with the prisoners and promised to return with arms and ammunition before leaving at about 1700 hrs. Both Admiral Jerram, C-in-C China Station, and the Governor stated in their initial reports that rifles were actually handed to the Germans.[61] But this does not appear to have been the case. After the sepoys departed, the prisoners of war tended to the dead and wounded. It seems they actually had their own plans for escape. The more enterprising Germans had actually been digging an escape tunnel for some time. On the day of the mutiny, the tunnel was only a yard short of the barbed wire entanglements and the Germans would have reached the surface the next day.[62] An hour and a half after the sepoys departed, when it was dark, seventeen prisoners took the opportunity to escape.[63] Six were subsequently recaptured. The remaining eleven crossed in canoes to the Dutch Carimon Islands. The Germans had truly prepared for their escape as they had plenty of money and the canoes were ready for them.[64] Among the Germans who escaped were four crewmen from the *Emden*, led by the navigation officer, Lt. Jules Lauterbach, who made their escape in an epic journey all the way to Shanghai.[65]

Two of the sepoys went on a lone killing frenzy. They shot two Royal Garrison Artillery officers in the vicinity of Sepoy Lines at Outram Road. They also killed a police inspector's horse and wounded two Chinese. They then went to New Bridge Road and stopped two cars carrying British civilians. Four British men and one Malay chauffeur were killed, but two British women were allowed to escape. Cars carrying Chinese were allowed to pass. The two sepoys then made their way to the Central Police Station at Hill Street where they fired at the Sikh guards, wounding two. The two sepoys then disappeared. The band of sepoys making its way to Keppel Harbour were content at first to turn back Europeans along the road. Two Europeans escaped before the mutineers turned violent, killing three men (including a district judge) and a woman for not turning back. The mutineers then showed up on the grounds of a bungalow at Pasir Panjang Road. The British occupant made the mistake of demanding to know what the sepoys were doing, giving as authority his status as a Volunteer. The sepoys promptly shot him and his two guests.[66]

While all this was going on, Martin, the regiment's Commanding Officer, was holed up in his bungalow with three of his officers and one woman, the wife of the regiment's Major Cotton. Four officers and 81 men of the Malay States Volunteer Rifles, who had been in a nearby camp training, joined him and helped beat off repeated attacks by the mutineers.[67] The Malay States Volunteer Rifles were raw troops, having only just begun their training on 9 February, but they were eager and intelligent.[68] Eighty sepoys had in fact also offered assistance to Martin in his besieged bungalow but they were not trusted. On 16 February, a relief force of 176 men, led by Lt.-Col. C.W. Brownlow, Commanding Officer of the Royal Garrison Artillery, advanced along Alexandra Road to relieve Lt.-Col. Martin. They retook Alexandra Barracks and reached Martin's house, where they routed the mutineers. Their mission accomplished, this force retired in good order to Keppel Harbour, clearing Keppel Golf Course of mutineers along the way. Brownlow took about 90 prisoners and an estimated 11 mutineers were killed in the fighting.[69] On the same day, the Veteran Company of the Singapore Volunteer Corps retook Tanglin Barracks unopposed.[70]

Martial law was declared on the first day of the mutiny and Major A.M. Thomson was appointed Provost Marshal. European women and children were ferried out to the transports *Ipoh, Recorder, Nile,* and *Penang* for safety. Members of the Singapore Volunteer Corps were mobilised. Two sections of the Singapore Volunteer Artillery's Maxim Company had an exciting time at Cemetery Hill behind Alexandra Road Police Station. The gunners under Capt. H. Tongue arrived to take up positions on the hill. One section under Lt. T.C. Hay remained at the foot of the hill. During the night, heavy rustling was heard. The sentries received no response to their challenges. Thinking that the mutineers were attacking, the section opened up with their Maxim machine-gun and routed the enemy with a few bursts of fire. Yet throughout the night, the enemy kept returning stubbornly and the Maxim clattered through the night. Next morning, the gunners searched around their positions and discovered that they had massacred a number of pigs. Later that day, armed civilians reinforced the position but a Japanese volunteer party came by and mistook the gunners for rebels. Both sides exchanged fire before the mistake was discovered. Fortunately, there were no casualties, although one civilian almost scored an own goal by putting a bullet through the shirt of the man in front of him.[71]

In putting down the mutiny, the Sikh police, the Singapore Volunteer Corps, a detachment of the Johore Military Forces (commanded by the Sultan in person), and a naval force from HMS *Cadmus* reinforced the regular forces and armed Europeans. As soon as Admiral Jerram heard of the mutiny, he telegraphed nearby ships for help. (The wireless telegraph stations at Singapore and Penang had only been erected a few months earlier by the Marconi Company.)[72] In addition, the Japanese Consul raised 190 Japanese Special Constables who joined 149 other Japanese sailors from the cruisers *Otawa* and *Tsushima,* French sailors from the French cruiser *Montcalm* and Russian sailors from the *Orel* in hunting down the mutineers. In this truly international effort, the Japanese contributed the largest foreign contingent of 339 men.[73]

One of the Japanese involved, M. Tsukada, wrote a book about his stay in Singapore. Tsukada was on the staff of the Japanese newspaper *Nanyo Shimbun.* Printed in Tokyo and published in March 1916, the book gave Tsukada's own account of the mutiny, which today adds a touch of comic relief to an otherwise sad episode. The book was translated and notes sent to the Admiralty. In a riveting account, Tsukada wrote of armed white-haired old men in their everyday clothes guarding the roads "as the sun was declining in the western hills." Hundreds of cars were commandeered as the sound of rifle fire grew louder. The Indians "when in a good temper are easily managed, like little children, but when they are angry they become as fearful as fierce tigers, or demons." According to Tsukada, the Malay troops fled when their officer was killed, and the Malay police were too scared to go out on the night of the 15th. The Malays lacking the fighting efficiency, it was up to the British and the "unorganised Volunteers" to deal with the sepoys, who were "savages, it is true." By the 16th, Tsukada reported that the Indian police were suspect, the Malay police had all been sent to battle, and the Chinese, "who are noted for taking such an opportunity as this which is like burgling from a house on fire" gave every likelihood of "acts of rascality." The British were in as much peril as a pile of heaped-up eggs. Who were to rescue them? Tsukada humbly admitted, "Yes, there were the Japanese."[74]

Tsukada and other chief members of the Japanese community were summoned to the Japanese Consulate at midnight on 15 February. The Japanese naval attaché, Lt.-Cmndr. Araki, addressed them. Araki, at the Governor's request, had earlier telegraphed the naval station in the Pescadores and asked for Japanese naval assistance. At 2000 hrs that night, he was informed that the *Otawa* and *Tsushima* were on their way. The Governor's secretary had also approached the Consul, Mr. Fujii, for 200 Japanese volunteers. Mr. Fujii, after "the fruit of a thousand thoughts and ten thousand reflections", decided to seek advice as to whether to respond and "make manifest the gallantry of the Japanese." At this moment, Tsukada records that the Governor telephoned and said that the British were unable to cope with the situation. The Japanese decided to ask for volunteers. The Japanese laid down four conditions for service. They would assist in guarding the town only, and they were to be treated in exactly the same way as the British volunteers. Furthermore, Japanese volunteers would serve only under their own officers. Finally, they would serve only until the Japanese ships arrived. Tsukada noted with some glee that the British "until recently so arrogant, now had their tails down and their wings tucked in, and had come greatly to love and fondle us. Was ever anyone in such a pitiable state?" Three hundred Japanese assembled in front of the Consulate at 0800 hrs on 16 February. Araki and retired Surgeon General Suzuki, late of the Imperial Japanese Navy, examined the men. Retired Lieutenant Wada Yoshimasa was placed in command and the men sent to the Volunteers headquarters by 1000 hrs. Retired Japanese soldiers peppered the ranks of the volunteers and fell into ranks in a variety of dress. Apparently, the Japanese looked so brave in their faultless ranks that Sir Arthur was moved to decide to send them into battle at Pasir Panjang. Tsukada witnessed the furious objection expressed by Mr. Fujii to Brigadier Ridout, who agreed to stick to the earlier agreement. The Japanese were then sent off from the sea front to their positions around the town in boats. Tsukada remained behind and joined fellow Japanese in giving their heroes a great send-off, shouting "*Banzai!*" Tsukada was certainly beside himself with joy:

> Up till now, slighted both by the British and the natives, and regarded as contemptible in trade, it now devolved upon us to protect the feeble and pitiable British, what joy and pride we onlookers felt.[75]

On 17 February, the French cruiser *Montcalm* under Rear-Admiral Huguet, which had just left Singapore for Colombo, returned and landed seven officers and 180 men along with two machine-guns. Despite these reinforcements the British refused to attack, according to Tsukada. He alleged that Brigadier Ridout said to Consul Fijii, "We will assume the offensive after the arrival of the Japanese ships." Again this filled Tsukada's heart with pride:

> Thus from first to last, the British officials were relying upon the strength of our Empire — these British who had filched the territories of others by means of their oily tongues, are very cunning, but now for once they were in a position where the power of the tongue could not avail, and there was a disgusting revelation of consternation and panic.

The French sailors were in fact sent to Seletar in the north to engage the mutineers there. Before the French arrived, most of the mutineers up north fled to Johore. Another 61 mutineers surrendered to the Sultan, who presumably returned home after delivering his troops.[76]

At 1800 hrs on 17 February, the *Otawa* arrived and landed five officers and 75 men. The next morning, *Tsushima* entered the harbour with the Japanese squadron commander, Rear-Admiral M. Tsuchiya, on board. Tsukada records that Tsuchiya at first declined to land a force. Apparently, his argument was that the Anglo-Japanese treaty of alliance made no provision for either party to interfere in local disorders. Tsuchiya supposedly requested that the Governor make formal representations for aid through normal diplomatic channels. Tsukada gives the impression that the Japanese ships were only in Singapore to protect Japanese civilians. However, as a result of the Governor's pleas, Tsuchiya eventually relented. On the morning of 18 February, the Japanese force landed with Lt.-Cmndr. Lida in command. The Japanese volunteers were all also placed under Lida's orders. By noon that day, the Japanese were in Alexandra Barracks. The Russians, on their own initiative, ordered the Russian Volunteer Fleet ship *Orel* from Penang, where she was engaged with the wreck of the *Zhemchug* (sunk the previous year by the *Emden*). The *Orel* arrived late in the afternoon on 18 February, and landed two officers and 40 men.[77]

Tsukada happily reported that — two days after Brownlow's relief force cleared out the mutineers — the Japanese force "broke up the main strength of the enemy, and [took] possession of their headquarters." Furthermore, not a shot was fired, "for in anticipation of the arrival of the Glorious flag of the Rising Sun, some had surrendered and the rest had dispersed." With the threat to the town eliminated, "the faces of the British began to assume their natural colour again." Tsukada failed to mention that the Japanese troops were actually accompanying Lt.-Col. Brownlow's force and that Brownlow was in overall command. The Japanese detachment continued to Normanton Barracks where it did come under fire. But the Japanese took the Barracks, capturing 12 camp followers and hospital patients of the 5th L.I.[78]

By this time, the British felt confident enough to issue an official announcement that the situation was completely in hand. The Provost Marshal, Major A.M. Thompson, also declared that the residential area of the town was safe and even made preparations for families to return to their homes. Brigadier Ridout took time to appoint a preliminary Court of Enquiry consisting of a member of the Legislative Council, Sir Evelyn Ellis, as President, the Inspector-General-of-Police, Mr. A.R. Chancellor, and Lt. Strover, Adjutant of the 5th L.I. But the British were taking no chances. The 21 German prisoners of war released on parole in the Federated Malay States were collected and brought to Singapore. Major Thompson also offered rewards on 20 February. Information on the movements of bands of mutineers was worth $200 and the recovery of a rifle was worth $5. The small number of Germans who escaped from Tanglin may have been one reason why $1000 was offered for the capture of any German, and the abundant supply of armed mutinous sepoys priced them at $20 per head. The same day, a proclamation was issued under martial law requiring all Indians to report at the police stations to obtain passes. They also had to satisfy the authorities that they were not soldiers in mufti.[79]

The crisis was all over by the time 600 men in six companies of the 1/4th King's Shropshire Light Infantry (1/4 KSLI) arrived from Rangoon on 20 February. All that was left to do was to round up the small groups of sepoys still at large. Three days later, the French ship *D'Iberville* arrived from Saigon but as its services were not required, the ship was asked to proceed to intercept the Norwegian steamer *Selun*, which had left Bangkok with some German passengers. *D'Iberville* returned on 26 February, with three prisoners: the Austrian Chancellor of the Legation at Bangkok and two Germans. The French destroyers *Pistolet* and *Fronde* also arrived from Saigon.[80] These French sailors saw no action. On 24 February, the whole residential district was declared safe, although small bands of sepoys were still hiding in the outlying areas. The Russians from *Orel* encountered one such band of mutineers on 25 February and suffered two casualties.[81] But Johore at least was reported free of mutineers. All those who fled there were captured or had surrendered. To make doubly sure, the Johore Court issued a warning that anyone helping a mutineer faced seven years imprisonment. In Singapore, the sepoys were thought to be masquerading as milkmen or cattle keepers. Searches concentrated at the Paya Lebar and Macpherson districts where there were many Indian cattle keepers.[82] As at 3 March, 49 mutineers and two Muslim Malay States Guides remained unaccounted for.[83]

The Muslims in Singapore were understandably eager to show their loyalty to the Crown. On 27 February, prominent Muslims including S.A. Alsagoff, Serang Mohamed Yusof and Mohamed Eunos met at the Alsagoff residence to propose a declaration of loyalty to King George V. Subsequently, on 6 March, thousands of Muslims gathered at the Victoria Memorial Hall. There was standing room only for the Malays, Arabs, Javanese, Indians, Egyptians, Parsees, and Malabaris who came. Syed Omar bin Mohamed Alsagoff chaired the meeting in the presence of the Colonial Secretary, R.J. Wilkinson, and the Clerk of Councils, M.S.H. McArthur. The meeting proposed sending a telegram to the King, expressing "the absolute loyalty of all Mahomadians in the Colony, a loyalty which has never changed, and never will change."[84] The mutiny was deeply deplored and mutineers were regarded by the meeting with contempt and abhorrence.

The butcher's bill for the British included ten officers, 34 soldiers and civilians, as well as three Chinese and two Malay civilians. One Volunteer gunner, P. Walton, was shot at Mount Faber when he failed to answer a sentry's challenge. It seems Walton had been sleepwalking.[85] Fifty-six sepoys were killed in the fighting, and the subsequent summary court-martial gave the death sentence to 41 sepoys. Executions began as early as 23 February, when two sepoys were shot outside the prison at Outram Road. Brownlow, Major Edge of the 1/4 KSLI and Capt. Ball of the 5th L.I. made up the summary court-martial. Court-martials continued throughout March and the Singapore Volunteer Corps provided 110 men for the firing party, commanded by Capt. Tongue of Cemetery Hill fame. A further 126 other sepoys were sentenced to exile or imprisonment.[86]

The mutiny had no hope of succeeding as the mutineers were without an effective leader or coherent plan. As one report put it, they were on the defensive after the first day, and fugitives thereafter.[87] The end of the mutiny also quashed disquiet elsewhere. Brigadier Ridout had placed secret agents among the Indians in the Federated Malay States. On 1 March 1915, Ridout received a report from Ipoh. Although agitators had been active, the report said that there was no danger of any trouble as the mutiny in Singapore had been crushed, "but the Northern Indian Mahommedans are not to be trusted." The Malay States Guides were also closely watched. Their commandant reported that the men were quiet but apprehensive of the fate of their fellow Muslims involved in the mutiny.[88] Nevertheless, the colonial authorities were not having any seditious elements around. On 3 July, the remnants of the 5th L.I. embarked for the Cameroons. They were disbanded in 1922.[89] The Malay States Guides embarked at Penang on board the transport *Arankola* bound for Aden. Nine British officers, 16 Indian officers and 681 men with a battery of four 10 pounder guns made up the force.[90]

The result of the mutiny, as far as Tsukada was concerned, was that attitudes towards the Japanese changed:

> All races without exception, gave way to the Japanese on the footpath...we were in military possession of a Portion of the British territory—it is true only for a very brief period, but what is the significance to be attached to the fact that the flag of the Rising Sun was set up in the centre of Singapore? Alexandra barracks are in the heart of Singapore Island, and Singapore is *the heart of Nanyo.*

Reading this with the benefit of hindsight, one can only chillingly acknowledge the prophetic ring in Tsukada's words.[91]

There is no doubt that the sepoys stormed Tanglin during the mutiny first to free their fellow "Muslim" Germans and second because the Germans were in any case the enemies of the British. But were the Germans involved in instigating the mutiny? W. George Maxwell, Acting Colonial Secretary in 1916, did not think so. In his report, he agreed that German money and German agents were active. An Admiralty report stated that Germany tried all in its power to "raise and arm the Mohammedans "particularly" in Singapore and the Malay States."[92] On the other hand, it was unlikely that any German prisoner of war at Tanglin could find a common language to speak to a member of the 5th L.I. Few in the 5th L.I. could speak Malay. Moreover, the Germans had not expected the mutiny at all. No bribe money was found on any of the mutineers and a search of their personal effects unearthed no letters that showed any German influence. Not that the Germans did not try. The German prisoners of war at Tanglin were quick to exploit the gullibility of the sepoy sentries guarding them. The Germans went so far as to imitate the Muslim practice of saying prayers at sundown and even pretended to recite the Koran. The 5th L.I. were completely taken in and came to think that the Germans were Muslims. However, the British soon got wind of this and prevented the Germans from coming within speaking distance of the 5th L.I. sentries.[93] Despite that, there was some contact. On the day of the regiment's departure for the Cameroons, one sepoy was heard to remark that it was "a thousand pities that they had blackened their faces by listening to those who had foolishly taken German money."[94] Looking at all the evidence, it is improbable that the Germans had a direct hand in the mutiny. Still, as the Governor noted, German agents would only be too happy to claim credit for it.[95]

Other contributory causes have been noted. The Governor felt that the primary cause of the mutiny was jealousy concerning promotions.[96] The unit's senior Indian officer, the Subadar Major, has also been blamed. On the Friday before the mutiny, the usual prayer for the officers and men was not offered at the mosque. The Subadar Major pointed out that this should not have been omitted. In doing so, he fomented some resentment among the Muslims, who disliked any interference in their religious affairs.[97] Yet it must be concluded that the fault was with the regiment and the Court of Enquiry made that clear. The Court of Enquiry's report into the mutiny ran to 994 pages. It naturally provoked cries of cover-up from the colonials in Singapore. The accompanying comments of the Governor and GOC threw an unpleasant light on the regiment, showing all the British officers to be "at loggerheads among themselves" and that Lt.-Col. Martin was a "hopeless C.O."[98] Among the civilians in Singapore, there was widespread complaint that the colonial government had early warning of the mutiny but was incompetent. Popular belief was that the Colonial Secretary was pro-German, German prisoners of war were able to leave camp to buy revolvers and ammunition, and everybody in the streets just knew that Singapore was a hotbed for sedition.[99]

Newspaper articles appearing in England that drew on the rumour mill further compounded the matter. The Governor felt aggrieved enough to draw the CO's attention to several articles. For example, an article that appeared in the *Morning Post* on 12 August 1915 published extracts of a private letter, alleging that a German prisoner had a wireless set and had been invited to dinner with the Governor. The previous month, the same newspaper alleged on 13 July that an important official in the colony was related to the Germans, that the authorities had foreknowledge of the mutiny, that interned Germans had unrestricted access to their bank accounts and that prior to the mutiny there was grave doubt over the loyalty of a portion of the 5th L.I. The *Central China Post* went so far as to say that the Governor's wife was a German and the Colonial Secretary's wife was an Austrian. Young found these allegations libellous and angrily denied them all. He asked the Colonial Secretary, Andrew Bonar Law, to make representations to the *Morning Post*.[100] Bonar Law did have a word with the editor, but the officials in the CO felt that newspapers, to get ahead of other papers, were compelled to publish "what is known to be not true, or at any rate is not known to be true." A denial would only fix the false story in the heads of the readers.[101]

Nevertheless, the talk about German agents was not without basis. Away from the public eye, the British managed to catch a German secret service agent in Singapore in 1915. George Frederick Vincent Kraft, born 1888 in Sumatra, was a member of an extensive organisation for stirring up rebellion in the East. He had served a year in the German army. His interrogation revealed that the organisation's headquarters, the *Hellverthetender Grosser Generalstab* based in Berlin, had an Indian committee that ran spy rings in Persia, Bangkok and Batavia. Arms were provided from Washington by the German ambassador there. The agents were certainly active. Eight thousand rifles were reportedly imported into Burma from the U.S. A general uprising in Burma was planned for October and German reserve officers were already waiting in Bangkok to head the revolt.[102] Kraft was a member of the spy ring at Batavia. He left Berlin on 17 May and reached Batavia on 14 June. There he awaited the arrival of the SS *Maverick* from Los Angeles, carrying 7000 rifles, 2000 revolvers and ammunition. On the way to Batavia and in his trips around the region, Kraft stopped off in Singapore three times (Singapore came under the Bangkok department of the German organisation). On his way to Shanghai to confirm instructions with the German consul there, he again passed through Singapore on 2 August 1915. This time the British were ready and quietly picked him up. They worked fast. The very next day, Kraft revealed secret recognition signs — a brooch with the Chinese colours worked upside down — secret naval signals for vessels landing arms — three white lights answered by two red lights — and invisible ink (5% ferro-cyankalium solution, visible when developed in 2% iron chloride solution).[103] The British successfully turned Kraft into a double agent and sent him on his way to Shanghai accompanied by a British agent. At Shanghai, Kraft began work to obtain complete details of the German organisation.[104]

The British also managed to arrest the purser of the *Maverick* when he passed through Singapore in November 1915 on board a Japanese steamer. Storr Hunter was an American with German sympathies. He was less cooperative than Kraft and denied all knowledge of smuggling activities. Hunter did let slip how lucrative the trade was for his crew. Although they signed on for a dollar a month in wages, they were in fact paid a bonus of 450 to 650 Dutch guilders. The British found Hunter's protests of innocence too incredible and notified the American Consul General in Singapore. He agreed that Hunter, a neutral in the service of the enemy, could justifiably be retained as a prisoner of war in Singapore.

The mutiny clearly did not dampen war fever in Singapore. Again, as in previous times of war, there was a complete change in attitudes on the part of the colonials. The eagerness of Singapore to assist in the war effort can also be seen in the exchange of telegrams between Brigadier Ridout and the WO. The Shropshire Light Infantry remained in Singapore after the mutiny. Two hundred of these men were offered without relief to fight in the war, as "the whole tendency [in Singapore was] in favour of the colony bearing as much as possible of its defence." The WO suggested that two companies of troops with the regimental headquarters could be sent to Hong Kong. The GOC replied that his proposal "emanated from strong feeling existing in the colony to release all troops possible for actual fighting, and the colony's readiness to bear any additional burden as required." Moreover, the "colony would feel resentful at the transfer of troops to another colony for garrison duty." As it turned out, the Chief of the Imperial General Staff (CIGS) wrote to the GOC to say that the Shropshire Light Infantry was to remain in Singapore, and to record his appreciation for the feeling in the colony expressed by the GOC.[105] Later in 1916, one havildar and 16 gunners from the RGA at Singapore, as well as 24 gunners from Hong Kong, were sent on board the transport *Malta* to join the 1st Mountain Battery at Egypt.[106]

Governor Sir Arthur Young could therefore with great satisfaction sum up the manner in which the colony had contributed to the war effort. Sir Arthur noted that the Straits Settlements sent to the front every man it could spare. Every local recruit was provided with money to buy passage to Europe. Furthermore, the colony arranged its finances to invest in the War Loan and contribute to the military expenditure. Sir Arthur went so far as to say, "The needs of the war dominate[d] all our finance."[107] It was estimated that more than 1000 British men in Malaya left to fight in the war.

The war and the mutiny stimulated recruitment into the Singapore Volunteer Corps, which doubled its strength in two years. The Reserve Force and Civil Guard Ordinance of 1915 made it compulsory in Singapore for all British males of military age not already serving in arms to be included in a volunteer force.[108] Throughout the war, detachments of the Singapore Volunteer Corps were permanently mobilised. About 100 Volunteers at a time were employed in various tasks around the island.

For example, the Singapore Volunteer Artillery assisted in the Examination Batteries; the Volunteer Engineers assisted in running the defence electric lights; the Volunteer Rifles, and the Chinese and Malay Companies helped in the general defences and looked after the prisoners of war; and the Singapore Field Ambulance Company assisted in the military hospitals. In addition, the Sultan of Johore provided three officers and 90 men for general duties on Pulau Brani and Blakang Mati.[109] It is interesting to note that the Army Council felt that a proposal to relieve territorial forces in the Straits Settlements by Australians not eligible for front-line duty was not likely to be acceptable to the government of Australia, or to the Australian troops.[110] There would be time enough in the next war to send Australians to Singapore.

When World War I ended on 11 November 1918, the British immediately began to reconsider the defences of the Empire. On 29 November 1918, the Director of Military Operations submitted a memorandum on *post bellum* imperial defence. The strategy was not to defend against traditional enemies as the Great Powers in Europe were all exhausted. Instead, preparations were made to defend against attacks by powers likely to attack the British Empire. The U.S.A. and Japan were identified as powers least affected by the war. In this light, it was recommended that the defences of the Straits Settlements should be "very materially strengthened and brought up to date."[111] The watch on the wall must continue, even after victory.

The period after 1892 now appears as a relative lull in the development of the defences of Singapore. Threat assessments were not stable. Potential enemies came and went rapidly. But it was mostly a period of peace in Singapore itself. The Anglo-Japanese Alliance coupled with the collapse of a Russian naval threat meant the withdrawal of British forces home, nevertheless a sense of safety grew in the British colonies in the Far East. This sense of security gave civilian and military authorities time to bicker over trivial matters. But there was also time to upgrade the guns and streamline the artillery organisation. Fewer guns were mounted but more gunners were available to fire them. There would be no more complaints of a lack of gunners. The quality of the native infantry, on the other hand, left much to be desired. Although the colony was rudely shocked by the sepoy mutiny in 1915, it rallied quickly to put down the mutiny in a grand example of inter-service and international cooperation. That and the forays of the *Emden* were the only direct experiences of the Great War for the defences and defenders of Singapore. But on another level, the war swept aside all petty quarrels and allowed the colonials in Singapore to demonstrate their loyalty and sense of duty. Colonials in Singapore took up arms in His Majesty's Forces at the front or enrolled in volunteer units in the colony. Disputes over contributions ended and Singapore gave generously to imperial defence. There was a real eagerness to assist the war effort in every way. This was clearly, if not always consciously, an expression of the perception in the colony that in the last resort Singapore's security rested on the power and security of the mother country itself. The accuracy of this feeling was all too starkly revealed in the postwar years.

Notes

1. PRO, CO273/178, Minute from WO to Under Secretary of State, CO, 5 January 1891. See also WO 20027/89, Despatch from Lord Knutsford to Governor, Straits Settlements, 13 December 1889.

2. PRO, CO537/47, Amended Report of the Local Defence Committee, Section X111, 26 January 1891. The Colonial Engineer, H.E. McCallum, signed the report subject to reservations.

3. PRO, CO273/178, letter from GOC Straits Settlements to Governor Straits Settlements, 24 February 1891.

4. PRO, CO273/178, Minute from the Major-General Commanding Troops to the Governor, Straits Settlements, 11 November 1890; Minute from the Colonial Secretary to the Deputy Assistant Adjutant General, 17 November 1890; Minute from the Under Secretary of State, WO to the Under Secretary of State, CO, 15 January 1891.

5. T.M. Winsley, *A History of the Singapore Volunteer Corps 1854–1937 being also An Historical Outline of Volunteering in Malaya*, Singapore, 1938, 29, 31.

6. PRO, CO537/47, Report on the Military Position and Aims of France in Indo-China, from the Director of Military Intelligence to Under Secretary of State, CO, 28 August 1891.

7. PRO, CO537/47, no. 648, p. 301, 29 February 1892.

8. PRO, CO273/200/2888, to Sir C. Mitchell, 24 February 1894.

9. PRO, CO273/204 / 10993, Report of Naval and Military Committee with Protest Against the Ever-increasing Demands, 22 May 1895.

10. PRO, CO273/210/8891, no.4, pamphlet on The Straits Settlements and Imperial Defence, 1895.

11. PRO, CO273/203/10993, confidential letter from Mitchell to Marquess of Ripon, 22 May 1895. The European artillery would be stationed at Fort Canning and the native auxiliary artillery with one company of infantry would be quartered at Blakang Mati. Pulau Brani would be home to the submarine mining establishment, the Royal Engineer detachment and the men of the Ordnance Store Department. Tanglin would house one company of infantry.

12. PRO, CO273/225/16036, letter from Mitchell to Chamberlain, no. 213 dated 28 June 1897.

13. PRO, CO273/293/18265, copy of telegraphic correspondence from Vice-Admiral Cypian Bridge to the Governor of Singapore, 26 February 1903.

14. PRO, CO273/293/18265, copy of telegraphic correspondence, memo to Chamberlain, 5 February 1903.

15. R. Grenfell, *Main Fleet to Singapore*, Oxford, 1987 (reprint), 21.

16. I. Nish, *The Anglo-Japanese Alliance: The Diplomacy of two Island Empires 1894–1907*, London, 1985, 92, 263ff. The Japanese had also been negotiating simultaneously for a Russo-Japanese alliance, which came to nought.

17. PRO, CO273/276/24768, letter from Chairman, Straits Settlements Association to Chamberlain, 17 July 1901.

18. PRO, CO273/280/32046, Report of the Straits Settlements 1901, p. 72.

19. Winsley, 2. See also Gabriel Chan Eng Han, "The Volunteer Corps; Contributions to Singapore's Internal Security and Defence 1854-1984," in *Pointer*, November 1990 Supplement, 1.

20. Winsley, 27. Unfortunately, the Maxim guns were not manned as there were not enough men and the Mountain Screw guns proved more popular. Winsley says modern 2.75" breech-loading Screw guns replaced the original muzzle-loading guns in 1903.

21. PRO, CO273/305/40033, Minutes regarding Japanese Plots against Russian Fleet, 25 November 1904; CO273/300, Telegram from Sir John Anderson to Mr. Alfred Lyttelton, MP, 27 December 1904.

22. PRO, ADM116/942, Confidential Paper on the Genesis of the Home Fleet, attached to secret letter from Sir John Fisher to HRH The Prince of Wales, 23 October 1906.

23. Ibid.

24. PRO, CAB11/118, Addendum to the Colonial Defence Committee's Memorandum No. 405 M, 8 July 1909.

25. PRO, CAB11/118, Secret Report on Standard of Defences at British Defended Ports in Distant Seas, 7 April 1909.

26. PRO, WO106/45, memo on Imperial Defences, General Principles affecting the Overseas Dominions, CDC417M, undated. The Japanese terms could have included the repeal of acts against "yellow" immigration and a guarantee for the unmolested return of any invading Japanese army to Japan.

27. PRO, CAB11/128, Confidential Report on Details of the Garrisons of Fortresses and Defended Ports Abroad, 30 May 1910.

28. PRO, CAB11/150, Secret Report on State of Completion as regards Works, Armaments and Defence Lights on 1 July 1910.

29. PRO, WO33/592, secret memo A1557, 13 June 1912. The Quick Fire guns were classified as examination batteries.

30. PRO, WO106/1412, copy of telegram received at WO from Editor, *Straits Times*, 27 October 1914.

31. PRO, WO106/1412, telegram from WO to the GOC Straits Settlements, 30 October 1914.

32. PRO, WO106/1412, secret telegram from Earl Kitchener to GOC Straits Settlements, 19 November 1914.

33. PRO, CO273/435/4564, telegram from GOC Straits Settlements, to WO, 27 November 1914.

34. PRO, CO273/416/50961, secret telegram from GOC, Straits Settlements to WO, 13 December 1914; See also WO106/1412, Secret telegram from GOC, Straits Settlements to WO, 19 November 1914.

35. PRO, CO273/420/3002, letter to Sir G. Fiddes, 19 January 1915.

36. PRO, CO273/262/31973, Memorandum by the Colonial Defence Committee "Straits Settlements; Military Force of Native States," 21 February 1901.

37. PRO, CO273/425, testimony of Lt.-Col. C.H.B. Lees at a Court of Enquiry, 14 January 1915.

38. PRO, CO273/425, testimony of Capt. S.J.G. Beaumont, 14 January 1915.

39. PRO, CO273/425, testimony of Capt. T.B. Minnikem, 14 January 1915.

40. PRO, CO273/425, testimony of R.C.F Schomberg, 14 January 1915.

41. PRO, CO273/425, Opinion of the Court of Enquiry, 14 January 1915.

42. PRO, CO273/423, "The Singapore Mutiny," in *Morning Post*, 26 November 1915.

43. PRO, CO273/420/3002, telegram from Governor Straits Settlements to Secretary of State for the Colonies, received by CO 19 January 1915.

44. Winsley, 61. See also Harfield, 355.

45. PRO, CO273/423, GOC's Comments on the report of the Court of Enquiry into the Mutiny, 27 August 1915.

46. PRO, CO273/423, Memorandum of GOC on Attitude of Officers towards their C.O., 27 August 1915. It was rumoured at one time that his successor, Col. Barrett, would not recommend Martin for promotion. Martin was therefore sent away from the regiment to be independently evaluated by a GOC elsewhere. After three months absence, he returned to be promoted.

47. Ibid. It seems that Lt. Strover, already adjutant under the previous commanding officer, was accused by Martin of trying to prevent Martin's promotion so that Strover's

brother-in-law (Major Stooks) could be promoted instead. Lt. Elliot had also fallen into Martin's bad books for no apparent reason.

48. PRO, CO273/408, telegram from Sir Arthur Young to Secretary of State for the Colonies, 14 December 1914.

49. PRO, CO273/416, Secret Minute from WO to Secretary of State for the Colonies, 12 December 1914.

50. PRO, CO273/435/1229, letter from WO to the Secretary of State for the Colonies, 7 January 1915.

51. Harfield, 357.

52. PRO, CO273//423, confidential letter from Sir Arthur Young to A. Bonar Law, 27 August 1915.

53. Reade had left for home, and Ridout, the former Commanding Royal Engineer, took over on 5 February.

54. PRO, CO273/420, secret letter from Governor Straits Settlements to Lewis Harcourt M.P., CO, 17 February 1915.

55. PRO, CO273/423, GOC's Comments on the Report of the Court of Enquiry into the Mutiny, 27 August 1915.

56. Harfield, 357.

57. PRO, CO273/423, GOC's Comments on the Report of the Court of Enquiry into the Mutiny, 27 August 1915.

58. Harfield, 357. See also Winsley, 70.

59. PRO, CO273/420, secret letter from Governor Straits Settlements to Lewis Harcourt M.P., CO, 17 February 1915; CO273/429, General Letter no. 36 from C-in-C China Station to Admiralty, 27 February 1915.

60. PRO, CO273/441, Report of W. George Maxwell, Acting Colonial Secretary Straits Settlements, 24 April 1916. The remainder of the Malay States Guides retreated as a group to Johore.

61. PRO, CO273/420, secret letter from Governor Straits Settlements to Lewis Harcourt M.P., CO, 17 February 1915; CO273/429, General Letter no. 36 from C-in-C China Station to Secretary of Admiralty, 27 February 1915.

62. PRO, CO273/441, Report of W. George Maxwell, Acting Colonial Secretary Straits Settlements, 24 April 1916.

63. PRO, CO273/420, narrative from a preliminary account by Mr W.G. Maxwell, Acting Secretary to the High Commissioner for the Malay States, 7 March 1915.

64. PRO, CO273/429, General Letter from C-in-C China Station to Secretary of the Admiralty, 27 February 1915.

65. Harfield, 358-59.

66. PRO, CO273/420, narrative from a preliminary account by Mr W.G. Maxwell, Acting Secretary to the High Commissioner for the Malay States, 7 March 1915.

67. PRO, CO273/429, General Letter no. 36 from C-in-C China Station to Secretary of Admiralty, 27 February 1915.

68. PRO, CO273/423, GOC's Comments on the Report of the Court of Enquiry into the Mutiny, 27 August 1915.

69. Harfield, 356-562. The C-in-C China Station says that 30 mutineers were killed. See PRO, CO273/429, General Letter no. 36 from C-in-C China Station to Secretary of Admiralty, 27 February 1915.

70. PRO, CO273/441, Report of W. George Maxwell, Acting Colonial Secretary Straits Settlements, 24 April 1916.

71. Winsley, 67. Today, the hill has long since been levelled. It was across the road from the Singapore Armed Forces Reservist Association's Bukit Merah Clubhouse and opposite Alexandra Hospital.

72. PRO, CO273/413, letter from Crown Agents to Under Secretary of State, CO, 29 April 1914.

73. Winsley, 64-66.

74. PRO, ADM125/66, Notes on a book entitled *From Nanyo* by Tsukada M., undated.

75. Ibid.

76. Harfield, 362.

77. PRO, CO273/429, General Letter no.36 from C-in-C China Station to Secretary of Admiralty, 27 February 1915.

78. Harfield, 362. See also Winsley, 69.

79. PRO, CO273/420, narrative from a preliminary account by Mr W.G. Maxwell, Acting Secretary to the High Commissioner for the Malay States, 7 March 1915; see also Harfield, 362, and Winsley, 68.

80. PRO, CO273/429, General Letter no. 36 from C-in-C China Station to Secretary of Admiralty, 27 February 1915.

81. PRO, CO273/441, Report of W. George Maxwell, Acting Colonial Secretary Straits Settlements, 24 April 1916.

82. PRO, CO273/420, narrative from a preliminary account by Mr W.G. Maxwell, acting Secretary to the High Commissioner for the Malay States, 7 March 1915.

83. PRO, CO273/421, Confidential Report from Sir Arthur Young to CO, 31 March 1915.

84. PRO, CO273/421, extract from the *Malaya Tribune*, 8 March 1915.

85. PRO, CO273/420, narrative from a preliminary account by Mr W.G. Maxwell, Acting Secretary to the High Commissioner for the Malay States, 7 March 1915.

86. Harfield, 363.

87. PRO, CO273/441, Report of W. George Maxwell, Acting Colonial Secretary Straits Settlements, 24 April 1916.

88. PRO, CO273/435, Secret Report from GOC the Troops Straits Settlements to WO, 3 March 1915.

89. PRO, CO273//423, Confidential Letter from Sir Arthur Young to A. Bonar Law, Secretary of State for the Colonies, 27 August 1915; Harfield, 363.

90. PRO, WO106/1413, secret cipher from the GOC Straits Settlements to WO, 15 September 1915.

91. PRO, ADM125/66, Notes on a book entitled *From Nanyo* by Tsukada M., undated. In February 1942 the Japanese did indeed return to the Alexandra area, where they committed the most notorious atrocity of the Malayan campaign; see chapter 8.

92. PRO, ADM 125/64, Minute to the Admiralty, 23 October 1915.

93. PRO, CO273/441, Report of W. George Maxwell, Acting Colonial Secretary Straits Settlements, 24 April 1916.

94. PRO, CO273/423, GOC's Comments on the Report of the Court of Enquiry into the Mutiny, 27 August 1915.

95. PRO, CO273/423, Confidential Letter from Sir Arthur Young to A. Bonar Law, 27 August 1915.

96. PRO, CO273/420, secret telegram from Sir Arthur Young to Secretary of State for the Colonies, 16 February 1915.

97. PRO, CO273/420, Confidential Report from Sir Arthur Young to Mr. Lewis Harcourt, CO, 25 February 1915.

98. PRO, CO273/423, Secret Minutes on the Court of Enquiry's Report, 23 September 1915.

99. PRO, CO273/423, copies of letters from Singapore and Federated Malay States forwarded to A. Bonar Law, 21 September 1915.

100. PRO, CO273/423, letter from Sir Arthur Young to A. Bonar Law, 16 September 1915.

101. PRO, CO273/423, Internal Minutes on charges against the colonial government, 2 November 1915 and 5 November 1915.

102. PRO, WO106/1413, Secret Report from Brigadier Dudley Ridout to the WO, 3 September 1915.

103. Ibid., Statement No. 2 by Kraft. It transpired that the German spying techniques were not too secret. There were no special communications systems. Agents sent messages using Arabs and Chinese as couriers or by normal telegraph. Only important letters were coded and letters sent through the mail had messages in invisible ink. Telegrams were sent in plain language, but the words had another secret meaning.

104. PRO, WO106/1413, Secret Report from Brigadier Dudley Ridout to the WO, 3 September 1915.

105. PRO, CO273/450/40173, telegram no. 963 from GOC Singapore, to WO, 14 August 1916; telegram no. 21630 from WO to GOC Singapore, 16 August 1916; telegram from GOC Singapore, to WO, 18 August 1916; and telegram no. 21765 from CIGS to GOC Singapore, 19 August 1916.

106. PRO, WO106/1413, secret telegram from GOC Singapore to WO, 14 April 1916.

107. PRO, CO273/423, Speech by Sir Arthur Young to Legislative Council, 24 September 1915.

108. PRO, CAB 11/166, Secret Report on Special Measures taken in the Straits Settlements to deal with internal civil difficulties due to the war, 23 March 1920.

109. PRO, CO273/456, Report from GOC the Troops Straits Settlements to Governor and C-in-C Straits Settlements, 16 January 1917.

110. PRO, CO273/435/43481, letter to Under Secretary of State for the Colonies, 20 September 1915.

111. PRO, CAB11/168, Secret Memorandum from Director of Military Operations to Overseas Defence Committee, 29 November 1918.

6

A Keystone of Imperial Defence or a Millstone around Britain's Neck? Singapore 1919-1941

Singapore's presumed role within the scheme of British imperial defence grew markedly after the First World War as Anglo-Japanese relations declined sharply in these years. Unfortunately, this presumption of importance was rarely, if ever, matched by a commensurate expansion in the means given to either achieve or sustain Singapore's newly acquired status, let alone secure the objectives sought by the British in the Asia-Pacific region. Harsh though this judgement appears at first sight — particularly given the building of the naval base at Sembawang — the spectacular collapse of Malaya and Singapore in late 1941 and early 1942 indicates that something was dreadfully awry in British foreign and defence policy east of Suez in the inter-war period. It is the function of the next three chapters to investigate the background to this military disaster in order to reveal just what went wrong and why the so-called fortress of Singapore fell so swiftly and dramatically in February 1942.

The Genesis of the "Singapore Strategy"1918-1929

Several months before hostilities with the Central Powers ended, the delegates to the Imperial War Cabinet at their meeting in June 1918 had already decided that a review of the whole system of regional defence was timely.[1] Apart from anything else, the state of Anglo-Japanese relations caused more than momentary concern at this time. Notwithstanding its bellicose attitude towards China, expressed through the infamous Twenty-One Demands of May 1915, and territorial expansion into the Western Pacific in the early months of the war, Japan seemed set on becoming a major naval power within the next decade and a force to be reckoned with in East Asian affairs in the post-war world.[2] All the while the Anglo-Japanese Alliance remained in existence, however, tension between London and Tokyo could, on the whole, be contained — but it was extremely difficult to be as sanguine about the future if this pragmatic diplomatic arrangement was to come to an end for any reason. In that event the prospects for a deterioration in relations between the two governments were likely to rise accordingly with potentially dire strategic consequences for the peoples of the British Empire living in the Asia-Pacific region. Not surprisingly, therefore, the British were reluctant to dispense with a diplomatic compact that had largely served its purpose in the past even though many felt that the alliance had been exploited far more by the Japanese than by their erstwhile friends in the west. Despite the professed shortcomings of this contentious alliance, however, the British government was still of the opinion that a renewal was probably in its best short- to medium-term interests.[3] Unfortunately, not all Britain's friends thought similarly. Unquestionably the greatest power in the world in 1919 — the United States — was in the forefront of those nations who viewed a prolongation of the Anglo-Japanese Alliance with acute distaste.[4] Apart from Japan's somewhat unsavoury record in the war, which was not lost on the Americans, the unveiling of Japanese plans to expand their naval arm substantially in peacetime seemed designed to promote a more active involvement in the Pacific — an ocean that was seen in the U.S.A. at least as being quintessentially a sphere of American interests. Even if the Imperial Japanese Navy (IJN) was not being built up to either intimidate, let alone tackle, the U.S. Navy (USN) or the RN in mortal combat, the Americans chose to see its development as being inimical to the fostering of good relations between Tokyo and Washington. Moreover, a belief was gaining ground in the United States that the Japanese had a hidden agenda of commercial expansion in the Asia-Pacific region which was in danger of putting it on a collision course with that of the Americans, particularly in China. Much the same view was held about the British too. According to this theory, a direct clash of commercial interests involving one or other of the allies with the United States might tempt the other ally to join the fray and result in some military action.[5] Whether this was a classic case of paranoia or a realistic assessment, the result was the same — a growing tide of suspicion experienced by both the Wilson and Harding administrations towards the two members of the Anglo-Japanese Alliance. Since the British government had no intention of going to war with the Americans on any conceivable matter in the foreseeable future, its leaders sought to ameliorate the concerns of its wartime associate even if, ultimately, that was to cost them very dear.

In this fluid geo-strategic situation, the British and Empire governments turned for advice on imperial defence to a prominent naval authority, the former First Sea Lord at the time of the Battle of Jutland, Viscount Jellicoe. He was instructed to lead a fact-finding mission to India and the Dominions to study the plans made by the individual governments for both local and regional naval defence.[6] While Admiral Jellicoe was many things, he was not the unobtrusive apparatchik the British government would have preferred to have undertaken this mission. In some ways, therefore, it was an incongruous appointment. Apart from being a highly autocratic figure, Jellicoe was strongly opinionated and self-confident, someone unlikely to be intimidated or overawed by the size and complexity of the task confronting him. So it proved to be in reality. Armed with rather ambiguous instructions, Admiral Jellicoe left on his imperial grand tour in the battle-cruiser HMS *New Zealand* on 21 February 1919. As the author of many precise rules of engagement in the past, Jellicoe had little difficulty in moulding the vague instructions he had been given on this occasion to his benefit. As a result, he took it upon himself to advise and cajole his various hosts on the dangers and obligations confronting them. In this way, Jellicoe imperiously arrogated to himself the role of the Admiralty in laying down what the various colonial and dominion governments ought to do to improve their security in local waters and on the high seas. Jellicoe's performance touched many nerves around the globe and proved to be highly embarrassing for the British government.[7]

Admiral Jellicoe's scheme — expensive and provocative as it was — could hardly have been more out-of-phase with the British coalition government's overall strategic thinking in the immediate post-Versailles period. Pledged to an expensive programme of domestic economic re-habilitation, the penurious Lloyd George administration was extremely reluctant to spend large sums of money on other new ambitious projects, least of all those drawn from the overseas military realm. This factor was an important determinant in the adoption by the Cabinet of the crucially important "Ten Year Rule" on 15 August 1919.[8] By taking this momentous decision the cabinet ministers essentially accepted the administrative notion that the British Empire would not be involved in a major war for the next ten years. Although this executive decision had both serious financial and strategic consequences, it stood in stark contrast to the tenor of the report that its prominent public servant issued to the Australian government a day later. That report, unencumbered by the necessity for administrative convenience, promptly identified the Japanese as a serious potential threat to the British Empire in the Asia-Pacific region.[9] Jellicoe's call for the stationing of a huge modern battlefleet in the Far East to deter the Japanese from embarking upon a southward advance in the future would necessarily involve the expenditure of vast sums of money not only on the provision of that fleet but also, significantly, on the establishment within the region of a first-class naval base capable of supporting it. If the former First Sea Lord could be believed, the future defence of the British Empire was contingent upon its members being willing to match the vast naval building programme proposed by the Japanese. His predictions about the potentially aggressive nature of the IJN were to prove uncannily accurate two decades later.[10] At the time, however, his observations and recommendations merely incited anger and resentment within the Admiralty establishment in London, not least because it suggested that a major naval force must be based in the Far East to thwart the ambitions of the IJN in that region. Although his views received a hostile reception in London, Jellicoe's suggestions for a more comprehensive system of naval defence were listened to with appreciation elsewhere within the Empire and particularly in the Australasian Dominions. For them, of course, what the British were inclined to describe as the Far East might be more accurately termed the near north. If the Japanese were to be such a potential threat to the Empire in the years ahead, those countries lying in the way of their strategic and economic objectives would become the most vulnerable targets for some form of military assault by a predatory foe.[11]

It was evident from the outset that the "Ten Year Rule" and Jellicoe's scheme of massive rearmament could not possibly co-exist and that the latter would almost certainly have to be forsaken for the requirements of the former. Despite its disavowal of Jellicoe's reports, the Admiralty was aware that there was more than a grain of truth in them. If the Japanese proved to be unreliable friends in the future, a more likely scenario if the Anglo-Japanese Alliance was not renewed, Britain would be forced into taking some hard strategic decisions in the medium to long term.[12] Even if maintaining a massive battlefleet somewhere in the Far East was likely to be ruled out for reasons of economy, the British would still need to have a first-class naval base in the region to which modern warships could be sent on occasion if the situation required it. Unfortunately no such base existed at this time. Although Hong Kong had some advantages, it was thought to be too vulnerable to a landward assault to become anything other than a forward operational base.[13] If Hong Kong was passed over for reasons of security, therefore, the most obvious alternative candidates were either Sydney or Singapore.

Sydney's candidacy was ruled out by the newly reconvened CID in the early summer of 1921 on the grounds that the Australian base was situated too far from Southeast and East Asian waters to be effective as the main regional hub for a large Far Eastern fleet that would be sent there in an emergency to do battle with the IJN.[14] This left Singapore as the only viable port in the region that could be developed into the main base for such a fleet. Jellicoe described Singapore in 1919 as "undoubtedly the naval key to the Far East" and the Admiralty in its *War Memorandum (Eastern)* in 1920 agreed that it was essential for the British Empire that Singapore be held in the event of war with Japan.[15] Once again its renowned geographical location as a maritime link between the Indian and Pacific Oceans had come to Singapore's aid, boosting its image in the eyes of strategic planners in Whitehall. This chorus of approval merely foreshadowed the official decision in favour of Singapore. At its meeting on 16 June 1921 the Lloyd George Cabinet accepted the recommendation of the CID that Singapore should be developed into a naval base sufficient to receive and handle the main fleet which the British would send there in the event of a future war in the Pacific.[16]

Before any base could be developed in Singapore, however, another matter with an important bearing on naval affairs in the region had to be resolved. This concerned the fate of the whole question of disarmament which the Americans were sponsoring at a conference to be held in Washington later in the year. By the time Charles Evans Hughes, the U.S. Secretary of State, officially opened the proceedings on 12 November 1921 it was an open secret that Harding's Republican administration was determinedly in favour of arms limitation. Nonetheless, few, if any, of the international delegates could have been mentally prepared for the revolutionary scheme of disarmament that Hughes proposed in his opening speech. Seizing the initiative on this occasion, the wily American statesman never lost it thereafter.[17] From that point onward the international powers found themselves in the uncomfortable position of having to debate someone else's political agenda knowing that the chances of establishing their own claims on these subjects were severely restricted. When the dust settled after the conference drew to a close in February 1922 the traditional naval scene had been transformed throughout the world. Gone was the Anglo-Japanese Alliance, a victim of American antipathy, and gone too were the days of the RN's much sought-after "two power naval standard."[18] From a position of numerical superiority in 1918 the RN was forced to accept that at most it would have ostensible global equality with the USN in the future. This situation arose directly from the Five-Power Naval Limitation Treaty which stipulated that the major naval powers would henceforth be limited by a comparative 5:5:3:1.75 ratio. As a result of this agreement the British and the Americans would only be allowed to retain or construct a maximum of 15 capital ships (battleships and battlecruisers of more than 10,000 tons), the Japanese would be allowed to build and maintain nine such ships and the French and Italians five each. Although the British delegation managed to resist any such quotas for cruisers and destroyers, the savage reduction of the RN's battlefleet was sufficient in itself to undermine, if not seriously compromise, the government's ability to provide an effective defensive shield for the British Empire under any and all circumstances. Moreover, by tacitly accepting a future Japanese dominance in the western Pacific, the naval limitation treaty ensured that the RN faced actual regional inferiority in these Asiatic waters.[19]

Whatever the legacy of the Washington Conference was for the other participants, it was almost wholly bad for the British government and the peoples of the Empire. From this time forward the curse of what historians now call "imperial overstretch" afflicted British defence policy overseas.[20] It was now a moot point whether the Royal Navy was strong enough in the post-1922 period to resist extreme pressures mounted by hostile forces thousands of miles from the mother country. Although there were no immediate potential threats in Europe, the abrogation of the Anglo-Japanese Alliance did leave the British government with the possibility of a strategic headache in the Far East if a serious breach in relations between Tokyo and London became apparent in the future and led to war breaking out between the two former allies. In such a grave situation the British would be forced to respond by sending a significant proportion of the main fleet to Singapore in order to cope with the menace of the IJN. If the Japanese fleet had reached its Washington treaty limit of nine capital ships, the RN task force could not afford to dispatch a fleet to the Far East substantially less in terms of quality and quantity than that committed to action by the IJN. If it did so, the British government would stand the chance of seeing its naval force routed by its Japanese opponents.[21] Aware that the business of assembling such a task force and sending it more than 8000 nautical miles to Singapore would take some time to implement, the Admiralty war planners built a six-week "period before relief" into Far Eastern defence policy. In other words, Singapore was meant to withstand any and all attempts to subdue it during this interval before the main fleet arrived to defend it. This minimum "period before relief" was revised upwards several times over the years as global risks increased. By 1941 the Singapore fortress was supposed to survive unaided for six months before it could be relieved.[22]

A commitment to some form of "Singapore Strategy" was, therefore, to be an enduring feature of British defence planning in the inter-war years. Although it would be radically revised once the European war broke out in earnest in 1940, the concept was never totally rejected. Nowadays, of course, it is dismissed by historians with the type of scathing criticism normally reserved for the equally bankrupt appeasement policy.[23] Such is the price of failure on the international stage. In the immediate aftermath of the Washington Conference, however, the "Singapore Strategy" had a certain vitality not least because the British had been granted permission under the naval limitation treaty to develop their only first-class naval base in the region on this small equatorial island situated some 2888 nautical miles from Tokyo. Yet in 1922 Singapore was only a thriving commercial port; it did not have the facilities to service a major battlefleet. Before a naval base could be developed on the island to give the "Singapore Strategy" some credibility, much time, effort and money would have to be lavished upon it by the British.

To begin with, of course, a suitable site had to be chosen for this base. Several possibilities existed, none of which were ideal. A deep water base was proposed a few miles southwest of the main island of Singapore in the roads at Selat Sinki. While a large enough anchorage to accommodate any size of fleet that might be sent there from Britain, it did not possess the shelter of a natural harbour and lay exposed to both submarine and air attack. In order to remedy these two deficiencies an eleven-mile breakwater would have to be constructed around the site at an estimated cost of £20 million. Additional fixed anti-aircraft defences would also have to be installed to protect the fleet anchorage and an air base would be needed either on the mainland or on the small offshore island of Blakang Mati. Further appreciable sums would have to be spent on building the necessary workshops, stores and other base facilities, none of which existed at this time. Expenditure of this magnitude proved a prohibitive factor in the case of Selat Sinki.[24] Of the two other "cheaper" sites that were considered, Keppel Harbour, the busy commercial port in the heart of the city district on the southern coast of the island, was a distinct possibility but for the disruption it was likely to bring to the large amount of mercantile traffic and the burgeoning entrepôt trade that used this facility.[25] This left the Strait of Johore at the northern tip of the island as the only other viable option for the establishment of a major naval base in Singapore. Barely a mile wide at its narrowest part, the Strait separated Singapore from the southern tip of the Malayan peninsula. Sheltered by the Johore coastline, the Strait had distinct possibilities as the Admiralty survey ship HMS *Merlin* discovered in October 1920.[26] Apart from having reasonable depth in its main channel and requiring some additional dredging work closer to shore, the survey revealed that various places in the eastern Strait could be utilised by the Admiralty for its Far Eastern fleet anchorage —

one that was capable of handling up to 20 capital ships and some 226 vessels in all.[27]

At the same time the Admiralty began to focus its attention on the Strait, a causeway and rail link was being built across it between Woodlands and Johore Bahru for the Federated Malay States Railway. Supported by the CO for its economic potential, the causeway's existence was bound to have a bearing on the final choice of site for a naval base if one was finally going to be selected in the Strait. Although various suggestions were made as to the design of the bridge so as to facilitate the passage of ships through an elevated portion of it, in the end financial considerations won out again and this expensive refinement was dropped in favour of a permanent structure that would effectively block off the Strait for all naval vessels once it had been completed.[28] Sites west of the causeway were not even considered by an important Admiralty committee of technical experts which came out to Singapore in November 1921 charged with responsibility for selecting possible locations for the naval base. Four sites to the east of the causeway were, however, found to have the necessary development potential: Sungei Senoko and Sungei Sembawang, both situated at the mouth of small rivers close to the actual causeway, and two more easterly sites, those at Ponggol and Tampines. Ultimately, Senoko's high foreshore, Ponggol's massive reclamation needs, and Tampines' vulnerability to attack counted against these sites and in favour of Sembawang. Despite having to alter the course of the Sembawang river so that it would drain into the Strait at a more westerly point, the Sembawang site was chosen by the Learmouth-Power committee as it appeared to possess more advantages than disadvantages.[29]

Although Sembawang may well have been the best of the four sites in the Strait, it did not inspire universal acceptance amongst British officials some of whom still hankered vainly after Keppel Harbour for reasons of defensive security. In the opinion of Sir Alexander Duff, C-in-C China, and supported by representatives from the WO, the Admiralty's choice of a site in the Johore Strait complicated rather than eased Britain's defence problems in Southeast Asia.[30] From the outset the WO went on record stating that the establishment of the naval base at Sembawang made it imperative in wartime for the British armed forces to establish at least a 30-mile [50km] defensive perimeter around the naval facility in the Johore Strait, to create a secure bridgehead that would protect it from hostile artillery bombardment or attack from enemy infantry landed anywhere along the southeastern shore of the Malayan peninsula.[31] Despite the severe reservations held by some British military officials, however, by the close of 1922 the Sembawang site had been approved by the CID as the official site for the Singapore naval base.[32]

While it may have been fine in theory to postulate the need for a defensive perimeter around the proposed naval base, the key to developing such a military redoubt in practice depended upon the Sultan of Johore's mercurial temperament.[33] If Sultan Ibrahim could be persuaded that the British naval base and the defensive preparations to accompany it were in the best interests of himself and his state all

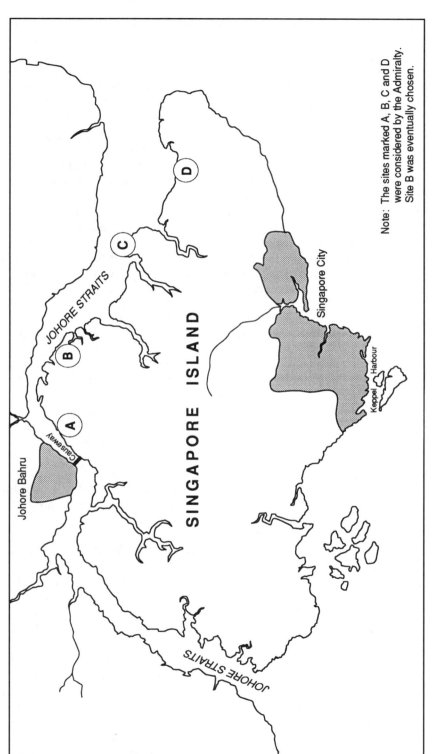

Note: The sites marked A, B, C and D were considered by the Admiralty. Site B was eventually chosen.

The siting of the naval base

would be well. From the outset, the independent Malay ruler was at his most accommodating. From the beginning of 1921 when mention was first made of the building of a British naval base in the Johore Strait, Sultan Ibrahim's haphazardly Anglophile tendencies came to the fore. Apart from having no objections to such a base being built, Sultan Ibrahim warned the British authorities that Japanese activities and interests in Johore were growing and that their leasing of 30,000 acres of state land for rubber cultivation could add an interesting dimension to the naval project if it ever came to fruition. Although this issue of Japanese land holdings in Johore was certainly a negative feature, the British authorities preferred to downplay its significance. Whether it was prudent to do so, however, is a moot point.[34]

One of the decisive factors in favour of the Sembawang site was its hitherto unexploited potentialities. It remained a large undeveloped area of mangrove swamps which, if cleared and filled in, would provide sufficient ground for the construction of a major dockyard and repair base. What Leopold Savile, the Admiralty's leading civil engineer, had in mind initially was a facility that would have at least 10 docks, a floating dock, an inner basin measuring some 609m by 487m that would be sealed off by two locks which themselves could be used as additional graving docks, together with a variety of workshops, over 3000m of wharves, substantial fuel tanks and other storage facilities, offices, together with flats and houses that could accommodate up to 2000 RN personnel, a hospital, and recreational facilities for those using the base.[35] In addition to this massive naval establishment, the Admiralty wished to provide a seaplane base at Seletar a few miles to the east of the Sembawang site. Savile's proposal became known as the "Green Scheme."[36] In a different age and financial environment it might have made sense. Alas, in the immediate post-Geddes era when money was tight and budgets were being slashed across the board, it looked and indeed was over-ambitious. As the "Green Scheme" stood very little chance of being accepted by either the Treasury or the Cabinet, the Admiralty Board's sub-committee was forced to think again and substantially modify Savile's original proposal. It finally proposed a revised and scaled-down version of the dockyard layout in March 1923. This was dubbed the "Red Scheme" and was designed to a very different specification than Savile had worked towards. Instead of being sufficient to meet the needs of a full battlefleet and its auxiliary vessels, the "Red Scheme" was supposed to be sufficient to cope with the demands of any peacetime fleet (roughly 20% of the full battlefleet) that might be sent out to Singapore in the aftermath of the Washington treaties. This modified plan retained a floating dock and a single graving dock, but was to dispense with the enclosed basin and most of the other docks that Savile proposed. It also reduced the original wharfage area by 40%, and made sweeping reductions in all other areas of the "Green Scheme." Even so the "Red Scheme" was still estimated to cost £14.8 million to construct. Once defence costs (£1.25 million) and those of establishing the seaplane air base at Seletar (£400,000) were added to the figure, together with a likely £9 million fee for accumulating the necessary oil reserves for use by the fleet once it arrived in Singapore, the overall cost even of the smaller naval base was, therefore, a hefty £25.45 million.[37]

Unfortunately, while the "Red Scheme" may have made good economic sense and fulfilled the Treasury's criteria for financial stringency, its military value was doubtful from the outset — and was always likely to be fatally compromised if peacetime conditions swiftly degenerated into war with the Japanese and the British government was forced to implement the "Singapore Strategy" by sending the main fleet out to the Far East. If it was forced to do so, the Admiralty assumed as late as April 1937 that at least seven battleships and an appropriate number of auxiliary vessels would have to be involved, since anything less might encourage rather than deter the IJN from embarking upon its long anticipated southward advance. Upon arrival in Singapore, however, the British Far Eastern fleet would have to manage with a range of facilities in Sembawang grossly inadequate for a naval force of its size.[38] Since the "Red Scheme" could not be transformed into something much larger without a considerable infusion of money, time and effort — a project mooted at the outset but never reconsidered — the concept of sending the main fleet to Singapore looks, and indeed was, inherently flawed. Moreover, the strategic concept was inexplicit on the question of what would happen once the Far Eastern fleet arrived in Singaporean waters. Inconceivable or not, this situation arose because the Admiralty planners felt that the overall strategic picture was almost infinitely variable in the future and given that only the actual disposition of forces ranged against them would ultimately determine the nature of the British response, contingency planning for a war with the IJN became fitful, at best, in these years. Consequently, the British were likely to be reactive rather than proactive towards the threat posed by the Japanese. Whatever the role assigned to the Far Eastern fleet would be, whether it was to be engaged in war or in some deterrent capacity, the fact remained that it would have to fulfil this assignment with wholly inadequate naval facilities at its disposal.[39]

Notwithstanding its serious weaknesses, the "Singapore Strategy" remained a touchstone of British defence and foreign policy for the 1920s and 30s. To admit that the RN was incapable of coming to the aid of the British Empire would have been unthinkable at this time. Yet the unpalatable truth was that through the ravages of disarmament and budgetary controls, the British armed services could not be strong everywhere and if faced by a simultaneous threat in two (or more) widely different theatres, stark choices would have to be made according to the strategic priorities involved. On the whole, few in the British "establishment" wished to think about the nature of this dilemma and the years passed with little amendment to the notion that if all else failed Singapore, being the key to the survival of the British Empire-Commonwealth, would have to be defended by a large contingent of RN warships sent out from home and Mediterranean waters for just this purpose. It was, as Ian Hamill so graphically describes it, a strategic illusion — but one that was to endure far longer than it ought to have done.[40]

Once the Cabinet agreed in principle in February 1923 to the construction of the naval base in Singapore, the British government began to pester Sir Lawrence Guillemard, Governor of the Straits Settlements, for a suitably appreciative gesture of support for this project from the colonial authorities. Guillemard was left in little doubt as to the type of practical assistance required by the British. In essence, they expected the Straits Settlements to offer the land needed for the construction of the naval and air bases at Sembawang and Seletar, some 2845 acres, free of charge. Since this land had a notional value of 1.25 million Straits dollars — equivalent to £145,833 — it was a significant token of support.[41] Whether it would encourage the rest of the Dominions to part with equally large sums of money to subsidise the cost of building the bases was uncertain. If New Zealand's response was anything to go by the prospects were quite propitious. A preliminary gift of £100,000 towards the cost of the base was announced in Parliament in Wellington on 3 July 1923. William Massey, the New Zealand Premier, indicated later that more money might be forthcoming as the project proceeded.[42] For his part, Stanley Bruce, the Australian Prime Minister, led a government that was basically sympathetic to the defence scheme but had still to make a definitive decision on the scale of its contribution towards the Singapore base.[43] Not all the Commonwealth leaders, however, were as supportive as both Massey and Bruce. South Africa's Prime Minister, the incomparable General Jan Smuts, was by far the most skeptical about the value of the entire "Singapore Strategy," especially if the British were engaged in a simultaneous war in Europe and the Far East.[44] Criticism from such a source as Smuts was a serious blow to the British cause and had to be rebutted at all cost. Leopold Amery, First Lord of the Admiralty, was chosen to disarm the delegates to the Imperial Conference of 1923 with a speech that mixed candour with wishful thinking, invoking the reassuring prospect of American aid should the disturbing scenario sketched in by Smuts come to pass in the future.[45] Needless to say, Amery could not call upon any substantive evidence to sustain his contention. It remained a figment of his imagination — a reassuring chimera that was invoked by the Admiralty and by other members of the British and Commonwealth establishments in the years to come with little or no encouragement from the Americans themselves.[46] Nonetheless, it succeeded in deflecting Smuts' harsh but perceptive criticism and the majority of the principal delegates returned home from London comforted by the notion that even in the worst-case scenario, help would lie at hand.

Just after the Singapore base survived its first test, another more immediate danger loomed with Baldwin's unfathomable decision to test his Conservative administration's approval rating with the British electorate. When the results of the December 1923 general election were finally tabulated political instability was assured with the Tories losing their overall majority in the House of Commons. Supported by the

Asquithian Liberals, J. Ramsay MacDonald was appointed as Britain's first socialist Prime Minister in January 1924. This would have been significant in any case; it was made more so because MacDonald was known to be a fervent advocate of pacifism and disarmament and someone, therefore, who was disinclined in principle to support the building of a major naval base east of Suez.[47] It did not take long for his minority government to establish a Cabinet sub-committee to review the matter. Within a month the Clynes Committee had taken evidence from a range of witnesses and come to the conclusion that the government should ignore the advice of Admiral Beatty, the First Sea Lord, and make an executive decision not to proceed with the Singapore base. After receiving the Cabinet's approval for this step on 17 March 1924, an announcement was made in Parliament on the following day to the effect that no expenditure would be approved for the development of the Sembawang base in the 1924-25 estimates. Although dominion reaction to this news was mixed, the three service departments were heartened that the Clynes Committee accepted their request that they should be allowed to finish the preparatory drainage work on the site that had already been started.[48] While this decision had more to do with public health concerns than anything else, it could be construed as revealing something of a fissure in the government ranks on this project. It was to be cunningly exploited by all concerned in the months which followed. For the service departments and Governor Guillemard, small-scale work would continue unobtrusively on the Singapore base in the hope that, at worst, the project would be merely postponed by the Labour government rather than cancelled altogether.[49]

Whether this policy would have achieved much success in the long run had the Labour government remained in office for any length of time is extremely debatable, but the political climate in Britain was such that MacDonald's administration was undermined by various scandals and fell into disarray in October 1924, to be replaced by a Conservative administration headed by Stanley Baldwin. What Labour had basically suspended, the Tories were anxious to restore in one form or another and a commitment to reactivate the scheme for a Singapore base was made by Baldwin's Cabinet on 26 November 1924.[50] Despite a new gift of £250,000 from Hong Kong's Legislative Council on 16 December 1924, the hiatus brought about by Labour's lack of commitment to the original scheme had had bitter consequences. Apart from the sum of £100,000 offered by the New Zealand government which had been withdrawn, the Australian government opted to divert what would have been a sizeable contribution into paying for warship construction. Although the New Zealand government reversed its decision and approved a donation of £1 million, over eight instalments, to the Singapore base fund in April 1927, the Australian money was lost to the scheme. Nevertheless, the Federated Malay States were persuaded to help make up for this shortfall with a grant of £2 million on 23 June 1926.[51]

By then Baldwin's government had reviewed the nature of the entire project and under relentless pressure from Winston Churchill, in his capacity as Chancellor of the Exchequer, the Admiralty had scaled down the size of the dockyard facilities that would be offered at the naval base and thereby reduced the overall cost of what would, in effect, become a "truncated" version of the "Red Scheme." In essence, this meant that while docking and oil storage would proceed as planned, repair facilities would not be provided at Sembawang. Ships needing repair would have to proceed to the commercial dockyard at Keppel Harbour instead. Although the revised scheme could be enlarged if circumstances warranted it, the old pious hope that the "Red Scheme" might be upgraded to the "Green Scheme" was now lost forever. Whatever economies Churchill may have insisted upon for the good of the nation's finances, one is tempted to say that from this point onward the "Singapore Strategy" became ever more impractical and its corollary, the naval base, an unsuspecting hostage to fortune.[52]

Despite the parsimonious behaviour of the Chancellor, the Admiralty was determined to give the project some momentum. After toying with and then finally rejecting the idea of using an old German floating dock for the Sembawang base, the Admiralty eventually awarded a contract in November 1926 to Swan Hunter, a Wallsend firm of shipbuilders, for the construction of a large new 50,000-ton floating dock that would be built in two halves each containing several sections. Once completed the two halves of the dock would be towed out to Singapore by a group of Dutch tugs.[53] Both halves of the dock reached Singapore without mishap in mid-October 1928, a few weeks before the parts for a 1913 vintage, giant floating crane arrived. This substantial piece of equipment would take up to six months to be assembled, consisting as it did of 80 boxes of electrical material, eight kilometres of electrical wiring, and 25,000 nuts.[54] Of the £7.75 million that the Cabinet allocated in August 1926 for the completion of the first phase of the "Red Scheme" by 1935, a sum of £3.9 million was set aside by the Admiralty for the main construction work on the graving dock and the wharves for the Sembawang base that would begin in the 1928–29 financial year and was scheduled to last for seven years. Various internationally established civil engineering firms tendered for this contract before it was secured in September 1928 by the lowest bidder, Sir John Jackson (Singapore) Ltd., whose estimate undercut even the Admiralty's figure for this work by more than £170,000.[55]

Although the tempo of the work on the Singapore naval base was at last being increased, the question as to what represented the best means of defending it remained to be settled. Essentially the crux of the matter revolved around the relative merits of a mix of heavy, medium and light artillery pieces as opposed to a combination of torpedo bombers, fighters and seaplanes in providing the most effective defensive screen of protection. A contentious dispute in the Chiefs of Staff Committee (COS) pitting the Admiralty and WO on one side against the Air Ministry on the other lasted for much of the inter-war period. It became increasingly acrimonious and was only temporarily resolved in July 1926 when Baldwin urged a compromise between the service departments.[56]

As a result of this decision, three 15" guns were to be installed on the island; one at Tanah Merah near Changi, roughly 19 km from the naval base, covering the causeway, Johore Bahru, the eastern part of the Johore Strait, and out to sea, and the other pair near the intersection of Ulu Pandan Road and what is now Clementi Road in the southwest of the island, known as the Buona Vista Battery. Although the 15" gun at Changi had a full arc of fire of 360 degrees, one of the pair of guns at Buona Vista was to be given a Mark I mounting which would restrict its capacity to bear on targets to roughly 180 degrees. While adequate for the task of shelling any enemy vessels seeking to attack from the western or southern approaches, it could only bear on part of the Johore coast lying well to the west of the causeway. It was planned to provide the other 15" gun assigned to the Buona Vista Battery with a Mark II mounting which would give it a 240-degree traverse and the possibility of being increased, if need be, to 360 degrees. All three 15" guns had a maximum range of about 32 km.[57]

Despite the compromise solution reached in 1926, the crucial issue of what constituted Singapore's best system of coastal defence in the long term was still anything but settled. After the technical proficiency of some, admittedly pre-war, 9.2" guns was suddenly called into question by their unsatisfactory performance in artillery trials held at Portsmouth and Malta in 1928, the controversy between the service departments on the subject of coastal defence threatened to ignite once more. Sir Laming Worthington-Evans, the Secretary of State for War, was so appalled by the results of the artillery trials that he wasted little time in communicating his level of concern to the CID. As a result of his intervention, the CID and the Cabinet responded by embargoing all spending on both the 9.2" and 15" guns until the 1929–30 financial year.[58] While the government had no intention of investing its meagre financial resources in heavy guns that were both demonstrably slow in their rate of fire and inaccurate to boot, the obsolescence of the veteran pieces used in the trials had certainly been a factor in their dismal performance. Later versions of both the 6" and 9.2" guns and their mountings, were radical improvements on their forerunners. As a result of increasing the elevation at which shells were fired from these guns from 15 degrees to 35 degrees, and by slightly raising their muzzle velocity using a shell that the experts would describe as a "better ballistic shape", the maximum range for both types of gun was improved massively. By the 1930s the 9.2" gun had increased its maximum range from 15,000 yards (13.7km) to twice that range or a little over 17 miles (27.4km), while the maximum range of the 6" had risen from 11,000 yards (10km) to 25,000 yards (22.8km).[59]

As the WO wrestled with the task of overcoming the technical deficiencies of its medium guns, the entire Singaporean project was stalled once more by a political crisis in Britain. After defeating Baldwin's Conservative government in the general election of May 1929, the Labour Party, under Ramsay MacDonald's leadership, returned to power in Westminster in early June. Given its previous policy on Singapore in 1924, it came as no surprise to anyone that the new government began an immediate policy review of the proposed naval base and its defences.[60] Unlike 1924, however, the government found itself enmired in a situation which was far more complicated than the one it had encountered when it was last in office. While it was opposed to extravagance, the government quickly discovered that its hands were tied to some extent by financial commitments to the Singapore project that could not be easily broken. Apart from the gifts the previous Conservative government had already received from Commonwealth sources for the base and the money already spent on the floating dock and site preparations for permanent naval structures at Sembawang, MacDonald's administration was well aware of the financial implications that would be incurred if it reneged on the Jackson contract and the extent of the refunds that would have to be made to its colonial and dominion donors. If significant economies could have been made from either abandoning or cancelling the Singapore project, the government might well have been tempted to do so. When the figures were drawn up, however, the cost-benefit analysis made such a policy remote.[61] Instead the government played for time, operating if not quite a "stop-go" policy, one that used a de-acceleration technique favoured by those who cannot quite make up their mind on what to do for the best and hope that circumstances will come to their rescue in due course.[62]

Developments on the International Stage 1929–37

MacDonald pinned his faith on the wiles of diplomacy and the appeal of disarmament to effect change in international relations. Knowing that Anglo-American naval relations had reached a glacial level at the ill-fated Geneva Conference of 1927 and realising that unless checked this antagonism could pose real problems for Britain in the future, MacDonald sought ways of establishing much closer links with President Herbert Hoover than Baldwin had been able to cultivate with Calvin Coolidge.[63] Heartened by the success of his visit to Washington in the late autumn of 1929, MacDonald saw his opportunity to build on this promising beginning by agreeing to a revision of the Washington treaties in ways favourable to the United States. He hoped that if he gave the US Navy some satisfaction on the issue of "heavy" cruisers, the Americans would drop or at least amend their naval building plans and embrace the concept of disarmament once more. MacDonald's faith in the London Naval Conference held from January-April 1930 was upheld by the success of the proceedings and the improvement in Anglo-American relations that resulted from these deliberations.[64] Even so, the Japanese could be said to have fared even better than the other two major naval powers in the final provisions of the London treaty.[65] Much, therefore, depended on the future quiescence of Japan. As long as democracy prevailed, the military threat of Japan was likely to be curtailed. If, however, Taisho democracy was to fall from grace, the danger exhibited in the East Asian region from a militarily resurgent Japan was likely to be very great indeed.

Important though the London Naval Conference was for Anglo-American relations in particular, the Commonwealth countries needed to be reassured at the Imperial Conference which convened in London in October 1930 that the British government had not compromised their defensive security in its quest for *realpolitik.* Lulled by promises to complete the Singapore naval and air bases in due course, the delegates agreed to a suspension of expenditure on all work not covered by the Jackson contract for a period of five years. This meant, in effect, that no actual investment in either the defences of the base or its essential dockyard equipment could be undertaken from official sources.[66] While this did not preclude the WO from running further artillery trials and making improvements to its medium and heavy guns, the fact that the Admiralty's floating dock in the Johore Strait and the island's oil stocks, some 759,000 tons on 31 May 1931, could now be considered defenceless enabled the Air Ministry to steal a march on the more senior service departments, by establishing an aerial presence in Singapore to provide defensive cover for these installations before any crucial decision about coastal defences would be made by the next Imperial Conference.[67]

Despite their international significance, both of these conferences were overshadowed by the shock waves of the Wall Street Crash. In the weeks and months that followed the eclipse of the New York Securities Exchange in October 1929, the world's economic picture became distorted beyond belief as the Great Depression set in. Colossal financial ruin and indebtedness, massive unemployment and contraction of trade, the collapse of credit and prices, together with the rise of economic stagnation and inflation, destroyed confidence, lives and governments around the world. In Britain the economic blizzard grew more severe in 1930 and became worse still in 1931. MacDonald's Labour government faltered under these ruinous economic conditions and yielded power in controversial circumstances to a MacDonald-led, but Tory-dominated, coalition government which felt it had little option but to come off the gold standard in September 1931.[68]

In the same month a fresh crisis provoked by the Japanese military erupted in East Asia. Using the Mukden incident as a pretext for a concerted attack on Manchuria, Japan issued a clear warning that its days of restraint were passed. In the coming months that impression was consolidated by its action in Shanghai and Jehol. Although international action was forthcoming in response to the threat posed by the Japanese to foreign investments in and around the commercial city of Shanghai and in defence of the burgeoning riverine trade on the Yangtze, the new strategic outlook for the British Commonwealth was disturbing to say the least.[69] If Japan could not be trusted to behave itself and was committed to a radical policy of militarism rather than democracy as now seemed certain, the dangers to the countries in the East and Southeast Asian region were stark. A more depressing catalogue of defence unpreparedness was difficult to imagine. To begin with, Hong Kong's vulnerability had been acknowledged for years and it remained basically indefensible by land; Singapore's new naval base was nothing more than a large construction site and years from completion; while British Malaya relied mainly on its dense physical vegetation rather than a functioning and integrated defence system to deter any invasionary force that might seek its natural riches. Further afield in the Asia-Pacific region, the Australasian Dominions were aghast at the implications of a powerful and dynamic Japan aggressively seeking imperial glory at the expense of those weaker nations standing in its way.

Something clearly had to be done to remedy these deficiencies and for once the British government responded by establishing a Cabinet sub-committee to advise the CID on the most appropriate coastal defence measures to be taken in the Far East. Its findings were evaluated and supported by the CID on 9 June 1932.[70] Baldwin's committee had not only plumped for the retention of the heavy gun, supported by suitable aircraft, but had also made a strong case for the completion of work on the first stage of Singapore's defences.[71] By this time the National government had distanced itself from the "Ten Year Rule," cancelled on 23 March 1932, and on 11 October it formally approved the recommendation of the CID and COS that the Singapore naval base should be turned into something worthy of the name. Additional money, £380,000, to that already budgeted for under the terms of the Jackson contract was to be found to make the graving dock operational.[72]

Despite Japan's aggressive intentions in East Asia, Ramsay MacDonald still pinned his considerable faith in the outcome of the Disarmament Conference at Geneva to provide a suitable forum to compose differences and agree upon a formula for peaceful co-existence between nations in the future. By March 1933, however, even he had little cause for optimism. Apart from Japan's announcement of its impending withdrawal from the League of Nations, a diplomatic impasse in Geneva threatened to ruin the dreams of those who had seen the Disarmament Conference as a force for good in international relations.[73] In the wake of these threatening developments, the Cabinet came under extreme pressure from the COS and CID to reduce the time taken to complete the work on the first stage of Singapore's defences by the summer of 1936, eighteen months earlier than planned. It accepted this advice and agreed on 12 April 1933 to support a resumption of the "truncated" version of the "Red Scheme," to build a second airfield on the island, and to dispatch a second torpedo bomber squadron, No. 100, from Britain to Singapore to join the squadrons of torpedo bombers, No. 36, and flying boats, No. 205, already stationed there. Not to be outdone by this activity, the Admiralty responded by announcing that it was about to overhaul and recommission the 15-year-old monitor HMS *Terror* — bristling with a variety of small guns, a pair of anti-aircraft guns, and ominously two 15" guns — before sending it out as a temporary depot ship for the Sembawang naval base. It would be joined in Singapore by the minelayer, HMS *Adventure*.[74]

Germany's withdrawal from both the Disarmament Conference and the League of Nations in October 1933 confirmed the impression that the world was becoming a more dangerous place to live in and that the

British Empire was exposed to risks from potential adversaries in at least two continents simultaneously. It was a threat that could not be ignored, but few National government ministers greeted the challenge with any sort of relish. Financial austerity programmes were still very much in vogue, money was tight, and the Treasury was unwilling to abandon its tough stance on government spending in a time of high unemployment and economic misfortune. Even so, the COS and CID were determined both to carry out a review of imperial defence to take account of this new strategic situation and to urge the Cabinet to appoint a specialist committee to evaluate the defence requirements of the British and reveal any deficiencies that existed in the realm of their service departments. Unfortunately, what the Defence Requirements Committee (DRC) most exposed was the schism which existed within the National government on what to do about the global predicament that Britain found itself in at this time. Those of a frugal disposition looked to keep defence expenditure as low as possible by seeking a diplomatic solution to their current difficulties, while the defence experts needed little encouragement to paint a gloomy picture of service inadequacy on a large scale which, in their opinion, could only be remedied by implementing an immediate five-year period of rearmament costing an estimated £82.38 million.[75] Finding it difficult to reconcile this acute division of opinion within its ranks, the government prevaricated and sent the DRC report to the Ministerial Committee on Disarmament for its considered opinion. Neville Chamberlain, who had consistently opposed any extensive programme of disarmament, once more took up the cudgels on behalf of the Treasury. He pointed out that Britain's dire financial situation was such that the government did not have the monetary resources to prepare for a simultaneous war on two fronts against Germany and Japan at any stage in the near future. While even Chamberlain conceded that it was desirable to retain Commonwealth support by completing the Sembawang base, he maintained his hearty dislike for the "Singapore Strategy" and much preferred to think of the dockyard as a home for light craft and submarines rather than as a first-class facility for the main fleet. As the Treasury's leading advocate, Chamberlain carried considerable weight in the Ministerial Committee on Disarmament and his vigorous defence of the necessity for financial restraint had an effect in cutting the deficiency programme recommended by the DRC to a sum of £50.3 million.[76] In slashing the DRC estimates by as much as 39%, and yet retaining the National government's overall commitment to the "Singapore Strategy," the Ministerial Committee's strategic expectations comfortably exceeded the means given to achieve those ends. It was nothing new. British defence planning had been beset by this type of problem for years as adherence to the *War Memorandum (Eastern)* without having the necessary resources at their disposal to do so showed only too well.[77]

By March 1935, however, the "muddling through" approach that had typified so much of British defence planning in the 1920s and 30s was in danger of being totally exposed. Once Germany's intention to ignore the disarmament restrictions of the Treaty of Versailles and build up its armed forces appreciably in the future had been announced by Hitler, the deterioration in Britain's strategic position was made apparent for all to see. Coming as it did after the excesses of the "Night of the Long Knives"' of 30 June–2 July 1934, and the failure of the Nazi putsch in Vienna later in that month, this latest news bulletin from Central Europe indicated that Hitler was in no mood for restraint. Now real, as distinct from purely nominal, potential threats existed on two widely scattered fronts. Britain's answer to this strategic dilemma was entirely self-serving. It sought to arrange a mutually satisfactory naval agreement, concluded in June 1935, to eliminate the prospect of a naval construction race between the RN and its German counterpart. While the Anglo-German Naval Agreement may have bought off its North Sea rivals at least temporarily, it did untold damage to Britain's diplomatic credibility.[78]

As Britain's stock fell internationally in the months which followed, so the threats to world peace grew steadily both in number and menace. Fascism, or some military variant of it, was definitely on the march. Italy took the imperial plunge by invading Abyssinia in October 1935. Japan followed by refusing to accept any further naval disarmament and withdrew from the London Naval Conference in January 1936. Germany then proceeded to tear up both the Treaty of Versailles and the Locarno agreement by re-occupying the Rhineland in March 1936.[79] Added to these upheavals was the constitutional crisis that enveloped Republican Spain in the summer of 1936, touching off a bloody civil war with the right-wing Falangist movement led by Francisco Franco who could count upon military help from both Italy and Germany in his quest for power in the Iberian peninsula. If one also took into account the formation of both the Rome-Berlin Axis in October 1936 and the Anti-Comintern Pact between Germany and Japan in November 1936, the overall picture was dark and brooding.[80] Despite being long on rhetoric, the British failed to take decisive action in the wake of any of these crises because they wished to avoid provoking any of the belligerents into committing hostile acts against them or their interests.

The Acid Test for the "Singapore Strategy"

By the beginning of 1937, therefore, all but the most myopic of ministers could see what the fraught global situation actually meant for the "Singapore Strategy." Only two basic questions needed to be answered. First, how could Britain afford to send off the bulk of its capital ship fleet on a foray into Southeast Asian waters for an indeterminate period of time to confront the IJN when a potential military foe of some substance existed just across the North Sea and could launch a surprise attack on the United Kingdom at any time? Second, if war erupted in Europe before it did in the Far East, was there any chance that the "Singapore Strategy" would still be implemented once war with Japan broke out? These were vital questions that went right to the heart of the concept that had underpinned imperial defence for more than a decade. When the COS and the Naval Staff addressed these questions in two important memoranda in the early months of 1937, their candid and authoritative answers were not appreciated by those in the Cabinet who preferred the portrayal of a less bleak outlook on matters of defence and foreign policy.[81] While the British statesmen indulged in a bout of being conservative with the truth in their discussions with the delegates to the Imperial Conference, the COS remained very defensive about an automatic British commitment to the "Singapore Strategy" in their *Far East Appreciation* of June 1937.[82]

Whatever ambiguity surrounded this contentious strategic concept, the shadow cast by militarism — with its penchant for international banditry and terrorism — was sufficient to act as an essential catalyst for change bringing about an abrupt end to the National government's hitherto languid attitude towards the completion of the Singapore naval base and its defences and replacing it with a new-found determination to get the job done as expeditiously as possible. If deterrence was going to be a key factor in future British Far Eastern defence policy, the base and the island's defences, both artillery and aerial, had to be operational. Even before Sultan Ibrahim's timely Silver Jubilee gift of £500,000 in May 1935 — £400,000 of which was used by the WO for the provision of two more 15" guns at Tanah Merah near Changi, with the balance being given to the Air Ministry for work on new airfields at Sembawang and Tengah, and additional accommodation at Kallang — defence preparations had been pushed forward with increasing momentum.[83] This was seen both in terms of the burgeoning strength of the Singapore garrison, which had risen by this time to over 3000 officers and men, and in the military-related construction works that had transformed the area between Sembawang and Changi from an undeveloped, marshy bog into a sprawling service installation that apart from the naval base itself

Sembawang naval base

boasted new concrete gun emplacements, airfields, hangars, workshops, stores, pumping stations, power stations, a hospital, barrack blocks, semi-detached, and detached housing units.[84]

Another key factor in helping to promote change in British military thinking on the defence of Singapore was the appointment of Maj.-Gen. Sir William Dobbie as GOC Malaya Command in November 1935. His views on the nature and complexity of the task confronting him differed fundamentally from the established WO doctrine that had held sway in London for more than a decade. Principally, Dobbie contested the comfortable — and flawed — assumptions that the British military had entertained for so long, to the effect that the Japanese would find it virtually impossible to penetrate the natural terrain and tropical vegetation of the Malayan peninsula even if they succeeded in putting their troops ashore, and that because of these perceived difficulties the Japanese were most likely to carry out a naval assault on Singapore if war broke out between them and the British. According to this orthodox view, the British would react to such a threat by invoking the "Singapore Strategy" once war had been declared and would appear in sufficient force to thwart any attempt by the IJN to subdue the fortress of Singapore and establish a naval dominance in the area. In the pre-Dobbie days the British erroneously believed that any attempt to land troops in Malaya would be impossible during the monsoon season. They also thought that the Japanese would be unable to establish a chain of forward air bases close enough to Singapore to serve as a bombing threat to the island and its inhabitants. Furthermore, the British never seemed to doubt that their intelligence-gathering was sophisticated enough to provide advance warning of any and all Japanese movements as and when they happened in the region.[85]

Dobbie's tenure in command shook up this fatal air of complacency. After studying the problem and travelling around Malaya, Dobbie came to the firm conclusion that the "Singapore Strategy" rested on shaky foundations — with the official "period before relief" unrealistically set at 42 days — and that an overland, as distinct from seaward, attack by the Japanese on Singapore was not only possible but also quite likely in the future. Apart from commenting upon the considerable improvements the Japanese had made in their landing craft and operations in recent years, he also pointed out that contrary to ill-informed opinion, Malaya was no longer the dense area of inhospitable jungle and mosquito-infested swamps it had once been. While it was true there were still areas that conformed to this description, a number of good new roads had been built across the length and breadth of the country to avoid these natural hazards and improve communications. Dobbie had little doubt that these new roads would certainly be used with great effect by Japanese infantry and artillery to speed up their advance southwards down the peninsula towards the island fortress of Singapore. As he grew more familiar with the myriad problems of orchestrating an effective defence of his operational theatre against a likely Japanese foe in the future, Dobbie began to articulate a new and revolutionary thesis, namely, that the successful defence of Singapore was actually dependent upon the defence of Malaya as a whole.[86] With this in mind he sought to establish a coordinated defence of Malaya in which more men and matériel would be needed up-country in the northern states as well as in the southern state of Johore to slow or halt a Japanese advance. Contending that he would be between eight and eleven regular battalions short of what he needed for this purpose even with the troops promised by the WO in an emergency, Dobbie urged the British authorities in July 1938 to increase the planned level of reinforcements. In addition, he requested an additional 16 armoured cars (he already had four), 15 tanks (he had none at this stage), and the erection of a suitable defensive perimeter in the state of Johore on a line strategically drawn from Kulai to Kota Tinggi to ensure that the defenders would reap maximum advantages from the local topography and be far enough away from the causeway to prevent the Japanese artillery from shelling the naval base at Sembawang. Dobbie estimated that it would cost £250,000 and take 12 months to complete the initial work on these defensive positions. Despite emphasising the urgency of the problem, he was unable to convince the WO to part with more than £60,000 for this defensive perimeter. Although a start was made on this work, the project eventually lost its impetus and stalled with only £23,000 spent on the entire project.[87]

Dobbie was not alone in considering that action was needed to improve the defensive posture of the British in Malaya. RAF Far East Command had also reached that conclusion by 1936 and had begun to construct a network of airbases in northern and eastern Malaya which could be used by a strike force of bomber aircraft to destroy and scatter any IJN fleet far out to sea before it had a chance to launch an invasion of either the Thai or Malayan coastlines. While this idea was sound in principle, RAF Far East Command did not have either the bombers assigned to them or even a promise that they would be so deployed in future. Unfortunately, the mere existence of these airbases posed a new and menacing dilemma for Malaya Command since it could not risk any of them falling into the hands of the Japanese. If such a disaster occurred, the Japanese would be in a position to use these bases to mount aerial attacks on the defensive positions of the Allies both throughout the peninsula and on the island of Singapore itself. Clearly the airbases had to be defended at all cost. Malaya Command fully appreciated this fact yet simply did not have the forces at its disposal to do so.[88]

By the time Dobbie relinquished command as GOC Malaya to Maj.-Gen. L.V. Bond in August 1939, the huge King George VI dry dock at Sembawang had been opened with considerable fanfare by Sir Shenton Thomas, Governor of the Straits Settlements, on 15 February 1938, the official "period before relief" had been raised twice (April 1937 and June 1939) to stand at 90 days (it would be raised again and doubled to 180 days at the outset of the European War in September 1939), and the artillery defences of Singapore — 18 x 6" guns, 6 x 9.2" guns, and 5 x 15" guns — had been largely completed, making it one of the most heavily defended pieces of territory in the entire British Empire.[89] Given the controversy that has dogged the issue of whether the guns were sited properly for more than fifty years, it is as well to remember that all 18 of the 6" guns, all six of the 9.2" guns and three of the five 15" guns were on mountings that enabled them to traverse 360 degrees so that they could fire landward (northwards) into Johore as well as out to sea in any other direction.[90] A solitary pair of 6" guns (Pasir Laba Battery) were situated on the west coast of the island, the northeast was well-served with four pairs of 6" guns (Changi, Beting Kusah, Sphinx [Pulau Tekong Besar], and Pengerang [Johore] Batteries), three 9.2" guns (Tekong Besar Battery), and three 15" guns (Johore Battery), while the south enjoyed protection from four pairs of 6" guns (Silingsing [Pulau Brani], Serapong Spur [Blakang Mati], Siloso [Blakang Mati], and Labrador Batteries, three 9.2" guns (Connaught Battery [Blakang Mati]), and two 15" guns (Buona Vista Battery).[91] As the threat to Singapore was historically perceived as coming from the sea and since the commercial hub of the island lay in the south, the majority of the traditional coastal artillery was also to be found in that part of the island protecting the harbour at Keppel and its approaches. Of all the guns situated in the south, the Buona Vista Battery may have been the least effective. While a pair of its guns could indeed train on the western approaches to the Strait of Johore, their arc of fire was restricted and proved insufficient to bombard targets either on the causeway or to the east of it.[92] Even so, the biggest drawback of the guns undoubtedly was not their siting but the type of ammunition with which they were stocked. Instead of having adequate high-explosive rounds for use against Japanese invasion forces, the 15" guns were supplied instead with 1200 armour-piercing shells primarily designed for use against shipping targets rather than for destroying enemy infantry or artillery. By early 1942 the 9.2" and 6" guns were stocked with 150 and 900 high-explosive rounds respectively, while the 15" guns had none.[93]

Internationally the last years of the 1930s were sombre ones for the democracies. After the much-publicised failure of appeasement in Europe, coupled with the military invasion of China by the Japanese, the hideous threat of a global war appeared an ever likelier prospect. Yet just when the British Commonwealth looked as though it would be confronted with a triple alliance of Germany, Italy and Japan against it, the strategic situation was unexpectedly and dramatically transformed to its advantage. Germany's astounding revelation on 22 August 1939 that it was to become associated with its sworn enemy, the Soviet Union, in a military pact abruptly ruptured the German-Japanese condominium and when Italy declined to declare war after Germany attacked Poland on 1 September 1939, the war was more confined than the leaders of the British Commonwealth had any right to expect only a few days before it broke out.[94] Moreover, after the collapse of Poland the nature of the Phoney War was such that the Commonwealth was afforded a few more months to make good its preparations before the European War took off in earnest. An eerie calm before the storm, it ended with the Norwegian débâcle in April 1940. A new phase in the European War was then struck

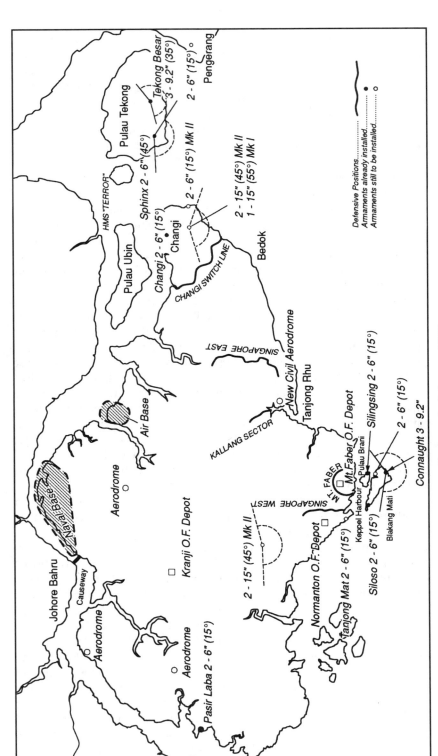

Singapore's defences, 1937

by Germany's devastating attack on the Low Countries and France in May 1940 and Italy's belated contribution to the Pact of Steel on 10 June 1940.[95]

Despite Winston Churchill's accession to power as British Prime Minister on 10 May 1940, the news for the beleaguered Commonwealth continued to go from bad to worse. By mid-June France appeared on the verge of collapse and on 19 June Viscount Caldecote, the Secretary of State for Dominion Affairs, finally admitted that as things stood his government saw no hope of being able to despatch a fleet to Singapore.[96] If the "Singapore Strategy" was still not officially dead, it had become distinctly comatose. Nine days after his first momentous announcement on this score, Caldecote contacted the Menzies government in Canberra again and indicated that while the complex naval situation was difficult to circumvent in the short term, the British recognised the need to improve the land and air defences of Malaya.[97] In truth, a good deal needed to be done. Maj.-Gen. Bond had indicated as much in his paper on the defence of Malaya of 13 April 1940. His impressive memorandum revealed the weak overall state of British defence preparations in the peninsula. Bond's thesis pulled few punches and basically reiterated the theme that the whole of Malaya would have to be held and that it was inappropriate to think of holding only a handful of states. In order to accomplish this objective successfully, Bond estimated that he needed a vastly increased infantry garrison strength of between 39 and 42 battalions. At the time his report was being written he had only nine regular battalions at his disposal![98] Bond was, however, a realist and believed that he was neither going to get the garrison that he needed to hold Malaya nor receive sufficient help from the RN to disrupt or deter the Japanese from launching an assault on the country. Therefore he recommended that the British should put their faith in the RAF to take on a substantially increased role in the defence of Malaya as this would reduce the number of British infantry troops to a total of 25 battalions supported by a company of armoured vehicles and by three anti-tank batteries. Unfortunately, as late as September 1940 there were still only eight air force squadrons with some 90 first-line aircraft in the whole of Malaya even though the COS in their *Far East Appreciation* of August 1940 basically agreed with Bond's analysis, if not with all of his figures, and stated that 22 squadrons with some 336 first-line aircraft and 18 battalions were needed to hold Malaya and Singapore. Until such time as the air force strength for Malaya reached this anticipated level, the COS were in favour of reinforcing the infantry garrison to a strength of three divisions or roughly 27 battalions.[99]

By the time American, British and Dutch representatives gathered in Singapore to begin discussions on a tactical appreciation of the regional defence situation in late October 1940, the strategic picture greeting them looked ever more forlorn with the Japanese move into Tonkin on 22 September 1940, followed by the announcement of the Tripartite Pact linking Germany, Italy and Japan five days later. When the top-secret Singapore Defence Conference report was finally written up and distributed to interested parties, it made grim reading for those opposed to Japanese expansionism within the region. Highlighting the prodigious scale of the military deficiencies in the defence of Malaya and Singapore, the bleak report served notice to all concerned that unless something dramatic happened, and soon, to cope with these problems the fate of the region could well be sealed.[100] Left bereft by the apparent failure of the "Singapore Strategy" to come to their rescue, some of the Commonwealth leaders began to regard the Americans from this time forward as being their only hope of military salvation.[101] Unfortunately, wishful thinking was no substitute for actual defence preparations and by early 1941 the Americans had intimated that they were not going to pull the British, Dutch or French chestnuts out of the fire in the Far East.[102] If the European colonial powers and their territories in the region were going to survive they would have to do so largely, if not exclusively, on their own.[103]

Notes

1. W.D. McIntyre, *The Rise and Fall of the Singapore Naval Base*, London, 1979, 3-4.

2. I. Nish, *Alliance in Decline: A Study of Anglo-Japanese Relations 1908-1923*, London, 1972, 115-57.

3. Ibid., 249-367.

4. M.H. Murfett, "Look Back in Anger: The Western Powers and the Washington Conference of 1921-1922," in B.J.C. McKercher (editor), *Arms Limitation and Disarmament: Restraints on War, 1899-1939*, Westport, Conn., 1992, 84.

5. M.H. Murfett, "'Are We Ready?' The Development of American and British Naval Strategy, 1922-39," in J.B. Hattendorf and R.S. Jordan (editors), *Maritime Strategy and the Balance of Power*, London, 1989, 214-42.

6. S.W. Roskill, *Naval Policy Between the Wars. Vol.I. The Period of Anglo-American Antagonism 1919-1929*, London, 1968, 275-88.

7. McIntyre, 21-23.

8. N.H. Gibbs, *Grand Strategy. Vol.I. Rearmament Policy*, London, 1976, 3-6.

9. J. Neidpath, *The Singapore Naval Base and the Defence of Britain's Eastern Empire, 1919-1941*, Oxford, 1981, 29-31.

10. Roskill, 279.

11. I. Hamill, *The Strategic Illusion: The Singapore Strategy and the Defence of Australia and New Zealand*, Singapore, 1981, 286.

12. McIntyre, 23.

13. Neidpath, 34-54.

14. Ibid.

15. McIntyre, 22-23.

16. PRO, CAB23/286, Cabinet Conclusions 50/21(3), 16 June 1921.

17. Murfett, "Look Back in Anger," 83-103.

18. The term "two-power naval standard" refers to a desire on the part of the RN to be of a size at least equivalent to the fleets of its two most formidable naval adversaries combined. Given the global distribution of the British Empire, this strategic gauge was seen by many within the Admiralty as being a minimum level of security for the mother country. As time went on, however, the concept became associated with the bygone age of *Pax Britannica*. When the term was initially proposed in the late nineteenth century the RN's two main rivals were France and Russia. This changed with the destruction of the Russian Fleet at the battle of Tsushima Strait in May 1905 and the

rise of the German High Seas Fleet. By 1921, however, the RN's two closest challengers were the USN and the IJN.

19. One of the key features of the Five Power Naval Limitation Treaty was the acceptance by all the signatories of a non-fortification clause which ensured that neither the British nor the Americans could build or maintain a first-class naval base closer to Japan than Singapore or Pearl Harbor respectively. Singapore stood 2888 nautical miles distant from Tokyo and Pearl Harbor, on the island of Oahu in the Hawaiian chain, was 3374 nautical miles from the Japanese capital. As a result of this clause, the British could not bring Hong Kong up to first-class standard even if they wished to and the Americans faced similar restrictions with Subic Bay and Cavite on the island of Luzon in the Philippines, or any of the islands in the Central Pacific, such as Guam, Midway, Truk, or Wake Island.

20. For an examination of the strategic problems facing the British after the Washington Conference, see Murfett, "'Are We Ready?,'" 214-42.

21. M.H. Murfett, *Fool-proof Relations: The Search for Anglo-American Naval Cooperation During the Chamberlain Years, 1937–1940*, Singapore, 1984, 4-12.

22. See the table charting the changes made in the "period before relief" in Ong C.C., "Major General William Dobbie and the Defence of Malaya, 1935–38," *Journal of Southeast Asian Studies*, Vol. XVII, No.2, 1986, 288.

23. See Hamill, 314; McIntyre, 213-14; P. Haggie, *Britannia at Bay*, Oxford, 1981, 209; P. Lowe, *Great Britain and the Origins of the Pacific War in East Asia, 1937–1941*, Oxford, 1977, 281; A.J. Marder, *Old Friends, New Enemies: The Royal Navy and the Imperial Japanese Navy. Vol.I. Strategic Illusions 1936–1941*, Oxford, 1981, 506; J. McCarthy, *Australia and Imperial Defence 1918–39: A Study in Air and Sea Power*, St. Lucia, Queensland, 1976, 55-63; M.H. Murfett, "Living in the Past: A Critical Re-examination of the Singapore Naval Strategy, 1918–1941," in *War & Society*, Vol.II, No.I, 1993, 97. For a less ascerbic treatment of the "Main Fleet to Singapore" concept, see Neidpath, 221-22.

24. Murfett, "Living in the Past," 80.

25. Roskill, 347-48.

26. McIntyre, 26.

27. Ibid., 31.

28. R. Cheong, "The Singapore Naval Base: A Local History," *The Pointer, Supplement*, August 1991, 11-12.

29. McIntyre, 31-33.

30. Roskill, 347-48.

31. Neidpath, 153-55.

32. PRO, CAB2/3, CID 165th meeting, 30 November 1922, & 168th meeting, 14 December 1922.

33. C.S. Gray, "Johore, 1910-1941, Studies in the Colonial Process," Unpublished Ph.D. dissertation, Yale University, 1978, 17-24, 33-37, 45. McIntyre, 11-12, 28. See also Zaimiah binte Mohd. Adam, "Sultan Ibrahim of Johore 1873-1959," Unpublished B.A. Hons. Academic Exercise, University of Malaya in Singapore, 1961.

34. Ibid., pp.24, 361; E. Robertson, *The Japanese File: Pre-War Japanese Penetration in Southeast Asia*, Singapore, 1979, 27. For a useful guide to the available literature on Japanese investments in Malaya, see Ong C.C., *The Landward Defence of Singapore [1919-1938]*, Singapore, 1988, 18-19.

35. Contrast the figures quoted by McIntyre, 31, 33, with those used by Neidpath, 103-04.

36. Cheong, "Singapore Naval Base," 15-16.

37. Neidpath, 104.

38. PRO, CAB16/182, Admiralty Memorandum, A New Standard of Naval Strength, 26 April 1937, submitted to Defence(Plans)Policy Committee, DP(P)3, Appendix to Enclosure, paragraphs 6-14.

39. For an interesting slant on the "Singapore Strategy," see I. Cowman, "Main Fleet to Singapore? Churchill, the Admiralty, and Force Z," in *The Journal of Strategic Studies*, Vol.17, No.2, 1994, 79-93.

40. Hamill, 314.

41. McIntyre, 55.

42. Ibid., p.56; Hamill, 63-70.

43. McIntyre, 56; Hamill, 66-67.

44. Murfett, "Living in the Past," 82.

45. Ibid.

46. For another blatant example of this type of policy that was tried later in the 1930s, see Murfett, *Fool-proof Relations*, 14-161.

47. Hamill, 71.

48. Ibid., pp.71-98.

49. McIntyre, 39-45.

50. Hamill, 99.

51. McIntyre, 55-66.

52. Ibid., 45-51; Hamill, 124-34.

53. *Straits Times*, 17 November 1926, 3 January 1928.

54. *Straits Times*, 13, 16 October, 3 November 1928.

55. McIntyre, 67.

56. Ibid., 69-85.

57. E.R. Alfred, "The Famous `Wrong Way' Guns of Singapore. Where Are They Now?," *Pointer*, Vol.12, No.1, 1985, 91-102; Ong, *Landward Defence*, 7-17. It is interesting to note, however, that in an entry dated 9 February 1942 in the War Diary of Faber Fire Command, the point was made that neither 15" gun at the Buona Vista Battery could bear on the enemy approaching from the north. In a further handwritten note written in the War Diary by the same officer the following observation was made: "...the 15 inch equipments at Buona Vista could not bear further north than 30 degrees (ie. Sungei Penda on the southern Johore coast west of Pasir Laba)." PRO, WO172/180, War Diary, Faber Fire Command, 9 and 11 February 1942. This certainly suggests that even with a Mark II mounting the second 15" gun could not traverse more than 240 degrees at most.

58. Hamill, 121-22; Neidpath, 115-16.

59. Alfred, "Famous `Wrong Way' Guns," 102.

60. Neidpath, 117-21.

61. Ibid., 118.

62. Selwyn Lloyd became infamous for this technique when he was Chancellor of the Exchequer in Macmillan's Conservative administration in the early 1960s.

63. R.W. Fanning, "The Coolidge Conference of 1927: Disarmament in Disarray," in McKercher, 105-27; D. Marquand, *Ramsay MacDonald*, London, 1977, 501-09.

64. G.C. Kennedy, "The 1930 London Naval Conference and Anglo-American Maritime Strength, 1927–1930," in McKercher, 149-71.

65. Neidpath, 118-19.

66. McIntyre, 99-102.

67. Although the oil reserves being accumulated in the storage tanks at the Normanton depot in the southwest of the island might be considered sufficient for peacetime purposes, they would have been wholly inadequate had a prolonged war broken out. As early as 1924 Lord Beatty had informed the CID that the Eastern Fleet in wartime would use 3.3 million tons of oil annually. Neidpath, 53, 116-17, 120-21.

68. Marquand, 518-670.

69. Haggie, 144-52.

70. PRO, CAB2/5, CID 256th meeting, 9 June 1932.

71. PRO, CAB5/7, CIC Paper 370C, Report of the Coastal Defence Committee, 24 May 1932.

72. McIntyre, 110.

73. Marquand, 694-98, 716-19, 724, 747-49, 751-56.

74. McIntyre, 111-12; *Straits Times*, 13 June, 9 December 1933; C. Shores and B. Cull with Yasuho Izawa, *Bloody Shambles. Vol.I. The Drift to War to the Fall of Singapore*, London, 1992, 16.

75. Murfett, "Living in the Past," 84.

76. Ibid., 84-85.

77. Ibid., 82-84.

78. Gibbs, 133-85.

79. Ibid., 187-272; Haggie, 78-101.

80. Murfett, "Living in the Past," 86.

81. PRO, CAB24/268, COS 560, Review of Imperial Defence, 22 February 1937; CAB2/ 6, CID 288th meeting, 11 February 1937; CAB16/182, Admiralty Memo, A New Standard of Naval Strength, 26 April 1937, DR(P)3.

82. PRO, CAB 16/182, COS 596, Far East Appreciation 1937, 14 June 1937, DP(P)5.

83. McIntyre, 120-22.

84. *Straits Times*, 7 April 1934, 22 March, 25 May 1935; S. Kathiravelu, "Fortifications of Singapore 1819–1942," Unpublished Academic Exercise, University of Malaya in Singapore, 1957, 49-53.

85. Ong, "Major General William Dobbie," 282-83.

86. Ibid., 282-306.

87. Ibid.; P. Elphick, *Singapore: The Pregnable Fortress: A Study in Deception, Discord and Desertion*, London, 1995, 27-31. See also A.C. Bell, *History of the Manchester Regiment: First and Second Battalions 1922-1948*, Altrincham, 1954, 39-42.

88. PRO, AIR23/7761, RAF Far East Monthly General Summary of Work, January 1937– July 1939; WO172/2, War Diary, GHQ Far East, June 1940; H. Probert, *The Forgotten Air Force: The Royal Air Force in the War Against Japan 1941-1945*, London, 1995, 16-17; C. Kinvig, *Scapegoat: General Percival of Singapore*, London, 1996, 116-17.

89. B. Montgomery, *Shenton of Singapore: Governor and Prisoner of War*, London, 1984, 59.

90. Ong, *Landward Defence*, 12-17; Neidpath, 223-25; Hamill, 213-14.

91. Gabriel G. Thomas, "Fortress: A Military History of Blakang Mati Island," Unpublished BA Hons Thesis, NUS, 1996/97, and particularly Map 8, xvii.

92. Ibid.; Alfred, 91-102.

93. Ong, *Landward Defence*, 14-15.

94. Murfett, *Fool-proof Relations*, 41-268.

95. Ibid., pp.269-94; McIntyre, 160-65; Hamill, 304-06.

96. Lord Caldecote to Sir Geoffrey Whiskard, No. 406, in H. Kenway, H.J.W. Stokes and P.G. Edwards (editors), *Documents on Australian Foreign Policy 1937–49. Vol. III: January–June 1940* [hereafter *DAFP.III*], Canberra, 1979, 460. See M.H. Murfett, "When Trust is Not Enough: Australia and the Singapore Strategy," in C. Bridge and B. Attard (editors), *Between Empire and Nation: Australia's External Relations, 1901-39*, Melbourne, forthcoming 1998.

97. Lord Caldecote to Commonwealth Government, 459, 28 June 1940, *DAFP.III.*, 517-18.

98. Neidpath, 168-70.

99. Ibid., pp.171-72; McIntyre, 169-70.

100. McIntyre, 173-74; Commonwealth Govt. to Lord Cranborne (Secretary of State for Dominion Affairs), 212, 1 December 1940, in W.J. Hudson and H.J.W. Stokes (editors), *Documents on Australian Foreign Policy 1937-49. Vol.IV: July 1940–June 1941* [hereafter *DAFP.IV*], Canberra, 1980, 14.

101. Arthur W. Fadden (Acting Prime Minister) to Lord Cranborne, 285, 12 February 1941, *DAFP.IV*, 383.

102. Alan S. Watt (First Secretary of the Legation in Washington) to Dept. of External Affairs, 294, 13 February 1941, *DAFP.IV*, 400; Richard G. Casey (Minister to the United States) to Dept. of External Affairs, 318, 24 February 1941, *DAFP. IV*, 440-42.

103. As an example of what this appeared to involve, see Ong C.C., *Operation Matador: Britain's War Plans against the Japanese 1918-1941*, Singapore, 1997, 89-250.

7

Too Little, Too Late: Preparing for War 1941–1942

In the early evening of Sunday 15 February 1942, the defenders of Singapore surrendered the island to the Imperial Japanese Army (IJA). This was the most dramatic day in the history of Singapore, and it marked the end of a campaign which changed both the course of the war against Japan and the future of the British Empire itself. In a mere 70 days, the Allies lost their most important position in Southeast Asia. The British were pushed onto the periphery of the war against Japan, and Singapore was left at the mercy of a most brutal conqueror. The main cause of the fall of Singapore is clear: the military power of the British Empire was gravely overextended. Compromised by decisions dating back over twenty years, heavily engaged in a now global war, the British could not reinforce Singapore fast enough to hold it. In this clash of empires, the Japanese used to full effect the advantage of choosing the time and place for war and concentrating the necessary forces. But the real disaster was not that Singapore fell, but rather how fast and how feebly its defences crumbled. The campaign itself was decisively influenced by command decisions and leadership at the highest level and by the theatre commanders themselves. British grand strategy for war against Japan, and plans for the defence of Malaya and Singapore, were both fatally disjointed and then mishandled. The Japanese, on the other hand, proved that sometimes fortune does indeed favour the bold.

Strike South

Three points stand out when comparing how the Japanese and the Allies prepared for a possible struggle for Singapore from 1940. The first is an irony: both drew very similar conclusions about how Malaya and Singapore could best be attacked, and what the most tempting defensive response might be. Both protagonists also found themselves working in great haste to prepare a campaign plan and the necessary forces almost from scratch. But whereas Japanese preparations, while hasty, were crisp, efficient and focussed, Allied preparations were marred by cross-purposes, indecision and conflicting priorities. The Japanese sent well-prepared forces into battle with a clear idea of their objective and how to pursue it. The defenders failed utterly, at every level of command, to prepare a coherent defence of Singapore. The end result was clear: Singapore was all but lost before a shot was fired. If one cause for this stands out above all other factors, it must be the failure of British commanders to resolve a fatal contradiction in their plans for defence.

In July 1941, the Japanese government and high command decided on a fateful course of action: Japan would pursue its goal of imperial self-sufficiency by establishing control over Southeast as well as East Asia. Given that this might make a war with the Western Powers unavoidable, the Japanese armed forces stepped up their ongoing preparations for a possible clash with both the U.S.A. and the U.K. Planners decided that Japan must launch a strategic offensive aimed to overwhelm all Western forces in the western Pacific and Southeast Asia in five months, before they could dig in and be reinforced. The plan hinged on strategic surprise, speed, economy of force, and the success of two pivotal assaults: an air attack on the main base of the main Western force, the USN, in Hawaii, and the rapid conquest of the main Western military base and hub in Southeast Asia — Singapore.[1]

If Japanese forces could overwhelm Singapore before strong reinforcements arrived from the west, they would gain the advantage of the central position. This would deprive the Allies of the only operational base of any importance in the region. It would also allow the Japanese to push them apart by striking into Burma, the Philippines and the Dutch East Indies, isolating each Allied force and defeating it in detail. That would separate the British positions in India from Australia and from the American forces in the Central Pacific. The Japanese could then dig in to repel any counteroffensives, exploit the resources of Southeast Asia, and finish off their long war in China. The occupation of bases in southern French Indochina brought Japanese forces within striking distance of Singapore in late July, and provoked an economic embargo by the Western Powers in response. That brought Japan to the point of no return. Unwilling to abandon their imperial dream, the Japanese authorities moved in autumn 1941 towards war with the West and an assault on Malaya and Singapore.[2]

Contrary to lingering mythology, serious Japanese plans for an attack on Malaya and Singapore dated only from the autumn of 1940. Nor did the IJA have any experience in making war in the equatorial jungle terrain and climate of the area. But it did have much combat experience, notably in amphibious operations, and it enjoyed the luxury of choosing where and when to fight. Preparations for the conquest of Singapore began in earnest in January 1941, orchestrated by a small planning staff dominated by the brutal but efficient Lt.-Col. Tsuji Masanobu. Tsuji produced a crash course of intense and focussed training, based on extensive intelligence-gathering, culminating in large-scale exercises in amphibious and jungle warfare conducted in Taiwan and Hainan. His team produced a manual designed to guide the army specifically for operations in Malaya, entitled *Read This Alone — And the War Can be Won.* By the time Japanese strategic plans took shape, Tsuji's staff was ready to provide a battle doctrine tailored to the task at hand.[3]

The Japanese strategic offensive was so ambitious it stretched both armed forces to their limit. The IJA could not provide enough divisions to complete all operations with separate forces, so some formations were designated to move on to help with a second task after completing the first. This included formations assigned to the *25th Army*, which was assigned to conquer Singapore. But as Singapore was such an important objective, that army was given priority in selecting personnel, units and supporting arms. It was also placed under the command of the tough, dynamic and very experienced Lt.-Gen. Yamashita Tomoyuki, regarded as Japan's best field commander. Tsuji, the man most familiar with the theatre and the plan, was appointed Director of Operations at Yamashita's headquarters. Yamashita also received two of the IJA's toughest veteran formations, the *5th* and *18th Divisions*; they were reinforced by the untested but highly regarded *Imperial Guards Division*, and the *56th Division*. Supporting arms included a Tank Brigade boasting over 200 medium and light tanks, ample artillery — particularly light field guns, mobile and therefore very useful in close country — and strong engineering support, led by specially equipped bridging units. This amounted to over 80,000 combat troops. Yamashita counted heavily on his air and naval support, with good reason. The veteran *3rd Air Group* was ready to commit 450 combat aircraft. They were reinforced by naval air forces including the *22nd Naval Air Flotilla*, specially trained and equipped to destroy enemy warships. This gave the Japanese over 600 combat-ready aircraft for the campaign, led by the formidable *Zero* type single-engined fighter. The *Southern Fleet* deployed the battleships *Kongo* and *Haruna*, six modern heavy cruisers, and ample smaller vessels. With all this force, Yamashita was expected to overrun Malaya and take Singapore in less than 100 days, then release formations for further duty elsewhere.[4]

Speed and economy of force also shaped the campaign plan for Malaya and Singapore. Japanese planners knew the defenders were weak in the air and at sea, and rated the British-led troops as second-rate. But *25th Army* could not mount a deliberate advance with concentrated forces. It did not have enough ships to advance in full strength at once, but if it moved too slowly enemy reinforcements might arrive. Nor could it pay a heavy price for Singapore, with other tasks ahead. Planners decided to emphasise mobility over mass. Light striking forces would advance relentlessly, taking calculated risks with supply lines, to seize the initiative and keep the enemy off-balance. Lightly equipped infantry could move fast through the jungle, so it would be the main mobile and strike arm. Tanks would dominate the roads, to control the lines of supply, and of advance in any battle that ensued. Whenever the defenders made a stand, the infantry would move off the road to make deep flanking and encircling moves to dislodge or destroy them without slowing down. The navy would give the army the ability to strike wherever it wanted from the sea. The air forces would win command of the air and assist

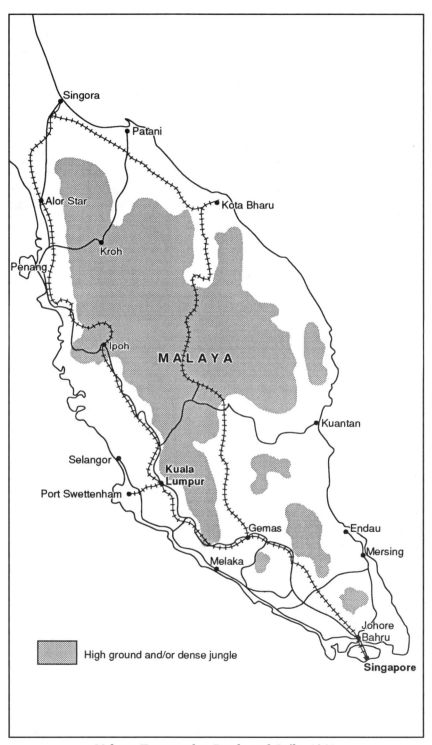

Malaya: Topography, Roads and Rails, 1941

the land battle. With this help and using its jungle warfare doctrine, *25th Army* would knock the enemy off-balance and keep him that way.

The Japanese expected the jungle-dominated terrain to favour a bold and mobile attacker over a defender trying to hold fixed positions. Restricted visibility in dense country would hamper efforts to use dug-in heavy firepower weapons to full effect. Providing the crucial first battle was won, the attackers could exploit the advantages of speed and mobility. If the defenders could be kept off-balance and prevented from regrouping in strength, there would be no need to mount deliberate set piece attacks. That would keep the advance moving and ease the strain on Japanese supply lines. It might also allow the Japanese to destroy the enemy army piecemeal, negating any threat from superior overall numbers.[5]

Japanese planners assumed from the start that any direct attack on Singapore and its great guns was a pointless gamble. The best way to take Singapore was to move through Malaya and assault it from the undefended north. In 1941, peninsular Malaya was thickly covered with jungle of varying density. An extensive mountain range ran like a spine through the centre of the peninsula. On the east coast, one railway line ran south from Kota Bharu into the interior, and one road ran west from Kuantan. There were no other routes of advance for large forces north of Johore, which itself was distant from Japanese air cover. West of the mountains on the other hand, the terrain was more mixed and a good deal more developed. The main trunk road and railway line ran south from the Thai border, through rice paddies and jungle in the north, mixed plains, plantations and jungle in the centre. There were extensive road networks in the central and southern regions. This all but forced an invader not willing to strike directly at Singapore or Johore to advance west of the mountains. Geography provided an opening: ports and airbases in southern Thailand had direct road and rail connections to the vulnerable areas in Malaya, and were within range of Japanese air cover. If the British did not violate Thai neutrality in a pre-emptive strike, the risky first landings could be made in the face of little or no opposition, a base could be secured, supplies and air cover moved up. The Japanese could then launch a two-pronged advance, down the road from Patani and along the road and railway from Singora, into Malaya.

This secure position was so enticing that Yamashita's planners insisted it must be seized immediately, coupled with a simultaneous direct assault on Kota Bharu to split the defenders and seize the airbases there. This would protect Japanese forces and bolster their own air support. Naval planners objected, arguing the enemy air force must be neutralised before the risky assault landings were attempted. Yamashita supported his staff, arguing the risk was acceptable given the weakness of the enemy air force, and time was a factor — the east coast monsoon would rule out landings after mid-December. The navy accepted this calculated risk and plans were finalised in late November. Attacking in Thailand would cover the first landings. Naval and air supremacy would isolate and distract the defenders. Speed, mobility and audacity would offset superior numbers. Yamashita directed his army to divide the enemy and defeat him in detail, as early and as far north as possible. His aim was to prevent the defenders from making any serious last-ditch stand in Singapore. To ease the strain on his supply lines, Yamashita left *56th Division* in Japan in reserve. When the Japanese forces were ordered to move on 2 December, they were as ready as they could reasonably be.[6]

Disjointed Defence

The same could not be said of the forces preparing to defend Malaya and Singapore. British, Indian, Australian, New Zealand, and Malay soldiers, sailors and airmen, supported by volunteer units drawn from the expatriate and Asian communities, had the advantage in only one respect — sheer numbers. Two major factors combined to leave the defences badly off-balance by December 1941: policy and grand strategy decisions made by the British government; and the interpretation of these decisions, and their own priorities, made by authorities on the spot. Disjointed grand strategy left authorities in Singapore in a compromised position. They made it worse by not sorting out cross-purposes and preparing ruthlessly for war.

Despite the situation in Europe in the summer of 1940, the British government did not change its policy regarding Malaya and Singapore. Local authorities were directed to concentrate on the production of rubber and tin for the Imperial war effort, two commodities which were strategic raw materials and valuable earners of American dollars. The COS appreciation in August 1940 confirmed that the naval base must be held — despite the fact the RN would not likely be able to use it — which meant all of Malaya must be held, and agreed the RAF should take the lead role in the defence. But British airpower was so overstretched it would not be possible to build up the RAF to the required strength until the end of 1941. In the meantime, Malaya Command must hold the line. The theatre commanders submitted their tactical appreciation in response in October. They stated that in order to take the lead the RAF would need 566 first line aircraft for Malaya and Singapore, with ample reserves. Until these were deployed, Malaya Command needed four divisions to fill the gap.[7] The decisions in London planted the seeds of disaster. The tactical appreciation provoked a spectacular feud between the service commanders in Singapore.

Bond argued that trying to hold all of Malaya without the necessary troops would lead to certain defeat as his forces would be spread too thin. Therefore he proposed to concentrate on the defence of Johore and Singapore, until reinforced. The new defence plan was based on the assumption that from the northern bases the RAF could decisively batter any invading force well before it reached Malaya. But in order to defend the bases Malaya Command would have to spread its small forces out in weak detachments. Yet the RAF was not strong enough to deal any such blow to an invader, and would not be for many months at best. If the enemy came first, Malaya Command would inevitably carry the brunt of the defence, on land. But it would be compromised from the start, spread out defending airbases. Bond insisted that if the Japanese attacked before full reinforcements arrived there would be risks no matter what strategy was adopted. If the army had to carry the fight, it would be better for it to concentrate to defend what it could. The RAF replied that this would allow the enemy to seize its northern bases, from which they could easily isolate and inexorably overwhelm Singapore. The argument reached the point where the service authorities in Singapore barely spoke to each other.[8]

Imperial authorities were unable to resolve these problems. Reinforcements were sent to Malaya Command from various quarters, more than doubling its strength by April 1941. Unfortunately, none of the formations was complete or combat-experienced, none had ever operated in the tropics, and some were far from fully trained.[9] Efforts to solve the command feud by establishing a new intermediate authority did as much harm as good. In October 1940 General Headquarters Far East Command was established, under Air Chief Marshal Sir Robert Brooke-Popham. The new headquarters was made responsible for operational control and the coordination of defence plans in Malaya/ Singapore, Burma and Hong Kong. Unfortunately, the RN was not placed under Brooke-Popham's direction, on the grounds that it had wider responsibilities in a larger area. Yet it controlled the Far East Combined Bureau (FECB) which all services relied on for intelligence on Japanese activities and capabilities. GHQ Far East was given only a tiny operations staff and no administrative staff. Brooke-Popham did not have the authority to change the defence strategy for Malaya. He saw the problem identified by Bond, but was not the kind of man ready to step on toes to force a reconsideration, or take action on his own. Now aged 63, years away from his last active command, having just completed a term as Governor of Kenya, Brooke-Popham was instead relied on to soothe ruffled feathers and provide an impression of stability and authority. His main mission remained to hold the naval base, for a service over which he had no control, and which could not promise to use it, but on which he relied for intelligence. The plan Brooke-Popham inherited called for his army to compromise itself to defend airbases his air force was too weak to use.[10]

This absurd situation indicates that the strategic dilemma confronting Singapore was not now seen as a major priority by the hard-pressed central direction of the war in London. Prime Minister Churchill made this clear in a comment to the COS on 13 January 1941 objecting to proposed RAF reinforcements for Malaya. Arguing that "the political situation in the area at that time" did not warrant such a diversion of forces badly needed in active theatres of war, Churchill pressed an alternative formulated in response to the COS paper of August 1940. He saw Singapore as a well-defended "Fortress," felt the Japanese would not attack unless the British were paralysed by the war in Europe, and insisted the Americans would almost certainly intervene right away even if they did. Because the Prime Minister also saw air and naval forces as very mobile, and the strain of the war in Europe as grave, he saw no point in tying up forces now to defend all of Malaya for fear it might eventually be attacked. This implicit support for Bond's ideas was part of an extended on-again off-again discussion between the Prime Minister and the COS which unwisely led to no real conclusion. The COS supported the strategy of defending all of Malaya as the only way to protect Singapore, despite being unable, for the moment, to provide the means. Only the CIGS, General Sir John Dill, went so far as to argue Singapore should be a higher priority in grand strategy than the Middle East. Churchill replied that the best policy was to build up large forces in the Middle East, which could prosecute the war there but respond rapidly to any crisis in the Far East. In April the Prime Minister directed that defence plans against Japan must assume American assistance would be available from the start, and ample warning would be provided — how was not made clear — of any Japanese attack. Churchill did not stop the COS from planning to defend all of Malaya, but did reduce the RAF reinforcements sent east.[11] The dilemma Bond spelt out, the contradiction between the strategy for the defence of Malaya and Singapore and the means on hand, would be solved by relying on time to make it possible to close the gap. The British Empire must concentrate on fighting Germany; it could not yet provide adequate forces for defence against Japan, but it would not abandon any positions.

This failure to close the gap between grand strategy and the local situation, or to at least take full responsibility for the real dilemma the Singapore authorities faced, was a grave oversight which must be laid at the feet of both the Prime Minister and the COS. This made it more apparent than ever that Far East Command could expect little help. The Americans remained reluctant to make any commitments for common action in advance. Both home governments expressly confirmed the strategy of concentrating against Germany first in spring 1941. The Dutch colonial authorities were keen to help but could offer little. British policy was to stay in step with the Americans, to avoid any confrontation with the Japanese unless the Americans were in the lead.[12] Unable to end the argument, unwilling to change plans on his own, all Brooke-Popham could do was change the atmosphere. In April and May 1941 he engineered the arrival of new service commanders in Singapore. Air Vice-Marshal C.W.H. Pulford became AOC Far East Command. Lt.-Gen. Arthur E. Percival took over as GOC Malaya Command. The new GOC soon welcomed Lt.-Gen. Sir Lewis Heath and his staff to take command of the Indian Army's III Corps, his major formation. Other important subordinates included Maj.-Gen. H. Gordon Bennett, commanding 8th Australian Division, and Maj.-Gen. Keith Simmons, Commander Singapore Fortress. These steps were meant to strengthen the defences, especially the appointment of Percival. Dill knew Percival well, rated him highly, and selected him for the post over the heads of several more senior officers. Dill knew Percival was more familiar with local conditions than anyone else, having served as Dobbie's GSO1 in 1936–37. Percival was in fact the main author of the appreciation in which Dobbie warned that the jungle of Malaya was not impassable to determined infantry, the east coast could be invaded during the monsoon, and the only way to defend Singapore was to defend the whole peninsula.[13] On these men, together with the Governor of the Straits Settlements and High Commmissioner for the Malay States, Sir Shenton Thomas, now rested the defence of Malaya and Singapore.

Percival returned to Singapore with a good idea of the low status of his command in British grand strategy and the plans and preparations being made for its defence.[14] In some ways, he was well-suited to his task. No one knew the defence problems of the area better. Percival was an experienced soldier, one of the sharpest staff officers in the army, personally courageous, a hard worker, and not inclined to waste time passing blame or bickering. Under Brooke-Popham's direction, he faced four main tasks. First, settle on an overall defence plan and deploy accordingly. Second, train the army to fight in this difficult terrain and climate. Third, establish mutual confidence with peers and senior subordinates. Finally, press ahead with general war preparations, including defence works and civil defence. Unfortunately, all these tasks were urgent matters at best left very unfinished by his predecessor. Worse, there were ramifications and complexities which brought out the weaknesses in Percival as a commander. In general, the GOC left contradictions unresolved rather than take a hard decision or accept a calculated risk, in the hope time would bypass or resolve them. To be fair, Percival could not be sure how much time he had to prepare his army for war. Yet in the end it must be said the GOC acted more as the staff officer he had been rather than the army commander he now was.

The situation Percival inherited was only too familiar to the man who first warned that Singapore could not be held by holding the island alone. In all his decisions, Percival was heavily influenced by a familiar military maxim: never lose sight of the mission assigned by higher authority. That mission he defined correctly: hold the naval base for friendly use, deny it to the enemy. That meant an invader must be kept as far away from Singapore as possible. But Percival believed that he could not safely rule out an attack anywhere along the coast, even directly at Singapore itself, if the Japanese commanded the sea. That meant Malaya Command must defend all vulnerable areas, including the scattered airbases. Any defender facing assault from the sea in World War II was forced to choose between two broad strategies: leave only a thin screen of defenders on the coast and concentrate the main forces inland, in order to launch a counteroffensive once the main enemy threat was identified; or, concentrate as strongly as possible on the beaches, to fight the main battle there and repel the invasion outright. Brooke-Popham and Percival opted for the latter despite the fact this would scatter their inadequate forces from Kota Bharu to Singapore.[15] Two factors seemed decisive. First, they wanted to fight the main battle as far from Singapore as possible. Second, they had a plan designed to pre-empt any Japanese advance.

The most painful irony of the Malayan campaign is that the defenders guessed exactly where and how the attackers would invade. The British plan, codenamed *Matador* in its final draft, aimed to forestall the Japanese by seizing the southern Thai ports from which they planned to launch their advance. If it worked it could keep the enemy well at bay. But the plan had one grave weakness: to execute it, the British might very well have to violate Thai neutrality first, to beat the Japanese to the targets. And the Thais insisted they would defend their territory against any invader. That raised concerns in London about a Japanese feint to draw out the British and make them look like the aggressor, which might complicate any move by the U.S. government to intervene. Yet time was of the essence; for the plan to work the troops must reach the ports first and dig in, or the chance of stopping the Japanese advance would be too small to warrant the risk involved. As it was, shortage of troops, plus the lack of any tanks, forced planners to scale down the proposal. The final draft called for the main force to seize Singora, but a smaller force would merely advance to and hold a good defensive position called The Ledge, south along the road from Patani. Despite a long lobby from Brooke-Popham, the COS remained unwilling to grant him the authority to launch the operation on his own if necessary, insisting he refer back to London first. Given that London seemed likely to approve only if the Japanese were already approaching the Thai coast, in which case they would very likely win the race to Singora, this made *Matador* a dubious proposition. Unwisely, Brooke-Popham and Percival opted to retain it as the basis of the overall defence plan. They directed the lead formation, 11th Indian Division, to train accordingly. It did so with enthusiasm, to the detriment of preparations for its other task: the defence of northern Malaya.[16] This was the "Singapore Strategy" error in miniature: the defenders prepared on a basis which might make sense if and when the means were ever provided, but as it stood compromised efforts to face the enemy if he came first.

On 2 August, Percival spelt out the basis of his plans and his estimate of the ground forces he required for an effective defence. These plans were based on an RAF estimate that they would be able to reduce any invading force by up to 40% by attacks on the incoming invasion fleet, with their *existing strength*. Officially, Malaya Command would "mop up" the invaders who made it ashore, even if the enemy attacked before RAF Far East Command reached its authorised strength. In that optimistic light, Percival called for some 48 infantry battalions, plus two tank regiments and additional artillery and anti-aircraft units — the equivalent of five full divisions. At that point, Malaya Command had barely half the required number of field forces, and no tanks at all. The COS accepted this estimate, but warned Percival they could not supply it "in the foreseeable future." Nevertheless reinforcements did continue, including more infantry, artillery and air defence units.[17] This did not meet Percival's needs — tanks remained a glaring omission — but it did allow the GOC to revamp his plans and deployments. By November 1941 Malaya Command boasted 10 brigades, with five assigned to III Corps and two under the 8th Australian Division of the AIF. These two main field formations were now assigned larger and clearer roles.

Percival made the AIF responsible for the defence of Melaka and Johore. This relieved the commander of Fortress Singapore, allowing him to concentrate his two brigades — plus the fixed defences of the Fire Commands — on the defence of the island. III Corps was directed to defend Malaya north of Johore, including handling *Matador*. That allowed Percival to move his best formation, 12th Indian Brigade, into command reserve. Each component of Malaya Command now at least had a clear task; albeit only Fortress Singapore, with the great guns, was really in any shape to face an assault in the near future. Stretched as it was defending from Kota Bharu to Singapore, let alone adding on *Matador*, Percival's plan provided a framework for a defence by 48 battalions. With only 32 available, it looked gravely thin. Yet the GOC remained committed by the need to defend airbases and convinced he could not leave any area uncontested.[18]

The switch in late July to a policy of deterring Japan, following the American lead in imposing an economic embargo, made it only prudent to assume war might well be near. But the British government did little to help relieve Singapore's situation. The government did send out a cabinet minister, Duff Cooper, to report on any problems regarding defence and administration in the Far East. But it did not give him any authority to act. The Joint Intelligence Committee (JIC) continued to argue the Soviet Union was the likely first target of any Japanese move; Far East Command agreed. On that basis, in September the Cabinet decided to divert large numbers of tanks and aircraft, some designated for Singapore, to the Soviets, to urge them to fight on. Duff Cooper convened a conference of local authorities in Singapore on 29 September. The meeting decided "it was improbable" Japan was preparing any imminent attack, and in any case the seasonal monsoon made it unlikely Malaya would be attacked before February. This baffling conclusion not only ignored the evidence of deteriorating relations charted by interceptions of Japanese diplomatic telegrams, plus menacing Japanese activities in Indochina, it also contradicted Percival's own appreciation of 1938. It remains hard to understand why the sense of urgency required to galvanise war preparations in both London and Singapore was so slow to develop, especially in the latter.[19]

The confusion over how the defence of Singapore could realistically fit into a sensible grand strategy produced one last unwise pre-war decision in London. Naval planners hoped to build up by spring 1942 a balanced Eastern Fleet strong enough to deter a Japanese sortie south, or to work effectively with the USN to confront the Japanese on two fronts if war came. The ultimate intention was to deploy a fleet led by six battleships, a battlecruiser, and one or two aircraft carriers. This all depended on the situation in the Atlantic and the Mediterranean remaining under control. But in August Prime Minister Churchill met President Roosevelt for personal discussions on common strategy and policy. The Americans remained reluctant to make any prior commitments for joint defence in the Far East, not least because of their doubts about the defence of Singapore. Churchill feared the Western Powers could wind up at war with Japan without a common strategy. He also felt the aim should be to deter Japan period, not just to ward off any move into the Indian Ocean. Speed seemed of the essence. On 25 August Churchill called for a change of plan, urging the Admiralty to make an early deployment of a small but strong force of fast modern capital ships, poised to act from Singapore.[20] This set off an argument with the COS which lasted two months and exposed the very essence of British grand strategy and the role of the naval base. In that sense, it was the culmination of two decades of debate on the "Singapore Strategy."

The Prime Minister argued that a force of fast modern ships could use Singapore to deter war by their presence, or at least to pin down enemy forces by the threat they posed to their movements — as German ships were doing in Norway to the RN. The First Sea Lord, Admiral of the Fleet Sir Dudley Pound, insisted this force could not by itself deter war and argued the "fleet in being" comparison overlooked two points: in this area, the British were just as dependent on sea lanes of communication as the Japanese; worse, it was doubtful the naval base could be protected against air attack. The Admiralty was clearly opposed to allowing major fleet units it could not afford to lose to use the naval base at all. This amounted to claiming the Indian Ocean, not Singapore, was the last-ditch position in any war against Japan. But Churchill had other priorities. A highly visible early deployment would hearten the Dominions, impress the Americans, and reassure the local populace. The game was afoot, and the British needed an ante. The Prime Minister prevailed. In late October HMS *Prince of Wales* sailed east to join HMS *Repulse* in the Indian Ocean, flying the flag of Vice-Admiral Sir Tom Phillips, lately Vice-Chief of the Naval Staff, now C-in-C Eastern Fleet designate. In November, Force Z proceeded majestically towards Singapore. At the eleventh hour the naval base thus prepared to host not the "main fleet," nor even a balanced fleet, but a force too important to lose but too small to stand on its own.[21] This was Churchill's call — but of course he was not alone in believing the Japanese would not soon attack, or at least would not overwhelm the defences if they did so. In theory the "Singapore Strategy" was thus activated; in practice, Malaya Command was left to hold the line helped only by the odds and ends that could be spared if the enemy came before it was convenient.

Percival had plenty of problems in his second task as well: to train his army to defend Malaya and Singapore. None of his formations had combat experience, as units. Imperial troops had not operated in jungle terrain for decades. Some units were new to the country; others had been there too long and become enervated, especially some in the Singapore garrison. Crucial equipment was short, especially tanks and anti-tank weapons. Most Indian units were made up very largely of young inexperienced soldiers, led by unfamiliar officers; many had not even seen a tank.[22] Malaya Command's job was to mould its patchwork army into a fighting force ready to defend the ground it was given. That meant defining an effective doctrine for local conditions and making sure *all* units worked as hard as possible to become combat-ready. The lead could only come from the top. Unfortunately, Percival inherited a staff which reflected the low priority his command had in grand strategy. All were overworked, some were incompetent, too few had any energy, drive or sense of urgency. Studies of jungle warfare made in India and sent to Singapore were left to sit on the shelf. Units were virtually left on their own.[23] Percival decided to tackle the mess by putting first things first.

The GOC drew up a training schedule calling for units to work on standard individual and sub-unit training for six months. From December, with more artillery available, the focus could switch to formation-level combined arms training. This schedule called for units to train for war in general, without any specific attention to local terrain and conditions. But because Percival saw the need and believed he had the time, he felt this was the most prudent approach.[24] Yet it also called for close and careful supervision by Malaya Command to make sure all units marched hard to the same drummer. This was not forthcoming. Only two formations can really be said to have trained hard and intelligently for war in Malaya: 12th Indian Brigade, led especially by its best unit, 2nd Battalion The Argyll and Sutherland Highlanders (2nd Argylls), and the 8th Australian Division, driven hard by Bennett.[25] Despite the fact that he became very concerned over the tendency of units to become too dependent on roads for moving and fighting, Percival did nothing to pursue ideas about how to handle that very problem developed by Lt.-Col. I.M. Stewart, Commanding Officer of 2nd Argylls. Worse, the GOC stood by when his Chief of Staff, Brig. Torrance, wrote Stewart off as a crank. Yet Malaya Command let whatever ideas it had on jungle warfare sit in files, rather than at least pulling them together for commanders. Percival also forbade his Chief Engineer from briefing units on up-to-date methods for fighting from fixed defences, ordering him to stick to supplying equipment. The conclusion is stark. Percival did not do all he might have done to pull his army together to train for war, while he had some time.[26] Influenced by how his second-rate staff underestimated the enemy, the GOC followed the orthodox British Army training syllabus not only before but instead of training for the conditions at hand. Lacking a strong push from the top, too many units did not train hard or well.

Percival did enjoy some success in establishing good personal relations. Pulford and Percival accepted each other as partners in the struggle to secure more help from London, became friends, and worked well together. That ended the feud between the services. In November 1941 the COS decided to replace Brooke-Popham by a younger more up-to-date commander, yet Percival continued to work well with his now lame duck superior. Relations were not as smooth with Heath. Heath was senior to Percival in rank, had more command combat experience, and resented being subordinated to him. Percival on his part did not know the Indian Army but prejudicially did not think very highly of it. While there was no real clash between the two, no mutual confidence developed either.[27] The worst problem was with Bennett. Percival never clarified exactly how much authority he had over Bennett and the Australian forces, which was a mistake. But the two were never likely to get along, mainly due to Bennett. Percival was quiet and reserved. Bennett was prickly, obnoxious and loaded with baggage. He was a citizen soldier locked in public mortal combat with the permanent soldiers of the Australian staff corps over Australian defence matters. He badgered Canberra constantly, and assumed the worst whenever he did not get his way. Bennett virtually paralysed his own headquarters in feuds started by fears the permanent force officers, especially his Chief of Staff Col. J.H. Thyer, were out to undermine him. Bennett also destroyed relations with the commander of his 22nd Brigade AIF, Brig. H.B. Taylor, over the running of that formation. Finally, Bennett was not impressed by his unassuming British superior.[28] This was a loose cannon on the deck, something Percival clearly could not afford. Bennett was a fighter but given the crucial role the Australians had, much depended on whether he could be an effective commander as well — and the signs were not good.

Percival must face far more criticism for failure to bolster local defences more effectively, yet even here London made things harder for him. In May 1941 the WO appointed Brig. Ivan Simson to take over as Chief Engineer Malaya Command. Simson was efficient, energetic and right up to date on problems of fixed defences, having helped prepare defences in the U.K. He received verbal instructions to bring about what amounted to a complete overhaul of the fixed defences and fortifications of Malaya and Singapore. Simson arrived in Singapore on 5 August, having been assured the CIGS would explain his task in writing to Percival. For some reason never explained, Dill never sent the letter. Worse, Simson inherited a dispute with the staff of Malaya Command over the role of fixed defences in the defence plan. For some reason Percival never acted on Simson's many requests to clarify his orders with Dill. Without the letter, many gave Simson the impression they thought he was bluffing. Simson went ahead on his own to tour the area over six weeks. He found ample stocks of useful matériel but only two ongoing defence works projects: a short anti-tank line at Jitra in northern Kedah, and beach defences on the south coast of Singapore itself. Simson concluded that what was needed was an integrated system revolving around selected and well-prepared defensive positions.[29]

In a comprehensive proposal, Simson called for the following: anti-tank and machine gun positions in depth to cover all defiles along major roads; wiring and mining of bridges; mines and other traps on the flanks of the road positions, to channel an enemy advance or stop a flank move; the completion of Dobbie's program of defences in Johore, to keep an attacker out of gun range of the naval base; and the serious development of defences on the northern coast of Singapore. Simson saw fixed defences as a common-sense way to bolster a defensive battle, giving mobile forces cover and a secure base in contact. Like Stewart, he saw fixed defences as complementing, not replacing, a mobile defence. But this amounted to a major revision of the defence plan and battle doctrine, such as they were. Simson also overplayed his hand to a staff not well-disposed to his office or ideas in the first place and jealous of their prerogative.

Percival heard Simson out but decided, without explanation, not to act on his ideas. His attitude rippled through the army and Simson met rebuff after rebuff from unit commanders regarding fixed defences.[30] While office politics did not likely sway a man like Percival, three other things did: the restrictions still placed on his authority by London, Percival's unwillingness to flout them or demand their removal, and the views of the GOC and his staff on that vital but elusive factor, morale.

Malaya Command agreed that fixed defences could help in certain places, such as vulnerable beaches, but saw Simson's proposal as a plan to base their whole defensive campaign on fortifications and fixed positions. They felt this would signal to the troops that there was no confidence in existing plans and doctrine, and would drain them of the "offensive spirit" needed to fight aggressively. For a defender with so little air support, no armour, and facing a road and jungle battle, the best that can be said about that attitude is that it was sheer dogma. So too were the tight restrictions London still maintained on what changes Percival might make in the defence plan, and how much money he could spend making them. The labour problem was the worst fiasco. Without labourers, troops were forced to give up training time to work on the defences the plan did allow. Asking the same men to work like donkeys then fight like lions in tropical humidity was obviously asking for trouble. Percival took up where Bond left off, pressing for help. But not until 24 November did he finally in desperation inform the WO that he would raise labour companies on his own. Money was the issue, but the root of the problem lay elsewhere.[31]

Labourers could not be pressed by a colonial power wishing to appear benevolent, so competitive wages were needed. But the WO stupidly refused to authorise wages above the Indian scales, well below plantation wages then prevailing. The Governor and the civil service supported this, because they believed recruiting too much labour would disrupt general production and frighten the Asian communities. This was seen as more dangerous than unfinished defences. The local government went so far as to say defence works in the south were a threat to morale because they implied the north could not be defended — as well as being damaging to private property![32] With such an attitude, one can sympathise with Percival's post-war charge that the local government did not do enough to prepare for war. But he shared with the Governor the belief that was the root of the problem: that any indication the British gave to the Asian communities that all was not under control would provoke dangerous panic, shake confidence in British power, and jeopardise British rule in the long term. The government hid behind its directive to maximise production, and did painfully little to organise stocks of essential supplies or prepare emergency plans for evacuation. In Singapore, proper air raid shelters and trenches were rejected on the grounds the water table was too low for shelters and trenches would breed mosquitoes. Civil defence was instead based on dispersal sites in the countryside, which did not of course need to be built before war left no choice.[33] Both Percival and Thomas assumed the worst of their charges, let it hamper their efforts, and refused to demand more help from their superiors, preferring to proceed by the book and gamble there was time.

Time ran out on 1 December 1941, when a State of Emergency was declared in Malaya and Singapore. Yamashita had every reason to be confident. Percival should have been alarmed, but was merely concerned. The main reason was something which best explains the stark difference between the theatre commanders' preparations for war: intelligence about the enemy and perceptions of him. The Japanese knew where and when they would strike. Thanks to an intelligence windfall, they also knew how low the area rated in British grand strategy, and had a good idea how under strength the defenders were. The conclusions reached in the COS Far East Appreciation of August 1940, spelling out British grand strategy as relating to Malaya and Singapore, were sent out by ship to the new C-in-C Far East. The vessel carrying the document, the cargo liner *Automedon*, was intercepted in the Indian Ocean by the German Armed Merchant Cruiser *Atlantis* on 11 November. The Germans managed to seize the document intact and in due course passed it on to the Japanese high command. That meant the Japanese planners knew both the general weakness of Far East Command and the contradiction in its defence plans.[34] Complete strategic surprise was not possible, and the Japanese had their own matériel shortages and political feuds. But in addition to this windfall they did enjoy that crucial psychological readiness for war which is so much of an advantage for those preparing to start one, and they did not waste it. Espionage and preparations for subversion were stepped up and problems tackled. The Japanese expected a fight, but knew their enemy and did not fear them.[35]

British intelligence and attitudes made a depressing contrast. In London, all eyes were focussed on the war against Germany. No one expected war in 1941 until quite late that year; even then, it was felt the Japanese would be too absorbed with the USN to overwhelm Far East Command.[36] Military intelligence in the theatre itself was more controversial, not least because on this matter Percival was not subtle:

> It must be recorded that Headquarters Malaya Command was not well supplied with information either as to the intentions of the Japanese or the efficiency of their fighting services.[37]

Percival later agreed that from various sources his command received "sufficient warning" war was at hand, and knew that the Japanese were "intrepid fighters" well-trained and equipped for amphibious operations. Yet at a press conference on 3 December Brooke-Popham assured his listeners the Japanese were not ready to attack, and while he hoped to receive more fighter aircraft those on hand could handle the threat.[38] The fact is that much useful and accurate information on Japanese capabilities was available. The problem was how that information was appreciated, and here British *attitudes* proved decisive.

Notwithstanding Percival's post-war claims, by late 1941 commanders and staffs in Singapore generally regarded the Japanese forces as brave but rigid, badly led and predictable, particularly weak on the use of mechanical equipment such as aircraft and tanks — "approximately half as efficient as the Germans." For too long the easy explanation for this attitude was to describe it as simple racism; the problem was in fact more complicated. There were actually several different "British" appreciations of the Japanese by this time, all affected by a variety of factors. There were only a handful of British military intelligence experts on Japan and they worked in Japan or London. This group tended to rate the Japanese highly. Other intelligence officers generally agreed Japanese battle doctrine would not work against an army "which held its nerve and its fire." Racism played some part in this, but a more important factor was military ethnocentrism. Too many British observers rated the IJA by one theoretical standard and one dangerously misleading one. On the paper standard, based on an army equipped with European scales of heavy weapons, the IJA fell short; but this standard was based on operations in European conditions. More important, British Army doctrine was the standard against which any rival was measured. If the IJA did something differently, too many assumed it must be inferior.[39]

There were glaring flaws in this reasoning. The IJA did not plan to fight in Europe; if conditions differed enough, the "paper standard" might be irrelevant. And the British Army had never fought an industrial foe in Asia; what if IJA methods were better suited to local conditions than its own? These questions were too rarely asked. If anything, Japanese problems in the drawn-out war in China impressed British observers more than the difficulties the IJA faced, and their impression of it became more critical. This attitude was most prevalent among officers from the garrison in China and from India. Transfers in 1940 concentrated such men in Singapore, and their views took hold in Malaya Command to the point where they became a bastion of the critical British view of Japanese combat power. As a result, an undermanned and disorganised staff became predisposed to weed out such warnings as it did receive in favour of reports which fit the optimistic impression. The most spectacular and costly example was failure to take seriously a timely warning sent by Chinese sources about the specifications and potential of the *Zero* type fighter aircraft. Brooke-Popham's assurance that the *Brewster Buffalo*, a lumbering American cast-off supplied earlier that year to Far East Command because it was not important enough to receive more modern planes, was "quite good enough for Malaya," was based not on a lack of warning but on the fact that the warnings received did not filter through preconceptions. Simson found this underestimation of the enemy spread through much of Malaya Command.[40] Inevitably, it affected the crucial areas theatre commanders had some leeway to improve: campaign plans and training.

Beyond *Matador* and a successful stand on the beaches, Malaya Command had no clear idea of how to defend north of Johore. It knew only what it would not do: adopt Simson's call for an integrated network of fixed defences. The vague idea was that some sort of controlled fighting retreat could be conducted, stopping at good positions to punish an enemy expected to rely on rigid tactics of frontal assault. But surely this

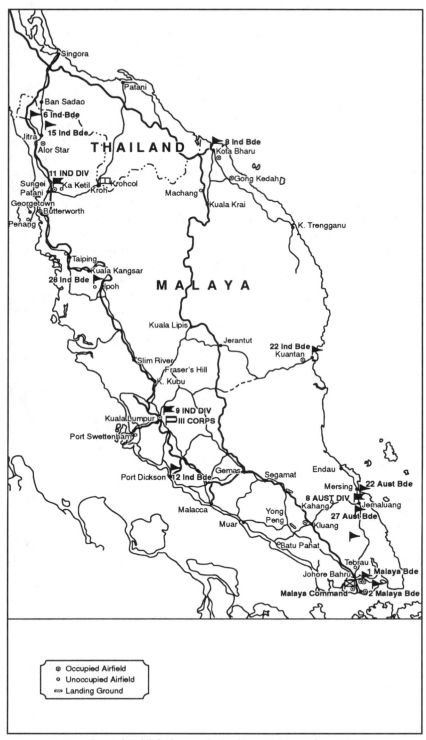

Location of British forces in Malaya, 8 December 1941

was the best reason to accept Simson's case? Behind well-sited fixed defences, the defenders could force the enemy to build up strength to mount deliberate assaults; that could prolong the defence, giving time for reinforcements to arrive from overseas. Instead, most units assumed the enemy was not coming yet, and anyway was not first-class. This image prevailed despite warnings provided by several field exercises of how easy it was for positions to be infiltrated through the bush and flanked by movement off the road; few expected the IJA to fight that way. The bottom line was that the defenders of Malaya and Singapore under-estimated the Japanese and overestimated themselves.[41]

The British dilemma was best summed up by one dramatic event: the arrival of Force Z in Singapore on 2 December. The progress of the two capital ships up the Straits of Johore was received with rapture by the civilian population, feelings not at all discouraged by the authorities. Here at last was the very expression of British power, the RN, underlining in a blaze of deliberate publicity the readiness of the Empire to defend itself. Nothing could have been more wrong, as the Admiralty and local commanders knew full well. With war looming, Force Z had just sailed into the most vulnerable position it could be in: sitting ducks within range of enemy air attack. Discussions were already underway about what it should do when the shooting started. But the ships could not now abandon the naval base without having the most damning effect imaginable on confidence in Singapore and the Dominions.[42] The RN completed the circle: all three services were reinforced for war, but deployed in the most compromised manner, with campaign plans marred by confusion and cross-purposes.

Even given the constraints on war preparations, it is hard to see how matters could have been much worse. The RAF was supposed to cripple any invading force at sea. Pulford had only 181 combat-ready aircraft, including no modern torpedo bombers, dive bombers, or transport aircraft, and obsolete fighters about to be very rudely surprised. There was no real air defence network apart from Singapore itself. Percival knew that even the new Eastern Fleet could not prevent a stronger enemy from striking wherever he chose along the east coast. Only two of Malaya Command's 10 brigades could be considered prepared, and the army had no tanks at all.[43] Prime Minister Churchill seems to have assumed the army would after all concentrate on defending Johore and Singapore. But Percival deployed his army to cover all posssible landing sites, airbases and good roads, all over the peninsula — with full support from the COS. Worse, with *Matador* still hanging in the air, the army was caught in the very trap the GOC feared: poised undecided between contradictory plans.

As they were deployed, the defenders could hope to beat off a strong assault only in Singapore — unless *Matador* was launched and worked. By trying to have at least some defence everywhere, the defenders were not strong enough anywhere. If the blow came in the north as expected, reserves were few and far away. Instead of taking a calculated risk to concentrate enough force to resist the most likely assault, Malaya Command was poised to contest any invasion but too weak to repel any.

Contrast this with the bold Japanese decision on the main landings. The one real concern the Japanese had was that the British might do exactly as *Matador* envisaged. In that case, they would land further north in Thailand and build up from there. But when the Japanese forces embarked on 4 December, Brooke-Popham was still waiting for an answer to his latest plea for clearance to launch the operation on his own authority.[44] The die was cast, and it was now down to the first contact and how effectively the two sides could size it up and react. Given that they at least now knew their own minds, the Japanese started off with a very distinct advantage indeed.

Notes

1. S. Falk, *Seventy Days to Singapore*, London, 1975, 18-31.

2. Tsuji, M. *Singapore: The Japanese Version*, Sydney, 1960, 18-24, argues that "serious preparations" did not begin until September 1941.

3. Tsuji, 9-24; Falk, 24-26.

4. US Army Center for Military History, Japanese Monograph No. 107, *Malaya Invasion Naval Operations* (Revised Edition) (hereafter called *Malaya Invasion Naval Operations*), p. 6. This was one of a series of monographs compiled immediately after the war by Japanese officers under the supervision of Allied occupation forces and the Japanese government, this volume being written largely by the naval general staff officer in charge of planning for *Southern Fleet* operations. It was completed in 1952, but revised and updated in 1958. Tsuji, 53; Falk, 28-30; H.P. Wilmott, *Empires in the Balance*, Annapolis, 1982, ch. 3.

5. Tsuji, 24-40; Falk, 26-27; Willmott, ch. 3.

6. *Malaya Invasion Naval Operations*, pp. 3-15; Tsuji, 25-40; J.D. Potter, *The Life and Death of a Japanese General*, New York, 1962, 44-45; Falk, 30-33.

7. PRO, CAB80/16, COS(40)592, 15 August 1941; WO172/3, 22412, War Diary, GHQ Far East, Appendix, Tactical Appreciation of Defence Situation in Malaya, 16 October 1940; *Operations of Malaya Command from 8th December 1941 to 15th February 1942*, paragraphs 24-26 (hereafter called *Operations of Malaya Command*). S.W. Kirby, *The War Against Japan. Vol.1. The Loss of Singapore* (hereafter called *The Loss of Singapore*), London, 1957, 31-36.

8. Ong, C.C., *Operation Matador*, Singapore, 1997, 115, n.86, 117, n.93; Probert, 16-17; C. Kinvig, *Scapegoat: General Percival of Singapore*, London, 1996, 116-17.

9. Two regular British battalions evacuated from China arrived in August 1940, two brigades of the 11th Indian Division arrived in November, the 22nd Brigade Australian Imperial Force (AIF) plus Headquarters 8th Australian Division arrived in February 1941, and two brigades of the 9th Indian Division arrived in March and April. *Operations of Malaya Command*, paragraphs 27-28; A.E. Percival, *The War in Malaya*, London, 1949, 48, 69-70; S.W. Kirby, *The Chain of Disaster*, London, 1971, 57, 71-72.

10. *Operations of Malaya Command*, paragraphs 9, 33, 115; Kirby, *The Loss of Singapore*, 50-51; Kirby, *The Chain of Disaster*, 42, 55-57; Probert, 7.

11. PRO, CAB120/615, Minister of Defence Secretariat Files, Churchill to COS, 1, 10 September, Churchill to Lord Cranborne, 15 December 1940, 5 January 1941; 120/517, 22 September 1940; CAB79/6, COS minutes, 4, 6, 9, 16-17, 19 September 1940; 79/7, 12, 19 November 1940; 79/8, 13 January 1941; CAB69/2, Defence Committee (Operations) minutes, 9, 29 April 1941; W.S. Churchill, *The Grand Alliance*, Boston, 1950, 188-92; A. Danchev, *Dill*, in J. Keegan, *Churchill's Generals*, New York, 1991, 57-58; Ong, *Operation Matador*, chs. 4, 5; Probert, 18.

12. Kirby, *The Loss of Singapore*, 48-50.

13. Imperial War Museum (IWM), Percival Papers, File 39, Deductions from Japanese Appreciation of the Attack on the Fortress of Singapore, December 1937; File 41, Memorandum on the Defence of the Fortress of Singapore, May 1937; *Operations of Malaya Command,* paragraph 21; Ong, *Operation Matador,* ch. 3; Kirby, *The Chain of Disaster,* 38-42, 73-76.

14. *Operations of Malaya Command,* paragraph 29; Percival, 36.

15. Percival, 58; J. Smyth, *Percival and the Tragedy of Singapore,* 1971, 71.

16. Liddell Hart Centre for Military Archives (LHCMA), Brooke-Popham Papers, V/4, Papers on Requirements of Army, RAF and GHQ Staff, contains numerous telegrams from GHQ FE to the COS pressing for reinforcements and outlining the need for authority to launch *Matador*—most important are V/4/26, Brooke-Popham to COS, 20 August, and COS to Brooke-Popham, FE43, 21 November 1941; *Operations of Malaya Command,* paragraph 29; Ong, *Operation Matador,* chs. 4-7, is the only systematic study of *Matador;* Kirby, *The Chain of Disaster,* 108-110.

17. *Operations of Malaya Command,* paragraphs 40-41, 47-48; J.M.A. Gwyer, *Grand Strategy. Vol. III. June 1941–August 1942 Part I,* London, HMSO, 1964, 278-80. Reinforcements included the 27th Brigade AIF which arrived in mid-August, 28th Indian Infantry Brigade in September, plus a heavy anti-aircraft regiment, a reconnaissance regiment, three field artillery regiments, and an anti-tank regiment, all arriving in late autumn.

18. *Operations of Malaya Command,* paragraph 49; Kirby, 111-15. Kirby argues that the plan and deployment was based on the assumption it might not be possible to launch *Matador.* But orders to 11th Division to prepare for *Matador* threatened to compromise the whole plan even if it was not executed, as shall be seen.

19. PRO, CAB79/14, COS minutes, 16 September 1941, records the COS consideration of JIC(41)362, an appreciation of Japanese intentions. The report correctly stated the embargo on Japan would now force it to make a cardinal decision whether or not to fight the Western Powers. Nevertheless, the JIC believed the Japanese were not yet ready to strike south and just as likely to move north. The COS took no action. The decision to send equipment to the Soviets was with hindsight cited by critics and supporters of British policy as a crucial obstacle to timely reinforcement of Far East Command. No supplies were earmarked for the Soviets before September and none sent before October, and the COS decided to reinforce the Middle East first with what remained: CAB80/59, COS(41)569, 14 September 1941. Kirby, *The Loss of Singapore,* 78-79, 285-89; Gwyer, 283-84; Kirby, *The Chain of Disaster,* 118-19; Ong, *Operation Matador,* 220-23; P. Elphick, *Far Eastern File: The Intelligence War in the Far East 1930-1945,* London, 1997, 310-12.

20. PRO, CAB79/13, COS minutes, 25 August 1941; S.W. Roskill, *The War at Sea 1939-1945. Vol. I. The Defensive,* London, 1954, 553-54.

21. The Force Z argument can be followed in PRO, CAB69/2, DC(O) minutes, 17, 20 October 1941; Gwyer, 270-74; Roskill, *The War at Sea,* 554-58.

22. *Operations of Malaya Command,* paragraph 52. Many Indian and some British units also suffered from "milking," the removal of experienced officers and NCOs to provide cadres for newly raised units. This problem is described in Bell, 39. The 12th Indian Brigade was the only Indian formation in Malaya Command whose units were mobilised before the frantic expansion of the Indian Army from 1940, and were not "milked."

23. Kirby, *The Chain of Disaster,* 91-94. Kinvig, 130-33, defends Percival. Elphick, *Singapore: The Pregnable Fortress,* 189-90, and Bell, 48, do not.

24. *Operations of Malaya Command,* paragraph 54; Kirby, *The Chain of Disaster,* 95-96; Kinvig, 134.

25. In *Operations of Malaya Command,* paragraphs 54-59, and Percival, *The War in Malaya,* Percival mentions that Malaya Command drafted a doctrine of jungle warfare—but he is vague on whether or not it ever made sure those ideas were taken on board and tested in training by its formations. A.B. Lodge, *The Fall of General Gordon Bennett,* North Sydney, 1986, 34, 50; G. Mant, *The Singapore Surrender,* Kuala Lumpur, 1992,

150-51; I.M. Stewart, *History of the Argyll and Sutherland Highlanders 2nd Battalion,* London, 1947, 2-5; Kirby, *The Chain of Disaster,* 96.

26. *Operations of Malaya Command,* paragraphs 54-59; I. Simson, *Singapore: Too Little, Too Late,* London, 1970, 122. See also PRO, CAB106/91, The Loss of Singapore: A Criticism, an undated postwar report by Lt.-Col. Stewart, for a devastating indictment of prewar training.

27. *Operations of Malaya Command,* paragraphs 96, 100, 101, 109; Percival, 30-31; Kirby, *The Chain of Disaster,* 119-20, 130; K. Simpson, *Percival,* in Keegan, *Churchill's Generals,* 263; Probert, 23; Kinvig, 126.

28. PRO, CAB106/162, Report on Operations of 8th Australian Division AIF in Malaya, compiled by Col. J.H. Thyer from narrative prepared by Col. C.H. Kappe, n/d, 1945 (hereafter called Thyer report), 191; L. Wigmore, *The Japanese Thrust,* Canberra, 1957, ch. 4, 65, 73; Percival, 34-35; Lodge, 34-41, 45-49, 50-58; Elphick, *Singapore: The Pregnable Fortress,* 174-75. Bennett was given a fairly typical directive for Commonwealth forces, subordinating him to Malaya Command for operations but reserving the administration and discipline of Australian forces to him. It also charged him with consulting Australian authorities if he received any order which in his view jeopardised his force, provided he took no action in the meantime which would endanger ongoing operations. Percival could and should have clarified this matter.

29. Simson, 24-33; Kirby, *The Chain of Disaster,* 116.

30. Simson, 33-38; Kinvig, 195.

31. *Operations of Malaya Command,* paragraphs 14-17; Percival, 15; Elphick, *Singapore: The Pregnable Fortress,* 197; Kirby, *The Chain of Disaster,* 96-99.

32. Kirby, *The Chain of Disaster,* 96-99; Kinvig, 131.

33. Compare *Operations of Malaya Command,* paragraphs 4, 80, 91-92, 96, to Percival, 86; Simson, 93-96, 122; I. Morrison, *Malayan Postscript,* London, 1942, 163; Kirby, *The Chain of Disaster,* 96-99, 188.

34. Elphick, *Far Eastern File,* ch. 14, has uncovered the full story of how the Japanese came to possess a copy of the War Cabinet minutes for 15 August 1940, addressed to Brooke-Popham. These minutes outlined the conclusions of the COS appreciation on grand strategy and the Far East, as noted above; see Chapter 6. The story was first raised by L. Allen, *Singapore 1941–1942,* U.K., 1993(1977), 2-4.

35. Elphick, *Singapore: The Pregnable Fortress,* ch. 4; Elphick, *Far Eastern File,* chs. 10-11; Tsuji, 29-32; Potter, 44-47. The most dangerous Japanese subversion operation was aimed at playing on nationalist feelings, with the help of the anti-British Indian Independence League (IIL), to subvert Indian troops. Operation *F-Kikan* was set up by Major Fujiwara Iwaichi in Bangkok in October 1941, who was ready to move when the invasion began. Japanese political problems centred around the enmity between Yamashita and the new Prime Minister, Tojo, a product of long years of factional feuding in the IJA. Many felt Tsuji was a Tojo plant; Nishimura, commander of the *Imperial Guards Division,* was openly pro-Tojo. Yamashita's personal position was thus anything but secure.

36. PRO, CAB79/15, COS minutes, 18 November, JIC(41)439, and 79/55, COS minutes 28 November 1941, indicate how late the JIC remained undecided about whether the Japanese would strike north or south. The JIC also expected the Japanese to invade Thailand first, to delay a direct confrontation with Western forces.

37. *Operations of Malaya Command,* paragraph 64.

38. *Operations of Malaya Command,* paragraphs 60-64, 99; Elphick, *Singapore: The Pregnable Fortress,* 82-88; J.R. Ferris, "Worthy of Some Better Enemy: The British Estimate of the Imperial Japanese Army 1919-1941 and the Fall of Singapore," in *Canadian Journal of History,* XXVIII, August, 1993, an excellent discussion, puts the crux of the matter well on page 247: "the army received assessments about the IJA from an organization controlled by the navy, through an intervening headquarters with the most nebulous of functions run by an RAF officer." Elphick, *Far Eastern File,* ch. 8, studies the FECB and the state of intelligence in some detail. O.D. Gallagher, *Retreat in the East,* London, 1942, 84-85, is evocative for Brooke-Popham's press conference.

39. Kirby, *The Chain of Disaster*, 74-75; Elphick, *Singapore: The Pregnable Fortress*, 82-83; Ferris, 227-37, 245-51; Allen, ch. XI, is the most important discussion of racism in British perceptions of the Japanese.

40. Simson, 26-27; Wigmore, 67; Probert, 27; Ferris, 236-51; Elphick, *Far Eastern File*, 95, 158-59, 166-68, discusses the compilation of a report entitled *Japanese Army Memorandum* by the FECB in 1940, available to military authorities in Singapore in 1941. The report did not survive in the papers of Malaya Command but is preserved in the India Office Records, British Library (IOR), L/Mil/17/20/24, a version reprinted with additions and modifications by General Staff India in March 1941. The report warns in some detail that the Japanese were well-equipped with good aircraft and tanks, very good at engineering in the field, and prone to use encircling tactics in attack. It specifically warns that the IJA was a threat to be taken seriously. Elphick notes that having interviewed over 100 officers who served in the campaign, he has yet to find one who read this report. On the other hand, the report also notes that the conclusions drawn about the IJA relied heavily on observations of operations in China "against an inferior enemy" and "should therefore be treated with some reserve" — a passage Elphick does not discuss. Ferris, 246-48, explains the difficulties of tracing through inadequate sources exactly what Malaya Command did and did not read, and how it handled the whole field of intelligence.

41. Ferris, 248-56.

42. Gallagher, 17-28, for a denunciation of the expatriate civilian mood in Singapore on the eve of war; Morrison, 16, for a more convincing portrayal; Percival, 95; Kirby, *The Chain of Disaster*, 73-74; M. Middlebrook and P. Mahoney, *Battleship: The Loss of the Prince of Wales and Repulse* London, 1977, 74-75.

43. *Operations of Malaya Command*, paragraphs 40-42, 101-09, Section XVI; Probert, 34-35; Stewart, 6, for an explanation of the difficulties unit commanders faced in late 1941.

44. PRO, CAB79/16, COS minutes, 28 November, 79/55, COS minutes, 28 November, 1, 2 December 1941; CAB65/24, War Cabinet minutes, 11, 12, 24 November 1941 make clear the deliberations of the central direction of the war on this problem. The key conclusion was that there must be no action that could be portrayed as provocative until the U.S. government promised it would intervene if the British and Japanese came to blows even without any Japanese attack on U.S. territory or forces. That meant Brooke-Popham would not be cleared to launch *Matador* until President Roosevelt agreed to support the British by force if it led to war with Japan. Long discussions are in Ong, *Operation Matador*, ch. 7, and Elphick, *Far Eastern File*, 310-17.

8

Bitter Harvest: The Defence and Fall of Singapore

W|ar came to Singapore from the air at 0430 hrs on 8 December 1941, as Japanese bombers attacked the city and airbases. The defence strategy was governed by the mission assigned: to prevent the enemy from capturing the Singapore naval base and preserve it for friendly use. Percival believed the enemy could not be held at bay without reinforcements, and Singapore could not be held on its own against an enemy concentrated on its doorstep. Making the enemy pay in time and men was not good enough; Singapore must not fall. But without strong reinforcements it would fall. Therefore Percival concluded he had no choice but to try to hold the Japanese as far north of Singapore as possible, to buy the time and space needed to bring in reinforcements. Yamashita assumed his foe would fight on that basis and drove his army hard, to prevent the defenders from regrouping and beat any reinforcements to Singapore. Three factors tipped the balance. The Japanese seized and maintained the initiative by outfighting the defenders on the ground. They won near total control of the air and used it effectively. Finally, the defenders were knocked off balance right away and lost their composure in what degenerated into an improvised piecemeal fighting retreat.

The Fall of Malaya

In the first four days, all the plans of the defenders were shattered by a combination of enemy pressure plus their own mistakes. On 5 December Brooke-Popham finally received clearance to launch *Matador* on his own authority if the Japanese were clearly moving towards Thailand in force. Unfortunately, still afraid of being blamed for starting a war, the now lame duck C-in-C dithered when air reconnaissance patrols spotted Japanese invasion fleets moving west the next morning. By the time definitive contact was regained with a Japanese fleet less than 160 km off the Thai coast at 1750 hrs on 7 December, it was too late to beat them to the target. Percival drew the obvious conclusion and advised the C-in-C to cancel the operation and put 11th Indian Division onto its defensive position. Instead, Brooke-Popham ordered the division to stand by to advance at dawn if necessary — then advised the Admiralty it was

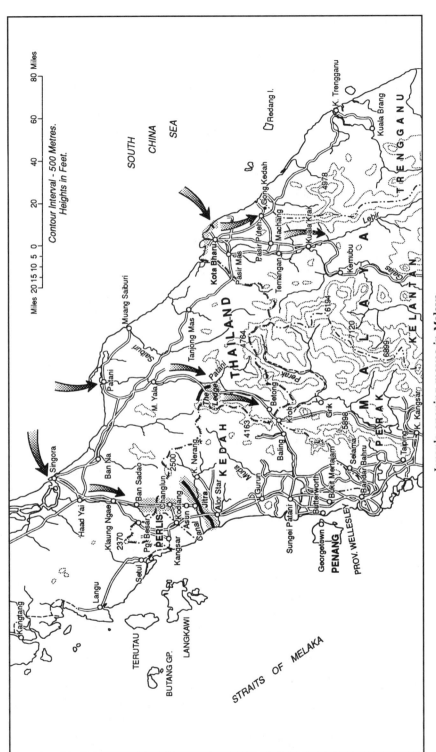

Japan's opening moves in Malaya

now too late to activate the plan! The C-in-C's next telegram informed London hostilities had begun in the early minutes of 8 December, with a Japanese invasion force assaulting Kota Bharu.[1]

Besides this feckless reluctance to shoulder his responsibility, Brooke-Popham also failed to grasp the tactical imperative of the advance into Thailand. Even if Singora could not be seized, the Ledge position on the road from Patani must be. That was the only place to block a Japanese advance which could outflank the main position the 11th Indian Division must now defend. But between them Brooke-Popham and Percival did not get the second force, *Krohcol*, moving until mid-afternoon on 8 December. It started too late, moved too slowly, and was beaten to the Ledge by the enemy. This left the back road vulnerable.[2] The main force moved back onto its defensive position seriously discouraged by the cancellation of *Matador*, made worse when the men were forced to work on incomplete defences in driving rain. A flying column sent into Thailand to buy time was brushed aside by the Japanese, who advanced boldly south to approach the outposts of the main position at Jitra on 10 December. The defenders should have been recovering their resolve by now but the division commander felt they were still a full day from being ready to fight. Worse, they were in a bad position to defend, chosen only because it was the only place available to screen the airbase just to the south at Alor Star.[3] Brooke-Popham's dithering thus ruined Malaya Command's plan to pre-empt the enemy advance, handed the initiative to the Japanese, and forced the defenders into the first battle on avoidably bad terms.

The idea that the RAF could deliver a telling blow to any invasion fleet, leaving the defenders manning the beaches to mop up what remained, was debunked in a day by the Japanese attack at Kota Bharu. Despite a stiff fight, the 8th Indian Brigade, under its dynamic commander Brig. "Billy" Key, was forced to retreat. Spread out over more than 50 km of beach defences, it could not stop a determined attack by a Japanese force willing to accept losses once it ran the RAF gauntlet.[4] The failure of that gauntlet was not due to lack of effort. Pulford threw his Air Striking Force at the invasions in full strength. Bomber squadrons attacked the enemy all day, but suffered heavily and in return scored only one real success by sinking one transport and damaging several others off Kota Bharu. *Brewster Buffalo* pilots found out the hard way their fighter was no match for their opponent, an unpleasant — and avoidable — surprise which left the bombers vulnerable.[5] Over the next three days, Japanese aircraft pummelled the northern airbases in a concentrated onslaught aimed to win control of the air over the battlefield. Pulford's force was undone by a scarcity of air defence equipment — which had to be concentrated at Singapore — plus a small dose of treason.[6] But the deciding factor was that the Japanese had more and better aircraft. By 11 December, with only 43 serviceable fighters ready to face over 300 Japanese aircraft moved forward, Pulford was forced to change his strategy. Bombing by day was abandoned, to conserve the force, and the fighters were concentrated at Singapore, to protect the naval base and reinforcement convoys. Panicky evacuations at some airbases, particularly Alor Star, unnerved the troops trying to protect them.[7] Coupled with the failure of Pulford's weak command to punish the enemy at sea, this left the plan to defend as far north as possible in tatters and the army in danger.

The only remaining force with a chance to salvage the original plan to repel invasion was the new Eastern Fleet. At midday on 8 December the C-in-C Eastern Fleet and his senior officers decided the situation, not to mention the traditions of the service, compelled them to engage the enemy. The Governor disagreed, but Brooke-Popham supported Phillips' decision to send the two capital ships on a raid, to catch the Japanese landing forces off Thailand by surprise and wreak havoc with the troop and supply ships. Phillips believed his ships could defend themselves at sea against aircraft, especially a supposedly second-rate air force such as the Japanese. Nevertheless, he asked Pulford to provide reconnaissance ahead of the fleet, plus fighter cover over the expected contact area on the morning of 10 December. The force sailed that evening, receiving Pulford's answer at sea early the next day. Reconnaissance would be arranged, but with the northern airbases already unusable fighter cover was no longer possible. Nevertheless Phillips sailed on, until discovery by Japanese aircraft forced him to turn back after nightfall rather than face great odds with no advantage of surprise. The *22nd Naval Air Flotilla* was actually in the air looking for him, alerted by a Japanese submarine which spotted the ships earlier on. But they missed the British force, which gave it a chance to slip away after all — until fate and bad judgement intervened.[8]

What later turned out to be a false alarm report of enemy landings near Kuantan persuaded Phillips to change course at 0052 hrs, hoping to catch the enemy off guard at dawn. Finding no trace of the enemy, the force headed out to sea on a detour before resuming course for Singapore. This almost but not quite eluded the Japanese sweep, which found the ships at 1000 hrs on 10 December. Eighty-five aircraft of the *22nd Naval Air Flotilla* attacked HMS *Prince of Wales* and HMS *Repulse* in waves starting about an hour later. In a little over two hours, both ships were sunk by repeated bomb and torpedo hits. Phillips might have had good reasons to sortie, but he failed to take some prudent steps to give his ships a fighting chance. It has been suggested the C-in-C would expect his Chief of Staff, left behind in Singapore, to assume the fleet would "sail to the guns" on the Kuantan report and arrange for fighter cover there at daybreak. But this cannot explain why Phillips did not break radio silence after the Japanese found him again that morning. RAF headquarters in Singapore did not receive any report the fleet was in trouble until noon, when the captain of the *Repulse* finally took it upon himself to radio for help. Eleven *Buffaloes* took off seven minutes later, arriving just in time to see the last Japanese plane disappear over the horizon as survivors awaited rescue. Phillips took the reason for his folly with him to a watery grave. His defeat left Malaya and Singapore open to whatever further attacks the Japanese cared to make from the sea, especially on the east coast.[9] "Main fleet to Singapore" was sunk, the Air Striking Force was hammered, and *Matador* was fumbled. Within 100 hours, the Japanese destroyed the basis of British strategy for the defence of Singapore. Now Malaya Command, already off-balance, had to fight by itself the vital battle to keep the enemy at bay long enough for reinforcements to appear.

Percival decided to fight that battle by a strategy which in the end only made matters worse. The GOC concluded that without reinforcements Singapore could not be held, but reinforcements would not arrive for a month, and not at all if Japanese forces cut Singapore off. The defeats of the RAF and the RN meant that the east coast and Singapore must remain defended. Therefore, Percival felt compelled to give 11th Indian Division contradictory orders: fight on in position, but do not allow itself to be destroyed, which would open the road to the enemy. And he was only willing to reinforce it by one brigade, the command reserve.[10] But the division was already off-balance, threatened from the flank, and deployed in a poor position meant to cover an airbase already evacuated. All might yet have been well had the defenders been able to stand at Jitra and force the enemy to make a deliberate assault. Unfortunately, 11th Indian Division was not well-prepared for battle and it did not fight intelligently.

Too many units were inexperienced, especially against tanks. Worse, the division tried to fight by holding rigidly to a long line of fixed positions, relying on firepower to beat off attacks. The Japanese advance guard of two battalions bounced the position in two days by an aggressive use of tank-led attacks blasting straight down the main road, infiltration in dense bush between defensive positions, and encircling moves around the flank. Percival resisted calls for a retreat, fearing such an early move from the only prepared position would greatly discourage the army and the civil populace. By the time he finally did authorise a retreat, the enemy was in close contact and it was dark. As a result the division was badly scattered, as well as being outfought by a smaller force.[11] Malaya Command now faced a very serious tactical problem: its main force was in retreat with no fallback positions prepared, while its troops were apparently unable to fight or move effectively without the road but could not stop tank attacks along it.

Percival and Heath met to discuss the problem on 18 December, having already been forced to give up Penang and all airbases to the north. Ominously, they strongly disagreed on how to fight on. Heath insisted his troops were too few and too tired to stand fast against an enemy advancing along two main routes, lacked anti-tank equipment or air cover, and now faced a threat from the sea. A careless evacuation allowed the Japanese to seize a flotilla of small boats in Penang; this plus boats they were bringing overland from Thailand would allow them to outflank any defensive position by attacking from the west coast. Given that Percival could offer no more reinforcements as he still refused to uncover the east coast, Heath argued there was now only one viable strategy: a long retreat down to Johore, behind the cover of delaying actions and demolitions at bottleneck positions. This would reduce the threat from the sea, shorten friendly and lengthen enemy supply lines, pull 11th Indian Division out of battle so it could regroup, and above all concentrate III Corps and the AIF on a more narrow front that could be more strongly held. In effect, Heath argued that the Japanese could not now be held in northern or central Malaya, so the army should pull back to where it might yet stand.[12]

Percival disagreed. His command decision was again swayed by broader considerations than the best tactical position for his troops. The GOC insisted III Corps must fight on to delay the Japanese as far north as possible for as long as possible. Percival knew how important relentless advance was to the Japanese and how hard-pressed the four brigades committed to battle already were. But he rejected the call for a strategic retreat on the grounds this would make it almost impossible to carry out the mission: to hold the naval base, period. To do that, the Japanese must be kept away from airbases in Central Malaya, from where they could interdict the vital reinforcement convoys. III Corps must fight on in the west and stand in the east.[13] Where Heath called for a calculated risk to be taken in order to give the troops a better fighting position, Percival decided the risk must be to keep the troops fighting in place in order to keep the mission alive.

This was one of the most decisive moves of the campaign. Percival was certainly not alone in believing only powerful reinforcements could save Singapore,[14] but his decision did not give his army the best chance possible to buy the necesssary time and space. 11th Indian Division was already too badly disrupted to fight on with so little help and not be shattered. That would open the road to Singapore faster than a long retreat. The place for the calculated risk was Pahang, not Perak, but Percival was too intimidated by complications to take that calculated risk. Given the misssion and the air threat, the gamble to fight on in the north was not inexplicable. Given the condition of the main forces, the failure to concentrate against the enemy was. This was made all the more poignant by a directive issued by the GOC on 20 December. Defences must be constructed in depth along the main routes of advance with particular attention to anti-tank cover. Holding groups should dig in at these positions to pin down the enemy attack. But there must be no more sitting passively in fixed positions nor automatic retreat in case of enemy infiltration or encircling moves. The defence must be fluid and aggressive, with striking groups poised on the flanks to counterattack.[15] One can only imagine Simson's reaction to this directive, and the belated order to prepare defensive positions south of Ipoh. Unfortunately, III Corps needed fresh troops, not just incisive orders. Leaving the next battle up to exhausted units already looking over their shoulder was not enough. Percival let the strategic threat to his mission persuade him to keep the army in the least likely array to keep it alive.

Only one formation enjoyed any real success against the Japanese in the effort to hold northern Malaya: 12th Indian Brigade, the command reserve. Sent in to stiffen 11th Indian Division, the brigade was forced to take on the job of stopping the Japanese advance along the interior road from Patani from getting in behind the main force and surrounding it. This it did with great skill, using tactics designed largely by Stewart of 2nd Argylls. The brigade fought not to hold ground but to hold up the enemy and punish him. It did this by striving to control the road, the only means of extended movement and supply, by fighting "for the road off the road." The Argylls in particular fought a battle of movement very similar to Japanese tactics, relying not on firepower and fixed positions but on infantry mobility.[16] Time and again they roughly handled the enemy in encounter battles in the second half of December. But had the brigade tried to stand and hold against tank-led attacks, as did the main force, it would have been beaten; therefore, it fell back. Percival's best formation could and did make it possible for 11th Indian Division to fall back below the Perak River into Central Malaya without being annihilated, but that was all.[17]

The speed and audacity of the Japanese advance reaped great rewards: moral ascendancy, gained by the victory at Jitra; the airbases; the Penang windfall; and a bonus of what the troops called "Churchill supplies," stocks of fuel, ammunition etc. which greatly eased the Japanese logistic position. Reinforcements moved up, allowing the Japanese to all but clear the RAF away from the battlefield by 19 December. From 23 December, Japanese airpower turned in force to assist the ground advance. Yamashita regrouped, to plan the next stage. Despite reinforcements he was still outnumbered on the ground, but Percival's strategy of holding everywhere played into his hands by dividing the defenders. That gave the Japanese a chance to defeat them in detail, made even more hopeful by the clear evidence that Japanese forces did not need superior numbers to overcome defended positions. Yamashita could afford to be bold, while reinforcements allowed him to rotate his units and keep the advance moving. On Christmas Eve Yamashita ordered his army to advance south of the Perak River, and to outflank by assault from the sea any major position on which the defenders tried to stand. The Japanese commander hoped to annihilate his enemy one division at a time north of Johore, then march into Singapore.[18]

III Corps escaped destruction in spite of its commanders, but the price it paid in Central Malaya brought the army to the last line of defence too soon, too weak. The troops fought well in places, but suffered from heavy pressure from the air, vulnerable sea flanks, fatigue, inexperience, poor deployments, unfinished defences — and above all from the dispute between Heath and Percival over strategy. Percival wanted to fight a lengthy delaying action in Perak, to cover Kuala Lumpur, Kuantan, the airbases, and the lateral road from coast to coast. So he ordered that III Corps would "fight the enemy wherever met and will NOT give ground until forced to" — but added the codicil "subject to the condition that the Corps must remain in being as a fighting formation." Heath still wanted to make a strategic retreat. This dispute had III Corps looking over its shoulder at every position, working to cross-purposes.[19] Heath and Simson agreed it was too late to hold north of Kuala Lumpur, but Heath refused to support Simson's effort to persuade Percival to authorise

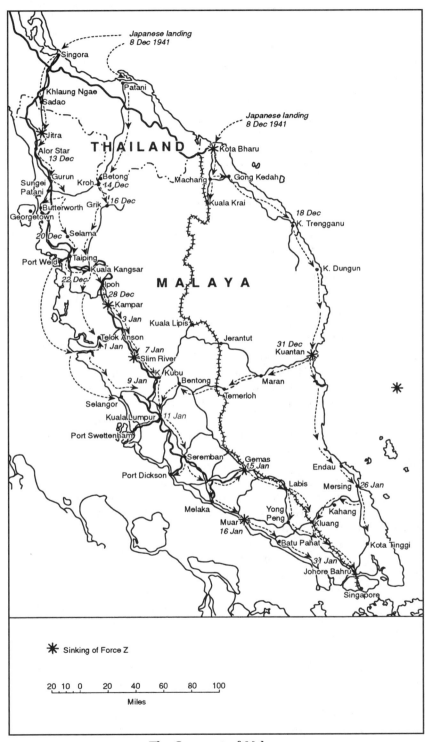

Japanese landing 8 Dec 1941

Singora

Khlaung Ngae
Sadao
Patani

Jitra
Alor Star
13 Dec

THAILAND

Japanese landing 8 Dec 1941

Kota Bharu

Gurun
Sungei Patani
Kroh
Betong
14 Dec
Machang
Gong Kedah

Butterworth
Georgetown
Grik
16 Dec

Kuala Krai

Selama
20 Dec

MALAYA

18 Dec
K. Trengganu

Port Weld
Taiping
22 Dec
Kuala Kangsar

K. Dungun

Ipoh
28 Dec
Kampar

3 Jan

Kuala Lipis

Telok Anson
1 Jan

7 Jan
Slim River

Jerantut

31 Dec
Kuantan

9 Jan
K. Kubu
Bentong

Maran

Selangor

Temerloh

Kuala Lumpur *11 Jan*

Port Swettenham

Seremban

Gemas
15 Jan

Endau

Port Dickson

Labis
Mersing
26 Jan

Melaka

Yong Peng

Kahang

Muar
16 Jan

Kluang

Batu Pahat

Kota Tinggi

31 Jan
Johore Bahru

Singapore

✳ Sinking of Force Z

20 10 0   20   40   60   80   100
Miles

The Conquest of Malaya

the immediate erection of a network of defensive positions further south, while there was still time. Percival agreed only to arrange for Public Works Department work teams to build obstacles, especially anti-tank obstacles, along the main axes of advance — without Simson's direction. III Corps was thus forced to fight on under a commander who objected to its orders but would not have it out with his boss.[20]

Percival had his reasons, which he spelt out on 30 December:

> To achieve our object of protecting the Naval Base it was necessary to fight the main battle on the mainland and it was hoped to be able to deploy all the reinforcements due to arrive in January for that purpose. Therefore the longer we could delay the enemy in central Malaya the better.

That suggested the "main battle" should not be fought *until* those reinforcements arrived. But here was the fatal contradiction again: 11th Indian Division must buy the time and space — but it was also needed to help fight the "main battle." Now at least Percival defined a precise task: hold the axis Kuantan-Kuala Kubu-Kuala Lumpur for 15 days. III Corps must not fall back more than 120 km for that time, and must not be destroyed.[21] This left the fate of Percival's strategy, and thus Singapore, in the tired hands of 11th Indian Division.

To give that division a chance to regroup and dig in at a good position at Kampar, 12th Indian Brigade fought a dogged running battle by itself for over a week. When it moved back into reserve on 29 December, it was badly depleted. Unfortunately, with no fresh units available Heath was forced to deploy it to cover the west coast, instead of regrouping.[22] That undid a good stand made by 11th Indian Division in a tough three-day battle at Kampar, from 31 December through 2 January, where the ground at last favoured the linear defence plus firepower tactics of the defenders. But the Japanese not only pressed that position hard, they also landed two separate forces on the coast and drove inland, threatening to come in behind the main force and cut it off from the lateral road and Kuala Lumpur. Superior fighting power allowed Yamashita to divide his forces yet still move forward. This doomed Percival's gamble of making a stand against the main advance without concentrating his forces. This was no rout, but by 6 January 11th Indian Division was again at full stretch in the last defensible area north of the lateral road, in a battle it must fight for at least eight more days.[23]

This threat to the lateral road forced a decision on the use of 9th Indian Division. Percival wanted it to deny Kuantan airbase as long as possible, especially with a reinforcement convoy then approaching Singapore. Heath made a new proposal, trying to combine Percival's orders to fight on with his desire to concentrate his forces. Heath suggested pulling 9th Indian Division together near Kuala Lumpur, then launching its two brigades in a counterattack to hit the Japanese from the flank as they moved through Selangor. This was certainly a gamble. Only a small party could be left to demolish the Kuantan airbase and delay its fall. And if the counterattack failed III Corps might find it difficult to disengage and retreat south. But it was at least a calculated risk. 11th Indian Division was not holding on its own, indeed would now be lucky to avoid disaster. If the counterattack worked, the enemy might be thrown off balance and delayed. Sadly, Percival refused to take the chance. Worse, the argument left 9th Indian Division torn between conflicting orders to hold the airbase but keep itself intact. By 3 January the base had to be abandoned anyway, under pressure from the Japanese regiment advancing along the east coast. 9th Indian Division extricated itself, but came back too late for Heath to either counterattack or hold the west coast properly.[24]

It is impossible to say what would have happened had Heath counterattacked, but the result of Percival's decision was clear. Both III Corps divisions were forced to retreat because neither could hold off the enemy on their own. The four brigades committed to the main battle in the west were now three depleted formations again facing heavy pressure in improvised positions. The only gain for this divided defence was the denial of the central airbases for a month. Against this enemy, with his aggressive jungle warfare tactics and tank spearhead, as long as the defenders were ordered to stand and fight, but deployed piecemeal, they were vulnerable. In this respect, the campaign must be seen in the broader perspective which so influenced Percival: the race between Allied reinforcements and the Japanese advance.

Only Churchill and the COS could provide two things essential to the defence of Singapore: reinforcements, and clear orders to military and civil authorities which related local defence to broader grand strategy. Churchill's reaction to the outbreak of war and the loss of the capital ships was this: while the situation was serious, it was outweighed in global terms by British advances in North Africa, Soviet success, and above all by the entry of the U.S.A. into the war. The Prime Minister decided to travel to Washington, to work out a firm grand strategy for global war. Far East Command must hold on while the new coalition worked out its plans.[25] Events and the Japanese moved faster than the Prime Minister. Along the way, the central direction of the war failed to reconnect grand strategy and the conduct of the defence of Singapore.

One thing which could not be changed was time and space. Reinforcements were far from Singapore and there were demands for forces elsewhere, while the enemy was approaching the doorstep. One thing Churchill and the COS agreed must not be changed was the basis of grand strategy: Germany must be defeated first. Any "excessive pull" of reinforcements to Singapore must be resisted. The Admiralty acted accordingly, authorising the Eastern Fleet on 20 December to abandon the Singapore naval base and retreat to the Indian Ocean when it became untenable — insisting unconvincingly it did not expect Singapore to fall. This of course terminated the "Singapore Strategy," the very basis of planning for war against Japan. But the early defeats did prompt the COS to divert some forces to Singapore, to prevent it from collapsing: the 18th Division, en route to Egypt, two brigades from India, *Blenheim* and *Hurricane* squadrons from the Middle East, and some crated *Hurricanes* en route at sea.[26]

This was not enough to overturn the "Germany first" policy, but enough to compel the COS to review the fast-moving Far East situation. The Prime Minister, at sea en route to the U.S., raised the key point:

> After naval disasters to British and American sea power in Pacific and Indian Oceans we have no means of preventing continuous landings by Japanese in great strength in Siam and the Malay Peninsula. It is therefore impossible to defend, other than by delaying action, anything north of the defensive line in Johore, and this line can itself only be defended as part of the final defence of Singapore Island fortress and the naval base. The C-in-C should now be told to confine himself to defence of Johore and Singapore, and that nothing must compete with maximum defence of Singapore. This should not preclude his employing delaying tactics and demolitions on the way south and making an orderly retreat.

This was exactly the point Heath made around the same time, and the same point the Prime Minister raised but then dropped months before. Because the matter was dropped, Churchill did not know there was no real line in Johore, nor full defences in Singapore. But his instinct remained to concentrate the army where it had a fighting chance. Gen. Sir Alan Brooke, newly appointed to replace Dill as CIGS, inherited the conventional wisdom that close defence of Singapore would inevitably fail. In a rapidly changing situation, his advice was that commanders on the spot were best placed to assess the situation and any decision should follow their report.[27]

That report was duly submitted on 22 December. The COS approved Percival's decision to fight a major delaying action in northern Malaya to buy time and space for reinforcements, giving him authority to fall back at his discretion. There was no misunderstanding here. This was not the strategic retreat with small rearguards suggested by Heath and Churchill. Percival's superiors in Singapore and London approved his decision to order III Corps to stand north of Kuala Lumpur.[28] A distracted Prime Minister again let the matter drop, and the COS again demurred from fully reviewing the state of defences in Johore and Singapore. The COS did not change Percival's mission, despite the fact the RN was now ready to abandon the naval base, and they left it to him to decide how to carry it out despite being unable to send reinforcements which could arrive in time to join any battle north of Johore. The cold truth is that the central direction of the war was simply overwhelmed by the pressure of events and the speed of the Japanese advance, and reacted hesitantly.

On Christmas Day the COS finally decided urgent steps must be taken to hold Singapore. But this was spelled out as a "minimum but essential redeployment" to hold the so-called "Malay Barrier" — the line Burma-Singapore-Java, the link between India, Australia and the Central Pacific. The basis of grand strategy remained to concentrate on Germany. After some debate, the British agreed to establish a unified Allied command in Southeast Asia, under a Supreme Commander with control over all Allied ground, sea and air forces in the area. The new command was named ABDA, or American-British-Dutch-Australian Command. Gen. Wavell, lately C-in-C India, took over the new command effective from 7 January, replacing Far East Command as Percival's superior. Wavell inherited the strategy of fighting a major delaying action north of Johore — and an express warning that only the early arrival of first-class fighter squadrons and an experienced division would give Malaya Command any chance to hold long enough for further reinforcements to mount a counteroffensive. Wavell, now responsible for pulling the several Allied defensive campaigns together into one coordinated battle, knew that as no battlefleet would arrive in time any counteroffensive to save Singapore must be led by ground forces. It would require even more air reinforcements, plus two more fresh veteran divisions and a tank brigade. But the Japanese were nearing the bases which would give them a chance to isolate Singapore. So the reinforcements needed for the main defensive stand must arrive soon, intervene fast, and be effective — or there would be no counterattack.[29]

Fifty-eight *Blenheim* bombers, 99 *Hurricane* fighters, two Indian brigades, Australian and Indian replacement troops and the 18th Division were all due in Singapore in January. That would meet the immediate requirements on paper, but only if the battle at hand went well. That now seemed to depend on reducing Japanese air superiority. On these grounds Percival concluded that the arrival of the *Hurricanes* was his best hope for salvation. That clinched his decision to keep fighting for Kuantan and Kuala Lumpur as long as possible.[30] Unfortunately the enemy advance had already cut the route by which fighter aircraft could be flown in from India, by seizing Victoria Point airbase in southern Burma. This debunked the claim air forces could be rapidly reinforced from elsewhere if necessary, the same sort of fallacy which grounded the entire "Singapore Strategy." Everything had to move in by ship. Worse, the final decision of the Washington conference was to send only the "minimum necessary forces," yet order Wavell to hold the "Malay Barrier." On 5 January, the Eastern Fleet moved its headquarters to Java. On 8 January Wavell warned the COS the situation was "becoming critical." The same day, Churchill and the COS settled the final reinforcement programme for the area: the 6th and 7th Australian Divisions and the 7th Armoured Brigade, all tough veteran formations returning from the Middle East, exactly what Percival needed. But they could not arrive before the end of February. Meanwhile, Percival's mission remained unchanged and his strategy was not challenged. Singapore was not expendable.[31]

What can explain this? One reason was the Prime Minister's persistent faith in a siege defence of Singapore. But the COS knew better. Their silence is better explained by the tensions of Imperial politics. On Christmas Day V.G. Bowden, Australian government representative in Singapore, sent a blunt telegram to his government. It spelt out the already dire straits of Malaya Command and the need for early reinforcements of quality. With the Japanese on the move and most of their own veteran units still in the Middle East, the Australian government lashed out. A very public argument erupted between the two Prime Ministers, the product of the years of British ambivalence about the "Singapore Strategy." The Australians made it clear they saw the defence of Singapore as the basis of their own defence and British commitment to it as the guarantee of British good faith in imperial defence — quid pro quo for Australian help in the European war. The British needed Dominion support too badly to dismiss Australian complaints. Churchill and the COS agreed to send I Australian Corps back to the Far East and fight on for Singapore.[32] That amounted to a gamble: that Malaya Command could hold Singapore with improvised reinforcements, without the strategic counteroffensive the "Singapore Strategy" always envisaged. Percival thus fought on in the north even though his mission now no longer really fit British grand strategy. This rupture compromised his army, accelerating the very collapse he was ordered to prevent.

Wavell's warning of 8 January was a reaction to the disaster that had already brought the army to the brink of that collapse. 11th Indian Divison tried to make one last stand north of Kuala Lumpur at a defile near Slim River. Only two exhausted brigades, led by 12th Indian Brigade, were available to deploy. On 7 January they were ripped apart by a Japanese tank attack which blasted through the road blocks, rampaged for 19 miles [35km] until stopped by artillery fire at point-blank range, destroyed two battalions, and helped follow-up infantry scatter the rest of the defenders far and wide by nightfall. What caused this disaster? The enemy advanced relentlessly, giving Percival and Heath no time to send up fresh units. His air attacks deprived the defenders of rest and shelter. Tired commanders deployed their units poorly, failing to use most of the anti-tank obstacles which were available and overlooking tracks the Japanese used to get around positions. Placed in a difficult position by the GOC, poorly deployed by its commanders, 11th Indian Divison was shattered, with only 1200 men still under command when it finally broke contact.[33]

Percival's gamble of leaving the brunt to 11th Indian Division, plus two reserve brigades, was lost at Slim River. Wavell took one look at the situation, then ordered what was left of III Corps to retreat to Johore without delay and sent his warning to the COS. III Corps passed through Australian advance positions and into the rear in Johore on 14 January, three days after the enemy captured Kuala Lumpur against little resistance.[34] While this was only four days ahead of Percival's timetable, the problem was not the speed so much as the way Malaya Command lost the battle to hold north of Johore. First, the final line on which there could be any hope of holding Singapore was northern Johore. The whole point of Percival's strategy was to deny the central airbases long enough to bring in reinforcements which would make Malaya Command strong enough to fight and win the "main battle" to hold that line. But the battle for the north cost the army two brigades destroyed, with two others severely battered; 12th Indian Brigade, by far its best formation, met its real end at Slim River and was never fit to fight as a brigade again. Malaya

Command would now only be replacing numbers, not increasing them. Second, the new formations were neither battle-experienced nor familiar with the area. Percival would have no choice but to throw them into battle as they arrived, ready or not, as 11th Indian Division plus his reserve was spent. This was avoidable. Percival had committed to the battle up north more strength than he could afford to lose, but not enough to hold or to avoid disaster. This was due in part to enemy pressure, but also a product of the foolish tactics of rigidly defending fixed lines which the defenders too often employed. Percival now found himself facing the "main battle" effectively weaker, not stronger.[35] This was not the situation Heath or Churchill envisaged after a retreat to Johore. Slim River was one battle, one disaster too many — and it undid the "main battle" before that clash even started.

Wavell's decision to fall back to Johore only confirmed plans Percival was already making. The last defensible line on which to stand to keep Singapore from being isolated was in northern Johore, on a line from Muar on the west coast to Endau on the east. This line had a good position developed by the Australians on the east coast, and the roads were flanked by belts of swamp, jungle and rugged Mt. Ophir in the west. On 10 January Percival directed his army to fight the main battle and stop the enemy here, on this "Johore Line." Unfortunately, as a keen observer noted this "Johore Line" was really a "certain area in north Johore where, if we had enough properly trained and equipped fighting men, we could have exploited the terrain to sufficient advantage to check the Japanese advance."[36] The ground was good, but the army was now too weak to hold it properly. When it was poorly deployed, this created an Achilles heel which proved fatal.

Percival's original plan was to concentrate III Corps on the main road and the west coast, leaving the Australians to hold their positions in the east. Bennett complained vigorously enough to impress Wavell. The Supreme Commander arbitrarily overruled Percival, directing him to place Bennett in command of the main defence on the main road.[37] Bennett planned to stop the Japanese dead in their tracks by springing a major ambush, then fighting an aggressive defence in depth between Gemas and Segamat. But Percival insisted on keeping one Australian brigade in the strong position on the east coast. 11th Indian Division regrouped to the south. 53rd Brigade, the lead formation of 18th Division, arrived in Singapore as the battle began and was sent forward immediately. That left Bennett four brigades to fight the "main battle." Bennett placed his 27th Brigade AIF in the lead, backed up by the 9th Indian Division. That left only the raw and newly arrived 45th Indian Brigade to cover Muar and the west coast. Bennett was wise to plan an aggressive encounter battle rather than hold a fixed line. But he undid this by leaving his weakest formation to hold the flank by itself, then forcing it to spread out too much to hold. Bennett simply counted on the enemy making only one major advance, down the main road, and assumed he could be stopped cold — and Percival and Wavell confirmed all his plans.[38]

The ambush at Gemas on 14 January went well, but not well enough to stop the Japanese advance. The Australians and Indians then put up a tough four-day fight which slowed the Japanese down. Unfortunately, Yamashita now had the entire *Imperial Guards Division* available for battle. This allowed him to mount two major advances in the west. The *Imperial Guards* hit 45th Indian Brigade hard. Bennett and Percival sent reinforcements in one battalion at a time, before they finally discovered late on 18 January how strong the threat on the west coast was. It was too late. After one of the most bitter fights of the campaign, by 22 January 45th Indian Brigade was destroyed, two Australian battalions sent in to help were shattered, and the west coast was now held only by the raw 53rd Brigade and the tired units of 11th Indian Division. That hard fight put up in retreat allowed Bennett's main force to pull back in good order, but the poor deployment and defeat at Muar forced a general retreat in the first place — and undid the "Johore Line." After only one week of the "main battle," a final retreat to Singapore was now clearly unavoidable.[39]

The quick collapse of Malaya Command in this "main battle" affected Allied grand strategy in Wavell's entire theatre. Wavell relied on a long stand in Johore as the basis of his plan to defend the whole ABDA area. If Singapore could even be held for two more months, tying down Japanese forces, this would buy time for vital reinforcements to hold Sumatra and Java. If things went well enough it might even be possible to direct I Australian Corps to Singapore, to lead a counteroffensive. On 15 January Wavell warned London the race would be a "near run thing," but reported Singapore could still be held if reinforcements were timely and effective.[40] Wavell counted on Bennett and the AIF, and on the reinforcements already converging. These amounted to the *Hurricane* squadrons, the already deployed 45th Indian Brigade, the 44th Indian Brigade, 18th Division, and the drafts of Indian and Australian replacements. The air situation was so important it is discussed separately. To suggest these troops could make the difference should have been seen for the wishful thinking it was. The rest of the Indians arrived on 22 January, all so raw they needed more training immediately. The Australians arrived on 24 January. A machine-gun battalion was assigned to Singapore; the replacements were now needed to repair the battalions smashed in Johore, but they too were far from fit for battle. The rest of 18th Division arrived on 29 January. That was too late, and in any case its lead brigade performed poorly in the fighting in Johore. Wavell should have realised by 15 January that if the "main battle" was joined before these troops arrived they could not help.[41]

Wavell was also swayed by sheer desperation. If he lost Singapore, the Japanese could strike at will towards any area of his command, from the central position. As long as it held, their attention was held there. But the question of how much help should now be sent to Singapore, to try to buy time to dig in elsewhere, could only be settled at the highest level. Churchill had already promised the Americans Singapore would be held. Wavell's warning set off an inquiry which at last made the Prime

Minister realise a cardinal fact: Singapore's own fixed defences were not designed to repel an attack from the north and very little had been done to bolster them after the war started. Churchill finally understood that Singapore was not in any sense a true "fortress" and would not likely be able to withstand a close siege for very long. On 19 January he warned the COS of the crux of the problem:

> Seaward batteries and a naval base do not constitute a fortress, which is a *completely encircled* strong place. Merely to have seaward batteries and no forts or fixed defences to protect their rear is not to be excused on any ground. By such neglect the whole security of the fortress has been placed at the mercy of ten thousand men breaking across the straits in small boats. I warn you this will be one of the greatest possible scandals that could possibly be exposed.[42]

Later that day, the Prime Minister accepted responsibility for the decision to withhold forces before the Japanese attack, but demanded immediate steps to bolster the defences — plus an inquiry into how the gap was allowed to fester. Churchill then told Wavell in no uncertain terms that he "expected every inch of ground to be defended."[43] On 21 January Wavell replied that a retreat to the island could now not be long delayed, and "I must warn you however that I doubt whether island can be held for long once Johore is lost." The shock hit the Prime Minister hard. As noted, before the war he did discuss with the COS defence plans for Malaya and the defences of Singapore — but both agreed to disagree and let matters evolve. That allowed the Prime Minister to base all his calculations on a false assumption: that the defenders could if necessary retreat on to an island bastion with all-round defences that would force the enemy to bring up heavy artillery in great strength, to bombard the fortress. That would take time, enough for Allied moves elsewhere to take effect. Now that hope was gone and the careless failure of the COS and Prime Minister to coordinate their plans before they had no choice took its toll. Churchill put the issue squarely: if Singapore could not be saved, would it not be better to cut losses by diverting the en route reinforcements elsewhere, where they might still help?[44]

The Defence Committee shrank from accepting this burden. The Australians, when they heard of the discussion, did not. On 24 January Prime Minister Curtin sent Churchill a telegram which did not mince words: "After all the assurances we have been given, the evacuation of Singapore would be regarded here and elsewhere as an inexcusable betrayal." Australians were putting their lives on the line to protect the U.K. The British would not be allowed to shrink from that blood debt. Churchill was angry, but also cornered, especially with the war in North Africa now taking a turn for the worse also. No doubt the Prime Minister would have insisted on a fight for Singapore regardless, but he sent in the rest of 18th Division, rather than divert it to Burma or Java, because the bluff of the "Singapore Strategy" was now called by an ally.[45] Rather than admit its pledge could not be honoured and insist it was better to send troops to fight to hold what could be saved, the British government sent them into a lost battle to preserve its face. Rather than accept the need to adjust to circumstances, however unjust it seemed, the Australian government insisted on the sacrifice. This collapse of leadership at the top left the defenders of Singapore with a final, bitter, belated and half-written "mission": to die well, and take their time doing so.

Percival's last real hope, the *Hurricane* squadrons, fell short, albeit through no fault of the men. The aircrews now experienced the same limitations as the army reinforcements. They did not know this enemy or area, had no time to learn about either, and were too few to absorb losses. Their machine was at best no more than a match for the Japanese *Zero*. The *Hurricanes* gave the IJA some difficult moments in ground attacks, but were rarely able to break through strong fighter escorts to break up bomber attacks. Their own mounting losses could not be replaced. RAF Far East shot its bolt in a gallant attack on a Japanese supply convoy approaching Endau on 26 January. More than half the bombers were lost, to little effect. On 30 January Wavell ordered all aircraft out of Singapore, except one *Hurricane* squadron left at Percival's request to defend the island.[46]

For Yamashita, speed remained the overriding imperative. With its supply lines now badly strained, *25th Army* opted to leave *56th Division* in Japan and bring up more munitions instead. Nevertheless, even stretched as they were by the last week of January the Japanese could have finished off the defenders on the mainland. They failed to do so, partly because of supply problems, plus caution brought on by several sharp rebuffs from the defenders, but even more due to failure to exploit their dominance of the air. Jealous of his success, Yamashita's rivals in superior authority transferred some of his air support to assist operations in Borneo. The remainder of *3rd Air Group* concentrated on bombing incoming convoys and Singapore; incredibly, it made no attempt to knock out the causeway, let alone go all out to help finish off Malaya Command before it got there. This perfect bottleneck was left intact, with no request from army headquarters to take it out.[47] That allowed Malaya Command a last chance to fall back intact, perhaps leaving it strong enough to put up a fight for the island itself.

That last chance was fumbled, due to command blunders. While the forces in the east fell back in good order and kept the enemy at a respectful distance by delivering some sharp blows, yet another brigade was lost due to avoidable mistakes. Percival knew as early as 20 January that there must be a final retreat. But the GOC insisted on holding positions until Wavell authorised the retreat. That left everybody trying to hold with one nervous eye over their shoulder, the other on the formation on the flank.[48] One brigade tried to hold Batu Pahat on the west coast too long, was encircled, and narrowly escaped destruction — many men being evacuated by sea. Worse, 22nd Indian Brigade was cut off by a premature retreat by the jumpy commander of its neighbour, not discovered until too late. Wavell finally authorised a full retreat on 27 January. Only 63 men from 22nd Indian Brigade emerged from the jungle and made it to Singapore.[49] Once again, reinforcements allowed

Percival only to replace numbers with less experienced troops, not to increase them—and now there was nowhere else to retreat.

The retreat into Singapore early on 31 January was an anti-climax. Stewart led the remainder of his Argylls out to fight to the death as a final rearguard, but the enemy was nowhere in sight. The rearguard marched across behind two of their pipers blaring defiance, Stewart the last to cross before demolition charges blew a hole in the fixed link. Malaya Command now found itself digging in for the last time, once again weaker rather than stronger after reinforcement. The troops had themselves to thank for being able to retreat, after several tough close-quarter actions. Their commanders had more to answer for. Bennett's plan for defence was seriously flawed, and when it failed he all but gave up on the battle in shock and feuded with his peers and staff. Wavell intervened without knowing the full situation, then left Percival in command even after signalling he had no confidence in him by changing his plan. Both men approved Bennett's bad plan. Finally, Percival clung too stubbornly to his assigned mission even after it put his army in positive danger by forcing it to stand in positions already untenable. When finally cleared to retreat, the GOC noted this must be done "despite the fact this meant failure to achieve our object of protecting the naval base."[50] In the process, he let Malaya Command entangle itself by trying to defend in place yet launch a full retreat at the same time.

It was not for the GOC Malaya Command to make grand strategy, but Percival did make two decisions here which now cost Singapore dear. The first was to interpret his orders by pursuing a strategy which cost his army too much in the north to make a real stand on better ground in the "main battle" in the south. The second was not making sure his superiors saw and acknowledged the possible broader consequences of ordering him to carry out a mission for which he had not the strength. This was not a matter of passing the buck. Churchill and the COS should have sorted out their differences on how to defend Singapore in December at the latest—January was much too late. The final and inexplicable conclusion is this: left almost on his own to pursue a militarily unrealistic strategy, Percival conducted a fighting retreat so as to preserve his army for a final battle it had virtually no chance to win—rather than take any calculated risk to try to avert this dilemma, let alone spell it out to those who allowed it to develop. Blinded by a sense of duty, Percival let events sweep Malaya Command along rather than challenge them. His superiors did not intervene. The defenders of Singapore now paid the price not for two months but for two decades of contradictions and wishful thinking in imperial defence.

The Naked Island

The situation that confronted the defenders of Singapore on 1 February 1942 was not retrievable. Nevertheless, Yamashita did not take this final challenge lightly. For the only time in the campaign his army faced defenders able to dig in behind a clear and unavoidable front line:

the Straits of Johore and Singapore. The Japanese must cross the water to attack. Supply lines were now long and badly strained, but large amounts of artillery ammunition might be needed to blast the defenders into submission. Finally, Yamashita needed to keep his commanders in check. Rivalry and thirst for glory threatened to upset any plan which gave pride of place to one division and relegated another.

25th Army staff started planning the attack on Singapore right after the fall of Kuala Lumpur. They expected Percival to fight stubbornly, but not to the last ditch in the city itself. The Japanese anticipated resistance from the equivalent of two divisions. This was an underestimate, but their other intelligence was better. Japanese planners respected the menace of the fixed defences and never intended to invade the south or east coasts. They opted to launch a concentrated assault on the northwest coast of the island, across the narrowest stretch of the Straits of Johore. The idea was to launch a hammer blow as soon as possible, to break through and overwhelm the defenders before they could dig in. The Japanese believed the defences being hurriedly built up were well-sited but not formidable. They expected to smash them with their own artillery, cross, and crush the defenders before they could regroup.[51]

Supply lines were a concern for exactly the reason Churchill noted. Only firepower could break the defensive crust, so extra allotments of heavy artillery ammunition were required. *25th Army* assembled 168 guns of all calibres to do the job. But only the arrival of the supply convoy at Endau allowed it to build up barely sufficient stocks. Speed remained of the essence. Given Japanese grand strategy plus the jealousy of his rivals, Yamashita could not afford to starve Singapore out in a long siege. So he took risks with his supplies in order to overrun it rapidly. Covered by their powerful air support, the Japanese assembled over 300 boats of various types, concealed their forces along the coastline and removed all civilians from it. Guns were deployed, targets registered. *5th* and *18th Divisions* would launch the main assault. They would blow through the beach defences, then overrun the area between the Kranji and Jurong Rivers. Feints would lead the enemy to expect an attack east of the causeway. On the second night the *Imperial Guards Division* would attack just west of the causeway, then advance to cut the defenders in two and prevent any retreat to defensible positions on the high ground near Bukit Timah. The water reservoirs and key supply dumps were in this area, near the centre of the island. When the Japanese took it they would overlook the city and its defenders. Yamashita assumed Percival would then surrender rather than fight it out in the city itself. Final orders were cut on 4 February. The assault was on for the night of 8 February.[52] That gave *25th Army* three days to keep its date with destiny.

Singapore was in fact already under attack, from the air. Japanese bombing attacks resumed from 29 December and steadily increased in weight. The radar network helped the fighters intercept nearly every raid, but they were first stretched by the double duty of protecting convoys, then hampered by the loss of mainland radar stations. At first the enemy bombed from altitudes over 20,000 feet, which made all but the heavy anti-aircraft guns ineffective. As resistance weakened, they came in lower and hit harder. Night attacks on Japanese airbases did little damage. Japanese efforts were more affected by the transfer of some bombers to operations in Borneo. Wavell finally warned Churchill that with three out of four island airbases now in range of enemy artillery, little could be done to bolster Singapore's air defence.[53] The Japanese had won the race against the reinforcements.

Passive air defences were no help. The decision to rely on dispersal rather than shelters backfired when refugees flooded onto the island. The normal population more than doubled, which put great strain on stocks of supplies and made the congested city a better target. Only on 7 February, too late, did the government decide to dig shelters. The almost unprotected population suffered the consequences, especially in the crowded Chinese districts. The full death toll will never be known, but it must have exceeded 10,000. Only the Japanese tendency to use high explosive rather than incendiary bombs saved the city from a holocaust by fire. As it was, by the time the siege began the body count was already unmanageable.[54]

More certainly could have been done to bolster civil defence. Given the controversy over accusations that labourers constantly scattered under fire in panic, never to return, it must be noted that the shortfall in civil defence was not caused by the civil population. People of all races behaved under attack as people in large numbers behaved nearly everywhere else in such conditions: some acted heroically, others broke in panic, most persevered. Expatriates and Asians volunteered in large numbers for duty as air raid wardens, fire fighters, and medical rescuers. Chinese leaders organised a civil defence network from the Chinese Secretariat offices, and it functioned to the end. But even willing hands could only do so much without leadership and organisation. Neither met the challenge.[55]

The roots of the problem were depressingly familiar: personal intrigue, plus the clash between needs of the moment and fears of consequences for the future. Between them, Duff Cooper and the Governor all but paralysed the central executive body, the Far East War Council, and thus civil defence, by a running argument over policy and authority in which many others took sides.[56] Under great pressure the Governor finally issued a directive on 15 January calling on the civil service to set aside normal procedure and take emergency measures boldly and rapidly. This was greeted with sarcasm in the press and skepticism in the military. Sadly both were justified, as habits of routine were not abandoned and the Governor did little to enforce his order.[57] The consequences were severe. The government decided on its own not to carry out mass evacuations ordered by London, fearing that a scuttle of Europeans would enrage the Asian population. Ships left in January with empty berths, leaving many "useless mouths" eating precious food and drinking even more precious water when Singapore fell under siege.[58] It took too long for the Chinese leaders to bury the hatchet between the Communist and KMT factions; not until the last week of December did a Chinese Mobilisation Council emerge, led by the respected businessman Tan Kah Kee. But the government, still influenced by fears of both Communist subversion and of appearing weak, remained reluctant to bring it into the war effort as a full partner, which gravely hampered efforts to secure and maintain labourers for essential war work.[59]

The root of the problem was the persistent reluctance of the local government to upset the Asian communities, and jeopardise British prestige, by taking any action which suggested the situation might get beyond control, or disrupt Asian interests. In its moment of peril Singapore needed a leader of the first rank, a man ready to take drastic measures and inspire their execution. Only Thomas and Percival were in a position to do this. Neither had the right personality or charisma to be an inspirational leader — but they also had too little faith in their charges to find the courage to reach beyond themselves. Both were men who would do their best according to procedure but not, even in extremis, make their own rules. Precious time was thus lost, the civilian population was more of a liability than it should have been, Singapore was more vulnerable than it might have been, due in no small measure to the shortcomings of those directly responsible for its defence.

The final most painful product of this failure of leadership in Singapore was the plans and preparations made for the defence of the island itself. Yet again, the story is of a bad hand badly played. Percival had no illusions. The Japanese had him cut off, under fire, and could attack where they chose. The best he could hope for was a prolonged fight. Wavell and Malaya Command made plans based on a siege lasting two to three months.[60] Circumstances gave the GOC only two choices of defensive strategy. Neither offered much hope for success. But the choice Percival made was the penultimate nail in the coffin, for three reasons. First, it relied on work which was not complete. Second, it threw away his own potential advantages, such as they were. Finally, it called for the kind of battle Percival was most reluctant and therefore least likely to fight: to take the calculated risk.

Percival expected an early attack, to keep him off-balance. He assumed Yamashita would assault the island with three divisions, then deploy four in reserve to follow up. This grossly overestimated the Japanese reserves, and had important effects on Percival's conduct of the battle. Malaya Command had perhaps 85,000 troops on the island, but too many formations were raw, spent or in disarray. While the defenders had no tanks fit for battle, they did have 226 guns of all calibres, including the Fortress guns. But there was a dangerous shortage of ammunition for the 25 pounder field guns, and there were limits on how effective the coastal batteries could be against an attack from the north.[61] Given his estimate of the enemy, Percival felt they could attack, and he must defend, all 72 miles [120km] of the island coastline. The GOC believed that the island was too small to take the risk of concentrating forces in the interior for a counterattack, leaving only a thin screen on the beaches. The enemy was likely to reach the vital central area, which

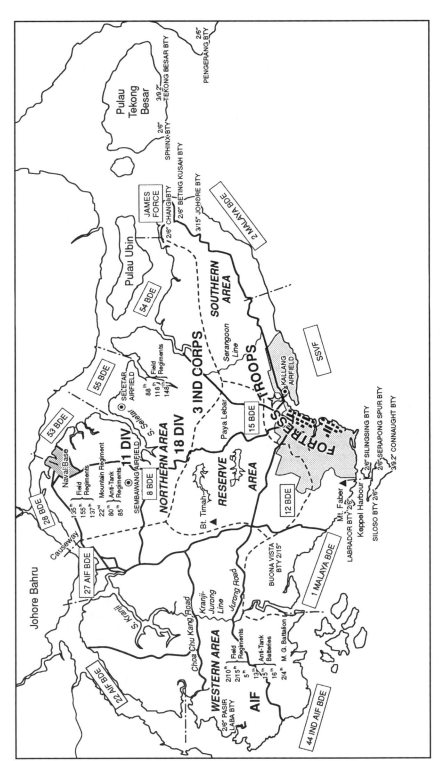

Deployment for the Defence of Singapore

must not be lost, before that attack could be mounted. That decision dictated the choice of strategy:

> The basis of the defence was that the enemy must be prevented from landing or, if he succeeded in landing, that he must be stopped near the beaches and destroyed or driven out by counterattack.[62]

The island was divided into three defence commands. Northern Area covered the coastline from just east of the causeway to just west of Changi Point, including Pulau Ubin. Western Area covered the coastline from the causeway to just west of the Jurong River. Southern Area covered the coastline from the Jurong River through Changi, including the city itself, Pulau Tekong, and the southern islands. The islands were part of the fixed defences, except Ubin, which was covered by patrols and observation posts. The supply dumps at Bukit Timah and Malaya Command field headquarters at Sime Road were in a Reserve Area in the centre of the island. Wavell expected the Japanese to attack in the northwest, so he advised Percival to deploy 18th Division, his largest and freshest formation, there. Percival concluded the enemy would more likely attack east of the causeway, where the terrain between the coast and the city was more open, so he ignored this advice and assigned it to Northern Area.[63]

Because of the losses in Johore, Percival had to deploy the freshly arrived Indian and British brigades directly in the front line. III Corps took over Northern Area. Heath deployed four brigades along the coast and left the 8th Indian Brigade in reserve; he also received the lion's share of the supporting artillery. Bennett took charge of Western Area, adding the raw 44th Indian Brigade to his two Australian brigades. All three were deployed along the coast, with no general reserve. Simmons and Fortress Headquarters took over Southern Area, deploying the Fortress troops and the Singapore garrison: 1st and 2nd Malaya Brigades plus the SSVF. Percival had only the very depleted 15th and 12th Indian Brigades in command reserve. The GOC intended to let his commanders fight the battle, but the crucial decision was his: when to commit forces to what kind of counterattack, if the invasion was not repelled outright. In that contingency, two stop lines were planned to provide a last-ditch line on which to cover the city and the central area. In the west, the narrow strip of land between the Kranji and Jurong Rivers was marked out as the "Kranji-Jurong Line." In the east, the rolling ground from the head of the Serangoon River to the southeast coast was marked as the "Serangoon Line." No plans were made for a last-ditch battle in the city itself; the battle would be won or lost before that.[64]

Percival could not change the fact the island was merely a defended base, not a fortress with all-round fortifications. Nor could he change the pre-war decisions which left it vulnerable in the first place, or the propaganda which persuaded the world it was another Gibraltar. But the GOC did have the means to improve the defences in the north; he cannot be excused for failing to make them as strong as they might have been in the time available. This was an error the Japanese found so incredible they blamed it on the Governor, assuming no soldier could have made such a blunder. But Percival did have reasons, and they need to be understood. One is well-known: concern for morale. Percival first considered steps to bolster the defences on 20 December. Simson made a comprehensive proposal for doing so on 26 December, when much might yet have been done. Simson's argument was that the best way to defeat an amphibious invasion was to destroy it on the water, failing that to pin it on the beaches then wipe it out. For that, a systematic network of fixed defences was needed, to help the defenders stand up to enemy bombardment. Percival curtly rejected Simson's plea with the words, "Defences are bad for morale — for both troops and civilians." Simson left this meeting "convinced Singapore was as good as lost."[65]

Matters did not rest there. Percival did order work on defences to begin, but no great activity ensued. Simson even gave Cooper a list of suggestions which was in the end returned to Percival by Churchill, in a long telegram insisting on measures to strengthen Singapore's defences. The last real chance to improve the position came on 9 January when an angry Wavell, standing near the causeway, insisted that Japanese troops pouring across an undefended Straits of Johore would do more to harm confidence than would building defences to stop them, and ordered Percival to bolster the defences forthwith. But the Supreme Commander did not in the end make sure his order was actually carried out.[66] Percival always insisted much work was done on Singapore's defences before the siege began* and blamed inadequate labour supply for the work left unfinished. Unfortunately for the GOC, the evidence is compelling: beach defences and the stop lines were all marked out on maps, but few positions were erected on the ground, and neither Percival nor Bennett did much about that in the first week of February. Percival later acknowledged the effect this shortfall had on his army and his under-stated style does not mask the truth:

> It is certain that the troops retiring from the mainland, many of whom had never seen Singapore before, were disappointed not to find the immensely strong fortress which they had pictured.[67]

During the retreat, the rumour mill convinced most units their role was now to delay the enemy to give the "Fortress" time to complete its defences. The truth which dawned on all when they arrived to find little or no work done on the area they must now defend was devastating. As before, the troops were now forced to try to do the job themselves, under enemy fire. Percival shied away from building defences in Singapore as insurance for fear he would create a self-fulfilling prophecy by undermining the army's will to fight on the mainland. Now he and the army had the worst of both worlds, and all formations were shaken by this evidence of neglect. Percival was right to blame the WO for failing to complete the pre-war plans for defences for Johore and Singapore advised by Dobbie. But it was he who chose a final defence strategy

---

* See Appendix 2.

which hinged on all but non-existent defences, which might have been made more formidable had he only acted in time.[68]

Percival's insecurity regarding morale does not by itself explain his neglect of Singapore's defences. Surprisingly few have noted how strongly his perception of the mission of Malaya Command influenced his preparations for the defence of Singapore itself. The point is frighteningly simple. Percival, brilliant staff officer and analyst that he was, pursued the axiom "maintenance of the aim." His aim, until 26 January, was to *hold the naval base*, rather than Singapore as a whole. The base was on the north coast, facing the mainland. If the Japanese came close enough to shell it and make it useless, the mission would fail. Building a major network of defences in and around it meant accepting that failure before the enemy arrived. Labour was scarce and morale appeared shaky. So Percival concentrated on the task at hand and resisted calls to increase work which might never be needed, could spark panic, and in any case would mean he had failed. Frighteningly simple — and frighteningly pedantic!

Percival was right to argue that Singapore let alone the base could not be held against an enemy across the Straits of Johore with command of the air and sea. But his decisions removed what chance there was the siege might last as long as Wavell intended. Percival's narrow strategy left the defence of Singapore itself against attack from the north an almost complete improvisation, rather than the reorganisation, albeit hasty, that was still possible from late December. Percival himself noted the general dismay caused by the clumsy final evacuation by the RN of the naval base, begun even as the final retreat ended. Demolitions shook troops from Bennett on down, all having been told it was their job to protect the base the navy was now blowing up in their face. Percival did almost nothing either to explain the change of mission to the troops or inspire them to accept the demolition of the base as a resolute military act of defiance, rather than a sign of doom.[69] Percival could not have simultaneously fought all out up-country and prepared Singapore for a siege. But he did not have to. All Simson needed was the GOC's authority and support, to provide the army with enough cover to make some sort of stand. When Percival decided to fight on the beaches, this was indispensable. But his obsessions with morale and narrow construction of the mission reinforced each other in making him back away from acting the only way anyone intending to hold Singapore now could: to fight like a cornered animal, with ruthless desperation. So sudden was the shift to improvising against an attack from the north, Malaya Command had no chance to pull itself together for a coherent defence of the island itself.

The Australian situation was particularly serious. Heavy losses in Johore forced Bennett to replenish his battalions with the reinforcements that arrived on 24 January, before they could do any further training. Wild stories persist about these men; some were said to be pressed men or convicts, others to have had barely two weeks training. Whatever the case, they were certainly not ready for battle. Every battalion received at least a platoon; 2 / 18 received 90 men, 2 / 19 370, 2 / 29 a whopping 500. This so heavily diluted these units, their fighting power was nothing like that they displayed in Johore.[70] Worse, after Johore Bennett lost the will to fight on come what may. He went to the island with one eye on escaping it, distracting him from preparing his division to defend it. The 8th Australian Division, sitting right in the path of the main enemy assault, was no longer really fit to fight as a division.[71]

Singapore also had an unavoidable Achilles heel: its water system was designed for a city, not an island fortress. The island reservoirs were fed by a larger supply in southern Johore, lost to the enemy on 27 January. The demolition of the causeway cut the flow in any case. With careful rationing the reservoirs held enough water to last for some months, but as the season was unusually dry no increase was expected. The distribution system was also exposed to enemy air and artillery attack, as most pipes were above or barely below ground. Malaya Command now had to defend greater numbers than expected with no secure water supply. At least the need to improvise here was placed in Simson's capable hands.[72]

Improvisation also marked Malaya Command's response to calls to organise a Chinese guerrilla force. As early as 1940 Lt.-Col. John Dalley of the Federated Malay States Police had suggested organising such a force, to be activated if the Japanese invaded. Dalley knew better than anyone the dangers and opportunities involved in such a move; not a few of the tough men he expected to be useful had been incarcerated thanks to him. But Dalley's suggestion was buried by political caution, and only acted on in mid-December 1941. It was too late to do very much, but backed by Heath and the Orient Mission of the Special Operations Executive (SOE) Dalley hastily organised a force. The Japanese moved faster; by the time the retreat ended, Dalley had only 4000 men available — many more volunteered. A handful of stay-behind parties were left to operate on the mainland, while the rest mustered under Dalley in Singapore. Dalley organised them into a scratch fighting formation, dividing the men into a KMT unit and a Communist unit under his command. The fighters made up a cross-section of the Chinese community, from students to hard-core gangsters. Unfortunately there were not enough weapons to equip them properly; most took the field on 5 February with shotguns, some with as few as seven rounds of ammunition. Percival sent detachments to each Area Commander, to act as fighting or covering patrols. The rest of *Dalforce* was deployed just west of the Kranji River, covering a gap between the two Australian brigades. Of all the defenders of Singapore *Dalforce* was certainly the most eager to fight the Japanese. As Percival noted, it is a pity it was forced to do so in such poor conditions.[73]

The final and most controversial feature of preparations for the last stand also required Malaya Command to improvise: to use the great guns of the Fire Commands to help beat off an attack from the north. The myth of the guns pointing the wrong way was discussed in Chapter Six. Most guns which could be brought to bear by improvisation were, including three of the 15" guns, all the 9.2" guns, and six of the eighteen 6" guns. Urgent requests were made for more high explosive ammunition, but none arrived in time. The essential fact is that the guns were never designed to defend against an attack from the mainland; such an attack was to be stopped up-country. When that attack was not stopped, it was not possible to use the coastal guns at anything like their full effectiveness against it because they were laid out to face a threat from the sea. The great irony is that in a crucial sense all the money invested on the fixed defences paid off, because the Japanese did not dare to attack by sea.[74] Percival could and should have taken this into account. He made a mistake by not taking advantage of the one success of pre-war preparations in his own final defence plan.

There was no need to garrison the south coast in strength. It was covered by the coastal batteries and the network of defences built from 1940. 22nd Brigade AIF, in the path of the enemy, was spread out over a front of three miles per battalion — much too much in close country, especially for weakened units. By trying to cover everywhere the army was again not strong enough anywhere, even though Percival knew the enemy would concentrate in force at his chosen target. His planned response was to send the now very weak 12th Indian Brigade to help the beach defenders pin the enemy down, then strip units from other sectors to launch a general counterattack once the main enemy invasion was identified. This made very little sense. It was unlikely the first reserve would arrive in time to help pin down a massive assault, and even if it did it was now too weak to reverse the tide itself. This problem need not have arisen so acutely. The SSVF and fortress troops were enough to cover the south coast; a risk could have been taken there, backed up by the great guns. This would have freed 1st and 2nd Malaya Brigades to either beef up the reserve or thicken the coast defences. Percival decided instead to overinsure in the south, thus wasting the investment on the guns. That left him with forces spread too thin to hold the coast, reserves too weak to rescue them, and only one last option if things went wrong: to throw everything into an all or nothing counteroffensive. Nothing Percival had done up-country made it very likely he would do this. The stop line plan suggests the reverse — but they were not ready either.

To be fair, it is true that from 1 February no plan Percival made would have stopped the Japanese. But even at this late stage, he could not bring himself to take a calculated risk to be bold rather than backpedal cautiously. By assuming the enemy was stronger than he was, then overguarding his back door, Percival settled on the strategy least suited to his situation and abilities. Percival was resolute and determined to do his duty, but he was not the street fighter Singapore now needed to have any chance to survive the onslaught. One episode underlines this point. In early February engineers began to drain the massive stocks of oil held in storage tanks for the naval base, to deny them to the enemy. One measure the Japanese truly feared was that a fire trap might be set up by creating oil slicks on the water and lighting them when their boats approached.[75] Simson pleaded to be allowed to do just that. No serious action was taken — other than by the Japanese, who bombed and shelled the storage tanks, to help drain them. Everyone in Singapore that February remembered the thick pall of black smoke created by the fires, which hung over the island throughout the battle. For the defenders and those they protected, it symbolised the inferno about to smother them. Yet surprisingly few now concluded the situation was hopeless. This was partly due to ignorance about how naked the island really was.[76] But it also suggests the Governor and the GOC were wrong to assume their charges were not ready to face possible disaster with defiance, if only they had a lead to follow. Probably not even a Great Captain could have held Singapore by this point. But it would not have taken a Great Captain to make it a tough proposition, taken only at real cost. By the time the enemy was ready to attack, that chance was gone.

The Fall of Singapore

The battle for Singapore lasted longer than the Japanese expected but was shorter than the Allies required. The defence was disorganised but far from token. The island saw the most intense battle of the campaign. The city itself escaped destruction by a narrow margin. The Japanese had the initiative, the confidence of victors, overwhelming air superiority, tanks, and a determined leader. The only thing Yamashita feared was a drawn-out defence which might drag him into a costly street battle in the city and overtax his supply lines. The defenders were not broken but were certainly shaken. The "backs to the wall spirit" did some good, but yet again the readiness of many troops to fight on was wasted by commanders who sped up defeat by making grave blunders. This time in fact command and control in Malaya Command all but collapsed; initial confusion became final chaos. The battle was lost as fast as it was because yet again, for the last time, the defenders were outgeneralled.

The systematic pummelling of Singapore began on 4 February, when *25th Army* artillery added its weight to the air attacks. Because Malaya Command planned to hold out for at least two months, it restricted counterbattery fire to mobile batteries, to avoid giving away fixed positions. It also imposed a strict limit of 20 rounds per day per gun, neither transferable nor saveable, to conserve ammunition. There may have been some point to this, but it was taken too far. The Australians were forbidden to fire on the tower of the Johore administration building, being used by the enemy for observation, until late on 5 February; headquarters was reluctant to annoy the Sultan. More incredibly, Malaya Command instructed all formations to notify it in advance before "making warlike noises," so it could warn the civil population and prevent panic.[77] With bombs and shells now raining down from Orchard Road to the docks at Keppel, what does this say about the state of mind at GHQ?

The Japanese bombardment did not hurt many troops, but it did impede work on defences and drain their energy. While most enemy guns were lined up to cover their main assault, Malaya Command left its batteries scattered all over the island to defend all approaches.[78] This was a crucial error too often overlooked. Trying to ration ammunition for a siege was obviously tempting, but the basis of the defence strategy was to destroy the invader in crossing or repel him on the beach. For this, the guns were indispensable. Artillery was the main punch in the battle doctrine of British Empire armies, especially on the defence. Only the guns could inflict enough slaughter when the attackers were most vulnerable out on the water, or trying to establish themselves ashore, that they might be overcome by infantry counterattack. At the very least, the guns must be unleashed in full strength against a determined invasion, or it would likely succeed. To do that, they had to be concentrated as much as possible in the right place, and brought to bear at the right time. But Percival felt the enemy could mount more than one serious invasion. Arrangements for gun positions and target registration were swayed by this. The Australians were badly outgunned at the key point. The enemy bombardment did the rest.

Needing a fast victory, Yamashita defied his lean stocks by unleashing a massive bombardment on 8 February. The shelling reminded some Australian veterans of the worst days in the trenches in World War I. Eventually most landlines were cut, leaving the forward infantry under terrific strain and almost cut off from commanders who assumed the bombardment would last for days — despite the fact that by late afternoon the island was so obscured by smoke the Japanese resorted to firing on plotted targets.[79] In such circumstances, 22nd Brigade AIF had little chance to repel the concentrated Japanese assault which hit it from 2130 hrs on 8 February. Three battalions, 2/18, 2/19 and 2/20 AIF, were spread out defending nine miles of coastline. Many company positions were separated by mangrove swamps or deep vegetation, ideal for Japanese infiltration. All three units were of course heavily diluted with

Japanese assault troops landing in Singapore

recently arrived replacements. The brigade had only the defences it managed to improvise in a week, backed up by two field artillery batteries. It was hit by the full weight of the *5th* and *18th Divisions*.[80] Even the friction of battle itself turned against the Australians, due in part to decisions made by their own commanders.

The near-total collapse of phone and radio communications proved disastrous. Because Taylor ordered that no searchlights could be lit up without permission, but communication was then lost, the enemy crossed in darkness. Nor could the artillery be reached in time, even with signal flares. Some companies stood their ground stubbornly, but in the face of little more than infantry fire the enemy kept coming. Too late the artillery responded to a volume of requests for fire, one battery being told to "bring fire down everywhere." By 0100 hrs the coast defences sagged, as defending units started to fall back.[81] The failure to illuminate the searchlights and bring the guns to bear made it impossible to destroy the invasion in crossing. Now the second crucial moment was at hand.

After 0100 hrs, it was becoming clear the Japanese were breaking the crust and penetrating inland. Now was the moment for command decisions. According to the plan, Taylor's job was to fight to contain the enemy at or near the coast, at all cost; Bennett and Percival must organise the counterattack aimed to exploit that stand and repel the enemy. None worked according to plan. Bennett and Percival sent what little help they could, in the form of 2/29 AIF and 12th Indian Brigade respectively. But Percival delayed until 0830 hrs — until he could be sure another enemy assault was not coming in elsewhere. Sixteen enemy battalions were now moving against Taylor, three times more than he first estimated, and no other attack was possible that night. No help reached Taylor until 0600 hrs. Hours of confused and desperate fighting at close quarters convinced Taylor around dawn that to have any hope of contesting any further advance his brigade must fall back, to form a covering line.[82] This fateful decision conceded a beachhead to the enemy. That left only the stop lines and an all-out counterattack, against an enemy now established inland, in the defence strategy.

In these early hours the man who mattered most was Taylor. He made the most fatal decision before the battle started. He was forced to spread his battalions out along the coast. He had not deployed the guns, nor was it his fault the defences were so meagre. But he chose to pursue the crucial battle — when defenders and invaders would be all mixed up in dense vegetation in pitch darkness with chaos all around — by a strategy which both defied his orders and was in any case more than his diluted units could manage. Taylor privately told his unit commanders that if their positions were hard-pressed they should not stand and fight but rather fight their way back to an area covering Ama Keng and the axes of advance towards the city. This meant giving up the crust — but the defence plan assumed instead that if penetrated 22nd Brigade AIF, or any other formation, would stand and fight in position as best it could, to tie down the Japanese and hold them for the counterattack. That meant a desperate fight, but these were already dire straits. By retreating, Taylor helped transform an unavoidable first defeat into an early collapse, one with fatal repercussions.[83]

A fighting retreat at night with enemy all around is the most difficult operation of war, one which 22nd Brigade AIF was not in any shape to attempt. It did not make it. By mid-morning two battalions were reduced to remnants, the rest of their troops scattered far and wide by enemy attacks. Taylor's plan was meant to preserve his brigade, to allow it to slow down the enemy. Instead it led to its dispersal, which allowed Japanese follow-up formations to move inland faster than they otherwise would have, nearly unimpeded. Twice on 9 February Taylor tried to improvise a stand, but by mid-afternoon he decided to fall back to an area screening the "Kranji-Jurong Line," apparently hoping to find help there. The Japanese let him go while they regrouped, having thus not only solidly established themselves inland but also scattered the only formation yet standing in their path.[84]

This brought Malaya Command to the last moment to make the command decision needed to have even a slim chance to repel the invasion. Unfortunately for the defenders, their command and control now steadily fell apart. To be fair, no account written in the light of hindsight can fully capture the sheer turmoil of the fighting in Singapore. Battle is notoriously a messy and confusing affair. To any commander, timely and accurate information is the difference between life and death. Percival had precious little in Singapore, starting with his own stubborn overestimate of enemy strength. Then again, neither he nor too many of his commanders tried hard enough to tackle this problem — nor did they make the best use of the information they did receive.

Bennett found out about Taylor's retreat too late to countermand the order. By the time he met Percival in late morning, they faced three choices: concentrate most of the army to deliver the general counterattack, post haste; have 44th Indian Brigade attack the enemy from the south; or mount a defensive stand in front of and on the "Kranji-Jurong Line." The first choice meant stripping all other sectors; Percival would not do this while he expected another major enemy invasion. The last was the easiest. It fit into existing plans for a last stand, and it matched Percival's tendency to backpedal and play for time. Percival duly ordered Bennett to form a line facing west from the Jurong River to the causeway.[85]

With this choice, Percival lost the second and decisive stage of the battle by default and threw away the last slim chance to execute his original strategy. Falling back could only prolong the battle, not throw the Japanese off the island. By opting not to attempt a general counterattack before the enemy was fully established, Percival was left with only the "Kranji-Jurong Line" to delay, let alone prevent, defeat. That left only one real remaining hope — the defence could be stubborn enough to drain Japanese supplies, forcing them to regroup.[86] This was already a very long shot, given how disrupted the defenders now were on the western flank. At the very least it required most careful coordination between commanders. Unfortunately, this became yet another plan compromised before it even took shape.

There was in fact no "Kranji-Jurong Line." Regardless of Malaya Command's intent to use it as a last-ditch defence, almost no work had been done on it. The Australians had only eight days to do so, and were under orders to concentrate on the coast. Nevertheless, what happened in that last week is inexcusable. On their own initiative Bennett's staff reconnoitred the position, based on Thyer's perceptive assumptions the coast would not be held and there would be no timely general counterattack. Thyer drafted a plan to make the line as defensible as possible at such short notice. Bennett rejected it with a tirade about retreat complexes and defensive mentality and forbade any serious work on the line. As a result, when units fell back late on 9 February they found a handful of gun emplacements, trenches, and a few anti-tank mines, but little else.[87]

Percival did not know how desperate the position really was, but he did appreciate the crisis was at hand. But instead of organising a general counterattack, the GOC spent the late hours of 9 February drafting a contingency plan for a final all-round perimeter, on which to mount a last defence of the city itself. Even now Percival decided not to strip the other coasts unless he needed forces to repel an attack on Bukit Timah. The final perimeter would then be formed around the city and the vital central reservoirs and supply dumps, anchored by high ground in the west and north.[88] This was a recipe for final defeat. It was produced by Percival's persistent suspicion the enemy could still mount an even stronger invasion against Northern Area, with non-existent reserves. By keeping the rest of the army waiting for the "main invasion," Percival left the Australians to be defeated by that attack, already well underway.

That defeat was compounded by a fiasco in the north, when the *Imperial Guards Division* launched the follow-up assault just west of the causeway that same evening of 9 February. 27th Brigade AIF was compromised before the attack even started. Its commander, Brig. D.S. Maxwell, a doctor in civilian life, decided the battle was already lost and gave himself orders authorising him to pull back after oil storage tanks in his sector were destroyed.[89] The formation was in the process of gearing up to move when the enemy attacked. From good positions, the Australians made the Japanese pay a price. But only one battery was still deployed in support, the other having moved out already, so there was not enough firepower left to hold. Due to a lucky accident all might yet have been retrieved. Around 0400 hrs the oil tanks were drained and the flow set alight. It swept into *Imperial Guards* units moving along the mouth of the Mandai Kechil River and in a spectacular inferno incinerated many of them. The division commander panicked and demanded the attack be scrubbed, but Yamashita was more resolute and had the situation investigated. The Australians, instead of digging in, retreated, Maxwell leaving the whole sorry business to a trusted subordinate as he remained at a very far back headquarters, out of touch.[90] That gave the Japanese the chance to launch the converging attacks which Yamashita hoped would split Malaya Command in two and force a surrender.

That chance loomed very large when in the early morning of 10 February Taylor made another error which undid the "Kranji-Jurong Line." Percival's warning order regarding a last-ditch perimeter went out that morning. Its intent seemed clear: "in the event the enemy could not be held, a perimeter would be formed." But it also spelt out sectors to occupy, ordered commanders to have them inspected now, and permitted them to make arrangements for the move which would not interfere with the battle at hand. Sending out such a signal, with its clear tilt in an ultimate direction, to tired hard-pressed men was asking for trouble. Taylor received it by hand at 0900 hrs. Dead on his feet, expecting to retreat, Taylor missed the caveats and saw only the intent — one which, given the state of his formation, made sense. Taylor ordered what was left of his brigade to retreat forthwith to its designated perimeter sector, along Reformatory Road. This left a huge hole in the "Kranji-Jurong Line."[91]

Bennett found out about the retreats of both his brigades only after they were well-advanced. He lost his temper, but neither countermanded them nor issued any other orders. When the other formations in the west came under renewed enemy attack, they drifted back to close ranks. By the evening of 10 February there was again a line of sorts, stretching from Bukit Panjang to Pasir Panjang, but it was very makeshift and most formations were quite bewildered.[92] The command decision finally came in mid-afternoon. Wavell, in Singapore for his last visit, lost patience and pressured Percival into ordering a counterattack. Percival duly directed Bennett to rally his forces and mount a three-stage attack, to drive the enemy back to the west coast. But neither of his superiors offered the Australian the help he needed to make this attack anything other than a farce. Instead, Wavell ordered the last serviceable RAF aircraft to retreat to Sumatra; Percival ordered the demolition of the main oil reserves near Bukit Timah. Wavell published an order of the day rebuking the troops for not fighting harder against an enemy they outnumbered. Percival added his own warning of lasting disgrace, and said, "In some units the troops have not shown the fighting spirit expected of men of the British Empire... There must be no further withdrawals without orders. There are too many fighting men in the back areas." Yet if this was to be the last-chance counterattack, Western Area needed reinforcements, not lectures. It was already probably too late to take the bold calculated risk, to throw the whole army into a counterattack before it was backed into the city itself. Instead, Percival did no more than order Heath to pull three of his 15 battalions off the coast defences and send them to help protect Bukit Timah.[93] The attack was left to Western Area, which was so evidently disorganised that, after a shouting match with Taylor, Bennett lapsed into self-pitying anger and made no real effort to pull his forces together. To make his day complete, Bennett was forced to note reports that a serious problem was developing in the city as large numbers of stragglers, including Australians, moved in that direction, away from the battle.[94]

Given that only 8th Indian Brigade saw serious fighting that day, in an effort to retake the ground abandoned by Maxwell, it is clear that

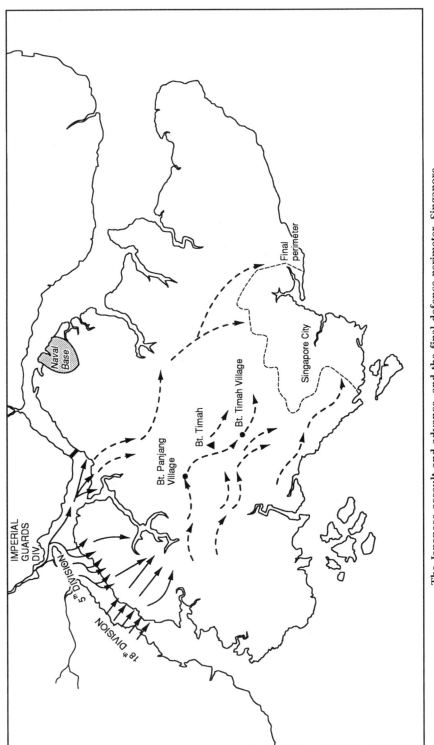

The Japanese assault and advance, and the final defence perimeter, Singapore

10 February was the day the high command of the defenders lost any real grip on their battle. Taylor's careless blunder, Maxwell's willful disobedience, and Percival's decision to launch no more than a piecemeal counterattack by badly disrupted forces together handed the Japanese a chance to finish the battle once and for all. Yamashita ordered an all-out attack for that night. *5th Division* would move east along the Choa Chu Kang Road, *18th Division* along the Jurong Road, and the *Imperial Guards* would take Mandai Village and advance southeast. The main attack would culminate in a bayonet attack to take the heights at Bukit Timah by storm. What a contrast this makes with every order issued by his counterparts that day — even Wavell did not follow up his order to make a serious counterattack possible.[95] The Japanese attack caught Bennett's units moving up to prepare their own advance and shredded several of them. Tanks led an assault which blasted through the defences at Bukit Panjang, allowing the enemy to overrun the high ground and many of the supply dumps at Bukit Timah. Only supply problems and a road block at the Bukit Timah road junction kept them from barrelling straight down that road towards the city. But their advance went far enough to force the gunners of the 15" battery at Buona Vista to destroy their guns, and compel Percival to abandon Malaya Command's field headquarters at Sime Road at 0745 hrs on 11 February.[96]

The Japanese were now poised to drive into the city itself. Percival knew that if he could not stop them and regain the Bukit Timah area the battle could not last. Yet even now the GOC did not throw caution to the winds. Heath was directed to assume charge of the line down to Bukit Timah, but only two more battalions were sent in that direction. The vital counterattack was left to the only formation at hand: the just-arrived three-battalion battlegroup, *Tomforce*. *Tomforce* did its best in what turned out to be the only serious counterattack of the battle of Singapore. It fought all that morning of 11 February, aiming to retake the Bukit Timah area, culminating in a bayonet charge witnessed by admiring Japanese officers from the nearby hill. But the attack could not move past the railway line, beaten back by enemy air and artillery support hastily moved forward.[97]

This turned out to be the last throw. Maxwell stalled on orders to retake Bukit Panjang, a move probably aimed to converge with the *Tomforce* attack, long enough to make the operation pointless. Later that day 27th Brigade AIF was dispersed in two directions and moved well south and east.[98] That forced Heath to give up the naval base at 1800 hrs — but even then he still held positions on the northeast coast. Three more 18th Division battalions arrived in late afternoon, and *Masseyforce* now took charge of the defence behind Bukit Timah. Yet again a continuous line was improvised. But now the defenders had lost the central high ground, several battalions, and most of their ammunition, petrol and military rations. Percival bravely ignored an elaborately worded demand for surrender dropped by a Japanese aircraft that afternoon, but he knew that the loss of the main supply dumps left his army with at most two weeks of food.[99] The GOC had let his army fall between two stools. The Australian defences fell apart too fast and too seriously, help came too little too late. Units were fed piecemeal into encounter battles. The counterattack was too weak to succeed, the improvised perimeter now too weak to hold.

Enemy attacks on 12 February finally convinced Percival and Heath to abandon the rest of the coast defences and pull into the now-compromised perimeter. That final line took shape on the morning of 13 February, stretching from Kallang, through Woodleigh, then Thomson Village, MacRitchie Reservoir, Adam Road, Tanglin Halt, and from there to Pasir Panjang. Percival had no illusions about this new reduced perimeter. The latest retreats cut the supply of rations down to a week, reduced stocks of mortar and artillery ammunition to dangerously low levels, abandoned coastal batteries hitherto most useful in support, and now made the water supply a grave problem. The whole city was now in easy range of enemy guns, and the water distribution system started to collapse as breaks in the pipes outpaced the ability of Simson's men to repair them.[100] A possibly even greater danger was the mood of the army. Units brought off the beaches now for the first time grasped how close they were to disaster. Bennett decided on his own to form his division into an all-round perimeter, to guard its own flanks and rear for a final battle — but the Australian units had been badly rocked, prompting real concern over how many men remained under command. Such concerns were rising over Indian and British troops as well, sparking Bennett to justify his decision by arguing there was no longer any real resistance being offered anywhere.[101]

The Prime Minister was not impressed by the rapid deterioration of Singapore's defences. Day after day he bombarded the COS and Wavell with queries about the battle. On 10 February, Churchill sent a telegram spelling out what he "felt sure" Wavell also felt, in order to "share your burdens." The government expected a determined resistance. They were told Percival had over 100,000 troops under command, half British and Australian. Churchill did not mince words:

> The honour of the British Army and the British Empire is at stake. I rely on you to show no mercy to weakness in any form. With the Soviets fighting as they are and the Americans resisting so stubbornly at Luzon, the whole reputation of our country and our race is involved. It is expected that every unit will be brought into close contact with the enemy and fight it out.[102]

This thinly veiled threat was the basis of the warning passed on by Wavell and Percival to the troops. Neither man made any effort to temper its tone to realities on the ground, nor explain these to the Prime Minister. Above all, it was a stark warning to Wavell and Percival not to surrender too soon. What Churchill really wanted was a dogged street battle in the city which would pin down the Japanese in a grinding fight and save British face.

On 11 February a Japanese invasion fleet heading for Sumatra cut Singapore off by sea, completing its encirclement. Two days later Wavell warned the COS Singapore would soon fall and the enemy was about to attack Sumatra. His whole defensive strategy for the theatre must be reconsidered immediately.[103] Most people in Singapore concluded before the Supreme Commander that the writing was on the wall. Daily life in Singapore was reduced to a struggle for sheer survival. The credit of the *tuan* had already disappeared, when merchants and clubs stopped accepting chits for payment. Now the defences crumbled, and the city with them. Shells and bombs wrecked houses and shops and set fires on Orchard Road, Beach Road, along the Singapore River, and in the Tanglin area. The last meeting of the Far East War Council was held on the morning of 9 February; after that the military and civil leaders were simply overwhelmed by disasters. That day the Governor finally ordered the destruction of civilian enterprises. The next day he ordered the expatriate staff of the Harbour Board to evacuate. That did more harm than good. Over the next few days some key government and police officials left their posts without permission; civilian labour now all but vanished. Yet many businessmen resisted the demolition of their facilities, and the Governor continued to exempt Chinese-owned property. Only the destruction of liquor supplies went ahead with general support, spurred by fears of the sort of Japanese rampage reportedly suffered by Hong Kong. By 12 February police control was at last cracking, especially at the port. Mr. Bowden reported to his government that all merchant ships under naval control were now gone and "except as a fortress and battlefield Singapore has ceased to function."[104]

Hospitals became hopelessly overcrowded with casualties, so many other buildings were pressed into service: for example, schools, St. Andrew's Cathedral and the Cathay Building. Deaths from enemy bombing and shelling outpaced efforts to dispose of the bodies, adding their smell to the chaos. A direct hit on the Istana drove the Governor and his wife into the Singapore Club on the waterfront. With the end in sight, people tried to escape on their own and under official auspices. A final official evacuation was organised on 13 February. Designated evacuees included nurses, technical and staff experts, Lt.-Col. Dalley and members of his force, other Chinese known to be wanted by the Japanese, Lt.-Col. Stewart, and even Pulford, under strong protest. But all departures were marked by progressively uglier scenes, as Japanese aircraft strafed crowded piers and deserters rushed ships at gunpoint. Tragically few ships made it through the gauntlet now ringing the island, but their departure underlined how close the end now was.[105] There could be no Dunkirk here, the army had no place left to go.

The other group with no way out was the great mass of Asian civilians. In the last days, Percival remembered their attitude as "with few exceptions...apathetic." Surely one such exception was *Dalforce*, roundly praised by British and Australian units it worked with as tough and brave. Workers did desert en masse as men fled home to tough it out, but troops recorded examples of civilians doing what they could to help wounded soldiers. "Fatalistic" is a fairer word to describe how the civilian population pulled into itself, to weather the storm. Many civilians who had boats tried to make money ferrying people to nearby islands. Others carried on with civil defence work to the bitter end. Most concentrated on surviving.[106]

On the afternoon of 13 February Percival met his senior commanders in conference at Fort Canning, proposing to counterattack. They all insisted it would fail and urged surrender instead; emotions boiled over as Heath argued bitterly with the GOC over who was responsible for landing the army in this mess. Percival decided to fight on, but warned Wavell the army could not hold longer than two more days, and raised the key question: could the possible benefits of fighting on in Singapore still outweigh or even equal the likely costs? This was not a question Percival could answer, absorbed as he was with the collapse of his own position. Only his superiors could gauge whether it was so important to impose any possible delay on the Japanese that the risk of a total collapse in Singapore and the sacking of the city should be accepted. Wavell's reply next day did not flinch, ordering Percival to fight it out house-to-house, but at the same time he warned Churchill Singapore was on the point of collapse.[107] Wavell already knew the answer. That same day, 14 February, the Japanese invaded Sumatra. Two more weeks of resistance in Singapore might have been useful to defenders elsewhere. Two days were strategically pointless. But the code of military discipline applies to all ranks. Percival and Wavell did not have the authority to surrender Singapore on their own volition. That decision rested at the only vantage point able to and responsible for considering the widest- and longest-term strategic and political consequences in the war as a whole. Only Churchill could authorise the surrender of Singapore. While he pondered the matter, Malaya Command must fight on.

That fight was already underway. Speed was more important than ever to Yamashita. Losses on the island were already heavy, supplies of artillery ammunition were dwindling, and stout resistance was still being offered in several areas. Yamashita threw his army into relentless attacks, aiming to crumble the perimeter and force the enemy to surrender outside the city. *25th Army* and the *3rd Air Group* attacked with all their force. The biggest attack came in the southwest, aimed at the barely blooded troops of 1st Malaya Brigade. The *18th Division*, having launched the first set piece attack of the campaign at Kota Bharu, now launched the last one at Pasir Panjang Ridge. The division was manned mostly by tough coal miners from Kyushu, a region famous for providing good soldiers.[108] Resisting it was a brigade led by The 1st Battalion The Malay Regiment (1st Malays) — regular soldiers with British and some Malay officers, the only Asians from Malaya and Singapore who fought as regular soldiers in defence of their own land, assisted by their incomplete and weaker 2nd Battalion. They were in improvised positions but on high ground, bolstered by pillboxes on the coast road and the twin 6" guns of the battery at Labrador Park. The brigade fought stubbornly, assisted by the coastal guns. But the Japanese veterans pushed doggedly forward, the guns were knocked out late in the afternoon, and by dusk the position became untenable and the brigade had to retreat overnight.[109]

The Japanese kept up the pressure with three large attacks the next day, 14 February. With the causeway repaired, the remaining heavy guns and tanks rushed up to join the battle. The defenders at last reached the crisis point regarding ammunition. When Bennett was told he would receive no more, he ordered his gunners and machine-gunners to conserve their supply by firing only in direct support of Australian positions under attack. This was despite the fact his men captured a Japanese map indicating their main attack that day would again hit the Malays — intelligence confirmed when that attack went in, presenting its flank in full view of Australian machine gunners who sat still. Ammunition shortage or not, this was worse than obtuse; it can only indicate Bennett had opted out of the common battle against the common enemy.[110] The *18th Division* faced tough resistance all day. C Company of the 1st Malays made an epic stand at Point 226 overlooking Buona Vista Village, and was all but wiped out. But in late afternoon a major tank-led assault pushed back the British, Indian and Malay defenders to the edge of the city. The stiff defence provoked the Japanese into a cruel rampage when they overran Alexandra Hospital. Staff and patients, including one on the operating table, were bayoneted; 150 people were forced into a small shed overnight, and most were murdered the next morning. The tough two-day battle also provoked Percival into paying a post-war tribute to the stand of the 1st Malays — but at the time it left his army backing into the city itself, staring in the face the kind of disaster just experienced at the hospital.[111]

The battering Singapore's defenders and infrastructure received that day in fact proved fatal. Simson warned Percival in the morning that the water distribution system would fall apart in 48 hours at the most. An epidemic would likely follow, very rapidly. Percival pressed Wavell, hinting that while the fight continued he may "find it necessary to take an immediate decision." Bennett on the other hand took matters into his own hands by informing his government that he had concentrated the AIF and would surrender on his own if it was cut off. Bennett neglected to inform Percival, his immediate superior. Far from being a "most extraordinary procedure," this indicated Bennett had indeed given up on the rest of Malaya Command — "a house divided..." indeed.[112]

Fortunately, Churchill at last concluded no amount of rhetoric or threats would stiffen the defence enough to fight on to any purpose. Therefore, he and Brooke agreed it would be wrong to enforce "needless slaughter" and the "horrors of street fighting" on the civil population just to gain some hours of delay. With the defenders now holding the outskirts of the city itself, and all order and services collapsing under direct attack, it did not seem before time. Wavell received permission to spare Singapore a final horror that evening: "You are of course sole judge of the moment when no further result can be gained at Singapore, and should instruct Percival accordingly."[113] The Japanese kept up the pressure which produced this state of affairs the next morning, 15 February. But by now they had their own misgivings. Artillery ammunition was now down to barely 100 rounds per field gun, not enough for counterbattery fire, and fighting was raging on as the battle neared the city. Tsuji waited impatiently all day for signs the defence was cracking.[114] But all the defenders could see was the starkness of their own position, not the concerns of their enemy.

Percival convened the decisive conference at Fort Canning at 0930 hrs. It was noted the water system was about to collapse, there was very little food left, no petrol, and artillery ammunition was almost exhausted. The next big enemy attack seemed likely to break into the city itself. Percival at last concluded that it was pointless to just fall back and defend — was this decision six days or six weeks too late? It was unanimously agreed a counterattack would fail. Fortunately, a telegram from Wavell granting permission to surrender arrived just as Percival decided there was no alternative.[115] He might have reflected bitterly that this was his only decision Wavell had approved of in five weeks of defeat after defeat.

After some parleying, posturing and general confusion, Percival at 1730 hrs arrived at Japanese headquarters, set up at the Ford factory on Bukit Timah Road, to surrender his army. The British party carried, as instructed, a Union Jack and a white flag. Yamashita, fearing Percival might be stalling for time to prepare a street battle, laid on massive security to intimidate the British party. After a discussion hindered by poor interpreting, Percival agreed to surrender, a ceasefire to take effect at 2030 hrs that evening. Having gained his main point, Yamashita shrugged off the news heavy weapons were already destroyed, agreed to allow Percival to keep 1000 men under arms to keep order overnight, and — above all — agreed to keep the main body of his army out of the city, and keep those who entered under strict control. Even in this awful moment, Percival remained in control, reporting to Wavell with dignity: "Owing to losses from enemy action, water, petrol, food and ammunition

Percival surrenders Singapore

practically finished. Unable therefore to continue the fight any longer. All ranks have done their best and are grateful for your help."[116]

So fell Singapore, 30 days faster than its attackers had planned, four months faster than the final "period before relief." The problem had started and ended with the "Singapore Strategy." Never very credible to begin with, it became impossible from 1940. But neither it nor plans for local defence were either adjusted effectively to changing circumstances or reconciled with each other. Buckling under the strain of a war being lost, the British authorities gambled that Singapore could be held by bluff and improvisation. Problems and contradictions which raised unwanted complications were deferred, not resolved. Singapore received only what could be spared — in terms of leaders, forces, equipment, and even attention from the top. It was not enough. The final gambles were that this enemy would be too distracted elsewhere, or not tough enough to take Singapore while it was weak. Both gambles failed. The central authorities left Singapore vulnerable. It fell as fast and painfully as it did because their gambles and neglect were aggravated by theatre commanders who were outgeneralled, and troops who were outfought, by an enemy tougher than themselves. These failures of policy and command produced lasting controversy in the U.K.,[117] but more immediately left Singapore at the mercy of a conqueror whose behaviour left it with scars it would never forget.

Notes

1. PRO, CAB65/24, War Cabinet minutes, 5 December 1941; LHCMA, Brooke-Popham Papers, V/5/28, C-in-C China and C-in-C Far East to Admiralty and WO, 6-7 December 1941; *Principal War Telegrams and Memoranda 1940-1943*, vol. 1, Lichtenstein, 1976 (*PT* vol. 1), C-in-C Far East to Admiralty, C-in-C China to Admiralty, 7 December 1941; *Operations of Malaya Command*, paragraphs 120-24; Percival, 109-110; Ong, *Operation Matador*, ch. 8.

2. *Operations of Malaya Command*, paragraphs 128, 130.

3. *Operations of Malaya Command*, paragraphs 129-31, 137; Percival, 112-13. Tsuji, 89, 110-11, described the initial encounter battles as follows: "We now understood the fighting quality of the enemy. The only things we had to fear were the quantity of munitions he had and the thoroughness of his demolitions." For an eyewitness account of the mood of 11th Indian Division on the eve of its first battle see G. Chippington, *Singapore: The Inexcusable Betrayal*, UK, 1992, 21, 27-30, 33-35.

4. *Operations of Malaya Command*, paragraphs 125-26, 132, 147; Tsuji, 94-96; Elphick, *Singapore: The Pregnable Fortress*, 221-22.

5. *Operations of Malaya Command*, paragraphs 125, 127; Probert, 41-42, puts the Japanese losses in air attacks off Kota Bharu at one transport destroyed, two damaged, 24 landing barges sunk, but wildly overestimates the number of Japanese killed. The correct figure is given in US Army Center of Military History, Japanese Monograph No. 54, *Malaya Operations Record November 1941–March 1942* (hereafter called *Malaya Operations Record*), f.54, a volume based largely on the notes of *25th Army's* intelligence, operations and rear echelon staff officers. It admits 320 killed and 538 wounded in the battles for and around Kota Bharu, which still makes this one of the most costly battles of the campaign for the Japanese. This suggests the RAF might indeed have done much damage to an invader, had it been properly equipped. But Probert argues convincingly that these efforts were misdirected — the all-out onslaught should have

been made against the main Japanese landings in Thailand, not the secondary assault at Kota Bharu. The opportunity was not repeated. The Japanese record of their ship losses at Kota Bharu is in *Malaya Invasion Naval Operations*, p. 20, and it does confirm Probert's figures.

   6. *Operations of Malaya Command*, paragraphs 42, 152, 157-58; Probert, 30-32, 42-45; Percival, 61-62. P. Elphick and M. Smith, *Odd Man Out: The Story of the Singapore Traitor*, London, 1993, discussed the case of Captain Patrick Heenan. They identified Heenan as the key man in a Japanese spy network which also infiltrated Indian Army units, some assigned to airbase defence duties. As an Air Liaison Officer at Alor Star, Heenan was able to feed the Japanese information regarding RAF strength, deployment, and operations. This information, plus incidents such as the mutiny of an Indian battalion guarding an airbase near Kota Bharu, at least did not help RAF Far East Command in its struggle to cope with the Japanese onslaught. Probert, ch. 3, n. 23, accepts the case against Heenan but notes that it remains impossible to determine just how important his treason was in asssisting the Japanese air attacks. Elphick sheds a little more light on this, and considerably more on subversion and espionage in general, in *Singapore: The Pregnable Fortress*, and *Far Eastern File*.

   7. PRO, WO172/18, War Diary, GHQ Malaya Command, Appendix V.1, 10 December 1941; *Operations of Malaya Command*, paragraphs 132, 152, 158-60; Probert, 48-50, is candid and critical on the panicky evacuation of several airbases; Tsuji, 94-96; Elphick, *Odd Man Out*, ch. 12.

   8. Roskill, 559, 563-64; C. Barnett, *Engage the Enemy More Closely: The Royal Navy in the Second World War*, London, 1991, 406-13; Middlebrook, 100-45; B. Montgomery, *Shenton of Singapore*, 6-9. The Japanese account of the action against the capital ships can be found in *Malaya Invasion Naval Operations*, pp. 23-29.

   9. Roskill, 564-68; Barnett, 411-21, notes that the change of course was picked up by a Japanese submarine barely two hours after Phillips turned towards Kuantan, which gave *22nd Naval Air Flotilla* its opportunity; Middlebrook, 148-57. The source of the "false alarm" is discussed in an account by an officer of 22nd Indian Brigade: D. Russell-Roberts, *Spotlight on Singapore*, UK, 1965, 35-36. Earlier accounts attributed the alarm to stray goats or water buffaloes setting off minefields. Elphick pointed the finger at espionage in *Odd Man Out*, but reversed himself in a more careful study in *Singapore: The Pregnable Fortress*, 235-39, which summed up the account started by Russell-Roberts, circulated in the unit War Diaries, later accepted by Kirby, *The Chain of Disaster*, 138, and Falk, 98-100. Based on air reconnaissance sightings of barges being towed, the discovery of three small boats washed up on shore days later riddled with bullet holes and full of Japanese gear, and the claim of a rare Japanese POW that probes were launched in the area, it was concluded that 22nd Indian Brigade overreacted to a Japanese pin prick scouting foray and unwittingly drew the battlewagons in for nothing. PRO, WO172/18, War Diary, GHQ Malaya Command, Appendices B.1, D.1, K.1, M.1, N.1, 9-10 December 1941, indicate that 22nd Indian Brigade believed it had beaten off an enemy probe. Yet Falk points out that Japanese records make no mention of any such probe, making this one of the mysteries of the campaign which may never be fully resolved. Middlebrook, ch. 15, is a careful account of Phillips' conduct of the last battle. It was reasonable to act on the Kuantan reports, but not signalling for air cover after being discovered was inexcusable. It can perhaps be explained by Phillips' overconfidence about anti-aircraft defence, his view of the Japanese, and lack of command experience at sea.

   10. *Operations of Malaya Command*, paragraphs 136, 155; Percival, 124. Heath also sent his corps reserve, 28th Indian Brigade, to reinforce the position at Jitra. That gave 11th Indian Division two brigades in place and two moving up to contest two Japanese advances.

   11. PRO, WO172/18, War Diary, GHQ Malaya Command, Appendices N.3, W.3, Y.3, Z.3, 11 December, Appendices C.4, G.4, K.4, 12 December 1941; *Operations of Malaya Command*, paragraphs 139-40, 165-73; Tsuji, 116-28; Kinvig, 152-57; Chippington, 67, notes as an eyewitness that the division was so badly dispersed by the confusing night retreat it could have been annihilated then and there. This overlooks the fact the Japanese

"bounce" attack was mounted so fast the main forces were not yet even in contact. The energies of the battlegroup were absorbed taking well over 1000 prisoners and seizing useful supply dumps. Some of these prisoners provided the foundation of the anti-British Indian National Army (INA) quickly organised by Maj. Fujiwara.

12. PRO, WO172/18, War Diary, GHQ Malaya Command, Appendix Q.8, 15 December, Appendix V.8, 17 December, Appendices G.9, O.9, 18 December 1941; WO172/15, War Diary, GHQ Far East, 15 December 1941 entries, Appendix, 23 December 1941; IWM, Percival Papers, File 26, Heath comments on Percival draft narrative of campaign, n/d, written in captivity; *Operations of Malaya Command*, paragraphs 177-93; Tsuji, 130-32; Kirby, *The Chain of Disaster*, 157-58.

13. *Operations of Malaya Command*, paragraphs 196-204; Percival, 152-54; Kinvig, 170; Kirby, *The Loss of Singapore*, 232.

14. H.G. Bennett, *Why Singapore Fell*, Sydney, 1944, 73, arrived at the same conclusion simultaneously. More to the point, the strategy was confirmed by Brooke-Popham and the Far East War Council in Singapore: *Operations of Malaya Command*, paragraph 202.

15. *Operations of Malaya Command*, paragraph 205; Percival, 157-58.

16. *Operations of Malaya Command*, paragraphs 208-211; Percival, 160; Tsuji, 141; Stewart, 2-6, 33-36.

17. *Operations of Malaya Command*, paragraphs 175, 192, 208-211; Stewart, 5, 36, 44-46.

18. *Malaya Operations Record*, f.57-60; Tsuji, 128-30, 142-47; *Operations of Malaya Command*, paragraphs 196, 218; Stewart, 47; Probert, 50-51; Falk, 141-43.

19. PRO, WO172/18, War Diary, GHQ Malaya Command, Appendix K.13, 22 December, Appendices L.13, H.14, 23 December, Appendix W.15, 28 December, Appendix R.16, 29 December 1941; Smyth, 256-57.

20. PRO, WO172/17, War Diary, GHQ Malaya Command, serial 1651, 29 December 1941; IWM, Percival Papers, File 42, comments on draft chapters of official history, 8 January 1954; Simson, 54-56, 62-63, 67-71; Bennett, 77-78; *Operations of Malaya Command*, paragraph 219.

21. *Operations of Malaya Command*, paragraph 260; Percival, 192.

22. PRO, WO172/18, War Diary, GHQ Malaya Command, Appendix J.14, 23 December, Appendices J.15, M. 15, 27 December, Appendix R. 16, 29 December 1941; *Operations of Malaya Command*, paragraphs 212-13; Stewart, 58-61.

23. PRO, WO172/20, War Diary, GHQ Malaya Command, Appendix P.18, 1 January, Appendix X.19, 2 January, Appendix F.21, 5 January, Appendix W.21, 6 January 1942; *Operations of Malaya Command*, paragraphs 257, 276-80, 283-88; *Malaya Operations Record*, f.62-67; Tsuji, 151-52, 157-61; Stewart, 65-71; Percival, 198; Kinvig, 172-73; Falk, 148-49.

24. PRO, WO172/20, War Diary, GHQ Malaya Command, Appendix R.18, 1 January, Appendix F.21, 5 January 1942; IWM, Heath Papers, LMH7, writer unknown, to Heath, 15 September 1947; *Operations of Malaya Command*, paragraphs 262, 268-75; Russell-Roberts, 42-43; Falk, 154-55.

25. PT, vol. 1, C-in-C Far East to COS, #4236, 8 December, COS to C-in-C Far East, COSFE53, COSFE54, 9 December 1941; PRO, CAB65/20, War Cabinet minutes, 10, 12 December 1941; 65/24, War Cabinet minutes, confidential annexes and conclusions, 8, 10 December 1941.

26. PRO, CAB79/55, COS minutes, 11 December 1941; 79/16, COS minutes, JP(41)1050, 12 December 1941; CAB69/2, DC(O) minutes, 19 December 1941; CAB80/60, COS(41)277(O), 14 December, COS(41)280(O)(revise), 20 December 1941; PT, vol. 1, C-in-C Eastern Fleet to Admiralty, 13 December, Admiralty to C-in-C Eastern Fleet, 14, 17 December, COS to C-in-C India, C-in-C Far East, 17 December 1941.

27. Churchill, *The Grand Alliance*, 636-39; J.R.M. Butler, *Grand Strategy. Vol. III. June 1941–August 1942. Part I*. London, HMSO, 1964, 413.

28. PRO, CAB69/2, DC(O) minutes, 19 December 1941; CAB79/16, COS minutes, 22-23 December 1941; PT, vol.1, WO to C-in-C India, COS to C-in-C Far East, 22 December 1941; Butler, 413-14.

29. PRO, CAB79/16, COS minutes, 25 December 1941; 79/17, 1 January 1942; CAB69/2, DC(O) minutes, 27 December 1941; LHCMA, Brooke Papers, 3A/V, 20, 24, 25 December 1941 diary entries; CAB80/61 and CAB99/17 document the establishment of ABDA Command; LHCMA, Pownall Papers, 20, 30 December 1941, 2, 5 January 1942 diary entries; PT, vol. 1, Pownall to Brooke, 27 December, C-in-C Far East to WO, 29 December 1941.

30. *Operations of Malaya Command*, paragraphs 196, 254-56; Probert, 51-52; Smyth, 145.

31. PRO, CAB99/17, COS-JCS minutes, 31 December 1941; CAB80/61, COS(42)7(O), 5 January 1942; PT, vol. 1, ABDA to COS, 8 January 1942; *Operations of Malaya Command*, paragraph 229; Kirby, *The Chain of Disaster*, 162-63, 184.

32. PRO, CAB69/2, DC(O) minutes, 31 December 1941; CAB99/17, summary of telegrams, 1 January 1942; CAB79/17, COS minutes, 7 January 1942; Wigmore, 164, 182-90; W.S. Churchill, *The Hinge of Fate*, Boston, 1950, ch. 1.

33. PRO, WO172/20, War Diary, GHQ Malaya Command, Appendices W.21, G.22, 6 January, Appendices J.22, L.22, N.22, Q.22, U.22, 7 January 1942; *Operations of Malaya Command*, paragraphs 293-94; Percival, 191, 206; Stewart, 75-86; *Malaya Operations Record*, f.68-70; Tsuji, 171-75, 182; Simson, 61-66; Kinvig, 175; Kirby, *The Chain of Disaster*, 177; Falk, 149-53.

34. PRO, CAB106/38, *Despatch on Operations in South-West Pacific, January 15th–February 25th 1942*, paragraphs 5-6 (hereafter *Operations in South-West Pacific*); *Operations of Malaya Command*, paragraphs 296-97.

35. Percival, 205-06, is unrepentant about his strategic gamble; Smyth, 156, 184-85; Kirby, *The Chain of Disaster*, 180.

36. PRO, WO172/20, War Diary, GHQ Malaya Command, Appendix Y.21, 5 January, G.22, 6/1, H.23, 8 January, Q.23, 9 January 1942; *Operations of Malaya Command*, paragraphs 290-91, 301-02; Percival, 211; Morrison, 140-41.

37. PRO, CAB106/38, *Operations in South-West Pacific*, paragraphs 7-8; WO172/20, War Diary, GHQ Malaya Command, Appendix Q.23, 9 January 1942; *Operations of Malaya Command*, paragraphs 290-91, 299; Percival, 208-210; Bennett, 16, 47-48, 100; Wigmore, 198-203; Kinvig, 178-79.

38. PRO, CAB106/38, *Operations in South-West Pacific*, paragraphs 9, 14; IWM, Percival Papers, File 43, Wavell comments on draft despatch by Percival, n/d, 1948; *Operations of Malaya Command*, paragraphs 301-03, 315, 330, 332, 336-46; Bennett, 47-48, 101-04; Tsuji, 190-92, 199; Wigmore, 203, 211-12; Lodge, 109-110; Kinvig, 178-79, 184; Smyth, 155-56.

39. The ambush at Gemas is described in PRO, WO172/20, War Diary, GHQ Malaya Command, Appendix U.26, 15 January 1942, *Operations of Malaya Command*, paragraph 347, *Malaya Operations Record* f.78-79, Wigmore, 214-218, Falk, 167-168 and J. Uhr, *Against the Sun: The AIF in Malaya, 1941-1942*, ch. 5, 1998. The fighting between Gemas and Segamat, the loss of Muar, the bitter fighting retreat of the 45th Indian Brigade and the two Australian battalions, the failure to relieve them, and the undoing of the "Johore Line" are all described in WO172/20, *Operations of Malaya Command*, *Malaya Operations Record*, Tsuji, Percival, Bennett, Wigmore, Lodge, Uhr, and Kinvig. Lt.-Col. C.G.W. Anderson, commanding officer 2/19 AIF, earned the Victoria Cross for his inspired leadership in the failed attempt to retreat from the Muar area. The retreat produced the most sustained close quarter combat of the campaign, followed by the cold-blooded murder of over 100 helpless wounded prisoners by the *Imperial Guards Division* after the force scattered, in retaliation for losses sustained in that fighting. An account of this repulsive episode is G. Mant, *Massacre at Parit Sulong*, New South Wales, 1995, passim.

40. PT, vol. 1, Wavell to COS, 9, 12, 14, 15 January 1942; PRO, CAB106/38, *Operations in South-West Pacific*, paragraphs 13-14.

41. *Operations of Malaya Command*, paragraph 407; Willmott, 320-21. Wavell acknowledged that he knew the Indian brigades were not combat ready: IWM, Percival Papers, File 43, comments on draft despatch by Percival, n/d, 1948.

42. W.F. Kimball, *Churchill and Roosevelt: The Complete Correspondence*, vol. 1, Princeton, 1984, telegram C-153x, 7 January 1942 (hereafter *Churchill-Roosevelt Correspondence*); PT, vol. 1, Churchill to Wavell, 15 January, Wavell to Churchill, 16 January 1942; Churchill, *The Hinge of Fate*, 38-45.

43. PRO, CAB65/29, War Cabinet minutes, confidential annex, 19 January 1942; CAB79/17, COS minutes, 19 January 1942, notes that Brooke ordered the inquiry but stipulated for the record the Prime Minister had been informed of the lack of fortress defence preparations at Singapore; PT, vol. 1, COS to Wavell, 20 January 1942; Churchill, *The Hinge of Fate*, 46-47.

44. PT, vol. 1, Wavell to Churchill, 19, 21 January 1942; PRO, CAB106/38, *Operations in South-West Pacific*, paragraphs 18, 21; CAB80/61, Churchill to Ismay, 21 January 1942; Churchill, *The Hinge of Fate*, 47-50; Kinvig, 187-88, 194; Kirby, *The Chain of Disaster*, 214-17.

45. PRO, CAB80/33, COS(42)37, 20 January 1942; CAB79/56, COS minutes, 21 January 1942; CAB69/4, DC(O) minutes, 21 January 1942; CAB65/25, War Cabinet minutes, 22, 26 January 1942; 65/29, confidential annex, 26 January 1942; PT, vol. 1, Churchill to Wavell, 23 January 1942; vol. 5, Auchinleck to Churchill, Churchill to Auchinleck, 24 January 1942; vol. 6, COS(W)19, Curtin to Churchill, COS(W)20, COS comments on same, 28 January 1942; *Churchill-Roosevelt Correspondence*, vol. 1, telegrams C-159x, 27 January, R-78x, 30 January 1942; Churchill, *The Hinge of Fate*, 49-52; Wigmore, 285-87.

46. PRO, CAB106/38, *Operations in South-West Pacific*, paragraph 21; *Operations of Malaya Command*, paragraphs 254, 338, 388, 397, 401-03, 405, 408; Percival, 217-18; Tsuji, 197-98; Probert, 56-60; Kirby, *The Loss of Singapore*, 323-24, 331-32.

47. *Malaya Operations Record*, f.87-88; Falk, 188, 194-95, 271; Morrison, 94.

48. *Operations of Malaya Command*, paragraph 346; Kirby, *The Chain of Disaster*, 202, 205; Kinvig, 187-89; Falk, 185-86, 189-90.

49. The final battle for southern Johore, the retreat to Singapore, and the loss of 22nd Indian Brigade, are discussed in PRO, WO172/20, War Diary, GHQ Malaya Command, CAB106/38, *Operations in South-West Pacific, Operations of Malaya Command*, Percival, Russell-Roberts, Bennett, *Malaya Operations Record*, Kinvig, Falk, and Elphick, *Singapore: The Pregnable Fortress*. While opinions differ as to who was primarily responsible for the loss of 22nd Indian Brigade, all agree the conduct of Brig. Lay, commanding 8th Indian Brigade, was inexcusable and led to the disaster.

50. The final rearguard is discussed in *Operations of Malaya Command*, paragraphs 391-92, 396, and Falk, 190-91, 196-97. Chippington, 151, Falk, 185, and Morrison, 138-39, all discuss the superiority of the defenders in close quarter and especially hand to hand combat. Percival's explanation of failure is in *Operations of Malaya Command*, paragraphs 346, 390.

51. *Malaya Operations Record*, f.91-101; Tsuji, 220-21; Falk, 223-25.

52. *Malaya Operations Record*, f.92-102; Tsuji, 187-89, 221-33; Falk, 223-27; Potter, 76-77; Allen, 187-88; Kirby, *The Chain of Disaster*, 223-25.

53. PT, vol. 1, Wavell to COS, 29 January, Wavell to Churchill, 3 February, Churchill to Wavell, 4 February 1942; *Operations of Malaya Command*, paragraphs 397, 669-70; Probert, 71; Elphick, *Singapore: The Pregnable Fortress*, 211-12; Kirby, *The Chain of Disaster*, 211-12.

54. *Operations of Malaya Command*, paragraph 672; Simson, 93-96; Morrison, 166-67.

55. *Operations of Malaya Command*, paragraph 400; Morrison, 169-70; Simson, 192-94.

56. PRO, CAB106/38, *Operations in South-West Pacific*, paragraph 9; *Operations of Malaya Command*, paragraphs 243-44; Simson, 78-89; Percival, 181-82; Montgomery, 105-06, 114, 117-19; Kirby, *The Chain of Disaster*, 139-40, 190-96.

57. Simson, 78-91; Percival, 182; Montgomery, 114-24, 193; Kirby, *The Chain of Disaster*, 191-96; Smyth, 99; Elphick, *Singapore: The Pregnable Fortress*, 65.

58. *Operations of Malaya Command*, paragraphs 238-40; Simson, 100-05; Kirby, *The Chain of Disaster*, 229; Montgomery, 105-06; Elphick, *Singapore: The Pregnable Fortress*, 274-75.

59. *Operations of Malaya Command*, paragraphs 247-53, 486, 673-75; Simson, 83, 87, 89-95; Allen, 247-52; Morrison, 30-31, 145-46, 158-59, 164-70; A.H.C. Ward et al (editors), *The Memoirs of Tan Kah Kee*, Singapore, 1994, 151-58; Kirby, *The Chain of Disaster*, 229-31; J. Kennedy, *British Civilians and the Japanese War in Malaya and Singapore 1941-1945*, London, 1987, 33, 38-39. The Chinese Mobilisation Council took charge of the drive to provide labourers with its Labour Service Department, and organised a Protection Department to help maintain law and order. Its third bureau, the Arms Department, soon also known as the Overseas Chinese Volunteer Army, had a different fate described below. Other information can be found in Foong C.H. (editor and compiler) *The Price of Peace: True Accounts of the Japanese Occupation*, Singapore, 1997(1995), 216-94.

60. PRO, CAB106/38, *Operations in South-West Pacific*, paragraph 24.

61. *Operations of Malaya Command*, paragraphs 443, 451-58; Percival, 261-62. See above, Chapter 6.

62. *Operations of Malaya Command*, paragraphs 460, 462, 465; Percival, 263-64; Kinvig, 203; Kirby, *The Loss of Singapore*, 363.

63. PRO, CAB106/38, *Operations in South-West Pacific*, paragraph 24; IWM, Percival Papers, File 43, Wavell comments on draft despatch by Percival, n/d, 1948; *Operations of Malaya Command*, paragraphs 437, 456, 459-68. Percival, 261, Smyth, 215, and Kinvig, 199-205, all contradict Wavell, claiming the GOC correctly anticipated where the Japanese would attack. Kirby, *The Chain of Disaster*, 220-21, rejects this, citing the conversation between Wavell and Percival on 20 January and a postwar letter by Percival to Kirby admitting his claim was incorrect and based on hindsight. That letter is in IWM, Percival Papers, File 48, Percival to Kirby, 2 December 1953, comments on official history draft. In that letter, Percival in fact claims that he did not settle on any specific area as the most likely to be attacked and made his deployments for logistic reasons. But PRO, WO172/21, War Diary, GHQ Malaya Command, for February 1942, makes it clear that the largest and freshest division, the bulk of the field artillery, and until the last moment most of the defensive materiel were deliberately stationed in Northern Area — suggesting this was where Percival, at the time, concluded the main attack would come.

64. *Operations of Malaya Command*, paragraphs 434, 461-67, 471-77; Kirby, *The Chain of Disaster*, 220-22.

65. *Operations of Malaya Command*, paragraphs 206, 219, 420-36, Appendix C; Percival, 259; Simson, 68-72, 106-07; Tsuji, 187; Kinvig, 195-97.

66. PRO, CAB106/38, *Operations in South-West Pacific*, paragraphs 9, 21; LHCMA, Pownall Papers, diary entry, 8 January 1942; *Operations of Malaya Command*, paragraph 436; Simson, 86-89, 106; Churchill, *The Hinge of Fate,* 45-46; Falk, 206-07; N. Barber, *Sinister Twilight: The Fall of Singapore*, London, 1968, 78-79. Percival does not mention his conversations with Wavell or Simson in his private correspondence with Kirby about the official history draft chapters, let alone his published despatch or memoirs. Wavell does, in IWM, Percival Papers, File 43, comments on draft despatch by Percival, n/d, 1948.

67. *Operations of Malaya Command*, paragraphs 436-37, 439; Percival, 254-56, 259; Kirby, *The Loss of Singapore*, 360-71; Kirby, *The Chain of Disaster*, 221-22; Lodge, 140-41. Bennett shared Percival's skepticism about the value of fixed defences, to the extent of thinking they might make his troops soft and lazy and resisting pressure to provide them with more. As a philosophy of beach defence, this was sheer idiocy.

68. Chippington, 174-75, 237; Russell-Roberts, 113; Percival, 254-56.

69. *Operations of Malaya Command*, paragraphs 390, 419, 435-36, 451, 458, 594-99, 612; Percival, 257; Morrison, 149-53; Bennett, 165; Wigmore, 294-95; Kinvig, 195, is the only other study to note the effect his perception of the mission had on Percival's

decisions on defences for Singapore. On page 246, Kinvig suggests bias in favour of Wavell led Kirby to blame Percival unfairly on this issue in the British official history. See Appendix 2.

70. Wigmore, 258, explains the decision by the Australian government to send these men, without making excuses; Elphick, *Singapore: The Pregnable Fortress*, 288-89.

71. Bennett, 165-71; Kirby, *The Chain of Disaster*, 223; Lodge, 129-33.

72. Percival, 258; Simson, 111-14.

73. PRO, WO172/21, War Diary, GHQ Malaya Command, Appendix D.47, A.48, 1 February 1942; *Operations of Malaya Command*, paragraph 469; Chapman, 27-29, 46; Morrison, 170-74. *Dalforce* appears to have absorbed the Overseas Chinese Volunteer Army in early January. Personal accounts of its deployment are in Foong, *The Price of Peace*, 46, 264-89.

74. Morrison started this in 1942 with these sentences: "The huge naval guns which protected it[the base] pointed out to sea. They were embedded in concrete and could not be turned to point inland"; Morrison, 153. Percival dealt with this in his 1948 despatch and 1949 memoirs, Kirby sorted it out in *The Loss of Singapore*, 361, in 1957, Falk made the truth crystal-clear in 1975, 202-04, Elphick updated the issue in *Singapore: The Pregnable Fortress*, 206-08, in 1995. After all that ch. 2 in Ong, *Operation Matador*, 1997, should be seen as definitive on the entire controversy. But it will not be, because the myth is simpler and more melodramatic than the truth, so it will live on.

75. *Malaya Operations Record*, f.91-92.

76. G. Rocker, *Escaped Singapore Heading Homewards*, Singapore, 1990, 46-59; Morrison, 145-53; Simson, 70-75, 98, 109; Tsuji, 219-21.

77. *Malaya Operations Record*, f.101; PRO, WO172/21, War Diary, GHQ Malaya Command, Appendices S.47, A.48, 1 February, Appendix Q.51, 5 February 1942; *Operations of Malaya Command*, paragraph 487; Wigmore, 299-300; Falk, 226-28.

78. PRO, WO172/21, War Diary, GHQ Malaya Command, Appendices A.54, C.55, 8 February 1942; *Operations of Malaya Command*, paragraphs 487-88; Wigmore, 304-07; Falk, 228-29.

79. Australian War Memorial (AWM), 52/8/2/22, War Diary, 22nd Brigade AIF, 6, 8, Appendix B 8 February 1942 entries; 52/8/3/18, War Diary, 2/18 AIF, 8 February 1942 entries; PRO, CAB106/151, Interview with Brig. Taylor, 30 January 1953; *Operations of Malaya Command*, paragraph 489; Wigmore, 306-311; Falk, 226-30.

80. *Operations of Malaya Command*, paragraph 490; *Malaya Operations Record*, f.102; Wigmore, 298-99, 302-09.

81. AWM, 52/8/2/22, War Diary, 22nd Brigade AIF, 8, 9, Appendix B 8 February 1942 entries; *Operations of Malaya Command*, paragraphs 491-94; Percival, 269; Wigmore, 309-316.

82. AWM, 52/8/2/22, War Diary, 22nd Brigade AIF, 8, 9, Appendix B 9 February 1942 entries; PRO, WO172/21, War Diary, GHQ Malaya Command, serials 4180-81, February 1942; *Operations of Malaya Command*, paragraphs 496, 498; Stewart, 102; Wigmore, 309, 316-19; Kirby, *The Loss of Singapore*, 376-77; Falk, 231.

83. AWM, 52/8/2/22, War Diary, 22nd Brigade AIF, 8, 9, Appendix B, 1, 8 February 1942 entries; PRO, CAB106/151, Taylor interview, 30 January 1953; *Operations of Malaya Command*, paragraphs 490, 494-95; Percival, 270; Wigmore, 309, 312-20.

84. AWM, 52/8/2/22, War Diary, 22nd Brigade AIF, 9 and Appendix B 9 February 1942 entries; *Operations of Malaya Command*, paragraphs 494-97; Wigmore, 312-23; Kirby, *The Loss of Singapore*, 377-78; Falk, 231-32.

85. PRO, WO172/21, War Diary, GHQ Malaya Command, serial 4207, Appendix W.56, 9 February 1942; *Operations of Malaya Command*, paragraphs 498-501; Wigmore, 325-27; Kirby, *The Loss of Singapore*, 378-79.

86. Kirby, *The Chain of Disaster*, 235.

87. AWM, 52/8/2/22, War Diary, 22nd Brigade AIF, 2 and Appendix B 1 February 1942 entries; J. Wyett, *Staff Wallah*, New South Wales, 1996, 90-96; Kirby, *The Loss* *of Singapore*, 370; Wigmore, 301-02; Elphick, *Singapore: The Pregnable Fortress*, 283-85.

88. *Operations of Malaya Command*, paragraph 502; Percival, 273.

89. AWM, 52/8/2/27, War Diary, 27th Brigade AIF, 6, 9 February 1942 entries, Appendix C, 8 June 1942; 67/3/25, Part 1, Bennett Diary, 1, 6 February 1942 entries; PRO, WO172/21, War Diary, GHQ Malaya Command, Appendix L.56, 9 February 1942; *Operations of Malaya Command*, paragraph 500; Wigmore, 328-29; Kirby, *The Loss of Singapore*, 381-82.

90. AWM, 52/8/2/27, War Diary, 27th Brigade AIF, 9, 10 February 1942 entries, Appendix C, 8 June 1942; *Operations of Malaya Command*, paragraphs 503-04, 507; *Malaya Operations Record*, f.103; Tsuji, 243-45; Wigmore, 331-33; Kirby, *The Loss of Singapore*, 382; A. Swinson, *Defeat in Malaya: The Fall of Singapore*, New York, 1969, 135.

91. PRO, WO172/21, War Diary, GHQ Malaya Command, Appendix M.57, 10 February 1942; AWM, 52/8/2/22, War Diary, 22nd Brigade AIF, 10 February 1942 entries. The relevant entry for 0900 hrs is terse: "Capt. Morrison, Div. LO [Liaison Officer], arrived with typewritten order for 22 Bde AIF to take up position forward of Reformatory Road." That in Taylor's personal Appendix B is no help either: "I received a long typewritten order from Div (Capt. Morrison, LO) in regard to holding a position north of Reformatory Rd... ." In an interview with British and Australian official historians in 1953, Taylor implied that when he met Bennett the order had not yet been promulgated and the movement could have been stopped if necessary: PRO, CAB106/151, Taylor interview, 27 January 1953. The brigade War Diary contradicts this claim: the battalions received "Orders issued based on Div. order" at 1000 hrs, Taylor left to meet Bennett at 1030 hrs. Wigmore, 336-37; Kirby, *The Loss of Singapore*, 384.

92. PRO, WO172/21, War Diary, GHQ Malaya Command, Appendices R.57, S.57, 10 February 1942; CAB106/117, Ballentine Account of 44th Indian Brigade operations for British official historians, 26 March 1951(Ballentine account); *Operations of Malaya Command*, paragraphs 511, 517-19; Percival, 275; Wyett, 97; Kirby, *The Loss of Singapore*, 383-87; Wigmore, 338-40.

93. PRO, WO172/21, War Diary, GHQ Malaya Command, Appendix V.58, 10 February 1942; CAB106/38, *Operations in South-West Pacific*, paragraph 27; AWM, 52/8/2/22, War Diary, 22nd Brigade AIF, 10 and Appendix A and Appendix B 10 February 1942 entries; *Operations of Malaya Command*, paragraphs 513-15, 519, 522; Kirby, *The Loss of Singapore*, 387-88.

94. Bennett, 178-81, mistakenly records events of 10 February as being the next day; Wyett, 97-98; Wigmore, 338-45.

95. PRO, CAB106/38, *Operations in South-West Pacific*, paragraph 27; *Malaya Operations Record*, f.104; Tsuji, 248-50; Kirby, *The Loss of Singapore*, 386; Falk, 236.

96. PRO, WO172/21, War Diary, GHQ Malaya Command, Appendices Q.59, X.59, 11 February 1942; AWM, 52/8/2/22, War Diary, 22nd Brigade AIF, Appendix A, 11 February 1942; *Operations of Malaya Command*, paragraphs 520, 525, 527; Stewart, 104-112; Kirby, *The Loss of Singapore*, 391-94; Wigmore, 346-52.

97. PRO, WO172/21, War Diary, GHQ Malaya Command, Appendix F.60, 11 February 1942; *Operations of Malaya Command*, paragraph 524, 526, 531; *Malaya Operations Record*, f.104-06; Tsuji, 255-56; Kirby, *The Loss of Singapore*, 394-97.

98. AWM, 52/8/2/27, War Diary, 27th Brigade AIF, 11 February 1942, entry for 0730 hrs: "Bde. Comd. to HQ 11th Ind. Div. Received orders that GOC Malaya Command has directed that Bt. Panjang village shall be recaptured, and directs that the task be fulfilled by 27th Bde. AIF. The attack will be lodged immediately and the village will be held at all costs," is confirmed by PRO, WO172/21, War Diary, GHQ Malaya Command, Appendix X.60, 11 February, a personal telegram from Percival to Wavell, and Appendix G.61, 12 February 1942; Appendix A.60, 11 February 1942, confirms that GHQ was aware Bennett lost touch with Maxwell. This clears up the uncertainty expressed by Wigmore, 354, and Lodge, 165-66.

99. PRO, WO172/21, War Diary, GHQ Malaya Command, Appendices J.60, O.60, GHQ to ABADCOM #456, 11 February 1942; AWM, 52/8/2/22, War Diary, 22nd Brigade AIF, 11 and Appendix B 11 February 1942 entries; *Operations of Malaya Command*, paragraphs 530, 533-35, 537; Kirby, *The Loss of Singapore*, 395-98; Wigmore, 352-53.

100. PRO, WO172/21, War Diary, GHQ Malaya Command, Appendices M.61 through W.61, 12 and Serials 4409-10, 12 February, Appendix Z.62, 13 February 1942; *Operations of Malaya Command*, paragraphs 539-47; Percival, 281; Kirby, *The Loss of Singapore*, 398-401; Falk, 247-48.

101. Bell, 68; Bennett, 183-84, should not be relied on for exact dates, but seems to have decided no later than 12 February to form an Australian perimeter. His comment on resistance and concerns about desertion are pursued in Appendix 3.

102. PRO, CAB66/21, War Cabinet situation report, 12 February 1942; PT, vol. 1, Churchill to Wavell, 10 February 1942; Churchill, *The Hinge of Fate*, 82-87; Kinvig, 209.

103. PT, vol. 1, Wavell to CCS, 13 February 1942; PRO, CAB106/38, *Operations in South-West Pacific*, paragraphs 28-29.

104. *Operations of Malaya Command*, paragraph 586; Simson, 97-99; Kirby, *The Loss of Singapore*, 408-09; Wigmore, 366, 370, 372-73.

105. *Operations of Malaya Command*, paragraphs 506, 540, 552, 558, 560; Barber, chs. 8-10, H. Sidhu, *The Bamboo Fortress*, Singapore, 1991, and Foong, *The Price of Peace*, are the most vivid descriptions of the daily ordeal Singapore's populace endured during the battle; Kennedy, 56-59; R. Gough, *The Escape from Singapore*, Singapore, 1994 (revised edition), Part One. *Malaya Operations Record*, f.107, records that the *3rd Air Group* and supporting units flew 4700 sorties over Singapore from 4 February, dropped 773 tons of bombs, and mounted an all-out effort to destroy all vessels attempting to escape.

106. *Operations of Malaya Command*, paragraph 571; M. Moore, *Battalion at War: Singapore 1942*, Norwich, 1988, 28-30; R. Holmes and A. Kemp, *The Bitter End*, Chichester, 1982, 174; Foong, *The Price of Peace*, 264-92.

107. PT, vol. 1, Wavell to Churchill, 14 February 1942; *Operations of Malaya Command*, paragraph 553; Percival, 286; Bennett, 186; Churchill, *The Hinge of Fate*, 90-91; Kinvig, 213-14; Kirby, *The Loss of Singapore*, 409-410; Wigmore, 371-72.

108. *Malaya Operations Record*, f.106; Tsuji, 263-64; R. Storry, *Japan and the Decline of the West in Asia, 1894-1943*, London, 1979, 140.

109. PRO, CAB106/155, Precis of the account of Brig. G.G.R. Williams on the operations of 1st Malaya Brigade, 8–15 February 1942 (Williams account); IWM, Miscellaneous files, Malaya and Singapore, diary, Lt. A. Mackenzie (officer commanding Carrier platoon, 1st Malay), February 1942; *Operations of Malaya Command*, paragraphs 548-50, 556; Chippington, 216-21; Kirby, *The Loss of Singapore*, 410-11; Falk, 249. WO172/180, War Diary, Faber Fire Command, entries for and reports on 13 February 1942, indicate the coastal defence guns at Labrador Park did their best to assist the defenders of Pasir Panjang Ridge but, due to concrete overhead cover, could not bear on the enemy after they advanced beyond Pasir Panjang Village. That meant the Japanese faced the infantry alone once they reached the ridge itself. An accessible but quite unreliable and unattributed account of the Malay Regiment action is in Foong, *The Price of Peace*, 295-307. Its many errors are revealed in the less accessible but more authoritative accounts of the officers noted above, especially that written by Williams while in captivity and submitted to the official historian.

110. AWM, 52/8/2/22, War Diary, 22nd Brigade AIF, 14 February 1942 entries; *Operations of Malaya Command*, paragraphs 562-65; Percival, 290; Bennett, 189; Wigmore, 375; Kirby, *The Loss of Singapore*, 411-12; Lodge, 172-73; Falk, 251-52.

111. *Operations of Malaya Command*, paragraph 561; Percival, 284, 290; Chippington, 223-27; Wigmore, 374; Falk, 252. There is controversy over whether or not Indian troops in retreat fired on the Japanese from the hospital grounds. An unpublished report held in the IWM, Miscellaneous File 168, Item 2588, P. Burton, "Narrative Report on Alexandra Hospital Massacre," based heavily on interviews with survivors and written in 1989, suggests convincingly that they did. This does seem plausible given the complaint noted by Brig. Williams that the withdrawal of his brigade was not reported in time

to the neighbouring 44th Indian Brigade, which inadvertently left the hospital in the front line that morning: PRO, CAB106/155, Williams account. But all this in no way excuses either the prolonged rampage of the Japanese troops inside the hospital or the atrocious mass murder they perpetrated the next morning.

112. PRO, CAB106/153, Bennett to Sturdee, 14 February 1942; *Operations of Malaya Command*, paragraphs 567-68, 570; Percival, 284, 289; Simson, 114; Bennett, 190; Kirby, *The Loss of Singapore*, 411; Wigmore, 374-75; Lodge, 172.

113. PRO, CAB79/18, COS minutes, 13 February 1942; PT, vol. 1, Churchill to Wavell, 14 February 1942.

114. *Malaya Operations Record*, f.104; Tsuji, 260-62.

115. *Operations of Malaya Command*, paragraphs 574-76; Percival, 291-92; Bennett, 191-92; Churchill, *The Hinge of Fate*, 91-92; Simson, 115-16; Kinvig, 216-17.

116. PT, vol. 1, Percival to Wavell, 15 February 1942; *Operations of Malaya Command*, paragraphs 577-82; Percival, 292; Wigmore, 378-80; Potter, 88-90; Allen, 175-84; Kinvig, 217-20.

117. The humiliating photograph of the Union Jack flying next to the white flag, over a surrendering British general, is easily the most memorable image of the campaign and had worldwide impact at the time. It undoubtedly was one reason why Percival's reception after the war by officialdom at home was so unjustifiably cold. That reception was indeed scapegoating, as Kinvig argues with much justice in his chapters 19 and 20. Given how difficult the mission assigned to Percival was, and how badly the central direction of the war fumbled its own job — to co-ordinate grand strategy with realistic theatre plans — laying the burden almost solely on Percival was one of the least honourable actions we must associate with Churchill. The idea of pursuing an inquiry into the fall of Singapore after the war was quietly buried after a lengthy investigation by the Joint Planning Staff in 1946. The COS tried to restrict the focus of an inquiry to the conduct of the campaign itself, but the JPS demurred. Their conclusion was that any public inquiry could not be restricted but must lead to a searching and unflattering probe of British grand strategy as a whole, prewar intelligence and its handling, colonial administration, command and policy decisions made by all higher authorities involved, civil and military, in both London and Singapore, the character and ability of higher commanders, and above all the system which produced all the above and still governed the U.K. The review is documented in the only recently released PRO, CAB119/208, culminating in JP(46)56(Final), Malayan Campaign — Limitations of a Public Inquiry, 6 May 1946.

9

Living under the Rising Sun: Singapore and the Japanese Occupation 1942–1945

There is little doubt that the Japanese Occupation of Singapore became one of the most contentious, emotive and harrowing periods of this island's chequered history. Almost as soon as it was over the Occupation began generating a massive literary and scholarly output from a vast array of sources. Much of this work has been written in the form of graphic personal recollections and many of these tales are, as one might expect, overwhelmingly hostile to the Japanese military administration. As a result, the new rulers of Singapore from mid-February 1942 to mid-August 1945 are often depicted as being demonic, violent, ruthless, arbitrary, and almost totally devoid of compassion, consideration and benevolence. Despite the ghastly nature and scale of human suffering that resulted from the Japanese Occupation, however, few local survivors of this troubled era doubt that it was to be a significant watershed in Singapore's political and constitutional development. Out of dire adversity sprang momentous change. Since the Occupation was such a multifaceted experience, this chapter will seek to portray it from four different perspectives, namely, that of the local Singaporean population, the Allied prisoners of war, the civilian internees, and finally, the Japanese administrators themselves.

Coming to Terms with the Occupation: The View of the Local Singaporeans

An eerie calm seemed to have settled over the harbour and city sectors of Singapore on 16 February 1942. In particular, the area around Raffles Place had become a magnet for a large number of Allied troops — some dishevelled, others kitted out in incongruous clothing — who were using the time afforded to them by the non-appearance of the Japanese military to play cards, smoke, drink, and chat with one another as they awaited news of their impending imprisonment.[1]

Fear of the unknown, or perhaps a grim foreboding of their own likely fate at the hands of the Japanese, kept many Chinese Singaporeans indoors on the morning after the British surrender. Most shops and businesses stayed closed, their owners sheltering behind boarded-up premises too anxious or circumspect to venture forth on this first day of a new and uncertain epoch. While some looters were out on Orchard Road and in other shopping areas on that Monday morning, the vast majority of the population took the day off. Some of the more enterprising or venal managed to procure or make Japanese flags which they eagerly displayed as welcoming signs to the all-conquering army of *Dai-Nippon*. Most of the Chinese population, however, refrained from doing so.[2]

It is not uncommon for war-weary soldiers of some nations to celebrate their hard-earned victory by engaging in an orgy of rape and looting once the enemy has surrendered. Singapore was a witness to these familiar excesses as some of the Japanese troops sought to garner the spoils of war by creating havoc amongst the civilian population of the fallen island. If faced with a choice most people were prepared to give up a few of their possessions to these unruly representatives of the Japanese military if they could prevent their family being despoiled by them. So for many people living on the island the early days of peace were just as laden with anxiety and tension as the final days of the campaign had been.[3]

From the outset, however, the Japanese military administration sought to operate a policy of divide and rule amongst the local civilian population of Singapore which numbered roughly 1.4 million in February 1942.[4] While the Japanese encouraged both the Malay and Indian communities and sought their active cooperation, they dismissed the minority Eurasian population with both contempt and distrust on the grounds that its members were tainted by association with the West.[5] Of all the ethnic groups in Singapore, however, the Japanese reserved their foulest treatment for the majority Chinese population of over 700,000 which they regarded as being inherently untrustworthy and a source of implacable hostility to all that *Dai-Nippon* stood for. Little effort was, therefore, expended by the Japanese officials on seeking an accommodation with the Chinese. Instead they proceeded to take steps almost immediately to decimate and strike fear into the heart of the community with a series of *sook ching* or purification-by-elimination exercises that were supposed to target and destroy all known anti-Japanese elements, such as Communist sympathisers, financial supporters of Chiang Kai-shek, members of *Dalforce* and volunteer military associations, civil servants, intellectuals, students, secret society members, and other assorted criminals.[6] While the net certainly closed around some of these suspects, the *sook ching* ended up being more of an exercise in ethnic cleansing than anything else. After ordering the Chinese population to congregate in a number of specified concentration areas within the city, the Japanese *Kempeitai* (military security police — the Japanese equivalent of the *Gestapo*), assisted by some local informers who wore hoods to mask their features, would proceed to check the identity of each person in their sector. This was a long drawn-out process lasting several days in exacting temperatures and high humidity. Those whose names were known to the *Kempeitai*, or were picked out by the informers as suspects, faced almost certain death by firing squad. Those who were fortunate enough to be cleared by the authorities received a chop or sign on their arm or piece of clothing and were allowed to return to their homes. Estimates of those implicated and swiftly exterminated by the Japanese in these *sook ching* range from a very conservative 5000 to at least 50,000. It is unlikely that one will ever know the extent of this appalling genocide.[7] It is poignant to think, however, that what have now become some of the most pleasant recreational spots on the island were once the scenes of mass murder.[8]

The *sook ching* round-up

By setting a brutal tone from the outset, the Japanese authorities confirmed the worst fears of the Chinese population. Fear of falling into the hands of the sadistic *Kempeitai* was real for those communities acutely at risk and it endured throughout the Occupation. Few doubted that the methods of torture used to interrogate suspects and extract information from them were depraved and barbaric besides defying every human rights convention that had ever been established. All seemed agreed that if the *Kempeitai* wanted to break anyone, they probably had the means to do so. Consequently, the aim of the endangered communities was to avoid doing anything which could draw attention to themselves; anonymity was preferable to public exposure since this could alert the dreaded authorities in 3 Oxley Road and 6 Oxley Rise or at other *Kempeitai* addresses in the city to investigate the individual concerned.[9] Wariness outside the family circle became a key element in a person's continued survival. "Careless talk costs lives" — a popular British poster of the period — was given a frightening new edge in Singapore.[10] For careless talk in the tropics was likely to cost the life of the person engaged in it.

If the Chinese community had not been sufficiently cowed by the *sook ching* massacres and the grim prospect of suffering from the injustice and perversion of the *Kempeitai*, there was to be yet further misery inflicted upon it in the form of a forced financial donation to the Japanese war effort. As early as March 1942 leading members of the Chinese communities in all the Malayan states were made aware of Japanese expectations in this matter. It was decreed that $50 million was to be raised as a "gift" to be given to the Japanese military as a gesture of loyalty to the new rulers of *Malai* and *Syonan-to*. Singapore's capacity to pay was considered to be greater than that of any Malayan state other than Selangor and each was expected to collect $10 million from their members. In Singapore an 8% tax was levied on all those Chinese who owned property worth more than $3000. As this measure proved to be insufficient to raise the required sum, ultimately the Chinese were forced to go to the Yokohama Specie Bank for a bridging loan to make up the difference.[11] This deliberate anti-Chinese policy naturally did not endear the by now subdued majority population to their new masters. Hatred mixed with fear became dominant emotions for many who had hitherto little knowledge of what the Japanese could be capable of in both war and peace.

Immediately following the Japanese takeover of Singapore, a determined effort was made by the new administration to rid the island of all vestiges of British colonial rule and institute Japanese equivalents in their place. A prompt start was made in changing both the calendar and the time of the day and was extended to replacing the currency too. From henceforth the year 1942 was replaced by the Japanese year 2602 and reference to Greenwich Mean Time was abandoned in favour of advancing Singapore time by ninety minutes to bring it in line with Tokyo time. Colonial banks and money also went the way of the time and the calendar; those banks associated with the old regime were summarily closed down and had their assets seized, while the Straits Settlements currency was replaced by the introduction of a new currency issued by the Bank of Japan ostensibly on a 1:1 basis. In order to be universally accepted any currency must become a store of value but the new monetary units failed in this crucial test because they were issued without the necessary economic safeguards against inflation. Predictably inflation soared as both the number and volume of the notes in circulation far exceeded the level of the island's economic productivity. This would have been bad enough without the vast number of forgeries that also began appearing in the market place at the same time. Soon the new medium of exchange became derisively known as "banana currency" (because of the illustration of a comb of bananas on the front of a ten-dollar note). Few of those paid in it had much confidence that it would ever accrue in value, as the steep price rises of goods on the black market indicated with telling effect. Nonetheless, it represented the official medium of exchange even if it was a flawed one.[12]

By the end of May 1942 the colonial legal system had been replaced with a remarkably similar set of institutions bearing Japanese names — surely, a case of old wine in new bottles? What had formerly been district, police and coroner's courts were now gathered together to form the

Syonan Keizi Tihohoin (Criminal District Court). By the same token the Civil District Court was to be called the *Syonan Minzi Tihohoin*, whereas the highest court in the land — the Supreme Court — was to be known as the *Syonan Kotohoin*. As was to be expected, Japanese judges filled the most important positions on the bench, but local legal experts were elevated to high office as well. M.V. Pillai, for example, was appointed a criminal district judge. Moreover, all local advocates and solicitors (unless specifically proscribed from so doing by the Japanese authorities) were allowed to resume their old legal practices upon the downpayment of $500 to the military administration.[13]

While the use of the English language could not be proscribed — for business still needed to be conducted on the island — it was hoped that in time it would wither away as the local population came to learn and achieve fluency in *Nippon-go*. A vast campaign to teach the local people the Japanese language was therefore mounted from as early as 21 February.[14] Although the population was cajoled into memorising the *Katakana*, the simplified Japanese characters, that were the key to an understanding of *Nippon-go*, various incentives were on offer to those who could master the new language of the ruling elite. Workers and professionals could expect greater job security, swifter promotions, or an increase in their basic rate of pay if they conformed, took their language lessons seriously and passed their subsequent examinations. Obviously school pupils were most likely to be the richest source of new adherents to *Nippon-go* if sufficient qualified language teachers could be obtained to provide this basic level of instruction. School curricula would be changed dramatically to enable the students at least a couple of hours of Japanese language study a day.[15]

Yet for several weeks all schools remained closed. When the first of them reopened for registration under new guises (all old colonial names being dispensed with) in late March and early April 1942, the response from the general public was hugely disappointing. Many Chinese parents were initially wary of the form of education that might be on offer. As life was hard and likely to remain so for the foreseeable future, many families preferred that their children should help them scratch a living at work rather than allow them to go to school and become indoctrinated by the Japanese.[16]

New Japanese words entered the vocabulary of the local population of Singapore from the time that the Japanese military administration (*Gunseikan-bu*) took over the island from the British forces and delegated civilian control to the municipal authority (*Tokubetsu-si*), the secret service (*Tekkikan*) and the dreaded *Kempeitai*. All parts of the newly installed bureaucratic machinery were known by their Japanese names so in due course the general public was to become familiar with other terms such as the Bureau of Welfare (*Minsei-bu*) and the Police Bureau (*Keisatu-bu*). It soon became clear, however, that until *Nippon-go* became the *lingua franca* of the residents of Singapore, the Japanese would have to compromise and romanise the individual *Katakana* characters. This meant in effect that the use of English, while still not officially encouraged, remained in everyday existence. Naturally, in instances where Japanese words could be substituted for the original English equivalent without spreading confusion, however, the linguistic transfer was made with great relish. Hence, the English daily newspaper the *Straits Times* was duly renamed the *Syonan Times.*[17]

Few could doubt that the Japanese felt inherently superior to all other ethnic groups and that they felt it was their duty to impose and inculcate an awareness of their national spirit (*Nippon-Seishin*) amongst the civilian population of Singapore.[18] This was to be achieved through showing the appropriate mark of respect for all Japanese institutions and officials. This extended from participation in daily ceremonies celebrating the national flag (the *Hinomaru*) and the national anthem (*Kimigayo*), to compulsory mass physical fitness drills accompanied by music provided by *Radio-Taisho*. Moreover, everyone was expected to bow to any official of the Imperial Japanese administration or members of their armed forces. If this was only done perfunctorily, or without the requisite finesse, the individual concerned was likely to be beaten or slapped by an irate servant of *Tenno Heika*, the son of heaven, the ruler of the Chrysanthemum throne, Emperor Hirohito. Unfortunately, even those who were not ethnically Japanese but who worked for them demanded the same mark of respect from the rest of the population and were just as likely to exact some retribution from those who failed to give it to them.[19]

Japanese propaganda, which never ceased to extoll the virtues of *Dai-Nippon*, and heavy censorship was all-embracing in Singapore. Direct control was exercised over what the local populace could read, listen to, or see on the big screen. In the event all the different language newspapers that were printed in Singapore during the Occupation became virtually unreadable — their literary content being a mix of official proclamations, dreary stories on the staging of local events and, particularly from the middle of 1942 onwards, mostly exaggerated articles on the progress of the Pacific war. As a result, this dull and tedious journalism made many people anxious to obtain authentic and more objective sources of information from any means at their disposal. To this end those people who had radios continued to tune in to the BBC World Service short-wave broadcasts from Bush House in the Strand. In an effort to stop this illegal acquisition of foreign news items, the Japanese authorities demanded that all those who owned radio sets must hand them in so that their short-wave reception capability could be sealed off. Those who did not avail themselves of this opportunity and were found in possession of short-wave radio sets were virtually guaranteed an indeterminate period of interrogation and confinement in the squalid and fetid cells of the *Kempeitai*.[20] Although possession of medium-wave radios was not in itself illegal, the fact that the only programmes offered on these sets were Japanese-censored productions meant that the demand for them was lukewarm.

Although the *Nipponisation* of Singapore's institutions was plainly the intention of both the military and civil organs of the Japanese administration regardless of local opinion, some of the more discerning senior officials were also aware of the need to obtain a measure of genuine public support for their programmes. While the imposition of Japanese values was considered essential in some areas, it was recognised as being not always the most appropriate policy in others. For this reason, therefore, the devotional, customary and sporting habits of the people were less subject to imperial control than most other things.

Whatever the intolerance level of the Japanese authorities may have been towards the cultural norms of the British colonial establishment, therefore, they were careful not to interfere with religious observance on the part of the majority of the people of Singapore. Pragmatism dictated that no herculean effort should be expended on trying to convert the entire population to either the Shintoist or Buddhist faiths. Instead the Japanese adopted a largely "hands-off" policy on the emotive question of religious devotion. This meant that most of the residents of Singapore were free to continue to worship in their chapels, churches, mosques, synagogues, and temples in a relatively unrestricted way. In fact, the Japanese used this as an example of their benign rule. Nonetheless, as the war progressed so adherents of both the Anglican and Jewish communities, in particular, found the authorities far less accommodating towards them and a number of these individuals were, alas, to suffer hideously at the hands of the *Kempeitai*.[21]

Local religious and secular customs or rites — particularly those of Malay and Indian origin — were actually encouraged by the Japanese administration, which also continued to observe the traditional public holidays of both communities. Nonetheless, when the Japanese eventually offered a number of polite suggestions to the Malays for certain reforms in their customary practices — promoting the concept of mass weddings, or changes in dress style, for instance — these proposals were largely ignored and the Japanese-inspired ideas never caught on. In the end, the Japanese learnt that it was probably safest and best to leave the Malays well alone since their interference was simply not appreciated and risked alienating them as both an ethnic and religious group.[22]

Traditional sports, such as athletics, badminton, boxing, football, rugby, *sepak takraw*, swimming, tennis, and wrestling were revived with the blessing of the Japanese authorities who saw mass participation in these recreational pursuits as being an essential way of convincing the local population that "normal service" was being resumed on the island. Both the results and highlights of these sports meetings were reported in the local press in perhaps the only unbiased coverage printed in the entire *Syonan Times* and the *Syonan Sinbun* (from 8 December 1942).[23] While sport mainly catered to the young and the fit, there were many residents of Singapore who did not fall into either of these two categories. For these people the Japanese reopened amusement parks and centres, such as "Great World" and "New World", cinemas (offering a restricted bill of fare) and theatres with an admittedly limited repertoire. A heavy enveloping censorship prevailed on all things judged prejudicial to the interests of the Japanese administration. As a result, all creative entertainment that originated in any of the Allied countries — classical works or not — was eventually banned in Singapore during the Occupation period.[24] This attitude was extended to the type of music that could be played or listened to on the island. Western music of all types was seen as being totally decadent and banned entirely. All Chinese and Russian musical scores were viewed with even more vitriol by the censors. This trenchant prohibition on non-Japanese works did not extend, however, to those classical composers who hailed from nations deemed friendly to Japan. While the works of Beethoven and Mozart, for instance, were allowed to be performed in Singapore, those of Tchaikovsky and Delius would never be heard while the Japanese authorities remained in place.[25] Instead the local people were provided with a largely unleavened diet of Japanese music. Whether many ever succeeded in acquiring a taste for this type of music is, nonetheless, very debatable. Although the possible avenues of entertainment in Singapore were clearly of mixed quality, virtually anything was better than nothing. By offering the general public a variety of entertainment the Japanese sought both to lift the siege mentality on the island and dispel the popular view that saw the Occupation as being merely a short, transitory stage before the eventual return of the British colonial authorities.

By the end of May 1942 the Japanese had decided upon the adoption of yet another measure designed to appeal to the local population. This latest initiative concerned the establishment of a state lottery. Much was made of the proposal because it was thought of as a uniquely acceptable device for saving purposes and for soaking up surplus amounts of cash in circulation — hints here surely of an already persistent and alarming degree of inflation being present in the economy. Material incentives are as welcome in wartime as they are in peace and since the local Singaporeans were anxious to improve their financial circumstances if they could, the lure of winning the lottery persuaded many of them to gamble a dollar note on the outcome of the draw. Although a gross generalisation, it still may be true to suggest that many Chinese people, in particular, have a penchant for gambling. For those who would bet even on the most inconsequential of things, the state lottery proved to be irresistible. Many a dollar note would therefore be passed over in exchange for a lottery ticket and a hopeful passport to future riches.[26]

While the existence of the state lottery was supposed to assist the economic reconstruction of Singapore in an indirect way, more direct methods had to be taken immediately to rehabilitate those vital parts of the island's infrastructure which had been damaged or destroyed by military action or sabotage in the early part of the year. A massive clean-up operation to repair the docks, oil tanks, streets, bridges, and buildings was embarked upon by the Japanese administration using a large pool of cheap labour drawn from the ranks of the Allied prisoners of war in Changi. Although using enemy prisoners to fulfil these tasks actually violated the Geneva Convention, the Japanese saw no earthly reason why they should respect these provisions and so they did not.[27] Although the Allied troops provided a useful source of unskilled labour throughout the war for their Japanese hosts, their work did not prove to be a key element in the resuscitation of Singapore's economy. Instead of reviving, the economy stubbornly failed to regain the vitality it had shown in the pre-war days when its status as a regional entrepôt port had been so striking. As international trade patterns were broken or warped by the war, the port of Singapore — the engine of the island's economy — languished.

In addition, Singapore's lack of mineral resources and poor soil inhibited all efforts to establish a Japanese-sponsored programme of autarky. Great and continuing emphasis was placed by the Japanese on various schemes to grow more food on the island. Gardening became an important part of the school curriculum and the press was used to launch a series of propaganda campaigns and incentives designed to increase substantially the total area of Singapore under cultivation. Accordingly, many a playing field or open space was immediately converted from recreational to agricultural use. Yet few vegetable crops thrived on Singapore's clay-bound soil. So the much sought-after spectacular boost in crop yields either failed to materialise or remained below the level required for island-wide self-subsistence.[28]

It would seem to be an economic truism that self-sufficiency can only work effectively in resource-rich areas. For an island that was used to importing its vital supplies — even water — from its trading partners, the war distorted this once cosy relationship and made autarky all the more improbable to achieve. As the war proceeded, imports of all commodities (and particularly foodstuffs) into Singapore fell precipitously as Allied submarines in the area began preying ever more profitably on all mercantile traffic plying between enemy-held ports. What supplies did get through were likely to be raided extensively by the Japanese who reserved the right to stockpile considerable quantities of these imported goods for their own purposes. What was left would be rationed amongst the rest of the population. For this purpose a whole administrative structure was erected.[29] Approved wholesalers and retailers were brought together to form distributors' associations (*Kumiais*). So-called "Peace Living Certificates" were initially issued to households whose members were thought to be of good conduct. Possession of these certificates would thereby entitle the holder to a number of ration cards. Essential commodities, such as rice, sugar, salt, and pork, were subject to strict rationing from the outset and became even more rigorous as time passed.[30] Nonetheless, these commodities and other articles could be found at a high price on the Singapore black market which flourished, as a result of indigenous entrepreneurial skill and tacit Japanese complicity, from the very start of the Occupation.[31]

Linked to the declining food situation, the general health of the community plummeted too. By the end of 1942 what had once been staple foods had become either rare and costly or non-existent. Milk, for instance, fell into this category. A substitute commodity — a type of rice gruel — was introduced by the Japanese authorities on 29 December 1942. Bread was made from a variety of unappetising substances, such as tapioca and ragi, once the wheat flour stocks were depleted. Food however decently prepared was rarely appetising or sufficient. As the war continued, vitamin deficiencies soon began to take their toll on the most vulnerable members of society. Beri-beri, for example, threatened to become a scourge for those lacking Vitamin B1. Although two katties of rice polishings were made available per month in early 1943 to provide this essential vitamin and all school children received a dose of pure red palm oil to bolster their immune system, the magnitude of the task of keeping 1.4 million people from starving or succumbing to a wide variety of diseases proved to be an enormous problem for the Japanese military administration.[32]

Almost paranoid about cleanliness and the spread of diseases, the Japanese were acutely aware of the risk of combatting epidemics in a crowded urban environment. As a result, from the very beginning of their rule the Japanese Military Administration instituted a compulsory mass inoculation programme against typhoid (27 February 1942) and cholera (2 July 1942). A series of anti-malarial drives to eliminate the breeding grounds of the *Aedes* mosquito were put in hand periodically throughout the Occupation period. These health care programmes were largely successful in Singapore, but as stocks of medicine ran down on the island and replenishment supplies could never be guaranteed to arrive, so the common forms of illness and disease became more difficult to treat and correspondingly claimed more victims.[33]

Even before it became obvious that the means of food production could not be raised sufficiently to cope with the demands of the population, the Japanese had been keen on repatriating those people who were non-Singaporean to their own states on the Malayan peninsula. A notice appeared in the press as early as 3 March 1942 indicating that those Chinese people seeking to return to Johore or Melaka by foot were given permission to gather at the causeway from 4-7 March, while those going by train to Seremban in Negri Sembilan were to meet at the central railway station on 5-6 March. All those seeking to leave Singapore had to bring along an adequate means of identification and a few belongings. Cars could not normally be used for repatriation purposes, although exceptions could be made by the Japanese authorities on a case-by-case basis. This voluntary repatriation was followed almost immediately by an order issued by the Japanese authorities (8 & 9 March) instructing all people from Malaya, regardless of racial origin, to return to their homeland by 14 March.[34]

Another method of reducing the population of Singapore was to create farming settlements up-country in Johore and Negri Sembilan or on offshore islands, such as Batam or Bintan. In August 1943, as the food situation grew more critical, members of the Chinese community in Singapore were encouraged by the Japanese authorities to emigrate to a new settlement at Endau in Johore. Those that were prepared to make the move were promised a fair degree of freedom in their new environment.[35] Living beyond the gaze of the dreaded *Kempeitai* proved to be one of Endau's main attractions for a community that had been ill-served by this notorious police force in the recent past. *New Syonan*, as the settlement at Endau came to be known, had numerous advantages over the Eurasian and Roman Catholic-designated site that was carved out of the hilly jungle slopes at Bahau in Negri Sembilan. *New Syonan* at least had both a plentiful supply of water and good peaty soil. Neither could be said of the Eurasian community's malaria-infested, infertile stretch of land at Bahau.[36]

Supported by the Oversea Chinese Association (OCA) to the tune of $1 million, *New Syonan* offered a fresh start to those families who wished to try their hand at farming. Roughly 12,000 members of the Chinese community made the move up-country and were awarded with individual plots of land that amounted to four acres in size. They were also provided with basic farming implements and seeds to begin their planting operations. Their settlement acquired a level of sophistication — it even had a school, several restaurants, a hospital, and some shops — that was never matched by the emigrés at the much smaller settlement at Bahau. Until guerilla operations in the last few months of 1944 threatened to undermine the whole scheme, the agricultural success of *New Syonan* was quite marked. While sufficient rice was grown in the padi fields to sustain the population, good-quality fruit and vegetables were cultivated on the 300,000 acre settlement.[37]

While feedback from the emigrants at *New Syonan* is mixed, the story is far bleaker from those who managed to survive the harrowing experience at the Bahau settlement. Despite glowing promotional statements that appeared in the press and enthusiastic reports delivered at public meetings about the state of the new settlement, members of the Roman Catholic and Eurasian communities had not been overwhelmingly inclined to leave their island home for a new start in Malaya.[38] Whether they did not believe the propaganda or were merely being cautious and conservative, the fact was that the 30,000-acre settlement in Negri Sembilan was never the success of the OCA-sponsored one in Johore. Using a site previously rejected by the OCA, the leaders of the Roman Catholic community in Singapore had opted for Bahau despite the fact that its water supply was inadequate, the soil quality was indifferent and preliminary excavation work was rudimentary.[39] Initially seen as a haven from *Kempeitai* persecution, the Bahau settlement (which was also known as *Fuji-go*) was home to roughly 300 Eurasian families and 400 Chinese Catholic families at its outset at the end of 1943. In addition, the Reverend Mother and the Sisters of the Convent of the Good Shepherd and the Canossian Convent as well as members of the Roman Catholic priesthood went to Bahau.[40] Despite providing devotional and spiritual guidance, as well as *de-facto* leadership to the members of the community, the clergy and the nuns did not possess much, if any, farming experience. Sadly, in this case, faith alone was not sufficient to make the *Fuji-go* settlement a success. Without either the organisational flair or the financial support of the OCA, the Bahau project in Negri Sembilan started badly and proceeded to get much worse as time wore on. Lacking infrastructural support from the Negri Sembilan authorities, as well as the necessary agricultural skills, equipment, seeds, and good fortune, the settlers had not made much progress in clearing their site before they soon had to contend with the onset of devastating illnesses, such as malaria, dysentery and beri-beri. At least two hundred members of this ill-starred community — mainly babies or the elderly — succumbed to one or other of these diseases. Bishop Devals, the Roman Catholic leader of the settlement, was one of those who failed to survive the grim ordeal of *Fuji-go*.[41]

By June 1945 the voluntary resettlement plan, which the Japanese authorities had originally hoped would siphon off up to 300,000 of the population in Singapore, had failed to attract more than a mere fraction of that number. As the Allied grip on the Pacific War increased and sightings of American aircraft became common over the skies of Singapore, the Japanese, fearing that it was shortly to become a war zone, began to issue orders for a forced evacuation of non-essential workers from the island. These civilians were encouraged to join their relatives or friends in parts of nearby Malaya or Indonesia. Those without familial or friendly links in these countries were still required to leave Singapore and make the best of the situation. They were allowed to take both money and food supplies with them. Those that did not have cars to make the journey up-country, the vast majority, were provided with special excursion trains that were added to the existing rail schedule to take the evacuees to a series of destinations in Malaya.[42]

In the end, of course, external events overtook the ominous situation in Singapore. Once the Allies had dropped the two atomic bombs on Hiroshima and Nagasaki on 6 and 9 August 1945, Emperor Hirohito felt compelled to ignore the advice of some of his ministers who wished to fight on and sued for peace instead on 14 August. Therefore, despite all the dire predictions of those who saw the island engulfed in war once more, Singapore was not to be battle-scarred again. Peace had returned to the island city-state.

Life as a Prisoner of the Japanese

Lt.-Gen. Percival's action in signing the instrument of surrender on 15 February 1942 had profound and immediate repercussions for the more than 100,000 Allied troops under his command. Not all of these troops were to be treated similarly by the Japanese however. A clear distinction was made in the case of the approximately 45,000 Indian troops that had fought on the side of the British in the Malayan campaign. They were ordered to congregate in Farrer Park on 17 February, where they were informed that the Japanese forces sympathised with their plight, wished to see them as friends rather than past foes and were anxious to help them in casting off the yoke of British rule and gaining their rightful independence. It was heady stuff, yet the concept of joining the INA under Capt. Mohan Singh and fighting for what was described as the cause of national liberation drew a mixed response from the assembled troops.[43]

While the Indian troops were to be billeted in the Nee Soon, Seletar, Bidadari, Tyersall Park, and Kranji camps for the time being, the Japanese regarded the other 50,000-plus British and Australian troops disdainfully as being prisoners of war (POWs) who would have to be confined for the duration of the war. These men were ordered to make their own way out to the Changi peninsula by the evening of 17 February. As little or no transport was made available to them, the vast majority of these troops had no option but to walk the nearly 25 km from the city in the tropical heat and humidity carrying a variety of clothes, food and gadgetry in their bulging kit bags.[44] It was both psychologically and physically draining for them. Defeat can sometimes be inspirational, but not on this occasion. For many of these troops this forced march into captivity through the streets of Singapore and past the ranks of the people that they were supposed to defend was to be a humiliating experience. Whether by accident or design, the Japanese had contrived to create a situation that would make an indelible impression on those who watched the ranks of the dejected Allied troops pass before them on their sweaty journey to Changi.[45] Since those days many commentators and politicians have chosen to see in this muted procession a metaphor for, or symbol of, British decline in the East.[46]

Before the invasion the purpose-built Changi military base had been one of the most modern and well-equipped in the entire Commonwealth and covered some 2000 acres. Apart from a host of barrack blocks, the base had various types of accommodation for married officers and men, several messes, cookhouses, guardrooms, storerooms, equipment sheds, power stations, a clubhouse, and a variety of facilities for a wide range of sporting and social pursuits. In addition to the base, the complex included Changi Village which had been cleared of all civilians and was to be home to members of the 11th and 18th Divisions.[47] From the very beginning the allocation of accommodation to the POWs was handled in an orderly and disciplined fashion by staff of Malaya Command Headquarters with very little input from the Japanese military who were content to allow the British to assume this task. It was decided to use Roberts Barracks (southeast of Fairy Point and due south of Temple Hill) as a hospital. By 11 March 1942 the Australians had moved their sick and incapacitated into Roberts Barracks too on orders from the Japanese. Selarang Barracks (south of Roberts, straddling the Changi Road about a mile from Changi Jail) was to be the home of the remaining Australian POWs. Kitchener Barracks (comprising the area west of Changi Village and covering the Fairy Point promontory) was allocated to the troops that had formed the Singapore Fortress contingent. Officers of III Indian Corps were housed at Temple Hill, while those members of 18th Division that were not in Changi Village occupied the barrack blocks and huts of what were known as India Lines. For their part, the Japanese forces supervising the POW camps established their own headquarters at Half Moon Crescent (just beyond the perimeter of Changi Jail).[48]

To many a POW who was to experience prison conditions elsewhere within the newly acquired Japanese empire, the Changi cantonment was something of a haven and in the early weeks more of an enforced rest camp than a place of incarceration. In these relatively unrestricted days, prisoners were able to mingle freely with those from other barracks, take long walks in the Changi area, organise swimming parties and generally enjoy their leisure activities. Such was the lack of pervasive scrutiny that both Lt.-Gen. Heath and a senior medical officer were able to smuggle their wives into the camp and live with them there undetected for several weeks before the women were discovered by the prison guards and sent to the civilian internment camp at Changi Jail.[49] Subsequently, of course, conditions deteriorated, a far more restrictive regime was imposed upon the inmates by the Japanese, food rations (always small) were reduced still further and dietary inadequacy left the weaker POWs prone to a growing incidence of illness and disease.[50] Moreover, the Japanese very quickly discovered that in the large number of British and Australian troops at their disposal they had a rich source of cheap labour which could be put to work repairing damaged dockyards, godowns, buildings, roads, and equipment. Work parties were soon formed for these and other high-priority tasks, such as bomb loading, or the sorting, packing and re-shipment of stores. Once assigned to a work party operating out of the Changi area, POWs would find themselves housed in temporary camps, such as those in Havelock Road, Pasir Panjang, River Valley Road, Serangoon Road, Sime Road, and Tanjong Rhu. Within a few weeks other POWs were sent to clear ground for the growing of crops and in the latter months of the war, many were engaged upon the building of a new aerodrome at Changi.[51] According to the Geneva Convention, POWs were not supposed to be engaged in assisting their captor's war effort. Clearly, some of these tasks contravened this principle. This fact was blatantly ignored by the Japanese. Their defiant and stubborn refusal to conform to these internationally approved rules of behaviour, despite being signatories to the Geneva Convention, was reprehensible. Whatever the arduous nature of the work in Singapore may have been, however, it was nothing in comparison to the horrendous situation awaiting those POWs who were unfortunately sent up-country to work — and many to die — on the infamous Thailand-Burma railway.[52]

Those who became POWs in Singapore immediately discovered that imprisonment did not blur the chain of command as the distinction between officers and other ranks was steadfastly maintained in the camps. Military discipline was regarded as being essential if the camps were not to degenerate into a chaotic shambles. Apart from establishing a camp office to liaise with the Japanese prison authorities, officers expected to be saluted by subordinates and those who did not conform to this customary practice were charged with a breach of discipline and punished accordingly. Allied military police units were not disbanded and some of the more unruly POWs soon found themselves in the rather ironical situation of being confined to a punishment cell as they became prisoners of the POWs! Court-martials and inquiries were also held in the camps by the POWs.[53] Although some prisoners deeply resented this old elitism and the absurd lengths some officers were prepared to go to enforce their superiority over others, there is little doubt that military discipline brought more than a semblance of order and efficiency to the life of the POWs. Irksome and unfair though it might have been on occasion, on balance re-establishing the military chain of command was probably a sound principle and far better than allowing a selfish individualism to pervade the camps.[54]

It was evident from the very start that the members of the IJA who took overall responsibility for running the prisons were profoundly disinterested in exercising internal discipline within the POW camps and were more than content to leave this tiresome matter to the prisoners themselves. There is little doubt that all prisoners were looked upon disdainfully by the Japanese military authorities. Many Japanese soldiers could identify with the rigorous *Bushido* code of honour and morals developed by the *samurai*. For them the idea of being captured in war was regarded as an unworthy act — it was considered far better to fight and die for the Emperor than to be captured and live in dishonour. Psychologically predisposed to viewing the POWs as being beneath contempt, the Japanese prison authorities saw the task of feeding and administering such huge numbers of prisoners as being a thorough nuisance and a handicap to the war effort. Nonetheless, as genocide was ruled out (though some members may well have been in favour of it) something had to be done to keep the camps running but at minimum cost and disruption and where possible maximum assistance to the Japanese war machine. For this purpose, policy initiatives and directives would emerge from the Japanese camp commandant's office and be enforced by the motley assortment of guards — Japanese, Korean, Taiwanese, Sikhs, and Bengalis — with enthusiasm. Sadly, many of the non-Japanese guards both at the camps and on work fatigues behaved with the same mean ruthlessness that was displayed by some of their Japanese colleagues. There were many cases of savage personal assaults being made upon the prisoners by unscrupulous guards. Sometimes they were administered for a range of infractions — such as a POW not saluting them properly — but often these vicious attacks were examples of un-provoked aggression. Slappings were considered both commonplace and light in comparison with some of the punishments inflicted upon the POWs by the more sadistic guards who needed no second bidding to indulge their primitive whims for violent conduct against those for whom they had no respect. Their war crimes remain a stain on the reputation of the IJA.[55]

Individual acts of brutality continued throughout the period of captivity but the most serious collective punishment was meted out to the prisoners shortly after Maj.-Gen. Fukuye took over as camp commandant in August 1942. At the end of that month the Japanese Headquarters peremptorily demanded that the by now 18,790 Changi POWs sign a pledge not to escape. Defiantly refusing to do so, the POWs soon faced the consequences of their unwillingness to cooperate with the new regime. On 2 September all the POWs, save those in the hospital in Roberts Barracks, were ordered to assemble in Selarang Barracks without delay. Those who had failed to arrive by 1800 hrs that evening would be shot. Selarang consisted of seven barrack blocks and was originally designed for roughly 800 troops. Once all the Changi POWs had arrived, Selarang became in every sense a concentration camp. Space was at such a premium that the troops were forced to take it in turns to sleep wherever they could secure a cramped position; a series of slit trenches had to be cut in the parade ground to provide a rudimentary toilet facility; no food or shelter was provided by their Japanese hosts and only one gallon of water per day was issued for use by the entire compound. Amazingly perhaps, the morale of the POWs withstood this extraordinary ordeal.[56] If anything, their spirits seemed to be lifted by it.[57] Even so the unrelenting equatorial heat exacerbated the already foul conditions that existed at Selarang and accounted for upwards of three hundred cases of diphtheria by Friday 4 September. One did not need to be a doctor to recognise the warning signs. If the POWs remained intransigent, refusing to sign the no-escape form, the already alarming health situation would worsen with deadly effect. For this reason and with the Japanese threatening to cut off the entire water supply, Col. Holmes, the senior Allied officer, ordered his men to sign the no-escape form. Next day Saturday 5 September the non-Australian POWs were ordered back to their barracks so bringing an end to what became known as the Selarang Incident.[58] There seems little doubt that Fukuye was determined not only to win this test of strength with the POWs but also signal by so doing his intention of adopting an even more resolute policy towards them in the future. This attitude was maintained by those who succeeded him as Japanese commander, Maj.-Gen. Arimura and Maj.-Gen. Saito.

Despite their perpetual hunger, the POWs showed a resourcefulness and industry that often belied their physical state. Such was the level of intellectual talent within the camps that within days of their confinement, the POWs had managed to establish what became known as "Changi University." A range of lecture courses were offered to the men on a variety of subjects ranging from mathematics and physics to languages and law. Staggeringly, library collections were unearthed as were blackboards, tables and chairs. For about four months (April to August 1942) "Changi University" had an enrollment of several thousand POWs. It was not to last, however. As the Japanese began despatching the fit inmates to form work parties both in Singapore and abroad, the number of prisoners at Changi dropped appreciably. By November 1942 there were only roughly 11,000 left in the cantonments. As many of the lecturing staff and students had been among those sent away, "Changi University" was forced to cut back on its services. Thereafter it became more of an education centre than a tertiary institute.[59]

One of the most enterprising and useful of pursuits and also the most painstaking was Changi's Bureau of Record and Enquiry (BRE) which was the only information centre of this type established behind Japanese lines in the Second World War. Its members faithfully recorded the name, regimental number, rank, and current status/location of individuals drawn from units in all three services. Information on all those injured, reported missing, killed in action, or who died subsequently as POWs, were listed on a series of master rolls that were kept meticulously up-to-date by the dedicated team of officers and men to whom this task was entrusted. Similarly, all movements of POWs were tracked by these members of the BRE. It was to be an invaluable resource that would be used constantly by POWs seeking news of the fate of relatives or friends who had been serving with the Allied forces in Southeast Asia. By December 1942 the BRE had also become the official mail-sorting office for the Changi camp since its members were the only ones who really knew the whereabouts of all the men in captivity.[60]

Entertainment also figured prominently at Changi. A surprisingly high standard of theatrical, cabaret and operatic performance was mounted by the POWs on a frequent basis drawing huge crowds of wildly appreciative prisoners and on some occasions groups of bemused Japanese officials. Despite the movement and transfer of prisoners from one camp to another, the quality and sophistication of the entertainment programme steadily improved as did the production of these myriad cultural events. Each camp produced their own shows: the Australians largely concentrating upon vaudeville, the British tending towards the staging of more conventional plays. Both achieved their purpose of boosting morale among their fellow prisoners.[61] After the POWs were transferred from their separate barracks and the Sime Road transit camp into Changi Jail in May 1944, it made sense for these two extraordinarily talented groups of entertainers to combine forces and become the Concert Party. Faced with the constraints of space and the lack of a converted stage, the members of the Concert Party immediately set about convincing Japanese officialdom that it made sense for the POWs to build a proper playhouse in which they could stage their concerts and virtuoso performances. Scrounging materials from all over the island and using the innate resourcefulness of the men themselves, the Concert Party erected the Playhouse. This was a remarkable construction and much more grandiose than the original plans had suggested that it would be![62] After a number of outstanding productions, including a Christmas pantomime, however, the Concert Party staged a cavalcade of song in February 1945 in which the crowning achievement was a new song entitled "On Our Return" — the lyrics of which, proclaiming great confidence in an impending Allied victory in the war, irritated Maj.-Gen. Saito, the guest of honour, to such an extent that he closed down the Playhouse for the duration of the war.[63]

Tactless though the lyrics undoubtedly were, they reflected the fact that the POWs were either merely engaged in frenzied wishful thinking or were genuinely aware of what was going on beyond the confines of their prison existence. Actually camp life produced both vast quantities of speculative gossip as well as reliable informed comment. Rumour-mongering was only to be expected and could not be forestalled. Guesswork, intuition and exaggeration all played a part in touching off a new wave of stories, but sometimes the inmates learnt news that did not come from an imaginative source on the lines of latrines known as the bore holes! Genuine news was gleaned by short-wave radio contact with the outside world. At extreme personal risk to themselves, a small number of POWs had secretly maintained at least one such battery-operated link for much of their confinement. BBC World Service news bulletins provided the POWs with the latest information about the state of the European and Pacific wars. A summary of this news was then passed round the camp — often undergoing a type of hyperbolic transformation as it passed from one group of prisoners to the next.[64]

While they remained deprived of their freedom, the POWs found expression for their talent and abilities in various ways — artistic, intellectual, sporting, and practical. Moving from the Changi cantonments into the grim and forbidding jail in May 1944 did not diminish the fervour with which these pursuits were embraced. Many POWs also discovered a love for literature that had been dormant before. Books became a passport to another and better world outside the gates of the prison camp. There is little doubt that religion too played a vital part in the lives of many POWs. It proved to be a source of great solace to those in need.[65]

Life in the overcrowded circumstances of Changi Jail could have been horrendous without these diversions. A gaunt symbol of incarceration, Changi Jail had been built in 1936 to hold a maximum of 600 prisoners. From May 1944 to March 1945, however, the figure of POWs housed in the jail and in the atap huts hastily built in its outside compounds stood at more than 10,000. Thereafter the numbers dwindled to roughly 6500 by July 1945 as more and more POWs were sent to satellite camps in and around the city. Ironically, many would be forced to make a temporary return to Changi once the war was over and before they were finally repatriated in the weeks after the Japanese surrender on 14 August 1945.

Life as a Civilian Internee

Once Singapore had been surrendered the fate of the Allied civilian expatriates on the island was speedily resolved. Those individuals who were regarded by the Japanese as fulfilling vital roles in Singapore's administrative, economic or physical structure were required to remain at their posts for the time being until they could be replaced by suitably qualified or trained Japanese personnel.[66] All others, including dependants, were instructed to proceed to the Padang on 17 February taking with them what clothes and food they could carry for the commencement of their life in internment. After listening to a harangue from a Japanese officer on the iniquities of the Allied troops and their savagery to Japanese civilians in various countries, the implication appeared to be that the same fate might well befall this largely Caucasian group of colonial imperialists amounting to 1197 men, 145 women and 37 children. Thereafter, a representative of each nationality was chosen to liaise with the Japanese officials and be responsible for their own group of civilians who were to embark on their exhausting trek down Beach Road and on towards Joo Chiat and the east coast.[67] Their first stop would be at the far from salubrious Karikal Mahal Camp along Still Road South. Eventually after spending more than a fortnight in Karikal and having been joined by several hundred more civilian internees, the entire company was told on 5 March that it would be expected to leave for Changi Jail the following morning. Four lorries would be provided for the transport of food and clothing as well as for the elderly or infirm who could not be expected to make the journey to Changi on foot. Beginning with a civilian population of over 2000 the jail became home eventually to over 3500 internees by April 1944.[68]

Divided into two separate camps for the male and female internees, the prison boasted four blocks each with a dining room and two workshops on the ground floor and three upper storeys each of which contained 44 cells. Designed for one inmate but often home to three or four, a typical prison cell measured 12 feet long by 8 feet wide [3.7x2.46m] and was hemmed in with high whitewashed walls, the outside one of which was topped with an iron grill window. A toilet bowl lay in one corner and in the centre of the cell was a raised concrete slab, nicknamed the sarcophagus, that was designed to be a bed.[69] In these relatively cramped quarters, the need for personal space and privacy could hardly be entertained. Even firm friendships were tested by this type of confinement. While an astonishing amount of camaraderie was developed under the most testing of conditions, not all was sweetness and light in Changi Jail.[70]

In this unpromising political environment the concept and practice of democracy flowered. Internees were encouraged to elect their own floor or group representatives from which a floor or group council would then be formed. Those elected would then choose one of their number to be the chairperson and he / she would then automatically become a member of the block council. A further electoral contest involving the representatives of this elite would then be held to see who would emerge as the block commandant. Those reaching these dizzy political heights could only do so after a direct vote had been taken of all the internees in a particular block / group. These block commandants would then become members of the camp council. At the top of this pyramidal structure was a camp commandant who would be elected by a direct vote of the entire camp. All elections were by secret ballot. Once elected, the representative would have a two-month period of office. If re-elected he / she would then serve a term of four months. Naturally, the main task of these various political representatives was to raise issues of substance, complaints, requests and so forth from the internees and pass them up through the system and finally to the attention of the Japanese themselves. Equally, the Japanese authorities used this structure to inform the camp council of any decisions they had made which would affect the internees. Liaison was not a dirty word in Changi. Some links needed to be forged between the captives and those that held them so that life could be improved or made less harsh for the internees. Whether the frequency of such elections served the best interests of all concerned, however, is more doubtful. By the same token, if an elected representative proved to be either incompetent or unsuitable, the opportunity for removing them from office was never far away. Perhaps, in the end, this safety valve outweighed even the negative aspects of what some might say was an overabundance of democracy.[71]

In many ways the life of the civilian internee was similar to that of the POW. Work and hunger went hand in hand. Fatigue parties were formed for a variety of tasks both inside and outside the prison compound. All those internees under the age of fifty who were in reasonable health were assigned to these work groups. Those whose skills fitted them to perform specialist duties, such as engineers and craftsmen of various kinds, were engaged on the provision and maintenance of essential services, such as electricity and water supply. All others were engaged upon routine unskilled work, i.e., cutting and stacking wood, grinding rice for bread, gardening, carrying food supplies, mopping and cleaning the corridors, courtyard and communal toilet — known affectionately as the "Wailing Wall" — and flattening empty tins for recycling purposes. Although professional help was forthcoming in some areas, for example, in the women's camp some 50 fully trained British nurses looked after the hospital patients on a rota basis, it was much more difficult to get adequate numbers of volunteers to tackle the singularly unattractive daily task of washing the hospital laundry.[72] By far the most popular of all fatigue parties were those that went beyond the prison compound, since they provided a taste of freedom for the internees and an opportunity for them to interact with the local population. News and food items were gleaned in this way and both were coveted in Changi.[73] Despite a Japanese prohibition on trading with the local population, a thriving black market existed in Changi. A mixture of canny native ingenuity and stealth ensured that the streetwise internees always managed to flout these regulations. They were often assisted in their illegal operations by the Japanese sentry guards themselves. It was often they who would be prepared to sell off contraband goods to those internees with the money to buy these items. As a result, all manner of goods and provisions were available at a price both inside and outside the compound.[74]

Whatever work the internees did, food, or the lack thereof, dominated their very existence. It is doubtful whether anyone, whatever their connections, had enough to eat. What amounted to an obsession with food grew apace as rations were cut and inmates suffered an appreciable weight loss over the course of their internment. Boiled rice at every meal, sometimes adorned with a thin gruelly soup or stew, a little fruit when available and a couple of cups of tea represented a typical day's menu in both the men's and women's camp.[75]

Although a sense of gnawing hunger was a perennial affliction, the internees showed as much resourcefulness in providing as wide a range of entertainment and pursuits as the POWs did in their camps. Journalistic ventures, such as the *Changi Guardian, Changi Times* and *Pow-Wow*, were published to varying degrees of acclaim, lecture courses were run on a bewildering number of subjects, literary and debating societies flourished, as did a mock parliament. For those with a competitive edge, bridge tournaments and sporting fixtures were held (especially soccer and cricket). Musical entertainment was always popular with the internees and they enthusiastically supported all concerts, variety shows and choral works that were usually staged in the evenings by their fellow inmates for their benefit.[76]

Unfortunately, most of the camp guards and officials had little compassion or understanding of the plight of those incarcerated and placed in their care. Bullies had little compunction in abusing their authority with internees of both sexes regardless of whether an infraction of the prison rules had been committed or not.[77] In the wake of Operation *Jaywick*, however, the Japanese authorities became even greater disciplinarians. Believing that the successful Allied commando raid on six Japanese cargo vessels and an oil tanker lying at anchor in three different locations in Singapore on 27 September 1943 could not have been carried out without the benefit of local intelligence, the *Kempeitai* became convinced that the guilty parties were to be found amongst the internees at Changi Jail rather than in the POW cantonments.[78] On 10 October (the Double Tenth) the *Kempeitai* launched their own raid on Changi. All internees were expected to gather in the prison compound for a roll call and were not dispersed for 13 hours. During this time search parties combed through their belongings looking for evidence, such as short-wave radio sets, that could have been used for communicating with the enemy from within the camp. At the same time *Kempeitai* officers began conducting a preliminary interrogation of those internees who were suspected of complicity in the affair. By the end of that day 57 internees were taken away for questioning.[79] As the days passed so an increasing number of internees of both sexes were taken into custody for further spells of interrogation and torture.[80] Even those that avoided this fate, soon found that their privileges were curtailed. Life at Changi became significantly worse for the internees after the Double Tenth Incident than it had been before it took place.

Eventually in May 1944 the internees moved out to the Sime Road Camp next to the Chinese graveyard opposite the Bukit Timah Golf Club (now the Singapore Island Country Club, Bukit Course) off Lornie Road. Built on an old rubber estate of some 70 acres, Sime Road Camp had served as Malaya Command Battle Headquarters before the fall of Singapore. In the Occupation period it was pressed into service both as temporary quarters for parties of POWs working in the vicinity and as a staging post for those prisoners being sent up-country to work on the Railroad of Death.[81] It was also home to the malaria-laden *Anopheles* mosquito and a particularly nasty mite that carried the Tropical Typhus disease. Until their breeding grounds were wiped out, these insects attacked the camp occupants persistently, a fact reflected in the spiralling rates of infection among the internees.[82]

Although Sime Road represented a markedly different environment from that of Changi, many of the female internees wondered whether the move was wholly positive, particularly given the dilapidated state of some of the old RAF huts into which the internees were crowded. Much work would have to be done by them to patch up the buildings and tame the overgrown grounds to make these compounds more congenial than they appeared early in May 1944. Once again, the gender division was maintained — the women's camp being closest to Lornie Road. An old road linked the two camps with only a barbed-wire fence and a sentry post marking the boundary between them. While the outdoors life suited many of the internees, the irony was that living space was even more restricted than at Changi. Consequently, all sense of personal privacy was forsaken.[83] Another unwelcome feature soon arose as a few of the Japanese guards began to exhibit a fondness for prowling around the women's camp at night. Some established sexual liaisons with a few of the female internees and a small cottage, known as the White House, was built as a brothel or comfort house for these troops.[84]

Life lurched on in a familiar way at Sime Road. Those fit enough to work were expected to do so. Much time and effort continued to be put in on cultivating plots of land scattered both within the camps and outside their perimeter in an attempt to improve the food supplies of the camp. As crop yield became a matter of serious concern to those toiling on this stubbornly marginal land, those agricultural plots that were successful became a magnet for those wishing to plunder these crops. Despite all this animation for small-scale market gardening, food supplies dwindled still further in the early months of 1945. Nevertheless, as the European phase of the war came to an end and Allied pressure increased in the Pacific, the attitude of the Japanese authorities towards the internees began to change slowly. Red Cross parcels would occasionally appear and food rations, which had been cut earlier in the year, received a temporary fillip. On the whole, however, the promise of a better life in internment was barely fulfilled before the news came through of Japan's capitulation in mid-August 1945.[85]

The Japanese Administration's Role during the Occupation

After the impressive success of the *25th Army* in capturing Singapore, the task of managing the island and its cosmopolitan population was assigned to a military administration — *Gunseikan-bu* — which delegated non-military matters to a special municipality — *Tokubetsu-si* — headed by a Japanese Mayor installed for the purpose by the authorities in Tokyo.[86] Initially at least the principal quest was the establishment of peace and order. What nowadays is referred to as "the smack of firm government" was applied by the military ruthlessly in the early days. In a spirit of *pour encourager les autres*, punitive disciplinary action was taken against all those who actually infringed the rules set by the occupying power or were deemed likely to threaten the aims and objectives of the military administration on the island. Severed heads on public display along some of the arterial roads in various parts of the city and suburbs were a sober and grim reminder that summary justice was very much in vogue.[87] Along with their infamous *sook ching* operations, the Japanese military undoubtedly succeeded in getting its blunt and uncompromising message across to the people of Singapore. It may be safely assumed that the marked absence of urban guerilla warfare conducted by secret societies or resistance groups in Singapore during the Occupation bears testimony to this fact.

Once peace and order had been restored to the island, it was essential that this condition should be maintained thereafter at minimal cost to the occupying power. Singapore's lack of natural resources meant that there was little for the Japanese administrators to exploit, except its stock of prisoners, to aid their war machine. While its strategic location remained its principal asset, Singapore was much less useful to the Japanese than, say, either Malaya or the Dutch East Indies were. A further serious liability existed, namely, that the Japanese suspected, with good reason, that the majority Chinese population were overwhelmingly hostile to them. Contrary to many of the Malays and Indians, the Chinese did not see the Japanese as colonial liberators but as oppressors in their own right — a legacy of Japanese militarism in recent Chinese history. Since the Chinese were unlikely to be won over by the Japanese Military Administration, the policy towards this ethnic group was, as we have already seen, to cow them into a sullen subserviance.[88]

If racial harmony could not be attained in *Syonan-to*, the Japanese were determined to reward those who were amenable to their presence in Southeast Asia. As a result, the Malays and Indians became the major beneficiaries of this policy. Apart from extending a far more humane and considerate attitude to them, promises were made to assist both ethnic groups in their drive for greater self-development and a measure of political independence in the post-war world. Notable efforts to recruit the Indians into the INA were successfully made by Mohan Singh with the active support and blessing of Major Fujiwara's intelligence group and this level of assistance continued regardless of leadership changes in the INA throughout the war.[89] After Mohan Singh fell out of favour with the Japanese authorities in December 1942, and was sent into exile on St. John's Island, the person courted by them was Subhas Chandra Bose, a leader of the Indian independence movement and a believer in military action rather than passive resistance to secure his aims. He arrived in Singapore on 2 July 1943 to great acclaim. Two days later at a conference of the Indian Independence League in the city, Bose was formally elected chairman of the Provisional Government of Free India. On the following day, 5 July, he reviewed 15,000 INA troops gathered in front of the Singapore Municipal Building and inaugurated them into the *Azad Hind Fauj* (Free India Army).[90] Using the INA/*Azad Hind Fauj* to fight the Allies in Burma made eminent good sense to the Japanese military even if the contribution of the INA to the campaign was not as profound as some hoped it would be.[91]

As far as the Malays were concerned, the Japanese placed much less emphasis on the political aspects of nationalism but showed respect for Islam and sought to improve and extend the religious and ethnic links between the Malays and other Islamic groups in *Malai*, Sumatra and *Syonan-to*. As mobilising Malay sympathy for their cause was a central tenet of Japanese policy throughout the region, so the needs of the Malay community were directly addressed by the promotion of job creation and training schemes. Malays were also encouraged to join either the Malay Volunteer Army (*Giyu-gun*), the Volunteer Corps (*Giyu-tai*) or the Auxiliary Services (*Hei-ho*) and fight for a better future than the one which the British had bestowed upon them in the past. As a general rule, the Japanese policy of extending the hand of friendship to the Malay community was successful and met with little sustained resistance from an ethnic group that had much to gain from its involvement with the occupying power.[92]

Eurasians, however, did not fare as well as either the Indians or Malays. Contemptuous of their racial mix, the Japanese regarded them with suspicion and treated them accordingly. Those with family members linked directly to any European country fighting against the Axis forces were interned, the rest were left their freedom but little else. Their usefulness to the British colonial authorities in the past now counted against them. Few were allowed to continue their former white-collar jobs and most had to seek employment in other fields altogether. In an effort to redeem themselves before the Japanese as a community that had collectively learnt its lesson, the Eurasians were required to provide eloquent public support for *Dai-Nippon* on a regular basis. Dr. C.J. Paglar, who became President of the *Syonan-to* Eurasian Welfare Association in October 1942, became the official spokesman for this disadvantaged group. After the war was over the British authorities took a dim view of Dr. Paglar's performance during the Occupation. They took him into custody and put him on trial for collaborating with the enemy. After an impassioned plea by Mamoru Shinozaki at Dr. Paglar's trial in late January 1946, the accused was released and his trial was postponed *sin'è di'è*.[93]

Japanese communal policies were hardly altruistic in the accepted sense of that term since they always looked for a suitable *quid pro quo* from those they assisted. Aiding the war effort, by direct or indirect means, was the driving force behind most, if not all, of their policies in *Syonan-to*. This economic and military imperative is clear in their vain attempts to make the island autarkic, so as to cut down on imported foodstuffs from the region. Try as they might through cajoling or competitive means, investment in new industries or the production of *ersatz* commodities, the Japanese authorities were still unable to achieve the desired level of self-sufficiency from *Syonan-to* and its inhabitants.[94] Despite exerting a very intrusive measure of administrative control, the Japanese failed to dampen deep-seated inflationary tendencies within the economy or to prevent the existence of a thriving black market.[95] In fact, their monetary policies managed to encourage both and by so doing undermined the very economic programme that they sought to fulfil.[96]

While their economic policies left much to be desired, breeding as it did contrary influences to those originally intended, the administration of "justice" was definitely more efficient, even if many of its exponents paid little or no attention to the rule of law or basic jurisprudence. Mastery of forensic skill was not necessary when arbitrary justice was commonplace, torture and intimidation were rampant and where corruption was pervasive. Any system dominated by the *Kempeitai* was bound to inspire fear and loathing among the ordinary people of *Syonan-to* and with good reason. While judges (both Japanese and local) may have exercised the highest standards of probity in those cases coming before them, many people fell victim to a cruel and barbaric system of internal security that recognised no boundaries to its authority and dispensed its own brand of justice as and when it liked.[97]

Unrestrained and excessive, the *Kempeitai* provided the behavioural norm for the 4000-strong regular police force which had little compunction in tilting the scales of justice against anyone that was brought to its notice. Since its primary task of protecting the community was largely subordinated to intimidating the population in various ways, the necessity for a proper policing of Singapore became vital in mid-1942. As a result, the Japanese authorities encouraged the establishment of an auxiliary police force from among the ordinary inhabitants of the city. In an early version of the neighbourhood watch committee system nowadays employed in many countries, some 21,000 families were involved in this auxiliary scheme which grew to include the provision of night patrols by all males between the ages of between 16 and 45 in June 1944. Apart from the prevention of crime, the auxiliary police were also used for a range of other tasks, including the distribution of food supplies.[98]

In addition to the arrangements made for auxiliary policing, the Japanese military authorities unveiled plans in December 1943 for a total mobilisation of manpower throughout *Malai* and *Syonan-to* to meet the anticipated demands of the war and the Allied plans for an invasion of the peninsula and the island. Labour Service Corps were thereafter established to provide an embryonic civil defence organisation. Initially a male preserve, females were permitted to form their own groups at a later stage. Their existence provided the Japanese military authorities and their civil counterparts with a substantially increased labour force for any task which either of these organisations might set them. While some groups donated their services free of charge, most Labour Service Corps members were paid wages and received a higher rice ration than those who were not involved in these duties.[99]

Within a few months the Japanese had decided that new regulations governing the type of occupations that could be undertaken by men were required so as to divert labour from non-essential tasks to those deemed vital for the war effort. In September 1944, therefore, a Change of Trade Committee, headed by the Mayor and consisting of community leaders and auxiliary police officers, was set up to realise this aim. On 30 December 1944 labour regulations were tightened even further with the implementation of the Male Employment Restriction Ordinance. Males between the ages of 15 and 40 were henceforth forbidden from working as cooks, dhobies, hawkers, lift attendants, peons, salesmen, tailors, telephone receptionists, and waiters. They were basically given two choices: either to find a job in an essential sector of the economy or to go to one of the offshore islands, or resettlement colonies, to farm. As the war entered its final phase, the Japanese authorities became even more restrictive and began closing down a number of non-essential firms or businesses, such as restaurants and cabaret establishments.[100]

One furtive way in which the Japanese on *Syonan-to* were making preparations to withstand a future Allied invasion was through the work of their top-secret biological research laboratory on the grounds of the Singapore General Hospital. Much of the work of this laboratory has been shrouded in mystery — its very existence being denied for decades by the Japanese — but revelations published in books such as *Unit 731* by Peter Williams and David Wallace and *The Bamboo Fortress* by H. Sidhu, and repeated in a series of articles by Phan Ming Yen in *The Straits Times*, suggest a sinister import. Although no definitive work has appeared either in Japanese or in English on the Japanese *Southern Army's No.1 Central Pathological Research Laboratory* in Singapore, what little information that has reached the public domain is ominous. Major W.E. Tyndall, of the Medical Directorate of Allied Land Forces SE Asia, for example, has publicly acknowledged the extent and expensive nature of the medical facilities which he discovered in the laboratory at the end of the war. According to him, the inordinately large number of hand centrifuges that were found in one room alone indicated that the laboratory may have employed several hundred technicians during the Occupation. It has been alleged by a number of individuals that the staff of the laboratory were actively engaged in the production of plague and the classification of other diseases, such as paratyphoid, for germ warfare purposes. At this stage, fortunately, we have no documentary evidence which would suggest that any biological experiments were carried out in Singapore by Japanese scientists or medical researchers using either hospital patients, POWs or civilian internees. Nonetheless, Norman Covert, Chief of Public Affairs at Fort Detrick, Maryland, has gone on record as suggesting that contaminated rats and monkeys were found in Singapore during the Occupation and that their contamination was probably caused by biological experimentation. Clearly, much remains to be discovered about this shadowy and deadly establishment and its contribution to the Japanese war effort.[101]

Oblivious to whatever their scientists may have been up to in the war, the Japanese civil authorities — sensing an increasing beleaguerment — belatedly recognised that they needed a greater measure of indigenous support than they had received previously. While they resorted to rules and orders as one means of obtaining manpower, they also began to move tentatively along the road to a more participatory approach to local government. In this respect, the establishment of the first Consultative Council on 7 December 1943 broke new ground. Consisting of six prominent and influential Chinese, four Malays, three Indians, a solitary Eurasian and an Arab, and chaired by the Japanese Mayor of *Syonan-to*, this body was required to offer advice on general matters to the *Tokubetsu-si*. Naturally its powers were strictly limited, but its mere existence was a sign that change was in the air. It was soon followed by the introduction of an Information and Publicity Committee at the end of March 1944, in which prominent members of the local community were asked to provide feedback to the Mayor on current issues and were required to explain government decisions to the general public.[102]

While fear of the enemy was a predominant emotion among many local Singaporeans, civilian internees and Allied POWs during the war — and with good reason — there were some Japanese officials, such as Mamoru Shinozaki, Lt. Andrew Ogawa, Mr. Kinoshita, Mr. Naito, and Yoschichika Tokugawa, who behaved with courtesy, decency, helpfulness, and sincerity towards the non-Japanese in *Syonan-to*.[103] Their behaviour, sadly, was untypical of so many of their fellow countrymen who displayed an abhorrent cruelty and vindictiveness to those who were subject to their overbearing authority.[104] And it is the scars and impressions left by these benighted individuals that endure. Stories of Japanese inhumanity to those they encountered in the Occupation period are legion. Not the least disadvantaged in this regard were the "comfort women," who were either brought into *Syonan-to* from overseas or were "recruited" from the local population for the physical enjoyment of the troops. Their harrowing experiences ought to weigh on the consciences of those who abused them so thoroughly in wartime.[105] When taken together these images of despoilation and bestiality, provide a very negative psychological legacy for Japan and one that has stubbornly refused to lift in the post-war period despite the proferring of official apologies by several of its leading figures in recent years.

Notes

1. K. Caffrey, *Out in the Midday Sun: Singapore 1941–1945*, London, 1974, 183-84.

2. N.I. Low, *When Singapore Was Syonan-to*, Kuala Lumpur, 1973, 2-3.

3. Ibid., 3-5, 9-10.

4. Although the population of Singapore in 1941 has been calculated at 769,216, the total number of civilians in the city in February 1942 is usually depicted as being approximately 1.4 million. Professor Eunice Thio suggests the difference was accounted for by the large number of refugees who had fled across the causeway from the advancing IJA in Malaya. While generally accepted, these figures could well be substantially inflated. Nonetheless, in the absence of a reliable census for the 1942–45 period, the total civilian population will be given throughout this chapter as 1.4 million. See Eunice Thio, "The Syonan Years, 1942–1945," in E.C.T. Chew & E. Lee (editors), *A History of Singapore*, Singapore, 1991, 95; P.H. Kratoska, *The Japanese Occupation of Malaya 1941–1945*, London, 1998, 318.

5. C.M. Turnbull, *A History of Singapore 1819–1988* [2nd Edition], Kuala Lumpur, 1989, 196-97; letter from Rudy Mosbergen to the author, 1 March 1998.

6. C.S. Lan, *Remember Pompong and Oxley Rise*, Singapore, 1969, 185-207; Kang Jew Koon, "The Chinese in Singapore During the Japanese Occupation 1942-1945," Unpublished BA Hons. Academic Exercise, NUS, 1981, 14-17; Archives & Oral History Department, *The Japanese Occupation: Singapore 1942-1945*, Singapore, 1985, 37-44.

7. Chen, *Remember Pompong*, 187-88; Sidhu, 79-89; Low, *When Singapore Was Syonan-to*, 22-25; Kang, "The Chinese in Singapore," pp. 83-5; National Heritage Board, *The Japanese Occupation 1942-1945*, Singapore, 1996, 67-73. Ian Ward is convinced that the real architect of the *sook ching* massacres was Tsuji. See his detailed account, *The killer they called a god*, Singapore, 1992.

8. Some of the killing grounds were located at Changi Point, MacRitchie Reservoir, Ponggol and off the coast of Sentosa. See Chen, *Remember Pompong*, 185-91; Sylvia Foo Mei Lian, "The Japanese Occupation of Singapore 1942-45: Socio-Economic Policies and Effects," Unpublished BA Hons. Academic Exercise, NUS, 1987, 41.

9. Ibid., 144-63. See also Zhou Mei, *Elizabeth Choy: More than a War Heroine*, Singapore, 1995, 67-83.

10. In the U.K. this poster was aimed at reminding the population to be careful about revealing any information which spies could pass on to enemy states and which could be used to damage the British war effort.

11. Chin K.O., *Malaya Upside Down*, Kuala Lumpur, 1976, 69-81; Low, *When Singapore Was Syonan-to*, 44-55; Kang, "The Chinese in Singapore," 17-22.

12. Archives & Oral History Department, *The Japanese Occupation*, 114.

13. *Syonan Times*, 26, 28 May, 3 June 2602(1942); Lee Ah Chai, "Singapore Under the Japanese 1942-1945," Unpublished BA Hons. Academic Exercise, University of Malaya, 1956, 19-20.

14. *Syonan Times*, 21 February 2602(1942).

15. Interview with Soh Guan Bee, Reel 03, 34-5, 42-3; Interview with Lim Choo Sye, Reel 07, 95-6, Oral History Archive, Singapore.

16. Some of the segregated schools for Malay children were reopened on 7 April 1942 and a few of the schools serving the Indian student population resumed operations three days later. More Chinese schools were opened in late April and early July 1942. *Syonan Times*, 25 March, 2, 7, 10, 24 April, 1, 5 July 2602(1942); Sidhu, 94-96; Archives & Oral History, *The Japanese Occupation*, 74-81.

17. Thio, 95-97; Lee Ah Chai, 6-8. See endnote 23 below.

18. In many ways this belief was redolent of the old and largely discredited racial policy identified by Kipling as the "White Man's Burden."

19. Thio, 97; Chin, 140-42.

20. *Syonan Times*, 6 August, 16 October 2602(1942).

21. Information provided for the author from the Jewish and Methodist communities by Madelaine Marcus and Victor Wong respectively. For a personal account of the Occupation from a member of the Jewish community, see E. Nathan, *The History of the Jews in Singapore 1830-1945*, Singapore, 1986, 100-151.

22. Thio, 98-101; Turnbull, 196.

23. For examples of early sports journalism, see the *Syonan Times*, 3, 14, 21 July, 5 November 2602(1942); *Syonan Sinbun*, 16 January 2603(1943). *The Syonan Times*, the English daily newspaper during the Japanese Occupation, underwent two further changes of name. It became *The Syonan Sinbun* on 8 December 1942 and *The Syonan Shimbun* on 8 December 1943.

24. Perhaps, surprisingly, the ban was not implemented immediately across all sources of entertainment. For instance, it was only on 1 September 1943 that the ban on Western films was imposed on all cinema operators. See Kratoska, 141-43.

25. As examples of these policies see the *Syonan Times*, 15 October 2602(1942);

Syonan Sinbun, 1 February 2603(1943); letter from Rudy Mosbergen to the author, 1 March 1998.

26. First news of the state lottery was given in the *Syonan Sinbun* of 19 February 2603(1943). For illustrations of some of the lottery tickets available, see Archives & Oral History, *The Japanese Occupation*, 113.

27. Prisoners were placed on work fatigues throughout the war. Tasks ranged widely as did the effort needed to complete them. A large number of prisoners were still engaged on the construction of Changi airfield when the war ended in August 1945. See R. Braddon, *The Naked Island*, London, 1952, 157-61, 232-34, 244-46, 260.

28. *Syonan Times*, 10 July, 7 August 2602(1942); *Syonan Sinbun*, 6 January, 10, 24 June 2603(1943); Lee, "Singapore Under the Japanese," 21-23; Interview given by Soh Guan Bee, Oral History Archive, Reel 03, p.34.

29. Kratoska, 249-55.

30. Ultimately, a Census-Taking List was drawn up for the same purpose and superceded the "Peace Living Certificates." For more information on these matters, see Thio, 105-06; Chin, 82-87.

31. *The Straits Times*, 9 September 1945, includes a table of 19 staple food prices both before and during the Japanese Occupation. In this list bean curd posted the smallest price rise of 400% on the black market, whereas the price of onions shot up by 3214%. Fish was 1600% more expensive, the price of pork rose by 1,333% and beef by 750%. There are numerous accounts of the black market in the available literature. See, for example, Sylvia Foo Mei Lian, "The Japanese Occupation of Singapore 1942-45," 54-59; Low, 56-66; Thio, 103.

32. *Syonan Sinbun*, 29 December 2602(1942), 30 January 2603(1943).

33. *Syonan Times*, 27 February, 2 July 2602(1942).

34. *Syonan Times*, 3, 6, 9 March 2602(1942).

35. Shinozaki M., *My Wartime Experiences in Singapore*, Singapore, 1973, 66-88.

36. Ibid.; Interview with Brian Bogaars, 17 November 1996.

37. Shinozaki, 73-81.

38. Interview with Rudy Mosbergen, 22 February 1998.

39. R.P. Balhetchet & J. Brophy, "Church in the Wilderness: Bahau," in R.P. Balhetchet (editor), *From the Mustard Seed*, Singapore, 1996, 69-89.

40. Ibid., 81-86. In Stephanie Kwok Siu Fun's, "Extraordinary Lives: Catholic Missionaries During the Japanese Occupation of Singapore 1942–1945" (Unpublished BA Hons Honours Thesis, NUS, 1995), 25-41, the author clearly states that the only Roman Catholic congregations not represented in Bahau were the Carmelite nuns and the Little Sisters of the Poor. Ms. Kwok also suggests that there were approximately 3000 settlers in Bahau. This figure is roughly a thousand higher than the figure usually associated with the *Fuji-go* settlement.

41. Ibid.; *Syonan Shimbun*, 18 January 2605(1945); Archives & Oral History, *Japanese Occupation*, 95-102; Interview with Brian Bogaars, 17 November 1996.

42. *Syonan Shimbun*, 16 July 2605(1945).

43. Professor Turnbull indicates that approximately 20,000 troops volunteered to join the INA. She points out that many Indian Muslims refused to join what they imagined would be a Hindu-dominated organisation. They preferred to establish an Indian Muslim Association to look after their special interests. Turnbull, 188, 196. According to Fujiwara, however, the response of the Indian troops was overwhelming. See Fujiwara I., *F. Kikan. Japanese Army Intelligence Operations in Southeast Asia during World War II*, Singapore, 1983, xv, 185-86. H.N. Pandit, *Netaji Subhas Chandra Bose*, New Delhi, 1988, 83-84, neither confirms nor denies either thesis. Professor Turnbull does receive support from both J.C. Lebra, *Japanese-Trained Armies in Southeast Asia: Independence and Volunteer Forces in World War II*, Hong Kong, 1977, 6-10, 19-38 and Joginder Singh Jessy,

"The Indian Army of Independence 1942–45," Unpublished BA Hons. Academic Exercise, University of Malaya, Singapore, 1958, 12-16, who quotes S.N. Khan, *I.N.A. and its Netaji*, New Delhi, 1946, 20. See also Lee Su Yin, "The Indian National Army Trials, 1945–46: The British Imperial Dilemma," Unpublished BA Hons. Academic Exercise, NUS, 1985, 18-19.

44. Chan Kin Sang, "Soldiers in Captivity: P.O.W. Experiences in Changi 1942–1945," Unpublished BA Hons. Academic Exercise, NUS, 1986, 14-18.

45. According to one authoritative source, it was estimated that 41,500 POWs reached the Changi cantonment area by 17 February and that this number swelled to 52,200 by the evening of Wednesday 18 February 1942. See David Nelson, *The Story of Changi Singapore*, Perth, 1974, 10.

46. Singapore's long-time Prime Minister (now Senior Minister), Mr. Lee Kuan Yew, has often expressed this feeling in speeches recalling the marked effect this visible demonstration of Britain's defeat had upon him and others of his generation. See, for example, Han F.K., W. Fernandez & Sumiko Tan (editors), *Lee Kuan Yew: The Man and His Ideas*, Singapore, 1998, 21-22, 31, and Lee Kuan Yew, *The Singapore Story: Memoirs of Lee Kuan Yew*, Singapore, 1998, 50-53, 55.

47. H.A. Probert, *History of Changi*, Singapore, 1970, 22-34; Chan, 20-24.

48. Chan, 22-24.

49. Ibid., 29-31.

50. Food scarcity was a habitual problem for all POWs. Even though a considerable amount of leafy vegetables and root crops were cultivated by the prisoners themselves, the survivors of the Changi years have little difficulty in remembering the constant gnawing feeling of hunger they experienced in the camps. For an account of the rationing system, black market operations and medical problems that beset the prisoners at this time, see Chan, 36-53.

51. Braddon, 153-70, 223-60; Caffrey, 190-95. See below, ch. 10.

52. Caffrey, 195-265.

53. Chan, 26-29.

54. Russell Braddon, an Australian POW, was particularly scathing about the maintenance of this distinction between officers and other ranks. See Braddon, 153-54; Chan, 62-70.

55. Caffrey, 230-33; Chan, 75-77.

56. David Nelson described the scene as something of a cross between Dante's Inferno, the Caledonian Market and the Epsom Downs on Derby Day! See Nelson, 43.

57. Chan, 77-80.

58. On the day that the Selarang Incident began (2 September) senior Allied officers witnessed the shooting of four prisoners found outside the camp perimeter, charged with escaping and sentenced to death. See ibid., 40-45.

59. It is clear that two distinct levels of courses were offered to the POWs. Southern Area College, which was established in Kitchener Baracks, provided more advanced courses, while 18th Division College aimed to take its students up to matriculation standard. See Probert, 44.

60. A revealing account of the work of the BRE is given by David Nelson, 29-240.

61. Probert, 44-45.

62. Ibid., 55-56.

63. Braddon, 254-57.

64. Discovery of such a radio set would guarantee the person/s responsible severe punishment at the hands of the *Kempeitai*.

65. This also became a marked feature of the life of the civilian internees many of whom developed an eclectic taste for literature.

66. Some were allowed to continue with their pre-surrender tasks for several weeks. Customs officials, engineers, nurses, priests and others were eventually

278   *Between Two Oceans: A Military History of Singapore*

forced to make the same wearisome march from the city to Katong and eventually to Changi Jail in March 1942. A few were more fortunate and remained free to continue their pre-war professional work. For a fascinating insight into the life of one such individual who worked in the Botanical Gardens, see E.J.H. Corner, *Marquis, a tale of Syonan-to*, Singapore, 1981.

67. T. Thompson, *Freedom in Internment: Under Japanese Rule in Singapore 1942–1945*, Singapore, 1990, 1-11.

68. Probert, 52; Thompson, 29; M. Thomas, *In the Shadow of the Rising Sun*, Singapore, 1983, 55-56.

69. Nearly 40% of the internees assigned to each block, however, ended up by being lodged in the dining room, workshops and hallways of the prison. M.H. Murfett, "Extracts From a Changi Diary," *Commentary*, vol. 6, nos. 2 & 3, August 1985, 70. In the Womens' Blocks the normal allocation to a cell was a more satisfactory two. See Thomas, 60.

70. Thomas, 72.

71. Thompson, 34.

72. Murfett, "Extracts from a Changi Diary," 71; Thomas, 105-06.

73. Outside working parties lost some of their popularity once scrounging was officially restricted by the Japanese in mid-1942. Any internee found guilty of trafficking in food or goods with any member of the local population thereafter would be punished and the entire camp would lose its tobacco and cigarette ration for an unspecified period of time. See Murfett, "Extracts from a Changi Diary," 71.

74. Ibid., 72.

75. Ibid., 71; Thomas, 62. Cases of thiamine deficiency were legion and oedema was a familiar scourge. Letter E.P. Hodgkin to author, 17 May 1998.

76. Thompson, 112-26; Murfett, "Extracts from a Changi Diary," 72.

77. Ibid., 72-74.

78. For further information on Operation *Jaywick* see B. Connell, *Return of the Tiger*, London, 1960. For the notorious aftermath see C. Sleeman & S.C. Silkin (editors), *Trial of Sumida Haruzo and Twenty Others: The "Double Tenth" Trial*, London, 1951.

79. Fifteen of these internees failed to survive the ordeal meted out to them at the hands of the *Kempeitai* in its grotesque torture cells in the city. Two radio sets were discovered as a result of the search in the Men's Camp and those responsible for owning and operating them were to be among those who suffered a cruel fate in custody. Those who did not die were so ill-treated that their lives were wrecked thereafter. See Probert, 54; Murfett, "Extracts from a Changi Diary," 75-77; Thomas, 134-44.

80. Montgomery, 156-57, 159. Bishop Leonard Wilson, the Anglican Bishop of Singapore, was one of those subsequently taken into custody and subjected to sustained interrogation and torture. See J. Hayter, *Priest in Prison*, Worthing, 1989, 157-71; F. Bloom, *Dear Philip*, London, 1980, 113-37.

81. Ibid., 175.

82. Thompson, 129-31. See also S. Allan, *Diary of a Girl in Changi 1941–1945*, Kenthurst, N.S.W., 1994, 111-37. Professor E.P. Hodgkin, formerly a medical entomologist in Kuala Lumpur, believes the Sime Road Camp was subject to the less virulent Urban Typhus. Letter E.P. Hodgkin to author, 17 May 1998.

83. Thomas, 146-47, 157-58.

84. Ibid., 151.

85. Hayter, 226-41.

86. Shigeo Odate (March 1942–June 1943) and Kanichi Naito (19 July 1943–14 August 1945) were the only two mayors appointed to this office during the whole of the Occupation.

87. According to Shinozaki, more than 15 people tried to loot a military warehouse in Keppel Harbour. Eight of these looters were caught and immediately beheaded. Their heads went on display in various prominent locations, such as Newton Circus, Holland Road and near Tanjong Pagar Police Station. Shinozaki, 19.

88. For an interesting analysis of Japanese writing on the Occupation see H.P. Frei, "Japan Remembers the Malaya Campaign," in P.H. Kratoska (editor), *Malaya and Singapore During the Japanese Occupation*, Singapore, 1995, 148-68.

89. For an interesting account of Japanese involvement with the INA, see Fujiwara, 6-10, 19-38.

90. Fujiwara, 138-47. A view of the same events as seen from an Indian perspective is offered by Joginder, "Indian Army of Independence," 33-36, 44-47.

91. Fujiwara, 257-65. On the other hand Japanese support for its efforts did not come close to what the INA leaders hoped for either: C.S. Sundaram, "A Paper Tiger: The Indian National Army in Battle, 1944-1945," in *War & Society*, Vol. 13, #1, 35-59.

92. Thio, 98 – 101. For the social impact of the Japanese Occupation of Malaya, see Cheah B.K., *Red Star Over Malaya*, Singapore, 1983, 18-55.

93. Shinozaki, 115-17; Archives & Oral History Dept., *The Japanese Occupation*, 59; Thio, 102; Interview with Rudy Mosbergen, 22 February 1998.

94. Lee, "Singapore Under the Japanese," 21-26.

95. N.I. Low provides a number of examples of how seriously inflation eroded the value of the local currency and pushed up the price of all articles from luxury goods to staple foods on the black market. He indicates that the price of a piano rose from $200 in December 1941 to reach $15,000 in June 1945. At the other extreme, a picul of rice costing only $5 in December 1941 reached the excessive sum of $5,000 in June 1945. See Low, 61-62.

96. Ibid., 26; Thio, 103; Chin, 33-54.

97. Sidhu, 121-39; Lee, "Singapore Under the Japanese," 13-17, 19-20.

98. For the basic structure of the auxiliary police force see Lee, "Singapore Under the Japanese," 17-19; National Heritage Board, *Japanese Occupation*, 104-05.

99. Ibid., 31-32.

100. Ibid., 32-33.

101. See P. Williams and D. Wallace, *Unit 731*, New York, 1989, 94-95, 108-111. Othman Wok's story of his involvement with the Japanese anti-plague, biological research laboratory, *Okai 9420 Butai* in *Syonan* from late-1942 to mid-1944 is recorded briefly in Sidhu, 175-79. His story and Norman Covert's allegations lend a certain credence to the suspicions of Phan Ming Yen, a former journalist with Singapore Press Holdings, who believes that the Japanese were actively involved in deadly biological experiments in *Syonan-to* during the war. See his articles in *Straits Times*, 19, 25 September, 11 November 1991.

102. Lee, "Singapore Under the Japanese," 9-12.

103. See Hayter, 83-85; Nelson, 114; Thomas, 82-83; Corner, 130; Shinozaki, passim.

104. Sadists, such as Capt. Mizuma and Sgt.-Major Toyoda Akichi of the *Kempeitai*, are described in Chen, *Remember Pompong*, 123-26. Some of the more notorious Japanese prison guards were given nicknames belying their brutality, hence "Puss in Boots," "Ice-Cream Man," and "Blue Stockings." These individuals were best avoided at all cost. See Braddon, 245-46; Murfett, "Extracts from a Changi Diary," 76; Thomas, 153-54.

105. Frei, 165-66; *Straits Times*, 30 August 1993.

10

Old Wine in a New Bottle: Singapore and British Defence Policy 1945-1962

On 12 September 1945 Vice-Admiral Lord Louis Mountbatten, Supreme Allied Commander Southeast Asia Command (SEAC), accepted the surrender of all Japanese forces in the area at the Municipal building in central Singapore. To much acclaim and nearly universal local relief, the British were back in military and political control of Singapore. For the next twenty years successive British governments tried to maintain at least that military control. They saw Singapore as a vital asset in the defence policy of a state determined to remain a global military power. To no avail. Formal British military control of Singapore ended with a ceremonial parade on 29 October 1971; full responsibility for the defence of the island was transferred to the government of what was now a sovereign city-state republic two days later. For the first time in centuries a political power in Singapore was again fully responsible for its defence.

This was the last phase of Singapore's military history before it became responsible for its own defence. The essential story of this phase is a clash of profound forces: the determination of British leaders to remain a military power in the area, for which they regarded the use of Singapore as pivotal; the erosion of both the financial means and general political will needed to do this; and the fundamental transformation of political will and the political status of Singapore and Southeast Asia, in the age of decolonisation. The final result was a remarkable irony. Singapore became an independent state responsible for its own defence, something neither British nor local leaders planned or intended. And British forces left Singapore faster than either their own leaders or those of Singapore wanted them to leave. This chapter will analyse the return of the British military to Singapore, the reworking of the place of Singapore in British grand strategy and defence policy, and the redevelopment of major base facilities on the island. The final chapter will consider both the political upheavals in Southeast Asia which affected the British military presence in Singapore after 1945 and the causes and circumstances of the British withdrawal.

Return to Singapore

There was never any doubt in the minds of the British authorities about whether to re-establish important military facilities in Singapore once it was reconquered. British rule was to be restored to those territories lost to the Japanese and Singapore remained the geo-strategic pivot it had always been for those territories between India, China and Australia. On the other hand, the U.K. had been pushed so far onto the sidelines in the war against Japan as a whole that no firm plans were ready regarding how to re-establish bases or what to do with them. To cap it all, the end of the war came so suddenly it caught SEAC completely off-guard building up forces for Operation *Zipper*, the reconquest of Malaya and Singapore starting with invasion from the sea in Central Malaya. To avoid snarling supply lines and plans the *Zipper* landings went ahead; to underline the political point of victory a task force rushed to Singapore to restore British control and prepare for the surrender. Fittingly however, the first British military return to Singapore actually occurred on 31 August, when a *Mosquito* aircraft on a reconnaissance mission developed engine trouble and had to chance a landing on the island, still in Japanese hands.[1]

This false start symbolised the crucial point. Mountbatten's triumphant ceremony rang somewhat hollow, as also seemed clear when Japanese soldiers had to augment the still small British presence by helping to guard the parade route. British forces limped back into Singapore courtesy of victories elsewhere, especially those of their U.S. allies. Singapore remained for the time being under military rule, as a British Military Administration (BMA) was established in Singapore and Malaya to evict the Japanese, restore law and order, and prepare the way for the restoration of civil government. This was a benevolent occupation Singaporeans were happy to exchange for the brutality, corruption and near-starvation of Japanese rule. Yet the fact of British defeat, the impact of Japanese occupation, and the less than overwhelming nature of the British return sowed political seeds for the future.[2] But for the moment there was no serious challenge to the British return. Repairing the damage of war, restoring a civil economy, and re-establishing a pivotal military base were the preoccupations of the new military administration.

By November 1945 the administrative structure for the transition period was in place. All three services were again occupying and assessing their former facilities on the island, and the BMA came under the supervision of SEAC as Mountbatten moved a large portion of his headquarters to Singapore. In April 1946 civil government was restored; in November, after a year in Singapore, SEAC was disbanded and replaced by a solely British military chain of command. During the fourteen months of military control then dominance in Singapore, all the issues which shaped the island's military history for the next generation emerged, at least in initial form. These included the place of Singapore in British defence policy and grand strategy, the type of facilities needed in Singapore, the role of the forces based here, and the impact of their presence on Singapore's political, social and economic development.

The first COS paper to discuss the military future of Singapore spelled out the basic problem very nicely in March 1945. For the U.K. to remain a military power in Southeast and East Asia, it needed a large, well-protected and established base in Singapore, for all three services. Yet the events of the war and occupation made the need for political reforms inevitable. In Singapore's case, the necessary reforms must be made without jeopardising British control over and use of the island as a military hub. The serious study of post-war political change in Singapore began in the CO as early as January 1945, but no firm plans were ready by the time British forces returned.[3] This did not prove fatal in the short run. The Malayan Communist Party (MCP) did at first emphasise urban revolution in Singapore in its almost immediate political effort to end British rule in Singapore and Malaya. It was fairly well-established in the Chinese community in Singapore by the end of 1945, working through a network of front organisations with much influence in the trade unions. The all but inevitable problems of rebuilding battered infrastructure — not enough food, jobs, housing — gave the communists the leverage to exploit popular frustration with the slow pace of recovery and instigate strikes and street unrest in January and February 1946. But this agitation never posed a serious threat to the BMA, nor seriously delayed the re-establishment of the bases or the shift to civilian rule. British control was secure by late 1945 and Singaporeans wanted recovery, not revolution.[4] This discontent indicated complications would arise in the future, but for now the work of redefining a military role for Singapore could proceed.

The recovery of Singapore was a top priority for its own sake, to restore some measure of prestige, to make it possible to restore British and Allied control in the rest of Southeast Asia by using it as an operating hub, and to establish a centre of gravity for future defence policy in the area. The over 77,000 Japanese troops on the island and in Johore caused almost no trouble and by the end of 1945 the 5th Indian Division held the island secure and repair work on the vital naval and air facilities was proceeding.[5] That work was subject to the central question: what was the object of British defence policy in the region for the future? That question became a matter of great urgency when by 1946 it was clear the new Labour government in the U.K., led by Clement Attlee, intended to end British rule in India as soon as the details of a transition could be settled. The "loss" of India was bound to affect defence policy as a whole, let alone Singapore, as will be seen. But the Attlee government and its military advisers were resolute in their determination to maintain the British territories in Southeast Asia, at least for the forseeable future. Singapore emerged almost by default as the military hub for the region, due to its location and in no small measure to the fact existing facilities were there on which to rebuild.[6]

The RAF regarded Singapore from the start as the obvious place for its main regional base. Its existing airfields were increased by the airstrip at Changi developed by the Japanese. Sabotage by prisoners of war used to build the strip left it incomplete, but the RAF took the facility in hand — with "help" from Japanese prisoners of war. In April 1946 RAF headquarters moved to the newly opened facility at Changi, which joined the already reactivated fields at Tengah and Seletar to give the air force the basis for a superbly balanced base facility. While much development was still required, plans were well-advanced to make the island complex a fully operational base in all respects. Tengah would house the air defence squadrons, Seletar would be the stores and maintenance depot, and the new facility at Changi, with room to expand the runway to take the heaviest aircraft, would become the air transportation hub. From this central position, the RAF would support policy and operations all over Southeast Asia.[7]

The RN situation regarding Singapore turned out to be more complicated. The famous base at Semabawang suffered heavily during the war, not least from Allied bombing in 1944 and 1945, and needed much repair. While there waṣ no intention not to revive the base, there were doubts about whether it should again become the principal naval facility in the Far East within the RN. But surveys and initial repair work on the damage raised local expectations, as naval officers took control of the work, a great many local workers were hired, and plans were made to rebuild large shore facilities. By December the *Straits Times* was talking confidently of the "return" of the Pacific Fleet.[8] A request for guidance on the priority of repair work in the area led the Admiralty that same month to decree Singapore must come ahead of Hong Kong, on several grounds. Singapore was less vulnerable to attack but still close enough to be both an operational and main repair base for fleet operations in East and Southeast Asia. It would cost less to rebuild the Sembawang base than to build another elsewhere from scratch. The civil war in China threatened British interests, so a fleet base was needed as fast as possible. Finally, the economies of Malaya and Singapore needed the boost the revival of the base would provide.[9]

This brought to a head the issue of whether Singapore should also again become the fleet's main support base. The Pacific Fleet objected to Singapore on three grounds: it was too vulnerable to air attack; the climate was too debilitating; and the infrastructure needed to develop a main support base was not there. Their suggestion was to establish such a base in Australia and/or New Zealand, where none of these objections were faced. The Admiralty rejected this argument in March 1946, insisting it was necessary to restore a visible and effective British naval presence in both East and Southeast Asia, to revive British trade and screen British interests — and only Singapore was close enough yet secure enough, and with a basis on which to build.[10]

This line of thinking reflected the consensus in London. That same month the Joint Planning Staff (JPS) suggested the establishment of new coordinating machinery for defence in Southeast Asia, based in Singapore. Singapore should be at least the main support base for the RN, the main base and regional headquarters for the Army and RAF, and the main facility from which British and friendly forces should deploy for operations anywhere in the region or strategic movements through it. This concept of reviving Singapore as the regional military hub was indeed settling in. By now the Army, expecting to lose both its vast Indian Army manpower pool and facilities in India, was looking at Singapore as the probable future main operations and supply base for imperial defence east of the Middle East.[11]

It was already clear that development on this scale would not be problem-free. Friction arose by mid-1946 between the army and civilians and within the services over the slow transition to peacetime routine. The demobilisation of troops did not move fast enough to satisfy either the citizen soldiers who wanted to go home or the local citizens who wanted the release of the housing, business and port facilities the troops were still occupying. Temperatures rose high enough for the Singapore Chamber of Commerce to complain in July 1946 that continued use of extensive facilities by the army was seriously retarding the restoration of the trade and commerce which was Singapore's lifeblood. The decision to develop a large facility in southwest Singapore for barracks, ordnance, hospital, and other uses, work on that facility, and the departure of soldiers to be demobilised eased the problem by late 1946.[12] The situation was stable enough by the time SEAC was disbanded, and the British chain of command fully restored, for the GHQ of the new Southeast Asia Land Forces (SEALF) to report "Malaya and Singapore: the reduction in manpower can be accepted as the political situation is expected to remain calm...", even though the Commander Singapore District still grumbled about the general turnout, deportment and black market tendencies of the by now about 20,000 troops on the island. The army however was in hand, as for the moment was Singapore.[13] The return of the British military was accomplished, if not complete.

British Defence Policy and the Role of Singapore

There is no doubt what the most important determining factor of the military position of Singapore was from 1945: the defence policy and related grand strategy of the U.K. That policy was shaped by a tug-of-war which began immediately and never ceased. On the one hand, the British economy failed to keep pace with the rising cost of maintaining a global defence policy and capability. On the other hand, British military and political leaders worked hard to maintain that very policy and capability. Affecting this tug-of-war were such factors as public opinion in the U.K. and the territories involved, the state of international relations, advances in technology, and the changing nature of the Empire/Commonwealth. Two central themes are clear. First, British governments instinctively assumed it was necessary to maintain an imperial military capability — full stop. Second, because of this, the more events forced changes in defence policy as a whole, the more important Singapore became in preserving British military power in the Far East. As far as Singapore is concerned, the evolution of defence policy can be broken down into three phases. From 1945 into 1952, the basis of a defence policy for a weaker, poorer but still ambitious U.K. was worked out, more by events and instincts than by calculation. From 1952 into 1959 efforts were made to transform the strategy by which that policy would be implemented; these efforts increased the significance of Singapore. From

1959 into 1962, the refining of changes in policy and strategy established Singapore as one of the "three pillars" of both — on the eve, ironically, of the events which finally made that policy untenable. Throughout, Singapore derived its importance in British defence policy from one objective fact above all: its location.

The reshaping of defence policy in general after 1945 rested on three constant factors. First, British public opinion consistently placed far greater weight on social reform and welfare at home than on maintaining an overseas empire. Only relative indifference to defence considerations kept this from aborting an imperial defence policy on the spot. Second, developments in science and technology set off a spiral which made weapons and other military equipment steadily more sophisticated but exponentially more expensive. Finally, the U.K. found itself eclipsed by the rise of the global economic and military superpowers, the U.S.A. and the U.S.S.R., but intimately involved from the start in the grave struggle for global power and influence which developed between them, generally known as the Cold War. Firmly embedded in the Western bloc led by the U.S., the British soon found themselves trying to maintain an overseas defence policy in the face of countervailing trends which pushed their priorities more and more towards Europe and home. In this context, two things provided by the early 1950s the basis for a reshaped defence policy and deployment affecting Singapore: the mere fact of being in residence, and the determination of political and military leaders to remain there.

Four events of overwhelming significance guided the course of British defence policy in the late 1940s. Wartime friction between the Soviet Union and the Western Allies deteriorated by 1949 into a rivalry so severe the Western powers decided the Soviets posed a grave threat, military and political, to their very survival. In August 1947 British rule ended in India, leaving behind two states with uncertain attitudes and policies. The Communist Party of China defeated its "nationalist" adversary in a civil war which ended in 1949 with the Communist takeover of the Asian giant. Finally, the U.K. fell far short in its attempt to launch a massive programme of social spending and reform at home, yet also revive an industrial and manufacturing economy able to maintain a global empire. All together, these events shaped decisions about the place of Singapore in British defence policy.

In April 1949 the U.K. became a founding member of the North Atlantic Treaty Organisation (NATO), a collective military alliance bringing together Western Europe, the U.S. and Canada for mutual defence against the perceived communist bid for global hegemony led by the Soviet Union. That only formalised what had always been true: in British defence policy, the direct defence of the home islands and the maintenance of a friendly balance of power in Europe were by far the most important objectives. The great bulk of British military striking power always remained committed to these objectives. British responses to military and political threats which arose elsewhere were in the end always conditioned by that priority. A new and crucial element was the development of nuclear weapons, especially with the success of the Soviet Union in developing its own bomb in autumn 1949. British defence policy increasingly had to balance the need to prevent a possible apocalypse yet contribute to an alliance strong enough to resist a superpower adversary if it launched a general war. When a shooting war broke out in Korea in June 1950, the U.K. rallied to the American-led effort to repel the communist attack, but British military and political leaders agreed the main threat remained the Soviet capability to launch a massive attack on Western Europe. The Korean War confirmed the importance of Singapore as a military base in the Cold War, as will be noted below; but it also underlined the British view that the main theatre of that struggle was in Europe, not the Far East.[14]

The British withdrawal from India immediately and massively affected British policy and prospects in Singapore and Southeast Asia. Without the manpower of the Indian Army it was hard to see how the British could maintain military forces strong enough to protect such large far-flung territories. Indeed, with the benefit of hindsight it is clear the withdrawal from India rendered the British Empire in the Far East militarily untenable. At the time the withdrawal of Indian units from the garrisons in Singapore and Malaya stretched the army to the danger point in the eyes of its commanders. But the British government concluded that the withdrawal made the British colonies in Southeast Asia, especially Singapore, even more important for their own sake. British investments and interests overseas remained huge, from Africa through Southeast Asia to China. Initial high hopes a friendly India would cooperate in maintaining a strong imperial defence were quickly dashed by an Indian government determined to keep their former masters at arms length. Still, the Attlee government sincerely believed an acceptable level of British power could not be maintained without the wealth provided by overseas interests. That wealth seemed as always to depend on maintaining secure trade routes and freedom if not control of the sea lanes. This did not seem possible unless a strong military presence was maintained in such a crucial strategic location as Singapore. Moreover, trade seemed to fuse with ideals in enlightened self-interest. The vital dollar-earning rubber and tin industries of Malaya and the port and transport facilities of Singapore were needed to maintain the strength of the Empire as a whole, but must also be denied to the Cold War adversary. At the very least, political change must develop along lines favourable to British interests. Therefore, withdrawal from India made British leaders more determined than ever to maintain their strong presence in Singapore.[15]

The Communist victory in the civil war in China only reinforced the perceived importance of Singapore. The new Communist government seemed certain to be at least an ally if not a proxy for Soviet policy, spreading the rivalry of the Cold War into Asia. An armed communist insurgency already being waged right next door in Malaya raised those fears, as did the war being waged between the French and the communist-led movement in Vietnam. The communist attack on Korea, followed in November 1950 by massive Chinese intervention in the war, only seemed to underline the apparent threat to Western interests in East and Southeast Asia raised by a possibly monolithic, certainly coordinated, communist bloc. For a time British leaders even considered abandoning Hong Kong as untenable, but in the end they decided to brazen it out. By 1951 the spread of the Cold War to the region, fuelled by the shooting war in Korea, entrenched Singapore as the principal base for the military forces British leaders believed must be deployed to protect this important region in the developing global struggle.[16]

It proved much easier to decide why Singapore must remain a principal overseas base than determine how it should best be used. Events simply moved too rapidly for the British government and its military advisers to conduct a searching reappraisal of defence policy and military strategy before the Korean War. Instead they made both up as they went along, relying heavily on instincts and traditions as well as existing assets. Singapore emerged by default as the obvious hub for the Far East, for the same reasons it was developed as such after the First World War.[17] In a morbid replay, plans for the defence of Singapore in regional and global conflicts developed along lines similar to those of the 1930s — and produced confusion and controversy between the U.K. and the Dominions similar to that which blew up so disastrously in 1941–1942.

What basis there was for British defence policy in the early post-war years was spelt out by the COS in January 1947. They insisted that to help deter another general war the U.K. must play a full share in collective security arrangements as a first-class military power with a global presence. The priorities of grand strategy were to preserve the U.K., maintain a firm hold on the oil resources of the Middle East, and preserve the sea lanes and lines of communication. This last item bore directly on Singapore and the Far East. While by this time the potential external threat to distant bases, especially in a general war, was clearly appreciated — 1942 was fresh in all minds — overseas bases were still regarded as indispensable in grand strategy. Imperial defence remained oriented around protecting the maritime and air lines of communication. This required stationing powerful forces in the area they were to defend. In the case of the Far East, forces needed to be acclimatised and familiar with the region, as well as have ample readily available stocks of equipment and weapons, to operate effectively. The RAF and RN simply could not operate without secure bases within range of anywhere they might need to intervene. The Army preferred to have such a facility in order to have units ready to react on the spot rather than have to beg London to send troops in response to any problem. Marshal of the RAF Lord Tedder, Chief of the Air Staff (CAS), spelt out the policy on a visit to Singapore in December 1946: the basis of grand strategy remained unchanged overall and regarding the Far East, and Singapore remained the focal point for the region.[18]

Plans for the defence of Singapore itself, and how it could be used to defend Malaya and the region, amounted to a reworking of the concept developed by 1941 — but with one interesting twist. Local resources would be used to help develop and protect the naval base, but this time the maximum production of tin, rubber and other materials would be subject to, not more important than, protecting the base. Moreover, the RAF again emerged as the force with the lead role in defence plans. It must take the lead in confronting the air threat to the base which aroused naval concerns. The Army, again, was to hold the base secure in order to allow the RAF and RN to cope with external threats to Singapore and the region. And only the RAF could provide the rapid transport the Army would need to deploy and operate in Malaya or elsewhere in the region. As Singapore was the only place from which such an air effort could be made, its importance was never in doubt to the soldiers and airmen.[19] Nevertheless two problems did make the rewriting of defence plans involving Singapore a drawn-out affair: a rearguard action by the sailors, and the unavoidable need to secure the support of allies in defending the region.

In June 1947 Singapore got a good scare when the *Straits Times* published reports that the battle in the Admiralty over the status of the base was still not settled. Suggestions that Sydney was being touted as a better main base for naval and indeed imperial defence in the region were very close to the mark, as both the C-in-C Pacific Fleet and the First Sea Lord were reluctant to locate fleet headquarters in Singapore. Both cited one rather colourful reason: "certain it is that the climate and atmosphere of Singapore make it a poor place for clear thinking in peace or war." But more substantial and familiar factors also influenced their views: Singapore might be fine for the Army but the RN had wider more far-flung responsibilities and must be mobile. Singapore was distant from the scene of likely operations yet still vulnerable to attack, and not necessarily well-suited to be the main base for coordinated operations with the allies — read the U.S. — without whom the Far East could not be defended. Indeed, reading between the lines it seems fair to suggest the sailors simply did not wish to entangle themselves in combined headquarters with the other services, where they might be tied to priorities they did not share. This visceral resistance could not however stop the counterforces which settled the issue. The CIGS and CAS forcefully insisted the advantages of locating all service headquarters and support facilities in the same location far outweighed any naval desire for mobility or even greater security. In meetings in August 1947 the defence authorities on station in Singapore supported this view. Singapore had facilities on which to build; Hong Kong and Sydney did not, Hong Kong was too close to danger, Sydney too far from it. Arguments dragged on but in September 1948 the issue was closed with the shift of Headquarters Pacific Fleet to the base at Semabwang.[20]

This brought all three area service commanders-in-chief together physically. Organisationally they had been together since the re-establishment of a British chain of command in November 1946. The service chiefs then joined the already operating British Defence Committee Southeast Asia, chaired by the Governor-General of Malaya. In due course it was renamed the British Defence Coordination Committee Far East (BDCCFE) when the duties of the service chiefs in the area were expanded to include Hong Kong and China. Its duty was to coordinate defence activities and prepare appreciations, not to make policy. Each service chief continued to answer directly to London. But their presence and the corporate presence of the BDCCFE in Singapore sealed its status as the defence hub of the Far East as far as the services were concerned.[21]

The service staffs in Singapore and their superiors in London did agree on another crucial issue with echoes from the past: no British military position in the Far East could be defended without the help of the U.S. and the Dominions, especially in a general war. The service authorities in Singapore worked on plans for coping with external threats posed by the Soviets or the Chinese, but pointed out no plans could be settled until the intentions of at least the Dominions were clear. The Attlee government discussed the whole question of imperial defence with Dominion Prime Ministers at a conference in April 1946, with an eye on the impact of changes in India, but no arrangements were made. Everyone was still demobilising, not looking forward to the next war. The COS lobbied as they always had for the Dominions to take a greater share of the defence burden as a whole, but now for the first time started to talk openly about ceding primary strategic responsibility for certain areas to their partners. That idea ran afoul of the direction of political change in the Empire. Given the withdrawal from India and the growing wealth and independence of the Dominions, that Empire was rapidly becoming the Commonwealth. More than ever the British found themselves obliged to persuade their erstwhile partners they shared common interests in defending colonial territories which required coordinated policy.[22]

The issue came to a head in autumn 1948 over preparations for another conference of Prime Ministers. The JPS submitted a paper proposing that strategic responsibility for taking the lead in imperial defence in the Far East should be offered to Australia. The COS supported the proposal, arguing it was the only way to entice more commitment from the Australians to the defence of the area. The FO objected, arguing the immediate threat to British interests in the area was political, such as the communist insurgency in Malaya; ceding leadership to Australia would fatally undermine British prestige as the Malay and other local peoples would conclude the British no longer had the will and ability to protect their interests. This view was supported by Malcolm Macdonald, now chairing the BDCCFE in the new post of Commissioner-General for Southeast Asia. Under pressure, the COS "clarified" their stand: Australia should be asked to take the lead in making strategic plans for the defence of this region up to and including general war.[23] From this debate and consultations in Australia and New Zealand on global and regional defence, a compromise JPS proposal was submitted in September 1949. The British would retain responsibility for internal security in the territories of Southeast Asia; the Dominions would take the lead in plans for securing the sea and air lines of communication; control of any operations against an external enemy would be shared. The COS and the BDCCFE had reservations about this scheme, but a general election in Australia in December 1949 returned a government under Robert Menzies much more willing to cooperate in regional defence arrangements than its predecessor. That allowed planners to get down to brass tacks.[24]

The Korean War galvanised action in this sphere as well. British strategic assumptions were spelled out with greater clarity in the second half of 1950. The U.K. still aimed to avoid general war, with China as well as the Soviet Union. The main threat remained in Europe. But now for the first time what became notorious as the "domino theory" made its appearance in British thinking. This theory was based on the premise that Southeast Asia was a vital region which must be denied to the communist bloc in the Cold War, but it was vulnerable to a combination of attack from without and subversion/insurgency from within. With active operations underway in Vietnam and Malaya, Indonesia having just won independence from the Dutch in a nasty conflict, and nationalism in general on the rise, one central idea emerged: if any one country fell to a communist takeover, that would gravely weaken the ability of its neighbours to stand firm. Ultimately, the toppling dominoes would take out Singapore. British planners believed the best place to meet an external attack remained in Vietnam, with the Kra Isthmus as a fallback stop line. The South China Sea must be held in order to screen Singapore, without which the forces needed to defend the region could not operate. But British plans for a general war did not allow for reinforcements to be sent to Southeast Asia. The British could not plan to defend the region without allied help, as any reinforcements must come from the U.S. and/or the Dominions.[25]

These points were thrashed out in several different rounds of talks in 1951 with the French, the Americans and the Dominions. The final British positions came out in bits and pieces. Southeast Asia was a secondary but important front in the Cold War. The Western Powers needed to work together to defend it; in due course a collective security pact might be required. The British might reinforce the region in a limited war, but could not undertake to do so in a general war. Under Australian pressure they insisted the threat would develop in full view over many months, at which time the "situation would be reviewed." The Australians had of course heard that song before. The two points on which everyone agreed were that Singapore was absolutely essential as the central position for the defence of the region, and that any general threat could only be faced with immediate and effective American assistance.[26] This was virtually the same position as had developed by 1941!

An important difference was that Dominion forces were not yet deployed in Singapore or Malaya. What did emerge was a loose arrangement which associated the Australian, New Zealand and British military authorities in common planning for the defence of Malaya and Singapore, it being understood operations against an external enemy would be coordinated — which implied Dominion forces would be deployed. This arrangement, known as ANZAM for Australia, New Zealand and Malaya, was seen as an interim step. The question for the British was whether it could be developed into a pact along the lines of the most important alliance Australia and New Zealand concluded in this period, the ANZUS Pact, which committed the U.S. to the defence of the Dominions. The overriding British military objective for Singapore was to commit allies, especially the U.S., to its defence. By the end of 1951 this governed the standing strategic plan: in any general war the RN would redeploy to the main theatre, the RAN would take the lead role in securing the regional lines of communication, and RAF and army forces on station would defend the island and its approaches.[27]

The development of the base at Singapore and plans for how to use and defend it very nearly fell victim to the most serious threat to British defence ambitions after the war: the exhaustion of the British industrial economy and its stubborn refusal to catch up to the demands made of it. As early as the first weeks of 1947 government ministers and the Treasury pressed for serious cuts in defence spending, cuts well beyond demobilising the bloated wartime forces. Opposition to any such cuts was spirited; regarding the Far East, the FO and the service departments agreed it was crucial to imperial defence and the base in Singapore was the most vital strategic position in the area. But a hard winter, a weak currency, and demands for social reform took their toll. In the autumn of 1947 the Cabinet decided the economic position required the U.K. to accept risks in grand strategy, in order to make cost-saving cuts in military strength. As risks would not be taken with home defence, the spotlight fell on overseas deployments.[28]

The service departments responded to this pressure by a clever piece of bureaucratic intrigue. A working party was formed to report to the COS on how the defence budget as a whole could be reduced to £700 million a year by 1950. The report, submitted in the spring of 1949, advised this could only be done by a wholesale gutting of the armed forces which would require a severe reduction in military commitments abroad, including abandoning the base at Singapore. The Army would have to cope without the national service which alone gave it the manpower to meet its numerous commitments; the RN would lose the bases which alone gave it the capability to operate in distant seas. Even this scaremongering might not have saved the armed forces from cuts serious enough to compromise plans for Singapore, given the fact the government was forced to devalue the pound sterling later that year. But the outbreak of the Korean War changed the political climate in which the debate unfolded. That plus the fact facilities were already there to be developed saved Singapore as a pivotal overseas base, at least for the moment. Work on rebuilding the base ran ahead of decisions on its future; already by late 1946 its facilities for acting as the main logistics hub in the region for all three services were about to surpass those developed before the war.[29]

Time and again over the next four years work was allowed to proceed on the grounds this was the cheapest way to provide the necessary infrastructure pending a definitive decision on defence policy. In the end the Attlee government never made any such decision. Rather than fight the divisive issue of defence versus economic risks through to an uncomfortable conclusion, the government made decisions in bits and pieces. The British remained in the Far East to show they were determined to remain a global power.[30] By the end of 1951 British defence spending was increasing sharply to meet the challenge of the Cold War and Singapore seemed well-established as the central position in a revived British defence commitment in the Far East.

In July 1952, a COS paper produced largely at the prompting of the CAS set out the basis of what in due course became an effort to revolutionise British defence policy and grand strategy. The U.K. must maintain a policy of Imperial/Commonwealth defence; in that policy, the position at Singapore was one of the "three pillars" of strategy. In fact, it was now regarded as higher in priority than the Middle East. On the other hand the burden of maintaining strong forces overseas might in future be eased by a major change in force structure. In 1946 the Attlee government decided the U.K. must develop its own nuclear weapons, in order to remain a first-class military power able to make independent decisions in the last resort. That effort now bore fruit as British bombs were tested successfully. The air staff-inspired paper hinted that major savings might eventually be realised by increasing British reliance on powerful nuclear forces to deter a major adversary — which might make it possible to reduce expensive large conventional forces and overseas bases.[31] For the rest of the decade Singapore's place in British policy and strategy was caught up in this larger tug-of-war: was it still necessary and possible to maintain large overseas bases, or was there a viable alternative? Changes in technology, politics and strategic thinking produced a bizarre answer.

Serious British debate over the strategic usefulness of major overseas bases began in 1953. In keeping with the desire to employ new technology and reduce overall costs, some voices called for building up a large mobile strategic reserve which could rapidly be deployed where and when required, instead of scattering forces in distant bases. But as far as the Far East was concerned there was no real push to reduce the British presence there. The war in Korea ground to a stalemate armistice that summer, but the conflict in Vietnam escalated and the insurgency in Malaya dragged on. The need for British military involvement in the region and thus for bases seemed all too clear. A review of the ANZAM arrangement later that year led to an agreement to establish a "Commonwealth Strategic Reserve" (CSR) of division size in Malaya, to underline the determination of the Commonwealth partners to protect their interests in the region. On the other hand Australia served notice its contribution to this CSR was contingent on a promise from the U.S. it would offer immediate support if a major external threat to the area developed.[32] The winding down of the French war in Vietnam provided an opportunity to press for this promise, as part of the reorganisation of collective security in the Far East.

In early 1954 the American government, anticipating a very possible French defeat in Vietnam, urged the British and French to join them in rethinking the strategic situation in Southeast Asia. British diplomats responded, helping first to broker the Geneva settlement which ended the war in Vietnam after the shattering French defeat at Dien Bien Phu, then to orchestrate talks which led to a collective security agreement reached at a conference in Manila in September. The pact, grouping the U.S., U.K., Australia, New Zealand, France, Pakistan, Thailand, and the Philippines, came to be known as the Southeast Asia Treaty Organisation (SEATO). SEATO was not exactly what the British wanted, as the Americans refused to support the Geneva agreement for a political resolution of the conflict in Vietnam. But in a tacit bargain they did not block the Vietnam deal and in return the British helped pull together the new collective security pact. The headquarters of the organisation was located in Bangkok, rather than Singapore as the British suggested. Unlike NATO, no integrated chain of command with standing forces was set up. Important opposition to the pact came from India and Indonesia, who argued it was meant to perpetuate colonial control in a new guise. And it proved difficult to distinguish clearly, for purposes of defining members' obligations, between the potential external threat which shaped the agreement, and the internal insurgencies which posed the actual threat of the moment — at least in Malaya. Nevertheless, the SEATO pact committed its members to mutual defence against any external threat to any of them.[33]

For the British, this meant above all that the defence of Singapore against a first-class threat was at last linked to a standing American commitment to protect the region. They also looked forward to being able to meet any foe well north of Malaya with allies in the field. Both situations seemed very great improvements indeed over the dark days of late 1941. The CSR took shape in 1955 as British, Australian and New Zealand units joined to form its ground component, the 28th Commonwealth Brigade, deployed in Malaya. SEATO now became the vehicle through which the British planned to confront any external — read Soviet- or Chinese-led or inspired — threat to Singapore and Southeast Asia. SEATO was not as its critics suggested an attempt to reverse the withdrawal from empire; it was a signal from the British of their determination to help make sure the communist bloc did not sweep up Southeast Asia in whatever political changes developed. British and Commonwealth forces in the area were not placed under SEATO command, and continued to operate in defence of British territory. But they were designated to operate as SEATO forces in any major conflict, and were directed to train and plan accordingly.[34] For physical and political reasons Singapore was central to these plans, as it was the only base through which major redeployments could be made and sustained.

Earlier in 1955 the search for ways to cut costs produced new proposals for reducing the size of the army. Three had a direct bearing on Singapore: abandon or reduce the size of some bases; transfer the burden of defence to colonies approaching political independence; rely more heavily on air transport in order to build up a larger strategic reserve at home. In the long run all three ideas would influence the military fate of Singapore. For now, they reflected a trend which was gaining strength in the U.K.: somehow, some way, British military power must be "modernised."[35] This trend was jolted by an event in 1956 which in retrospect signalled that the U.K. was indeed no longer strong enough to act as an independent global military power. The emergence of a strongly nationalist government in Egypt in 1952 led in 1954 to the reluctant British withdrawal from the massive Suez Canal Zone base, the centre of gravity of British military policy in the Middle East. Further friction in this area regarded by British leaders as vital to the U.K.'s economy and international standing led to a head-on collision in the second half of 1956, when the Egyptian government nationalised the Suez Canal. A series of poor judgements by Prime Minister Anthony Eden, plus poor coordination between military planning and diplomatic manoeuvring, led to a fiasco in November 1956. When Israeli forces attacked Egypt, an Anglo-French force moved in ostensibly to "separate" the combatants and protect the Canal. In fact the allied forces operated in clumsily orchestrated collusion with the Israelis. Under pressure from a furious American government and a bitterly divided public at home, the British government called off the operation. This visible humiliation set off grave reprecussions for British policy as a whole, let alone Singapore.[36]

First, Eden was forced to resign in January 1957. He was replaced by Harold Macmillan, who was determined to repair the damage done to relations with the U.S. and to take a searching look at the state of military forces which cost so much but when the call came moved so sluggishly. This was hardly fair given how much the military operation was at the mercy of the erratic direction of the government, but that was how Macmillan saw it and he was now in a position to make things happen. Suez suggested the U.K. might not be able, or even willing, to maintain strong military forces overseas very much longer. British confidence was badly shaken and change was in the air. This revived questions about the future of large overseas bases and commitments. It also made calls for ending national service and shifting priority to a nuclear deterrent more attractive. But it complicated the position of those who called for greater emphasis on air transport and a strategic reserve, not least because it provoked the erection of an "air barrier," refusal to permit overflying, by states in the Middle East and North Africa angry with the British operation—states straddling the air route from the U.K. to Singapore. In sum, the Suez fiasco jolted the search for new directions in British defence policy which first emerged with the air staff paper in 1952.[37]

Macmillan appointed as Minister of Defence a hard-charging politician, Duncan Sandys, ready to tackle vested interests to make changes. From the start Sandys was directed to restructure the armed forces and thus defence policy as a whole, especially by shifting priority to a nuclear deterrent and making large reductions in manpower and spending. Sandys produced a White Paper or statement of intent later that year which was presented as revolutionary but in fact summed up ideas for change developing over the past several years. The essence of

Sandys' plan was to change a large manpower-intensive military scattered all over the world into a more streamlined professional force, relying much more on nuclear weapons and a greatly expanded air transport capability, in order to meet the same global commitments with fewer men and for less money. National service would be ended, the RAF would take the lead in operating the nuclear deterrent forces, and no clear role was spelt out for the RN in any major war. Yet all existing military commitments in the Far East would be maintained, including the CSR and the bases in Singapore. Sandys' paper did not explain exactly how this could be done while still cutting costs; it just assumed a continued British presence was necessary. Singapore was specifically described as the pivotal base for the region, where heavy equipment would be stored and in any crisis reinforcements brought in. Here perhaps was the answer: increased air transport mobility could make it possible to reduce the sheer number of troops at home and overseas but still maintain all British facilities and commitments abroad.[38]

Sandys' paper set off the liveliest debate over British defence policy since the Second World War. Much of that debate bore directly on the future of Singapore. Critics charged that powerful nuclear forces designed to deter a possible World War III were useless in coping with the kind of operations British forces were actually then conducting, low-level conflicts in Cyprus, Oman, and of course Malaya. Cutting conventional forces too much might leave the Army in particular too small to handle the strain. Suggestions that SEATO would be included in a nuclear umbrella and British nuclear weapons might be deployed in Singapore did not really address those concerns, as SEATO itself was designed for the war that must not come rather than those at hand. The idea of replacing forces stationed overseas by greater strategic mobility also ran into difficulties. The RAF could not operate without bases. No matter what the range of its aircraft, the masses of support staff and equipment needed to operate them must be in the theatre; aircraft were supremely mobile, ground support all but immobile. The Army could not continue to operate on the scale it then was in the Far East without a supply base and depot the size of Singapore, especially for heavy equipment.[39] But the service which really focussed the connection between the "new look" defence policy and the Far East was the RN.

For the sailors the new strategic proposals were a threat to their survival. Without a clearly defined role in the largest possible war, the service risked being reduced to the handmaiden of the soldiers and airmen. In its own interest the Admiralty developed and pushed strategic doctrines underlining the need for general-purpose naval power in conflicts ranging from large nuclear wars to small-scale insurgencies overseas. It also made the point that without bases the RN would need to develop an even more costly fleet train of supply ships, to give it the capability to operate for long periods overseas.[40] The point was just as relevant for the Army. Given the "air barrier" and the physical limits on the size of the transport fleet, it could not hope to maintain anything like the strength now deployed outside Europe without its full service bases. The equation was stark: the only way to cut the cost of military expenditure on overseas commitments was to cut the commitments; it could not be done by cutting the capabilities alone.

By 1959 it was clear no revolution was yet underway. The CSR and the tri-service headquarters and large base facilities at Singapore were maintained not just because air transport could not yet replace them. They also stayed in place because this seemed to be the only way to address a commitment the British government would not relinquish: to remain a military power in Southeast Asia, in order to prevent political change from doing lasting damage to British and Western interests. Similar considerations kept British forces in the Middle East. The result, when combined with rising weapons costs, was that even though national service was winding down, overall economies fell far short of expectations. A harsh view would suggest the habit of acting as a world power was dying too slowly in British minds; a more generous view would note that there was a strong feeling that the British military presence in the area, visible and routine, was contributing more to preserving order in a time of change than any reserve held out of sight could ever do. A warning note on that very point was sounded in the British press. It was easier to keep a base in place than to rebuild one after it was gone, and easier to keep British forces in the area than to send in British forces to reinforce the area if the need ever arose. In the end the needs of the moment over-ruled schemes for the future. The Army led the way in the Far East because it carried the burden of current operations and future plans. Even without national service it must remain, to stabilise Singapore and its neighbour Malaya and stand ready for SEATO. Air transport could assist but not replace the base facilities and forces stationed at Singapore; there were no shortcuts. By the end of 1959, Sandys' "new look" may have changed much about British defence policy but it did not change the point which most affected Singapore. As long as the British government was com-mitted to remaining a military power in the Far East, its military advisers would insist they needed Singapore to execute that policy.[41]

The British government went into the 1960s still hoping to achieve the swingeing reduction in defence spending Sandys aimed for by refining the changes in strategy and force structure he sketched out. Events, their own policy assumptions, and the services combined to dilute their efforts very seriously. The strong RN lobby for maintaining general-purpose maritime power was assisted by threats to British interests overseas, especially in the Middle East, which still could not be met other than by maintaining bases and forces overseas. While media attention focussed on the end of national service in 1960 and the development of nuclear forces, the share of British forces deployed east of Suez actually increased slightly in 1960-61, in response to various troubles. The "air barrier," the slow expansion of air transport capability, and endemic trouble in southern Arabia and the Persian Gulf forced the services to deploy stronger more balanced forces east of Suez in this period, to respond effectively to threats. This included the deployment of at least one of the RN's four aircraft carrier groups in the Indian Ocean, leading a balanced fleet based in Singapore.[42]

The harder the efforts to reduce the dependence on major overseas bases, the more entrenched those bases became. In 1961 a threat by Iraq to its neighbour Kuwait, a British protégé and source of vital petroleum, sparked an impressive rapid build-up of ground, air and naval forces which deterred the Iraqis. While air transport was a factor, staff officers were quick to point out the build-up could not have been as fast and large without three things: the naval forces on station in the Indian Ocean; the ground forces deployed at Aden; and the air bases in the theatre. That same year the RAF made a determined effort to win government support for the development of a chain of island airfields in the Atlantic and Indian Oceans which would outflank the "air barrier." These airfields would be easy to secure, free from political complications, and enable British forces to move without hindrance along the lines of communication. The RN saw this as a potential threat to the survival of its main fleet units, the expensive aircraft carriers, which would soon need to be replaced. That set off the latest round of the endless battle over the relative merits of land- vs sea-based airpower. But as the argument dragged on, all parties agreed on one point: the island airfields chain could not replace major full service hub bases, it could only complement them, make them more accessible. The bases in question were Aden and Singapore.[43]

As far as overseas bases were concerned, Singapore was by this time the jewel in the crown. The only other remaining major bases east of Suez were Kenya and Aden, but neither had the full range of facilities or apparent stability and security that Singapore offered. British political and military leaders agreed Singapore remained the pivotal position for British defence policy and grand strategy in the Far East. With its facilities and location, it was essential for any deployment SEATO might need to make. And regardless of who won the battle over airpower, both needed Singapore. Sembawang had the only dry dock capable of taking an aircraft carrier east of Suez, so it must be the regional operations centre for the naval task force the RN saw as its main combat force of the future. As for the RAF, it saw Singapore as the only suitable base for the advanced long-range multi-role combat aircraft it hoped would make naval plans redundant. By 1962 RAF air transport capability was big enough to airlift an entire brigade group and its equipment from the U.K. to Singapore in nine days. But without the extensive facilities on the island, the brigade could neither come in that fast, nor move out very quickly to wherever it was needed when it arrived — and in any case it was designed to reinforce the forces stationed in the area who would respond first to the threat. British grand strategy remained heavily influenced by the current needs of the forces upholding commitments overseas the government would not relinquish. That put Singapore in a special category. Together with Aden and the U.K. itself, Singapore was designated in March 1962 as one of three tri-service hub bases from which British and friendly forces would deploy to meet contingencies on any scale.[44]

The pressure of events did not entirely derail the Sandys revolution. In addition to the unavoidable concentration on NATO, the expansion of nuclear and air forces, and the end of national service, important changes were made in the higher organisation of the armed forces themselves. These changes, pressed from 1959 by the new Chief of the Defence Staff (CDS), Lord Mountbatten, aimed to reduce the independence of the services and hopefully increase the efficiency of planning and policy decisions by concentrating power in a more centralised structure. The changes affected Singapore because Mountbatten decided the best way to proceed was by having the tail wag the dog: changes in overseas commands could be used to inspire the essential changes in the central machinery at home. As a hub command Singapore was a major target. Despite stiff service resistance Mountbatten had his way. In November 1962 the BDCCFE and the three service commanders-in-chief, with their separate chains of command, were folded into a unified Far East Command, under a single commander with authority over all three services, based in Singapore.[45]

Nevertheless, this triumph of the future only enhanced the importance of Singapore itself as a military position. Indeed, that same year no less an authority than Field Marshal Montgomery, speaking in the House of Lords, noted that as the position at home and in Europe seemed stable the current threats to British interests came from overseas, especially in the Far East. The COS agreed. In January they advised the government the most likely military threats to British interests over the next decade were in Africa and Asia. But the constraints on British defence spending meant that the forces would only be strong enough to mount one major operation at a time and per year. The government noted such advice in its White Paper on defence of that year, which singled out the Far East as an area of serious instability which required a continued British military presence.[46] Despite such upheavals as the acceleration of the withdrawal from Empire, signalled in 1960 by Macmillan in his famous "winds of change" speech, the intractable problem of rising defence costs and lagging economic growth, and even major political changes in Singapore itself, the equation, into 1962, seemed to be holding fast. The U.K. intended to remain a military power in the Far East. To do that, British ground, air and naval forces needed the unfettered use of a major base at Singapore. So there they stayed.

The Growth and Use of the Base and its Impact on Singapore

The re-establishment of Singapore as a major British military base influenced the development of the island and its people in several ways. First, the British military presence and the use of the facilities became a major issue in the political transformation which took Malaya and Singapore from colonies to independent states. Second, the expansion of the facilities reached the point where the military presence became a pillar of the local economy. Finally, the use of the base made a political, diplomatic, economic, and social impact on Singapore. The first problem is so important it requires a separate discussion.* The latter problems were intertwined enough to see them here as a coherent issue. Due to the special circumstances of re-occupation and military administration Singapore by late 1946 was, as noted, all but an armed camp. By the early 1960s the presence and impact of the military forces and facilities was less overwhelming, but extensive enough that it would be fair to describe Singapore then as a garrison island. No aspect of the life of its people was untouched by the military presence.

When the first stirrings of frustration with the military presence rose in 1946, they did not go unnoticed. Presumably with the authority of the home government, Mountbatten's headquarters issued a statement which outlined why Singapore was going to remain so pivotal a base and what impact that must have on the local economy and population:

> Singapore, as the geographical hub of the Southeast Asia area, must inevitably remain a considerable military base, but the Services, fully recognizing the urgent need for accommodation, are doing their utmost to see that this commitment shall not be a burden to the people of Singapore.[47]

Singapore had to come to terms with the effect a large military base with all its personnel must have on the local economy and society. The Singapore Chamber of Commerce accepted this at its annual general meeting in March 1947, but issued its own warning. Now that the "token garrisons" of peacetime pre-war routine were to be replaced by much larger forces in larger facilities, the work required to erect then maintain these facilities, and the personnel stationed there, was bound to cause a certain problem: inflation. Military building would drive up prices for labour, contractors and matériel, for both housing and industrial work. More military families would even drive up the cost of domestic servants. If the military base was to be a fixed and massive feature in the local economy, then government and military leaders in Singapore and the U.K. must do more to make sure this helped rather than hurt the effort to revive Singapore as a trading and commercial hub.[48]

By this time the problem was being both solved but changed. Demobilisation and progress on constructing new barracks allowed the forces to release buildings, albeit never fast enough to suit anyone. But the establishment of the regional headquarters of first the RAF and Army, then in 1948 the RN, plus the deployment of both combat and support units, created a long-term demand for facilities larger than those built before the war. By 1949, with the Malayan Emergency heating up, the requirements for facilities in Singapore took firm shape. As the Army seemed destined to carry the burden of operations short of general war, its needs would determine the supporting strength required from the other services. All three services now saw Singapore as the main

---

* See Chapter 11.

administrative, supply, maintenance, transit, and recreation facility for the region. For the RN and the RAF, Singapore was also an operational base for combat units. Each service took charge of expanding and maintaining its own facilities, returning most requisitioned property to the civil sector by the second half of 1948 and moving personnel into their designated areas. Sembawang again became the naval hub, the RAF spread out over the three facilities already noted, and the Army shifted its centre of gravity to the facility being developed at Pasir Panjang.[49]

1947 was the year RAF operations began in earnest. Tengah was re-opened after extensive upgrading. Jet fighter aircraft arrived that year for tests on how the facilities could be further improved to handle the most modern aircraft. By mid-1948 the peacetime establishment was complete and the Singapore airbases were home to 11 squadrons with over 100 aircraft and 8676 personnel. In June 1949 the command was upgraded to Far East Air Force (FEAF), controlling five regional head-quarters; one, AHQ Malaya, was located at Changi as well.[50] The first helicopter unit in the Far East began operating from Changi in April 1950, evacuating casualties from operations in the Emergency. Tengah was twice upgraded to handle the ever more sophisticated jet aircraft being deployed by the RAF, once from 1950–51, then from 1959 to 1961. The second upgrade cost £3 million, involved the levelling of several hills, and extended the runway to 9000 feet [2770m], producing in the end the most up-to-date RAF base outside the U.K. By that time the other airfields were also much expanded, and there were even plans to deploy the latest *Bloodhound* surface-to-air missiles for air defence. In 1962 eight RAF and two RNZAF squadrons were stationed in Singapore, under the direct operational control of 224 Group but at the disposal of FEAF for tasks ranging far beyond Singapore.[51]

The RN did not rebuild Sembawang on the same scale as the pre-war base. But once the Pacific Fleet headquarters moved to join the dockyard, the base became again in the 1950s what it was by 1939: the main operations and support base for the RN east of Suez. The floating dock, sunk again by American bombers late in the war, was salvaged, but sent home. The graving dock again hosted major vessels, supported by five smaller floating docks. Most of the substantial shore facilities were revived, then upgraded. Wholesale hiring of local labour stabilised in 1947 at a labour force of over 10,000, performing tasks ranging from major ship repairs to domestic service. Yet work outpaced resources, forcing the Admiralty to contract out repair work regularly to civil ship-yards in Singapore. Singapore found itself spared from serious cuts in RN strength and facilities after the "Sandys revolution," as the closing of facilities in Hong Kong and Ceylon left it the only possible hub for the RN to operate east of Suez. By the end of the 1950s the island hosted the only "balanced fleet" operating outside home waters, including a naval air component. Into the 1960s then, Singapore's north coast continued to be dominated, and its whole economy greatly boosted, by the naval base.[52]

The Army remained a more intrusive presence, with its facilities closer to the city itself and the fair-sized garrison more or less permanently stationed on the island. By the mid-1950s only one British infantry battalion was regularly stationed in Singapore; most personnel were from the plethora of support branches needed to maintain a Western army. The coastal artillery, partly manned by Malay soldiers, remained on Blakang Mati until 1956; Gurkha and Malay units maintained a training facility thereafter. Older facilities at Tanglin, Alexandra and elsewhere were joined in the early 1950s by the 2600-acre complex stretching from Alexandra to Clementi Roads. The WO picked up the building costs, local contractors and workers did all the work. By the middle of the decade a full-scale base, with barracks, warehouses, vehicle parks, workshops, etc. was the nerve centre of Far East Land Forces (FARELF).[53]

All three services regarded Singapore as a comfortable posting, especially by the early 1960s when a full range of amenities were available on base to supplement the charms of the city. The bases were virtually self-contained towns in themselves. The length of postings was determined by the view that operational efficiency had a minimum and maximum in this equatorial area. Without being acclimatised units and personnel would not perform at full efficiency; left here too long, their edge would dull. The Army posted personnel for three years, the RAF for two and a half. By 1959 the various bases took up 10% of the land area of the island and by the 1960s British military spending generated 25% of its GDP. Military demands for goods and services of all kinds were clearly a mainstay of the local economy.[54]

The most direct point of contact was with the local workers employed by all three services. By 1952 their combined totals exceeded 30,000, making the presence of the bases, and labour relations there, significant economic, social and political questions in Singapore. Labour relations were never dull, particularly at the naval base, but there were only two large strikes, in 1952 and 1956. Both were at the naval base, short-lived, and not more broadly political. Base employment was an important source of skills training for a developing economy. The services employed together close to 2000 skilled office workers in Singapore by 1956, and the naval base trained all manner of shipyard workers. But the dominant theme of labour relations was an endemic tug-of-war. The unions strove to improve conditions and keep full employment. The military authorities kept a watchful eye out for communist influence, strove to cut costs, and issued periodic warnings that the existence of the bases depended on reliable labour conditions. Yet into the early 1960s at least mutual dependence held fast and labour relations did not threaten the maintenance of the British bases.[55]

The three services used their facilities in Singapore extensively but not uniformly from 1947. The Army had wide-ranging responsibilities, from protecting Malaya and Singapore against a first-class enemy in a general war to assisting the civil power in maintaining law and order in Singapore itself. Fortunately the test of general war never came, but from the SEATO era ever more detailed plans and serious training envisaged deploying from Singapore units stationed in the area and Dominion reinforcements sent in. The soldiers always regarded the general war role as their prime mission. This created a bit of a tug-of-war when Malaya Command found itself on almost continuous active service from 1948 in the Malayan Emergency, a very low-level conflict. Troops did act in Singapore in support of the police in serious riots in 1950 and 1956, the second time with conspicuous success. But for most combat soldiers, Singapore was either a place to rest, be healed, train, or move through. Active service made the army the workhorse of the Far East commands. The British authorities recognised this in 1959 when they adopted the "major user principle" to streamline the control of logistics overseas. For the Far East the Army took charge, working primarily through Singapore.[56]

The RAF used Singapore as home, hotel, workshop, and combat platform. From late 1954 it took over the duty of moving personnel to and from Singapore for all three services; the RN left its vessels on station and rotated crews by flight. The airmen also saw general war as their main role, which caused an even worse clash of roles when the Emergency made extensive demands — so extensive that into 1957 RAF missions from Singapore in support of Emergency operations accounted for more activity than air transport. Detachments of heavy bombers from Bomber Command and the Dominions were regularly stationed at Singapore. Ostensibly they were to familiarise themselves with the area in case of general war, but often they too found themselves otherwise involved. But in this case the theoretical role at least did not clash with the air defence of Singapore, a duty shared from 1958 by the squadrons at Tengah with Australian squadrons stationed at Butterworth for the CSR. Squadrons from Singapore served by rotation in the Korean War. Facilities at Singapore were used extensively to support the air effort in that conflict. From 1955 Singapore was envisaged as the main base for a Commonwealth contribution to any SEATO-led deployment, with plans for the stationing of up to 500 aircraft plus American use of the base as well. The policy of stationing first-rate combat aircraft of all types was confirmed in the Sandys era. It paid off in 1962 when aircraft were flown up to Bangkok in the SEATO role to help deter an apparent threat to Thailand from its communist neighbours. For the RAF, Singapore was quite simply its all-purpose home in the Far East.[57]

The first real post-war occasion for the RN after its return to Singapore was to offer rest, refit and a hero's welcome to the gunboat HMS *Amethyst* in September 1949, on its way home after its ordeal on the Yangtze River.[58] The RN also played its role in the Emergency, operating of course from the base in Singapore. The Sembawang base acted as the main support base for fleet units operating in the Korean War, during which its Fleet Air Arm aircraft facility hummed with activity. The aircraft station was mothballed after 1955; in 1956, a newspaper report even suggested the naval base might be replaced by a facility at Labuan, on the grounds it was now too easy to neutralise its narrow approach lanes using modern weapons such as minelaying aircraft and submarines. This was soon dismissed, and by the end of the decade the Sembawang base hosted a Far East Fleet powerfully equipped for its perennial mission to keep the sea lanes and trade routes open. By 1961 the fleet boasted on station an aircraft carrier, commando/helicopter carrier, escort vessels, a submarine squadron, and its aircraft were ostentatiously equipped to deliver nuclear weapons.[59] All this force was needed to handle the largest command area in the RN, operating from the largest base outside the U.K. As noted, when put to the test in the Persian Gulf area in 1961, the fleet and its base proved more than adequate. Looking back from 1962, the decision to re-establish a major base at Singapore seemed more than vindicated — given how heavily all three services were engaged in various operations in the Far East, how critical the Singapore facilities were to their efforts, and how important their presence was in developing the local economy.

Notes

1. D. Lee, *Eastward: A History of the Royal Air Force in the Far East, 1945–1972*, London, 1984, 7, 26-27; R. Tanner, *A Strong Showing: Britain's Struggle for Power and Influence in Southeast Asia 1942-1950*, Stuttgart, 1994, 70, 80.

2. *The Straits Times*, 7-13 September 1945; P. Dennis, *Troubled Days of Peace: Mountbatten and Southeast Asia Command*, Manchester, 1987, 12-14; A. Lau, *The Malayan Union Controversy*, Oxford, 1991, 98; Turnbull, 219-21.

3. Lau, 91-92; Tanner, 70.

4. Tanner, 95-96; Lee, 33, 36; Turnbull, 223-24.

5. *Straits Times*, September to December 1945; Lee, 7, 27.

6. Lee, *Eastward*, 71.

7. *Straits Times*, 9 April 1946; Lee, *Eastward*, 32-36, 74-76. The RAF obtained Changi after a long discussion with the army, who were reluctant to give it up because of its location, next to the cool breeze coming in off the Straits. Ironically, the existence of the Japanese airstrip which could readily be improved was a deciding factor!

8. *Straits Times*, 12, 14 October 1945; M.H. Murfett, *In Jeopardy: The Royal Navy and British Far Eastern Defence Policy 1945-1951*, Kuala Lumpur, 1995, 5-7, explains the distinction between an operational naval and main support base.

9. Murfett, *In Jeopardy*, 13-15.

10. Ibid, 5-7, 15-18.

11. Ibid, 31-32.

12. PRO, WO268/2, Quarterly Historical Reports, G(Ops) Branch, GHQSEALF, October to December 1946, DCSEA minutes, 7th meeting, 9 December 1946; *Straits Times*, 21, 29 June, 11 July, 8 August, 10 December 1946; Lee, *Eastward*, 8-11.

13. PRO, WO268/2, Quarterly Historical Report, G (Ops) Branch, GHQSEALF, October to December 1946, DCSEA minutes, 8th meeting, 21 December 1946; WO268/693, Quarterly Historical Report, HQ Singapore District, July to December 1946; Lee, *Eastward*, 85. Maj.-Gen. Cox blamed the troops' apparent low morale primarily on being forced to wear five different types of uniforms, therefore losing uniformity and esprit de corps. The evidence of his own report among others suggests the slow pace of demobilisation and being forced to live in tents and other temporary quarters were far more important causes. As it was troop strength in Singapore was cut in half during 1946, making such problems clearly temporary.

14. P. Darby, *British Defence Policy East of Suez 1947-1968*, London, 1973, 44-45.

15. PRO, DEFE5/4, COS(47)99(O), 7 May 1947; Darby, 10-11, 25; Tanner, 128-29; Murfett, *In Jeopardy*, 65; Royal Institute of International Affairs (RIIA), *Collective Defence* *in Southeast Asia*, London, 1955, 33-34; J. Keay, *The Last Post: The End of Empire in the Far East*, London, 1997, 243.

16. C. J. Bartlett, *The Long Retreat: A Short History of British Defence Policy 1945-1970*, London, 1972, 14; Murfett, *In Jeopardy*, 100.

17. PRO, DEFE5/3, COS(47)5(O)Final, 23 January 1947; see above, ch. 6.

18. PRO, DEFE5/3, COS(47)5(O)Final, 23 January 1947; WO268/2, Quarterly Historical Reports, G(Ops) Branch, GHQSEALF, October to December 1946, Minutes, DCSEA 7th meeting, 9 December 1946; Darby, 32; Murfett, *In Jeopardy*, 38.

19. PRO, DEFE5/1, COS(47)9, 18 January 1947; WO268/2, Quarterly Historical Reports, G(Ops) Branch, GHQSEALF, October to December 1946; DEFE5/5, COS(47)167(O), 13 August 1947; Murfett, *In Jeopardy*, 49. Interestingly, the COS agreed there was still a use for coast defence artillery until more effective weapons became available, and Singapore remained vulnerable to the threat of hit and run attack from the sea which led to guns being deployed there in the first place. As a result Singapore retained five 6" guns and eleven 6 pounders: COS(47)181(O), 29 August 1947. Coastal artillery was declared obsolete and retired in 1956.

20. PRO, DEFE5/5, COS(47)161(O), 11 August, COS(47)165(O), 14 August 1947; Murfett, *In Jeopardy*, 46-49, 66-68.

21. PRO, WO268/2, Quarterly Historical Reports, G (Ops) Branch, GHQSEALF, October to December 1946; DEFE5/5, CCOS(47)161(O), 11 August 1947; Murfett, *In Jeopardy*, 48-49, 56-57.

22. PRO, WO268/2, Quarterly Historical Reports, G(Ops) Branch, GHQSEALF, October to December 1946; DEFE5/4, COS(47)99(O), 7 May, COS(47)101(O), 15 May 1947; *Straits Times*, 24 April, 28 May 1946.

23. Murfett, *In Jeopardy*, 75-79.

24. Ibid, 102-04.

25. PRO, DEFE5/4, COS(47)106(O), 16 May, COS(47)108(O), 21 May 1947, indicate the WO was aware the loss of the Indian Army would abort any hope of reinforcing Southeast Asia in a general war; Murfett, *In Jeopardy*, 120, 122, 125-136.

26. Murfett, *In Jeopardy*, 137-44.

27. Ibid, 153; Bartlett, 54, placed more emphasis on Dominion lobbying in working out the ANZAM arrangement.

28. Murfett, *In Jeopardy*, 144-45, 154-55.

29. Ibid, 35, 86-97, 118-19, 150-54.

30. Darby, 14-22.

31. Dockrill, 25-26, 45-46; Darby, 47.

32. Darby, 49-55; Tanner, 252; Bartlett, 87.

33. Darby, 61-64; RIIA, 144-45; Dockrill, 55; *Straits Times*, 8 December 1954; Chin K.W., *The Defence of Malaysia and Singapore: The Transformation of a Security System 1957-1971*, Cambridge, 1984, 39.

34. RIIA, xi-xii, 33, 145, 160; Dockrill, 55; Darby, 64; Lee, 161-62; H.B. Eaton, *Something Extra: 28 Commonwealth Brigade 1951-1974*, Durham, 1993, 159-61, 227.

35. M. Carver, *Tightrope Walking: British Defence Policy Since 1945*, London, 1992, 44.

36. W.S. Lucas, *Divided We Stand: Britain, the U.S. and the Suez Crisis*, London, 1991, is the best discussion of the Suez Crisis.

37. Johnson, 51.

38. Dockrill, 68; Bartlett, 137; Carver, 66; Darby, 118-19.

39. Darby, 68, 84, 121, 129-30; RIIA, 152-53, 158; Dockrill, 70, 82.

40. Darby, 112.

41. Darby, 88-92, 151-55, 175, 203; Dockrill, 127; Lee, *Eastward*, 163-64, rightly points out how SEATO plans came to rely on airlifted reinforcements for any major deployment, especially as RAF capabilities grew. But planners did not agree that this made forces in the region unnecessary — and of course the base into which reinforcements would fly was Changi.

42. Jackson, 174; Darby, 163-64, 175.

43. Darby, 263-65.

44. Bartlett, 162, 181-82; Keay, 187; Darby, 203, 211-12, 263-65, 276.

45. Johnson, xi, 74-76. Far East Command headquarters was located at Phoenix Park.

46. Keay, 184; Darby, 214-18.

47. *Straits Times*, 21 June 1946.

48. *Straits Times*, 29 March 1947.

49. *Straits Times*, 10 December 1946, 4 March 1948; Murfett, *In Jeopardy*, 154.

50. Lee, *Eastward*, 82-83, 86-87, 93.

51. Lee, *Eastward*, 124, 126, 150, 184-89; *Straits Times*, 15 September, 13 October 1959, 23 August 1961; Darby, 211-12. AHQ Malaya was disbanded in August 1957 when Malaya achieved independence, and replaced by 224 Group. Developments in aircraft technology outpaced airbase expansion, forcing combat aircraft to use the longer runway at Paya Lebar civil airport in the late 1950s. This forced the RAF to upgrade Tengah again.

52. *Straits Times*, 24 October 1952, 20 February, 1 October 1958, 15 March 1960, 31 May 1961; Darby, 197, 278; Murfett, *In Jeopardy*, 68-69.

53. Straits Times, 19 September 1949; R. Clutterbuck, *Conflict and Violence in Singapore and Malaysia 1945–1983*, Singapore, 1984, 117; Gabriel G. Thomas, "Fortress: A Military History of Blakang Mati Island," National University of Singapore, Unpublished Honours Thesis, 1997, 63. An important legacy of the establishment of this large facility around Pasir Panjang is what was then a canteen for base personnel but is now Singapore's only surviving civilised drinking establishment: the legendary *Colbar*.

54. Lee, *Eastward*, 177-82; Bartlett, 162; Clutterbuck, 335; D. Hawkins, *The Defence of Malaysia and Singapore: From AMDA to ANZUK*, London, 1972, 10.

55. *Straits Times*, 22, 24, 29 December 1952, 3, 18 January, 6 October 1953, 18 October, 13 November 1954, 10 August, 27 October 1955, 27 January, 2 February, 19, 28 September, 28 November 1956, 31 May 1961.

56. PRO, WO268/693, Quarterly Reports, HQ Singapore District, July to December 1946; *Straits Times*, 26 February 1953; Clutterbuck, 72-73, 123, 126, 129-35; Chin, 39; Johnson, 71.

57. Lee, *Eastward*, 96, 115, 128-30, 150-51, 190; Darby, 83, 230; *Straits Times*, 24 March 1948, 11-12 February 1955.

58. *Straits Times*, 15 September 1949. The best account of the *Amethyst* crisis is M.H. Murfett, *Hostage on the Yangtze*, Annapolis, 1991.

59. Darby, 197; *Straits Times*, 9 July 1955, 5 January 1956, 15 February, 26 August, 1 October 1958, 16 June 1959, 15 March 1960, 31 May 1961.

11
End of Empire: From Union to Withdrawal

T he British military presence in Singapore did not depend on British defence policy and grand strategy alone. British authorities never overlooked the fact that major changes in the political status of Singapore and its neighbours were bound to have great influence on whether the bases could, even should, be maintained. Another tug-of-war emerged in this sphere, as British desires to oversee political change floated uneasily with British determination to maintain effective control over a strategic position as vital as Singapore. Nationalist aspirations, communal friction, geography, money, and overlapping policy goals all raised the question of whether Singapore could remain a British military base even as it and its neighbours achieved self-government or more. Ironically, the final political upheaval underlined how wise it was to maintain strong British forces in such a well-established base, yet at the same time sped up the political changes which made its survival only a matter of time.

From Union to Confrontation

When the British returned to Singapore and Malaya in 1945 they no longer expected to remain indefinitely as the Imperial power. To the extent that there was a long-range vision, the ultimate intention was to bring the area towards self-government, preferably in friendly and profitable association with the U.K. From there, the questions began. How long would/should this process take? In the eyes of most British officials, it should be longer rather than shorter — and whenever the British finally did transfer power, it should be to friendly local authorities ready to remain within the Empire/Commonwealth and preserve British interests. Most of all, what would/should the relationship between Singapore and the mainland become? The British official mind began working on the problems in 1943, determined to stay ahead of or at least in step with any local pressures for change.[1] From the beginning, the issue of defence was a central feature of the discussion.

The CO took the lead in proposing plans for political change and their early views were heavily influenced by the belief that the hopeless tangle of administrations in the area before 1941 made the defence of Singapore more difficult. Ministers and service advisers agreed that defence would be bolstered by merging the Malay states, plus Penang and Melaka, into some form of union. But they disagreed about whether or not including Singapore in any union was strategically imperative or would also bolster defence. In the end the plan to construct a Malayan Union excluded Singapore, which became a separate Crown Colony when the Union was proclaimed in April 1946. Defence was a factor, the COS arguing that control of the base facilities must be kept as tightly in British hands as possible.[2] But a more important factor was communal friction.

It was undeniable that against any external enemy the physical defence of Malaya and Singapore was indivisible; after 1941–42, that was a settled issue. But the plan to form a Union raised grave internal questions such as the place of the Sultans, the balance of population and therefore power between the Malay and Chinese populations, and the social / economic relationship between Singapore and the peninsula. In the end the British planners decided that the addition of the large urban population of Chinese in Singapore plus the granting of citizenship to qualified residents in the new Union would provoke an unmanageable Malay backlash, in fear of losing political as well as economic control of their own country. This was the main reason Singapore was excluded; the desire to maintain tight control of the bases acted as further impetus.[3] But this raised the question of the long-term future of Singapore. Would it be possible to maintain a cohesive defence if politically the neighbours went in different directions?

The Malay reaction to the whole plan made the issue even more complicated. The Union plan was a shot of adrenalin in the arm for Malay nationalism, which emerged for the first time as a major organised political force. The political voice became the United Malay's National Organisation (UMNO), launched in 1946 with the first task of scuttling the Union plan. It succeeded, forcing the British to scrap the Union and replace it in 1948 with a looser Federation of Malaya. The British completely misjudged the impact of their wartime defeat and the Japanese Occupation on Malay thinking and underestimated the strength of the desire to end colonial control and achieve political independence.[4] The merging of the states into the Federation made *merdeka* a matter of time. Singapore's exclusion cast an ominous shadow on the future. The two neighbours were inter-dependent for defence and economic growth, but the successful management of communal politics and communist violence could be undone by the Singapore question. Communist strategy only made the problem worse.

In June 1948 the MCP changed policy and launched a new armed struggle in an attempt to drive the British out of Malaya by a campaign of terror in the countryside. The campaign to spark an urban revolution in Singapore moved into the background as a related but not coordinated struggle. Nearly all communists and their supporters were Chinese, which only exacerbated the friction between the communities. The communist onslaught stopped discussion of a proposal for a merger between Singapore and the Federation — raised in Singapore — for fear this would strengthen the communist position by expanding their Chinese power base, and thus aggravate race relations. Yet it also convinced the British that in order to prevent a communist takeover in either Malaya or Singapore the political leaders and security forces in both must work in close coordination.[5] A State of Emergency was declared in both areas that month, launching a counterinsurgency campaign which dragged on officially for twelve years.

The Emergency proved in the end to be the most successful counterinsurgency war waged by a Western country after World War II. But the single most important reason the victory was won was the British decision to bring the people of Malaya in as real partners in the war against the communists by accelerating the granting of political independence. That gave the inhabitants a direct and personal stake for which to fight.[6] Militarily, Singapore and its forces were an indispensable asset in Emergency operations. Singapore was a very secure rear base from which the Army sent combat units forward, the RN patrolled the coasts, and the RAF mounted an intense campaign ranging from heavy bomber attacks to aerial photography to moving troops in and casualties out of remote jungle areas by helicopter. At its height the Emergency pinned down over two divisions of British and Commonwealth troops, all dependent on the lifeline through Singapore. The British and Gurkha troops were all but invulnerable to communist subversion. Communist subversion, agitation and political warfare increased in Singapore from 1954, but was not coordinated with MCP operations and did not threaten the bases.[7] But it did underline the point that politically Singapore was part of the problem, not the solution, in the Emergency.

The emergence of a political alliance in 1952 forged by UMNO, now led by Tunku Abdul Rahman, and Chinese and Indian parties laid the basis for a political power bringing the races together and staunchly opposing the communists. That made it possible for the British to consider the transfer of real power. But it also aggravated the question of the place of Singapore. A compromise over citizenship for non-Malays in a future Malaya kept the alliance together and helped weaken the communists. The addition of the large Chinese population of Singapore seemed likely to threaten that tenuous bond and increase the communist menace to both areas — not least because of the upsurge in frustration, protest and violent agitation in the Chinese community in Singapore over colonial government policies. By 1956 the sophisticated counterinsurgency strategy developed by the British made the question of military victory a matter of time. That of course increased the importance of political problems, a fact underlined by the Tunku in a trip to London that year to press for the earliest possible transfer of power. In these talks all parties agreed independence must come in 1957 but that it was very difficult to separate the problems of internal and external security for Malaya and Singapore combined.[8] The threat really seemed to be a blend of both.

That conclusion was borne out by talks over the future of Singapore, which began in earnest with the election of the first local Chief Minister, David Marshall, in 1955. Marshall found himself caught between forces pulling in different directions. The demand for self-government was now very strong in Singapore. But the British insisted that the communists, now operating covertly, remained too much of a threat to hand over responsibility for internal security to a local government. They were in no mood to take chances with the security of the bases. The failure of talks on this issue in April 1956 helped provoke the severe riots in October which required the army to intervene. These riots were seen as communist-inspired, which reinforced the concerns of British and Malayan leaders over instability in Singapore and what ripple effects it might cause. That jeopardised the position of the People's Action Party (PAP), now emerging as a strong political challenger to Marshall, dedicated to a merger of Singapore and the mainland, but seen as heavily compromised by communist penetration.[9]

As if things were not complicated enough, the Malayan government-in-waiting regarded SEATO with suspicion as an organisation likely to compromise Malaya by dragging it into Cold War confrontation, especially with China. The Tunku made it clear that while he welcomed the help of British and Commonwealth forces in the Emergency, he would be less happy if after independence they undertook SEATO deployments from Malaya because Malaya did not intend to join SEATO. That made Singapore even more important as the position from which any deployment against a major external threat must be made. The strategy was to defend Singapore as far north as possible, and the CSR was dragged into the Emergency, not sent to Malaya because of it. The 28th Commonwealth Brigade remained in Malaya, but planned and trained to move into any SEATO role through Singapore. This only helped convince the British not to bend on the terms for self-government for Singapore. A disgusted Marshall resigned in June 1956, declaring that self-government for Singapore was vetoed in the interests of SEATO and broader British defence policy. This was true enough to be uncomfortable, as one British response to Marshall's resignation was to insist that on broader strategic grounds, "We need Singapore now more than ever."[10] That left the British in an intricate position in late 1956. The Emergency must be finished once and for all, in cooperation with a soon to be independent Malaya. A new defence agreement must be concluded with that new state, to allow British and Commonwealth forces to continue to deter external threats as well as operate against the Communist Terrorists (CTs). And a new political framework must be found to accommodate three things: the political aspirations of Singapore; British, Malayan and Singaporean desires to defeat any communist upheaval in Singapore; and the British desire to maintain unfettered use of the bases in Singapore.

The intention to reduce the number of overseas bases but maintain overseas commitments, which Sandys confirmed in 1957, only made it more important for the British to retain full use of Singapore and work out a sensible agreement with Malaya. The common interest in defeating the CTs and maintaining close ties brought the British and Malayans together on the main points. Malaya achieved *merdeka* in August 1957. In October a new defence agreement was reached, one which made it possible to maintain British and Commonwealth forces in Malaya even though it did not join SEATO. The Anglo-Malayan Defence Agreement (AMDA), to which Australia and New Zealand "associated themselves," used tortuous language to balance the new Malayan government's need for help in defence against its sensitivity to criticism over the colonial power keeping its forces in the country. Privately both parties saw the agreement as a mechanism by which the Emergency could be won and the British gradually disengage, leaving behind a stable and secure Malaya. The base in Singapore made it possible for the British and the Dominions to juggle AMDA and SEATO and leave their forces in place, thanks to an ambiguous clause regarding the redeployment of units based in Malaya.[11]

Things did not go so smoothly in the talks on the future of Singapore. The British needed Singapore so much for their broader strategy, and had such reservations about its internal stability, that they resisted any idea of granting genuine independence to the island by itself. The breakthrough came with an agreement to form a seven-member Internal Security Council to oversee that task: three British members, three Singapore members, and the member with the casting vote from the Federation government in Malaya. That acknowledged the indivisibility of the security problem for the neighbours and led to an agreement in April 1957 to grant Singapore self-government by 1959. The British would retain full control of defence and the bases, while internal security would be shared with the Federation, to contain communism. The British could use their troops and suspend the new constitution if it became necessary to maintain order. The PAP came out in favour of the agreement. It argued that British concern for the bases made full independence unlikely unless Singapore merged with Malaya, and Singapore needed Federation help in order to strengthen the anti-communist front, so shared control of internal security was necessary. Lee Kuan Yew took the decisive step forward in his political career by challenging David Marshall to a by-election on the self-government plan and winning.[12] All this made it possible to bring arrangements for defence against internal and external threats for both Malaya and Singapore back into some sort of harmony.

There were limits to what could be done. Malaya was now an independent state with its own agenda; Singapore remained a British possession, about to become largely self-governing. These limits were exposed by the controversy over Sandys' public statements about deploying nuclear weapons as Malaya celebrated *merdeka*. Tunku Abdul Rahman objected to the deployment of any weapons for SEATO purposes, but Singapore leaders acknowledged the British could well deploy the weapons in Singapore if they chose as there were no restrictions on the use of the bases. This increased the debate in Malaya over how British bases in Singapore really fitted into their new situation, especially with regard to a possible merger. Yet even as Singapore leaders such as Lee Kuan Yew hoped to outflank British qualms by arranging a merger, political tensions in Singapore hurt their efforts.[13]

Lee Kuan Yew adopted the strategy of working with the communists in order to win independence, looking to defeat them in turn when the time was ripe — better known as "riding the tiger." This high-risk approach kept the Tunku reluctant to entertain a merger for fear of adding to Malaya's own communist and race relations problem. In 1959 the PAP won a general election and Lee Kuan Yew became Prime Minister of the new self-governing Singapore. He supported British arrangements to expand the bases and adopted an agenda crowned by two items: a merger with Malaya, to give Singapore the political depth to crush the communists and the economic and military space to survive and thrive; and internal stability, in part to keep the British comfortable with the commitment to maintain large bases in Singapore. Lee regarded the British presence as essential to make Singapore more secure and boost its economy during the years of transition needed to bring about a successful merger.[14]

The shared security problem helped bridge the gap between the governments in Kuala Lumpur and Singapore. The successful ending of the Emergency in 1960 gave the Tunku some room to reconsider. Lee Kuan Yew was already on record as envisaging an eventual British withdrawal from Singapore "in the long run" after a successful merger, and with due notice. The Singapore Infantry Regiment (SIR), formed in 1957 in relation to the agreement on self government for Singapore, was seen as one part of a Singapore contribution to a future joint defence force with Malaya; the Royal Malayan Navy (RMN) already operated out of a base in Woodlands, next to the RN facility. All that helped in one direction.[15] Serious political tensions in Singapore in 1961, as the tiger bucked hard, helped in another. The Tunku now concluded that it was more dangerous to leave Singapore out than take it in. The two leaders then agreed on the basis for discussion for a merger: Malaysia, bringing Malaya, Singapore and the British territories in Borneo into one state. The British very much supported the concept in principle, and why not? Malaysia might be better able to defend itself, reducing the strain on them, and would help solve the issue of what to do with the Borneo territories. Above all it might at last repair the damage done by politically separating the economically and militarily interdependent Singapore and Malaya, with a strong anti-communist federal government helping Lee Kuan Yew finish off the tiger. The Tunku went to London to discuss all these matters, including what the status of the British bases and forces in Singapore would become in a new Malaysia.[16]

The parties reached an agreement on the base question and extending AMDA to cover Singapore in November 1961, one they deliberately made ambiguous. It was confirmed in spring 1962 by the ANZAM partners. Once Malaysia was formed, control of internal security would pass to the federal government. The British bases and forces would remain, but the British and the Tunku said different things about who would decide how the bases might be used, allowing them to keep everybody guessing. Nevertheless the Tunku and Lee Kuan Yew agreed that for the time being the British military must stay, to help stabilise the transition. On the other hand, the combination of politics in Singapore and the emergence of Malaysia made British public and official discussion about the future of the base in Singapore more pointed. The FO told the COS that year it estimated political conditions would enable the British to keep the base for "at least another seven years." Talk of shifting the base to Australia surfaced again. The creation of Malaysia was clearly going to force the issue and settle the military status of Singapore once and for all.[17] In the process, the plan to form the new state provoked an unfriendly reaction which put the British military presence in Singapore to its last and greatest test of the post-war era.

Tunku Abdul Rahman and Lee Kuan Yew campaign for merger and Malaysia

The plan to unite Malaya, Singapore and the British territories in Borneo received mixed reactions from the neighbours. The Indonesian government pursued a cautious policy at first. In public it stated that all of Borneo should naturally join Indonesia, but it would be willing to test the wishes of the people concerned with a plebiscite. Quietly, it organised fifth columns in Brunei, Sabah, Sarawak, and Singapore. In Brunei strong opposition to joining Malaysia sparked an armed revolt led by the People's Party in December 1962. The rebels expected to win rapid popular support in Brunei, Sabah and Sarawak.[18] Instead they faced what must have been the most effective military operation mounted by British forces in this century.

The British were aware that trouble was brewing in Brunei, but the rebellion did achieve tactical surprise as the intelligence services were able to provide only very short notice of the revolt. Nevertheless, the newly consolidated Far East Command reacted with impressive speed. Plans to respond by airlifting in forces from Singapore, codenamed *Ale*, were fully prepared. When the call came on 8 December, Gurkha companies were deplaning in Brunei within hours. 2000 troops from Singapore were on the ground within 60 hours. This led a 12-day airlift and the despatch of Royal Marine Commandos and their helicopter carrier. On 19 December the formidable General Walter Walker took command as Commander British Forces Borneo. By Christmas Day he had three infantry battalions, two Royal Marine Commandos, naval and helicopter support, operating under joint command, supported by the unified headquarters in Singapore. The rebels were routed with little loss. This spectacular success simply could not have been achieved without the facilities, forces and headquarters in Singapore.[19] It allowed the Malaysia project to proceed, albeit the Sultan of Brunei in the end decided to opt out. But it also provoked an Indonesian response which led to open if undeclared war.

In January 1963 the Indonesian government started to attack the Malaysia project in public. In February President Sukarno formally and bombastically declared that Indonesia opposed Malaysia and would not allow it to be formed. This set off a diplomatic dance over the next few months in which the Tunku succeeded in annoying all other interested parties, from Singapore, the U.K., the Philippines, and Indonesia, by swaying from one arrangement to another. Finally, a UN-sponsored plebiscite confirmed the wish of the majority in Sabah and Sarawak to join Malaysia; the new state was formed in September, automatically extending the AMDA agreement to cover the Borneo territories. As part of the campaign to pressure the Tunku, Indonesian armed men began in April to launch harassing raids across the border in Borneo. In response to the launching of Malaysia, Indonesian regular soldiers joined raiding parties which sought to penetrate deep into Sabah and Sarawak. The war known as *Konfrontasi* or "Confrontation," a term chosen by the Indonesian government, was underway.[20] For the next three years the Indonesians tried to prevent the consummation of Malaysia, at least in Borneo, by a combination of diplomatic and political pressure, threats and armed attacks by land, sea and air, ranging from small parties to groups of several hundred men. The Confrontation stretched from Borneo through Singapore to the peninsula itself. In every sense, Singapore was at the very centre of the whole struggle.

As early as February 1963 Indonesian bomber aircraft started what became an on-again off-again pattern by flying menacingly towards Singapore, forcing RAF fighters to scramble. Police rounded up over 100 suspected Indonesian agents in Singapore in the following months. At a tense moment in the diplomatic duel in July, Sukarno singled out the British military presence in Singapore as proof Malaysia was being manipulated for Western interests. Singapore was thus from the start not only the main support base for operations in Borneo but a front-line target in its own right. While a nerve-wracking war developed in Borneo, a war of jungle infiltration, raids and patrols between Indonesian-supported "volunteers" and mainly British forces, diplomacy could do no more than delay an escalation. Indonesia demanded the abortion of Malaysia; Malaysia demanded a full Indonesian withdrawal from its Borneo states. In the summer of 1964 the Indonesians ostentatiously built up forces in the Riau Islands and Sumatra, making threats about Singapore and the peninsula.[21] From August, they struck.

On 17 August an Indonesian raiding force landed in Johore, the troops told by their high command the "people" would rally to the cause of Indonesia upon their arrival. The first attack on Singapore came five days later, when a raiding party shot up Esso's island petroleum bunkering station. The threat increased on 2 September when the Indonesians dropped raiders by parachute into Johore. From August 1964 through March 1965 no less than 41 incidents involving infiltrators were recorded in Singapore and on the peninsula. A total of 142 Indonesians were killed in these actions. Singaporean fishing boats were seized by Indonesian gunboats; Indonesian saboteurs set off bombs in Singapore. All armed forces in Singapore and Malaysia, including the CSR, were put on war alert, and serious reinforcements were sent in: the RN's newest fleet carrier, HMS *Eagle*, *Javelin* fighter aircraft, *Bloodhound* Mark II surface-to-air missiles, even nuclear-capable V bombers from Bomber Command. Indonesian anti-aircraft units in the Riau Islands began firing on British aircraft in March 1965, followed by a ban on overflying. The cat-and-mouse game in the air continued, but Singapore was not attacked. A significant moment did occur in late May when a platoon of the SIR was sent to deal with a platoon of 25 Indonesian regulars holing up in an old Japanese-built bunker on the mainland, just across the strait from Changi. Unfortunately the dug-in Indonesians shot up the Singaporean troops badly enough that air strikes and reinforcements from the Malay Regiment and the police were needed to overcome them.[22]

While Borneo always remained the main theatre of the military Confrontation, Singapore was thus a very active combat zone at the peak of the struggle. There was of course no popular rallying to the invaders' cause and the infiltrating parties were all in the end rounded up. But the operations, and the scale of British reinforcements for the Confrontation as a whole, made Singapore once again a hive of military activity. The British government, supported by Malaysia and the Dominions, decided that a massive show of force was the best way to intimidate the Indonesians from making even more ambitious attacks, especially near Singapore. V bombers, "much of the strategic reserve," and over 25% of the RN brought the number of British personnel committed to the Far East to over 60,000 by 1966, all coming through Singapore. From November 1964 to October 1965 FEAF flew 200,000 men back and forth to Borneo and flew in 10,000 tons of supplies, nearly all from Singapore. Maintaining this deployment raised the expenditure on Far East Command from £70 million in 1964 to £250 million in 1966. Quite simply, without the Singapore base and forces the British-led forces could not have prevailed in Borneo, as they did by mid-1966.[23]

Politically, just as in the Emergency, Singapore became part of the problem — to say the least. The merger was a contract made by perceived necessity more than by conviction from the heart. Even without the immediate stress of Confrontation it would have been a challenge to fit urban Chinese-dominated Singapore into rural Malay-dominated Malaysia. Confrontation exposed the fault lines very rapidly. Singapore's government felt its trade and security were so much at risk that at first it tried to keep a low profile in the dispute. This of course upset the federal government. Indonesian provocations in and around Singapore produced a harder line and more Singapore-Malaysia solidarity in 1964,[24] but other problems were now getting worse. Malays in Singapore first supported the PAP in elections in 1963, but this provoked a backlash by UMNO which stirred up Malay demands for the same privileges their kinsmen received in Malaysia, plus resentment over many PAP plans for change and development. Lee Kuan Yew resisted federal government policies favouring the Malays and pressed hard for the common market promised as part of the merger. The PAP then ventured unsuccessfully into federal politics, which led both Malay and Chinese leaders on the mainland to conclude that it intended to become the main voice for the urban Chinese community — which would jeopardise the alliance between UMNO and the Malaysian Chinese that was seen as the basis of communal harmony. All these problems, helped on by Indonesian troublemaking, sparked off vicious race riots in Singapore in August 1964. These very riots in fact persuaded the Indonesian government to launch its raids on Singapore and the peninsula, to stir the trouble. Lee Kuan Yew and the Tunku worked hard to contain the violence and calm tempers, but the damage was done. The blunt fact was that Singapore and Malaysia were simply politically incompatible.[25]

The British regarded this friction as a potential disaster and tried to help resolve it, but their efforts were seen by the Malaysian government as favouring Singapore. By June 1965 there were serious concerns that Malaysian authorities might try to move against the PAP government in Singapore. Tempers were so high that the Tunku concluded the only way to avoid civil war was to expel Singapore from the Federation. This unilateral decision seriously upset the British, who after all were defending a Malaysia which was formed primarily as a means to bring Malaya and Singapore together. Singapore became an independent republic on 9 August 1965, amid high military alert and general tension. This was a serious political defeat for Lee Kuan Yew, who now faced the challenge of making the tiny island state with no natural resources a viable country.[26] It was also a major headache for the British.

Despite the common bonds of an ongoing Confrontation with Indonesia and economic interdependence, Kuala Lumpur and Singapore could not remain in step. This raised an obvious question: just how absolute was the very basis of AMDA, the assumption that the defence of Malaya and Singapore was indivisible? As AMDA underpinned the bases in Singapore, the whole complicated issue of whether or not the British should stay, and on what terms, was now reopened. In fact British forces now had no legal status in Singapore at all. This did not affect ongoing operations in support of the Confrontation. Singapore and Malaysia still needed British help to persuade their giant neighbour to accept defeat; British policy still sought to ensure friendly and stable authority in old colonies before any definitive withdrawal. But Sukarno was removed from power in 1966 and the "war" was formally ended by his successors with the Bangkok Agreement of August 1966. The Malaysian government was already pressing for British forces to withdraw from Borneo as soon as possible.[27] The Singapore government needed to work out new military relationships with both Malaysia and the British. And by now voices within the British government and high command supported growing calls from public opinion at large that it might be time to come home. The British bases in Singapore and the forces deployed there helped far more than hurt the development of an independent and secure Malaysia, and did not cause the expulsion of Singapore. But neither could they prevent it, or provide any other political solution. Victory in the Confrontation vindicated the defence policy that placed such emphasis on Singapore, but political changes there and in the U.K. cut the ground out from under that policy. The lack of any visible external threat plus the new political landscape left *all* principals wondering whether the British military should stay in Singapore much longer.

Withdrawal: End of an Era

When the Labour Party returned to power in the U.K. in 1964, it brought to government a faction which believed a contraction of British defence policy was long overdue. But the Prime Minister, Harold Wilson, and the Minister of Defence, Denis Healey, strongly disagreed. Wilson told his Cabinet in November 1964 that he regarded the maintenance of a broader military role, especially in the Far East, as an "article of faith." For several reasons — to uphold the Commonwealth and keep it friendly, stable and under British lead, to protect British trade, to bolster the "special relationship" with the U.S., to help preserve stability in general in tense times — Wilson and Healey tried hard to preserve the "east of Suez" military commitments.[28] Their resistance helped make matters worse when political and economic pressures finally made it impossible for the British to maintain those commitments. The ensuing shift in policy brought a chapter in Singapore's military history to an end in a conclusion which reared up over the island as a potential disaster — but in the end passed off as an anti-climax.

From the start Wilson and Healey pursued a defence policy which in retrospect seemed bound to fail because its two prime objectives were contradictory: to preserve the "east of Suez" role, but to cut defence spending overall, to the tune of £2 billion in five years. Initially and in the face of some opposition within their own party they hoped to do this by reducing the NATO role and replacing some expensive forces with new equipment. In particular Healey hoped the long-range *F111* multi-role aircraft could replace the RN's fleet carriers. But only about half the required cuts could be made by equipment reductions and replacements; the rest would have to be found from commitments. This set off what Healey himself accepted was a "rolling review" of defence policy from the end of 1965.[29] The Singapore bases were part of this review, but did not seem in jeopardy. Singapore was assured the review was part of a broader rethinking, not in response to its expulsion from Malaysia. And in 1966 the White Paper insisted British forces must remain in the Far East because it was the area most likely to see a military threat to Commonwealth interests over the next decade. The bases in Singapore would be maintained so long as the local government welcomed their presence and the conditions of their use remained acceptable. But there was a note of warning: talks were being held with the Australians regarding a possible relocation of the British bases if conditions in Singapore changed.[30] And other problems which challenged the political, economic and military assumptions on which Wilson and Healey were operating had already arisen.

Success in the Confrontation proved the British were indeed able to project military power effectively in the Far East, but the cost of that success accelerated the desire to rethink the whole policy. From the start the armed forces seemed dangerously stretched by even this low-intensity conflict. To handle the initial coup in Brunei, the Army had to detach a signals component from the main force in Europe, British Army of the Rhine (BAOR), and alert about half the Strategic Reserve in the U.K. in case the operation dragged on. By 1964 the Army was forced to dip into the pool of combat units in the BAOR to maintain its deployment in Borneo. This was mainly because the continued deployment overseas delayed the formation of a reasonable Strategic Reserve at home. Some planners believed there was nothing wrong with shifting forces to meet immediate needs, but the COS were most reluctant to dip into BAOR and the NATO pool. At the height of Confrontation they asserted that the forces, especially the Army, were so overstretched they would not be able to respond to a major crisis anywhere else. That same year, 1966, Healey's decision to build no new aircraft carriers, and retire those now in service by the mid-1970s, provoked the COS to note that this would make it all but impossible for Far East Command to repeat the operations it was able to mount since 1961.[31] The hint from the military professionals was clear: with fewer resources, it would be militarily impossible to maintain the command in its bases in Singapore.

The government was moving in the other direction. Healey dropped expensive aircraft projects, cut the fleet carriers, reduced the nuclear submarine programme, and pushed through the decision to withdraw from Aden. The administrative changes which produced a true Ministry of Defence in 1964, bringing all three services together, only increased Treasury influence over budget considerations which were the lifeblood of defence policy. The Treasury supported the Prime Minister and Healey in their drive to find savings. Yet still the government insisted on maintaining Far East Command and the bases in Singapore. Both the junior minister for the navy and the First Sea Lord resigned in 1966 in protest at this move to cut means without cutting tasks. This did not shake the Cabinet; Wilson in particular seemed emotionally rather than analytically determined to keep the flag flying in the Far East even with less money.[32] But deeper and more momentous political changes finally did shake this house of cards.

Sustained political debate in Parliament over the future of the "east of Suez" role began as early as March 1965. Critics of Cabinet policy reflected a fairly broad spectrum of motives, suggesting public opinion was not yet ready to reach any consensus. The expulsion of Singapore from Malaysia started fresh speculation on whether the region could and should fend for itself militarily. Early in 1966 British-Malaysian talks over future defence relations led to some candid pressure from the British, unhappy over the expulsion of Singapore and keen to broker a reliable defence cooperation between their ex-colonies. This only increased speculation at home over how long the British bases could remain. But by far the most dramatic and important shift in public opinion was regarding the general orientation of British foreign policy. Macmillan's failure to gain admission to the EEC was not taken as final. To this day the British cannot make up their minds about the nature of their relationship with the rest of Europe other than that there must be a close one; but by the mid-1960s there was a definite shift in public sentiment towards exploring closer ties, especially economic ties, with the neighbours. This shift was if anything fuelled by an ambivalent reaction to the prospect of a nuclear war; if the decisive front was NATO, why bother to keep expensive forces spread out overseas? This was not a new argument, but now it was an issue being more widely discussed. The government could not run against this grain, nor did it really want to. Closer ties with Europe, especially economic ties, were a must. That could not fail to affect defence policy. Up to July 1966 Wilson and Healey continued to argue they could do it all: cut costs, get closer to Europe, maintain Far East Command. Yet already the political issue had become not whether but when British bases overseas would be closed and the forces brought home.[33]

When his own MPs debated the question of leaving the Singapore bases in June 1966, Wilson resisted the idea, arguing the Singapore government still wanted a British presence, Singapore still needed it, and the U.K. needed a friendly, secure Singapore. But the end of Confrontation, plus some ominous pressure on the pound sterling and the balance of payments, kept the issue near the top of the agenda. For starters, the return of forces from the Confrontation was accelerated. 10,000 personnel left within months; by late 1967, the ground forces in Far East Command were back to little more than the Royal Marine Commando brigade and the British component of the CSR. Meanwhile, the annual conference of the Labour Party in October 1966 called for the bases to be closed and the forces pulled out by 1970. This was pressure Wilson and Healey could not continue to keep at bay. The political bickering was noisy but in reality it was only the backdrop. The really decisive problem was the economic strain. The U.K. economy continued to struggle to maintain an overvalued currency and produce an export surplus. Its problems were much deeper than could be solved by money redirected from defence spending, but this was an obvious and dramatic target. The Singapore bases alone cost £70 million per year to maintain. It was the economic factor which forced planners to consider the future of the bases from the beginning of Healey's efforts, partly against his will.[34]

The problem the government faced by 1967 has been well summed up by Michael Dockrill: "No doubt Britain could have kept her world role indefinitely if this had been the only way of preserving her vital interests and if she had been prepared to devote more resources to the task."[35] Many within and outside the government now disagreed the U.K. needed military forces stationed east of Suez to protect its vital interests. Those interests seemed to revolve more and more around Europe. In any event the American difficulties in Vietnam seemed to offer a stark warning the U.K. could not generate the amount of power needed to cope with a really serious distant crisis. On this point Wilson and Healey were forced to agree: the U.K. could no longer afford to spend what it had been spending on the armed forces. The conclusion seemed unavoidable and this time it was approached analytically. If the bases could not be properly maintained and used effectively, then they must be dropped. In April 1967 the Cabinet decided in principle to cut Far East Command in half by 1971 and terminate it by 1975. The reasons cited were the general economic position, the new focus on Europe, and the "lesson" of Vietnam. A slightly modified decision was announced to the world in Parliament in July: Far East Command and its bases to be terminated by 1973-77, and cut in half by 1970-71. In return the government expected to save £300 million, partly by reducing the services by 75,000 men.[36]

The expected return underlined a seminal point: whether the policy revision to this point was driven entirely by the Treasury and economic pressure, as some critics charge, or whether the Treasury merely focussed a broader debate, as seems more likely, Wilson and Healey did not give up the policy of maintaining military power in the Far East until they were forced to by overriding economic concerns. The considered decision which the government reached in the summer of 1967 to withdraw in stages from Singapore was at least 11 years overdue, in retrospect. But political leaders do not have the advantage of looking back. They must look forward into the unclear future and too often they tend to postpone unwelcome controversial decisions and hope something will turn up. This was especially true regarding defence and British pretensions to remain something more than a European power. Giving up the bases seemed tantamount to giving up any claim to more than a minor world role. That seemed dangerous in some vague but deeply felt sense and, more clearly, distasteful. As long as there were no major military challenges to British interests and there was hope of a deep and enduring economic "recovery," it seemed easier to make minor adjustments and postpone irreversible decisions. But the economy did not "turn up"; instead, it forced the Labour government to accept in a haste more apparent than real what we can now see as a sensible conclusion from the withdrawal from India 20 years before. The U.K. could no longer afford to remain a major military power in the Far East. The bases in Singapore were untenable.[37]

This shift in British defence policy regarding Singapore and the region naturally aroused concern and confusion in Singapore and among other interested British allies. The parties most directly concerned were Singapore, Malaysia, Australia, New Zealand, and the U.S. By late 1965 they were all wary of future British decisions regarding Far East Command, given the growing political and economic pressures in the U.K. Wilson and Healey were urged by the Americans and Australians to maintain the British military presence. The Americans argued that SEATO would not be credible without British assistance; their concern was influenced by their now rapidly growing involvement in the war in Vietnam. The Australians insisted that their policy of forward defence, deploying forces in Southeast Asia, relied on collective security arrangements which would not work without the British bases and forces. Such pressure caused the British leaders to waver, but it was not enough to offset their own more pressing concerns. When the withdrawals at the end of Confrontation were announced in mid-1966, Healey suggested to the Australians that the British might wish to shift what forces they retained in the region to a new base in Australia, assuming Singapore would not be available much longer. The Australians reacted coolly, hoping to convince the British to persist in Singapore. That made sense to Canberra, given the Australian policy to keep all trouble as far from Australia as possible. But of course it was not enough to offset the economic crunch in British eyes. When the British informed their Western allies in April 1967 of the decision to withdraw in stages from Singapore, they could not be deflected. The Americans, worried that regional allies might lose confidence in Western resolve to maintain the SEATO commitment — despite waging a now very large war in Vietnam which they saw as part of that mission — settled for urging Wilson to delay the decision as long as he could.[38]

The British decision was of course of even greater importance to Singapore and Malaysia. The discussions which produced it set off a complicated triangle of defence relations to sort out. In that triangle there was one constant: all three partners envisaged a British withdrawal from Singapore some time in the 1970s. In fact, Lee Kuan Yew found it expedient to assure the Indonesian government that the British would leave in ten years. But while the political opposition in Singapore called for a full and early British withdrawal, the government wanted the whole process to be much more careful. On the one hand the Singapore government asserted itself. It noted the British bases were not a sovereign enclave and claimed the right to control how they were used. Lee Kuan Yew expressed reservations about the usefulness of SEATO and the future of British policy. On the other hand it was impossible to settle the issue of the British presence without resolving the problem of the defence relationship with Malaysia. The Separation Agreement stipulated that the defence of the two parties was indivisible, and vaguely declared that for the moment the arrangements governing the use of the British bases would remain unchanged. The British agreed it was necessary to review the defence arrangements with a now independent Singapore and accepted the above as a basis for discussion. But they did not expect to be hurried, assuming the Singapore government still saw the British bases as a military and economic necessity and would not demand any early changes in the conditions of their use.[39] And indeed, the first problems blew up over relations with Malaysia.

As long as the Confrontation lasted, an external threat to both kept Singapore and Malaysia trying to work together — and persuaded both the British presence in Singapore remained necessary. Singapore joined the Joint Defence Council and Combined Operations Committee as a full partner, and sent 2nd SIR to Borneo. Malaysia agreed to help defend Singapore in return for facilities there. But when 2nd SIR returned in early 1966, a public argument erupted over Malaysia's desire to maintain combat units in Singapore. The waning of the Confrontation increased mutual suspicion over each others' dealings with Indonesia. Malaysian troops left Singapore, which then pulled out of the joint committees. Political friction and public emotions were too high, mutual trust too low. Together they reduced defence cooperation to little more than wary ad hoc moves by mid-1966. The rapid British reduction of forces was therefore welcomed by Malaysia regarding Borneo, but disturbing to both regarding Singapore as the British and Dominion presence now stood as the only contact point at best, or buffer at worst. Wilson tried to emphasise a distinction between reducing forces deployed for Confrontation and maintaining the bases in Singapore. But only the most delicate tightrope act now kept AMDA and the CSR alive in any form.[40] The trend was ominous enough by late 1966 to provoke a response in Singapore.

In March 1967 the Singapore government introduced national service, laying the foundation for a full-scale Singapore armed forces. In April Healey informed the Singapore government of the British decision to withdraw in stages. Soon after, a British team arrived in Singapore to discuss future assistance and the details of the transition. In June, Lee Kuan Yew went to London to take up the problem personally. While it was now clear the British would leave, the Singapore government felt it was imperative to persuade the British to proceed as slowly as possible, and to offer maximum and visible economic and military assistance to help Singapore fill the large holes that must be left. Given the stated British intention to move deliberately and the absence of any definite threat, there did not seem to be any imminent crisis. But there were many troubling uncertainties: relations with Malaysia, the need to develop a credible Singapore armed forces, and the economic impact of the withdrawal of British personnel.[41]

The British tried to be reassuring and in doing so Wilson demonstrated just how reluctant he still was to make the decision. Certainly the British would arrange to help develop and train Singapore forces. Perhaps even more important, the government also intended to maintain a part of the Strategic Reserve dedicated to operating in the region if the need arose — and therefore trained and equipped accordingly. But by now the very visible doubts in the U.K. about whether a role outside Europe was still desirable or possible were too clear for comfort. The stakes were too high. A clumsy British withdrawal might leave an economically gutted Singapore on very bad terms with its neighbours and unable yet to defend itself. Lee Kuan Yew tried hard to head this off. As the debate increased in the U.K., Lee used it to persuade the Tunku to agree they both needed the British to help manage a stable transition. The Tunku agreed not to interfere with Singapore sovereignty after the British left, and to cooperate in efforts to affect British decisions. Lee returned to the U.K. in October 1967 with more specific requests: British combat units to remain into 1975, especially those manning the air defence system; the stationing of Strategic Reserve forces, especially amphibious units, as close to Singapore as possible; help with training and equipment. That would buy Singapore the time to repair relations with Malaysia, build ties with other neighbours, revamp its economy, and build its own defence capability.[42] Unfortunately, an economic bombshell now threatened to destroy efforts by all parties to move as methodically as possible.

On 18 November 1967, after a long battle to avoid the unavoidable, the British government was forced to devalue the pound sterling. This judgement on the competitiveness of the British economy, plus the government's mishandling of the political furore which ensued, made it impossible to follow the policy of a methodical withdrawal from global military commitments. The government felt that only drastic and dramatic action would dispel the impression the British economy was in terminal decline. That meant deep cuts in government spending, including £100 million from the defence budget. Healey at first argued this could be done without changing the schedule laid down in July for withdrawal east of Suez. But the turbulent economic situation dictated otherwise. After "a month of urgent planning and abrasive argument" the COS forced the government to agree that commitments must be cut at the same pace as resources were reduced. This produced a decisive shift in policy. The writing was clearly on the wall by the turn of the year; in early January, *The Times* warned that the U.K. could no longer nursemaid Singapore indefinitely. Nevertheless, the new policy declared on 16 January 1968 was announced to the other parties concerned, not discussed with them. The Prime Minister stated that all aircraft carriers would be retired by 1971, the order for long-range *F-111* aircraft would be dropped, and all British forces would leave Malaysia and Singapore by April 1971.[43]

This was far more than just an acceleration in the schedule for withdrawal. Economic pressures forced the government to abandon a controlled withdrawal and launch a precipitate one. The most important move was the abandonment of plans to maintain a portion of the Strategic Reserve for future service in the Far East. That underlined the stark truth: the British were going to terminate their role as a military power in the Far East in three years, whether Singapore and Malaysia were stable and secure or not.[44] Lee Kuan Yew clearly understood what had happened but for once his initial reaction to a crisis was unproductive. Lee complained that he was told the schedule announced in the summer of 1967 was final and that these changes were made without any consultation. He tried to stop the changes by threatening to remove Singapore from the pound sterling trading area, boycott British goods, and even shift control of the commercial port to a Japanese firm. The problem was not the fact the British would leave but the manner and speed of their departure and the arrangements made for what would happen next. British military spending accounted for over 20% of Singapore's income and a hasty withdrawal threatened to create a mass unemployment problem. The relationship with Malaysia remained unsettled and the embryonic Singapore Armed Forces (SAF) were far from ready to take over the defence of Singapore — especially in the high-skill high-technology area of air defence. As all Lee's plans were based on a stabilising British presence during the difficult years of transition, the British change of course now forced him back to the drawing board.[45]

Lee tried to rally support from Malaysia, Australia and New Zealand to press the British to reconsider, but despite their concerns the Singaporean leader was left to press Singapore's case on his own. Lee returned to London to make counterproposals to Wilson. He asked for help to ward off any "mad dog attack," time to build up the SAF and help with its equipment and training, and above all help in developing an effective network for air defence. Overall, the Singapore leader called for a plan which would leave the British bases and forces in place a little longer, make clear and reliable arrangements to transfer equipment and expertise, and culminate in a looser arrangement which would still associate British and Commonwealth forces with the defence of Singapore. Wilson agreed to consider all these ideas, especially the need to strengthen air defence capability, and to delay the termination of Far East Command until the end of 1971. This nine-month postponement stemmed from Lee's belief that the driving force behind the decision to withdraw was pressure from within the Labour Party's own ranks, rather than dire economic straits. A general election would have to be held in the U.K. before the end of 1971 and the Conservatives insisted that if they regained power the decision to withdraw from the Far East would be reversed, a promise Lee took seriously. Lee turned out to be mistaken on both these points, but these were the last errors he made in facing up to Singapore's new military situation.[46]

Once the British decision had sunk in, the governments involved made increasingly pragmatic moves to cope with the change. In May 1968 the British and Singaporean governments settled the details of a package of British aid to address the transition: £50 million in cash, 25% of it an outright grant, commitments to transfer the facilities of the bases on generous terms, and significant assistance to the SAF, including the transfer of and help in operating the air defence facilities already developed, *Bloodhound* surface-to-air missiles, and *Hunter* trainer aircraft. Both parties also agreed to discuss transforming AMDA into a new arrangement which would keep the external partners involved in some way in the defence of Malaysia and Singapore. That was made possible by more realistic moves already made on bilateral cooperation between Malaysia and Singapore. The partners reaffirmed their agreement that mutual defence was "inseparable" on 21 January 1968, days after Wilson's definitive pronouncement. Defence relations were revamped by "functional co-operation." In March Malaysia and Singapore agreed to maintain a joint air defence system and use it as a basis for the rewriting of AMDA.[47] Meanwhile, the Singapore government took steps to prepare the island state to carry these new burdens.

After it regained its composure, the PAP government used the British decision to withdraw to launch what in due course became a fundamental transformation of Singapore's very structure as a state. Working on a base already prepared by the prior discussion of eventual British withdrawal, plus the establishment of national service and the SAF, the government bluntly warned the nation it must now take responsibility for its own security and this would involve sacrifice and change. To "clear the decks for action" the PAP called a general election for April 1968. Its victory paved the way for changes in economic policy, such as the tightening of government control over labour unions, which aimed to make Singapore politically stable and economically attractive. The Army was joined by an Air Force and Navy and spending on defence was tripled, reaching a level equal to 10% of the gross national product within six months.[48] Lee Kuan Yew determined to make Singapore prosperous and secure by tackling both problems head on and tying them together.

It proved more difficult to rewrite the AMDA arrangement to meet the new situation and the aims of five parties. On the one hand all agreed the defence of Malaysia and Singapore against an external foe was indivisible and concerned them all. On the other hand it was far from impossible that there might yet be trouble between Malaysia and Singapore. "Functional co-operation" did not prevent the Malaysians from taking exception to Singapore decisions to adopt a policy of "total defence," to bring in Israeli advisers to help develop it, and to buy main battle tanks. Yet the British, Australians and New Zealanders could hardly declare openly they would remain involved in order to keep the neighbours from attacking each other! Nevertheless, in June 1968 all five parties agreed in talks in Kuala Lumpur to work out a new collective security relationship — starting in the first instance with an Integrated Air Defence System (IADS) which would include British and Dominion units. But this new arrangement would be one in which the British were external partners, not principal guarantors. The change stood, and it was definitive. It also made AMDA obsolete, so Singapore and its partners moved forward to replace it by final arrangements which would end British military control of Singapore.[49]

The final arrangements emerged step by step, starting with the redeployment of British forces. Most of the naval dockyard was handed over to Singaporean control in December 1968. Seletar was handed over in April 1969; the Singapore government wanted Changi at the same time, planning to use it as the nucleus of an aerospace industry, but the British insisted on retaining it until their final withdrawal. Far East Command opposed the rapid withdrawal, arguing three years was not long enough to train the RMAF and RSAF to take over, but their arguments were overruled. A British fighter squadron was sent out to cover Singapore while the training of the local air forces proceeded. By 1970 224 Group was gone and Tengah was nearly empty. 28th Commonwealth Brigade was redeployed to Singapore in late 1969, but by now the SEATO arrangement was virtually obsolete, superseded by the massive American intervention in Vietnam, so its future was uncertain. Partly to encourage the British, Australia and New Zealand announced in February 1969 that their forces would remain in Malaysia and Singapore beyond 1971 — but their role needed to be determined, in a full-scale review of collective security arrangements.[50] The British nibbled, but did not really bite.

The Conservative Party was indeed returned to office in the British general election of 1970, but defence policy was a non-issue. In October 1970 the new government proposed changes in the plan to withdraw from the Far East, claiming a complete withdrawal was too dangerous in this unstable area and a British presence must be maintained. But the changes fell short of what Lee Kuan Yew had hoped for, in both the numbers of troops and the terms on which they would remain. The British proposed to maintain five naval vessels east of Suez, one battalion in Singapore as part of 28th Commonwealth Brigade, some helicopters and maritime patrol aircraft. No commitment was made regarding the Strategic Reserve. The whole force would not exceed 4000 men and cost no more than £10 million per year. The SEATO commitment would be continued, but AMDA must be replaced by a looser framework based on consultation rather than commitment. The British would maintain a presence but relinquish responsibility; their task would be to complement and support local forces, not replace them. The only real change the new government made was that small British forces would remain in Singapore itself; a request by Lee Kuan Yew for strike aircraft to remain was turned down.[51]

The arrangements for a new collective security framework were in fact already under review. In spring 1970 the British suggested talks to work out a new relationship, and organised military exercises in Malaysia, involving the AMDA partners, to lay the foundation. The exercises generated praise for the SAF but exposed some differences between Singapore and Malaysia. Malaysia did not react well to the presence of Singaporean troops or their focus on the defence of the island itself. Other differences developed over policy; Malaysia hoped that Southeast Asia would become a neutral zone excluded from Cold War rivalry, while Singapore wanted the Great Powers to balance each other in the area. Nevertheless an arrangement associating the British, Australians and New Zealanders with the collective defence of Malaysia and Singapore offered a chance to establish some common ground. For Singapore, it also offered a possible buffer between both its neighbours. Talks duly moved forward.[52]

Military arrangements were settled first. The Jungle Warfare School reverted to Malaysia, which would make the facility available to the distant partners but not to the SAF. The IADS was shifted to Butterworth, bringing together the two local air forces and the Australian squadrons under the overall command of an Australian officer. Singapore became the maritime and ground operations hub for a new three-party framework: Singapore, Malaysia and an integrated force designated ANZUK, combining the assigned forces of the distant partners. Political arrangements took longer, delayed by the vagueness of British policy and Malaysian desires for regional neutrality. But by April 1971 it was agreed that AMDA would be terminated at the same time as Far East Command was closed, in November, and replaced by a Five Power Defence Agreement (FPDA). This deliberately ambiguous agreement stipulated that the external defence of Malaysia and Singapore was indivisible and of concern to the U.K., Australia and New Zealand; the five parties agreed to consult each other in the event of any perceived external threat to the local partners. But the only organised "alliance" force was the IADS; ground and naval forces were not automatically pledged to defend the local partners.[53]

British facilities valued at £19 million were handed over to Malaysia and Singapore by late 1971. The ANZUK force moved into Singapore, but without any formal integration with the SAF. On 29 October 1971 FARELF (Far East Land Forces) paraded into history. Two days later FEAF and Far East Command followed it. On 1 November the renamed 28th ANZUK Brigade paraded at its new camp in Nee Soon to inaugurate ANZUK force, while an exchange of letters launched the new FPDA. The air component of ANZUK at Butterworth was directly assigned to integrated local defence, but the ground and naval forces were not. RAF helicopters and *Nimrod* patrol aircraft were already in place at Tengah, but were now guests at an RSAF facility. Small British forces thus remained in Singapore but as guests of a country they were not automatically committed to defend, other than in the air. The days of British responsibility were over and the British presence was now barely more than token. The defence of Singapore was now in the hands of its own people.[54]

It took almost another five years for the last British troops to leave Singapore, and New Zealand kept troops there until 1989. But 1971 was the turning point. ANZUK proved to be no more than a political footnote to a military story already concluded. ANZUK forces were quite active in the early 1970s, training hard for any SEATO call and even for internal security duties. Neither call ever came, because the new environment left both redundant. SEATO was undermined by the development of the Association of Southeast Asian Nations (ASEAN), formed in 1967 and making its presence felt by the 1970s. In 1971 Malaysia persuaded its partners in this forum to call for a neutral zone in the area, to be guaranteed by the Great Powers. Coupled with American moves to disengage from Vietnam, this left SEATO-designated forces at loose ends. Concerns that friction might yet arise between Malaysia and Singapore also abated, as both governments acted responsibly in handling issues. On the Singapore side, notable examples were Singapore's support for Malaysia in the face of territorial claims from the Philippines in 1968 and the quiet but firm manner in which the Singapore government used the security forces to prevent any backlash in Singapore during the race riots in Kuala Lumpur in May 1969. The FPDA was in any case only a lowest common denominator arrangement, a way to maintain minimal functional defence ties. Singapore's leaders never saw the continued presence of foreign forces as other than "a breathing space," and a source of valuable support and technical aid.[55] In such circumstances, and under the increased economic pressure of an energy crisis, the external partners acted accordingly.

The Australian government decided to withdraw its ground force from Singapore in 1973; the troops were gone by February 1974. British and New Zealand units remained as separate forces, but not for long. In 1974 another Labour government under Wilson directed that defence spending be reduced to a fixed ceiling of 4.5% of the GNP. The COS decided that to meet this target while maintaining the NATO commitment the assignments to SEATO and the FPDA must be terminated. The last naval units left Singapore in September 1975, 28th Brigade was disbanded two months later, and the last British soldier stationed in Singapore left in March 1976. The only foreign forces left in Malaysia and Singapore were the Australian air units in Butterworth and the New Zealand battalion in Singapore.[56]

This withdrawal was more symbol than substance. The definitive change was the termination of a British headquarters based in Singapore plus the decision not to maintain any special capability to intervene in the region in the Strategic Reserve. The FPDA was not really a commitment, it was only the loosest promise to consult made in the expectation the call would no longer come. The forces were no more than a gesture, a stay of execution. Except for air defence, the mother country pushed Singapore out of the nest when Far East Command stood down. The token presence was too small to deter an external threat but enough to be compromised by internal problems, so the economic crisis made the decision an easy one.

To the surprise of many and the relief of even more, this did not prove to be anything but an anti-climax. Singapore's strong leadership and its rapid economic growth helped it cope well with the changes. The need to develop a broader economy to replace the bases turned out in the long run to be a positive change for the country. On the other hand, the facilities themselves helped Singapore build up important shipping and air industries. The resulting economic boom brought stability as well as prosperity. Friction between Malaysia and Singapore declined to a tolerable level which did not raise the spectre of conflict; the RMN stayed quietly on at Woodlands, the IADS continued. The Singapore government invested heavily in defence but this did not prevent the general economic upsurge. The irony is that in retrospect Singapore benefitted more from the British withdrawal than did the British. The need to defend itself helped infuse Singapore's nation-building with a sense of responsibility. Whatever money the British saved by the withdrawal was not put to any effect in solving economic problems or maintaining strong forces. There were further crises, more reviews, more cuts.[57] On the other hand, the British left Singapore with a legacy of real value.

Singapore's location makes it strategically important; its lack of size makes it vulnerable. In 1941–42 Singapore's status as a key point in the British Empire made it a target; the British, overwhelmed at home, failed to defend it. But after 1945 Singapore survived the upheavals of communist subversion, the Malayan Emergency, the Confrontation, and even the failed merger with Malaysia — due in no small part to the presence and effective use of British forces. This last phase of British military control of Singapore was the most productive. The British military helped make it possible to build modern Singapore and did very little to add to its burdens; their presence and success bought the new republic the time to take its military baby steps. Yet when conditions changed, strategic imperatives and foreign policy ambitions that had held fast for over 20 years were steamrollered by economic pressures in six months. Even this withdrawal taught the Singaporeans a valuable lesson. When you are a distant bastion of empire, you may seem crucial today, but you can become expendable tomorrow. The only people who will always regard your security as the overriding priority are your own. That was the fundamental truth of the military relationship between the U.K. and Singapore and it is the basis of Singaporean defence policy today. Their shared military history is the most durable legacy the British left to Singapore.

Notes

1. Lau, 276-77; Turnbull, 216-17.
2. Lau, 37-39, 44-49, 56, 83; Tanner, 69.
3. Lau, 268-71, 282-84, is definitive on this point; Tanner, 70; Hawkins, 8-9.
4. Lau, chs. 7-9.
5. Lau, 270-71; Turnbull, 232-34; Clutterbuck, 265.
6. Important studies of the Malayan Emergency include A. Short, *The Communist Insurrection in Malaya 1948-1960*, London, 1975, and R. Stubbs, *Hearts and Minds in Guerrilla Warfare: The Malayan Emergency 1948-1960*, Singapore, 1989.

7. Clutterbuck, 269; Dockrill, 51; Lee, *Eastward*, 96-102, 130-50; M. Postgate, *Operation Firedog: Air Support in the Malayan Emergency 1948-1960*, London, 1992, passim, spells out in detail the importance of Singapore in Emergency air operations.

8. Chin, 25; Turnbull, 239-45, 255.

9. Turnbull, 247-58; Darby, 87-88; Chin, 39-40; Clutterbuck, 113-17; Keay, 316-18. The reinforcement of the garrison to handle the riots in October 1956 came from units operating up-country, which only underlined the connection between the two neighbours on the security question. Keay argues the successful quelling of the riots paved the way for two things: Lee Kuan Yew's "riding the tiger" strategy, and the 1957 agreement on a constitution for self-government.

10. Chin, 18, 22, 39-41; Darby, 88; Eaton, 227; Lee Kuan Yew, 225.

11. Carver, 64-65; Tanner, 252-53; Darby, 148-49; Chin, vii, 1, 31-32; Hawkins, 14-17.

12. Turnbull, 257-58; Tanner, 253; Darby, 149; Chin, 41-42; Clutterbuck, 145.

13. Chin, 33-34, 41-42; Darby, 121; Hawkins, 15; *Straits Times*, 21 August 1957, 11 September 1958.

14. Chin, 45; Turnbull, 262-268; Bartlett, 162; Han et al, 67.

15. Chin, 38, 42-44; *Straits Times*, 13 March 1956, 8 September 1957, 6 February, 16 April 1958.

16. Carver, 64; Darby, 212; Chin, 54; Hawkins, 10; Turnbull, 269-73; Han et al, 69-72, 279-84.

17. Darby, 88, 212, 276; Chin, 44, 51-52, 55-61; Hawkins, 18-20; Bartlett, 163, 168; Jackson, 189; *Straits Times*, 23 September 1961, 3, 4, 17 October, 14, 24 November, 6 December 1962.

18. Hawkins, 21-23; Jackson, 192; Lee, *Eastward*, 195-96; J.A.C. Mackie, *Konfrontasi: The Indonesia-Malaysia Dispute 1963-1966*, Kuala Lumpur, 1974, 103-117.

19. Mackie, 117-22; Lee, *Eastward*, 197-99; Hawkins, 22-23; Carver, 65; Bartlett, 183; Chin, 65; Darby, 233-34; Johnson, xi.

20. Mackie, 122-209; Hawkins, 22-23; Chin, 79.

21. Mackie, 210-17; Chin, 67, 79; Jackson, 204; Hawkins, 25.

22. The incidents in 1964 are catalogued and described in detail in Ministry of External Affairs Malaysia, *Indonesian Aggression Against Malaysia*, vols. 1-2, Kuala Lumpur, 1965; Mackie, 258-64; Lee, *Eastward*, 210-14; Bartlett, 187; Chin, 94-95; Hawkins, 25. Lee describes the firefight in which the SIR platoon was worsted. Bad intelligence might well have been significant here, the SIR force was not strong enough to overcome dug-in defenders of nearly equal strength. Mackie describes an incident in which some 80 Indonesian regulars landed in Kota Tinggi in March and bested an SIR force, but were eventually undone by lack of support and maps.

23. Lee, *Eastward*, 229; Hawkins, 25-26; Chin, 95-96, 101; Bartlett, 183, 186, 190, 281; Jackson, 205-07. Legally, Malaysia commanded operations in Borneo from September 1963, British and later Australian and New Zealand forces operating "in support." Commonwealth forces suffered just under 100 fatal casualties.

24. Chin, 76-77, 82-83, 90; Turnbull, 282.

25. Hawkins, 11; Chin, 103; Turnbull, 283-84; Jackson, 205-06. The PAP claimed that it aspired to represent urban interests only as a non-communal party, but the Malaysian Chinese Association in particular did not believe this. Han et al, 65-83, and Lee Kuan Yew, chs. 35-42, for Lee Kuan Yew's perspective.

26. Han et al,, 77-83, 285-309; Turnbull, 282-85; Chin, 103-06; Hawkins, 26-27; Lee Kuan Yew, 629-30.

27. Hawkins, 26-27; Lee, *Eastward*, 221; Chin, 113-14.

28. H. Wilson, *The Labour Government 1964-1970: A Personal Record*, London, 1971, 39-44; D. Healey, *The Time of My Life*, London, 1979, 279-80; Dockrill, 82, 86-87; Carver, 73-74.

29. Healey, 270-80; Darby, 285-86, 290; Dockrill, 92; Jackson, 231.

30. Chin, 115; Bartlett, 197; Carver, 77; Darby, 311.

31. Chin, 101; Darby, 234, 298-306; Jackson, 221; Dockrill, 79.

32. Healey, 270, 276-79; Johnson, 136-38, 166-68; Dockrill, 87.

33. Healey, 279-81, 292; Wilson, 41-42; Bartlett, 291; Darby, 309-312; Chin, 121; Jackson, 232; Johnson, 131; Carver, 76-79.

34. Wilson, 233, 243; Hawkins, 30; Carver, 79; Dockrill, 93-94; Darby, 314; Bartlett, 190, 296-98.

35. Dockrill, 90.

36. Healey, 289-93, notes that at the height of the Confrontation there were 80,000 British personnel east of Suez, more than in BAOR; Wilson, 297, 421-22, 433-35; Carver, 80-83; Darby, 317, 321.

37. Dockrill, 83, 87-90; Darby, 298; Hawkins, 28-29.

38. Healey, 291-93; Darby, 298, 312; Carver, 78-80.

39. Hawkins, 27; Turnbull, 271; Jackson, 211; Chin, 108, 113-14; Lee Kuan Yew, 652-55.

40. Chin, 111, 117-24, 132; Darby, 122-23; Hawkins, 27, 53; Han et al, 341.

41. Carver, 81; Darby, 318-19; Chin, 137.

42. Healey, 290-91; Darby, 317-21; Chin, 139.

43. Wilson, chs. 22-24; Healey, 293; Chin, 140; Dockrill, 95, 98; Bartlett, 226; Carver, 83-84; Darby, 322-23.

44. Darby, 324-26; Dockrill, 126.

45. Turnbull, 293-94, called the initial PAP reaction the "first surge of angry panic"; Hawkins, 30-31; Chin, 137, 140-41, notes that Singapore's unemployment rate at that time was 12%. Han et al, 107, 111, use the now received figure that British military spending by the end of 1967 accounted for 12.7% of Singapore's GNP. Lee Kuan Yew, 23, states that in 1965 the figure was about 20% of GDP. The difference might be explained if these figures are restricted to official British government expenditure on the bases and their personnel. *Straits Times* editions every day for the balance of January and all through February 1968 underline the enormity of the shock of Wilson's announcement on Singapore.

46. Healey, 293; Chin, 141-42; Darby, 325; Carver, 84; Han et al, 107.

47. Chin, 144-51; Hawkins, 31; Han et al, 96.

48. Turnbull, 294, 297; Clutterbuck, 335; Hawkins, 31-32; Han et al, 110.

49. Hawkins, 53-54; Chin, 153-56.

50. Hawkins, 35-36; Lee, *Eastward*, 237-47; Eaton, 297; Chin, 164.

51. Carver, 95; Bartlett, 254-56; Chin, 173.

52. Chin, 171-74; Hawkins, 40.

53. Chin, 175-76; Hawkins, 41-42.

54. Lee, *Eastward*, 249-50; Chin, 177-78; Eaton, 299-300; Hawkins, 42.

55. Eaton, 303-04, 309; Chin, 158-59, 178; Hawkins, 12, 48, 54; Turnbull, 298.

56. Chin, 193; Jackson, 257; Tanner, 253; Carver, 107-09; Dockrill, 107; Eaton, 314-21; Lee, *Eastward*, 252. The *Nimrod* patrol aircraft were the last British operational unit to leave. The New Zealand battalion stayed on as much because it would cost too much to send them home as for any foreign policy reason: J. Rolfe, *Defending New Zealand*, Wellington, 1993, 99-106.

57. Turnbull, 296-99; Keay, 325-26; Hawkins, 29-31; Han et al, 111. The RMN finally relinquished the facilities at Woodlands to Singapore in the autumn of 1997.

APPENDIX 1
Notes on the Forts of Nineteenth-century Singapore

Fort Canning

The 1871 defence review[1] judged Fort Canning's guns to be useless except in case of an internal disturbance. In the late 1870s Singapore's defences were redesigned. The building programme of the 1880s made Fort Canning's role as a bastion for harbour defence superfluous. In 1891 it was admitted that:

> Fort Canning is too retired to be of service for the defence of the roadstead, even if the work were remodelled to receive a heavy armament of long range...The fort, however, occupies a position from whence Singapore is well commanded on all sides; and in case of an insurrection of the coloured population, it would be a valuable place of refuge for the Europeans of the Settlement, whilst its fire would overawe the town.[2]

Thus much of the expenditure on Fort Canning beyond that necessary for an emergency would seem to have been wasted. It is ironic that the longest lasting and best known artifact in the historic defences of Singapore was this fort designed mainly to intimidate the majority of its own population — something never in the end necessary.

Fort Palmer

By the early 1860s, a system of fortifications centred around the New Harbour had appeared. This fort, constructed during the period 1859–62, was situated on Mount Palmer, near Telok Ayer, overlooking the eastern entrance to Keppel Harbour. Fort Palmer's armament in 1864 was five 56 pounder guns. A small battery already stood here in 1855. The fort at that time consisted of a small earthwork, a magazine and a guardroom. In 1866 two of the 8" guns at Fort Canning were moved to Fort Palmer for use in artillery practice.[3] The fort was in active service at least as late as 1892, when it is listed as having 26 Royal Artillerymen stationed there.[4] At that time, Fort Palmer constituted "a formidable defence", with four breech-loading cannon which were the first in Singapore to be fired by electricity. The fort was dismantled in about 1900, when the soil of the hill was used for the second phase of reclamation work at Telok Ayer.

Fort Faber

This fort, named after Captain Charles Edward Faber, Madras Engineers, who came to Singapore in September 1844 and became Superintending Engineer of the settlement, was built during the same period as Fort Palmer. This fort had sites for two guns on top of Mount Faber. At one time two 13" mortars were set up there; in 1867 there were also 56 pounder guns there.

According to Winsley, Fort Faber was "never a really good fort."[5] A description evocative of the contrast between the availability of weaponry hardware in early Singapore and the scarcity of manpower to exploit them uses Fort Faber as its theme:

> On the top of this hill are two mortars, and lower down is a battery of two 56 pounder guns, with barracks attached, forming part of the far-famed fortifications of Singapore. It is difficult to say whether the two gaping mortars on the top of the hill, or the two lonely guns below, convey the greatest feeling of desolation and decay. The very sepoys that guard the latter — for they don't man them — seem touched with the melancholy of neglect.

"With the development of the harbour facilities adjoining New Harbour Fort Faber was dropped from the plan put forward in 1885."[6]

Fort Teregah

Fort Teregah was built on the island of Brani, in Keppel Harbour. Samuel Best as early as 1843 indicated this as a good fortification site, but no works were built here until 1861. A gun platform was erected overlooking the entrance to the Singapore harbour area. According to Harfield, "After the forts on Blakang Mati had been converted into training establishments the fort on Pulau Brani was abandoned. Unfortunately during the 1973 reclamation programme on Pulau Brani all traces of Fort Teregah were obliterated."[7]

Fort Fullerton

This was located on the beach where the Fullerton Building, until recently Singapore's General Post Office, now stands. In the 1860s it had nine 68 pounder guns and one mortar.

This fort, built in 1830-32 at the mouth of the Singapore River, was enlarged in 1861 to three times its original size, so that it extended from the river to Johnston's Pier. Facilities in the fort included quarters for the commander, barracks for gunners, and 10 guns: nine 68 pounders and one 13" mortar.

Near Fort Fullerton was the settlement's main arsenal, which was rented from a private landowner. It was in a dilapidated state, poorly guarded, and in the middle of the town. In 1865 the arsenal began to be moved because of fear that its presence in time of battle would draw enemy fire on the town and the nearby warehouse area. It was also agreed that the recently-expanded Fort Fullerton should be demolished. According to Makepeace, Fort Fullerton's demolition began in 1875, ended in June 1873, and was only completed in 1890.

Scandal Point

This was Singapore's first fortified post. It was the only fort to be built in response to T.S. Raffles' original instructions. It was mainly used for ceremonial purposes until 1845 when it was upgraded as a result of the recommendation of Captain Samuel Best. Its official name was the Saluting Battery. When a sea wall along the shore was built in 1851, it disappeared. The site obtained its name from the custom of early colonists who used the slightly elevated spot near the shore to chat in the evenings. The location corresponds to the modern site of the Singapore Recreation Club, or perhaps the former Satay Club, near the junction of Connaught Drive, Stamford Road, and Nicoll Highway, at the northeast corner of the Padang. In 1841 it was described as "a convenient old battery, the low walls of which serve for benches ... The old battery beyond this one, is now a green mound, which the Institution boys use as a play ground."[8] It had disappeared by 1851.[9]

The Forts of 1878: Fort Pasir Panjang, Fort Tanjong Katong, Fort Connaught, Fort Siloso,[10] and Fort Serapong

These five forts were built as part of a large-scale extension of Singapore's defences. Pasir Panjang had been selected as a site for a fort by Best in 1843. Originally all transportation and communication with the fort had to be conducted by sea. The battery was active in World War II. It was abandoned after the war, but many elements of the fort are well-preserved in what is now known as Labrador Park. Fort Tanjong Katong stood at the the eastern end of the new defensive line. The fort was not well-constructed, since it stood on sandy soil. It was abandoned in 1910. The site is now marked only by the name of Fort Road. Fort Siloso became the headquarters of the Royal Artillery based in Singapore in 1907, and much of the fort has been preserved and restored. Fort Connaught, at the eastern end of the island then called Blakang Mati and now called Sentosa, was demolished for the construction of a golf course after Singapore became independent. Remains of Fort Serapong, overlooking Pulau Brani, also on Sentosa, in the 1980s could be reached by following a paved road through the forest, branching off to the left just before the Corallarium. Although overgrown with jungle, many of the fort's structures could still be observed.

Col. Harry St George Ord, Governor of the Straits Settlements 1867–1873

During Ord's governorship, the presence of 60,000 French troops in Indochina, the opening of the Suez Canal, and the increased use of steamships all influenced British strategic planning. Steamships required coal, and Singapore rapidly became one of the main coaling stations on the trade routes. Since the ships found it convenient to bunker here, a number of subsidiary businesses connected with refitting them also developed in Singapore. Ord's first proposals for changes in 1869, however, were not yet heavily affected by these developments. Instead, Ord saw Singapore as mainly a waystation on the route to China and a collecting and distribution centre for the Malay Peninsula and nearby archipelago. Desultory suggestions to station a potent warship plus three or four gunboats at Singapore continued to be rejected on grounds of cost. This entrenched the policy of relying on small forts and coastal artillery. Ord thus turned his attention there, proposing to maintain Fort Fullerton and indeed up gun it with five 68 pounders. Fort Palmer should also be retained, and a new fort built on Mt. Faber to hold six 68 pounders. Another battery at the western entrance to Keppel Harbour was proposed, to be equipped with four 8" guns. That site in due course became the batteries of Fort Labrador. Finally, Sandy Point was suggested as a site for a battery of four 56 pounder guns, to protect ships at anchor in the harbour. On the ground therefore, in spite of changes in the broader situation, very little changed during the early years as a Crown Colony.

Riots of 1871

In the same year as a new discussion of planning for Singapore's long-term defence was initiated, new rioting broke out among the Chinese community. Prior to 21 October there had already been an increase in robberies and burglaries among two of the Chinese dialect groups, the Hokkiens and the Teochew. A quarrel between members of the two groups on that date led to a major outbreak of violence. The Lt.-Governor received a request for 50 European troops to guard all the bridges. The rioting was accompanied by much looting and a few deaths. The police force was too weak to quell the riots. Troops were sent in, but the rioting continued for several days. Aid to the civil power was thus added to the tasks of the British military in Singapore, a mission which grew in importance in the next century.

Notes

1. See Chapter 4.
2. PRO, FO881/6252*A, 182; Intelligence Division, Horse Guards, War Office, *Precis of Information Concerning the Straits Settlements and the Native States of the Malay Peninsula*, London, 1891.
3. Harfield, *British and Indian Armies*, 203.
4. Harfield, *British and Indian Armies*, 279.
5. *A History of the Singapore Volunteer Corps*, quoted in Harfield, *British and Indian Armies*, 300.
6. Harfield, *British and Indian Armies*, 300.
7. Harfield, *British and Indian Armies*, 305.

8. W. Markpeace, "Singapore's Military History. Singapore Defences" in Makepeace et al., eds., *One Hundred Years of Singapore*, vol. I, 378-79.

9. Buckley, *Anecdotal History*, 363. It is not clear why two batteries should be referred to. According to Harfield, *British and Indian Armies*, 209, a Government Gazette order for 1858 stated that "'To prevent accidents and for general information it is hereby notified that until further orders all Salutes will be fired by the Artillery from the Esplanade near the large...' This site was adjacent to the old battery site that had been known as Scandal Point."

10. Information on these forts is condensed from Harfield, *British and Indian Armies*, 293-305.

APPENDIX 2
Wartime Preparations to Defend Singapore Island

1941

19 December	The COS direct Thomas and Percival to evacuate as many "useless mouths" as possible and report on future plans.
20 December	Martial law declared in Singapore, Fortress Commander designated the responsible authority.
	Percival directs his staff to consider preliminary steps to bolster the defences of the north coast.
	Admiralty authorises HQ Eastern Fleet to abandon Singapore naval base if it becomes untenable.
23 December	Percival orders Simmons to arrange for reconnaisance of the north coast, to identify likely landing sites and defensive positions.
26 December	Simson urges Percival to authorise the systematic erection of fixed defences on the north coast; the GOC refuses, citing concern for civilian and troop morale.
27 December	Simson puts the same case to Simmons and receives the same answer.
28 December	Percival authorises the formation of labour groups led by PWD engineers to build field defences, but does not inform Simson and does not direct the teams to work in Singapore.
	Percival orders Simmons to prepare a plan to demolish the causeway.
29 December	Japanese resume air attacks on Singapore.
31 December	Duff Cooper has Simson made Director General Civil Defence, with sweeping powers for Singapore and Johore and F.D. Bisseker as Deputy.
December	Engineer units carry on bolstering the beach defences of the south and east coasts.

Simson has matériel for fixed defences assembled and dumped at sites in northern Singapore west of the causeway.

Chinese community leaders form a united front in the Chinese Mobilisation Council, led by Tan Kah Kee, and offer their services for the war effort.

1942

1 January	Thomas forbids Simson to act as DGCD in Johore and orders him to refer all measures for official approval by the appropriate department.
	Jones refuses to give Simson and Bisseker any assistance.
3 January	Percival directs Simmons to treat work on the defences of Singapore "as an urgent measure."
5 January	HQ Eastern Fleet withdraws from naval base.
7 January	Simson complains to Cooper no work is being done regarding field defences on the north coast of Singapore.
	Cooper asks for and receives from Simson a list of measures that can and must still be taken to bolster the defences of Singapore; the Resident Minister then passes the information on to Churchill and the COS.
9 January	Simson briefs Wavell, telling him the most urgently needed step is the erection of field defences on the north coast of Singapore.
	Wavell and Percival tour the causeway area; the Supreme Commander, incensed by the lack of defensive preparations, directs the GOC to bolster the defences of the island immediately.
11 January	Duff Cooper leaves Singapore, ordered home after Wavell takes over as Supreme Commander ABDA Command.
15 January	Thomas issues a public directive to all civil servants to abandon routine procedure and accelerate all war measures.
	Churchill asks Wavell for a report on the defences of Singapore Island.
16 January	Wavell informs the Prime Minister the defences were not designed to repel an invasion from the north and very little has been done to bolster them since the outbreak of war. Wavell also sends a list of questions about the defences to GOC Singapore Fortress.

18 January	GHQ Malaya Command completes the first draft outline plan for the defence of Singapore Island by the entire army. Percival replies to Wavell's list of questions.
19 January	Wavell directs Percival to complete the plan for the general defence of Singapore.
20 January	Wavell meets Percival and suggests he deploy his largest formation, the en route 18th British Division, in the northwest, where the Supreme Commander expects the Japanese to attack, but gives the GOC a free hand on deployments.
	Churchill orders Wavell to make an all-out effort to bolster the defences of Singapore Island, forwarding a list of recommendations based on the Simson list; this includes the preparation of field defences on the north coast.
21 January	Churchill gives Wavell a direct order to defend Singapore Island to the utmost, including by fighting in the city if necessary.
22 January	44th Indian Brigade and reinforcement drafts of Indian troops arrive in Singapore.
23 January	Draft outline plan for the general defence of Singapore Island issued in secret to formation commanders.
	Percival makes the Fortress Commander responsible for the completion of the defence plan, and designates Brig. Paris to lead the planning staff.
24 January	The Australian 2/4 Machine Gun Battalion and reinforcement drafts of Australian troops arrive in Singapore.
	Prime Minister Curtin warns Churchill that Australia will consider any failure to defend Singapore to the utmost "an inexcusable betrayal."
27 January	Outline plan for the defence of Singapore is completed and passed to formation commanders.
	Wavell authorises Malaya Command to abandon the mainland and retreat to Singapore Island.
28 January	Rear Admiral Malaya begins the evacuation of the naval base, without informing Malaya Command it will now be responsible for demolition and denial.
29 January	11th Indian Division staff are told in a briefing the defences in the sector of the coast assigned to them are far from complete, there are no maps with details of the naval base area, and there is no plan for a final perimeter defence if the enemy lands successfully.

54th and 55th Brigades, HQ 18th British Division, and the 100th Light Tank Squadron arrive in Singapore.

Wavell notifies Churchill Malaya Command is in full retreat onto Singapore Island.

30 January   Wavell orders all RAF units except one squadron of *Hurricane* fighters out of Singapore.

31 January   A four-metre wide hole is blown in the causeway after the final rearguard of Malaya Command completes the retreat onto Singapore Island.

January   Some essential steps are taken to build up the all-round defences of Singapore: all strong points to be defended are identified and marked, headquarters locations are selected and communications equipment assembled, unit deployments are settled. On the north and west coasts, some fields of fire are cleared, some equipment is put in place and some fortifications are begun, arrangements are made to enable some batteries of the Fixed Defences to fire inland. Wavell on the other hand does not follow up Percival's reply of 18 January to his questions regarding defences on the north coast and never inspects the area again.

Percival concludes the Japanese will most likely make their main attack east of the causeway; the 18th British Division is assigned there, and the matériel dumped by Simson is transferred to that area.

1-8 February   Malaya Command orders all formation commanders to inform it in advance before making "warlike noises," in order to avert panic by notifying the civilian population in advance.

All formation commanders protest over the lack of field defences in their assigned sector and inform the GOC how shocked the troops are by this and the ongoing evacuation and demolition of the naval base and facilities.

In order to conserve ammunition for a long siege Malaya Command restricts counterbattery fire to mobile batteries, to a limit of 20 rounds per day per gun, not transferable from gun to gun nor day to day without command approval.

All formations do their best to bolster the coast defences of their sectors, often under Japanese air attacks and artillery bombardment.

The staff of 8th Australian Division reconnoiters the area

between the Kranji and Jurong Rivers, selected by Malaya Command as the Kranji-Jurong Line, the last position to be prepared for a defensive stand west of the city. Bennett angrily refuses to allow them to complete entrenching the position.

Japanese air raids and artillery bombardment add to the defenders' own demolitions of petrol storage tanks and important facilites to create a pall of thick black smoke, plus mounting physical damage and disruption all over the island.

APPENDIX 3
Controversies surrounding the Surrender of Singapore, February 1942

Almost from the day it happened, two major controversies made the surrender of Singapore seem anything but an understandable capitulation by a force with no other choice. Some sources still believe a story that the Japanese high command felt so hard-pressed by the last days of the battle it was seriously worried *25th Army* might even be defeated and forced to surrender. This suggests Percival was bluffed into surrendering before it was really necessary. Adding a great deal of smoke to this fire is the argument that the unspoken motive for the surrender had nothing to do with water or ammunition: Malaya Command was disintegrating by mass desertion, giving up on the fight. Taken together this suggests the Japanese, not the Allies, were bluffing in their daring attack on Singapore, and in the end its loss was caused by fecklessness more than grand strategy. But neither story is as it appears to its strongest supporters. The first is sheer misinterpretation. The second is misunderstood, in both cause and effect.

The first story was started by remembrances of Japanese staff officers, especially Major Fujiwara, and by widely quoted statements attributed to Yamashita. The Japanese were indeed surprised at how stubbornly the defenders fought on after the loss of Bukit Timah, especially at how heavy the defending artillery fire remained on the last two days. They were also caught off-guard by the sheer number of troops in Malaya Command, easily double their own numbers on the island. Given their own serious shortage of field artillery ammunition, this certainly produced real concern, as high up as in the person of Maj.-Gen. Suzuki, *25th Army* Chief of Staff.[1] But does this justify the claim that Yamashita himself believed at the time that if Percival had not surrendered when he did, the Japanese commander "would have had to give up his final assault on Singapore?" The very clear implication is that this might have saved the city from surrender after all. The Japanese could have been caught overstretched by a counterattack and routed. Or they would have had to pull back to Johore, buying time for reinforcements to arrive.[2] This does fit with Yamashita's definite concern over being dragged into a costly battle in the streets which would chew up two things precious to him: infantry and time. But in the main it rests on interpreting this

famous statement attributed to Yamashita, regarding his state of mind
that evening when discussing surrender terms with Percival:

> My attack on Singapore was a bluff — a bluff that worked. I had 30,000
> men and was outnumbered more than three to one (sic). I knew if I
> had to fight long for Singapore I would be beaten. That is why the
> surrender had to be at once. I was very frightened all the time that the
> British would discover our numerical weakness and lack of supplies
> and force me into disastrous street fighting.[3]

This statement was made after the war by Yamashita to his American
biographer. It is very specific and consistent with all records of
Yamashita's views during the campaign on the main point: *25th Army*
must not bog down in street fighting in the city of Singapore, given the
risks it took with troops and ammunition in order to advance as fast
as possible. At the time Yamashita faced the problem with his usual
boldness. An all-out attack led by tanks was laid on for that night, 15
February, to break through 18th Division and storm into the city;
meanwhile, the air support intensified its attacks in and around the city.[4]
But there is that seductive phrase "...I would be beaten," coupled with
the word "bluff." How have they been misinterpreted to suggest Yamashita
feared he, not Percival, might soon be surrendering? In three ways: by
misunderstanding what Yamashita meant in choosing those words, by
not appreciating the situation as he did at the time, and by using the
testimony of others to confirm something he supposedly felt.

Yamashita knew the British overestimated his numbers. He also knew
Japanese air and naval forces now had Singapore firmly isolated. If the
night attack did not break through, the worst situation he could really
have envisaged was a pause to regroup and bring up supplies. Meanwhile,
the air attacks must have been intensified to keep up the pressure. If
necessary Yamashita would surely have demanded the return of those
squadrons transferred from him by higher command and assistance from
the invasion fleet which the day before had landed a force on Sumatra.
And he would have received it. Speed was always of the essence to
Japanese grand strategy and the rapid conquest of Singapore was
absolutely essential to those plans. For Yamashita the real problem was
that his success only made his enemies, including Tojo, all the more
determined to clip his wings — as it was, even victory did not spare him
from being sent to an obscure command in Manchuria. But he knew very
well the high command would not cut off its nose to spite its face. He
would have received help to finish off Singapore, and the Japanese air
and naval forces deployed nearby would have done that in short order.
The price would have been immediate disgrace for Yamashita, not defeat
for his army; that explains his concern, his words and his relief. Fujiwara
describes vividly how concerned Suzuki and *5th Division* officers were
about the battle. *5th Division* made little headway that day and received
the brunt of the last bombardment Malaya Command guns could deliver.
But Suzuki was not Yamashita, and Fujiwara never even met the army
commander that day. Tsuji set the record straight long ago. If it came

to city fighting the army would need a new plan for a new battle, as Yamashita feared, but that was all. Whatever some of their colleagues assumed, the responsible officers feared loss, delay, above all repercussions — but not defeat.[5]

The "premature surrender claim" implies that even given incomplete intelligence on both sides Yamashita and Percival, experienced commanders both, would have believed this possible as of 15 February: after retreating some 800 km, losing heavily on the way, now with its back to the sea, cut off in a seething and disintegrating city, with no air support at all, Malaya Command could still turn like a cornered rat, catch the enemy off-guard, and knock him out in one blow — just because it had more men in uniform and Japanese field guns were almost empty. There is no credible evidence that Yamashita, not Suzuki or Fujiwara, reached this advanced stage of delusion — which is what it was, given the gauntlet Japanese air and naval forces had thrown around Singapore. Yamashita took calculated risks and the margin was a narrow one, but even though he did not know just how spent Malaya Command was he did know it was trapped. The important thing was to win according to plan, not just to win.

The men who surrendered to Yamashita were of course convinced they had no other choice. One British staff officer who during the conference snuck a peek at a Japanese map marking out the major attack for that evening — left there for him to see? — concluded it would break through the exhausted and spread-out defenders. Percival and his commanders all agreed the army was too broken to counterattack.[6] And with very little ammunition and no water left, it hardly seems worth questioning their conclusion. But it has been questioned, based on controversial accusations which appear more sensational if one believes the Japanese really were vulnerable. In its strongest form, the argument has been made as follows: Malaya Command was not just a beaten army breaking down in the always grim circumstances of losing a siege, it was rapidly becoming an armed mob as men walked out of the battle in great numbers. Percival surrendered while he still could before his army fell completely apart on its own. Desertion, not water, brought him to the table.

For the record, Percival's explanation of his surrender acknowledged how tired the troops were but did not go beyond that. Wavell on the other hand presented another explanation in his confidential report on the operations leading to the loss of Singapore, submitted later that year. Wavell insisted that the main reason the siege of Singapore lasted only two weeks instead of two months was that Malaya Command was unravelled by large-scale desertion — and he singled out the 8th Australian Division as the worst offender.[7] The stakes seemed high, even if Singapore was by 1 February doomed to fall sooner or later. ABDA Command was the northern buffer for Australia and the vital resource-rich target of Japanese grand strategy. Wavell based his plans on a two-month siege of Singapore, to give him time to regroup elsewhere. Its rapid collapse allowed the Japanese to beat him to the punch. ABDA Command was disbanded ten days later, on 25 February. The Dutch surrendered their whole vast archipelago on 14 March, and the Allies lost Burma and were pushed back to the frontier of India by early May. For a time in April the main fleet of the IJN rampaged in the Indian Ocean, forcing the Eastern Fleet to retreat to the east coast of Africa. This plus renewed agitation by the Congress Party seemed at the time to threaten British control of India itself. As it was, the British were forced onto the periphery of the war against Japan. The I Australian Corps went home, and later took the field not to defend the Empire but to fight as part of the American-led counteroffensive against the Japanese central position that now split the Allies. It is going much too far to suggest this was all due to the rapid collapse of Singapore, but so many Allied plans and interests were dependent on a long siege that its effects at the time seemed large indeed.[8] The Australians accused the British of deceiving them over the "Singapore Strategy," and thus their security against Japan, by covering up the risk they took in grand strategy to leave the area so weak. Now some Britons replied that the final defence of the island was fatally compromised by the collapse of the Australian division relied on to bear the brunt.

The question needs an answer: did Percival still have an army, however tired, responding to orders and battling on? Three problems arise in pursuing this question: the size and heterogenous composition of Malaya Command, the primary sources available, and the inherently confusing nature of the last battle on the island. Some units reacted to news of the surrender in shock and anger, apparently because they did not yet see the situation as truly hopeless.[9] And the war diaries testify that a majority of Percival's formations had the majority of their men still fit to fight under command and in position when the GOC surrendered. But there is no doubt that by the last four days of the battle a very serious problem had arisen as large numbers of troops drifted away from the chain of command and into the city — hiding out, trying to escape, or just waiting in resignation for the end. Numerous eyewitness accounts and many official records agree that thousands of men, including Australians, Indians and Britons, were during those days absent without permission. From there, nothing is yet clear. How many were stragglers cut off by the ebb of battle but seeking to regain their unit? How many were deserters, away for whatever reason but with no intention to rejoin their unit? In such confusion, how many were both at one time or another? What was causing the problem? Above all, how did the high command see it and what did it try to do about it?

The root of the problem was surely the army's belief that it was now trapped on the island in a hopeless fight it could not win. Such a situation called for leadership of the very highest order, from Percival down to the junior leaders in companies and platoons. Simply put, it was their bounden duty to inspire the troops to fight on doggedly, to keep the army together as a disciplined fighting force. Whatever reservations Malaya Command's officers had about the situation, the purpose of the fight was a problem for their superiors; their job was to defend Singapore with all their might. And the army looked to its commanders to make the decisions which gave it the best possible chance under the circumstances to fight on effectively. Instead, 18th Division officers arriving on 29 January were shocked to be told by GHQ staff receiving them how unfortunate it was they were too late, the battle was lost. This may have already seemed clear, but putting it so pessimistically could only undermine whatever fight the division would now put up. This grave failure of leadership spread like cancer throughout the army — and indeed beyond, given the disgraceful scuttle from duty of some senior police officers despite direct orders from the Governor to remain at their posts.[10] In the end the high command lost and was seen to lose control of the battle and the army as it retreated into the perimeter. When it became obvious to the troops their commanders could no longer restore any order to their position, the results were disastrous. Worst hit were several Indian units and above all the 8th Australian Division.

The Indian battalions which fought on Singapore Island were either completely raw or seriously depleted by losses on the mainland. Eight battalions were heavily diluted by replenishing them by up to at least 60% of their strength with the newly arrived reinforcements, troops the GSO1 of 11th Indian Division called "immature boys." The Indians were now also the target of an all-out effort by *F Kikan* to help win this "decisive battle," especially as resistance dragged on. Fujiwara employed a propaganda and three "pacification" teams to persuade Indian troops to rally to the INA banner. But the majority of Indian failures in this last battle were caused by the inability of raw troops to stand up to Japanese attacks. 4/19 Hyderabad, once a fine battalion of regulars, was now so heavily diluted its brigade commander warned Bennett it would do well to stand and fight, let alone participate in the counterattack organised on 10 February. Most of its men deserted before the Japanese attack that evening scattered the remaining 100 for good. A company of 6/1 Punjabi set off a stampede by the raw 44th Indian Brigade that morning. Australian records note that several companies of that brigade were only halted the next morning, and some were later disarmed when they panicked under enemy attack.[11]

On the northern flank, 11th Indian Division also saw some units falter. 1/15 Punjabi gave up a position for no reason on the night of 10 February. 1/8 Punjabi retreated without orders the next night under heavy mortar fire, and was rallied by Key himself, but the next day three of its companies disappeared. Three companies of 2/10 Baluch were enticed over to the enemy by Fujiwara's agents on 14 February; 11th Indian Division noted with some relish in its war diary that the "deserters" were the next morning spotted on a nearby hill and bombarded by their artillery. That same day 5/11 Sikh cracked under shellfire and dispersed, only the company under direct control of the commanding officer standing fast.[12] Many Indian units did fight doggedly until the end. 15th Indian Brigade was destroyed by overwhelming force during the aborted counterattack. 44th Indian Brigade and 11th Indian Division were still fighting formations as the army surrendered. But the final claim of the division history that "at this hour every post of the 11th Indian Division was intact, and every man was at his post," is demonstrably false. Six separate battalions from five different brigades cracked or were turned. Moreover, numerous eyewitness reports and several war diaries agree there were many Indian troops wandering aimless and leaderless around town in the last days. Witnesses from different units saw a large number of Indian soldiers resting at MacRitchie Reservoir with Japanese troops on 12 February.[13] Taken all together this evidence could point to only one conclusion in those last two command conferences at Fort Canning. Due to inexperience, fatigue, bad leadership, and politics, the large Indian component of the army was cracking up fast under the strain, one unit at a time.

Worse and more damaging was the general disaster which overtook the 8th Australian Division. There are contrasting interpretations, at either extreme, of its performance on the island. The Australian official history, written in 1957 by Lionel Wigmore and based on privileged access to official records, insists the division fought as such till the end and was overwhelmed by heavy enemy attack. In one paragraph Wigmore dismisses the whole question of collapse and desertion. 22nd Brigade AIF was disrupted by enemy pressure on 9–10 February, a situation aggravated by misunderstandings and poor organisation but rectified by division staff, who returned most men to their units. Only a residue of men, mostly inexperienced replacements, defied them and deserted. Only the best known and most widely reported incident, the boarding of the *Empire Star* at gunpoint by "a group of Australians and others," was specifically admitted. Wigmore implies that only a couple of hundred or so bewildered young troops gave up on the fight. On the other hand Peter Elphick, relying on documents only recently released for research in the Public Record Office in the U.K., argues that the division was disintegrated by uncontrollable desertion which began even before the Japanese attacked. He claims that over 8000 men left the chain of command, leaving only some 5000, 2000 from the combat units, under command in Bennett's final perimeter.[14] The truth lies somewhere in between these extremes, but closer to Elphick. Unfortunately, due at least in part to not consulting Australian archives, Elphick misunderstood when and how the desertion began — which meant he could not fully explain the far more important questions of why it happened and what impact it had on the final battle.

The following facts are not in dispute. 14,972 men of the AIF were in captivity in Singapore on 17 February, two days after the surrender. Thirty-nine AIF personnel left Singapore as authorised evacuees on 13 February. Approximately 2000 troops were in hospital by the final day of the battle; hospital and administrative personnel there and elsewhere might raise the total to 3000. That left Bennett, with all his units back under his command by 12 February, approximately 12,000 men for his final perimeter. But the highest claim made is that at most two-thirds of "those fit to fight" stood in that position; Bennett himself reported the now accepted round figures: around 2000 troops in combat units, 5000 all told.[15] That leaves possibly 7000 men who must be accounted for on the last four days, the majority by default men from the combat units.

The problem first surfaced in 22nd Brigade AIF and it was too glaring for even the official histories, British and Australian, to ignore. From midday 9 February both describe two of Taylor's battalions as remnants. Reports of stragglers reaching the city began that day. Every friendly unit in contact with Taylor's formation reported encounters with parties of Australians moving back on their own. By the next day things were serious enough for Bennett to record in his diary hearing of 100 such men. But why did so few require "Parties of Australian officers... constantly patrolling the city in trucks, picking up any Australians found and returning them to reinforcement camps"? Bennett laid the founations of the official explanation by claiming all Australian stragglers in the city were fresh untrained replacements from the depot. This is contradicted by the unit war diaries which report Australians leaving the battle area, not the depot which was miles to the east near the Island Golf Course.[16] Taylor counted at most 500 men under command late on 9 February, most from 2/18 AIF. That number fell to perhaps 250 early on 11 February, recovering to 400 that evening. All these numbers are far below the totals suggested in either official history, even considering casualties and personnel from X Battalion and other miscellaneous units.[17] What happened?

The most common Australian explanation is blunt: "the story of the first few days is simply one of a brigade overrun by weight of numbers and the nature of the close country with most action at night which enabled the Japs to bypass us more easily." This is supported by pointing to the fact the numbers under brigade control went up to 600 on 12 February and over 800 by the last day of the battle, as men regained their units. Elphick flatly rejects this argument, using a variety of personal and official sources led by what he cites as a smoking gun notation in the Malaya Command GHQ War Diary for 10 February:

> Reference reports of large numbers of Australian tps in Singapore. Gen. Gordon Bennett reports that approx 600 have been picked up *in the last three days* and have returned to their units and will be used in the attack. *Casualties are not by any means heavy and Gen. Gordon Bennett does not require reinforcements as yet.* He is however getting his reinforcements at G.B.D. formed into corps ready for use.[18]

Elphick interprets "the last three days" as indicating Australian combat troops were deserting in numbers the day *before* the Japanese attacked. This accepts the claim made in the Wavell report, based on the same reports Wavell drew on to reach his conclusion. These included war diary fragments brought out by survivors and some 60 eyewitness reports by escapees, including senior staff officers of GHQ Malaya Command, officers and men of regular and volunteer units, and influential civilians. Many reported seeing Australians desert or hearing from Australians their men had not stood to fight. To bolster accounts he acknowledges are hearsay and mostly non-Australian, Elphick turns in the end to a powerful report assembled during their years of captivity by senior staff officers of the 8th Australian Division. The report, in a section titled "Tactical Errors in the AIF sector," states:

> The Japanese crossed the Straits and landed in the AIF sector practically unopposed. There is considerable evidence to show that Brig. Taylor disobeyed Divisional Orders in not searching the Straits with B.E.L.'s [searchlights]. There are claims in the narrative that the Japanese suffered in crossing but such casualties to the enemy were very local and not general, over the AIF sector.

> Brigadier Taylor had given an order to his battalions that in the event of being pressed, they were to withdraw into defensive battalion perimeters. The result was that on the Japanese effecting a landing, the Brigade automatically commenced a withdrawal movement which could not be checked.[19]

From all this, Elphick argues there was no real defence at all on the west coast as 22nd Brigade AIF unravelled before the attack. The contagion pulled 27th Brigade AIF back and apart. The Australian defences were abandoned, not overwhelmed. The collapse of the division not only pushed Bennett into his final laager, but also ruined Malaya Command's defence strategy and forced Percival to capitulate.

There can be no doubt uncontrollable numbers of Australian troops abandoned their units and the battle before but especially as the AIF settled into its final perimeter. Australian military reports, British military and civilian reports, eyewitness accounts and postmortem comments are too numerous, consistent, and stem from too many vantage points to be either deliberate exaggeration or unconscious magnification of a few notorious episodes.[20] But Elphick makes a crucial error which weakens his explanation of the problem. Both Australian brigades fought for the beaches; neither broke as a formation *before* the Japanese attack. The weight and detail of evidence confirming this in the Australian war diaries, notwithstanding the fact many were compiled in a prisoner of war camp, is supported by Japanese admissions of painful casualties in these encounters. It far outweighs the hearsay second- and third- hand conversations Elphick places such stress on, and in any case misconstrues.[21] Worse, he also misinterprets his two most important documents, the war diary entry and the passage in the Thyer report.

The reference to the "last three days" in Malaya Command GHQ's War Diary for 10 February does not by itself prove large numbers of Australians were deserting before the attack. Thyer's report actually suggests the opposite, contrary to Elphick's view. The report supports the claim of the 22nd Brigade AIF War Diary that there was a confused but intense battle for the coast into the dawn of 9 February. When the Thyer report complained the Japanese were able to cross the Straits and land practically unopposed, it meant literally that the defenders did not bring down fire on the enemy when he was most vulnerable: *on the water itself*, crossing in small boats. This is why the report discussed the crossing and the retreat in separate paragraphs. It is consistent with artillery reports that many rounds were fired in support of the defenders yet infantry complaints fire was brought down too slowly, due to failures to turn on the beach lights and contact the guns. Thyer dismisses claims the Japanese suffered in crossing as local results; this is consistent with war diary reports that machine gunners off Lim Chu Kang and at the mouth of the Berih River were among the few able to engage the enemy for effect *before* he landed.[22]

The Malaya Command GHQ War Diary is Elphick's main source for the claim the 8th Australian Division fell apart before it moved back to the final perimeter. Elphick argues that if masses of Australian troops were adrift, but Bennett claimed casualties were small, then by default they must be deserters. This is again supported by the reports used by Wavell, reports made by naval commanders with access to information from Percival's headquarters, and by Bennett's own note regarding stragglers and officer patrols.[23] Once again the problem is distorted, for two main reasons. First, most troops set adrift before 12 February seem to have been stragglers rather than deserters. Second, Bennett could not have given an accurate report of his strength to headquarters at that moment — and he had a reason to be optimistic.

Three other Australian reports discuss the straggler problem on 9 and 10 February. For 2000 hrs on 9 February, 22nd Brigade AIF War Diary notes that AIF HQ reported over 2000 Australians were in Singapore at the ANZAC Buffett; they would be collected and returned to their units. This diary plus that of the Provost Company, 8th Australian Division, describe a search which found some stragglers of all nationalities but nothing like that number of Australians in the town; the Thyer report notes that several hundred of Taylor's men were being regrouped at the AIF depot.[24] Very likely this report was exaggerated and most combat troops adrift on 9–10 February were closer to the fighting west of the city, caught up in the general confusion. 22nd Brigade AIF, AIF HQ, 44th Indian Brigade and the Provost Company all agree there were many Australian stragglers on those days and the problem became worse not better.[25] But there is no direct evidence that as yet really large numbers of combat troops were crossing the line that divides straggling from desertion. That line was defined very clearly by the AIF in July 1940:

> Desertion is being AWL [absent without leave] in furtherance of an intention to quit the Defence Forces not to return or with the intention of escaping some particular important military duty...The only difference between desertion and AWL is a difference of intention. In the case of desertion the intention is not to return at all or not to return until some important military duty such as embarkation is over whereas in the case of AWL the intention is to return but after a period.[26]

In Singapore in February 1942, substitute "being cut off from the main body by enemy action but trying to return" for AWL. Substitute "trying to escape the island or hide in the city until the battle was over" for desertion. As of midday 10 February 8th Australian Division *was* suffering from a serious straggler problem, but not yet from uncontrollable desertion.

Bennett could not report on his formations because he was not in touch with either of them. He was surprised and furious to hear of the retreats by both Taylor and Maxwell that morning of 10 February. That afternoon he planned the counterattack ordered by his superiors in a haphazard and disinterested way, arguing with Taylor over the whole situation. Malaya Command GHQ War Diary notes the following reports from 8th Australian Division HQ for that day: at 0310 hrs, no contact with 22nd Brigade AIF; at 0355 hrs, the Australian GSOII said he believed the brigade was making use of the "prepared Jurong position," when in fact it was in front of it; at 0751 hrs Thyer reported the brigade was reorganising at the Racecourse — in fact it was nowhere near it — but admitted his information was sketchy; at 1345 hrs Bennett himself told Torrance the situation was "not so good," and he would have no troops for an attack *until 18th Division reinforcements arrived.*[27] But then Wavell and Percival paid their second visit and made their displeasure very clear. Suddenly, the next report Bennett made was the optimistic nonsense on which Elphick relied so heavily — in spite of noting how fluid the situation was that day and how little reliable information was available to either Bennett or Percival.[28] Elphick unjustly dismissed the fight put up against both invasions by the Australian brigades because he misread the evidence to pursue the unlikely claim the division gave up even before it was attacked. He then confused mass straggling for mass desertion to argue the division was finished even before Taylor finally settled in at Reformatory Road. Elphick's charge that the 8th Australian Division did not fight at all as such on Singapore Island is untenable.

Nevertheless, the division did indeed fall apart in the end because it did not bring the straggler problem under control. From 10 through 12 February mass straggling turned into mass desertion, and only a rump formation fought in the final perimeter. The problem did not start before the battle. Both brigades took up their positions in strength, a fact recorded by their war diaries. There were doubtless Australians stirring up trouble in the town before the enemy attacked, but the Provost Company War Diary, the only authoritative source, makes it clear they were few indeed. The troops were not happy. Due to the demolition of the naval base, the lack of prepared defences, the destruction of the air bases, and the inexperience of their reinforcements, there were "many misgivings."[29] But the units were in position. The trouble really started with Taylor's attempt to execute a fighting retreat in dense bush at night while being overrun by great numbers of enemy infantry.

Taylor claims he never issued written orders regarding a retreat and saw a brigade line in front of Ama Keng as a last resort. The Thyer report insists verbal orders were issued hours before the attack and battalion perimeters were always intended to form a brigade line. All parties agree it was generally understood the battalions were to fall back in the face of a major onslaught to perimeters designed to form a stop line hingeing on Ama Keng. Yet there was almost no work done to prepare this position, and the artillery was not warned it might be required to support it. Hard hit as they were by the enemy, with reinforcements still too far away to assist, Taylor's battalions all but disintegrated into small groups scattered all over the area. The first retreat was bad enough. 2/20 AIF was down to 100 men by midday 9 February, 2/19 to less than one company by 0900 hrs. The second retreat that afternoon — all but guaranteed by Taylor's failure to prepare his fallback line — produced the massive straggler problem, as small groups reached Ama Keng only to find their units gone.[30]

The confusion which descended on Western Area from this point became almost indescribable. Neither brigade nor division nor army staff made any prior effort to organise patrols or police posts to collect battle stragglers and redirect them. Taylor's failure to do this was inexcusable, given that he at least knew what he intended, and how difficult this would be for his diluted units. His next move was fatal. Men who on their own or in groups streamed back overnight looking for their units were again left behind by the premature decision to retreat to the designated final perimeter. That scattered the brigade beyond recovery. Only some timely tough fighting by its rump, especially the remnants of 2/20 and 2/19 AIF now led by Maj. Merrett, enabled Taylor to regroup on Reformatory Road on 11 February with any sort of formation at all.[31]

The steps taken by Bennett's headquarters made this problem worse, not better. The men of 22nd Brigade AIF who were found back at the AIF depot on 9 February were sent there by division staff, who ordered the military police to collect stragglers regaining friendly lines and send them back in trucks. There the men were told "the whole Brigade was being reformed." No effort was made to separate those still under their own junior leaders and those on their own with little or no gear. At 0800 hrs the next day 500 men were told they would be sent back to their own unit shortly. Instead, the senior officers were told an hour later a composite battalion was being formed. This was the ill-fated X Battalion. Depot staff, not their own officers, assigned the troops to companies. The battalion moved out to its death that night, with the stunt already being repeated as 200 more stragglers were grouped in Y Battalion under Maj. Robertson, acting commander of 2/19 AIF, when he reached the depot. Just when 22nd Brigade AIF desperately needed to retrieve its own scattered men, to reunite companies under their own leaders, staff officers of another command arbitrarily redirected them into unfamiliar teams, under unfamiliar leaders, and sent them out piecemeal. No Australian record explains why this was done. Circumstantial evidence suggests that Bennett no longer trusted Taylor to fight. As far as divisional headquarters knew, Taylor had only one battalion headquarters left, and had already made two unauthorised retreats from crucial positions.[32] Whatever the reason, this failure by division headquarters to even try to rebuild its units helped the fog of war finish 22nd Brigade AIF as a fighting brigade.

These grave command errors undid the stiff fight 22nd Brigade AIF and its reinforcing units put up on the first two days. From 8 through

10 February, the brigade plus 2/29 AIF, 2/4 MG AIF, and the 2/10 Field Regt. AIF suffered 625 battle casualties — more than 200 in 2/20 AIF alone. This not only confirms the fact there was a fight for the northwest, it also underlines how Taylor's formation was undone by its dispersal on two consecutive nights. It was a disastrous chain reaction: massive enemy pressure, ill-conceived and unwisely concealed first retreat, darkness and dense bush, dispersal, enemy pressure, miscommunication between commands, regrouping mishandled, further retreat, more dispersal. Maxwell made it worse by pulling his own brigade back without orders, losing touch with it, then allowing it to be split in two.[33] The result was that by midday 11 February both Australian brigades had a massive straggler problem on their hands and many stragglers were on the verge of giving up the chase to rejoin their units or find someone who knew what to do.

Malaya Command became aware of the problem late on 10 February. After Bennett's report at 1600 hrs, its war diary became inundated with reports of "stragglers." Percival included that pointed reference to too many fighting men in the rear areas in his call to arms that afternoon. Two reports of Australians trying to leave by boat were logged that evening. Key told GHQ at 2115 hrs that Maxwell had not closed the gap, and insinuated he would not. The most sensational report was logged at 0415 hrs 11 February by Brig. Newbigging, Percival's chief administrative officer. Newbigging went on a tour of sentry posts in the city in which he proceeded "in fear of his life."[34] For 11 February, the diary is one long repetitive report of troops causing trouble, especially by rushing boats at the docks. The majority concerned Australians. That day Newbigging set up posts at all entry points into the city. In a confusing and ugly situation it is too simple to say that before a certain time most troops were stragglers; after it they became deserters. But the mood of the troops and their behaviour did respond to the course of the battle. At first the military police reported that most troops wanted food, rest and redirection.[35] On 11 February the balance started to shift. More and more, men cut off twice from their own units stopped looking for help and started trying to escape or just to hide. Those whose actions were logged by GHQ were deserters.

Against this backdrop, Bennett and Taylor had a final, ugly and important confrontation the morning of 12 February. When an exhausted Taylor reported to Bennett on the way to hospital for a rest, the fiery divisional commander cracked:

> He then went on to say that the 22nd Bde had run away from the enemy when he landed on the island, that we had let down the remainder of the force, that both I and the Bde were a disgrace to Australia and the AIF, and that he would relieve me of my command.

Taylor walked out in anger but was duly relieved. A witness on Bennett's staff described this as a vengeful act provoked by Bennett's rage over the collapse of his command, which made him look bad to Wavell and Percival — especially when they ordered him to launch an attack that was no longer possible.[36] Bennett was of course mistaken; 22nd Brigade AIF did not "run away." But it was scattered to the four winds by enemy pressure plus its own poorly planned and ill-advised retreats, especially the first. This reaction by Bennett confirms what must be seen as a crucial fact in the whole disaster: both Bennett and Percival *did not know* 22nd Brigade AIF was not going to stand and fight it out on the coast at all costs.

Percival also did not know that Bennett had prevented any work to prepare the Kranji-Jurong Line. There can be no excuse for these failures. Both commanders should have known, ought to have asked, should have taken precautions such as organising police patrols. But neither did, so both were caught off-guard when both Australian brigades fell back in disarray.[37] That left them floundering when the chain of command should have swung into action to regroup the division. When the men suffered twice from this in two days, many gave up. The total failure of Percival, Bennett, Maxwell and Taylor to even work together put the 8th Australian Division in a position to be destroyed as a formation. By the time Bennett sacked Taylor, the damage was done.

The collapse of an army is never tidy. When it happens in a crowded city with no hope of escape there will always be scenes of cowardice, brutality, even horror. Fear is the ugliest emotion. In Singapore in the last four days the thin line that divides an army between a disciplined force and an armed mob faded badly, and per capita the Australians suffered more than the others. No important reliable eyewitness report or official source fails to mention how completely order in the city broke down, and that many troops gave up on the battle. This is what so impressed Wavell when he signed his report. But the principal cause is also singled out consistently and clearly: the loss of confidence in their leaders by too many troops.[38] Too few commanders found ways to persuade their men to fight on as a disciplined force, too many troops were allowed to give up in a *sauve qui peut*. As far as the Australians are concerned, the definitive evidence comes from within.

Bennett provided the first indication with his after action report, submitted six weeks after the surrender. The GOC noted down that disturbingly low figure for troops in the final perimeter and confessed the morale of the army collapsed as many units buckled under mass desertion at the end. Bennett singled out Indian troops but did not confine his remarks to them. He admitted that towards the end it was all but impossible to return men to their units. In 1946 an advance copy of Percival's despatch was sent to Australia for vetting. Callaghan — who took over the Australian force after the capitulation — was asked to compare it with that submitted in 1942 by Bennett. Callaghan recommended that on any clash Percival's report be accepted as more reliable. Then he singled out the "dangerous statement" in Bennett's report about the number of troops in the final AIF perimeter, noting it was now clearly impossible to identify all missing men as casualties or prisoners. Regarding the many reports of Australians hiding in town or trying to escape, Callaghan bluntly admitted "there is a certain amount of truth in both these statements...This temporary lapse of the Australian on the island and the criticism it has invoked has caused me a lot of uneasiness." Callaghan advised his superiors to accept Percival's proposed defence of the AIF performance on the island gratefully and bury Bennett's report quietly. His advice was accepted.[39]

This sense of guilt and embarassment was very evident in the Thyer report. The authors went to great lengths to unravel the story of the collapse of 22nd Brigade AIF, grilling all survivors with great care. They did not shrink from discussing how and when each unit was scattered. They also admitted categorically there were too many AIF troops in town rather than at their posts, from 9 February on. The authors took every chance to excuse the troops' performance by bringing up other considerations, an indication of how sensitive the issue was. But in the end they admitted only two thirds at most of those fit to fight manned the final perimeter. Above all, they argued that all of Malaya Command failed to rise to the challenge to do their dogged best in a poor position on Singapore Island.[40]

Such reports were so threatening to the Australian reputation that at some point the official historian prepared a draft, marked "end of chap15?," to explain away the confessions made by Australian officers about the collapse of the division. This undated eight-page report was a proposed whitewash, which aimed to discredit the Thyer report by smearing its authors. Thyer's confession of bias against Bennett and the feud between the two were singled out in a report which argued that criticisms of Bennett came from men who detested him, blamed him for their defeat, and spoke when their spirits were at their lowest ebb and the desire for revenge at its peak.[41] But this draft was never used in the published volume — perhaps because the picture it painted was of a dysfunctional division headquarters. That might well have backfired, making stories of command blunders and morale collapse seem more, not less, credible. Wigmore instead resorted to the pathetic paragraph noted above. With that the Australians hid behind Percival's despatch and let the truth hibernate.

This only allowed the controversy to simmer, and excuses for the final days to fester. The most emotional and amusing was the charge that large numbers of British troops wore Australian slouch hats, leaving the Aussies to take the fall when they broke and rampaged. The 8th Australian Division Provost Company War Diary is the only reliable primary source which discusses this issue, albeit for 4 February. Two British units did officially adopt such hats when their own ran short, 2nd Loyals and 5th Sherwood Foresters. 2nd Loyals lost men, but fought on as a unit until the end. 5th Sherwood Foresters on the other hand were dispersed in unimpressive fashion by an attack by five Japanese tanks on the morning of 12 February. They never fully regrouped. But they are the only U.K. *unit* recorded to have cracked outright on Singapore Island. Certainly many British troops were back in the city without permission, but it is fantastic to suggest there were so few Australians that all slouch hat incidents were a case of mistaken identity. The only senior Australian to comment directly on British straggling was the reliable and much-admired "Black Jack" Galleghan. After he left hospital on 13 February, Galleghan was directed to round up stragglers — itself an indication of the problem. He did not see any British stragglers and later estimated one-third or less of the total could have come from British units.[42] British troops wearing slouch hats probably did desert, but not nearly enough to explain away all the Australians.

The crowning piece of evidence in Australian records regarding the collapse of the 8th Australian Division on Singapore Island is the war diary of the unit directly responsible for keeping the troops in the chain of command: the Provost Company. The diary was carefully typed, submitted in point form for February 1942 with every paragraph corresponding to a date, and every paragraph was initialled and the whole signed by the unit commander, Capt. A.G. Menz. It traces clearly and concisely the deterioration of the defence as the battle wore on. And it is a crucial source for helping to explain the all important "why" as well as the "what." As early as 9 February it uses the word "panic" to describe the situation just behind the battle area. As early as 11 February it uses the word "stragglers". For the last four days of the battle it is so devastating and important that it must speak in full for itself:

> **12.** Many soldiers of all Units finding their way into Singapore saying they needed a sleep and a meal, and giving panicky accounts of the front line actions. Under the circumstances, as much food as possible was provided by us, after having being [sic] collected by members of this unit from the wharves, under shell fire and aerial bombing. Soldiers are becoming very sullen, and they are so numerous that it is very difficult to collect and return them to Assembly Area.

> **13.** Conditions as on the previous day. Enemy air activity increasing. Some AIF soldiers very reluctant to return to the line, saying "There is no organisation there." British and Indian troops wandering aimlessly about. Representations made to APM Malaya Command to provide directional information for British troops, but with no result.

> **14.** More and more soldiers in Singapore, morale very low. All imagineable excuses being made to avoid returning to the line. Arms and equipment being discarded all over Singapore. Wharves crowded with soldiers viewing chances of getting off in boats.

> **15.** Enemy air and artillery action on Singapore greatly increased. Water mains severed, electricity cut off, and town very badly battered. Soldiers everywhere. Daily requests to Malaya Command to collect and direct British soldiers, but nothing done. AIF soldiers collected by this unit and transported to Botanical Gardens, but morale shocking. A lot of men hid themselves to prevent and avoid return to the line. Very heavy air raids and shelling about 1600 hrs. Fires in several parts of the town, vehicles on fire along the whole length of streets, general pandemonium and confusion. Rumour that "cease fire" would be at 1600 hrs caused troops to throw away arms and ammunition, and all guns in Singapore

to stop firing. Rumour proved false. Great activity then in getting troops
out of town and to take up arms again to hold the line until 2030 hrs,
when "cease fire" really became operative.[43]

Wigmore and Kirby had access to this and all other sources cited
in this study; as for Percival, he was there at the time. There can be only
one conclusion: British and Australian authorities decided not to admit
Malaya Command was disintegrating into an armed mob as it tried to
hold a final perimeter in Singapore. The two collapses of the Australians
were so striking because they undid *all* their combat units, then carrying
the brunt of the battle. They also undermined all of Percival's plans:
coast defence, "Kranji-Jurong Line," final perimeter to hold Bukit Timah.
The unravelling of Indian formations looked more like the toppling of
dominoes but also drained the army because it was concentrated in
combat units. Clearly there were also large numbers of British deserters,
many of whom must have been from the vast impedimenta of etcetera
with which the British Army encumbered itself in war. Overall Percival
may well have been missing 40% of his "still fit to stand" strength from
the final perimeter, by educated guess. So much for any counterattack,
lost opportunity or not.

Some causes of desertion were particular to one group. While some
Indian troops were turned by the enemy, this did not happen to
Australians or Britons. No British units faced an assault as massive as
that which hit 22nd Brigade AIF, nor did any suffer such incompetent
attempts by higher commands to respond as did that formation. 18th
Division, inexperienced as it was, was at least fully trained. Some
Australian replacements had not fired a weapon, nor received any training
in fieldcraft. One reliable source described such men as "a positive menace
to anyone near them and to any commander who expected his orders
to be carried out." 2/19 and 2/29 AIF in particular were in no way ready
for battle, let alone the fight they faced on 8–9 February. Of course this
affected their performance, so much so that Wigmore did publish a
scathing indictment of the decision to send such men rather than better-
trained militia troops.[44] And of course these men were numerous among
the stragglers and deserters. Yet in the end the most important cause
of the collapse of Malaya Command was a factor common to all its parts,
varying only in degree. High command at army, division and brigade
levels lost the confidence of and control over so many troops that GHQ
was forced to surrender while it still could.

The connection between leadership and performance was crucial
and direct. Heath and Key never lost control of their formations, but
could not stop the haemorrhaging of their units. Heath personally
confronted an unnamed "lot of stragglers" on the afternoon of 11
February and was aware of the deterioration of his corps. III Corps could
not have lasted much longer, which explains his attitude at the last
conferences. 18th Division remained cohesive until the end, but when
poorly led units came under pressure their inexperience showed. One
British brigade *headquarters* reacted to Japanese firecracker scare tactics

by "several hours" of pandemonium and firing. That same brigade reported on the last day that two of its units were spent and the other — 5th Sherwood Foresters — was undone by news of a white flag and abandoned its positions.[45] 18th Division could not stand on its own. But the command failure which most affected the defence was that which undid the Australians.

Maxwell should have been court-martialled for defeatism. As early as late January Bennett reprimanded him repeatedly for complaining about the situation and his tired troops, warning him to stop "wet nursing" his soldiers. Instead of removing this dangerous influence, Bennett left him in command. The GSO1 of Malaya Command claims that on the morning of 8 February Maxwell urged Percival in person to surrender Singapore, rather than waste lives in a hopeless fight. Thyer remembers Maxwell telling him the next evening that as a doctor his job was to save lives. Bennett told the official historians that Maxwell and his ADMS, speaking as doctors, asked him — after the final retreat — to use his influence to "have the show called off." Maxwell gave up the causeway in what Australian officers agreed was an unnecessary withdrawal. The official historians forced him to admit this was contrary to Percival's standing order. Maxwell simply refused to answer when they asked him if he knew the Japanese were attacking when the retreat began. Maxwell left his brigade in the hands of an officer he placed that day in command of 2/26 AIF, and who did not have the confidence of his subordinates but who could be relied on to retreat. Then he made little effort to regain control of his units. Maxwell denied giving up on the fight, but it was the weight of evidence to the contrary which provoked the official historians to ask the question in the first place.[46] The commander of 27th Brigade AIF gave up on the battle of Singapore before it started, made no attempt to stiffen or lead his men, and the minority who fought on until the end were there in spite of him.

Taylor's behaviour was less craven but had greater consequences. Asked by the official historians why the Thyer report insisted he failed to make sure the Japanese crossing was contested while the enemy was on the water, Taylor in the end could not do so and accepted responsibility. The Thyer report made it clear over 50 years ago that Taylor's decision to retreat from the coast under pressure was not only unwise in itself but the first step down the slippery slope, particularly because it was unauthorised. Taylor kept it quiet because he knew this directly contradicted, and would compromise, Malaya Command's defence plan. After the battle he did not deny this, as Callaghan noted in his comments on the Percival despatch. If Taylor did this because he doubted Percival would at least use a sacrificial stand to organise an all-out counterattack, then one can feel some sympathy for him. And Percival and Bennett have no excuses for not asking the right questions and being ready to cope with the unexpected. But the fact remains that Taylor not only ruined his own plan by not spelling it out in order to conceal it from his superiors, he also ruined their plans by that concealment. Double jeopardy — quadrupled when Taylor gave up the "Kranji-Jurong Line" and moved back to the perimeter.[47] None of these three commanders had any confidence in the other two. The troops paid the price.

The Thyer report put the blame for the Australian collapse squarely on command failures. In doing so, it underlined how massive that collapse was. Too many men were so raw they needed exceptional leadership to fight at all. The collapse was "mainly due to faulty direction." The authors singled out the sturdy fight put up by the hardy remnants under Maj. Merrett to show "that if given resolute leadership, stray parties from disintegrated battalions could be welded into an efficient fighting detachment capable of engaging superior forces." The stand made on Reformatory Road on the morning of 11 February "by tired and hungry troops against an aggressive and triumphant enemy" showed that "any criticism of the rank and file of those Brigades for the happenings on the 9th and 10th must be completely refuted."[48] Lt.-Col. Dalley personally witnessed Lt.-Col. C.F. Assheton hold his 2/20 AIF together by calm cool example and doggedness. Hours after Assheton was killed on the morning of 9 February, the battalion was reduced to a remnant. On the negative side, the complaints noted by Capt. Menz of the Provost Company were marked by the troops' loss of all confidence in their leaders in the line: "there is no organisation there."[49] How could there be, when officers such as Assheton and Merrett were let down by Maxwell, Taylor, and above all Bennett and his headquarters.

Bennett lost confidence in both his brigadiers before Singapore was attacked, but left both in command. He gave Percival 75% of the blame for faulty dispositions. The rest he awarded to Taylor, for his retreats, and Thyer. Bennett blamed Thyer for developing the "Kranji-Jurong Line" without his knowledge, and for pointing it west instead of north. These were ridiculous criticisms, especially as the enemy came from the west. Bennett then accused Thyer of skulking off to hide from the battle in GHQ Malaya Command. He did not offer one word of repentance or accept any blame for the loss of Singapore. The official historians rightly dismissed his slanderous accusations and in the end gave up their effort to obtain a considered analysis from him, after eight years of correspondence.[50] Bennett took his failure to hold in Johore — for which he blamed everybody but his Australians and himself — so hard that he assumed his troops were no longer willing to fight either. It was a vicious circle, but Bennett held the rank and the responsibility, so the blame is his. He never threw himself into the fight for Singapore, and his troops suffered accordingly.[51]

Instead of fighting for Singapore Bennett escaped it, leaving his troops to the mercy of the enemy. He planned the escape as early as 28 January; when the time came, he ordered his troops to stand fast, but made off himself. This decision was so controversial Bennett faced a post-war court of enquiry to explain it. His obsessive vendetta against the staff corps drove him to make two egregious blunders. First he virtually paralysed his headquarters in order to prevent his staff from undermining him. Then he gave up on the last battle in order to escape and make sure his rivals at home could not take over the army completely.

In later years Bennett was seen as a hero by many of his men.[52] Rarely has such regard been so ill-deserved.

The most wounding and controversial accusation made against the Australians on Singapore Island was that they were "known as daffodils — beautiful to look at but yellow all through."[53] Of course there must have been individual cases of cowardice. But on the whole this is slander, even to the great majority of those who gave up on the battle in the last four days. The GOC was barely functioning, looking instead to escape. One brigadier was defeatist. The other made plans based on the assumption the main plan would not succeed. The rank and file of the 8th Australian Division were tired, but not stupid. They could not have failed to note the attitudes of their commanders and the lack of clear direction and harmony in the chain of command. As Percival himself admitted, when no one told them otherwise they decided the battle was futile.[54] When the front fell apart and no one stepped forward to restore the situation, many — twice provoked — gave up. Mass desertion there was, but the main cause is also clear: left to fend for themselves by an incompetent command, the troops did just that.

This almost certainly tipped the balance when it came to the decision to surrender. Accounts of the last meetings note the emphasis on plummeting morale and the shortage of reliable troops. In his own report, Bennett rated this as equal to the water and supply position in swaying Percival. The weight of evidence supports him.[55] Malaya Command surrendered not only because it was out of water and supplies but also because too many troops were no longer willing to fight. Percival and his staff cannot escape a large share of the blame for this result. No questions were asked about Taylor's plans or the "Kranji-Jurong Line." No action was taken against Maxwell. Percival never tried to master the situation by taking the kind of drastic measures which alone might have inspired an all-out battle by the army as a whole. Staff officers who said the battle was lost before it started should have been arrested. Deserters who tried to hijack ships should have been summarily executed, while there were still few enough to handle. Percival was not the type of charismatic leader whose personality could inspire men to fight on against all odds. But this was the kind of leadership the army required in its dire straits. The very least he could have done was ask the right questions, if not take charge himself when 22nd Brigade AIF started to unravel. Taylor was not the only soldier to sense the lack of iron and fire at the top, where it was needed most.[56]

Rather than take charge in no uncertain terms and take the calculated risk to be bold, Percival settled for the improvised piecemeal measures which had already lost him the mainland. He also allowed his staff to exhort the troops in ways which reduced rather than raised their confidence. In addition to warning everyone not to make "warlike noises," GHQ refused to allow Alexandra Hospital to be flagged with a Red Cross because "it was unfair to the enemy to have a hospital marked with a Red Cross so near to the main oil and petrol installations!!"[57] This Colonel Blimp attitude reached the troops on 3 February. Just as they were working desperately to build the defences that had not been erected for fear of harming their morale, they received this war-winning advice from Lt.-Col. Phillips, GSO1 Malaya Command:

> Experience has shown that the Japanese soldier will not stand up to bayonet charges. This therefore is the best way to beat him. All ranks must be imbued with the spirit of the attack. It is no good waiting for the Japanese to attack first. The endeavour of the soldier must be to locate the enemy and, having located him, to close with him. The soldier should, if exposed, cover his advance with fire, either from Tommy gun, rifle or light automatic, until he is able to attack with the bayonet. If every soldier is determined to kill at least one Japanese the enemy will not have a chance.[58]

Faced with such a feeble high command, it is a wonder the army fought as hard as it did on Singapore Island. No extenuating circumstances or grand strategy decisions can conceal the final hard fact. Singapore was lost as fast as it was because too many of the commanders responsible for defending it did not, or could not, do their duty.

Notes

1. *Malaya Operations Record*, f.104; Tsuji, 260-66; Fujiwara, 173-74; Allen, 173-74. Both Fujiwara and Tsuji note how heavy enemy shellfire was on the last day of the battle in the area the *5th Division* was operating in, and how concerned this made them. The War Diary of the HQ Royal Artillery 18th Division, contained in PRO, WO172/91, entry for 15 February 1942, notes that a divisional concentration rising to a "crescendo" was brought down on that very area in the early afternoon — around the time noted by the two Japanese memoirs. It should be noted that 18th Division guns had more ammunication left that morning than other formations because they had not been in action from the first day of the Japanese attack on the island. But the War Diary goes on to note that the divisional shoot left the guns in a very serious position as less than a day's supply of ammunition was left with no chance of replenishment — and that the shoot was in response to an enemy bombardment which seemed to be growing in intensity.

2. Hall, 192, Ward, *The killer they called a God*, 93-95, and Elphick, *Singapore: The Pregnable Fortress*, 111, 364, all suggest Yamashita feared defeat and surrender.

3. This is the statement as quoted in Ward, *The killer they called a God*, 95. Longer and less incriminating versions are found in Potter, 89-90, and Allen, 181-84.

4. *Malaya Operations Record*, f.106; Potter, 89.

5. Elphick, *Singapore: The Pregnable Fortresses*, 111, 364, chooses his words carefully, saying Yamashita later stated that if Percival had not surrendered when he did the Japanese commander "would have had to give up his final assault on Singapore" — but then quotes Fujiwara to imply this might have saved the city from surrender. Fujiwara, 173-74, 176-77, 180, receives too much attention; Tsuji, definitive on this issue on page 262, receives too little. The *Malaya Operations Record* supports him with this controlled statement on f.104: "As the battle progressed towards the area surrounding Singapore city the enemy resistance suddenly increased while our ammunition decreased heavily with only about 1 to 2 standards [out of 10.5 standards allotted for the entire battle for the island: f/97] left. Therefore, the Army studied the preservation of ammunition and the progress of battle hereafter."

6. Allen, 175-84; Kirby, *The Chain of Disaster*, 249-50.

7. *Operations of Malaya Command*, paragraph 618; Percival, 292; Elphick, 322. Compare the published PRO, CAB106/38, *Despatch on Operations in the South-West*

Pacific from 15 January 1942 to 25 February 1942, paragraph 34, with the only recently released PREM2/168/3, *Report on Operations in Malaya and Singapore*, 1 June 1942; see also below, note 20.

8. Wavell blamed the rapid fall of Singapore for what he obviously saw as the imminent collapse of his whole theatre and Allied defensive strategy against Japan: PRO, CAB106/163, Wavell to Brooke, 17 February 1942.

9. Chippington, 237-40; Stewart, 115-16; Moore, 72.

10. Moore, 11; Elphick, *Singapore: The Pregnable Fortress*, ch. 14.

11. PRO, CAB106/162, Thyer report, 91, 128, 137, 141; CAB106/58, History of 11th Indian Division, ch. xxv, 516; Fujiwara, 167-72; AWM, 54/553/16, Report on Malayan Campaign by Maj.-Gen. H.G. Bennett, 2 March 1942 (Bennett Report), 13; AWM52/8/ 2/22, War Diary, 22nd Brigade AIF, 11 February 1942 entries. In PRO, CAB106/152, Ballentine replies to questions from official historians, Brig. Ballentine agrees a panic among young troops in 6/1 Punjab started the retreat. But he denies it ever became an uncontrollable rout and argues it was due at least as much to the news the Australians were retreating to a perimeter.

12. PRO, CAB106/58, History of 11th Indian Division, ch. xxv; WO172/21, War Diary, GHO Malaya Command, Appendix V.61, 12 February 1942; CAB106/71, Diary of events, 54th Brigade in Singapore 29 January–15 February 1942 (54th Brigade Diary), 14 February 1942 entry; Fujiwara, 172-73, claims nearly a thousand Indian troops defected by the evening of 13 February; Elphick, *Singapore: The Pregnable Fortress*, 338-43.

13. PRO, CAB106/58, History of 11th Indian Division, ch. xxv; CAB106/117, Ballentine account; AWM, 52/8/2/22, War Diary, 22nd Brigade AIF, 11-12 February 1942 entries; 52/18/2/21, War Diary, Provost Company, 8th Australian Division, 12-15 February 1942 entries; Elphick, *Singapore: The Pregnable Fortress*, ch. 13, 352.

14. Wigmore, 365-66; Elphick, *Singapore: The Pregnable Fortress*, chs. 12-13.

15. AWM, 54/554/11/39, War Diary, AIF Changi, 17 February 1942 entry; 54/553/ 5/16, Bennett Report, 40; 54/553/3/4, AGH Report, 8th Australian Division Operations Reports; PRO, CAB106/162, Thyer report, 193.

16. Wigmore, 312-30, 343-45, 366, needs to be read with great care regarding the reorganization of 22nd Brigade AIF; Bennett, 178-91; Elphick, *Singapore: The Pregnable Fortress*, 290-93.

17. AWM, 52/8/2/22, War Diary, 22nd Brigade AIF, 9–11 February 1942 entries; PRO, CAB106/162, Thyer report, 112, 125, 153; Bennett, 178-81; Wigmore, 335-45, 366; Kirby, *The Loss of Singapore*, 384-91. On the eve of the battle 22nd Brigade AIF, its supporting arms, plus 2/29 AIF accounted for over 5000 men. By late 10 February, Kirby had the total down to 1600 still under command; Wigmore stated the number was 1200. Battle casualties for these units from 8 through 10 February were listed as 376 killed, 201 wounded. 200 of the men under command arrived after the battle started, with the X Battalion; the Special Reserve Battalion was not under Taylor's command. That leaves 1400 men, if Kirby is correct. Wigmore argues that the casualty count should be increased to 1200, on the basis of a normal ratio of two and a half wounded for every battle death in similar engagements. That would still leave 2400 men, nearly half the total, unaccounted for.

18. AWM, 54/553/5/14, Interview with Maj. C.B. O'Brien 2/18 AIF, 23 September 1845, 12-14 (O'Brien interview); 52/8/2/22, War Diary, 22nd Brigade AIF, 12-15 February 1942 entries; WO172/21, War Diary, GHQ Malaya Command, AIF Sitrep, 1600 hrs 10 February 1942, Appendix V.58, my emphasis; Elphick, *Singapore: The Pregnable Fortress*, 300, does not quote the last sentence.

19. CAB106/162, Thyer report, 198; Elphick, *Singapore: The Pregnable Fortress*, 290-91, 303-33; Montgomery, 129-35.

20. Eye witness reports of Australians — and others — retreating in disarray, roaming the streets, rushing boats, above all behaving badly can be found from the following quarters: GHQ Malaya Command, 11th Indian Division, 18th Division, 1st Cambs, 44th Indian Brigade, the British Battalion, 2nd Loyals, Bennett, Taylor, members of their staffs, the 8th Australian Division Provost Company, and many expatriate civilians.

A larger list, well summarized by Elphick, can be illustrated by PRO, WO208/1529, Enclosure to Captain on Staff's Letter No. 1184/081 of 5 March 1942 (Seabridge Report) and WO208/1529, Malaya and Singapore: Report drawn up by Maj. H.P. Thomas, 30 May 1942 — the report countersigned by Wavell — plus FO371/35924, Malayan Experiences, report drawn up by F.L. Cave-Penny of the Shell Company, 12 January 1943 (Cave-Penny report), as well as Chippington, 197-98, Gallagher, 92, Pancheri, 51-52, Moore, 25-27, Montgomery, 135.

21. *Malaya Operations Record*, f.102-03, does exaggerate for effect — claiming the defenders counterattacked with tanks for instance, which was not done — but also clearly records that all three Japanese divisions met with resistance on their landings and overcame a defence which was not prolonged but also no mere token. Final casualties in the battle for the island were admitted as 1714 killed, 3372 wounded, ie. some 15% of *25th Army* combat troops committed — casualties admitted for the fighting on the peninsula were 1793 killed, 2772 wounded. Elphick concludes that the Colonel who supposedly confessed to Molly Reilly his men broke and ran like rabbits was Broadbent, leader of the authorized AIF escape party and the only Australian of that rank on board the ship. But as DAAG or principal administrative officer at Bennett's headquarters, Boardbent could not have done or seen what this man described. He had no field command, no combat troops to rally or watch collapse. Elphick is rash to assume Brig. Blackburn spoken to Taylor. Given their actions, he could have spoken to either 8th Division brigadier and been so advised. Elphick, *Singapore: The Pregnable Fortress*, 290-91, 303-06, 330-33.

22. AWM, War Diary, 22nd Brigade AIF, 9 February 1942 entries; 54/553/5/16, Bennett Report, 12; 54/553/5/14, O'Brien interview, 12; PRO CAB106/162, Thyer report, 104-21; CAB106/117, Ballentine account. All these sources report Australian resistance on the coast and problems in bringing artillery to bear. Ballentine reports that in 44th Indian Brigade's area sounds of machine gun and small arms fire from the Australians were audible past midnight.

23. Elphick, *Singapore: The Pregnable Fortress*, 291, 300-03, 319-20.

24. AWM, 52/8/2/22, War Diary, 22nd Brigade AIF, 2000 hrs 9 February 1942 entry; 52/18/2/21, War Diary, 8th Australian Division Provost Company, 9-10 February 1942 entries; PRO, CAB106/162, Thyer report, 125; Bennett, 181.

25. AWM, 52/8/2/22, War Diary, 22nd Brigade AIF, 9-10 February 1942 entries; 52/8/2/22, War Diary, 8th Australian Division Provost Company, 9-10 February 1942 entries; PRO, CAB106/117, Ballentine account, 6; WO172/21, War Diary, Malaya Command GHQ, Appendix S.56, 9 February 1942.

26. AWM, 54/249/1, Notes on Desertion, 7th Australian Division Circular, 12 July 1940.

27. AWM, 52/8/2/22, War Diary, 22nd Brigade AIF, 10 February and Appendix B 10 February 1942 entries; Wyett, 97-98; PRO, WO172/21, War Diary, GHQ Malaya Command, Appendices P.57, Q.57, W.57, M.58a, V.58, 10 February 1942.

28. Elphick, S*ingapore: The Pregnable Fortress*, 295. Percival, 276-77, admits he gave the order for the counterattack without much idea of the real situation of the units involved.

29. AWM, 52/8/2/22, War Diary, 2nd Brigade AIF, 1-8 February 1942 entries; 52/8/2/27, War Diary, 27th Brigade AIF, 1-8 February 1942 entries; 52/8/2/21,War Diary, 8th Australian Division Provost Company, 4 February 1942 entry; 54/553/5/116, Bennett Report, 11; 54/553/5/14, O'Brien interview, 9; PRO, CAB106/162, Thyer report, 93.

30. AWM, 52/8/2/22, War Diary, 22nd Brigade AIF, 8-9 February and Appendix B 8-9 February 1942 entries; PRO, CAB106/162, Thyer report, 97, 104-22.

31. AWM, 52/8/2/22, War Diary, 22nd Brigade AIF, 9-10 February and Appendix B-9 February 1942 entries; PRO, CAB106/162, Thyer report, 97, 125-40; CAB106/117, Ballentine account, 8; CAB106/58, History of 11th Indian Division, ch. xxv, 513.

32. AWM, 52/8/2/27, War Diary, 22nd Brigade AIF, Appendix A, X Battalion, 10-11 February 1942; 54/553/5/14, O'Brien interview, 13-16.

33. AWM, 54/171/2/27, List of Casualties, 8th Australian Division, Malaya; PRO,

WO172/21, War Diary, GHQ Malaya Command, Appendix L.56, 9 February 1942, spells out the agreement between Percival and Bennett that Maxwell's brigade was supposed to stand at the causeway.

34. PRO, WO172/21, War Diary, GHQ Malaya Command, Appendices Y.58, B.59, L.59, 10/2, Z.59, 11 February 1942. In the original document a handwritten note claims that Newbigging "found all alert" at the posts. The phrase quoted in the text was that originally typed in at the time, then incompletely scratched out.

35. PRO, WO172/21, War Diary, GHQ Malaya Command, Appendices N.60, R.60, W.60, Serials 4353, 4354, 4269, 4376, 11 February 1942; CAB106/162, Thyer report, 125; AWM, 52/18/2/21, War Diary, 8th Australian Division Provost Company, 11 February 1942 entry.

36. AWM, 52/8/2/22, War Diary, 22nd Brigade AIF, Appendix B 12 February 1942 entry; Wyett, 98-99.

37. *Operations of Malaya Command*, paragraphs 495, 500.

38. PRO, CAB106/58, History of 11th Indian Division, ch. xxv, 530, for a vigorous if pompous indictment of "evacuitis" and "absenteeism," clearly directed against the Australians; WO208/1529, Seabridge report and Thomas report, both agree the collapse of morale produced by bad leadership was general by 12 Ferbruary. Elphick cites many accounts on this theme.

39. AWM, 54/553/5/16, Bennett Report, 39; 54/553/1/16, Callaghan comments on Percival and Bennett reports, 29 January 1947 (Callaghan comments). Callaghan's comments were supported in writing by Thyer.

40. PRO, CAB106/162, Thyer report, 100, 125, 144-45, 155, 193.

41. AWM, 54/554/11/38, Notes by Col. Thyer and Col. Kappe on the departure of General Gordon Bennett from Malaya and conditions in Changi pow camp during the pow period, n/d. The mistitling is obviously deliberate.

42. AWM, 52/18/2/21, War Diary, 8th Australian Division Provost Company, 4 February 1942 entry, concludes its report of the investigation of disturbances in the town that day as follows: "Nearly all British troops are wearing Aust. style slouch hats, which is apparently why AIF troops have been blamed for all disturbances involving troops." It is easy to see how this impression could then be magnified by the grapevine. Bennett, 212-13, used this excuse in telephone conversations with Wavell after his escape from Singapore. PRO, WO172/21, War Diary, GHQ Malaya Command, Appendices P.61, R.61, S.61, T.61, W.61, 12 February 1942, describe how 5th Sherwood Foresters "broke," the commanding officer reporting only 20 men under command by early afternoon. Some stragglers were regrouped, but the battalion failed again in its final ordeal, described below. CAB106/151, Galleghan interview with official historians, 22/1/1953, 4. One other British unit also balked briefly: on 13 February a company of the 5th Battalion Bedfordshire and Hertfordshire Regiment abandoned its position on Pt. 125 at Pasir Panjang "without orders or necessity" after its commanding officer was killed by heavy enemy shelling. But the unit returned to the hill under brigade orders and held fast the rest of the day: CAB106/155, Williams account. Roy Connolly and Bob Wilson, *Cruel Britanna: Britannia Waives the Rules 1941-1942. Singapore Betrayed, Australia Abandoned*, New South Wales, 1944, an almost incoherent response to the release of the Wavell report, give the slouch hat alibi in the form the troops accepted it, 6. See also Elphick, *Singapore: The Pregnable Fortress*, 303.

43. AWM, 52/18/2/21, War Diary, 8th Australian Division Provost Company, 12-15 February 1942 entries.

44. AWM, 54/553/5/14, O'Brien interview, 10; PRO, CAB106/153, draft note on Australian Reinforcement Problem for Kirby, n/d, later appeared in Wigmore, 258n.

45. PRO, WO172/21, War Diary, GHQ Malaya Command, Appendix N.60, 11 February 1942; CAB106/71, 54th Brigade Diary, 11, 13-14.

46. AWM, 67/3/25 (Part 1), Bennett diary extracts, 28-29/ January, 1 February 1942 entries; PRO, CAB106/162, Thyer report, 198; CAB106/151, Bennett interview, 30 January 1953, Thyer interview, 26 January, Galleghan interview, 22 January, Maxwell interview, 26 January 1953. Kirby said to Thyer, "It does look as though he had decided that the battle was finished so far as he was concerned." Neither official history squared up to this issue in the end.

47. PRO, CAB106/162, Thyer report, 97, 104, 198; CAB106/151, Taylor interview; AWM, 54/553/1/16, Callaghan comments.

48. PRO, CAB106/162, Thyer report, 90, 101, 140, 156.

49. PRO, CAB106/58, History of 11th Indian Division, ch. xxv, 513; AWM, 52/18/2/21, War Diary, 8th Australian Division Provost Company, 13 February 1942; Elphick, *Singapore: The Pregnable Fortress*, 318.

50. AWM, 67/3/25, part 2, Gavin Long Papers, correspondence to and regarding Bennett, 1949-57.

51. AWM. 54/553/5/16, Bennett Report; 67/3/25, part 1, Bennett diary extracts, 30–31 January 1942 entries; PRO, CAB106/58, History of 11th Indian Division, ch. xxv, 526; Lodge, 164-65, considers that Bennett lost control and gave up on 10 February.

52. AWM. 67/3/25, part 1, Bennett diary extracts, 28 January 1942 entry; Elphick, *Singapore: The Pregnable Fortress*, 177; Lodge, 186-90, is cautious about the accusation that escape plans distracted Bennett from doing his duty before 10 February, arguing it came from Percival — but he admits Bennett was a disastrous failure as a division commander. A discussion of the change in attitude towards Bennett and his escape is on 246-47. Bennett, 198, 218-19, discusses his own escape. The Ligertwood Commission found that Bennett acted legally but not wisely in leaving his men. Good discussions of the controversy are in Lodge, chs. 11-13, and M. Clisby, *Guilty or Innocent? The Gordon Bennett Case*, Sydney, 1992, passim.

53. The accusation was made by Maj. J.K.C. Marshall, an expatriate officer in the Malayan Volunteer Force, in one of the reports received in 1942 and released in 1993: Elphick, *Singapore: The Pregnable Fortress*, 326-27.

54. *Operations of Malaya Command*, paragraph 495; Percival, 270. Seabridge also argues forcefully that the troops fought poorly because they were so badly led: PRO, WO208/1529, Seabridge report.

55. AWM, 553/5/16, Bennett report; PRO, CAB106/58, History of 11th Indian Division, ch. xxv, 538; Bennett, 186, admitted in print during the war that the fact the "streets were crowded with battle stragglers" influenced the surrender discussions.

56. Percival's pre-battle press conference seems to have sapped rather than boosted confidence, his performance was so bland: Morrison, 158-59. One very interesting report is PRO, WO172/16, War Diary and Appendices, GHQ Far East, Report #7, Information about certain aspects of GHQ Malaya Command during the last few days in Singapore, A/Maj. W.R. Waller, GSOII Malaya Command, n/d. This report by an authorised escapee was another used by Wavell. It is an interesting if self-incriminating account of how Malaya Command lost control of the army, not least by failing to prevent its national components from degenerating into separate contingents blaming each other for their fate.

57. AWM, 54/553/5/7, War Diary, ADMS, 8th Australian Division.

58. PRO, WO172/21, War Diary, GHQ Malaya Command, Appendix M.49, 3 February 1942.

BIBLIOGRAPHY

To 1819

Archival Sources

Public Record Office

CO273 series:	Straits Settlements Original Correspondence
FO881 series:	Confidential Print, Numerical Series
WO55 series:	Miscellaneous

East India Company Records
Bengal Secret Consultations

Singapore national archives

Straits Settlements Records, Series A–Z, AA–FF:
      Letters to Bencoolen
      Correspondence, Governor and Bengal
      Government

Tamil Nadu Archives, Madras

East India Company Public Works Department Consultations

Indian National Archives, New Delhi

East India Company Public Works Department Consultations

West Bengal State Archives, Calcutta

Narrative Abstracts of General Letters to and from the Court of Directors, III, in the Judicial Department 1793–1858

Published Sources

Andaya, L. (1975) *The Kingdom of Johore 1641–1728*. Kuala Lumpur: Oxford University Press.

Anderson, J. (1840) *Acheen, and the Ports on the North and East Coasts of Sumatra*. London: Allen.

Bastin, J. (1965) *The British in West Sumatra 1685–1825*. Kuala Lumpur: University of Malaya Press.

Birch, W. de G. (1875–1884) *The Commentaries of the Great Afonso Dalboquerque*. 4 vols. London: Hakluyt Society.

Bronson, B., M. Basoeki, M. Sukadi, and J. Wisseman. (n.d.) *Laporan Penelitian Arkeologi di Sumatera 20 Mei–8 Juli 1973*. Lembaga Penelitian Purbakala Nasiona, University of Pennsylvania Museum, Mimeographed.

Brown, C.C. (translated and annotated) (1970) *Sejarah Melayu or Malay Annals.* Kuala Lumpur: Oxford University Press.

Caldwell, Ian and A.A. Hazlewood. (1994) "'The Holy Footprints of the Venerable Gautama': A New Translation of the Pasir Panjang Inscription," in *Bijdragen tot de Taal-, Land- en Volkenkunde* 150, 3.

Cameron, J. (1965) *Our Tropical Possessions in Malayan India.* Kuala Lumpur: Oxford University Press (Reprint; Original: London: Smith, Elder and Co, 1865).

Charbonneau, A., Y. Desloges, and M. Lafrance. (1982) *Quebec the Fortified City: From the 17th to the 19th Century.* Ottawa: Parks Canada.

Coedes, G. (1968) *The Indianized States of Southeast Asia.* Honolulu: University of Hawaii.

Cortesao, A. (editor and translator) (1944) *The Suma Oriental of Tome Pires. 2 vols. 2nd Series, #89.* London: Hakluyt Society.

Crawfurd, J. (1823) *History of the Indian Archipelago.* Edinburgh.

— (1967) *Journal of an Embassy from the Governor-General of India to the Courts of Siam and Cochin China.* Kuala Lumpur: Oxford University Press [Original edition: London, 1828].

Darby, H.C. (1932) "The medieval sea-state," in *Scottish Geographical Magazine,* 48/3.

Fox, E.W. (1971) *History in Geographic Perspective: The Other France.* New York: W.W. Norton.

Gibson-Hill, C.A. (1955) "Johore Lama and other ancient sites on the Johor River," in *JMBRAS,* 28, 2.

— (1954) "Singapore: Notes on the history of the Old Strait, 1580–1850," in *JMBRAS,* 27, 1.

— (1956) "Singapore Old Strait and New Harbour, 1300–1870," in *Memoirs of the Raffles Museum,* 3.

Groeneveldt, W.P. (1987) *Historical Notes on Indonesia & Malaya Compiled from Chinese Sources.* Jakarta: Bhratara, 1960, p. 37.

Guillemard, F.H.H. (1886) *The Cruise of the Marchese to Kamschatka & New Guinea.* London: J. Murray.

Hamilton, A. (1930) *A New Account of the East Indies.* 2 vols. London: Argonaut Press.

Harfield, A. (1984) *British and Indian Armies in the Far East 1685–1935.* Chippenham: Picton.

Hervey, D.F.A. (1885) "Valentyn's description of Malacca," in *Journal of the Straits Branch of the Royal Asiatic Society (JSBRAS),* 15.

Hill, A.H. (1955) "The founding of Singapore described by 'Munshi Abdullah'," in *JMBRAS,* 28/3.

Hirth, F. & W.W. Rockhill. (1911) *Chau Ju-kua: His Work on the Chinese and Arab Trade in the Twelfth and Thirteenth Centuries.* St. Petersburg: Imperial Academy of Science.

Indrapala, K. (1971) "South Indian merchant communities in Ceylon, 950-1200," in *Ceylon Journal of Historical and Social Studies,* Nos.1/2.

Kathirithamby-Wells, J. (1977) *The British West Sumatran Presidency (1760–85): Problems of Early Colonial Enterprise.* Kuala Lumpur: University of Malaya Press.

Marsden, W. (1966) *History of Sumatra.* Kuala Lumpur: Oxford University Press [reprint of 1783 edition].

Maxwell, W.E. (1879) "The founding of Singapore," in *JSBRAS,* 4.

Miksic, J.N. (1985) *Archaeological Research on the 'Forbidden Hill': Excavations at Fort Canning, 1984.* Singapore: National Museum. See also Kwa, C.G. "Appendix. Records and Notices of Early Singapore."

Miksic, J. (1995) "Hubungan sejarah antara Srivijaya Palembang☐dan Lembah Bujang," in *Tamadun Melayu*, volume 3., ed. Ismail Hussein, A. Aziz Deraman, and Abd Rahman Al-ahmadi. Kuala Lumpur: Dewan Bahasa dan Pustaka, 894-917.

Miller, H.E. (Trans) (1941) "Letters of Col. Nahuijs," in *Journal of the Malayan Branch of the Royal Asiatic Society (JMBRAS)*, 19.

Mills, J.V.G. (1930) "Eredia's description of Malacca, Meridianal India, and Cathay," in *JMBRAS*, 8, 1, 1930.

— (1970) *Ma Huan, Ying-yai Sheng Lan: The Overall Survey of the Ocean's Shores.* Cambridge: Cambridge University Press, Hakluyt Society.

Moore, E. (1988) *Moated Sites in Early North East Thailand.* Oxford: British Archaeology Reports, International Series, No. 400.

Naerssen, F.H van. (1977) "The administrative and economic history of early Indonesia," in *Handbuch der Orientalistik, Dritte Abteilung, Siebenter Band.* Leiden/Koln: E.J. Brill.

Pigeaud, T.G.Th. (1960) *Java in the Fourteenth Century: A Study in Cultural History. Vol. III.* The Hague: M. Nijhoff.

Pintado, M.J. (1978) "Some Portuguese historical sources on Malacca history," in *Heritage*, 3.

Reid, A.R. (1988, 1993) *Southeast Asia in the Age of Commerce 1450-1680. Vol. 1: The Lands below the Winds. Vol. 2: Expansion and Crisis.* New Haven: Yale.

— (editor) (1993) *Southeast Asia in the Early Modern Era: Trade, Power, and Belief.* Ithaca: Cornell University Press.

Robertson, J.A. (1906) *Magellan's Voyage Around the World.* 3 vols. Cleveland: A.H. Clark.

Rockhill, W.W. (1915) "Notes on the relations and trade of China with the eastern archipelago and the coast of the Indian Ocean during the fourteenth century. Part II," in *T'oung Pao*, 15.

Rouffaer, G.P. (1921) "Was Malaka emporium voor 1400AD, genaamd Malajoer?" in *Bijdragen tot de Taal-, Land- en Volkenkunde*, 77.

Rutter, O. (1984) *The Pirate Wind.* Singapore: Oxford University Press [original edition 1910].

Sopher, D. (1977) *The Sea Nomads.* Singapore: National Museum.

Tambiah, S.J. (1977) "The galactic polity: the structure of traditional kingdoms in Southeast Asia," in S. A. Freed, (editor), *Anthropology and the Climate of Opinion.* New York: Annals of the New York Academy of Sciences No. 293.

Tarling, N. (1963) *Piracy and Politics in the Malay World.* Singapore: Donald Moore.

Trocki, C.A. (1979) *Prince of Pirates.* Singapore: Singapore University Press.

Warmington, E.H. (1928) *The Commerce Between the Roman Empire and India.* Cambridge: Cambridge University Press.

Wheatley, P. (1961) *The Golden Khersonese.* Kuala Lumpur: University of Malaya.

Wolters, O.W. (1967) *Early Indonesian Commerce.* Ithaca: Cornell University Press.

— (1971) *The Fall of Srivijaya in Malay History.* Ithaca: Cornell University Press.

— (1982) *History, Culture and Region in Southeast Asian Perspectives.* Singapore: Institute of Southeast Asian Studies.

Wurtzburg, C.E. (1986) *Raffles of the Eastern Isles.* Singapore: Oxford University Press [1954].

1819-1918

Archival Sources

National Archives of India, New Delhi

East India Company Public Works Department Consultations
Military Department Consultations, 1854-60
Public Works Consultations, 1855-58
Proceedings of the Government of India in the Public Works Department, 1860
Public Works Department, 1861

Public Record Office

ADM116 series:	Cases of the Admiralty and Secretariat
ADM125 series:	Station Records: China, Correspondence
CAB7 series:	Colonial / Oversea Service Co: Minutes
CAB11 series:	Colonial / Oversea Defence Co: Defence Scheme
CO273 series:	Straits Settlements Original Correspondence
CO537 series:	Straits Settlements Original Correspondence
FOCP series:	Foreign Office Confidential Print
WO10 series:	Artillery Muster Books and Pay Lists
WO33 series:	Committees: Reports and Papers
WO106 series:	Directorate of Military Operations and Intelligence

Tamil Nadu Archives, Madras

East India Company Public Works Department Consultations
Military Index 1857, 1860, 1861, 1867
Military Department Consultations, 1858-59
Military Department Proceedings, 1868

West Bengal State Archives, Calcutta

Narrative Abstracts of General Letters to and from the Court of Directors, III, in
    the Judicial Department 1793-1858

Published Sources

Brice, M. (1984) *Stronghold; A History of Military Architecture.* London: B.T. Batsford
    Ltd.
Buckley, C.B. (1965) *An Anecdotal History of Old Times in Singapore.* Kuala Lumpur/
    Singapore: University of Malaya Press.
Carver, M. (1986) *The Seven Ages of the British Army.* London: Grafton Books.
Chan E.H.G. (1990) "The Volunteer Corps: Contributions to Singapore's Internal
    Security and Defence (1854-1984)", in *Pointer,* November Supplement.
Fox, G. (1940) *British Admirals and Chinese Pirates, 1832-1869.* London: Kegan
    Paul, Trench, Trubner and Co.
Fuller, W.C. (1992) *Strategy and Power in Russia, 1600-1914.* New York: The Free
    Press.
Gibson-Hill, C.A. (1954) "Singapore: notes on the history of the Old Strait, 1580-
    1850," in *JMBRAS,* 27, 1.
— (1956) "Singapore Old Strait and New Harbour, 1300-1870," in *Memoirs of the
    Raffles Museum,* 3.
Glover, M. (1973) *An Assemblage of Indian Army Soldiers and Uniforms.* London:
    Perpetua Press.

Graham, G.S. (1978) *The China Station; War and Diplomacy, 1830-1860.* Oxford: Clarendon Press.

Grenfell, R. (1987 reprint) *Main Fleet to Singapore.* Singapore, Oxford and New York: Oxford University Press.

Harfield, A. (1984) *British and Indian Armies in the Far East 1685-1935.* Chippenham: Picton.

Hibbert, C. (1980) *The Great Mutiny: India 1857.* London: Penguin Books.

Hopkirk, P. (1990) *The Great Game: On Secret Service in High Asia.* Oxford: Oxford University Press.

Lee, E. (1991) *The British as Rulers Governing Multiracial Singapore, 1867-1914.* Singapore: Singapore University Press.

Makepeace, W., G.E. Brooke, and R.St.J. Braddell. (editors) (1921) *One Hundred Years of Singapore.* London: J. Murray.

Mills, L.A. (1966) *British Malaya 1824-67.* Kuala Lumpur: Oxford University Press, 1966 (First published in *JMBRAS* 1925.)

Moore, D. & J. (1969) *The First 150 Years of Singapore.* Singapore: D. Moore.

Nish, I. (1985, second edition) *The Anglo-Japanese Alliance: The Diplomacy of Two Island Empires 1894-1907.* London: Athlone Press.

Philips, C.H. (1961) *The East India Company 1784-1834.* Bombay: Oxford University Press.

Reith, G.M. (1985) *Handbook to Singapore.* Singapore: Oxford University Press [original edition 1907].

Sarty, R.F. (1988) *Coast Artillery 1815-1914.* Bloomfield, Ontario: Museum Restoration Service.

Scott, H.L. (1968) *Military Dictionary.* New York: Greenwood Press.

Sheppard, Tan Sri Dato' Mubin. (editor) (1982) *Singapore 150 Years.* Singapore: Times Books International for the MBRAS.

Singapore Free Press. (1885) *The Defences of Singapore: being a series of articles reprinted from the Singapore Free Press.* Singapore: Singapore and Straits Printing Office.

Song, O.S. (1967) *One Hundred Years History of the Chinese in Singapore.* Singapore: University Malaya Press.

Stephen, L., and Lee, S. (editors) (1922) *The Dictionary of National Biography,* Vol. 21. London: Oxford University Press.

Tarassuk, L., and Blair, C. (editors) (1982) *The Complete Encyclopaedia of Arms and Weapons.* London: B.T. Batsford.

Thompson, E., and Garratt, G.T. (1934) *Rise and Fulfilment of British Rule in India.* London: MacMillan.

Turnbull, C.M. (1975) *A History of Singapore 1819-1975.* Singapore: Oxford University Press.

Westwood, J.N. (1987) *Endurance and Endeavour: Russian History 1812-1986.* Oxford: Oxford University Press.

Winsley, Capt. T.M. (1938) *A History of the Singapore Volunteer Corps, 1854-1937, being also An Historical Outline of Volunteering in Malaya.* Singapore: Government Printing Office.

Wurtzburg, C.E. (1986) *Raffles of the Eastern Isles.* Singapore: Oxford University Press [1954].

Yapp, M.E. (1987) *The Making of the Modern Near East.* London, New York: Longman.

1918-1971

Archival Sources

Australian War Memorial

AWM52 series:	War Diaries, 8th Australian Division, formations and units
AWM54 series:	Written Records, 1939–1945 War
AWM67 series:	Official History, 1939–1945 War: Records of Gavin Long, General Editor

Birmingham University Library

Earl of Avon Papers
Neville Chamberlain Papers

Cambridge University Library

Viscount Templewood Papers

Churchill College, Cambridge, Archive Centre

The Chartwell Papers (W.S. Churchill)
Admiral Sir R.A.R. Plunkett-Ernle-Erle-Drax Papers
Hickleton Papers (1st Earl of Halifax)
Viscount Caldecote (Sir Thomas Inskip) Extracts from Diaries 1938–1940
Sir V.A.L. Mallet Memoir

Imperial War Museum

Heath Papers
Percival Papers
Wards Papers
Wild Papers
Miscellaneous Files (Subject Heading Malaya and Singapore)

India Office Records, British Library

L/Mil/17 series, Indian Army Records

Liddell Hart Centre for Military Archives, Kings College, London

Brooke Papers
Brooke-Popham Papers
Pownall Papers
Vlieland Papers

National Maritime Museum, Greenwich

Baron Chatfield Papers

Public Record Office

ADM1 series:	Admiralty and Secretariat Files
ADM116 series:	Cases of the Admiralty and Secretariat
ADM167 series:	Board of the Admiralty: Minutes and Memoranda
ADM181 series:	Navy Estimates
ADM205 series:	First Sea Lord Files
AIR23 series:	RAF Overseas Commands, Far East

CAB2 series:	Committee of Imperial Defence Minutes
CAB5 series:	Committee of Imperial Defence Memoranda
CAB16 series:	Ad Hoc Sub-Committees of Enquiry: Proceedings and Memoranda
CAB23 series:	Cabinet 1919–39 Minutes, CC series
CAB24 series:	Cabinet 1919–39 Memoranda
CAB32 series:	Imperial Conference 1937 Minutes and Memoranda
CAB53 series:	Chiefs of Staff Minutes and Memoranda
CAB54 series:	Deputy Chiefs of Staff Minutes and Memoranda
CAB55 series:	Committee of Imperial Defence Joint Planning Committee: Minutes and Memoranda
CAB64 series:	Minister for Coordination of Defence Registered Files
CAB65 series:	War Cabinet 1939–45 Minutes
CAB66 series:	War Cabinet Memoranda 1939–45 WP and CP Series
CAB69 series:	Defence Committee (Operations) Files
CAB79 series:	Chiefs of Staff Minutes 1939–45
CAB80 series:	Chiefs of Staff Memoranda 1939–45
CAB82 series:	Deputy Chiefs of Staff Minutes and Papers 1939–45
CAB84 series:	Joint Planning Committee Minutes and Memoranda 1939–45
CAB94 series:	Oversea Defence Committee Minutes and Papers 1939–45
CAB99 series:	Commonwealth and International Conferences 1939–45
CAB106 series:	Cabinet Office Historical Section Files
CAB119 series:	Joint Planning Staff Files
CAB120 series:	Minister of Defence Secretariat Files
CAB128 series:	Cabinet Minutes from 1945
CO273 series:	Straits Settlements Original Correspondence
DEFE5 series:	Ministry of Defence Files, Chiefs of Staff Memoranda
DO3 series:	Dominions Office Registers of Correspondence
DO35 series:	Original Correspondence
DO114 series:	Confidential Print — Dominions
FO371 series:	Foreign Office General Correspondence, Political
FO436 series:	Far Eastern Affairs: Further Correspondence
PREM1 series:	Prime Minister's Office: Correspondence and Papers to 1940
PREM3 series:	Correspondence and Papers 1940–42
T160 series:	Treasury Correspondence and Finance 1937–40
T172 series:	Chancellor of the Exchequer: Miscellaneous Papers
WO33 series:	War Office Committees: Reports and Papers
WO172 series:	War Diaries 1939–45, GHQ Far East, Malaya Command, formations, units, sub-units
WO208 series:	Directorate of Military Intelligence Files
WO268 series:	Quarterly Historical Reports, Far East Land Forces

US Army Center for Military History, Japanese Monograph series

Monograph No. 24	History of the Southern Army 1941–1945
Monograph No. 54	Malaya Operations Record November 1941–March 1942
Monograph No. 107	Malaya Invasion Naval Operations (Revised Edition)

Other Primary Sources

Cabinet Office, U.K. (1976) *Principal War Telegrams and Memoranda 1940–1943.* 7 volumes. Nendeln, Lichtenstein: KTO Press.

Colonial Office, U.K. (1949) *British Dependencies in the Far East 1945-1949. Cmd. 7709*. London: HMSO.

Dept. of External Affairs Malaysia. (1965) *Indonesian Aggression Against Malaysia. Vols. 1-2*. Kuala Lumpur: Government Press.

Hudson, M. (1969) *East of Suez*. London: Conservative Research Department.

Hudson, W.J. and H.J.W. Stokes. (editors) (1980) *Documents on Australian Foreign Policy 1937-49. Vol.IV. July 1940-June 1941*. Canberra: Australian Government Publishing Service.

— (1982) *Documents on Australian Foreign Policy 1937-49. Vol.V. July 1941-June 1942*. Canberra: Australian Government Publishing Service.

Kenway, H., H.J.W. Stokes and P.G. Edwards. (editors) (1979) *Documents on Australian Foreign Policy 1937-49. Vol.III. January-June 1940*. Canberra: Australian Government Publishing Service.

Kimball, W.F. (editor) (1984) *Churchill and Roosevelt: The Complete Correspondence*. 3 volumes. Princeton: Princeton University Press.

Koh, D. (compiler) (1976) *Excerpts of Speeches by Lee Kuan Yew on Singapore 1959-1973*. Singapore: University of Singapore Library, 1976.

Medlicott, W.N. and Dakin, D. (1973-82) *Documents on British Foreign Policy 1919-1939. Second Series, XIII, XVIII, XIX*. London: H.M.S.O.

Neale, R.G. (editor) (1975) *Documents on Australian Foreign Policy 1937-49. Vol.I. 1937-38*. Canberra: Australian Government Publishing Service.

— (1976) *Documents on Australian Foreign Policy 1937-49. Vol.II. 1939*. Canberra: Australian Government Publishing Service.

Operations of Malaya Command from 8th December 1941 to 15th February 1942. Supplement to the London Gazette, 26th February 1948.

Report to the Combined Chiefs of Staff by the Supreme Allied Commander, Southeast Asia, 1943-1945. London: HMSO, 1969.

Royal Institute of International Affairs. (1956) *Collective Defence in Southeast Asia*. London: RIIA.

Department of State. (1954-59) *Foreign Relations of the United States, 1937-1940*. Washington, D.C.: USGPO.

Stockwell, A.J. (editor) (1995) *Malaya. British Documents on the End of Empire. Series B. Vol. 3*. London: HMSO.

Woodward, E.L. and R. Butler. (1949-55) *Documents on British Foreign Policy 1919-1939. Third Series, II-IX*. London: H.M.S.O.

Ziegler, P. (editor) (1988) *Personal Diary of Admiral the Lord Louis Mountbatten, Supreme Allied Commander Southeast Asia 1943-1946*. London: Collins.

Published Sources

Aldrich, R. (editor) (1992) *British intelligence, strategy and the Cold War 1945-51*. London: Routledge.

Alfred, E.R. (1985) "The Famous 'Wrong Way' Guns of Singapore. Where Are They Now?" in *The Pointer, 12, 1*.

Allan, S. (1994) *Diary of a Girl in Changi 1941-1945*. Kenthurst, NSW: Kangaroo Press.

Allen, J. de V. (1967) *The Malayan Union*. New Haven: Yale University Southeast Asia Studies.

Allen, L. (1993) *Singapore 1941-1942*. United Kingdom: Frank Cass and Co. Ltd. [original edition 1977].

Archives and Oral History Department. (1985) *The Japanese Occupation: Singapore 1942-1945*. Singapore.

Balhetchet, R.P. and J. Brody. (1996) "Church in the Wilderness: Bahau," In R.P. Balhetchet (editor), *From the Mustard Seed*. Singapore: Cathedral Reprographic Services.

Bassett, D.K. and V.T. King. (1986) *Britain and Southeast Asia. Special Issue, Occasional Paper #13*. University of Hull: Centre for Southeast Asian Studies.

Barber, N. (1988) *Sinister Twilight: The Fall of Singapore*. London: Arrow Books Limited [original edition 1968].

Barnett, C. (1991) *Engage the Enemy More Closely: The Royal Navy in the Second World War*. New York: W.W. Norton and Company.

Bartlett, C.J. (1972) *The Long Retreat: A Short History of British Defence Policy 1945-1970*. London: The Macmillan Press Ltd.

Bell, Lt.-Cmmndr. A.C. (1954) *History of the Manchester Regiment First and Second Battalions 1922-1948*. Altrincham, U.K.: John Sherratt and Son.

Bell, R.J. (1977) *Unequal Allies: Australian-American Relations and the Pacific War*. Melbourne: Melbourne University Press.

Bennett, H. Gordon. (1944) *Why Singapore Fell*. Sydney: Angus and Robertson Ltd.

Bhargava, K.D. and K.N.V. Sastri. (1960) *Campaigns in South-East Asia 1941-42. (Official History of the Indian Armed Forces in the Second World War 1939-45)*. India: Combined Inter-Services Historical Section India & Pakistan.

Bloom, F. (1980) *Dear Philip*. London: The Bodley Head.

Braddon, R. (1952) *The Naked Island*. London: Werner Laurie.

Caffrey, K. (1974) *Out in the Midday Sun: Singapore 1941-1945*. London: Deutsch.

Callahan, R. (1977) *The Worst Disaster: The Fall of Singapore*. London: Associated University Presses.

Carver, M. (1989) *Out of Step: Memoirs of a Field Marshal*. London: Hutchinson.

— (1992) *Tightrope Walking: British Defence Policy Since 1945*. London: Hutchinson.

Chan, H.C. (1971) *Singapore: The Politics of Survival 1965-1967*. Singapore: Oxford University Press.

Chapman, F.S. (1963) *The Jungle is Neutral*. London: Chatto & Windus.

Cheah, B.K. (1983) *Red Star Over Malaya*. Singapore: Singapore University Press.

Cheong, R. (1991) *The Singapore Naval Base: A Local History*. Singapore: The Pointer Supplement.

Chen, S.L. (1969) *Remember Pompong and Oxley Rise*. Singapore: Chen Su Lan Trust.

Chew, E.C.T. and E. Lee. (editors) (1991) *A History of Singapore*. Singapore: Oxford University Press.

Chin, K.O. (1976) *Malaya Upside Down*. Kuala Lumpur: Federal Publications.

Chin, K.W. (1983) *The Defence of Malaysia and Singapore: The Transformation of a Security System 1957-1971*. Cambridge: University Press.

Chippington, G. (1992) *Singapore: The Inexcusable Betrayal*. United Kingdom: Self Publishing Association Ltd.

Christie, R.W. (editor) (1991) *A History of the 2/29th Battalion — 8th Australian Division AIF*. Victoria: High Country Publishing (Second Edition).

Churchill, W.S. (1948-53) *The Second World War*. 6 volumes. Boston: Houghton Mifflin. [Volumes 2 through 4, *Their Finest Hour, The Grand Alliance, The Hinge of Fate*, all have important material regarding the Malayan campaign, the fall of Singapore, and the conduct of the war by the British government.]

Clisby, M. (1992) *Guilty or Innocent? The Gordon Bennett Case*. Sydney: Allen & Unwin.

Clutterbuck, R. (1984) *Conflict and Violence in Singapore and Malaysia 1945-1983*. Singapore: Graham Brash.

Connolly, R. and B. Wilson. (1994) *Cruel Britannia: Britannia Waives the Rules 1941-42. Singapore Betrayed, Australia Abandoned*. New South Wales, Australia: privately published.

Coopey, R., S. Fielding and N. Tiratsoo. (editors) (1973) *The Wilson Governments 1964-1970*. New York: Pinter Publishers.

Connell, B. (1960) *Return of the Tiger*. London: Evans Brothers.

Connell, J. (1969) *Wavell: Supreme Commander 1941-1943*. London: Collins.

Corner, E.J.H. (1981) *Marquis, a tale of Syonan-to*. Singapore: Heinemann Asia.

Cowman, I. (1994) "Main Fleet to Singapore? Churchill, the Admiralty, and Force Z," in *The Journal of Strategic Studies*, 17, 2.

— (1996) *Dominion or Decline: Anglo-American Naval Relations in the Pacific, 1937-1941*. Oxford: Berg.

Darby, P. (1973) *British Defence Policy East of Suez 1947-1968*. London: Oxford University Press.

Darwin, J. (1988) *Britain and Decolonisation: The Retreat from Empire in the Postwar World*. London: Macmillan.

Day, D. (1989) *The Great Betrayal: Britain, Australia & the Onset of the Pacific War 1939-42*. New York: W.W. Norton.

Dennis, P. (1987) *Troubled Days of Peace: Mountbatten and Southeast Asia Command 1945-1946*. Manchester: University Press.

Dockrill, M. (1988) *British Defence Since 1945*. Oxford: Basil Blackwell Ltd.

Donnison, F.S.V. (1956) *British Military Administration in the Far East 1943-1946. (History of the Second World War, United Kingdom Military Series)*. London: HMSO.

Drysdale, J. (1984) *Singapore: Struggle for Success*. Singapore: Times Books International.

Eaton, H.B. (1993) *Something Extra: 28 Commonwealth Brigade 1951 to 1974*. Durham: The Pentland Press Ltd.

Elphick, P. (1995) *Singapore: The Pregnable Fortress. A Study in Deception, Discord and Desertion*. London: Hodder & Stoughton.

— (1997) *Far Eastern File: The Intelligence War in the Far East, 1930-1945*. London: Hodder & Stoughton.

Elphick, P. and M. Smith. (1994) *Odd Man Out: The Story of the Singapore Traitor*. United Kingdom: Coronet Books.

Falk, S. (1975) *Seventy Days to Singapore: The Malayan Campaign 1941-1942*. London: Robert Hale.

Farrell, B.P. (1998) *The Basis and Making of British Grand Strategy 1940-1943: Was There a Plan?* Lewiston, N.Y.: The Edwin Mellen Press.

Ferris, J.R. (1993) "Worthy of Some Better Enemy: The British Estimate of the Imperial Japanese Army 1919-1941 and the Fall of Singapore," in *Canadian Journal of History*, XXVIII, August.

Foong, C.H. (1997 translation) *The Price of Peace: True Accounts of the Japanese Occupation*. Singapore: ASIAPAC Books Pte. Ltd.

Fraser, D. (1983) *And We Shall Shock Them: The British Army in the Second World War*. London: Hodder & Stoughton Ltd.

Frei, H.P. (1991) *Japan's Southward Advance and Australia: From the Sixteenth Century to World War II*. Melbourne: University Press.

Fujiwara, I. (1983) *F. Kikan. Japanese Army Intelligence Operations in Southeast Asia during World War II*. Singapore: Heinemann Asia.

Gallagher, O.D. (1942) *Retreat in the East*. London: G.G. Harrap.

George, T.J.S. (1973) *Lee Kuan Yew's Singapore*. London: Andre Deutsch.

Gibbs, N.H. (1976) *Grand Strategy. Vol. I. Rearmament Policy. (History of the Second World War, United Kingdom Military Series)*. London: HMSO.

Gilbert, M. (1976) *Winston Churchill. Vol.V. 1922-1939*. London: Heinemann.

— (1983) *Winston Churchill. Vol.VI. 1939-1941*. London: Heinemann.

Gill, G.H. (1957) *Royal Australian Navy 1939-1942*. Canberra: Australian War Memorial.

Gough, R. (1985) *Special Operations Singapore 1941-42*. Singapore: Heinemann Asia.

Gwyer, J.M.A. (1964) *Grand Strategy. Vol. III, June 1941-August 1942 Part I. (History of the Second World War, United Kingdom Military Series)*. London: HMSO.

Haggie, P. (1981) *Britannia at Bay: The Defence of the British Empire Against Japan 1931-1941*. Oxford: Clarendon Press.

Hall, T. (1983) *The Fall of Singapore*. Sydney: Methuen Australia.

Hamill, I. (1981) *The Strategic Illusion: The Singapore Strategy and the Defence of Australia and New Zealand 1919-1942*. Singapore: University Press.

Han F.K., W. Fernandez and S. Tan. (1998) *Lee Kuan Yew: The Man and His Ideas*. Singapore: Singapore Press Holdings and Times Editions.

Harries, M. & S. (1991) *Soldiers of the Sun: The Rise and Fall of the Imperial Japanese Army*. New York: Random House.

Hasluck, P. (1952) *The Government and the People 1939-1941*. Canberra: Australian War Memorial.

Hawkins, D. (1972) *The Defence of Malaysia and Singapore: From AMDA to ANZUK*. London: Royal United Services Institute.

Hayter, J. (1989) *Priest in Prison*. Worthing: Churchman Publishing.

Healey, D. (1989) *The Time of My Life*. London: Michael Joseph.

Hodgkin, E.P. (n/d) Changi Diary, Unpublished wartime diary.

Holmes, R. & A. Kemp. (1982) *The Bitter End*. Chichester: Antony Bird Publications Ltd.

Horner, D.M. (1982) *High Command: Australia and Allied Strategy 1939-1945*. Sydney: George Allen & Unwin.

Hough, R. (1963) *The Hunting of Force Z*. London: Collins.

Hoyt, E.P. (1993) *Three Military Leaders: Togo, Yamamoto, Yamashita*. New York: Kodansha America Inc.

Huxtable, C. (1988) *From the Somme to Singapore: A Medical Officer in Two World Wars*. Tunbridge Wells: D.J. Costello.

Jackson, W. (1986) *Withdrawal from Empire: A Military View*. London: B.T. Batsford Ltd.

Johnson, F.A. (1980) *Defence by Ministry: The British Ministry of Defence 1944-1974*. London: Duckworth.

Josey, A. (1993) *Lee Kuan Yew: The Crucial Years*. Singapore: Times Books International (1980).

Keay, J. (1997) *Last Post: The End of Empire in the Far East*. London: John Murray.

Keegan, J. (editor) (1991) *Churchill's Generals*. New York: Grove Weidenfeld.

Kennedy, J. (1987) *British Civilians and the Japanese War in Malaya and Singapore 1941-45*. London: MacMillan Press.

Kennedy, Maj.-General Sir John. (1957) *The Business of War*. London: Hutchinson.

Kinvig, C. (1996) *Scapegoat: General Percival of Singapore*. London: Brassey's.

Kirby, S.W. (1957) *The War Against Japan. Vol. 1. The Loss of Singapore. (History of the Second World War, United Kingdom Military Series)*. London: HMSO.

— (1971) *Singapore: The Chain of Disaster*. London: Cassell.

Kratoska, P. (editor) (1995) *Malaya and Singapore during the Japanese Occupation*. Singapore: University Press.

— (1998) *The Japanese Occupation of Malaya: A Social and Economic History*. Sydney: Allen & Unwin.

Lau, A. (1991) *The Malayan Union Controversy 1942-1948*. Oxford: Oxford University Press.

Leasor, J. (1968) *Singapore: The Battle that Changed the World*. Garden City, N.Y.: Doubleday.

Lebra, J.C. (1977) *Japanese-Trained Armies in Southeast Asia: Independence and Volunteer Forces in World War II*. Hong Kong: Heinemann Educational Books.

Lee, C. (1994) *Sunset of the Raj: Fall of Singapore*. London: Pentland Press.

Lee, D. (1984) *Eastward: A History of the Royal Air Force in the Far East 1945-1972.* London: HMSO.

Lee, K.Y. (1998) *The Singapore Story: Memoirs of Lee Kuan Yew.* Singapore: Times Editions.

Lewis, J. (1988) *Changing Direction: British military planning for postwar strategic defence, 1942-47.* London: Sherwood Press.

Lodge, A.B. (1986) *The Fall of General Gordon Bennett.* North Sydney: Allen & Unwin Australia.

Low, N.I. (1973) *When Singapore was Syonan-to.* Kuala Lumpur: Eastern Universities Press.

Lowe, P. (1977) *Great Britain and the Origins of the Pacific War in East Asia, 1937-1941.* Oxford: Clarendon Press.

Mackie, J.A.C. (1974) *Konfrontasi: The Indonesia-Malaysia Dispute 1963-1966.* New York: Oxford University Press.

— (1986) *Low-level Military Incursions: Lessons of the Indonesia-Malaysia Confrontation Episode, 1963-66.* Canberra: Research School of Pacific Studies.

Mant, G. (1992) *The Singapore Surrender.* Kuala Lumpur: S. Abudl Majeed & Co.

— (1995) *Massacre at Parit Sulong.* New South Wales: Kangaroo Press.

Marder, A.J. (1981) *Old Friends, New Enemies: The Royal Navy and the Imperial Japanese Navy. Vol.I. Strategic Illusions 1936-1941.* Oxford: Clarendon Press.

Marquand, D. (1977) *Ramsay MacDonald.* London: Jonathan Cape.

McCarthy, J. (1976) *Australia and Imperial Defence 1918-39: A Study in Air and Sea Power.* St.Lucia: Queensland: University of Queensland Press.

McGibbon, I. (1981) *Blue Water Rationale: The Naval Defence of New Zealand 1914-1942.* Wellington: P.D. Hasselberg.

McIntyre, W.D. (1979) *The Rise and Fall of the Singapore Naval Base 1919-1942.* London: MacMillan Press Ltd.

McKercher, B.J.C. (editor) (1992) *Arms Limitation and Disarmament: Restraints on War, 1899-1939.* Westport, Conn: Praeger.

Middlebrook, M. and P. Mahoney. (1979) *Battleship: The loss of the Prince of Wales & the Repulse.* London: Penguin.

Montgomery, B. (1984) *Shenton of Singapore: Governor and Prisoner of War.* Singapore: Times Books International.

Moore, M. (1988) *Battalion at War, Singapore 1942.* Norfolk: Gliddon Books.

Morrison, I. (1942) *Malayan Postscript.* London: Faber and Faber Limited.

Murfett, M.H. (1984) *Fool-proof Relations: The Search for Anglo-American Naval Cooperation During the Chamberlain Years, 1937-1940.* Singapore: University Press.

— (1985) "Extracts from a Changi Diary: The Secret Diary of T.P.M. Lewis," in *Commentary*, 6, 2.

— (1989) "'Are We Ready?' The Development of American and British Naval Strategy, 1922-39," in J.B. Hattendorf and R.S. Jordan. (editors), *Maritime Strategy and the Balance of Power.* London: Macmillan.

— (1993) "Living in the Past: A Critical Re-examination of the Singapore Naval Strategy, 1918-1941," in *War & Society*, II, I, 1993.

— (editor) (1995) *The First Sea Lords: From Fisher to Mountbatten.* Westport, Conn: Praeger.

— (1995) *In Jeopardy: The Royal Navy and British Far Eastern Defence Policy 1945-1951.* Kuala Lumpur: Oxford University Press.

— (1998) "When trust is not enough: Australia and the Singapore Strategy," in C. Bridge and B. Attard (editors), *Between Empire and Nation: Australia's External Relations, 1901-39.* Melbourne: Scholarly Press.

Nathan, E. (1986) *The History of the Jews in Singapore 1830-1945.* Singapore: Herbilu.

Neidpath, J. (1981) *The Singapore Naval Base and the Defence of Britain's Eastern Empire, 1918-1941.* Oxford: Clarendon Press.

National Heritage Board. (1996) *The Japanese Occupation 1942-1945.* Singapore: Times Editions.

Nelson, D. (1974) *The Story of Changi Singapore.* Perth: Changi Publication Co.

Nish, I. (1972) *Alliance in Decline: A Study of Anglo-Japanese Relations 1908-1923.* London: The Athlone Press.

Ong, C.C. (1986) "Major General William Dobbie and the Defence of Malaya 1935-1938," in *Journal of Southeast Asian Studies,* vol. XVII, #2, September.

— (1988) *The Landward Defence of Singapore 1919-1938.* Singapore: Heinemann Asia.

— (1997) *Operation Matador: Britain's War Plans against the Japanese 1918-1941.* Singapore: Times Academic Press.

Owen, F. (1960) *The Fall of Singapore.* London: Joseph.

Palit, D.K. (1971) *The Campaign in Malaya.* Uttar Pradesh: Palit and Dutt [original edition 1959].

Pancheri, P.G. (1995) *Volunteer! The Story of One Man's War in the East.* Singapore: P.G. Pancheri.

Pandit, H.N. (1988) *Netaji Subhas Chandra Bose.* New Delhi: Sterling Publishers.

Parkinson, C.N. (1955) *Britain in the Far East: The Singapore Naval Base.* Singapore: Donald Moore.

Patterson, G. (1993) *A Spoonful of Rice with Salt.* Durham: The Pentland Press Ltd.

Percival, A.E. (1949) *The War in Malaya.* London: Eyre & Spottiswoode.

Pimlott, B. (1992) *Harold Wilson.* London: Harpercollins.

Postgate, M.R. (1992) *Operation Firedog: Air Support in the Malayan Emergency 1948-1960.* London: HMSO.

Potter, J.D. (1962) *The Life and Death of a Japanese General.* New York: Signet Books.

Probert, H. (1970) *History of Changi.* Singapore: Prison Industries in Changi.

— (1995) *The Forgotten Air Force: The Royal Air Force in the War against Japan 1941-1945.* London: Brassey's.

Reed, B. and G. Williams. (1971) *Denis Healey and the Policies of Power.* London: Sidgwick and Jackson.

Robertson, E. (1979) *The Japanese File: Pre-War Japanese Penetration in Southeast Asia.* Singapore: Heinemann Educational Books [Asia].

Robertson, J. (1981) *Australia at War 1939-1945.* Melbourne: William Heinemann.

Robinson, A.O. (1964) "The Malayan Campaign in the Light of the Principles of War," in *Journal of the Royal United Services Institution,* CIX, August and November.

Rocker, G. (1990) *Escaped Singapore Heading Homewards.* Singapore: Graham Brash.

Rolfe, J. (1993) *Defending New Zealand.* Wellington: Institute of Policy Studies.

Roskill, S.W. (1954) *The War at Sea 1939-1945. Vol. 1. The Defensive. (History of the Second World War, United Kingdom Military Series).* London: HMSO.

— (1968) *Naval Policy Between the Wars. Vol.I. The Period of Anglo-American Antagonism 1919-1929.* London: Collins.

Russell-Roberts, D. (1965) *Spotlight on Singapore.* United Kingdom: Times Press and Anthony Gibbs & Phillips Ltd.

Shah N.K. (1946) *I.N.A. and its Netaji.* New Delhi.

Shinozaki, M. (1973) *My Wartime Experiences in Singapore.* Singapore: ISEAS.

Shores, C. et al. (1992) *Bloody Shambles. Vol. 1. The Drift to War to the Fall of Singapore.* London: Grub Street.

Short, A. (1975) *The Communist Insurrection in Malaya, 1948-1960.* London: Muller.

Sidhu, H. (1991) *The Bamboo Fortress: True Singapore War Stories.* Singapore: Native Publications.

Simson, I. (1970) *Singapore: too little, too late. Some Aspects of the Malayan Disaster in 1942.* London: Leo Cooper.

Sleeman, C. and Silkin, S.C. (1951) *Trial of Sumida Haruzo and Twenty Others: The "Double Tenth" Trial.* London: William Hodge.

Smyth, J. (1971) *Percival and the Tragedy of Singapore.* London: Macdonald.

Sopiee, M.N. (1974) *From Malayan Union to Singapore separation: Political unification in the Malaysia region 1945-1965.* Kuala Lumpur: Penerbit Universiti Malaya.

Stewart, I.M. (1947) *History of the Argyll and Sutherland Highlanders 2nd Battalion: The Malayan Campaign 1941-42.* London: Nelson.

Stockwell, A.J. (1979) *British policy and Malay politics during the Malayan Union Experiment 1945-1948.* Singapore: Malaysian Branch of the Royal Asiatic Society.

Stubbs, R. (1989) *Hearts and Minds in Guerrilla Warfare: The Malayan Emergency 1948-1960.* Singapore: Oxford University Press.

Sundaram, C.S. (1995) "A Paper Tiger: The Indian National Army in Battle, 1944-1945", in *War & Society*, Vol. 13, #1, 1995.

Swinson, A. (1969) *Defeat in Malaya: The Fall of Singapore.* London: Ballantine Books.

Tanner, R. (1994) *A Strong Showing: Britain's Struggle for Power and Influence in Southeast Asia 1942-1950.* Stuttgart: Franz Steiner Verlag.

Tarling, N. (1996) *Britain, Southeast Asia and the Onset of the Pacific War.* Cambridge: Cambridge University Press.

Thomas, M. (1983) *In the Shadow of the Rising Sun.* Singapore: Maruzen Asia.

Thompson, T. (1990) *Freedom in Internment: Under Japanese Rule in Singapore 1942-1945.* Singapore: Kefford Press.

Tinker, H. (1988) "The Contraction of Empire in Asia 1945-48: The Military Dimension," in *Journal of Imperial and Commonwealth History*, vol. 16, #2.

Trenowden, I. (1978) *Operations Most Secret — SOE: The Malayan Theatre.* London: William Kimber.

Tsuji, M. (1960) *Singapore: The Japanese Version.* Sydney: Ure Smith.

Turnbull, C.M. (1989) *A History of Singapore 1819-1988.* Singapore: Oxford University Press.

— (1995) *Dateline Singapore — 150 Years of the Straits Times.* Singapore: Singapore Press Holdings.

Uhr, J. (1998) *Against the Sun: The AIF in Malaya 1941-42.* Sydney: Allen & Unwin.

Wall, D. (1985) *Singapore and Beyond: The Story of the 2/20 Battalion as told by the Survivors.* East Hills: 2/20 Battalion Association.

Ward, I. (1992) *The killer they called a God.* Singapore: Media Masters.

— (1996) *Snaring the other Tiger.* Singapore: Media Masters.

Watt, A. (1967) *The Evolution of Australian Foreign Policy 1938-1965.* Cambridge: Cambridge University Press.

Wigmore, L. (1957) *The Japanese Thrust. (Vol. IV, Series One, Army. Australia in the War of 1939-1945).* Canberra: Australian War Memorial, 1957.

Williams, P. and D. Wallace. (1989) *Unit 731.* New York: The Free Press.

Willmott, H.P. (1982) *Empires in the Balance: Japanese and Allied Pacific Strategies to April 1942.* Annapolis: Naval Institute Press.

Wilson, H. (1971) *The Labour Government 1964-1970: A Personal Record.* London: Weidenfeld and Nicolson.

Wong, L.K. (1982) "The Malayan Union: A Historical Retrospect," in *Journal of Southeast Asian Studies*, vol. 13, #1.

Wyett, J. (1996) *Staff Wallah: At the Fall of Singapore.* New South Wales: Allen & Unwin.

Yap S.Y., R. Bose and A. Pang. (1995) *Fortress Singapore: The Battlefield Guide.* Singapore: Times Books International [original edition 1992].

Yeo, K.W. (1973) *Political Development in Singapore 1945-1955.* Singapore: University Press.

Yong, C.F. and R.B. McKenna. (1990) *The Kuomintang Movement in British Malaya 1912-1949.* Singapore: University Press.

Yong, C.F. (1992) *Chinese Leadership and Power in Colonial Singapore.* Singapore: Times Academic Press.

Zhou, M. (1995) *Elizabeth Choy: More than a War Heroine.* Singapore: Landmark Books.

Ziegler, P. (1985) *Mountbatten: The Official Biography.* London: Collins.

Newspapers

The Straits Times
Syonan Shimbun
Syonan Times
The Times

Interviews and Correspondence

Bogaars, B.
Hodgkin, E.P.
Lim, C.S.
Marcus, M.
Mosbergen, R.
Phan, M.Y.
Soh, G.B.
Wong, V.A.

Unpublished Sources: Theses

Chan, K.S. (1986) "Soldiers in Captivity: P.O.W. Experiences in Changi 1942-1945." Unpublished B.A. Hons. dissertation. Department of History, National University of Singapore.

Chiang, M.S. (1993) "Military Defences and Threat Perceptions in Nineteenth Century Singapore, 1854-1891." Unpublished B.A. Hons. dissertation. Department of History, National University of Singapore.

Evans, B.L. (1961) "The Attitudes and Policies of Great Britain and China toward French Expansion in Cochin China, Cambodia, Annam and Tongking; 1858-1883". PhD Thesis, School of Oriental and African Studies, University of London.

Foo, S.M.L. (1987) "The Japanese Occupation of Singapore 1942-45: Socio-Economic Policies and Effects." Unpublished B.A. Hons. dissertation. Department of History, National University of Singapore.

Gray, C. (1978) "Johore 1910-1941, Studies in the Colonial Process." Unpublished Ph.D. dissertation, Yale University.

Joginder, S.J. (1958) "The Indian Army of Independence 1942-45." Unpublished B.A. Hons. dissertation. Department of History, University of Malaya in Singapore.

Kang, J.K. (1981) "The Chinese in Singapore During the Japanese Occupation 1942-1945." Unpublished B.A. Hons. dissertation. Department of History, National University of Singapore.

Kathiravelu, S. (1957) "Fortifications of Singapore 1819-1942." Unpublished B.A. Hons. dissertation. Department of History, University of Malaya in Singapore.

Kwok, S.S.F. (1995) "Extraordinary Lives: Catholic Missionaries During the Japanese Occupation of Singapore 1942-1945." Unpublished B.A. Hons. dissertation. Department of History, National University of Singapore.

Lee, A.C. (1956) "Singapore Under the Japanese 1942-1945." Unpublished B.A. Hons. dissertation. Department of History, University of Malaya in Singapore.

Lee, S.Y. (1985) "The Indian National Army Trials, 1945-46: The British Imperial Dilemma." Unpublished B.A. Hons. dissertation. Department of History, National University of Singapore.

Thomas, G.G. (1997) "Fortress: A History of the Defence of Blakang Mati." Unpublished B.A. Hons. dissertation. Department of History, National University of Singapore.

Zaimiah binte Mohd. Adam. (1961) "Sultan Ibrahim of Johore 1873-1959." Unpublished B.A. Hons. dissertation. Department of History, University of Malaya in Singapore.

INDEX

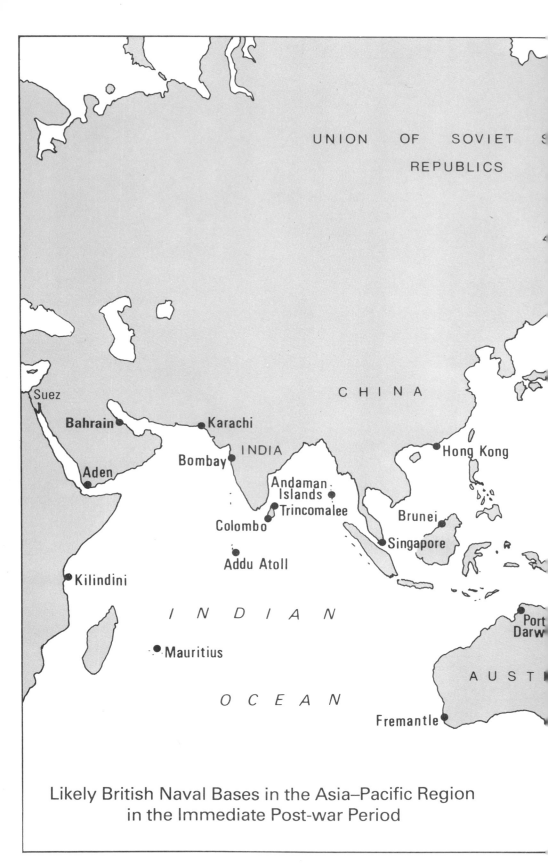

Likely British Naval Bases in the Asia–Pacific Region
in the Immediate Post-war Period